Modern Internal Auditing

MODERN INTERNAL AUDITING

Continuing Professional Education (CPE) Edition

ROBERT M. ATKISSON
Management Consultant—Internal Auditing

VICTOR Z. BRINK
Graduate School of Business
Columbia University

HERBERT WITT
Office of Inspector General
Department of Health and Human Services

A Ronald Press Publication

JOHN WILEY & SONS,   New York   Chichester   Brisbane   Toronto   Singapore

Library of Congress Cataloging in Publication Data:

Atkisson, Robert M.
  Modern internal auditing.

  "A Ronald Press publication."
  Includes index.
  1. Auditing, Internal. I. Brink, Victor Zinn,
1906–   . II. Witt, Herbert.

HF5668.25.A88 1986   657'.458   85-20380
ISBN 0-471-81882-8

Printed in the United States of America

10 9 8 7 6 5

*To Brad Cadmus
for pioneer professional leadership
and to our wives,
Alma, Dorothy, and Hiala,
for loyal support*

Preface

This new book—*Modern Internal Auditing: Continuing Professional Education (CPE) Edition*—is intended to serve the special needs of the internal auditing profession for its expanding education activities. A second purpose of this CPE edition is to have a shorter book—compared with the existing fourth edition. Hence it deals only with the matters of day-to-day concern to the practicing internal auditor.

In more specific terms, this new CPE edition:

Uses many of the chapters of the fourth edition, modifying them only to update references and to achieve maximum clarity

Expands the coverage in particular areas, including:

Technical approach of the internal auditor

Computer operations

Use of the computer as an audit tool

Reporting

Adds new teaching material, which includes:

Learning objectives at the beginning of each chapter to guide the reader and to help him measure later accomplishment

Use of meaningful side captions to highlight the many significant aspects of internal auditing

Review questions to test the reader's understanding of the content of each chapter (Author's responses are separately available.)

Case problems with each chapter for discussion and work assignment (Author's responses are also available, separately.)

In summary, this edition is a companion to *Modern Internal Auditing*, fourth edition. The two books overlap but serve different major purposes, the CPE edition focusing on educational use and the fourth edition providing more complete coverage of the various operating areas and of other relations of the internal auditor.

Since 1973, when the third edition of *Modern Internal Auditing* was published, the role of the internal auditor in all organizations has continued to expand. This has been due in part to the acceleration of social expectations for higher standards of professional conduct and for greater protection against inefficiency, misconduct, illegality, and fraud. One response to the greater needs for protection was the Foreign Corrupt Practices Act of 1977 and the related implementation of that act by the Securities and Exchange Commission. There has also been a more realistic recognition of the fact that the internal auditor can contribute importantly to satisfying the expanded protective needs. These observations about internal auditors are as true today as they were when the fourth edition was published.

There are three matters that require some explanation. First, throughout the text we have used the personal pronouns he and him in referring to internal auditors. This is for convenience only. Excellence in internal auditing is not limited by sex, color, race, or nationality. Second, the book is couched in terms of business organization. This is also for convenience only. In truth all organizations—business, nonprofit, and governmental—have protection and productivity needs that provide the common basis for the services of the internal auditor. All portions of the book have general application for all types of organizations. Finally, we make frequent reference to professional organizations, professional certifications, and laws, the majority of which pertain exclusively to the United States. It would not be practicable to list all of the excellent professional audit organizations and certifications in other countries. Insofar as the laws are concerned, it is incumbent upon internal auditors to be aware of the laws of their nation which affect their organization and professional activities.

In developing this edition, Victor Z. Brink and Herbert Witt, the authors of the fourth edition, now joined by Robert M. Atkisson, are again indebted to the host of practitioners, educators, writers, and others, who have provided comments and leadership in all areas. We are also especially indebted to Daniel P. Armishaw and Charlie Re, The Society of Management Accountants of Canada, L. Susan Dean, Arthur Young Educational Services, and Harold M. Korin, JC Penney Company, who, along with Richard G. Lynch, our editor at John Wiley & Sons, evaluated the need for this CPE edition and gave us valuable guidance.

Finally, we reaffirm our faith in the expanding service role of the internal auditor, our pleasure in being a part of that ongoing effort, and our sincere hope that this CPE edition will help to better provide the increasingly needed educational foundations.

ROBERT M. ATKISSON
VICTOR Z. BRINK
HERBERT WITT

Winter Park, Florida
Laguna Hills, California
Mill Valley, California

January 1986

Contents

Modern Internal Auditing

PART ONE

*Foundations for
Internal Auditing*

CHAPTER ONE

The Nature of Internal Auditing

Upon completing this chapter you should be able to:

- [ ] *Describe the nature and scope of internal auditing*
- [ ] *Give a general explanation of the internal auditor's focus on control*
- [ ] *Describe the relationship between internal auditing and other company activities*
- [ ] *Differentiate between internal and external auditing*
- [ ] *Understand the evolution of internal auditing and its current broad responsibilities*

WHAT IS INTERNAL AUDITING?

There is no better way to begin this book about modern internal auditing than to turn to The Institute of Internal Auditors, the professional association of internal auditors. In the Standards for the Professional Practice of Internal Auditing, released in May 1978, there is the following definition:

> Internal auditing is an independent appraisal function established within an organization to examine and evaluate its activities as a service to the organization.

We can, perhaps, make this statement more meaningful by focusing more directly on the key terms that have been used. The term "auditing" itself suggests a variety of ideas. On the one hand it can be viewed very narrowly as the checking of arithmetic accuracy or existence of assets, and on the other as thoughtful review and appraisal at the highest organizational level. In this book we use the term to include the total range of levels of service.

The term "internal" is to make clear that this is auditing work carried on by the organization and by its own employees. In this way the auditing work here is distinguished from such auditing work as may be carried on by outside

Internal means auditing carried out by employees of organization

public accountants or any other parties not directly a part of the particular organization.

The remainder of the statement covers a number of important key dimensions of the internal auditing work, as follows:

1. The term "independent" characterizes the audit work as being free of restrictions that could significantly limit the scope and effectiveness of the review or the later reporting of findings and conclusions.
2. The term "appraisal" confirms the evaluation thrust of internal auditors as they develop their conclusions.
3. The term "established" confirms the fact of definitive creation by the organization of the internal auditing role.
4. The terms "examine and evaluate" describe the action role of internal auditors first, as fact-finding inquiry, and second, as judgmental evaluation.
5. The words "its activities" confirm the broad jurisdictional scope of the internal auditing work as applying to all of the activities of the organization.
6. The term "service" identifies help and assistance as the end product of all internal auditing.
7. The term "to the organization" confirms the total service scope as pertaining to the entire organization—which includes all corporate personnel, boards of directors (including their audit committees), and stockholders.

Focus on Control

A better understanding of internal auditing can be obtained by recognizing that it is a kind of organizational control which functions by measuring and evaluating the effectiveness of other controls. When an organization establishes its planning at all levels and then proceeds to implement those plans in terms of operations, it must do something to monitor the operations to assure the achievement of established objectives. These further efforts can be thought of as "controls." The internal auditing function is itself one of the types of control used. However, there is a wide range of other controls, and it is the special role of the internal auditing work to help measure and evaluate those other controls. Thus internal auditors must understand both their own role as a control and the nature and scope of other types of controls.

Internal auditing measures and evaluates effectiveness of controls

All this means that internal auditors who do their job effectively become experts in what makes for the best possible design and implementation of all types of control. This expertise includes understanding the interrelationships of the various controls and their best possible integration in various ways in the total system of internal control. It is thus through the "control" door that internal auditors come to "examine and evaluate" all organizational activities and to provide maximum service to the organization. Internal auditors cannot be expected to equal—let alone exceed—the technical and operational expertise pertaining to the various activities of the organization. But internal auditors *can* help the responsible individuals achieve more effective results by appraising existing controls and providing a basis for helping to improve those controls.

Historical Background of Internal Auditing

It is normal for any activity—including a control activity such as internal auditing—to come into being as a result of emerging needs. We can also understand better the nature of the activity which currently exists if we know something about the changing conditions in the past which created the needs for that activity. What is the simplest form of internal auditing and how does it come into existence? How has internal auditing responded to changing needs?

In strict theory the internal auditing function can exist when any single person sits back and surveys something that he[1] has done. At that point the individual asks himself how well he has done the particular thing and, perhaps, how he might do it better if he were to do it again. When a second person is involved, the function is expanded to include the review of the second person's activities. In a small business the owner or manager will be doing this to some extent with all of his employees. In all of these situations the internal auditing function is being carried out directly as a part of the basic management role.

However, as the operations of the business become more voluminous and complex, it is no longer practicable for the owner or top manager to have enough contact with the various operations so that he can review satisfactorily the effectiveness of performance. Although he can build a supervisory system and try to keep an overview through that supervisory system, it becomes increasingly difficult for him to know whether the interests of the business are being properly serviced. Are established procedures being complied with? Are assets being properly safeguarded? Are the various employees functioning efficiently? Are the current approaches still effective in the light of changing conditions? The ultimate response to these needs is that he must have further help. This help is provided by assigning one or more individuals to be directly responsible for reviewing activities and reporting on the above-mentioned types of questions. It is here that the internal auditing activity comes into being in a formal and explicit sense.

The first internal auditing assignments usually originated to satisfy very basic and sharply defined operational needs. The earliest special concern of management was whether the assets of the organization were being properly protected, whether company procedures and policies were being complied

---

[1]We repeat here for emphasis, the use of the personal pronouns he or him, or any other words denoting gender, is for convenience only. Excellence in internal auditing is not limited by sex, color, race, or nationality.

with, and whether the financial records were being accurately maintained. There was also considerable emphasis on fraud detection and maintenance of the status quo. To a great extent also the internal auditing was viewed as a closely related extension of the work of the external auditor. The result of all of these factors was that the internal auditor was viewed as playing a relatively narrow role. At the same time the internal auditor himself was viewed as a person of relatively limited responsibility in the total managerial spectrum. He was the financially oriented checker and more of a policeman than a co-worker. Understanding this situation is important because it is an image which to some extent still exists for modern internal auditors, even when the character of the internal auditing function is now actually very much different.

Earlier internal auditors were financially oriented and more like police officers

Over a period of time, however, this situation has changed a great deal. The operations of the various organizations were increasing steadily in volume and complexity. The managerial problems thus created have resulted in new pressure on higher-level management. The managerial executive has therefore sought new ways of responding to these pressures. It was quite natural, then, that management would recognize the possibilities of better utilization of the services of the internal auditor. Here were individuals moving through the organization—in various departments and in various geographical areas—and there seemed to be every good reason for getting greater value from these individuals with relatively little increase in cost. At the same time, the internal auditors themselves were perceiving the existing opportunities and were more and more initiating new types of service. Thus internal auditors took on a broader and more management-oriented character. Because the earlier internal auditing was very much accounting oriented, this upward trend was felt first in the accounting and financial control areas. Subsequently, however, it was extended to also include the nonfinancial areas.

Internal auditors now more management oriented

The Situation Today

Internal auditing today, like any other evolving function, reflects a broad spectrum of types of operational activity and levels of coverage. In many organizations internal auditing—as a formal staff activity—is quite new and its more permanent role is still being defined. In other situations—for various reasons—the internal auditing is still functioning to a major extent at the more routine compliance level. In some other situations it still suffers from being integrated with regular accounting or other operating activities. In certain situations the internal auditing is carried out entirely or substantially only in the strictly financial areas. In other situations the focus has shifted to a varying extent to the more general nonfinancial operational areas. In most situations the internal auditing group has moved to very high levels in all operational areas and has established itself as a valued and respected part of the top management effort. To an increasing extent also the internal auditor is serving the board of directors—usually via the audit committee of that board. The overall situation, however, reflects major progress in the scope of coverage and the level of service in the individual areas. The internal auditing profession itself, through its own self-development and dedication, has contributed to this progress and has set the stage for a continuing upward trend.

Composite Nature of Operational and Financial Auditing

In recent years there has been a strong tendency on the part of many internal auditors to adopt the label of "operational auditing" in place of the traditional "internal auditing." The rationale appears to be that "internal auditing" as a term is tied too closely with the more basic financial auditing—including both basic financial control activities and the review of financial statements. There is a desire to focus more on the other operational activities that provide the greater opportunities for increased profit and overall management service. In its most extreme form the so-called operational auditor would like to disassociate himself entirely from the so-called financial areas. However, such a separation involves matters of both substance and self-interest for the internal auditor.

Financial reviews open door to operating activities

Traditionally the internal auditor has been concerned with accounting and financial matters, and some expertise in these areas has generally been considered to be essential. The coverage of these matters has also served to provide the opportunity of expanding the range of service into the broader operational areas. Since the accounting record directly or indirectly reflects *all* operational activities, the financial review has served to open the door to the other activities. This type of extension has been most advantageous and there are major doubts as to whether this advantage should be abandoned. There would seem to be no good reason why the level of the operational outreach should be limited because of the route taken.

Finally, in terms of strategy, the abandonment of the accounting/financial areas could well be to create a vacuum that would invite the emergence of other competitive groups. The organization certainly needs to have someone covering the accounting and financial areas, and whoever does that will inevitably spill over into the broader operational areas. Therefore, the internal auditor needs to cover the accounting and financial areas in his own long-run self-interest. It is recognized that there are some internal auditors who feel that a continuing connection with financial auditing hinders the effort to exhibit adequately the potentials of operational auditing. Still other internal auditors favor having the internal auditor do work in both areas but to deal with them separately. On balance it is reasonable to conclude that there is an important linkage between the so-called financial and nonfinancial areas and that it is desirable to recognize and to take advantage of that linkage. At the same time there is no reason why all of the internal auditing efforts cannot be shaped, with various types of emphasis, to serve organizational needs in the total operational area in the most effective manner possible. It is believed, therefore, that both modern operational auditing and financial auditing can find full expression within the framework of modern internal auditing. In a very real sense there no longer is operational and/or financial auditing but only good modern internal auditing.[2]

Increasing Recognition of Internal Auditing

New environmental factors generate need for internal auditing

Over recent years there has been a continuing expansion of business and nonbusiness activities. This in itself would have caused a continuing increase in the need for the services of internal auditors. But in addition there have been some new environmental forces that have created still further needs. These environmental forces are a part of the generally accelerated rate of social expectations in such areas as protection of natural resources, pollution, minority groups, higher levels of business responsibility, and moral standards. In the latter area we can include higher standards for corporate management, greater involvement of boards of directors (including the greater use of audit committees), a more active role for stockholders, and greater independence of the outside public accountant. On the legislative side one specific development in the United States has been the Foreign Corrupt Practices Act of 1977 and the supportive regulation on the part of the Securities and Exchange Commission. A second important legislative development has been the Inspector General Act. As a result of these new pressures, the services of the internal auditor have become more important to all parties of interest. This has been reflected in more and better qualified internal auditing personnel and higher-level organization status. During this period The Institute of Internal Auditors has grown from its charter chapter in 1941 with 25 members to an international association of about 28,000 members and 165 chapters. At the same time new and impressive literature has also been developed. It can well be said that the internal auditing profession has reached major maturity and is well positioned for continuing dynamic growth.

FUNCTIONAL ROLE OF INTERNAL AUDITING

Relationship of Internal Auditing to Other Company Activities

Internal auditors should not be assigned operating responsibilities

An essential basis for understanding the nature of internal auditing is to examine the relationship between internal auditing and other company activities. In the first place the work of the internal auditor needs to be detached from the regular day-to-day operations of the company. A good practical test is that if the internal auditing activity—partially or completely—was temporarily inactive, the regular company operations would go on for the time

---

[2]This integration of financial and operational auditing is more fully discussed in Chapter 6.

being in the normal manner. The reasons for this detachment are very practical. To the extent that the internal auditing group is charged with day-to-day activities—as, for example, validating disbursements, reconciling bank accounts, approving movements of assets, and the like—the separate and supplementary review has ceased to exist. Instead, the internal auditing activity has simply taken the place of regular accounting or other operational responsibility. At times there is a temptation on the part of management to assign such operational responsibilities to the internal auditor, but when this is done, it is based on a misunderstanding of the loss of the independent review.

A second important aspect of the relationship of internal auditing to other company activities is that the internal auditor is a staff man and that, therefore, he should not usurp the role and responsibility of other individuals. Thus the line manager or supervisor has the basic responsibility for his own particular sphere of the operations and he cannot shift the responsibility to the internal auditor. This does not mean that the internal auditor is without responsibility. The internal auditor has his responsibility to do a job that is competent in a professional sense. But if he were to relieve line personnel of their responsibilities it would indeed weaken the motivation of the line managers and to a considerable extent lessen the value of their roles. Thus the findings and recommendations of the internal auditor are always informative and advisory, and in no way carry any direct authority to command specific action. The latter must be determined by the line personnel based on the soundness and persuasiveness of the particular information and recommendations.

A final point concerns the unavoidable overlap of the internal auditing role with many other company activities. In principle, all personnel in an organization are committed to doing their particular jobs effectively and in helping to achieve maximum company welfare in an overall sense. This commitment increases as one goes up the organizational ladder, including the various staff areas. Thus a financial analysis group, an operations research group, or some other staff group might be very much concerned with operational analysis and assistance. Frequently special task forces will also be created to study designated organizational problems. What then is so unique about the role of the internal auditor in providing analysis and service? The answer here is that the internal auditing group is the one that is completely detached from both the operational components and the functional staff groups (finance, marketing, production, and the like) and which can look at the various problems independently in terms of overall control. Here also competence in the design and implementation of the control gives it a needed credential to round out its overall professional capability. No other group in the company so well combines the fact of detachment, the objectives of organizational service to the organization, and the major competence in the field of control. In the federal government this independence is further provided by the Inspectors General and the General Accounting Office.

Internal auditors detached from other organizational activities

Relationship of Internal Auditing to Board of Directors

As a result of the previously mentioned environmental pressures, the board of directors is playing a more active role and assuming increased responsibilities in its relationships with both corporate management and the stockholders. One of the ways in which the board has coped with these increased responsibilities is through the formation or expansion of the role of its audit committee. Although the proper role of the audit committee is still emerging, it normally includes an overview of the completeness and integrity of the financial statements, the effectiveness of the system of internal accounting control, and the adequacy of the total audit effort. The latter includes relations with both the outside independent auditor and the internal auditor. Although the more usual arrangement is for the internal auditor to report administratively to either the chief executive officer or chief financial officer, the need also exists for both defined reporting and assistance to the audit committee. The internal auditor customarily has a dual relationship to corporate management and to the audit committee, and in both connections appropriately coordinates his work with that of the independent public accountant—the external auditor.

Internal auditor coordinates with external auditor

Relationship of Internal Auditing to the External Auditor

Mention has been previously made of the earlier view that the internal auditing activity was in a major sense an extension of the external auditor effort. In fact, in many cases the internal auditing program was designed by the external auditor and utilized directly to serve the needs of the outside audit. Frequently also, the internal auditing personnel were recruited from the outside auditing profession and their internal assignments were all the more attuned to public auditing standards and interests. It is now, however, more clearly recognized that despite certain common interests, their priorities are quite different. The external auditor has a primary responsibility to parties outside the client organization, while the internal auditor is primarily responsible to the organization. The external auditor is interested more specifically in the soundness of the financial statements, whereas the internal auditor is concerned predominantly with the overall effectiveness of company operations and resulting profitability. But, although both audit groups have different primary missions, there are many common interests that provide the basis for an extensive coordination effort. Primarily, however, the common interest stems from the fact that the soundness of the system of internal accounting control is an important basis for each group achieving its primary mission. This common interest has also become especially important because of the requirement in the Foreign Corrupt Practices Act of 1977 that corporations maintain a system of sound internal accounting control, and by the interest of the Securities and Exchange

Priorities of internal and external auditors quite different

Commission in pressing for a report from management covering the adequacy of the system of internal control.

SOME PRELIMINARY CONSIDERATIONS

Universal Applicability of Internal Auditing

The development of internal auditing has to a major extent been centered in business organizations. This tie continues in the existing literature of the profession and the convenient treatment of problems within the framework of business organizations. These ties, however, unduly deny the universal applicability of internal auditing to all types of organizations. Moreover, they fail to recognize that some of the most progressive internal auditing is now being done by nonbusiness types of organizations. A related fact also is that many organizations are a blend of business and nonbusiness activities—as for example, where a governmental authority like the Port Authority in the New York area is created and charged with the responsibility for operating public service facilities.

Internal auditing applies to all types of organizations

All of these developments confirm the truth that the need for internal auditing exists in all types of organizations where the complexity of the activities, the volume of transactions, and the dependence on large numbers of people exist in some combination to create operational problems. Organizations can exist for a variety of purposes, but the very reason for their creation is that there are objectives to be achieved. It is then the common role of all organizations to utilize the available resources in the most productive manner possible to achieve the organizational objectives. In that endeavor all responsible managers require effective control and in all cases can utilize the assistance of the internal auditing group. Thus there is a need for internal auditing in all types of organizations and there is a common body of professional knowledge that applies to all of these varied internal auditing activities.

A second aspect of the universal applicability is that there is potentially a need for the services of the internal auditor at any organizational level in any particular company or organization. This means that there can be legitimate needs for internal auditing services by the stockholders, the board of directors, and by the responsible management at the corporate headquarters level, the subsidiary or divisional level, and other lower levels. The controlling principle here is that whenever given organizational responsibilities are established there are potential needs for internal auditing services which should be served in some way. It is possible that all of these needs might be served by a central internal auditing group, provided that the central group can structure and administer the total operation in a sufficiently competent manner. In other cases the lower-level organizational components may believe that their own needs are best served by an internal auditing

Internal auditing services can be needed at all organizational levels

group of their own—even though indirectly responsible to the central group. What is important, however, for our present purposes is to recognize that internal auditing needs are directly linked to all organizational components.

Problems of Terminology

Much variation in use of terminology

There is always the problem of how different terms shall be used and whether individual terms are viewed narrowly or broadly. This is especially a problem when the activities associated with the terms are undergoing major change and when new terms are being introduced. At the time of the first edition in 1941 the term "internal auditing" had just begun to emerge fully as describing the independent review activity of the type just described. Prior thereto the more commonly used term was "internal audit" and here the term was frequently used as a part of the term "internal audit and control," encompassing a combination of true internal auditing activities, internal accounting, and other regular operational procedures. Today the term "internal auditing" is believed by many to be unduly restrictive in describing the broad operational scope of the internal auditing effort. These individuals would prefer some broader term such as "management auditing," "management analysis," "operations analysis," and the like. Thus far, however, it has been concluded that there is more to be lost than gained by changing the name and we are therefore, left with the need to develop a new understanding of the broader scope of the internal auditing effort.

A similar problem of terminology exists in the case of the terms "internal check" and "internal control." At the time of the first edition in 1941 the term "internal check" was viewed as having reasonably broad coverage. By the time of the second edition in 1957, this particular term had come to have a fairly narrow application to lower-level types of cross check. "Internal control" had then become the broader term. There were also other new terms, such as "managerial control," "organizational control," and just plain "control." Different people of course use these terms in different ways.

More recently also a new term has been introduced by the American Institute of Certified Public Accountants, "internal accounting control." This particular term is intended to apply to that portion of the total internal control that pertains to the data in the financial reports about which the outside public accountant is expressing an opinion. The internal accounting controls, then, when coupled with internal administrative controls, are viewed as constituting the entire system of internal control. The term "internal accounting control" has also been used in the new Foreign Corrupt Practices Act of 1977 and by the Securities and Exchange Commission in its regulatory pronouncements.

Our own treatment will be somewhat along the following lines. Internal audit is viewed more as the individual audit review within the total field of internal auditing. When we come to the area of control we start with the recognition that the term "control" is the general term which covers all types of control and which needs further identification as to the particular type of control. "Managerial control" is then viewed as the broadest type of control, of which internal auditing is one part. "Organizational control" is then viewed as the part of managerial control that pertains to the assignment and direct coordination of organizational responsibilities. "Internal control" is used to describe internal procedures and practices that pertain to achieving organizational objectives better. "Internal check" will be hardly used at all, but where used it will apply to the lower-level cross checks between procedures, within the broader types of internal control. Finally, we will use "internal accounting control" in the same way as the American Institute of Certified Public Accountants and as used in the Foreign Corrupt Practices Act of 1977.

Internal controls are procedures and policies to achieve organizational objectives

Plan of the Book

Our overall plan in this CPE edition of the 4th edition of *Modern Internal Auditing*, will be to deal first with foundation concepts and other considerations that apply to all internal auditing assignments. These foundations include an analysis of the "Standards for the Professional Practice of Internal Auditing," issued by The Institute of Internal Auditors in 1978, an examination of the nature and scope of control, and other approaches and skills. In this edition we have included the first three Statements on Internal Auditing Standards, recently issued by the IIA.

The stage is then set for the coverage of the selected operational areas, which are common to most organizations and covered by internal auditing assignments. Be aware that there are numerous operational areas in any organization. Those we have chosen should be used as examples. The concepts and principles discussed in this book apply to any operational area. In each of these operational areas the objective is to identify the individual controls and combinations of controls that are important in achieving results in that particular area. The understanding of these controls then provides the basis for developing specific audit programs. In addition, however, audit guides are provided to further assist in the development of those specific audit programs.

Objectives of the Book

This book has been designed to serve a wide range of needs of internal auditors. There is on the one hand the objective of providing practical assistance to internal auditors as they carry out individual parts of their internal auditing assignments. Whether the particular need is for report writing, the review of computer operations, investigating fraud, or whatever, the book should serve as a helpful reference in taking particular action. Even at this level, however, the approach of the book is to provide basic information and guides rather than detailed instructions. At all levels the work of the internal auditor must be tailored to the particular operational or other type of organizational situation. At the same time there is the very serious intention

Book is information and guides, and not instructions

to develop a theory and philosophy of internal auditing that will generate depth thinking and professional development. Here too the objective is to provide a better understanding of the total environment of which the internal auditing effort is a part. To a considerable extent, therefore, the book requires thoughtful study. Hopefully, together the basis may thus be laid for an expanded range of service by professional internal auditors. Hopefully it will also help provide all other interested parties with a better understanding of what they may properly expect from internal auditors and of how they can relate to internal auditors more effectively.

REVIEW QUESTIONS

1. Describe in your own words the nature and scope of internal auditing.
2. What are controls and what is their function?
3. Why do you think the early development of internal auditing in business had the special character it did?
4. How do you perceive the present environment in which internal auditing operates?
5. How is internal auditing, in general, responding to the present environment?
6. How does the internal auditing activity relate to other company activities?
7. Compare the roles of the internal and external auditor, noting what appear to be common and special interests.
8. Why does internal auditing have general applicability to all organizations and at all levels of those organizations?
9. What is the significance of whether control is defined narrowly or broadly?
10. If you have an internal auditing department in your company, describe what you perceive that department's role to be and how you appraise its present and potential level of contribution to your organization.

CASE PROBLEMS

Problem 1-1

Cocktail conversation had turned to what each person did for a living. Sam Blesser said, "I am the head of the internal auditing department at the Home City Electronics Company." "That's a bit out of my line," said John Rose. "Its a good thing I am in sales because I was never good at figures." "Well," broke in Willie West, a concert pianist, "I have always had the impression that internal auditors just check lists of numbers to see that they were right— and I would think that could be pretty dull." "But," ventured Jerry Wilson, who was vice president, international operations for a large company, "my boss tells me that we had to set up an internal auditing department because the Foreign Corrupt Practices Act had legislated so many penalities for crime and corruption. But Sam, you don't look like a policeman. Rather, you give me the impression that you are more interested in the big picture. What do you really do?" "O.K.," chimed in Willie West, "I'm ready to be educated." "Me too," added John Rose. "But put it in words we poor laymen can understand."

Required. Assume the role of Sam Blesser and explain your work as an internal auditor, including specific reference to the perceptions expressed by Rose, West, and Wilson.

Problem 1-2

Ken Chubby, ABC Corporation's director of internal auditing, sensed that his boss, George Massey, vice-president–finance had something on his mind. Massey had earlier asked Chubby to drop by his office, and now both were sitting comfortably at Massey's small conference table. Massey began, "Ken, I know the effort you have poured into covering the internal auditing needs in our major subsidiary 'Chemical Inc.' However, their president, Rich Wille, has gotten the ear of our chief, Tom Burns. Wille says he needs more internal auditing services in areas where he can better guide the direction and the priorities. He wants to take over part of your staff and let Chemical do its own thing. Apparently he has convinced the old man that Chemical can then better meet the profit objectives Tom is pressing so hard for. Ken, I really don't know what is best for ABC, but I do think that Tom ought to have the entire story. Could you put together the pros and cons in a short memorandum? Also, I think it would be useful if you would describe your views as to just what your role would be at Chemical down the road if they do have their own internal auditing department. All in all, I think this is a good opportunity to give the boss some useful guidance. I don't want to disturb your schedule unduly, but—well today's Wednesday—do you think you could have the memo ready by next Tuesday?"

Ken Chubby did not hesitate. He said, "George, I'll do my best. I'm sure we can live with either approach, but I will be glad to help him better understand the effect of what he is considering and how the company can then be best assured of receiving full internal auditing services. Also, he must understand the continuing need of ABC headquarters for certain internal auditing services. In any event, we will try to support the set-up that Burns thinks will best serve his managerial needs but if we do go in Wille's direction, we will need the proper backing from Mr. Burns."

Required. Prepare the memorandum from Ken Chubby to Tom Burns.

CHAPTER TWO

Professional Standards for Internal Auditing

Upon completing this chapter you should be able to:

☐ *Explain the benefits of having professional standards for internal auditing*

☐ *Describe in your own words the five general standards*

☐ *Understand the importance of the standards as an authoritative reference source*

☐ *Recognize that the standards are subject to judgment and interpretation when applied to individual circumstances*

Standards approved 1978   The most authoritative statement about the nature and scope of internal auditing exists in the form of the "Standards for the Professional Practice of Internal Auditing."[1] These Standards were approved by The Institute of Internal Auditors in June 1978. They are described in the foreword to those Standards as being "the criteria by which the operations of an internal au-

---

[1]Prior to the approval of these Standards the most authoritative statement was the Statement of Responsibilities of the Internal Auditor, originally issued by The Institute of Internal Auditors in 1947, and subsequently revised in 1957, 1971, 1976, and 1981. That Statement of Responsibilities was believed to have continuing informational value as a summary of what internal auditing is all about, and was therefore revised in 1981 to eliminate inconsistencies with the new Standards.

Quite clearly it was important that the Statement be consistent with the Standards. It does mean, however, that the Statement is now subject to some of the same limitations as the Standards—to be described later in this chapter. One important loss is the elimination of language in the older Statement pertaining to the internal auditor's interest in *improving* all types of operational performance. On the positive side, however, the Statement expands the service role of internal auditing from operational management to the entire organization. Another gain is that in the first paragraph the revised Statement retains an earlier sentence "It [internal auditing] is a control which functions by examining and evaluating the adequacy and effectivess of other controls"—a sentence unfortunately omitted from the Standards. The revised Statement is attached as Appendix A.

diting department are evaluated and measured. They are intended to represent the practice of internal auditing as it should be, as judged and adopted by the Board of Directors of The Institute." In that foreword, it is stated that "Organizations which have already established an internal audit function or are planning to establish one, are urged to adopt and support the Standards for the Professional Practice of Internal Auditing as a basis for guiding and measuring the function."

In December 1983, The Institute issued the first Statement on Internal Auditing Standards (SIAS). The purpose of this and subsequent SIASs is to issue pronouncements on internal auditing matters. These Statements are authoritative interpretations of the Standards for the Professional Practice of Internal Auditing[2]. The three which have been issued at this writing are attached as Appendices D, E, and F.

It is appropriate, therefore, that we use these Standards and related Statements to expand our review of the foundation concepts of modern internal auditing beyond the brief coverage in Chapter 1.

Why Standards?

To qualify properly as a profession there are a number of requirements. These requirements include a recognized and well-defined area of service to society, special knowledge and skills for providing that service, standards of performance, a code of ethics, and a procedure by which the members can be disciplined. Because of the key role of standards it was therefore both appropriate and essential that The Institute of Internal Auditors develop and validate a set of standards for the professional practice of internal auditing.

The standards serve both the members of The Institute and the larger society served by internal auditors. Through properly developed standards the internal auditors—as individual members, as internal auditing departments, and as a professional body—can have a benchmark against which to measure the level and quality of their internal auditing activities. At the same time the standards become a basis for education and training to achieve the desired levels of excellence. For those outside the internal auditing profession—management, boards of directors, stockholders, investors, regulatory bodies, and all other interested parties—the standards serve as a useful measure of what they all should expect to receive in the way of internal auditing services.

Standards serve all internal auditors

Structure of Standards and Our Plan of Treatment

The Standards consist of (1) a foreword, (2) an introduction, (3) a summary of general and specific standards, and (4) five chapters covering five sectors

[2]In February 1983, The Institute began printing Professional Standards Bulletins in its journal, *The Internal Auditor*. These bulletins are prepared for information only by the standards information service subcommittee of The Institute of Internal Auditors' Professional Standards and Responsibilities Committee.

of concerns—in each case with the applicable general and specific standards plus supporting guidelines. In the foreword two points of special interest have already been quoted—in the definition at the beginning of Chapter 1 and in the opening of this chapter. A third important point of interest is the indication of the intent to modify the standards from time to time in response to the continuing change in business and society. The introduction in total appears to serve a dual purpose. On the one hand it is useful background for the standards and guidelines that follow. On the other hand some statements are anticipatory of the standards themselves. Although such anticipatory statements are not officially part of the standards, they do to a considerable extent take on the role of the standards, especially when they go beyond the coverage in the official standards and the supporting guidelines.

Individual standards and guidelines subject to varying interpretations

In discussing the above-mentioned standards and guidelines we need to recognize that they were developed by committee members based on their individual thinking and comments received from many other interested members, both inside and outside the internal auditing profession. In such a group of participants there was quite obviously a varying range of expertise, experience, and values. It was unavoidable therefore that the final language has some overlap, compromise, and incompleteness. As a result, individual standards and guidelines may be subject to varying interpretations. Our own approach will be to quote the text of each Standard, and then endeavor to develop an informed interpretation as to the particular issue involved. At the same time we will identify what we believe to be further needs and indicate our own views as to how those needs should be dealt with. Our overall objective will be to develop the best possible conceptual foundation for the more detailed treatment of modern internal auditing in the various chapters of this book.

THE INTRODUCTION

Opening Paragraph:[3] Definition

Internal auditing is an independent appraisal function established within an organization to examine and evaluate its activities as a service to the organization. The objective of internal auditing is to assist members of the organization in the effective discharge of their responsibilities. To this end, internal auditing furnishes them with analyses, appraisals, recommendations, counsel, and information concerning the activities reviewed.

The first sentence will be recognized as the definition of internal auditing quoted and interpreted at the beginning of Chapter 1. Reference should therefore be made to that discussion.

[3]Individual sections of the Standards will be quoted verbatim in this chapter. However, the complete Standards will be found in Appendix C.

The second sentence can be viewed as a further elaboration of the definition. In this connection there is the recognition of the fact that the way for the internal auditor to serve the organization is to *assist* the members. There is also the recognition of the fact that such assistance has as its end objective the *effective* discharge of their responsibilities by the members. We also believe that it should be more clearly stated that the objective should be for *maximum* effectiveness. This more fully recognizes that the organization should continuously seek the *best* possible utilization of its resources under the existing conditions. To help the organization achieve that "best possible" utilization of those resources is in our view the central core of the role of the modern internal auditor.

Objective is to assist members of organization in effective discharge of responsibilities

The third sentence is a further useful elaboration of the definition because it defines more specifically how the internal auditor actually renders the service previously mentioned. Quite clearly many ways exist in which information relative to the internal auditor's examination and evaluation of the activities of the organization is made available to the properly designated members of the organization. But these various ways do of course include the means thus identified.

Second Paragraph: Groups Served and How

The members of the organization assisted by internal auditing include those in management and the board of directors. Internal auditors owe a responsibility to both, providing them with information about the adequacy and effectiveness of the organization's system of internal control and the quality of performance. The information furnished to each may differ in format and detail, depending upon the requirements and requests of management and the board.

Internal auditing serves both management and board of directors

The paragraph is an introductory statement about issues with which we will deal in greater detail at various points. Especially important, however, is the clear statement that the organization served by the internal auditor includes both management *and* the board of directors.

Third Paragraph: The Charter as a Source of Authority

The internal auditing department is an integral part of the organization and functions under the policies established by management and the board. The statement of purpose, authority, and responsibility (charter) for the internal auditing department, approved by management and accepted by the board, should be consistent with these *Standards for the Professional Practice of Internal Auditing*.

Internal auditing authority based on charter

These sentences are also introductory statements about issues that will be dealt with in greater detail at a later point in the Standards and in our own analysis. However, a point made here, and not repeated later, is that the charter should be consistent with the Standards—a situation definitely desirable and necessary.

Fourth Paragraph: Content of the Charter

The charter should make clear the purposes of the internal auditing department, specify the unrestricted scope of its work, and declare that auditors are to have no authority or responsibility for the activities they audit.

This paragraph again covers an area to be dealt with at a later point. There is, however, some especially useful language, as follows:

1. "The charter should make clear the *purposes* of the internal auditing department." Presumably such "purposes" should be based on the language used in the opening paragraph.
2. To "specify the unrestricted scope of its work" parallels a later standard (110-.01-.4) but is especially definite and hence very useful.

Internal auditors have no authority or responsibility for activities audited.

3. The last requirement—that auditors have no authority or responsibility for the activities they audit—parallels a later standard (350-.01) but is an especially clear and useful statement covering the primary responsibility for the organizational activities reviewed by internal auditors.

Fifth Paragraph: Impact of Environment

Throughout the world internal auditing is performed in diverse environments and within organizations which vary in purpose, size, and structure. In addition, the laws and customs within various countries differ from one another. These differences may affect the practice of internal auditing in each environment. The implementation of these *Standards*, therefore, will be governed by the environment in which the internal auditing department carries out its assigned responsibilities. But compliance with the concepts enunciated by these *Standards* is essential before the responsibilities of internal auditors can be met.

These sentences are important because they recognize the wide range of situations and environmental influences encountered by individual internal auditing departments. Hence it is very properly concluded that the implementation of the Standards must also necessarily vary. But there is also the important conclusion that there must be compliance with the *concepts* enunciated in the Standards before the responsibilities of internal auditors are met. Just what that exactly means is not entirely clear. Presumably it is recognized that there will necessarily be differences in practice in differing organizational situations, but that these differences must not extend to concepts. But there is the question as to just what the concept is that must not be violated, and as to where that concept starts and stops as applied to practice. Quite clearly identifying that line will require considerable judgment.

Sixth Paragraph: Independence

"Independence," as used in these *Standards*, requires clarification. Internal auditors must be independent of the activities they audit. Such independence permits internal auditors to perform their work freely and objectively. Without independence, the desired results of internal auditing cannot be realized.

Independence permits internal auditors freedom and objectivity

These sentences are anticipatory of the further coverage in the standards pertaining to Independence—which we will discuss in more detail at that point. However, the last sentence is especially useful in linking independence to the realization of "the desired results of internal auditing."

Seventh Paragraph: Pertinent Developments

In setting these *Standards*, the following developments were considered:

Standards reflect important new developments

1. Boards of directors are being held increasingly accountable for the adequacy and effectiveness of their organizations' systems of internal control and quality of performance.
2. Members of management are demonstrating increased acceptance of internal auditing as a means of supplying objective analyses, appraisals, recommendations, counsel, and information on the organization's controls and performance.
3. External auditors are using the results of internal audits to complement their own work where the internal auditors have provided suitable evidence of independence and adequate, professional audit work.

These three important developments were discussed in Chapter 1. They are indeed very important and will be continuously recognized throughout this book.

Eighth Paragraph: Purposes of the Standards

In the light of such developments, the purposes of these *Standards* are to:

1. Impart an understanding of the role and responsibilities of internal auditing to all levels of management, boards of directors, public bodies, external auditors, and related professional organizations
2. Establish the basis for the guidance and measurement of internal auditing performance
3. Improve the practice of internal auditing

The *Standards* differentiate among the varied responsibilities of the organization, the internal auditing department, the director of internal auditing, and internal auditors.

Standards relate both to internal auditing department and to individuals

This listing of the purposes of the Standards parallels our own interpretations at the beginning of this chapter and differs only in the manner of classifying the several aspects involved. The last sentence is an especially useful recognition of the fact that the Standards have unique impacts on the several entities affected. It needs, however, to be also recognized that the "internal auditors" group covers a wide range of practitioners at various levels in an individual internal auditing department. As a consequence, the responsibilities of individual internal auditors will also vary greatly.

Ninth Paragraph: Format of the Standards

Standards consist of general standards, specific standards, and guidelines

The five general *Standards* are expressed in italicized statements in upper case. Following each of these general *Standards* are specific standards expressed in italicized statements in lower case. Accompanying each specific standard are guidelines describing suitable means of meeting that standard. The *Standards* encompass:

1. The independence of the internal auditing department from the activities audited and the objectivity of internal auditors
2. The proficiency of internal auditors and the professional care they should exercise
3. The scope of internal auditing work
4. The performance of internal auditing assignments
5. The management of the internal auditing department

This outline of the format to be followed is self-explanatory. Our own analysis and interpretations will follow that same outline.

Tenth Paragraph: Three Terms with Specific Meanings

The *Standards* and the accompanying guidelines employ three terms which have been given specific meanings. These are as follows:

Terms defined

The term *board* includes boards of directors, audit committees of such boards, heads of agencies or legislative bodies to whom internal auditors report, boards of governors or trustees of nonprofit organizations, and any other designated governing bodies of organizations.

The terms *director of internal auditing* and *director* identify the top position in an internal auditing department.

The term *internal auditing department* includes any unit of activity within an organization which performs internal auditing functions.

The explanations here are also self-explanatory. The extensions of the terms to cover both profit and nonprofit-type organization is also very important.

The designation "director of internal auditing" is somewhat cumbersome in repetitive use, while the single term "director" alone is sometimes not sufficiently precise. In actual practice the term "general auditor" is very frequently used to identify the head of the internal auditing departments, and in this book we will more often do the same.

The Introduction in Perspective

Introduction supports standards

As previously noted, the introduction to the more formal standards deserves careful consideration. In part it provides new concepts—as, for example, the definition of internal auditing in the opening paragraph, background in the form of developments considered and the purposes of the standards, basic definitions, and other substantive statements which in a very real sense overlap with and further extend the formal standards themselves. Whether or not the Introduction has the same authority as the formal standards can be subject to differing views. Professional Standards Bulletin 84-2 states in part that

> The foreword and introduction to the Standards were not considered to be part of the official authoritative material, that is, part of the Standards. However, they explain the role of the Standards, especially when they go beyond the coverage in the official Standards and the supporting guidelines.

The fact that substantive issues have to some extent been dealt with leads unavoidably to the conclusion that we need to give the Introduction serious attention.

SUMMARY OF STANDARDS

This summary, as shown in Exhibit 2.1, contains the general and specific standards. The standards are then repeated in the five following sections and serve as a foundation for the supporting guidelines. These standards and guidelines are discussed individually in the remainder of this chapter.

100   INDEPENDENCE

INTERNAL AUDITORS SHOULD BE INDEPENDENT OF THE ACTIVITIES THEY AUDIT

.01   Internal auditors are independent when they can carry out their work freely and objectively. Independence permits internal auditors to render the impartial and unbiased judgments essential to the proper conduct of audits. It is achieved through organizational status and objectivity.

In this summary standard the desired independence for the professional practice of internal auditing is defined as being independent of the activities audited. This general requirement is basic to all other specific standards and supporting guidelines.

The first sentence of the guideline (.01) parallels the second and third sentences in the sixth paragraph of the Introduction but more clearly links the existence of independence for internal auditors to whether they can carry out their work *freely and objectively*. The second sentence also parallels the last sentence of that same sixth paragraph of the Introduction but now more specifically establishes independence as essential to the proper conduct of audits. The third sentence identifies the two means by which independence is achieved—organizational status and objectivity.

EXHIBIT 2.1. Summary of Standards.

SUMMARY OF GENERAL AND SPECIFIC STANDARDS
FOR THE PROFESSIONAL PRACTICE OF INTERNAL AUDITING

100   **INDEPENDENCE** — *INTERNAL AUDITORS SHOULD BE INDEPENDENT OF THE ACTIVITIES THEY AUDIT.*

     110   **Organizational Status** — *The organizational status of the internal auditing department should be sufficient to permit the accomplishment of its audit responsibilities.*

     120   **Objectivity** — *Internal auditors should be objective in performing audits.*

200   **PROFESSIONAL PROFICIENCY** — *INTERNAL AUDITS SHOULD BE PERFORMED WITH PROFICIENCY AND DUE PROFESSIONAL CARE.*

     The Internal Auditing Department

     210   **Staffing** — *The internal auditing department should provide assurance that the technical proficiency and educational background of internal auditors are appropriate for the audits to be performed.*

     220   **Knowledge, Skills, and Disciplines** — *The internal auditing department should possess or should obtain the knowledge, skills, and disciplines needed to carry out its audit responsibilities.*

     230   **Supervision** — *The internal auditing department should provide assurance that internal audits are properly supervised.*

     The Internal Auditor

     240   **Compliance with Standards of Conduct** — *Internal auditors should comply with professional standards of conduct.*

     250   **Knowledge, Skills, and Disciplines** — *Internal auditors should possess the knowledge, skills, and disciplines essential to the performance of internal audits.*

     260   **Human Relations and Communications** — *Internal auditors should be skilled in dealing with people and in communicating effectively.*

     270   **Continuing Education** — *Internal auditors should maintain their technical competence through continuing education.*

     280   **Due Professional Care** — *Internal auditors should exercise due professional care in performing internal audits.*

300   **SCOPE OF WORK** — *THE SCOPE OF THE INTERNAL AUDIT SHOULD ENCOMPASS THE EXAMINATION AND EVALUATION OF THE ADEQUACY AND EFFECTIVENESS OF THE ORGANIZATION'S SYSTEM OF INTERNAL CONTROL AND THE QUALITY OF PERFORMANCE IN CARRYING OUT ASSIGNED RESPONSIBILITIES.*

     310   **Reliability and Integrity of Information** — *Internal auditors should review the reliability and integrity of financial and operating information and the means used to identify, measure, classify, and report such information.*

3

EXHIBIT 2.1 *(Continued)*

320 **Compliance with Policies, Plans, Procedures, Laws, and Regulations** — *Internal auditors should review the systems established to ensure compliance with those policies, plans, procedures, laws, and regulations which could have a significant impact on operations and reports and should determine whether the organization is in compliance.*

330 **Safeguarding of Assets** — *Internal auditors should review the means of safeguarding assets and, as appropriate, verify the existence of such assets.*

340 **Economical and Efficient Use of Resources** — *Internal auditors should appraise the economy and efficiency with which resources are employed.*

350 **Accomplishment of Established Objectives and Goals for Operations or Programs** — *Internal auditors should review operations or programs to ascertain whether results are consistent with established objectives and goals and whether the operations or programs are being carried out as planned.*

400 **PERFORMANCE OF AUDIT WORK** — *AUDIT WORK SHOULD INCLUDE PLANNING THE AUDIT, EXAMINING AND EVALUATING INFORMATION, COMMUNICATING RESULTS, AND FOLLOWING UP.*

410 **Planning the Audit** — *Internal auditors should plan each audit.*

420 **Examining and Evaluating Information** — *Internal auditors should collect, analyze, interpret, and document information to support audit results.*

430 **Communicating Results** — *Internal auditors should report the results of their audit work.*

440 **Following Up** — *Internal auditors should follow up to ascertain that appropriate action is taken on reported audit findings.*

500 **MANAGEMENT OF THE INTERNAL AUDITING DEPARTMENT** — *THE DIRECTOR OF INTERNAL AUDITING SHOULD PROPERLY MANAGE THE INTERNAL AUDITING DEPARTMENT.*

510 **Purpose, Authority, and Responsibility** — *The director of internal auditing should have a statement of purpose, authority, and responsibility for the internal auditing department.*

520 **Planning** — *The director of internal auditing should establish plans to carry out the responsibilities of the internal auditing department.*

530 **Policies and Procedures** — *The director of internal auditing should provide written policies and procedures to guide the audit staff.*

540 **Personnel Management and Development** — *The director of internal auditing should establish a program for selecting and developing the human resources of the internal auditing department.*

550 **External Auditors** — *The director of internal auditing should coordinate internal and external audit efforts.*

560 **Quality Assurance** — *The director of internal auditing should establish and maintain a quality assurance program to evaluate the operations of the internal auditing department.*

4

110   Organizational Status

The organizational status of the internal auditing department should be sufficient to permit the accomplishment of its audit responsibilities.

.01   Internal auditors should have the support of management and of the board of directors so that they can gain the cooperation of auditees and perform their work free from interference.

.1   The director of the internal auditing department should be responsible to an individual in the organization with sufficient authority to promote independence and to ensure broad audit coverage, adequate consideration of audit reports, and appropriate action on audit recommendations.

.2   The director should have direct communication with the board. Regular communication with the board helps assure independence and provides a means for the board and the director to keep each other informed on matters of mutual interest.

.3   Independence is enhanced when the board concurs in the appointment or removal of the director of the internal auditing department.

.4   The purpose, authority, and responsibility of the internal auditing department should be defined in a formal written document (charter). The director should seek approval of the charter by management as well as acceptance by the board. The charter should (a) establish the department's position within the organization; (b) authorize access to records, personnel, and physical properties relevant to the performance of audits; and (c) define the scope of internal auditing activities.

.5   The director of internal auditing should submit annually to management for approval and to the board for its information a summary of the department's audit work schedule, staffing plan, and financial budget. The director should also submit all significant interim changes for approval and information. Audit work schedules, staffing plans, and financial budgets should inform management and the board of the scope of internal auditing work and of any limitations placed on that scope.

.6   The director of internal auditing should submit activity reports to management and to the board annually or more frequently as necessary. Activity reports should highlight significant audit findings and recommendations and should inform management and the board of any significant deviations from approved audit work schedules, staffing plans, and financial budgets, and the reasons for them.

Internal auditor's effectiveness dependent on proper organizational status

The specific standard deals with the first of the two types of requirements —organizational status. It provides the general test that the organizational status "should be sufficient to permit the accomplishment of its audit responsibilities." This presumably means sufficient to permit accomplishment of proper audit objectives and to discharge the related responsibilities assigned by appropriate organizational authority.

The guideline (.01) identifies the support of management and the board of directors as a necessary basis for gaining the cooperation of auditees and performing internal auditing work free from interference. The six supporting subguidelines then interpret that more general guideline.

In the first paragraph (.1) we have a listing of the criteria by which we evaluate the adequacy of the authority of the individual to whom the director of internal auditing reports. The first of these deals with the individual's capability in promoting independence. The criterion is presumably that the director reports to someone who is sufficiently powerful to assure such backing for the director of internal auditing as may be necessary.

In the second paragraph (.2) the requirement of "direct" communication of the director of the internal auditing department with the board is first established. Coupled then with the second sentence there is the further indirect requirement that the communication also be *regular*. The rationale —presumably intended to apply to both of those requirements—is that this helps assure independence and provides a means of keeping both parties informed as to matters of mutual interest. Both the requirements and the underlying rationale are quite clearly sound.

Guidelines provide criteria for determining organizational status adequacy

In the next paragraph (.3) the point is made that when the board concurs in the appointment or removal of the director there is an enhancement of independence for the director. The standard thus clearly encourages the concurrence practice. Also the term "concurs" is used instead of "approves." This treatment appears to recognize the related fact that the primary reporting responsibility is more likely to be to management rather than to the board. The requirement of concurrence is very important because it gives the board an opportunity to question the appointment or removal action and thus have a better basis for evaluating the judgment of the management pertaining to the action. There is the further advantage that the board is alerted to the need to establish a proper working relationship with a new director of internal auditing. Thus on balance it is believed that the arrangement for concurrence is extremely important and should definitely be *required* practice.

The next recognized support action (.4) covers the very important need that the total role of the internal auditing department be defined in a formal written document (the charter). It parallels, but importantly extends, the coverage in the fourth paragraph of the Introduction. That charter should be *approved* by management and *accepted* by the board. It is also important what level of management does the approving. We believe that the approving officer should be the chief executive officer, so that all company officers are then clearly bound by the terms of that charter. The term "acceptance" used to define the board's involvement again suggests much the same logic as was previously discussed for the "concurrence" action. However, because the charter covers responsibilities to both management and the audit committee, we believe the approvals by both parties should be equally important. In the final sentence we then have some of the requirements for the content of the charter.

The next part (.5) concerns the range of the reporting of the director of internal auditing. The language "to management for approval and to the board for its information" again suggests a primary reporting responsibility to management. The final sentence in this part covers the very important need of keeping both management and the board properly informed as to the activities of the department, although presumably the information provided to the audit committee would be in less detail. This provides needed understanding and an opportunity to raise questions and shape the program to cover the needs of all recipients. The inclusion in this sentence, however, of possible "limitations" is a much more complex matter. Actually the coverage in the charter—as discussed in .4 above and in the Introduction—should have properly established the freedom from limitations. If there is a denial of that freedom later by members of management, it would usually lead to some kind of a confrontation. Then if any problems cannot be effectively dealt with, the audit committee would need to become involved.

The final paragraph (.06) also deals with current reporting to management and the board—in this case audit results and conformance to established plans. Although the standard again does not say whether the volume and detail of such reports should vary as between management and the board, we would reasonably expect that the reporting to the board would be in more summary form. These matters are dealt with later in the chapter dealing with the reporting.

Broader Aspects of Support

The six paragraphs just discussed are all presumably directed to showing the manner in which management and the board of directors provide sufficient support to the internal auditing department. It needs to be recognized, however, that support can also be provided in other ways. These other ways go beyond official organizational status, as shown in organization charts, charters, reports, and other formal stipulations. We refer here to the extent to which higher-level management and the board demonstrate their interest in internal auditing activities and the manner in which they interpret the various formal arrangements. It is a fact of life that individuals at all levels in the organization directly or indirectly continue to test whether formally stated arrangements have real higher-level support, and hence whether they should be taken seriously. It is therefore necessary that higher-level management and the board are continuously alert to this danger and that they continuously reaffirm their support for the internal auditing department. This support is especially critical when—as so often happens—a particular high-level officer resists evaluation by internal auditors and tries to convince higher-level management that internal auditing activitiies are having a detrimental impact on the achievement of his own organizational objectives. Such problems need to be promptly resolved through depth review by still-higher-level management, so that obstacles to effective internal auditing are properly eliminated.

High level management support needed for internal auditor

What Is Sufficient Authority to Assure Effective Internal Auditing?

In the standards quoted above it is stated that the director of the internal auditing department should be responsible to an individual in the organization with sufficient authority to assure effective internal auditing. This wording asserts a proper principle but it does not specify the organizational status of that individual. Some further discussion of this problem therefore is appropriate.

A good starting point is to review the results of several surveys of actual practice reported in *Research Report 24*, "Evaluating Internal/External Audit Services and Relationships," of The Institute of Internal Auditors (see Exhibit 2.2)[4]. These comparisons show very clearly the continuing trend toward a higher-level reporting responsibility for the internal auditing department. However, the greater number still report to a vice president. Typically, in actual practice, that vice-president is the chief financial officer.

Opinions relative to the merits of alternative reporting arrangements will vary as between the different parties of interest and particular individuals. On the one hand there is the very logical view that the higher the reporting authority, the greater the independence of the internal auditor as a basis for effective internal auditing. On the other hand, reporting to the higher level may deprive the internal auditor of important day-to-day support.

Pros and cons exist for alternative reporting responsibilities

EXHIBIT 2.2. Comparing Reporting Responsibilities with Previous Studies[a]

| | Year-End Percentages | | | | | |
	1957[b]	1968[c]	1975[d]	This Study[e]	1979[f]	1983
Board of directors	7	6	7	8	10	24
President	7	10	11	18	13	17
Vice president	16	31	32	41	46	30
Controller	42	32	20	23	11	11
Other	28	21	30	10	20	9

[a]The classifications were regrouped to facilitate comparisons.
[b]The Institute of Internal Auditors, Inc., *1957 Survey of Internal Auditing* (New York: The Institute of Internal Auditors, Inc., 1958), p. 17.
[c]The Institute of Internal Auditors, Inc., *1968 Survey of Internal Auditing* (New York: The Institute of Internal Auditors, Inc., 1969), p. 13.
[d]The Institute of Internal Auditors, Inc., *1975 Survey of Internal Auditing* (Altamonte Springs, Fla.: The Institute of Internal Auditors, Inc., 1976), p. 23.
[e]Survey questionnaire data used in this research effort was collected in 1977.
[f]The Institute of Internal Auditors, Inc., *1979 Survey of Internal Auditing* (Altamonte Springs, Fla.: The Institute of Internal Auditors, Inc., 1980), p. 20.
Source: The Institute of Internal Auditors, *Research Report 24* (Altamonte Springs, Fla.: The Institute of Internal Auditors, Inc., 1980), Table 21, p. 31.

[4]This exhibit has been extended to include 1983 data— see The Institute of Internal Auditors, Inc., *1983 Survey of Internal Auditing* (Altamonte Springs, Fla.: The Institute of Internal Auditors, Inc., 1984) p. 17.

Moreover, the merits are quite different in companies of different size and maturity. Because of the pressure of the Foreign Corrupt Practices Act and other considerations we can foresee in most organizations a vice-president status for the director of the internal auditing department and a primary reporting responsibility to the chief executive officer, but this does not mean that a reporting to a chief financial officer needs to be ruled out. Additionally there must always be defined secondary responsibilities to the board of directors. The typical and future versions of the reporting responsibility are shown in Exhibits 2.3 and 2.4, respectively.

120   Objectivity

Internal auditors should be objective in performing audits.

.01   Objectivity is an independent mental attitude which internal auditors should maintain in performing audits. Internal auditors are not to subordinate their judgment on audit matters to that of others.

.02   Objectivity requires internal auditors to perform audits in such a manner that they have an honest belief in their work product and that no significant quality compromises are made. Internal auditors are not to be placed in situations in which they feel unable to make objective professional judgments.

Guidelines for objectivity

.1   Staff assignments should be made so that potential and actual conflicts of interest and bias are avoided. The director should periodically

EXHIBIT 2.3   Typical Organizational Placement of Internal Auditing Department.

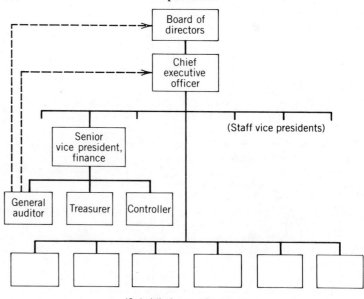

(Subsidiaries and Divisions)

**EXHIBIT 2.4. Future Organizational Placement for the
Internal Auditing Department.**

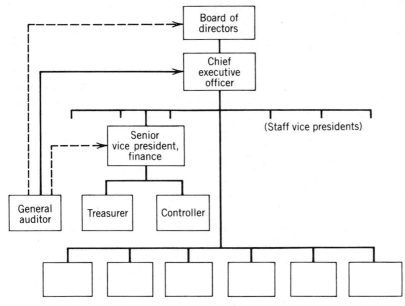

(Subsidiaries and Divisions)

obtain from the audit staff information concerning potential conflicts
of interest and bias.

.2   Internal auditors should report to the director any situations in which
a conflict of interest or bias is present or may reasonably be inferred.
The director should then reassign such auditors.

.3   Staff assignments of internal auditors should be rotated periodically
whenever it is practicable to do so.

.4   Internal auditors should not assume operating responsibilities. But if
on occasion management directs internal auditors to perform nonaudit
work, it should be understood that they are not functioning as internal
auditors. Moreover, objectivity is presumed to be impaired when
internal auditors audit any activity for which they had authority or
responsibility. This impairment should be considered when reporting
audit results.

.5   Persons transferred to or temporarily engaged by the internal auditing
department should not be assigned to audit those activities they previously performed until a reasonable period of time has elapsed. Such
assignments are presumed to impair objectivity and should be considered when supervising the audit work and reporting audit results.

.6   The results of internal auditing work should be reviewed before the
related audit report is released to provide reasonable assurance that
the work was performed objectively.

.03 The internal auditor's objectivity is not adversely affected when the auditor recommends standards of control for systems or reviews procedures before they are implemented. Designing, installing, and operating systems are not audit functions. Also, the drafting of procedures for systems is not an audit function. Performing such activities is presumed to impair audit objectivity.

This specific standard establishes the requirement that internal auditors "should be objective in performing audits." Although recognizing the need for objectivity in performing audits, we believe that the quality of objectivity is also important in every other phase of the internal auditor's activities.

In the first sentence of the first guideline (.01) the truth is recognized that there must be an independent mental attitude on the part of the internal auditors. This independent mental attitude is something that is directly up to the individual internal auditor, irrespective of organizational status. The second sentence then goes on to stipulate that the internal auditor, having reached conclusions through an independent mental attitude, must not compromise by yielding to the pressures of other affected parties. These pressures can come from people at all levels who either have strong contrary views about the judgment of the internal auditor, or who see possible embarrassment from the visibility that will result from the internal auditor's findings and conclusions. This does not mean that the internal auditor will not consider these other views. But it does mean that the internal auditor must do what he thinks is necessary and proper.

Requirements for objectivity   The special focus of guideline (.02) is on the way internal auditors carry out their various audit assignments. It stipulates that the audit must be made in a manner that makes possible honest belief in the work product on the part of the internal auditor. Hence the internal auditor must avoid shortcuts and compromises that block or dilute the adequate basis needed for the sought-after "honest belief." In the second sentence the related important point is then made that internal auditors should avoid being placed in situations where objective professional judgments are not possible. Six lower-level guidelines then identify specific requirements bearing on objective professional judgments.

The first of these requirements (.1) is that the staff assignments should be made in such a way that conflicts of interest and/or bias are avoided. It might well be that the particular internal auditor has enough character and objectivity that conflict of interest or bias would not be any problem. However, this is not enough. In addition all staff assignments should be avoided where the possibility *could* exist that conflicts of interest or bias might affect audit judgments. In the second sentence the director is also directly charged with the responsibility of obtaining information about existing conflicts or potential bias on the part of individual staff members. Such information can then be given appropriate consideration when actual staff assignments are made.

In the first sentence of the second requirement (.2) the same problem is then attacked via the internal auditor himself. Here the internal auditor is specifically charged with the responsibility to take the initiative and report any situation involving either actual or reasonably inferable conflict of interest or bias. In the second sentence the director of internal auditing is directed in such a situation to reassign that internal auditor. Thus there is the joint responsibility of the two individuals to prevent the existence of conflict or bias.

In the third requirement (.3) the director is charged with the further responsibility of periodically rotating the staff assignments of internal auditors. However, it is recognized indirectly that factors may exist which limit the practicability of such rotation. It is generally believed that the rotation of audit assignments is beneficial solely on the ground of providing fresh and often more effective approaches to particular audit assignments. However, the special significance in achieving objectivity is that a continuation of assignment to the same audit task may result in personal relationships that may somehow dilute the independence and related objectivity of the particular internal auditor. Auditees very often prefer the relative comfort of dealing with the same internal auditor, and in some cases will exert pressure for the continuation of that arrangement. However, on balance, rotation appears to be a very desirable practice in the total interest of the organization.

The fourth requirement (.4) covers a number of different important aspects of the total effort to generate and sustain needed objectivity. In the first sentence there is the basic truth that internal auditors should not assume operating responsibilities. The reasons for this, as previously discussed in Chapter 1, are that the internal auditor then becomes a line individual and no longer functions as an independent internal auditor. In the second sentence, however, the possibility very realistically is recognized that the internal auditor may be *directed* by proper organizational authority to take on a particular operating responsibility. However, it is soundly recognized that all interested persons should understand that the internal auditor is then not functioning as an internal auditor. Under those conditions, therefore, the director of the internal auditing department should also assign other staff personnel to provide the regular internal auditing service. All of the foregoing should of course be properly explained to management. The third sentence is concerned with a related but somewhat different problem. The threat to objectivity in this instance arises when an auditor goes back as an internal auditor to a particular organizational component for which he previously had authority or responsibility. Here there is the very real possibility that the internal auditor will be biased, based on his prior involvement. The final sentence then seems to presume that such an audit assignment has in fact been made and then goes on to caution the internal auditor to be especially careful of the possibility of loss of objectivity when he is developing his report.

The fifth requirement (.5) builds on the threat to objectivity just discussed

Further guides for objectivity

under (.4) and states that audit assignments covering activities previously performed should not be made until after a reasonable time has elapsed. Whether the activity involves previously held responsibilities or operational participation, the key factor is of course the amount of intervening time that has elapsed. A too strict interpretation here can unduly limit the availability of the particular auditor for various audit assignments. Moreover, there can also be some very real benefits in using such individuals because of their better understanding of the activity now being covered as an audit assignment. Nevertheless, the last sentence quite properly sounds the warning to the internal auditor to be aware of the potential danger of loss of objectivity, and to do all possible to guard against loss of objectivity.

The final requirement in this group (.6) is that the results of internal auditing work need to be reviewed before the release of the audit report. This entire problem is discussed in more detail in the section of the Standards pertaining to the performance and supervision of audit work.

Guideline (.03) has to do with a special problem that exists when major systems or procedures are developed in the organization and when the internal auditor needs to avoid any involvement that would undermine his independence when he later makes a regular internal audit of the completed project. The problem is that once a typical system or major procedure is operative it usually becomes very costly—in terms of time, cost, and impact upon the organization—to correct deficiencies identified by the internal auditor in his later internal audit of that system or procedure. It makes far greater sense in terms of total company welfare for the internal auditor to make available his expertise regarding controls, so that his counsel can be utilized in the design of that system or procedure. This guideline therefore recognizes the propriety of internal auditors providing such counsel as pertaining to *standards of control*. At the same time, however, internal auditors are cautioned not to get involved in designing, installing, operating those systems, or in drafting procedures—thus impairing their objectivity. Moreover, such involvement is time consuming and could be such a drain on the internal auditing resources that the regular internal auditing function would suffer. However, what is difficult is how and where the internal auditor draws the line in interfacing with the individuals directly charged with the development of the various policies and procedures. Here too, good sense and sound judgment are essential.

Internal auditors can provide counsel during systems design

Objectivity in Perspective

There is general agreement as to the desirability of objectivity by internal auditors and the utilization of all means practicable to protect such objectivity. To a considerable extent the means of achieving needed objectivity is in the hands of internal auditors themselves. In other instances, however, the arrangements that assure needed objectivity are in the hands of other individuals and groups in the organization. What is important in the latter situations is that internal auditors utilize every possible means to inform and guide the other parties in the organization about their impact on objectivity. By so doing, internal auditors can best assure the needed setting for achieving the proper levels of objectivity. In the last analysis objectivity is a state of mind on the part of the internal auditor, and the ability to develop that needed state of mind is one of the greatest challenges to the truly professional internal auditor.

Importance of continuing effort by each internal auditor

Independence in Perspective

We have seen how independence is an essential basis for effective modern internal auditing. We have seen also that independence is achieved both by the conditions imposed upon the internal auditing department by the organization and through the objectivity of the individual internal auditors. Therefore, a necessary continuing effort must be made to maintain and improve both kinds of the basic conditions that affect the achievement of the needed independence. We must, however, be fully aware of the truth that complete independence can never be achieved. This is true because there are always conditions that to some extent limit independence. For example, a board of directors is subject to the constraints of its accountability to government and society. A chief executive officer has the same constraints plus the constraint of the board itself. The outside public accountant can never fully forget that the client pays his fees and that these fees are necessary to maintain a viable public accounting firm. The internal auditor reports to someone in the organization and is dependent on that organization to a major extent for his own livelihood. It is also always something of a problem to resist pressures from organizational colleagues with whom the internal auditor wishes to maintain good working relationships. What all this means is that no person is an island unto himself and that independence is always a relative term—that is greater or less, but never absolute. This in no sense depreciates the value of independence or detracts from the various efforts to upgrade the extent and quality of the desired independence. In the case of internal auditors our continuing effort must always be to strengthen the needed independence even though there are and always will be substantive limitations to that independence. The internal auditor himself does this first, by doing effective work and having the courage to stand up for his convictions, and second, by exerting every effort practicable to induce and obtain the organizational arrangements that will best assure his independence. In both cases the worth of the effort lies in the contribution of that greater independence to providing effective internal auditing services, which can then make for maximum organizational welfare.

The many components of independence

200   PROFESSIONAL PROFICIENCY

INTERNAL AUDITS SHOULD BE PERFORMED WITH PROFICIENCY AND DUE PROFESSIONAL CARE

.01 Professional proficiency is the responsibility of the internal auditing department and each internal auditor. The department should assign to each audit those persons who collectively possess the necessary knowledge, skills, and disciplines to conduct the audit properly.

The second section of the Standards deals with the very necessary professional proficiency of the practice of internal auditing. The general standard properly establishes the requirement that proficiency and due professional care are essential qualities in the performance of internal audits.

In the first sentence of the supporting guideline (.01) professional proficiency is made the responsibility of *both* the internal auditing department and each internal auditor. This dual assignment is important because the department and the individual each has its own roles to play and each has differing opportunities to further professional proficiency. In the second sentence there is a specific supporting requirement pertaining to the role of the internal auditing department—to assign persons to each audit who possess the necessary knowledge, skills, and disciplines to conduct the audit properly. The further component requirements are covered in the specific standards and their supporting guidelines.

The Internal Auditing Department

210   Staffing

The internal auditing department should provide assurance that the technical proficiency and educational background of internal auditors are appropriate for the audits to be performed.

.01   The director of internal auditing should establish suitable criteria of education and experience for filling internal auditing positions, giving due consideration to scope of work and level of responsibility.

.02   Reasonable assurance should be obtained as to each prospective auditor's qualifications and proficiency.

This subsection deals in more detail with the responsibilities attributable to the internal auditing department—the first of which pertains to staffing. In the specific standard those overall responsibilities are described as providing assurance that internal auditors have the technical proficiency and educational background appropriate for audits performed. This is the normal managerial responsibility that staff personnel assigned to individual audits are capable of doing the required job.

Guidelines for achieving professional proficiency

In the supporting guidelines two ways to satisfy the above-mentioned responsibility are indicated. The first (.01) pertains to the director of the internal auditing department. This action establishes the criteria needed for filling the various staff positions presumably after giving consideration to the scope of work and level of responsibilities pertaining to those positions. The second way (.02) comes at the problem through procedures that identify the capabilities of individual applicants. These two ways together provide needed assurance that individual audit assignments will be carried out by properly qualified internal auditors.

We must recognize the fact that the nature and scope of particular audits carried on are always changing and that staff personnel previously having adequate qualifications may no longer satisfy the new needs. Hence the effort to assure the proper fit is never ending. But the internal auditing department must, according to the previously mentioned specific standard, provide assurance that the qualifications are appropriate for the audits to be performed. What "provide assurance" actually means is not entirely clear, but in addition to the actions just discussed it is reasonable to conclude that there should be adequate documentation covering both prescribed actions in .01 and .02 and the manner in which the matching is actually made in terms of individual capabilities and work assignments.

220   Knowledge, Skills, and Disciplines

The internal auditing department should possess or should obtain the knowledge, skills, and disciplines needed to carry out its audit responsibililies.

.01   The internal auditing staff should collectively possess the knowledge and skills essential to the practice of the profession within the organization. These attributes include proficiency in applying internal auditing standards, procedures, and techniques.

.02   The internal auditing department should have employees or use consultants who are qualified in such disciplines as accounting, economics, finance, statistics, electronic data processing, engineering, taxation, and law as needed to meet audit responsibilities. Each member of the department, however, need not be qualified in all of these disciplines.

The second type of responsibility of the internal auditing department deals with knowledge, skills, and disciplines. The related specific standard establishes the requirement that the department should possess *or obtain* staff personnel with those particular capabilities as necessary to carry out its audit responsibilities. In the first interpretative guideline (.01) the focus is on knowledge and skills. One further clarification is, however, the use of the word "collectively"—which presumably means that the particular needed knowledge or skill is *somewhere* among the staff members. The second qualification is that the knowledge and skills include proficiency in *applying* internal audit standards, procedures, and techniques—thus stressing the importance of effective managerial implementation.

Guidelines for knowledge, skills and disciplines

In the second interpretative guideline (.02) the focus is on the kinds of disciplines required. The examples cited include accounting, economics, finance, statistics, electronic data processing, engineering, taxation, and law; but presumably the listing is intended to be open-ended and must be reappraised in the light of the particular audit need. A further interpretation here is that consultants may be used if the needed capabilities are not available from staff personnel actually in the department. And a second related interpretation is that any one member does not need to be qualified in *all* the relevant disciplines.

230   Supervision

The internal auditing department should provide assurance that internal audits are properly supervised.

.01   The director of internal auditing is responsible for providing appropriate audit supervision. Supervision is a continuing process, beginning with planning and ending with the conclusion of the audit assignment.

.02   Supervision includes:

.1   Providing suitable instructions to subordinates at the outset of the audit and approving the audit program

.2   Seeing that the approved audit program is carried out unless deviations are both justified and authorized

.3   Determining that audit working papers adequately support the audit findings, conclusions, and reports

.4   Making sure that audit reports are accurate, objective, clear, concise, constructive, and timely

.5   Determining that audit objectives are being met

.03   Appropriate evidence of supervision should be documented and retained.

.04   The extent of supervision required will depend on the proficiency of the internal auditors and the difficulty of the audit assignment.

.05   All internal auditing assignments, whether performed by or for the internal auditing department, remain the responsiblity of its director.

Guidelines for supervision   This third type of responsibility of the internal auditing department deals with supervision. The related specific standard covers the responsibility for the proper supervision of internal audits. Again also there is the requirement to provide assurance—presumably including adequate documentation. In the first supporting guideline (.01) the same requirement for proper supervision is repeated. The second sentence, however, is an important clarification of the total span of the supervising responsibility—that is, from the initial planning to the conclusion of the audit assignment. We should also recognize the need for prior planning by the director himself.

In the second guideline (.02) five aspects of the supervisory process are identified. It is interesting to note that now there is no specific identification of the planning phase, even though planning personnel would also need to be supervised.

The third guideline (.03) very properly emphasizes the need for adequate documentation, and for the retention of that documentation, to provide evidence of proper supervision.

The fourth guideline (.04) is a useful recognition of the truth that the need for supervision is directly dependent on two key variables: (1) the proficiency of the particular audit personnel involved in varying audit assignments and (2) the difficulty of the particular assignments. Relevant also would be the significance of the activity being reviewed in terms of impact on organizational welfare.

The fifth and final guideline is a useful recognition of the truth that the individual at the head of any group can never escape ultimate responsiblity, irrespective of delegations to subordinates. This ultimate responsibility also extends properly to work which that group head may get done by obtaining audit assistance from persons outside his own departmental staff.

The Internal Auditor

240   Compliance with Standards of Conduct

Internal auditors should comply with professional standards of conduct.

.01   The *Code of Ethics* of The Institute of Internal Auditors sets forth standards of conduct and provides a basis for enforcement among its members. The *Code* calls for high standards of honesty, objectivity, diligence, and loyalty to which internal auditors should conform.

This next subsection deals with the responsibilities for professional proficiency that are attributable to the internal auditor as an individual staff person. Attention is also directed to the first type of responsibility—that of compliance with professional standards of conduct.

The supporting guideline (.01) is self-explanatory in its reference to the Code of Ethics of The Institute[5] as the standards of conduct to which the internal auditor is required to conform.

250   Knowledge, Skills, and Disciplines

Internal auditors should possess the knowledge, skills, and disciplines essential to the performance of internal audits.

.01   Each internal auditor should possess certain knowledge and skills as follows:

.1   Proficiency in applying internal auditing standards, procedures, and techniques is required in performing internal audits. Proficiency means the ability to apply knowledge to situations likely to be encountered and to deal with them without extensive recourse to technical research and assistance.

.2   Proficiency in accounting principles and techniques is required of auditors who work extensively with financial records and reports.

.3   An understanding of management principles is required to recognize and evaluate the materiality and significance of deviations from good business practice. An understanding means the ability to apply broad knowledge to situations likely to be encountered, to recognize significant deviations, and to be able to carry out the research necessary to arrive at reasonable solutions.

.4   An appreciation is required of the fundamentals of such subjects as accounting, economics, commercial law, taxation, finance, quantitative methods, and computerized information systems. An appreciation means the ability to recognize the existence of problems or potential

Guidelines for needed knowledge, skills and disciplines for individual internal auditor

---

[5]See Appendix B.

problems and to determine the further research to be undertaken or the assistance to be obtained.

The specific standard (250) reasserts the previously stipulated matching of professional efficiency (knowledge, skills, and disciplines) with audit assignment needs, but now focuses on the responsibilities in that respect of the *individual* internal auditor. The supporting guideline then outlines the specific dimensions of the needed proficiency in terms of knowledge and skills.

In the first specification (.1) there is the requirement that there be proficiency in applying internal auditing standards, procedures, and techniques. That proficiency is then interpreted as the ability to apply that knowledge to the individual audit situation likely to be encountered and to deal with those situations without extensive technical research and assistance. Needed also is the further ability to recognize just *when* further technical research and assistance may be needed.

The second specification (.2) covers the requirement for proficiency in accounting principles and techniques when the internal auditor works extensively with financial records and reports. There is the related truth, however, that all internal auditing work at some point usually relates to financial records and reports. It follows therefore that all internal auditors should have at least some understanding of that discipline.

In the third specification (.3) there is a major recognition of the truth that internal auditors need to understand management theory and to know how that theory applies to varying operational situations. Quite clearly that understanding is a basic foundation for carrying out internal auditing assignments in a manner that best contributes to management needs. In Chapter 3 we deal in greater depth with that type of knowledge.

Finally, in the fourth specification (.4) the broad knowledge requirements of 220.02 are outlined in terms of the individual internal auditor.[6] It also follows that each internal auditor need not have expertise in all categories. However, what is important is again the level of expertise in each, which enables the internal auditor to know when actual or potential problems may exist in the various areas. Put in other words, it is the capability to know when the point is reached when further information or special assistance is needed.

260 Human Relations and Communications

Internal auditors should be skilled in dealing with people and in communicating effectively.

Guidelines for working with people

.01 Internal auditors should understand human relations and maintain satisfactory relationships with auditees.

.02 Internal auditors should be skilled in oral and written communications so that they can clearly and effectively convey such matters as audit objectives, evaluations, conclusions, and recommendations.

[6]The areas specified here are similar but vary slightly from those specified for the internal auditing department, but again will depend on the specific work assignments.

In this specific standard the necessity for understanding people and communicating effectively is properly recognized. Clearly this need exists for the internal auditor in *all* of his audit activities.

The first guideline (.01) addresses itself to the first of these two areas by the requirement that internal auditors should understand human relations and maintain satisfactory relationships with auditees. With respect to the first part of the requirement—understanding human relations—it needs to be recognized that this is something exceedingly complex and never fully achieved. In Chapter 7 we deal with this problem in greater depth.

The reference to maintaining satisfactory relations with auditees is also sound but again should also include *all* other persons with whom the internal auditor has contact during his internal audit activities. The need for understanding human relations also applies to all of those contacts.

The second guideline (.02) now focuses on the importance of being skilled in both oral and written communications. The need for this expertise also applies to *all* individuals and groups which are either involved in or affected by the total internal audit effort. We also deal in greater depth with this problem in Chapter 7. There are also particular situations when the internal auditor will need to seek special assistance from communications specialists.

270   Continuing Education

Internal auditors should maintain their technical competence through continuing education.

.01   Internal auditors are responsible for continuing their education in order to maintain their proficiency. They should keep informed about improvements and current developments in internal auditing standards, procedures, and techniques. Continuing education may be obtained through membership and participation in professional societies; attendance of conferences, seminars, college courses, and in-house training programs; and participation in research projects.

Need for continuing education for internal auditors

This specific standard (270) clearly states the need to maintain technical competence through continuing education. In our dynamic and changing world it is self-evident that this is the only way for the professional internal auditor to avoid becoming obsolete and ineffective.

The supporting guideline (.01) in its first sentence reaffirms the need for continuing education but now for "proficiency"— a somewhat broader term than the previously used "technical competence" and one that we believe is more appropriate. The second sentence then focuses on the content of the continuing education. Again the question can be properly raised as to whether continuing education should not also extend to many nontechnical but related areas in terms of impact on the effectiveness of internal auditors. In the final sentence the various means are identified by which the continuing education can be obtained. Presumably, other ways would also be acceptable if proper relevance was established.

280   **Due Professional Care**

Internal Auditors should exercise due professional care in performing internal audits.

Guidelines for due professional care

.01   Due professional care calls for the application of the care and skill expected of a reasonably prudent and competent internal auditor in the same or similar circumstances. Professional care should, therefore, be appropriate to the complexities of the audit being performed. In exercising due professional care, internal auditors should be alert to the possibility of intentional wrongdoing, errors and omissions, inefficiency, waste, ineffectiveness, and conflicts of interest. They should also be alert to those conditions and activities where irregularities are most likely to occur. In addition, they should identify inadequate controls and recommend improvements to promote compliance with acceptable procedures and practices.

.02   Due care implies reasonable care and competence, not infallibility or extraordinary performance. Due care requires the auditor to conduct examinations and verifications to a reasonable extent, but does not require detailed audits of all transactions. Accordingly, the internal auditor cannot give absolute assurance that noncompliance or irregularities do not exist. Nevertheless, the possibility of material irregularities or noncompliance should be considered whenever the internal auditor undertakes an internal auditing assignment.

.03   When an internal auditor suspects wrongdoing, the appropriate authorities within the organization should be informed. The internal auditor may recommend whatever investigation is considered necessary in the circumstances. Thereafter, the auditor should follow up to see that the internal auditing department's responsibilities have been met.

.04   Exercising due professional care means using reasonable audit skill and judgment in performing the audit. To this end, the internal auditor should consider:

.1   The extent of audit work needed to achieve audit objectives
.2   The relative materiality or significance of matters to which audit procedures are applied
.3   The adequacy and effectiveness of internal controls
.4   The cost of auditing in relation to potential benefits

.05   Due professional care includes evaluating established operating standards and determining whether those standards are acceptable and are being met. When such standards are vague, authoritative interpretations should be sought. If internal auditors are required to interpret or select operating standards, they should seek agreement with auditees as to the standards needed to measure operating performance.

Related aspects of due professional care

This specific standard asserts the need for due professional care in performing internal audits.[7] Certainly, "due professional care" is one of the basic foundation components of the sought-after "professional effectiveness." At the same time the definition, measurement, and final evaluation of that profes-

---

[7]SIAS No. 3, Attached as Appendix F, provides an authoritative interpretation for standard 280 and Guidelines 280.01, 280.02, and 208.03.

sional care becomes extremely difficult. The five guidelines endeavor to come at that problem in different ways.

In the first guideline (.01) the first two sentences deal with basic substance. This substance is first, the concept of "a reasonably prudent and competent" internal auditor. The key problem here is how one should measure and evaluate "reasonably." Second, there is the recognition of dependence on the complexities of the particular circumstances—certainly a very necessary qualification. In the second sentence "complexities of the audit" is recognized as one type of variation between individual situations. However, one should also take into consideration the economic or operational significance of the activity subject to audit.

The remainder of this first guideline shifts from the basic concept of professional care to a number of somewhat different—although related—issues. In the third sentence the focus is on particular types of problems to which the internal auditor should be alert—specifically the possibility of intentional wrongdoing, errors and omissions, inefficiency, waste, ineffectiveness, and conflicts of interest. In the next sentence there is the further caution to be alert to those conditions and activities where irregularities are most likely to occur. Again in all these situations we would add that the extent of the alertness depends on the economic or operational significance of the activity being audited. The fifth and final sentence is a direct statement pertaining more appropriately to the scope of audit work, to be discussed later.

The first three sentences of second guideline (.02) together cover the unavoidable fact that all internal audits have limitations and cannot provide complete assurance that all noncompliance and irregularities have been disclosed. There are a number of reasons for these limitations, but they include the fact that the extent of audit work must be guided by costs and potential benefits, that audits of expanded scope will not always detect all regularities, and that internal auditing work is, like any other activity, subject to the limitations of human beings. But in the final sentence there is a more positive consolation prize for the audit recipients by requiring the internal auditor for each audit assignment to keep in mind the possibilities of material irregularities or noncompliance. Clearly, the internal auditor has *some* responsibilities in this area, and we discuss that in more detail in Chapter 16.

The third guideline (.03) deals with a somewhat different matter—the procedure for the internal auditor when wrongdoing is suspected. In the first sentence there is the requirement of informing the appropriate authorities. Quite clearly, some judgments will have to be made, including how significant the suspected wrongdoing, the extent of the belief that such a wrongdoing in fact exists, and the identification of the appropriate authority to advise. The second sentence then makes it permissive that there also be a recommendation for an investigation covering the situation, where wrongdoing is suspected. This involves still more judgment on the part of the internal auditor. Finally in the third sentence there is the requirement that

Role of internal auditor for fraud and wrongdoing

the internal auditor follow up to see that the internal auditing department's responsibilities have been met. What those responsibilities actually are and when they have been met involves still further judgments. Professional Standards Bulletin 83-5, February 1983, indicates that "When wrongdoing is suspected the auditor's responsibility extends to the appropriate level of management within the organization."

The fourth guideline (.04) focuses on the meaning of "exercising due professional care," and again comes back to the test of "reasonable" audit skill and judgment in performing the audit. However, the internal auditor is instructed to consider the four factors detailed in .1 to .4 inclusive. In this connection items .1, .2, and .4 appear to be the key considerations. The inclusion of item .3, "The adequacy and effectiveness of internal controls," is less clear because, as further confirmed in the next section of the standards, adequacy and effectiveness of the internal controls involved is itself the key objective of the audit work rather than being a determinant of due professional care.

The fifth guideline (.05) again deals with a problem that probably pertains more directly to scope of work. There is first, confirmation as to the internal auditor's concern with evaluating operating standards for acceptability and then as to whether those standards are being met. The second sentence then goes on to require the internal auditor to seek authoritative interpretations if the standards being used are vague. In the third sentence there is the further requirement that the internal auditor seek agreement with auditees when new interpretations or selections of standards are required. All of this raises some interesting questions. Since the internal auditor is typically always interpreting standards there is the question as to whether seeking agreement as to those interpretations is always required. A second question is the extent to which selection by internal auditors of operating standards for use by operating personnel is appropriate—since such selection is usually considered to be a responsibility of operational management. However, management will typically welcome assistance in setting operating standards.

Professional Proficiency in Perspective

Overview of professional proficiency

"Professional proficiency" is one of those interesting terms that can be viewed at varying levels. At its highest level the term encompasses the achievement of total effectiveness of the entire internal auditing effort. But as used in this section the term relates more to how the audit work is carried out for particular audit assignments. As such, professional proficiency becomes on the one hand the responsibility of the internal auditing department and on the other hand the responsibility of the individual internal auditor. This is true despite the fact that some responsibilities can be dealt with more effectively by either the department or the individual. But in total there is the common objective of matching staff personnel with audit assignments in a manner that best assures the desired high level of internal auditing service to the organization. To achieve this common objective there must somehow be adequate capabilities. But in addition to capabilities there must be due professional care. Here, however, the measurement and evaluation become very difficult and resort must ultimately be made to concepts of reasonableness depending on the significance of the activities being audited, the costs of audit work, and the benefits thought to be derived. Judgment thus becomes the final determinant, the soundness of which must be demonstrated over an adequate period of time.

The guidelines relating to due professional care for the most part focus on protective type concerns in such areas as fraud, compliance, and conservation of assets. This protective orientation should not, however, let us forget the equal relevance of professional care of internal auditors in carrying out the broader management improvement types of audit services. That is, the needs for proper professional care are just as compelling for identifying and properly recommending opportunities for potentially greater management effectiveness and profitability. We are again reminded that the dual protective and improvement objectives of the internal auditor are what distinguishes him so importantly from the external public auditor.

A final point that also needs to be made is that internal auditors as a group will be in varying stages of their professional career development. They will therefore have different levels of capabilities in terms of knowledge, skills, and disciplines, depending directly both on their different personal capabilities and the extent of their experience. All of these factors must be considered when individual internal auditors are assigned to particular audit tasks.

300   SCOPE OF WORK

THE SCOPE OF THE INTERNAL AUDIT SHOULD ENCOMPASS THE
EXAMINATION AND EVALUATION OF THE ADEQUACY AND
EFFECTIVENESS OF THE ORGANIZATION'S SYSTEM OF INTERNAL
CONTROL AND THE QUALITY OF PERFORMANCE IN CARRYING OUT
ASSIGNED RESPONSIBILITIES

.01   The scope of internal auditing work, as specified in this standard, encompasses what audit work should be performed. It is recognized, however, that management and the board of directors provide general direction as to the scope of work and the activities to be audited.

.02   The purpose of the review for adequacy of the system of internal control is to ascertain whether the system established provides reasonable assurance that the organization's objectives and goals will be met efficiently and economically.

.03   The purpose of the review for effectiveness of the system of internal control is to ascertain whether the system is functioning as intended.

.04   The purpose of the review for quality of performance is to ascertain whether the organization's objectives and goals have been achieved.

.05   The primary objectives of internal control are to ensure:

.1   The reliability and integrity of information
.2   Compliance with policies, plans, procedures, laws, and regulations
.3   The safeguarding of assets
.4   The economical and efficient use of resources
.5   The accomplishment of established objectives and goals for operations
or programs

Key aspects of total scope of work

The general standard (300)[8] covers the total scope of the internal audit and identifies its two key aspects—"the examination and evaluation of the adequacy and effectiveness of the organization's system of internal control" and "the quality of performance in carrying out assigned responsibilities." The first of these aspects thus deals with the kind of work to be performed and the second the quality of the performance pursuant to that established range. The two aspects have distinctive characters but are obviously closely interrelated.

In the first guideline (.01) we have a matter of major significance. In the first sentence the scope of work is tied to the coverage of the aforementioned general standard. In the second sentence, however, there is the qualification that the scope of the audit work and activities to be audited are subject to the general direction of management and the board of directors. This qualification might be interpreted as endorsing a situation where the internal auditing department was restricted in exercising its own judgment as to what kind of an internal audit program was appropriate—even if based on the Standards. The use of the word "general" avoids to some extent a possible contradiction between the two sentences, and hopefully provides an adequate basis for such management direction as is not inconsistent with the Standards. We must make that assumption because otherwise there would be a potential threat to the independence of the internal auditor.

In the second guideline (.02) the accomplishment of the organization's objectives and goals in an efficient and economical manner are tied directly to the adequacy of the system of internal control. This is indeed an important tie. It might suggest, however, that the system of internal control is the only means of assuring the accomplishment of the objectives and goals of the organization efficiently and economically. We do need to recognize, however, that other approaches can also be utilized.

Elements of internal control

The third guideline (.03) now defines the purpose of the review of the system of internal control as ascertaining whether the system is functioning as intended. This guideline may be too narrowly structured. Certainly the internal auditor is also concerned with identifying any additional means by which the system can be improved. That is, internal auditors should always search for betterment as well as protection.

The fourth guideline (.04) now defines the purpose of the review of performance as ascertaining whether the objectives and goals of the organization have been achieved. However, further elaboration is appropriate. Quite clearly the quality of performance pertains to the level of contribution being

[8]For an authoritative interpretation of General Standard 300, see Appendix. D

made to the ultimate achievement of the objectives and goals, but in addition management utilizes many means to achieve those objectives and goals, and does itself have the final responsibility for that achievement. Moreover in a very practical sense, goals and objectives are ongoing and never fully achieved.

In the fifth guideline the primary objectives of internal control are defined as assuring the five types of results. We can first note that the first three of these desired results pertain to the more protective services of the internal auditor and the final two to the higher-level constructive services. All are sound objectives. Although we are substantially in agreement with this guideline, a somewhat better approach might be to recognize that the five results sought are more directly the objectives of the internal auditor, and that the internal auditor utilizes his review of internal control as the major means by which he achieves those desired objectives. At the same time the internal auditor is endeavoring to assist management to achieve *maximum effectiveness* in the use of resources as well as economy, efficiency, and established objectives—a somewhat broader audit mission.

Basic Role of the System of Internal Control

The preceding comments may perhaps be better understood by a more integrated overview. What we believe should be avoided is a view that the organization approaches its achievement of goals and objectives exclusively through the system of internal control. Instead we favor the view that management and the board establish sound goals and objectives for the organization and then seek to achieve those goals and objectives in a variety of ways—a process we examine in more detail in Chapter 3. The system of internal control then becomes only one of the means—even though a very important one—by which that total achievement process is both protected and improved. The internal auditor at the same time endeavors to contribute directly to the total effectiveness of the management process. In this connection he utilizes his review and appraisal of the system of internal control as a major means by which he can assist management. What we then have is a major role for the system of internal control but without it constituting the total channel by which the organization effectively achieves its goals and objectives.

Overview of internal control

310 Reliability and Integrity of Information

Internal auditors should review the reliability and integrity of financial and operating information and the means used to identify, measure, classify, and report such information.

.01 Information systems provide data for decision making, control, and compliance with external requirements. Therefore, internal auditors should examine information systems and, as appropriate, ascertain whether:

.1 Financial and operating records and reports contain accurate, reliable, timely, complete, and useful information.

.2 Controls over record keeping and reporting are adequate and effective.

Evaluating reliability and integrity of information

In the specific standard above the internal auditor's concern for the reliability and integrity of financial and operating information—plus the means used to identify, measure, classify, and report such information—is confirmed. Now also this mandate is made *directly* to the internal auditor, rather than as an objective of internal control—an approach that more closely agrees with our own views.

In the supporting guideline the implementation of this internal auditing objective is usefully described. The first sentence expands on the importance of the data provided by information systems. The second sentence goes on to identify two key approaches of the internal auditor—first to focus on the records and reports produced by the system and second, to focus on the adequacy and effectiveness of the underlying controls.

The separate identification of "financial" and "operating" records and reports presents no problems, even though in practice both types of records are closely interrelated and very frequently either overlap or are integrated. Also any operational record or report eventually affects or becomes a part of other financial records.

320   Compliance with Policies, Plans, Procedures, Laws and Regulations

Internal auditors should review the systems established to ensure compliance with those policies, plans, procedures, laws, and regulations which could have a significant impact on operations and reports, and should determine whether the organization is in compliance.

.01   Management is responsible for establishing the systems designed to ensure compliance with such requirements as policies, plans, procedures, and applicable laws and regulations. Internal auditors are responsible for determining whether the systems are adequate and effective and whether the activities audited are complying with the appropriate requirements.

Assuring compliance for internal control

This specific standard deals with the second primary objective outlined above—that of the organization's compliance with existing policies, plans, procedures, laws, and regulations. The two means again utilized are through established systems and directly via the confirmation of compliance. Over the years compliance has always been one of the foundation concerns of the internal auditor. The concern expressed is protective—that is to avoid the various costs of noncompliance—but it should also include the search for improved controls and higher levels of compliance.

In the supporting guideline (.01) the first sentence reaffirms the basic responsibility of management for establishing the systems designed to ensure the various types of compliance. The second sentence focuses on the determinations by the internal auditor of both (1) the adequacy and effectiveness of the systems and (2) the ultimate compliance action. In total the compliance actions involve policies, plans, procedures, laws, and regulations, plus other specified actions authorized by management—formally or implicitly. These compliance actions apply to any level of organizational activity and again involve both protective and improvement aspects.

330 Safeguarding of Assets

Internal auditors review the means of safeguarding assets and, as appropriate, verify the existence of such assets.

.01 Internal auditors should review the means used to safeguard assets from various types of losses such as those resulting from theft, fire, improper or illegal activities, and exposure to the elements.

.02 Internal auditors, when verifying the existence of assets, should use appropriate audit procedures.

This specific guideline focuses on the third objective stated above and recognizes the two types of audit approaches.[9] The first of these approaches is through reviewing the means employed and the second through the direct verification of the existence of the assets involved. The safeguarding of asset activities of the internal auditor has again always been a foundation-type responsibility of internal auditors. As noted in Chapter 1, this and the two previous objectives of the internal auditor in the areas of reliability and compliance have combined to first generate the initial establishment of the internal auditing function in the typical organization.

Review and verification of assets

The first supporting guideline (.01) then focuses on the evaluation of the means employed by the organization to safeguard assets. The wide range of the safeguarding activities is of course directly dependent on the particular type of asset involved. Some of the various threats that need to be considered are also illustrated. The importance of safeguarding assets is also of course directly dependent on the extent and significance of the risk of loss to the organization. For example, cash is especially vulnerable and requires safeguarding actions that are very detailed and intensive. On the other hand the risk may be very low for another type of asset that is bulky and relatively immobile. Obviously, considerable judgment is required to determine the extent of risk and how best to deal with the related problems.

The second guideline (.02) focuses on the direct verification of the existence of the particular assets. The additional coverage, however, has to do with the requirement that appropriate procedures are used in carrying out that verification. The significance of the term "appropriate" is that verifying the existence of some assets involves important types of total verification control such as for the previously mentioned vulnerability and possibilities of cross substitution.

340 Economical and Efficient Use of Resources

Internal auditors should appraise the economy and efficiency with which resources are employed.

[9]See SIAS No. 3, Appendix F.

.01   Management is responsible for setting operating standards to measure an activity's economical and efficient use of resources. Internal auditors are responsible for determining whether:

.1   Operating standards have been established for measuring economy and efficiency.

.2   Established operating standards are understood and are being met.

.3   Deviations from operating standards are identified, analyzed, and communicated to those responsible for corrective action.

.4   Corrective action has been taken.

.02   Audits related to the economical and efficient use of resources should identify such conditions as:

.1   Underutilized facilities

.2   Nonproductive work

.3   Procedures which are not cost justified

.4   Overstaffing or understaffing

Guidelines for achieving best use of assets

This specific standard has to do with the predominantly constructive role and responsibility of the internal auditor in helping to achieve the economical and efficient use of the resources of the organization. The key word here is "appraisal" by the internal auditor as he seeks to assist the organization in this very important aspect of total organizational welfare.

The first guideline (.01) has to do with clarifying the respective responsibilities of management as compared to the internal auditor. It is first recognized that management has the responsibility to set the various operating standards. The responsibilities of the internal auditor are then indicated to be the determination of the four specifically enumerated implementing-type actions. These four aspects are essentially the range of the control cycle as applied in a variety of situations, and will be dealt with in greater depth in Chapter 4. However, at this point some further clarification of the respective management and internal auditing roles may be useful.

What needs to be more strongly recognized is that the total control cycle is basically the responsibility of management. The internal auditor's role then is to assist by providing further information as to how economically and efficiently the various parts of the control cycle are actually being carried out—and including also how those various parts can be improved. The interpretation of this guideline should therefore be subject to the aforementioned truth and at no point give the impression that the internal auditor is being given some special responsibility which either conflicts with or dilutes the basic management responsibility.

In the second guideline (.02) there is some further elaboration of the kinds of specific conditions which need to be identified—and presumably also appraised—by the internal auditor. All of the types of conditions indicated are definitely potential causes of the organization falling short of the proper level of accomplishing the economical[10] and efficient use of its various re-

---

[10]We prefer the term "effective" to "economical" because of its higher-level coverage of improvement.

sources. However, there can also be other causes. In total the internal auditor is challenged to use his various skills to identify and establish priorities by which he can best assist management to achieve the ever important objectives and goals of *best possible utilization* of resources. As dealt with further in Chapter 3, the most effective utilization of resources is the basic central thrust of all management efforts. That central thrust then in turn extends to the modern internal auditor.

350 Accomplishment of Established Objectives and Goals for Operations or Programs

Internal auditors should review operations or programs to ascertain whether results are consistent with established objectives and goals and whether the operations or programs are being carried out as planned.

.01 Management is responsible for establishing operating or program objectives and goals, developing and implementing control procedures, and accomplishing desired operating or program results. Internal auditors should ascertain whether such objectives and goals conform with those of the organization and whether they are being met.

Review of extent of accomplishment of goals and objectives

.02 Internal auditors can provide assistance to managers who are developing objectives, goals, and systems by determining whether the underlying assumptions are appropriate; whether accurate, current, and relevant information is being used; and whether suitable controls have been incorporated into the operations or programs.

This specific standard deals with the accomplishment of established objectives and goals for operations or programs. There is the specific concern that results are consistent with established objectives and goals and whether the operations or program are being carried out as planned. It is closely related to the preceding standard covering the economical and efficient use of resources and to a considerable extent overlaps with it. Indeed, the accomplishment of objectives and goals unavoidably involves the economical and efficient use of resources.

As in the preceding case, the first guideline (.01) distinguishes between the responsibilities of management and the internal auditor. To management is attributed the responsibility for establishing operating or program objectives and goals, developing and implementing control procedures, and accomplishing desired operating or program results. To the internal auditor is attributed the responsibility of ascertaining whether such objectives and goals conform with those of the organization and whether they are being met. Here again it needs to be recognized that internal auditors should also assist management in its continuous search for better and improved policies and procedures, and in turn higher objectives.

Participation role of internal auditor

The second guideline (.02) goes still farther in supporting a participative role of the internal auditor—this time to provide assistance to managers developing objectives, goals, and systems. The areas of assistance include whether the underlying assumptions are appropriate; whether accurate, current, and relevant information is being used; and whether suitable controls have been incorporated into the operations or programs. The first two types of assistance must again not go so far as to undermine basic management responsibilities. The third type of assistance—relating to the suitability of controls again involves the question discussed in connection with guideline 120.03.

Scope of Work in Perspective

Overview of scope of work

The central truth relating to scope of work is that the internal auditor accomplishes his objectives of assisting management through his reviewing and evaluating the various internal controls, both individually and collectively—even though that is not necessarily his only approach. Admittedly management can alter that scope, but such alteration should not prevent the aforementioned basic concentration on the system of internal control. The higher-level objectives thus accomplished are the protective services of sound compliance, and safeguarding of assets; and the constructive role of contribution to the improvement of resource utilization in terms of economy, efficiency, *and effectiveness* in terms of properly established and properly achieved objectives and goals. In all of these connections the role of the internal auditor is always advisory and never to relieve management of its basic responsibility for utilizing the resources for maximum organizational welfare.

400   PERFORMANCE OF AUDIT WORK

AUDIT WORK SHOULD INCLUDE PLANNING THE AUDIT,
EXAMINING AND EVALUATING INFORMATION,
COMMUNICATING RESULTS, AND FOLLOWING UP.

.01 The internal auditor is responsible for planning and conducting the audit assignment, subject to supervisory review and approval.

The fourth section of the standards deals with the actual performance of audit work. That performance is viewed as including the planning of the audit, examining and evaluating information, communicating results, and following up. These phases are the component work segments of the individual internal audit. The supporting guideline (.01) then goes on to stipulate that it is the responsibility of the internal auditor to plan and conduct the audit, presumably at all levels of audit responsibility and utilizing proper supervisory review and approval. This classification of the individual phases and the related concept of responsibility comes off as logical and acceptable.

410   Planning the Audit

Internal auditors should plan each audit

Elements of effective audit planning

.01 Planning should be documented and should include:

.1   Establishing audit objectives and scope of work
.2   Obtaining background information about the activities to be audited

.3   Determining the resources necessary to perform the audit

.4   Communicating with all who need to know about the audit

.5   Performing, as appropriate, an on-site survey to become familiar with the activities and controls to be audited, to identify areas for audit emphasis, and to invite auditee comments and suggestions

.6   Writing the audit program

.7   Determining how, when, and to whom audit results will be communicated

.8   Obtaining approval of the audit work plan

The specific standard properly confirms the necessity of planning each audit. The supporting guideline then provides in more detail the scope of that planning. The first item (.1)—establishing audit objectives and scope of work—is clearly the essential first step. Items .2, .3, and .4—as listed—cover important preparatory activities. Item .5—the on-site review, as appropriate—can be viewed as further preliminary work, but probably more as an integral phase of the audit itself. At this point the audit work has really begun and as a result definitive judgments will be made as to the more formal audit program. Item .7—determining how, when, and to whom audit results will be communicated—are interesting questions for preliminary consideration. It needs to be recognized, however, that these questions must be continually reappraised based on what the audit results actually turn out to be.

420   Examining and Evaluating Information

Internal auditors should collect, analyze, interpret, and document information to support audit results.

.01   The process of examining and evaluating information is as follows:

.1   Information should be collected on all matters related to the audit objectives and scope of work.

.2   Information should be sufficient, competent, relevant, and useful to provide a sound basis for audit findings and recommendations.

Sufficient information is factual, adequate, and convincing so that a prudent, informed person would reach the same conclusions as the auditor.

Competent information is reliable and the best attainable through the use of appropriate audit techniques.

Relevant information supports audit findings and recommendations and is consistent with the objectives for the audit.

Useful information helps the organization meet its goals.

.3   Audit procedures, including the testing and sampling techniques employed, should be selected in advance, where practicable, and expanded or altered if circumstances warrant.

.4   The process of collecting, analyzing, interpreting, and documenting information should be supervised to provide reasonable assurance that the auditor's objectivity is maintained and that audit goals are met.

.5 Working papers that document the audit should be prepared by the auditor and reviewed by management of the internal auditing department. These papers should record the information obtained and the analyses made and should support the bases for the findings and recommendations to be reported.

The specific standard deals with the collection, analysis, interpretation, and documentation of information to support audit results. Support necessarily pertains to the development of audit conclusions as well as the backup of those conclusions. That is, information must be first analyzed and interpreted as a basis of developing audit findings and related conclusions. Then as definitive conclusions and recommendations are developed, there is the further special need to be sure that there is adequate backup documentation to support those conclusions. Such backup is especially important when later those conclusions are studied and possibly challenged. This is made more *Guidelines for examining* clear in the supporting five components of the process for examining and *and evaluating information* evaluating information.

The first of these five components prescribes the nature of the desired information relating to audit objectives and scope of work. The second component is an important statement as to the adequacy of the basis for findings and conclusions. The qualities specifically enumerated are sufficiency, competence, relevance, and usefulness, and each of these qualities is then further defined. Again here we fall back on our previously introduced concepts of due care and reasonableness of content. The coverage of "useful" overlaps with the other three more definitive qualities and is really not a separate point. The third component is an important recognition of the need to expand or alter audit procedures in the light of the evolving circumstances. The fourth component reaffirms the importance of supervision as a basis for needed objectivity and accomplishment of audit goals. Finally the fifth component covers the importance of properly prepared and reviewed working papers. In total these five components constitute the basis for an effective examination and evaluation of information, the development of appropriate conclusions, and the supporting documentation for work done and conclusions reached.

430 Communicating Results

Internal auditors should report the results of their audit work.

.1 A signed, written report should be issued after the audit examination is completed. Interim reports may be written or oral and may be transmitted formally or informally.

.2 The internal auditor should discuss conclusions and recommendations at appropriate levels of management before issuing final written reports.

.3 Reports should be objective, clear, concise, constructive, and timely.

.4 Reports should present the purpose, scope, and results of the audit; and, where appropriate, reports should contain an expression of the auditor's opinion.

.5 Reports may include recommendations for potential improvements and acknowledge satisfactory performance and corrective action.

.6 The auditee's views about audit conclusions or recommendations may be included in the audit report.

.7 The director of internal auditing or designee should review and approve the final audit report before issuance and should decide to whom the report will be distributed.

The specific standard confirms the internal auditor's responsibility to report the results of his audit.[11] Quite obviously findings and conclusions are of very little value unless reported to those members of management who have the authority to take the actions that make possible the benefits potentially available to the organization.

Guidelines for effective communication of audit results

The supporting guidelines pertain to the form and content of the afore-mentioned reports plus the manner of their preparation and distribution. The first of these guidelines (.1) confirms the need for a signed written report and possible interim reports that can be written or oral, formal or informal, depending on the significance of the contents and the degree of urgency.

The second guideline (.2) mandates the preliminary discussion of conclusions and recommendations with appropriate levels of management, thus both assuring input which may be relevant and for building proper relations with auditees.

The third guideline (.3) properly describes the desired quality of reports—to be objective, clear, concise, and timely.

The fourth guideline specifies the coverage of purpose, scope, and results of the audit and, *where appropriate,* an opinion. The latter action is usually associated with financial statements but can apply also to some operational situations. In many cases, however, there is no formal opinion, even though any conclusion is to some extent an opinion.

The fifth guideline makes recommendations for potential improvement permissive. It would be better, we believe, to recognize that internal auditors should always seek to identify potential improvements. This same sentence also makes permissive the acknowledgment of satisfactory performance and corrective action. In most cases such acknowledgments are clearly desirable for the record and also because they help build a good relationship with the auditees.

The sixth guideline deals with a more complicated question—whether the auditee's views about audit conclusions or recommendations should be included in the audit report. Ideally the internal auditor reaches agreement with the auditee on all matters, and any still existing disagreement suggests that the several parties of interest may not have adequately reviewed the facts. However, there may be good reasons why the auditee has different views than the internal auditor and why those different views should be

---

[11] For an authoritative interpretation of Standard 430, see Appendix E.

reported. In any event, the application of this guideline needs to be handled with extreme care and objectivity.

Finally, the seventh guideline mandates appropriate supervisory review of the report before issuance and again comes back to the earlier point of now reappraising what the distribution of the report should be. Normally there is a standard distribution, but the unique findings and recommendations from a particular audit may justify a special distribution of all or part of the particular report.

440   Following Up

Internal auditors should follow up to ascertain that appropriate action is taken on reported audit findings.

.01   Internal auditing should determine that corrective action was taken and is achieving the desired results, or that management or the board has assumed the risk of not taking corrective action on reported findings.

Extent of internal auditor's follow-up responsibility

This specific standard provides that the internal auditor should follow up to ascertain that appropriate action is taken on reported audit findings. The supporting guideline (.01) restates that requirement as a determination but does go on to recognize more definitely the possibility that management may decide not to take the recommended corrective action, instead assuming the related risk. Again we have a similar issue to the one discussed under standard 340. Certainly, the internal auditor has an interest in the utilization of his findings and recommendations, and he will wish to assist in assuring that utilization in every practicable manner. That assistance must not, however, become so structured, or administered in such a way, that it impinges on or undermines the basic responsibility of management to give consideration to the audit results and to take appropriate action. It needs to be recognized that appropriate action may in management's judgment be no action at all.

Typically management uses one of its regular line or staff components to administer a formal program of monitoring responses, action, and ultimate clearance of all audit recommendations—including both the recommendations of the internal and external auditor. The internal auditor then periodically reappraises the effectiveness of that procedural program. As a part of the next audit he will also review action on previously made audit recommendations—again of both his own making and those of the external auditor—and incorporate noncompliance findings in the current audit evaluations. This procedure is we believe more consistent with proper roles and responsibilities of the internal auditor and other organizational components. It also avoids having the internal auditor take on a police image and thus endanger his own partnership relationship with the auditee.

Performance of Audit Work in Perspective

Overview of audit work responsibility

The section on performing audit work focuses more directly on the four sequential phases: planning the audit, examining and evaluating information, communicating results, and following up. It does of course build on the standards of independence, and it does unavoidably overlap with the sections on professional proficiency and scope of work. It is not surprising, therefore, that there is occasionally repetition of the same basic point, as well as situations where the coverage of a particular point could logically be in either of the other sections. This is not a serious problem, but it does mean that the various sections must be viewed as an integrated whole. Together the proper base is then established for the final section of the standards dealing with management of the internal auditing department.

500 MANAGEMENT OF THE INTERNAL AUDITING DEPARTMENT

THE DIRECTOR OF INTERNAL AUDITING SHOULD PROPERLY MANAGE THE INTERNAL AUDITING DEPARTMENT

.01   The director of internal auditing is responsible for properly managing the department so that:

   .1   Audit work fulfills the general purposes and responsibilities approved by management and accepted by the board.

   .2   Resources of the internal auditing department are efficiently and effectively employed.

   .3   Audit work conforms to the *Standards for the Professional Practice of Internal Auditing*.

The final major section of the Standards has to do with the management of the internal auditing department. The mandate here is that the director of internal auditing should properly manage the internal auditing department. All the specific standards and supporting guidelines are about the manner in which the director should accomplish that management mission.

Guidelines for managing internal audit department

The supporting guideline (.01) to the specific standard deals first with the end objectives of the internal auditor's management mission. The first of these objectives (.1) is to satisfy the established expectations of management and the board as officially approved and accepted by them. This assumes, of course, that such established expectations properly reflect the professional services of the range and level for which internal auditors have proven their capabilities. Obviously, the particular director of internal auditing is bound by the currently established general purposes and responsibilities, but there is also a professional responsibility of the director to somehow activate the forces that will result in sufficiently high level purposes and responsibilities.

The second objective (.2) then goes on to recognize for the director of internal auditing the same responsibilities that exist for all managers, that is, to make effective use of assigned resources. In best practice also the internal auditor should seek the *most effective* utilization of those resources that is practicable. All of this recognizes the fact that the director is himself a manager as he administers his own department.

Finally, the third objective (.3) properly confirms the need of audit work in the department to be consistent with the Standards for the Professional Practice of Internal Auditing—thus tying in the earlier statement in the foreword that the standards are intended to represent the practice of internal auditing as it should be, as judged and adopted by the Board of Directors of the Institute.

510   Purpose, Authority, and Responsibility

The director of internal auditing should have a statement of purpose, authority, and responsibility for the internal auditing department.

.01   The director of internal auditing is responsible for seeking the approval of management and the acceptance by the board of a formal written document (charter) for the internal auditing department.

Need for proper organizational charter   This specific standard deals directly with the responsibility of the director to have a statement of purpose, authority, and responsibility for the internal auditing department. In the supporting guideline (.01) there is also the further mandate of the director's responsibility for *seeking* a statement that is both approved by management and accepted by the board. Presumably also, the content of that statement (the charter) should be consistent with the Standards in total, as stated in the third paragraph of the Introduction. Presumably, that statement should also specify the unrestricted scope of the internal auditor's work, as stated in the fourth paragraph of the introduction. Presumably also, that statement should incorporate the high-level objectives of internal auditors—as stated in 300.05 of Scope of Work—which include services to the organization in the areas of the economical and efficient use of resources and the accomplishment of established objectives and goals for operations or programs. What perhaps needs to be more specifically covered by the current specific standard and guideline is that the charter should be of sufficiently high level in terms of purpose, authority, and responsibility. It is also part of the internal auditor's responsibility to help make that desired situation come to pass when it does not already exist.

520   Planning

The director of internal auditing should establish plans to carry out the responsibilities of the internal auditing department.

.01   These plans should be consistent with the internal auditing department's charter and with the goals of the organization.

.02   The planning process involves establishing:

   .1   Goals
   .2   Audit work schedules
   .3   Staffing plans and financial budgets
   .4   Activity reports

.03   The goals of the internal auditing department should be capable of being accomplished within specified operating plans and budgets and, to the extent possible, should be measurable. They should be accompanied by measurement criteria and targeted dates of accomplishment.

.04   *Audit work schedules* should include (a) what activities are to be audited; (b) when they will be audited; and (c) the estimated time required, taking into account the scope of the audit work planned and the nature and extent of audit work performed by others. Matters to be considered in establishing audit work schedule priorities should include (a) the date and results of the last audit; (b) financial exposure; (c) potential loss and risk; (d) requests by management; (e) major changes in operations, programs, systems, and controls; (f) opportunities to achieve operating benefits; and (g) changes to and capabilities of the audit staff. The work schedules should be sufficiently flexible to cover unanticipated demands on the internal auditing department.

.05 *Staffing plans and financial budgets*, including the number of auditors and the knowledge, skills, and disciplines required to perform their work, should be determined from audit work schedules, administrative activities, education and training requirements, and audit research and development efforts.

.06 *Activity reports* should be submitted periodically to management and to the board. These reports should compare (a) performance with the department's goals and audit work schedules and (b) expenditures with financial budgets. They should explain the reasons for major variances and indicate any action taken or needed.

Planning is the basis for achieving effective results in every organization. It is therefore to be expected that this specific standard should require the director of internal auditing to establish plans to carry out the responsibilities of the internal auditing department. It also follows, as covered in the first supporting guideline (.01), that those plans should be consistent with the internal auditing department's charter and with the goals of the organization. Again, however, it becomes important, as previously discussed, that the charter provide for sufficiently high-level professional internal auditing service. It is also important that the goals of the organization be at a sufficiently high level and be properly defined. *Guidelines for effective internal audit planning*

In the second guideline (.02) the span of the planning process is outlined. That planning process covers the planning of both the goals, covered by the first (.1), and the framework for the implementation, as covered by the other three subguidelines. We must recognize fully the critical nature of the planning process as a basis for later sound implementation, and in turn for best possible utilization of internal auditing resources for maximum organizational welfare.

530 Policies and Procedures

The director of internal auditing should provide written policies and procedures to guide the audit staff.

.01 The form and content of written policies and procedures should be appropriate to the size and structure of the internal auditing department and the complexity of its work. Formal administrative and technical audit manuals may not be needed by all internal auditing departments. A small internal auditing department may be managed informally. Its audit staff may be directed and controlled through daily, close supervision and written memoranda. In a large internal auditing department, more formal and comprehensive policies and procedures are essential to guide the audit staff in the consistent compliance with the department's standards of performance.

The specific standard properly recognizes the importance of written policies and procedures for guidance to the audit staff. Actually policies and procedures can be at either of the two levels—for planning or for implementation. At the planning level the policies and procedures become the basis for more detailed elaboration and execution as part of the following implementation. This means that such higher-level policies and procedures usually need to be formally developed.

Need for adequate internal auditing policies and procedures

The foregoing is important for the interpretation of the supporting guideline (.01). This guideline properly recognizes that the need for formal administrative and technical audit manuals will vary depending on the size and complexity of the organization. This is due to the fact that in smaller organizations enough can be accomplished through closer supervision. It is important to recognize, however, that this greater informality is applicable predominantly to the implementation phase. That is, formal definition is usually always desirable in the higher-level planning phase.

540   Personnel Management and Development

The director of internal auditing should establish a program for selecting and developing the human resources of the internal auditing department.

.01   The program should provide for:

Guidelines for selecting and developing internal auditing personnel

.1   Developing written job descriptions for each level of the audit staff
.2   Selecting qualified and competent individuals
.3   Training and providing continuing educational opportunities for each internal auditor
.4   Appraising each internal auditor's performance at least annually
.5   Providing counsel to internal auditors on their performance and professional development

Managerial results are accomplished through people. The director of internal auditing, like any other manager, must accomplish his managerial objectives through people. This specific guideline therefore very properly mandates the director to establish a program for selecting and developing the human resources of the internal auditing department.

The five supporting guidelines then go on to cover in more detail the significant components of such an adequate program. Several broad observations are appropriate at this point. One of these observations is that the personnel management process actually begins with the determination of personnel needs for the internal auditing department, based on the total needs of the organization, and then extends to the time when the individuals actually leave the internal auditing department. It follows that all intermediate aspects of the employment of the individual involve personnel management. In some cases these intermediate aspects are covered by definitive and special subprograms, and in other cases they are handled as a part of the regular managerial processes—as for example in the case of regular supervision.

Finally, there is also the need that the personnel management activities be related properly to those of the larger organization of which the internal auditing department is a part. In some cases personnel activities for the internal auditing department are handled by another organizational group, in other cases separately by the internal auditing department, and in still other cases together. Moreover, the policies of the larger organization are normally controlling. What this means is that the director of internal auditing must determine what he needs to be doing to supplement the policies and procedures of the organization to achieve his own proper objectives. But at the same time his own activities must properly conform to the established organization's activities.

Tie to other company personnel policies

550   External Auditors

The director of internal auditing should coordinate internal and external audit efforts.

.01   The internal and external audit work should be coordinated to ensure adequate audit coverage and to minimize duplicate efforts.

.02   Coordination of audit efforts involves:

.1   Periodic meetings to discuss matters of mutual interest
.2   Access to each other's audit programs and working papers
.3   Exchange of audit reports and management letters
.4   Common understanding of audit techniques, methods, and terminology

This specific standard deals with the responsibility of the director of internal auditing to coordinate his internal auditing efforts with those of the external auditor. While the coordination of the two audit efforts is becoming increasingly the role of the audit committee of the board of directors, it should be noted at this time that the internal auditor should do his part to assure the best possible two-way coordination of the two audit efforts. A similar responsibility exists on the part of the external auditor.

Need to coordinate internal auditing activities with external auditor

The first supporting guideline (.01) goes on to confirm the need for co-ordination and then to define the objectives of that coordination as ensuring adequate audit coverage and minimizing duplicate efforts. Both of these stated objectives perhaps suggest unduly a nice quantitative fit of the two audit efforts. A better overall objective would be "to best ensure maximum effectiveness of the total audit effort."

The second guideline (.02) then goes on to specify the major components of the aforementioned coordination effort. All of the components mentioned are certainly important to an effective coordination effort. However, it needs to be recognized more precisely that effective coordination begins with advance planning between the two audit groups. Such joint planning is also facilitated by (1) understanding and recognition by each audit group of the

Achieving effective internal–external audit coordination

other's primary roles and responsibilities, (2) a more definite acceptance of their major common interest in the effectiveness of the system of internal accounting control, (3) a demonstration of adequate professional competence on the part of the internal audit staff, and (4) the acceptance of an environment in which two mutually respected partners work together to exploit best total common interests. The total scope of this coordination effort is so far-reaching that overall coordination by the audit committee of the board is all the more desirable.

560   Quality Assurance

The director of internal auditing should establish and maintain a quality assurance program to evaluate the operations of the internal auditing department.

.01   The purpose of this program is to provide reasonable assurance that audit work conforms with these *Standards*, the internal auditing department's charter, and other applicable standards. A quality assurance program should include the following elements:

    .1   Supervision
    .2   Internal reviews
    .3   External reviews

Need for effective quality assurance

.02   *Supervision* of the work of the internal auditors should be carried out continually to assure conformance with internal auditing standards, departmental policies, and audit programs.

.03   *Internal reviews* should be performed periodically by members of the internal auditing staff to appraise the quality of the audit work performed. These reviews should be performed in the same manner as any other internal audit.

.04   *External reviews* of the internal auditing department should be performed to appraise the quality of the department's operations. These reviews should be performed by qualified persons who are independent of the organization and who do not have either a real or an apparent conflict of interest. Such reviews should be conducted at least once every three years. On completion of the review, a formal, written report should be issued. The report should express an opinion as to the department's compliance with the *Standards for the Professional Practice of Internal Auditing* and, as appropriate, should include recommendations for improvement.

This final specific standard deals with an aspect that has increasingly become an important dimension of the internal auditor's standards for professional practice—that of establishing and maintaining a quality assurance program to evaluate the effectiveness of the operations of the individual internal auditing department. Although quality as an objective is always in the mind of any manager, what is important is the recognition of the need for a definite supplementary effort to measure, protect, and generate the desired high levels of quality.

The first supporting guideline (.01) goes on to outline three levels or components of such a quality assurance program. These components are supervision, internal reviews, and external reviews—each of which is then further described in the subsequent three guidelines. The first of these components is the further recognition of the supervisory responsibility covered in the earlier specific standard (230). The specific recognition in the second guideline (.02), however, properly identifies that supervision as a definitive component of the total quality assurance program.

Achieving adequate quality assurance

The third guideline (.03) then deals with internal reviews. In actual practice the supervision at the various levels in the internal auditing department provides various types of internal reviews. The new kind intended, however, is a separate audit review conducted under the same procedures and standards as any other audit assignment.

Finally, in the fourth supporting guideline (.04) the nature and scope of the external review is outlined. The conditions enumerated include the adequacy of the qualifications of the external reviewer, independence from the organization, and freedom from any real or apparent conflict of interest.

Standards for the Professional Practice of Internal Auditing in Perspective

In this chapter we have endeavored to provide a better understanding of internal auditing as a total professional activity. In accomplishing this objective we have utilized the "Standards for the Professional Practice of Internal Auditing" as approved by The Institute of Internal Auditors. In using these Standards we have gone beyond them to develop related principles, concepts, and approaches. In so doing we have unavoidably identified areas where the coverage in the standards appears to be incomplete and where therefore further interpretation and elaboration appear to be needed. The recognition of such conditions is not unexpected when one considers the fact that the Standards were a joint effort of many practitioners and necessarily involved compromise and adjustment. This in no way detracts from the monumental significance of the Standards and the level of achievement on the part of those who produced them. Hopefully, however, the further interpretations and views expressed in this book can be useful in the further evaluation of the existing Standards.

Overview of professional standard

REVIEW QUESTIONS

1. Discuss the benefits of having professional standards. What are the limitations?
2. What are the advantages of the existence of a strong and comprehensive charter for internal auditing?
3. Why is "independence" important for the internal auditor? How im-

portant also is that "independence" for management and the board of directors?

4. To what extent should the internal auditor be involved with the development of systems and procedures? Why?

5. What types of responsibility for professional proficiency exist on the part of the internal auditing department and the individual internal auditor?

6. How does knowledge about human relations and the ability to work effectively with people help the internal auditor?

7. What is "Due Professional Care"? How can it be measured?

8. "The review and appraisal of the system of internal control is a means and not an end in itself." Do you agree or disagree? Why?

9. "The internal auditor provides two types of services, one being *protective* and the other *constructive*." Explain what is meant. To what extent are the two types of services interrelated?

10. What is the role of effective reporting?

CASE PROBLEMS

Problem 2-1

George Mason, director of internal auditing at Bolton Manufacturing Company, had been looking forward to meeting his new boss, Thomas Wilson. Wilson had just been brought in to fill the post of vice-president–finance, when Henry Jones had been wooed away to head a large conglomerate. But now there was a new development. Wilson said, "George, I really have my hands full working with the president on charting Bolton's future and then determining how finance can best support those plans. With the controller, treasurer, and administrative manager reporting to me, I think it might be better all around if you reported to John Fox, the controller. At the same time I would, of course, want to keep in touch with you." Mason had been pretty much caught off guard but did some quick thinking and instinctively wanted to stall for time. "Mr. Wilson," he countered, "I think I understand your problem. However, changing my line of reporting has more angles than might first appear—with a number of important pros and cons—and I would really appreciate it if you would keep an open mind on it until I can give you a more organized evaluation. I could do this in say, about three days." "That sounds fair enough, George," responded Wilson. "When I get your memo we will talk again."

Required. Prepare George Mason's memorandum outlining the advantages and disadvantages of the proposed move and his overall recommendation.

Problem 2-2

"My view is very clear," asserted Hugh Walker, National's vice-president–finance. "We must have the external audit opinion to comply with the SEC requirements, but we want it at the lowest possible cost. Therefore I consider the internal auditing department's primary role is to help our CPA firm, and thus to reduce the audit bill. I hear a lot of talk that the internal auditors should help management get better results, but I say that if we haven't got managers who can stand on their own feet, we had better get some new ones. Now don't get me wrong, I'll take anything the internal auditors turn up for increased profits, but I just don't think they should get diverted from their main assignment to get our external audit costs minimized." "I suppose you are right," said George Rush, the executive vice-president for administration, "but I understand Will Ross, our general auditor, has some other views. I think I would feel better if I gave him an opportunity to be heard. Also next month we have to put together next year's budget and we will want to be fairly sure that we are going in the right direction. We should also be sure that we cut Ken Barnes in—after all as CEO he has a right to have the final policy say."

Required.   Prepare a statement for Will Ross covering his view about the role of the internal auditing department, including its relationship with the company's external auditor.

CHAPTER THREE

Understanding Management Needs

After studying this chapter you should be able to:

☐ *Explain why it is important that internal auditors understand the management process*

☐ *Recognize the needs of management in determining the role of the internal auditor*

☐ *Define the term "management" and describe the management subprocesses*

☐ *Recognize the different aspects of the environment in which an organization operates*

☐ *Identify the important attributes of management*

☐ *Explain the model for management in action*

☐ *Describe the essential ingredients of a partnership role between the manager and the internal auditor*

Importance of Management Focus

In the three previous editions of this book, service to management was regarded as the controlling mission of the internal auditor. Initially the concerns were also with the narrower and more protective needs of management. There has, however, been a continuous upward trend over the years, both as pertaining to the level of those protective needs and now the more effective use of resources. At the same time the internal auditor's mission has been expanded to cover the board of directors and through that board the stockholders, government, and the total society. We therefore now properly refer to the controlling mission of the modern internal auditor as service to the organization.

Quite clearly many recipients of the more expanded internal auditing services have certain special needs—the exact nature of which are still evolving. The truth remains, however, that management effectiveness is still a major concern of *all* parties of interest. If organizations are not well-managed all members of society suffer. At the same time the management role is becoming more complex because of the rapidly changing external environment and the new tools available to managers. All of these factors combine to make it all the more important that the internal auditor assist managers in every way practicable.

To assist management properly, the internal auditor must continuously strive to understand management needs. We need to understand management objectives and how managers go about it to identify and solve problems as they seek to achieve those objectives. We need to learn to think like managers so that we can truly achieve a partnership relationship with them in their managerial endeavors.

Internal auditors should understand management needs

There is still another important reason why internal auditors need to understand good management theory and practice. This is because internal auditors themselves—as directors and supervisors—are managers of their own professional activities. Such individuals must develop objectives and apply managerial practice to achieve those objectives, working through people and with other resources, just as do all other managers. One can really not be a qualified counselor to managers if he himself cannot effectively manage his own operations. There is the need in fact to provide a model that can be observed and followed by all others.

In this chapter we look briefly at some of the more general concepts of management. In Chapters 4 and 5, we then probe more deeply into control and the other types of organizational control utilized by all managers. At the same time all the other chapters involve important management areas. Effective internal auditing in all respects involves understanding management needs and working with management to best serve those needs. That understanding is directly necessary to make possible the *capability* to serve management. But it is also an essential ingredient in providing *credibility* for the internal auditor. Recipients will then respect the internal auditor and listen to his counsel. Only then also will managers and internal auditors achieve effectiveness in all operational areas and thus best promote maximum organizational welfare.

What Is Management?

The mention of the words "management" or "manager" will suggest a variety of thoughts to different people. In its most simplistic form there will be an image of someone getting a job done and doing it in an effective manner. In other cases it may suggest an individual or a group of individuals dealing with large and complicated problems. Typically, however, there is the common thread of a more enlightened and more systematic accomplishment of some defined objective.

Management is the process
of achieving effective
use of resources

When we come to developing formal definitions of management—the actions of managers—we can again have a wide range of ideas in terms of nature and scope. Our own most compact definition is: "*Management is the process of achieving the effective utilization of resources.*" This definition recognizes-that management is an active *process*, that it deals with *resources* (including both human and nonhuman resources), and that the end objective is *utilization* of those resources in the *most effective* manner practicable. Maximizing the effective utilization of total resources is indeed the most basic aspect of what management is all about. Managers get the best possible results and they do it in the best possible manner. In business this normally means maximum profitability based on long-run standards and giving fair consideration to the rights of all parties of interest.

Expanding the Definition. If we go on to expand the basic definition of management, we would need to recognize that the resources exist in an environment and that managers seek to relate the strengths and weaknesses of the particular resources in terms of existing environmental restrictions and opportunities. Out of that analytical study the managers develop the highest goals and objectives to be accomplished that are practicable. Those determinations include consideration of the major strategy to be employed and this leads into the development of lower-level strategy policies and plans for implementation.[1] Finally, there is the actual implementation of all the preceding plans, by and through people, leading to the maximum achievement of established goals and objectives. This is an interrelated continuing process as we move through time. We will come back to this more defined process later in the chapter. We then develop in greater depth the management process as a model for application in all managerial situations through continuing reiteration and refinement. But first we need to recognize several other ways in which we can look at management and identify more precisely some of the key attributes that need always be given serious consideration.

Management as a Series of Subprocesses. Another very popular way to look at the management process is through breaking it down into a number of related subprocesses. Different students of management do this in different ways. Our own approach is, as follows:

1. *Planning.* This subprocess involves the studies and decisions pertaining to where we want the organization[2] to be at stated times in the

---

[1]Our usage of terms is that *goals* are the highest level ends we try to achieve, and that *strategies* are the means by which those goals are achieved. We then use the term *objectives* as lower-ranking goals, and the term *policies* as lower-level strategies, and finally the term *procedures* to describe the still lower means by which policies are made operative. In actual practice different people use the terms in a variety of ways. Also individual terms unavoidably take on different meanings depending on the organizational level of the user.

[2]The principles in all of these subprocesses can also be applied to any component of the organization.

future. It includes the total range of planning, from the highest-level determination of major goals and objectives, to the lower-level strategies and supporting policies, to the still lower procedures and methods for actual operational implementation. It is the foundation for all the other subprocesses.

Managers plan, organize, provide resources, administer, and control

2. *Organizing*. This subprocess has to do with breaking down the work of the organization into pieces and then bringing those pieces back together so that the total work of the organization can be accomplished. This also enables each individual in the organization to know what he is supposed to do and to whom he can go for direction and help. Developing all of these relationships is itself a kind of planning but more properly builds upon the previous planning.

3. *Providing Resources*. Overlapping into the planning and organizing is the particular subprocess of providing other needed resources. It includes the procurement of material resources—plant, equipment, and all types of materials and supplies—and the recruitment and development of people. The latter activities are to a major extent part of the modern personnel function, although all managers must be deeply involved.

4. *Administering*. This is the subprocess when work is actually done. It includes three different types of supportive action which are basic to the execution of work assignments. The first of these is "directing"—which has to do primarily with how instructions are communicated to subordinates, the second is "coordinating"—which has to do primarily with providing needed information between all workers; and the third is "leading"—which is essentially the motivation of workers through the example set by the leaders and the way those leaders work with the individuals who have subordinate responsibilities.

5. *Controlling*. Current work accomplishment is unavoidably affected by changing conditions and varying human capabilities. We must therefore identify deviations from plans and deal with such deviations effectively. Thus controlling is the necessary subprocess to help us to achieve best the established objectives. It is also the area in which the internal auditor has special expertise. We deal with this important subprocess in greater depth in Chapter 4.

Management in Functional Areas. We can also view management in terms of the functional areas of a typical organization. These functional areas refer to the various groups of work activity that are similar in character. The classification in this case will vary depending on the importance of the particular functional area in a given organization. Typical areas so recognized include research, engineering, production, marketing, administration, personnel, and finance. The management process in each area is subject to the same subprocesses previously discussed but the focus now is on achieving the performance of the designated function in the most effective manner practicable. When combined with general management, they comprise the total management of the organization. Because each of these functional areas also has its own relatively unique problems, the coverage of the internal auditor's concerns with controls have been similarly structured in the second section of this book.

Nature of the Environment

Organizations operate in a complex environment

The individual organization with its resources operates in a very complicated environment, requiring some elaboration as to the features contributing to that complexity. Part of this complexity arises because of the various types of environmental factors which are operative. A possible classification of these types of factors would include the economic, competitive, technological, political, and social. Each of these deserves some brief comment.

Economic Aspects.   A major portion of the environment has to do with the various economic factors. There are first of all the dimensions of the state of the economy in terms of the world situation, nation, and specific regional areas affected. Within this framework we are concerned with the more specific factors which relate to the products and services of the particular company. Who uses the products and why? How strong is that demand in terms of other needs? Where are the users of the product? How able are they to afford the use of the product? There are then, on the other hand, the factors relating to the supply of the product or service. Where do the materials and services come from that are needed to produce the aforementioned products and what is their availability? What kinds of facilities are needed to produce the products, and what kind of production processes are involved? What are the requirements in terms of capital, know-how, and costs? Finally, these factors relating to both demand and supply have to be equated in terms of whether there are acceptable profit potentials.

Competition exists both inside and outside industry

Competitive Aspects.   Coupled also with the economic aspects just described is the existing competitive situation. Who are the competitors? How many are there? How large are they in relation to our own company? What are their particular competitive strengths? And how easily do competitors enter the field and withdraw from it? All of these factors combine to determine the character of the competitive environment which bears on the industry in a broad sense, and on the particular firm in a more direct sense. Very often the competitive relationship has a number of dimensions. A can maker, for example, is subject to the competition first, of other can makers, and second, to makers of other types of containers—glass, plastic, paper, and the like. At a still broader level there is the competition for the consumer dollar from other products that do not require the use of any kind of a package.

Technological Aspects.   All organizations, by the nature of the kind of business they are in and the industry in which they operate, are subject to the technological factor in their own special way. A company in the aerospace industry is illustrative of a situation where there is a major technological impact. On the other hand a company in the restaurant business is illustrative of where the impact is relatively low. In the former situation changes in the technology can constitute both major risk and major opportunity. In the second case there may also be risk and opportunity, but not so much from the changes in the existing technology. The varying impact will be on the kind of people required, the extent of research, the time span of planning, and the like.

Political Aspects.   The political side of the environment refers to the extent to which there are laws or other kinds of governmental regulation that have important bearing on the operation of the particular organization. In the case of a public utility, the regulatory aspect is very significant. In the automobile industry the regulations covering safety and emissions represent a more recent type of regulatory development. In the steel industry the political factor may take the form of pressure on pricing or wage levels. All organizations, however, to some extent are subject to legal controls and restrictions of various types.

Laws and regulations have important bearing on organization

Social Aspects.   Back of existing law is the force of the society, which is expressed ultimately through the political process, and then in some cases in the enactment of various types of laws. Present also are the attitudes and views of the society, which themselves constitute important environmental forces. Here there is a wide spectrum of developments, including such important matters as decaying urban areas, minority rights explosions, attitudes toward pollution, and overall rising social expectations as to various types of conduct relating to the operations of both business and nonbusiness organizations. These social aspects represent some of the most difficult problems every company faces if it is to survive and prosper. This is especially true when there is an increasing demand for business organizations to assume a greater degree of social responsibility.

Increasing pressure for more social responsibility

Nature of the Environment at Lower Organizational Levels

Our discussion of environmental factors has been from the standpoint of the entire company or other independent organizational entity. But management entities also exist at lower organizational levels—subsidiaries, divisions, departments, and the like. In these cases the environmental factors previously discussed include additionally the authority and controls of the higher organizational levels to which the lower-level management entity is accountable. On the positive side there are the resources of the higher-level management organization which may be available to augment the already assigned resources. On the other side are the constraints of various kinds which may be imposed by the higher-level management authority.

Some Important Attributes of Management

As stated previously we need also to understand certain key attributes and truths about the management process before reviewing the major model of the total process. Those that we regard as being especially important are described next.

Dependence on People. We have seen that people are one part of the resources for which the effective manager is seeking the best possible utilization. Thus people can be resources in terms of their knowledge, skills, and experience. But people have a unique importance that goes far beyond those considerations. This importance stems from the basic truth that all management action is carried out by and through people. An effective manager, therefore, is directly dependent on people to make plans and to implement those plans through definitive actions. This means that we need to understand people so that we can relate to them in an effective manner and obtain their maximum contribution toward the achievement of managerial goals and objectives.

Management action is by and through people

But understanding people is not a simple accomplishment. People as individuals are human in that they have feelings and emotions and they must be properly motivated. Put in other words, there is a continuing challenge to find the best possible fit and integration of individual and organizational goals. That integration can never be perfectly achieved because individuals are human and are always subject to continuously changing conditions. It is something, therefore, that we must always keep working at.

Focus on Decision Making. If we go back far enough all managerial action is based on a decision of some kind. Some of these decisions are at a very high level—as in the case of a major strategic policy decision involving entry into a new kind of business. Other decisions are at relatively low levels— as in the case of the decision to purchase a piece of small equipment. There is, however, a commonality among all of such decisions as respects principles and methodology. The problem must be identified, alternatives explored, the use of all information available or reasonably attainable, and a judgment as to the selected type of action.

Continuing effort to make decision process more effective

What differs in decision making is the magnitude of the problem, the extent to which information is available, the criteria that are most appropriate, and the extent to which judgment be exercised. Thus there is a continuous effort to make decisions in a more effective manner. In addition, there are the factors of time available, risk levels that are acceptable, and the costs of improving the basis for the actual final decision. The quality of the implementation is also extremely important. But the necessary first requisite is always to identify the right problem and then to make the best possible decision covering its solution.

Effect of Risk Level.   The previously mentioned varying acceptability of the level of risk requires some further elaboration. To a considerable extent risk can be reduced or in some cases substantially eliminated by better information about operational and environmental factors. The limitations here are the costs of obtaining the various types and levels of information desired. But increasingly one is confronted with the fact that there are uncontrollable factors that affect our desired results. To some extent again we can reduce the aforementioned risk by statistical calculations of probabilities. However, here also there are increasingly substantive limitations. The overall result is that the total certainty is impossible because of both practical and absolute limitations. This means that decisions pertaining to management actions reflect the levels of risk deemed to be acceptable to the particular responsible manager. Usually, there is a correlation between the potentially available profitability and the extent of risk but there is also the varying capacity to survive failure and operational losses. There are also varying inclinations to take risk. Each manager must therefore make his own evaluations within the parameters of his own authority and preferences.

Total certainty not possible but managers determine acceptable levels of risk

Management Is Judged by Results.   This attribute is important in the first place because it is the truth that everything a manager does in the way of action is judged by how it furthers the achievement of his established goals and objectives. Managers are always primarily interested in results as opposed to letting an intermediate phase be an end in itself. But the significance of this attribute goes much deeper. Often there are different ways to achieve managerial objectives. And often, different approaches in individual situations can achieve the same desired results. At the same time, what appear to be similar approaches to management problems can end up with completely different measures of success.

Managers judged by results and extent of achievement of objectives

What this means is that there are always variables that cannot be fully predicted or adequately dealt with. These variables then often become of such force that they are controlling. Additionally, personnel effectiveness varies in dealing with similar obstacles. As a result, the merits of particular managerial decisions or approaches are often extremely controversial. In the last analysis, therefore, we must judge management competence mostly by the results achieved. It is quite possible that the good results actually achieved in a particular situation might have been better with what we think is a more enlightened management approach. On balance, however, we tend to equate managerial excellence with the quality of the results.

Time Span for Appraising Results.   The judgment of management by results as a general concept is quite clear. It does, however, raise a related question of the time frame in which the particular results are evaluated. In the typical situation a manager can show short-term profitability but attain that profitability by undermining the longer-run profits of the organizational component for which he is responsible. For example, quality can be temporarily sacrificed with resulting short-term profits, but be so damaging to customer satisfaction that future products are no longer purchased by consumers. Good managers therefore think in terms of long-term factors and resist tempting shortcuts that endanger longer term potentials.

Varying timeframes for appraising results

When all of the foregoing is understood by all parties of interest, the correct judgments are quite clear. More often, however, there are complicated factors involved. One of these factors is how long the time span should be for the decisions made today. How long will higher-level managers or stockholders wait for longer-run rewards? A second complicating factor is the difficulty of measuring the long-run effect. Managers often innocently make bad estimates in these areas and often also are victims of "wishful" thinking. In still other cases lower-level managers ignore long-run consequences because of the probability that they will not be around when the final outcome becomes evident. Moreover, even then the evaluation is usually controversial. In total this means that the evaluation of results must be made with great care and with all possible judgment.

Proper balance needed between change and regularity

Continuing Reconciliation of Change and Regularity.   One of the central truths of management is that conditions are always changing. A valued employee is lost to the organization, a new invention obsoletes existing practice, consumer preferences shift, or something else unforeseen develops. As a result, all dimensions of the management process must be reappraised and redirected. An organization's capacity to foresee such possibilities and to adapt to them once they come to pass is a measure of their ability to survive and prosper. But at the same time there are benefits of standardization and regularity that include lower cost and a more effective supervisory effort. We constantly seek to exploit the benefits and economies of regularity through mass production, standardizing services, and comprehensive policies and procedures. The benefits are the reduced cost of facilities, labor, and managerial involvement. But herein lies a conflict in that change may be needed for growth or even survival. Hence there is a continuing challenge to management to find the proper balance between the two types of pressure.

An example here is the extent to which capital investment should be made in a single-purpose machine when a change in product design will make that machine obsolete. It was also a problem faced by Henry Ford when he thought all motor cars should be black. It is a problem that is never properly solved at any one point of time and the reconciliation continues to be complex as conditions continue to change. It is, however, the ability to cope with this kind of challenge that identifies and measures managerial competence.

General Applicability of Management Concepts.   All of the theoretical and practical concepts of management need to be applied to individual managerial situations in a manner that recognizes the unique factors operative in the particular situation—an area we discuss in greater detail later in the chapter. But at the same time the basic principles and concepts of management are generally applicable to all managerial situations. These managerial situations exist whenever there are resources for which a particular individual is directly or indirectly responsible. The situation may be in any business organization or in government or any nonbusiness type of organization. Moreover the situation may be at the top of the organization—which may be as large as the General Motors Corporation—or it can be a very low operational unit far down in the organization. In all of these situations, however, the problems in principle are the same to the extent that all managerial concepts and practices are of use in evaluating resources and considering how to best achieve managerial objectives. This is true despite the fact that the character of the individual situation requires a different application of the concepts. All this is true even for a single individual as he or she seeks to maximize individual resources and have the most successful career possible.

Good management concepts are useful in all situations

Reconciliation of Economic, Personal, and Social Goals

In the typical business organization, the success of that organization is measured to a major extent by its ability to grow and be profitable. In our free enterprise system, a business organization that cannot be profitable over a reasonable period of time is either viewed as an organization no longer providing a needed product or service, or as an organization not being effectively managed. Although this profit measure does not exist in the governmental or other nonbusiness organization, there is a comparable yardstick available. This is the achievement of various types of service or impact objectives in terms of quantity or quality at minimal cost.

The determination and evaluation of these economic or other measurable goals can also, at the same time, be affected by personal goals. These are the very real—even though often denied—desires of managers to do something personally satisfying to themselves. Having the most impressive office facilities, being number one in unit or dollar volume, or favoring relatives for staff appointments over better qualified people are all common examples. Sometimes managers have the power to make such personal goals prevail, but in any event their cost should be known in terms of its effect on fully economic or other more rational goals.

The more significant conflict, however, exists in relation to socially oriented goals. Increasingly, there is the pressure from society on the business organization to act in a manner that achieves so-called social objectives. Examples are conservation of natural resources, improving the physical environment, special assistance for minority groups, and pressuring a country that violates human rights—all involving actions that may often go beyond existing legal requirements. The rationale here is that these are major re-

Management subject to conflicting pressures

sponsibilities of a business organization in this modern world. As a result
the manager in a business organization is subject to conflicting pressures.
Somehow he must assure the survival of the growth and profitability of the
organization. At the same time he must satisfy the society which, through
government, has legalized its organizational existence. The problem is how
to reconcile these pressures and to thus assure continuing healthy survival.
Here a balance must be found of what can be appropriately called "enlightened self-interest." That is an intermediate point where there can be needed
levels of profitability with concurrently adequate recognition of, and adjustment to, the social demands.

Is Management an Art or a Science?

*Management is both art
and science*

All the variables we have discussed lead to the question of whether management is an art or a science. The correct answer to this question is "probably both." To the extent that scientific surveys, analyses, and methodology
can be developed—as, for example, with the tools of management science
and electronic data processing—the practice of management moves in the
direction of being a science. However, information can never be complete
and there are always variables that are too complicated, diverse, and uncontrollable to be assessed adequately. At some point, therefore, management must depend on judgment and personal effectiveness. To that extent
management remains an art. Quite obviously, we are continually trying to
expand the scientific dimensions and thereby reduce the impact of the variables with their related risks. But the world continues to become increasingly
complex and we are usually hard pressed just to keep even.

A related question is whether management is a profession. By the standards outlined in the two preceding chapters, we can say that we are moving
in that direction. Also managers increasingly develop the kinds of capabilities
that enable them to move relatively freely from one organization to another
and from industry to industry. That freedom of involvement is also being
demonstrated. More and more professional managers exhibit a breadth of
responsibility for the needs of the larger society. We can therefore be proud
of the high professionalism of modern managers even though few would
claim that we have reached a fully satisfactory level. However, we are certainly moving in the "professional" direction.

Model for Management in Action

*Action flow covers use of
resources to achieve
objectives*

Thus far we have talked about management in terms of concepts and major
characteristics. We now propose to discuss the management process as a
defined sequence of various types of action. In doing this we again need to
recognize that all management action covers a great span of levels and scope.
We think, however, that the most useful way to look at management action
is at the highest level—that is, from the viewpoint of the top manager of a

large business organization. We do this because the principles involved are more clearly identifiable at that level, and lower-level situations differ only in that there is a degree of contraction of factors for which the manager has significant control. Moreover, it is always easier to understand one's managerial situation more clearly when that situation is viewed as a component of a larger situation for which we do have understanding.

The basic setting of our management situation is the existence of identified resources which are to be utilized over a future period of time to achieve established goals. This utilization takes place within an environment that is changing as we move through time. In graphic form the foregoing situation would look something like this:

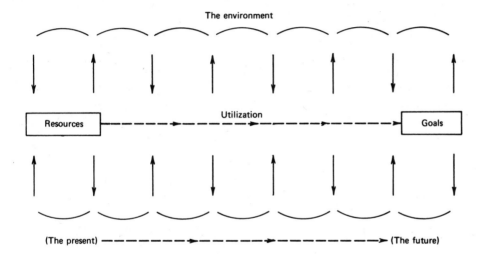

The two-way directions of the arrows between the environment and the goal achievement process is deliberate. Although for the most part the process is responding to the environment, the arrows directed outward recognize that to some extent the environment can be influenced by proper managerial action.

Resources as a Starting Point. In most cases the starting point for management action is the existence of specific resources. It is quite possible, however, that the recognition of a market or end product need can come first and that *then* we acquire the necessary resources. But in any event resources include both those we already have, plus those we can obtain, once we provide appropriate justification for the need. For our purposes it is satisfactory to start with the resources we have—their size, value, and service capabilities. At this point we seek to understand these resources in terms of both current and potential utilization.

Understanding the Environment.   A second logical necessity is to understand the environment in which we presently or potentially will use our resources. Here we seek to understand the environmental factors outlined earlier in this chapter as they are, how they are changing, how future changes can be influenced, and how the changing environmental factors involve risk with its various degrees of magnitude. Obviously, such an achievement is never fully possible. Moreover, the extent of achievement depends on how broadly we view the environment and how much time and money we are willing to devote to the effort of identification and measurement. But there can never be total certainty.

Elements of management process

We know that the general aspects of the total or larger environment cannot be ignored. However, we are especially concerned with the portion of the environment that relates more directly to our own resources. Here we seek to identify and evaluate the problems and opportunities which appear to exist in that more narrowly defined part of the total environment, and to appraise the strengths and weaknesses of our particular resources. At this stage we are concerned with relationships between our resources and the particular part of the environment that has potential for productivity and profitability in the face of competition and other types of risk.

*Identification and Evaluation of Alternative Product/Market Missions.*From the general overview given previously we now move to a more defined identification of alternative combined product and market choices. We seek the particular niches or sectors which indicate the greatest promise. We are at the same time evaluating those alternatives at the aggregate levels (as to quantification) of goals and supporting strategy. We are dealing at the aggregate level to facilitate the necessary breadth of the search without the expenditure of time and money that is necessary for more precise quantitative evaluation. But we are still using our knowledge and experience to weigh the merits and problems of the various alternatives. Basic to this evaluation is the fact that as we consider alternatives that involve new skills and new geographical areas, the degree of risk increases proportionately. It follows that with equal profit opportunities we give priority consideration to products and markets where we have knowledge and experience—thus achieving effective utilization of resources with lowest possible risk.

Choice of Major Product/Market Mission.   Out of the preceding evaluation now should come the tentative choice of the combined product and market combination that appears to promise the maximum rewards at acceptable levels of risks. At this point we are more precisely defining our goals, the supporting strategy, and planned implementation. At this time we are also reconciling personal, economic, and socially oriented goals and objectives— a conflict previously discussed—especially as to impact on the goals and strategy. The further definition of planned implementation also becomes

Mission refinement leads to strategy

important both for setting the stage for later to come actual implementation, and for further validating the soundness of goals and strategy.

Development of Supporting Strategy and Policies.   Management is now ready to move to the next lower level of developing the many needed supporting strategies and policies. These supporting plans are now developed in the various functional areas of finance, production, personnel, distribution, sales, promotion, procurement, and the like. They pertain also at the same time to the subprocess areas, such as organizing, providing resources, administering, and controlling—and go on to include the various types of procedural systems for information and control.

Continuing Planning Blended with Implementation.   At this stage, various types of procurement, training, construction, testing, initial production, market testing, preliminary promotion, and the like, are involving actual implementation. At this stage also, plans are developed for defined time periods—typically at something like a five-year span and then in more detail for the first year as an annual budget. These plans are quantified—at the five-year level on a more aggregate basis but with reasonable precision for the budget year—for operations and profit goals.

Full-Scale Implementation.   At this point, the organization is in full-scale operation applying planned policies and procedures and utilizing the previously acquired resources. During this actual implementation we are directly dependent on our administrative skills in the areas of directing, coordinating, and leading. At the same time the results accomplished are appropriately reported and compared to planned objectives at all operational levels. As a result of these comparisons, gaps and variances are identified and appraised, and such actions taken as appear best to assure the achievement of established goals.

Goal Achievement and Reappraisal.   The preceding stages have now achieved, to the maximum extent practicable, the desired goals of the total management process. However, there are normally deviations both up and down. These deviations may be due to various aspects of the planning and implementation which have been faulty in some respect. These deviations should of course be dealt with on their merits. Other deviations are due to new factors in the changing environment. The challenge here is to identify the causal factors and to take the new approaches that will best enable us to deal with the particular problems.

The Graphic Model in Expanded Form

As originally shown, the graphic management model emphasized the managerial action flow from resources to goals and objectives. The revised graphic model below is now in more detail and also stresses the circular action, which exists in two important ways:

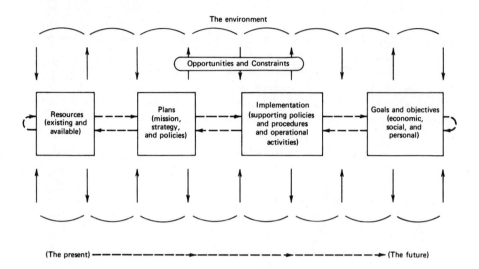

The first of these circular actions comes in the planning phase covered by the forward steps previously outlined. The circular action is the several cycles by which plans are studied and restudied at various lower levels of precision. Thus planning at the product/market mission level is in terms of broad aggregates, whereas planning in terms of the annual budget is at the level of operational precision. The second aspect of the circular action is in terms of repetitive planning as we move from one time period to the next.

Circular action is basic   Thus this year we have our five-year plan and annual budget, but at least a year later we repeat the same planning process, based on the then-existing conditions, and establish new budgets and five-year plans.

Adapting the Model to Situations at All Levels

In accordance with our earlier stated election, we have developed our model of the management process in terms of the top-level executive who is responsible for a large completely integrated organization. But management
Management action model   analysis and action takes place at all organizational levels. How then do we
similar at all levels   use our model to be helpful in all of these other situations? The variables in these different situations are twofold: the resources and the environment. In the case of resources the nature and scope can, as we have seen, be very much restricted at lower organizational level. Also to a greater extent resources are provided by high-level authority subject to established organizational policies and procedures. The manager must therefore deal with those resource facts as they are. In the case of environment there is again

a wide range of controls and restrictions with which the manager must contend. The restrictions become more and more substantial as we move to lower and lower organizational levels. Nevertheless, the *process* of relating the particular resources to the existing environmental factors to determine goals is the same in principle as it is for the top executive himself. It follows also that strategy and policy determination must be subject to the planning actions of the higher-level organizational managers. Finally also, the actual implementation will be subject to higher-level procedures and controls. At the same time, managers at all levels have an opportunity to reappraise the effectiveness of those higher-level organizational determinations and to make all efforts practicable to press for needed change.

Solving Management Problems

The graphic model just discussed shows the way the key components of resources, environment, plans, implementation, and goals relate to each other as an ongoing process over time. These same components can also be rearranged as in the accompanying diagram to better illustrate and facilitate specific management decisions:

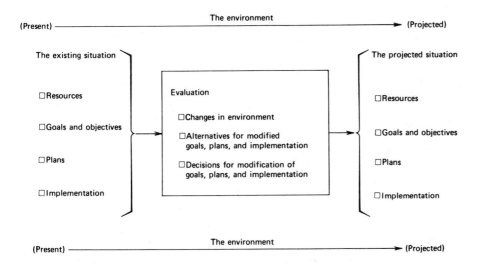

The approach is to start with the existing situation of all components and then to make the judgment of alternative modification actions as related to estimated projected outcomes. Again, this management decision model can be applied in any organization, at any organizational level, and to any management problem of any magnitude and substance.

Understanding Our Own Business

Management models must be adapted to our own business

What we have covered thus far in this chapter have been principles and concepts of a very general nature which apply for the most part to every managerial situation in all kinds of business and nonbusiness activities. These principles and concepts are basic and need to be the first foundation for all managerial activities. How they are applied, however, depends on the kind of business or nonbusiness activity in the particular managerial situation. Varying physical factors, technology used, nature and scope of processes to produce the product or service offered, capital investment, types of facilities, distribution, sales, maintenance, conditions of product usage, extent of risk, social visibility, and a host of other factors combine to make managing different in individual situations. As a result the various aspects of the management process need different kinds of attention with differing priorities and pertinent considerations. Effective managers must therefore be informed about these practical factors, and indeed the more they know the better, provided that the various factors are kept in proper balance.

Granted the importance of adequately understanding these pertinent factors, how do the manager and those who would serve management acquire the needed knowledge and understanding? There are also the related questions of how much one needs to know versus depending on others, and when the pursuit of such expertise is unduly costly as judged by other alternative utilization of available time. The resolution of these questions is obviously something that needs continuing judgment in the light of changing conditions. This resolution is also different for each manager in terms of his own ongoing career aspirations and utilization of his own resources in the most effective manner over future years.

Alternative Approaches for Developing Special Expertise. At the top of the alternative approaches for understanding the nature and scope of particular types of operations is certainly actual experience as a worker on the job. To the extent that an individual can have direct responsibility for particular types of operational activities, the more likely that individual is to become familiar with the types of problems that arise. The drawbacks are the amount of time required and the fact that much experience can become unduly repetitive—thus having diminishing value as a setting for desired levels of earning. A second alternative approach is through observation. Such observations may take the form of deliberately planned learning, but can also exist as a by-product of other responsibilities. The observations afforded by the conduct of internal auditing activities are illustrative. Finally, there is the alternative approach of actual study of the various areas pertaining to the production and use of the particular products. This too can take many forms and can involve a varying range of focus. In addition, in the case of all the alternative approaches just indicated, there is usually the further opportunity to combine the learning of unique aspects with the principles and concepts discussed in the earlier part of this chapter.

Partnership Role of the Internal Auditor

The accomplishment of the basic service role of the internal auditor to management starts with understanding management problems and needs, but then goes on to involve a partnership role between the manager and the internal auditor at all operational levels—a partnership role that extends to helping management achieve its managerial goals and objectives to the maximum extent possible. Such an effective partnership role can be achieved in many ways. We believe, however, that the following are essential ingredients of a sound program to achieve the desired results:

1. The ability to provide basic protective services but, at the same time, to help management achieve desired improvement. Moreover, the protective contributions often provide an important foundation for making the constructive contribution.

   Components of partnership role of internal auditor with management

2. Being continuously alert to use the point of detachment from actual operational responsibilities as a special capability to identify, evaluate, and support issues of significant management interest.

3. The capacity to interface in a persuasive manner with managers at all levels. This is a combination of operational understanding plus a manner of personal appearance and conduct.

4. Avoidance of the inherent temptation of auditors to use unduly available power with management and other operational auditees. Such actions generate auditee resistance that then blocks ongoing constructive relationships.

5. The strategic focus on control as the credential for the analysis and review of operational areas. Since the technical expertise of the auditee is typically always superior, the focus on control provides a more acceptable justification of the audit assistance offered.

6. The respect at all times during the process of assistance for the responsibility that managers have for operational results. Hence staff recommendations must stand on their own merits, as judged by those who have operational responsibility.

7. The continuing blending of the objectives of assistance at auditee levels with the necessity for upward disclosure within the framework of total organizational welfare. It is indeed the latter focus which neutralizes all lower-level conflict for the upward exposure.

8. The recognition that the success of the internal auditor is really measured by the extent to which managers manage better and not through the internal auditor being a policeman, adversary, critic, or seeker of independent credit.

Understanding Management in Perspective

The potential of service to the organization through assistance to management at all levels is a major goal for professional internal auditors. It is these potentials that justify every possible effort on the part of the internal auditor to see the management job through the eyes of management and to render all possible assistance for maximum goal achievement of all managers. The problems of management are very complex and are continually changing in the light of both internal and external environmental factors. This means that management increasingly needs the assistance of internal auditors and will in most cases welcome it when the ability and credibility of the internal auditor are established. It is a continuing challenge to internal auditors to render assistance which is in fact made productive through management acceptance and application.

*Understanding management
is a basic need*

Applying Management Concepts to Internal Auditing

The discussion of management concepts in this chapter has been in terms of any business or nonbusiness organization. It is also appropriate to recognize that these management concepts can also be used directly by individual internal auditing departments and by the total profession.

REVIEW QUESTIONS

1. There are two important reasons why internal auditors need to understand good management theory and practice. Explain.

2. Management is a process for achieving the most effective use of resources. Explain this definition in your own words.

3. What time period should be used in evaluating the most effective use of resources? Why?

4. The total management process consists of five subprocesses (or functions). Explain the interrelationships between each of the subprocesses.

5. What are the benefits of understanding the external environment of the organization?

6. How does the director of internal auditing view his or her environment?

7. Discuss the possible criteria to be used in determining the success of a particular management group.

8. What kind of conflicts can potentially exist between economic, personal, and social goals? In such cases who has the final say? Why?

9. Describe in your own words the revised graphic model for management in action.

10. How desirable do you think it is for an internal auditor to develop a partnership role with management? Explain in your own words the way in which this can be done most effectively.

CASE PROBLEMS

Problem 3-1

You are an audit supervisor with the XYZ Company. Until recently your internal audit staff has been concerned only with the narrower and more protective audit needs of management. The newly appointed general auditor for XYZ has just announced that from this time on the scope of every internal audit will include identifying improvement opportunities. The general auditor has advised you that his observation of staff activities left him with the impression that little has been done to attempt to establish internal auditing in a partnership role with the company managers. He believes that such a partnership is vital if the expanded scope audits are to be successful. He requested that you look into the matter and report back to him with suggestions on how to achieve such a partnership.

Required.   Prepare a response to the general auditor's request for suggestions to achieve a partnership role with managers.

Problem 3-2

Select a company with which you are most familiar—either as an employee or one you have studied—and describe the existing environment, resources, goals, plans, and adequacy of implementation. Then make your own evaluation of future environmental trends and the possible need for modification of goals, plans, and implementation. Assume that you have been engaged as a management consultant and are preparing a report covering the foregoing analysis and evaluation. Include, to the extent practicable, definitive recommendations for improvement and maximization of company welfare.

CHAPTER FOUR

Fundamentals of Control

After studying this chapter you should be able to:

- [ ] *Define "control" and describe the control process*
- [ ] *Explain the differences between the external and internal auditor's interest in control*
- [ ] *Distinguish between the protective and constructive dimensions of control systems*
- [ ] *Describe how control objectives are defined and established*
- [ ] *Understand the importance of cost considerations in control*
- [ ] *Recognize the desirable control specifications*
- [ ] *Explain the internal auditor's role in control*

NATURE OF CONTROL

Internal Auditor's Major Focus on Control

In Chapter 1 we saw that internal auditing is a type of organization control that functions by measuring and evaluating the effectiveness of other controls. In Chapter 2 we considered in greater depth the internal auditor's concern with the system of internal control. In Chapter 3 we recognized the importance of control in the total management process. The importance of the control function comes from the fact that the examination and appraisal of control are normally a part—directly or indirectly—of every type of internal auditing assignment. Moreover, the internal auditor's special competence in the control area is what justifies his review of a wide range of operational activities, even though he does not possess special knowledge about the substance of those activities. We need, therefore, to examine more closely the basic fundamentals of control so that we can apply the concepts

Competence in control justifies wide range of operational reviews

and principles more effectively in all operational situations. It is the purpose of this chapter to probe these underlying concepts and principles. We hope to identify a common framework and philosophy of the control process which is at the heart of the internal auditor's professional expertise.

Basic Nature of Control

Control as a process is needed in all areas of human activity, both inside the organization and for the total society. In most respects the concepts and principles used are the same. However, because the internal auditor's primary mission is to serve the organization, our own approach will be to focus on control as it applies to the activities of the organization. This more focused application is most often referred to as "internal control." It is the area of concern we intend even though we may often use the broader term "control."

Control as an organizational activity—or as a component of any organizational activity—exists at all organizational levels and is the concern of many different individuals in the organization. Its basic nature can best be understood in terms of the major phases of the total management process. That total process begins with planning and the related establishment of objectives. The planning is then supported by organizing and the necessary further providing of resources—including people. Managers then take the definitive operational actions to achieve the previously established objectives. But these operational actions will normally by themselves not be enough. Things seldom work out exactly as planned. Our underlying knowledge and estimates are never that good. Moreover, people are human and errors are made. Also environmental conditions change. We therefore need *supplementary measures and action to provide appropriate readings on our progress and to provide the basis for further actions which will better assure the achievement of our objectives*. We also need *procedures that assure desired types of action and prevent those that are not desired*. The control function is concerned with providing these supplementary measures, actions, and procedures.

Control is a concern with all organizational activities

It is of course apparent that the control function cannot exist unless we have objectives. If we do not know where we want to go, we can hardly know what kind of measures and actions should be taken to get us there. It is also apparent that the taking of the supplementary actions brings us back again into the actual management process as further managerial actions are taken. Thus control exists as an independent phase of the management process but at the same time an essential part of it.

Control function cannot exist without objectives

A very simple illustration of the control function is a boat setting sail for a given port with a planned arrival date. At interim points the progress is determined. Because of the prevailing winds, or engine problems, the boat may be off course. As a result changes in direction are made necessary, and possibly speeds may have to be modified. If necessary, there will be a revision of the scheduled arrival. The control function here is to consider and evaluate the impact of the new developments in actual progress, and to provide a proper basis for needed supplementary action. It thus contributes to reaching our destination on a timely basis and in the most efficient manner practicable.

Range of Interest in Internal Control

Concerns for control exist at all levels

The broad scope of the interest in control can be better understood by recognizing the range of control applications and relating that range to the varying levels of users. In terms of applications we can start at the highest level of organizational activity. Here, for example, there is the application of monitoring the various key factors that determine rates of profitability and growth. Another example is monitoring the factors that pertain to maintaining dividend policies and to attracting needed investment. At still lower operational levels is, for example, the monitoring of divisional profitability or the market acceptance of individual products. At still lower operational levels, for example, are applications to ensure the proper billing of sales to customers or the collection of accounts receivable. At the lowest level is the monitoring by each individual of his own daily work activities. Other low-level controls exist as specific procedural requirements.

To a considerable extent these varying levels of control applications parallel the interests of different types of users, although often in a varying range of combinations. For example, we have the high-level interests of a regulatory body such as the Securities and Exchange Commission, the special interests of the independent auditor, and the increasingly narrow interests of different individuals, as determined by their declining levels of organizational responsibility. These levels of organizational or other user interest interface with the range of control applications to provide and define the total universe of control activities. In all cases, however, there are objectives for which controls are needed to measure performance and to help guide us toward the objectives we have established. The control function is thus a multidimensional tapestry covering the entire range of organizational activities.

Types of Control[1]

While control is always tied directly or indirectly to objectives, and while the nature and scope of objectives can vary widely, the manner in which control is exercised can also vary. In general, there are three different types of controls.

1. *Steering Controls.* One major type of controls is through the identification of events which prompt us to take interim actions that will be contributory to the achievement of larger objectives. These interim

---

[1]This classification and discussion is based in part on one developed by William H. Newman in his book *Constructive Control* (Englewood Cliffs, N.J.: Prentice-Hall, 1975).

events can be very precise or very broad. However, the common characteristic is that they alert us to the need to take some type of managerial action on a timely basis. In the case of the driver of the boat previously mentioned, the drift of the boat to one side first indicates the need for definitive steering action. Various types of gauges in a manufacturing process indicate the fact of developing conditions that require particular processing actions. A drop in dealer orders triggers the carmaker's problem of declining market acceptance of his product and the related need to adjust production schedules. In still other cases a broad index of economic trends can alert us to changing conditions that spark protective or other opportunity-oriented actions.

Alert management to need for timely action

2. *Yes–No Controls*. Controls of this type are those designed to function more automatically to protect us or to otherwise help assure the accomplishment of desired results. In its simplest form it could be a quality control gauge through which only a product part of the exact specifications can pass. In another illustrative situation the control could be a required approval on a business form—thus ensuring that a particular individual had made a necessary review of the action involved. The design of organizational responsibilities also properly exploits opportunities to assure needed cross evaluation of major business decisions and implementing action. The common element is that there is a preestablished control device or arrangement that under normal conditions will more or less automatically help assure the desired protective, or improvement action.

Help assure protective and improvement action

3. *Post-Action Controls*. A third type of control overlaps with the two types just discussed but is distinctive in that the managerial action comes about some time later and takes the form of doing the best thing possible under the circumstances existing then. The action taken may be to repair a product that has been damaged, change a policy or procedure, or dismiss or reassign an employee. That after-the-fact action may be immediately feasible or require extended study and development. The analyses done by internal auditors are typically directed to determining the nature and scope of the most effective type of after-the-fact action, even though that action be very much future oriented. Control needs here are thus identified by looking at the past but always to the extent possible are oriented to improving future activities.

Oriented to improving future activities

Internal Control as Viewed by Certified Public Accountants

The definitions in the United States by the American Institute of Certified Public Accountants (AICPA) pertaining to internal control are of special interest because of their relationship to the work of the Certified Public

Accountant (CPA)[2] which underlies his expression of an opinion as to the fairness of the financial statements of his client company. As further discussed, these definitions have also been used as a guide by the Securities Exchange Act in developing regulations covering the enforcement of the Securities Exchange Act of 1934 and the Foreign Corrupt Practices Act of 1977. In the AICPA's codified standards covering auditing practice (320.09) there is the following definition:

> Internal control comprises the plan of organization and all of the coordinate methods and measures adopted within a business to safeguard its assets, check the accuracy and reliability of its accounting data, promote operational efficiency, and encourage adherence to prescribed managerial policies.

Two way control approach by CPAs

Other definitions in paragraphs 320.27 and 320.28 then further define the two sectors of that internal control as follows:

> **.27** *Administrative control* includes, but is not limited to, the plan of organization and the procedures and records that are concerned with the decision processes leading to management's authorization of transactions. Such authorization is a management function directly associated with the responsibility for achieving the objectives of the organization and is the starting point for establishing accounting control of transactions.

> **.28** *Accounting control* comprises the plan of organization and the procedures and records that are concerned with the safeguarding of assets and the reliability of financial records and consequently are designed to provide reasonable assurance that:

> a. Transactions are executed in accordance with management's general or specific authorization.

> b. Transactions are recorded as necessary (1) to permit preparation of financial statements in conformity with generally accepted accounting principles or any other criteria applicable to such statements and (2) to maintain accountability for assets.

> c. Access to assets is permitted only in accordance with management's authorization.

> d. The recorded accountability for assets is compared with the existing assets at reasonable intervals and appropriate action is taken with respect to any differences.

The overlapping relationship of these two types of internal control is then further clarified in paragraph 320.29:

Some controls are dual purpose

> **.29** The foregoing definitions are not necessarily mutually exclusive because some of the procedures and records comprehended in accounting control may also be involved in administrative control. For example, sales and cost records classified by products may be used for accounting control purposes and also in making management decisions concerning unit prices or other

[2]Although the focus here is on public accounting practice in the United States, the principles are generally applicable to the Chartered Accountant and other independent public accountants.

aspects of operations. Such multiple uses of procedures or records, however, are not critical for the purposes of this section because it is concerned primarily with clarifying the outer boundary of accounting control. Examples of records used solely for administrative control are those pertaining to customers contacted by salesmen and to defective work by production employees maintained only for evaluating personnel performance.

In both paragraphs 320.09 and 320.49 it is also made clear that the system of internal control extends beyond those matters which relate directly to the accounting and financial statements, but that the CPA's primary interest for purposes of the review of financial statements is with the internal accounting control. In paragraph 320.49 there is the specific statement that

> accounting control is within the scope of the study and evaluation of internal control contemplated by generally accepted auditing standards, while administrative control is not.

Although the interests of the internal auditor extend beyond internal accounting control to the effectiveness of the total system of internal control, the internal accounting control is part of the larger system, Moreover, the line of demarcation from the part to the larger whole is never exactly clear. Hence interpretations by both the Securities and Exchange Commission and AICPA relating to the system of internal accounting control are extremely important. Similarly, the voluminous interpretations and guidelines developed by leading CPA firms are of great value to the practicing internal auditor. These materials are discussed further in Chapter 6.

Internal auditors have broader interest in internal control

Impact of the Foreign Corrupt Practices Act of 1977

In 1977, responding to an increasing public concern with reported practices of U.S. business corporations, Congress enacted the Foreign Corrupt Practices Act. In this act the following requirements, based directly on the statements by the AICPA, were established:

> (2) Every issuer which has a class of securities registered pursuant to section 12 of this title and every issuer which is required to file reports pursuant to section 15(d) of this title shall—
> (A) make and keep books, records, and accounts, which, in reasonable detail, accurately and fairly reflect the transactions and dispositions of the assets of the issuer; and
> (B) devise and maintain a system of internal accounting controls sufficient to provide reasonable assurances that—
> (i) transactions are executed in accordance with management's general or specific authorization;
> (ii) transactions are recorded as necessary (I) to permit preparation of financial statements in conformity with generally accepted accounting principles or any other criteria applicable to such statements, and (II) to maintain accountability for assets;

(iii) access to assets is permitted only in accordance with management's general or specific authorization; and

(iv) the recorded accountability for assets is compared with the existing assets at reasonable intervals and appropriate action is taken with respect to any differences.

The special significance of these new requirements is that they establish more clearly the responsibility of management for an adequate system of internal accounting control. This responsibility overlaps with, but goes beyond, the CPA's concern with the internal accounting control to the extent that he relies on that internal accounting control for purposes of supporting his opinion as to the fairness of the financial statements of his client company. However, it is significant that the FCPA requirements use word for word the previously quoted definition by the AICPA.

Control Process

Another way to better understand controls and to be better able to apply them to all types of organizational activities is to focus on the control process. This control process, which to some extent underlies every individual operational application in the organization, has been broken down by various authorities in differing ways. However, our own interpretation is as follows:

Control process involves seven key steps

1. *Development of Objectives*. The first step is the determination of what it is we wish to achieve—some kind of an objective. This objective can be one which is at a very high level or it can be a very detailed and definitive sort of thing. In the latter instance it is commonly referred to as a standard. Thus the allowance of a given amount of time to carry out a particular operation on an automobile assembly line is thought of as a work standard. Low-level objectives also include specific procedural requirements—as, for example, an approval by a certain officer. The common characteristic in all cases is, however, that there is a determined objective. What is of greatest importance from the standpoint of the control process is the validity of the objective. This total quality includes how carefully the objective was determined, how specific it is, whether there is agreement as to its legitimacy, and the extent to which its achievement can be measured. Thus the effectiveness of the control process is linked directly to how well the underlying objectives have been established.

Lower level objectives take form of work standards

A further way to utilize objectives is to use available interim guidelines to provide faster response to problems that can significantly affect future results. Sometimes these interim guidelines are already available—as, for example, when initial sales at a new model car show can be used to appraise total customer response. In other cases, through controlled field tests we can make more scientific preliminary estimates of product acceptability. In still other cases the varying rate of accomplishment can be recognized in a series of programmed interim objectives—as, for example, to reflect cyclical patterns—to recognize more realistically changing interim conditions.

2. *Measurement of Results.* Assuming that the objective has been stated in the terms by which it can be measured, the second step of the control process is to provide the actual measures of current performance. We need to know what we are actually accomplishing in the way of progress toward the established objectives. Also this information as to performance needs to be available in the right places, at the right time, and to the right people. Thus while we need to know where we want to go, we must also know what we are doing through actual performance toward the achievement of those goals. Only in this way can we have the proper basis for the comparisons and analysis of what corrective or other managerial action may be needed on an interim basis.

Measurements show extent of progress toward objectives

3. *Comparison of Actual Performance Against Objectives.* We are now ready to match the data of actual performance against the previously established objectives. This makes possible the identification of the differences, frequently referred to as variances. This comparison can be both for current time periods and for longer cumulative periods. Although the comparison is a specific step in the control process, it is in practice often combined with the reporting of actual results. Clearly the making of these comparisons depends on actual performance and objectives being stated in the same manner—a need that must be anticipated when the objectives are established.

4. *Analysis of the Causes of Differences.* The next step is to determine what the causes were for the differences reported. This is the probing to identify the various causal factors, plus the efforts to measure the effect of each. The approach in part is to push backward for more detailed information about the various operational activities. There is also an effort to determine both immediate and more basic causes. At the same time there is a judgmental evaluation of how important individual factors actually are as causes. This is the essential step in utilizing the results portrayed in the three preceding steps. It is the responsibility of every manager, whether done by himself or by another party. It is also the typical work of the internal auditor, whether done directly from basic data or superimposed on previously accomplished analysis.

Causes of variance determined

5. *Determination of Appropriate Managerial Action.* The analysis of the causes of differences unavoidably blends to some extent with the determination of appropriate managerial action. In some cases the responsible manager will himself be making part or all of the analysis. In most cases, however, this will be done by a separate analyst, and this analyst may also make recommendations for management action.

Taking management action
responsibility of line
managers

The actual determination of management action in any event belongs to the person who has the line responsibility for the particular operational activities involved. Here the available alternatives must be evaluated and the very important judgment reached as to what, if any, specific action should be taken.

It is useful to note also that the responsibility for the proper analysis and determination of appropriate managerial action *is* the responsibility of the manager in charge and in turn of higher-level managers, irrespective of the extent to which those activities are delegated to subordinates or other staff groups. This is consistent with the fact of every manager's overall responsibility for final acceptance and utilization of all actions pertinent to the achievement of his own goals and objectives.

6. *Taking Action.* The judgment just reached as to appropriate managerial action must now actually be implemented. The needed instructions are now issued in a manner that gives consideration to the required urgency, the level of personnel being dealt with, and the complexity of the actions to be taken. The action to be taken may be something that can be accomplished quickly—like correcting an error —or it may extend over a long period—as, for example, modifying a complex system. In all cases, however, there is a further control problem as to what follow-up there should be to satisfy the responsible manager that action has been completed as desired.

In some situations the proper action determined to be taken may be to do nothing at all. Perhaps the cost of correction outweighs the risk. Or perhaps there is knowledge of future developments that will be adequate to cure the presently existing problem. It needs to be recognized, however, that taking no action is itself a decision, and hence a kind of responsive action.

7. *Continuing Reappraisal.* A final step in the control process is the appraisal of results after the aforementioned actions have been carried out. This in effect is a further check on the soundness of the earlier determinations of needed action and the manner in which the actions were actually taken. This final step now provides the necessary linkage of the original control cycle to the next cycle. This continuing appraisal thus blends into the next measurement of progress analysis, and determination of further managerial action. Indeed, post appraisal is a continuing action reflecting the input of changing conditions, more experience, and greater knowledge of all factors.

Thus the total control process can be conveniently reviewed in terms of the seven key steps. We will deal with some of the major problems that relate more specifically to the individual steps. First, however, we look briefly at some more general aspects of the control function in the total management process.

Relation of Control to Total Management Process

In our discussion of the nature of the control process we saw that the control function begins with the defining of objectives and ends with the achievement of those objectives. As applied to the conceptual framework outlined in Chapter 3, this control function has mostly to do with the effectiveness of the implementing actions whereby strategies are translated into action to achieve established goals and objectives. It is also useful to see in more depth how the control function interrelates with the major stages of the conventional management process—planning, organizing, providing resources, and administering.

Tie to Planning. As we know, planning is concerned with determining sound objectives for the company, both as a whole and for each operational component. These objectives in total, and in the case of each operational component, provide the points of reference for the supporting control activities. Complete and comprehensive planning thus provides the foundation for the control function. We know that management recognizes the need for good planning. But it needs to be emphasized also that anyone interested in developing or improving effective control must necessarily be concerned with both the adequacy of the design for planning and the effectiveness with which the planning is actually done. Our first interest, therefore, is to have sufficiently good planning throughout the total company.

Planning provides foundation for control

Tie to Organizing. The importance of organizing to the control function is that it is through organizing that work assignments are made, authority delegated, and accountabilities determined. In this way organizing provides the framework for control. More specifically, the organizational responsibilities of individuals and groups of individuals (including organizational components) make possible the more systematic identification of objectives and the measurement of operational results. Again this means that if we want effective control we must be concerned with improving the soundness of organizational design and related organizational arrangements.[3] Good organizing thus becomes a major building block for effective control.

Organizing supplies framework for control

Tie to Providing Resources. The acquisition, handling, and disposition of all resources involve problems of control. But in the case of human resources the problems are all the more critical because control—like the total management process of which the control process is a part—is done by people who are supposedly properly selected, trained, and administered. Also where there are capable managers, the administration of control functions will be done in a more effective manner. Thus the achievement of effective control must involve all of the key aspects of the staffing and personnel function.

Providing resources has special control problems

[3]See Chapter 5.

Administrative actions must
be supportive

Tie to Administering. We know that administering has to do with the issuing of instructions, supervising people, working with people, coordinating, and leading. At this stage managers also administer the control system and take the actions determined to be necessary as a result of the variations from planned performance. The manner in which this total directing role is carried out can either support the control system or hinder it. This means then that achieving effective control requires a close partnership with responsible managers so that actions in that area are supportive of control needs.

Design and Implementation

What, How, and How much
decisions key questions

Another useful way to approach the control function is in terms of the dimensions of design and implementation. *Design* has to do with the selection of the particular operational aspects to be controlled, the determination of the extent to which these aspects are to be controlled, and the choice of the way that control actions are to be carried out. Such a design effort of course takes into consideration the later implementation of the system, but it tends to focus more directly on the more basic dimensions of managerial needs. A particular type of standard is determined, a procedure for measuring results is developed, and a program is laid out for review and possible action. All of this involves a considered judgment as to benefits expected and costs to be incurred. The second part of the control system then has to do with the actual *implementation*, that is, the installation of the system and the subsequent administration of it. At this point we focus directly on actual performance and the people who are involved. Here the need is for administrative skill and judgment to deal with the many unforeseen developments and the unavoidable human problems. What is important here is that we recognize that there are two interrelated but still fairly separate problems areas. In both cases we must learn how to deal with them effectively.

Need to Blend with Management System

A closely related problem to the aforementioned design and implementation is the extent to which the control measures can be blended with normal managerial procedures and actions. What we are trying to do is to avoid as much as possible having the control measure as a supplementary and separate type of activity. Instead, we seek to achieve our control objective as much as possible through the regular operational procedures. The reason for this

Control should be built into
regular operating
procedures

is twofold. There is, first, the benefit of avoiding the extra cost which is otherwise necessary. Second, there is a lesser irritation to the persons who are directly or indirectly being controlled. For example, if the acceptance of a particular part by a using department from the producing department can be automatically determined by whether it fits into the larger assembly, then we may not have to set up an intermediate inspection group. Similarly, we seek to cover the administration of control as a part of normal management relationships rather than to deal with it as a separate type of problem. Every control specialist is always looking for these opportunities for achieving control as a part of regular operating procedures.

Protective and Constructive Dimensions

Another important way to look at control systems is to recognize their protective and constructive dimensions, and then to try to maximize the latter, as much as possible. To a major extent controls do serve to protect higher-level managers from what may go wrong at the lower levels. Some controls have as at least one of their major purposes the prevention of particular kinds of action not desired by higher-level management. Illustrative of such undesirable actions would be the improper use of company property, the making of commitments beyond an authorized level, or improperly preparing a particular form. Other controls are protective in the sense that higher-level management wants to know of particular types of developments so that they can take corrective or defensive action on a timely basis.

Protective controls provide alerts for undesirable developments

In other cases, however, the controls emphasize more the constructive possibilities. Here the control is viewed as a guide as to where we might improve some aspects of our operation. For example, a control in the form of consumer preference testing would enable us to develop new products or differently present existing ones to exploit new consumer trends. Part of this constructive approach can be achieved by emphasizing the positive benefits which normally follow control actions that are protective in the first instance. Illustrative would be the emphasis on customer satisfaction and company reputation which is a result of protective-type inspection measures. Frequently also, the control can be defined in a broader manner which will better motivate the persons subject to the control. Illustrative would be the use of profit performance controls over a subsidiary instead of detailed operational controls. In still other cases the constructive emphasis can come through a more understanding and sensitive administration of controls. In all of these situations the objective of the control specialist is to cover the protective needs in a manner which avoids the emphasis in that direction, and instead to stress the constructive potentials.

Risk Analysis for Protective Objectives

As we have just seen, the evaluation of effective internal control involves both protective and constructive types of objectives. The fact of that dual interest is especially important for corporate managers, and in turn for internal auditors who seek to serve the total range of management interests. Moreover the evaluation of controls in relation to constructive and broader improvement objectives are a higher level and more sophisticated type of evaluation—especially when improvement objectives involve increased corporate profitability. However, protective objectives are basically very important and need to be covered properly. As it happens also, the evaluation

Risk analysis helps achieve protective objectives

of internal control for protective objectives lends itself especially to more scientific and structured risk analysis.

Evaluation of risk for protective objectives focuses directly on (1) the nature and scope of the impact of the particular types of potential deficiencies, and (2) the feasibility and cost of the actual controls. This kind of evaluation must of course be made individually for each company and its various operational situations. But when so done it can be a useful guide as to what kind of controls, and the extent of their use, actually make good business sense. What does further complicate the evaluation, however, are the often existing conflicts between the reduction of potential direct losses with broader management needs and operational objectives. An example in a retail store would be the extent that merchandise for sale should be immediately available to the customer for examination. In this situation we can keep the merchandise locked up—and thus minimize theft—but we may thereby discourage examination of that merchandise and unduly restrict sales. What all this means is that risk analysis can be sound or unsound in management terms depending on the extent to which all related management objectives are properly recognized and evaluated.

Problem of Human Responses to Control

Individuals typically oppose controls

We have at various points noted the fact that people are involved in the control process and that this calls for special kinds of skills in dealing with them. At this point, however, we need to recognize the special problems that are raised on the human side in developing an effective control system. The basic source of the problems comes from the fact that most individuals instinctively like independence and freedom of action. The very fact that people are required to do something makes them tend to view such a control with aversion and even with hostility. The extent of the tolerance for controls depends to a considerable extent upon the individual himself—his intelligence, experience, cultural background, emotional stability, and the like. But we can say that there is a normal tendency to resent controls and to resist them to some extent. Much also depends on the way controls are developed and how they are presented and administered. Therefore, in our endeavor to achieve effective control we need to understand this normal human response and to try to do everything possible to minimize the existing problems.

How can we deal with these human barriers to effective control? We suggest the following types of action:

1. *Augmenting Total Company Image.* Undoubtedly the most basic approach to achieving effective control is to establish an overall company reputation for competence and integrity. This reputation must first be established at the top and then disseminated down through the entire organization. A greater general receptivity for control measures is thus established.

2. *Providing Adequate Rationale*. People especially resent any kind of control which they do not understand. Indeed, they are then tempted to interpret the control actions as arbitrary and unfair. This means that it is necessary to go out of one's way to explain the reasons for particular types of control. The rationale behind a "keep off the grass" sign may be sufficiently obvious, but in other cases the reasons for the particular restriction need to be understood to be acceptable to the people affected. Budgetary controls are, for example, better received if there is some understanding of the objectives of the budgetary process and how it needs to operate.

3. *Manner of Presentation*. In addition to adequate rationale there is much that can be done in the way the particular control is initiated. People respond to courtesy and to evidence of reasonable consideration. There is also the need for proper explanations of how the controls are to work and a reasonable opportunity for people to adjust to them.

4. *Legitimacy of Source*. People especially resent controls that are imposed by persons not believed to have the authority to impose them. The solution here is that the particular control be sponsored by a sufficiently high level of authority, where there is no question as to its being proper. Supporting details can then be supplied, where necessary, by a lower level of authority.

Guides for minimizing human problems of controls

5. *Participation*. In many cases it is not practicable for all parties who are to be subject to the control to be able to participate in the formulation of the control itself. We do know, however, that the further we can go in that direction, the greater will be the acceptance of the control. Thus the acceptance of budgetary controls requires a participation of the responsible manager with his superiors. Even in the case of work standards, the joint consideration between representatives of management and labor achieve important participation benefits.

6. *Manner of Administration*. Finally, much can be done in the way controls are administered. The need here is to avoid being arbitrary, to the extent possible, and to demonstrate understanding of the problems involved. For example, budgetary controls, which are applied in a mechanical manner not only destroy current motivation, but in addition lead to built-in protection when the next budget is developed. People being controlled need to know that there is an interest in operational problems and that there is a willingness to listen to subordinates. This important quality of the administration emphasizes flexibility rather than rigidity.

It is not claimed that the problems of human responses to controls can be completely eliminated by these approaches. But we can do much in these ways to make controls more acceptable to most people. Since controls do have a necessary role to play, our next best type of action is to learn to deal with them in the way that is most acceptable to the people being controlled.

PROBLEMS OF THE CONTROL CYCLE

We have thus far dealt with control in its entirety. We now go back to the seven steps in the control cycle and examine in greater detail some of the major operational problems which relate more specifically to each phase of the cycle.

Problems of Objectives

We have already discussed the fundamental role of objectives in the total control process. Our further interests now are the following individual features of process through which objectives are developed.

What Should Be Controlled?   In developing meaningful control we must first ask ourselves what it is we wish to control. This is a question that needs to be asked for the company as a whole and at each level of operational activity. Even though we may be dealing with a specific level of operational activity, we need to relate the particular needs there to other operational activities, and to the larger company activities as a whole. In making this determination it will be helpful to think in terms such as the following:

Sound decisions needed for what to control

1. *What are the key resources?* At each level of operational activity, and as required by the nature of the particular operational activity, there will be resources of people, machines, money, materials, customer loyalty, and the like. What resources are the most valuable in relation to the others, and what are the risks in each case of waste, misappropriation, or failure to be used productively? Where also are the most potential possibilities of effective utilization? What are the values of these resources in relationship to each other and to other company resources, both in terms of dollar value and operational impact?

2. *What are the key costs?* A related way to look at the particular situation is in terms of key costs. What are the largest types of expenditures? Which of these types of expenditure are the most controllable? Which offer the greatest potentials for saving, and which the greatest opportunities for other types of effective utilization? The solution here involves careful analysis and good judgment so that we can direct our control efforts where the results will be most rewarding.

3. *What are the critical issues?* Still another way to look at a particular operating activity (or group of activities) is in terms of their impact on the other company activities. What happens to other specific operational groups if this particular group does not do its job effectively? What is the impact upon total company welfare? Perhaps, for example, the later failure of a small part being produced can endanger the performance of the completed assembly, and even involve the lives of people.

4. *What combinations of control needs?* It is especially important to relate specific control needs to each other in proper combinations. There is the danger that particular controls will unduly overlap and be at odds with each other. For example, a control in the form of maintenance labor cost per mile of pipeline might overlap with additional controls over hours worked or rates paid. The overlap could easily restrict the manager's effort to use available types of labor most effectively. A second illustration is where controls over the level of bad-debt losses might conflict with efforts to increase profits through increased sales.

5. *Are control objectives consistent with decentralization policy?* A useful way to look at the problem of properly combining control needs is to ask ourselves whether the level of control objectives at each operational level is consistent with the intended decentralization of responsibility to the next-lower management level. This is especially important if the decentralization policy has been implemented by hiring managers of the higher-level capabilities. In such cases, too detailed objectives will waste the money expended as salaries to those capable managers.

How Can the Objectives Be Defined?   The determination of what should be controlled leads us to the question of how we should define the particular objectives. Our concern at this point is with the specific characteristics of such definition. These essential characteristics include:

1. *Need to Be Specific.* Our first need is to go beyond the level of generality and to be specific about our control objectives. At a high level, for example, it is not enough to say we want a company to be profitable. In addition, we need to specify the exact terms by which that profitability shall be measured. At a lower level it is not enough to say that we want a worker to be productive. We need also to specify the terms in which that productivity will be measured—units produced, hours per unit produced, sales achieved, costs incurred, and the like.

Operational objectives need adequate definition

2. *Maximum Quantification Practicable.* In addition to the need to be specific, there is the related need to express the objectives to the extent practicable in quantitative terms. If the objective is increased profits per share, how much of an increase? If the objective is increased sales, we need to specify the amount of that desired sales increase. In many situations the quantification is difficult and there is a reluctance to come to grips with it. We need to remember, however, that quantification provides a necessary degree of precision to the control effort.

3. *Fixing of Time Dimensions.* The specification of objectives in quantitative terms also involves a proper determination of the time dimension. If the objective is increased earnings per share, we need to specify the periods to be covered. In other cases the time dimension becomes the key quantitative dimension. Illustrative is the fixing of

target dates for the various stages of the installation of a new system. Again these time dimensions are essential to provide an adequate framework for control.

4. *Anticipation of Measurement Phase*. Finally the specification of objectives must anticipate the later need to measure performance against those objectives. At this point consideration must be given to the scope of the existing accounting system and other related operational reports. If new types of measurement are to be involved, consideration must also be given to the feasibility and cost of such supplemental procedures.

How Will the Objective Actually Be Established?   The determination of what is to be controlled, and how the objective will be defined, now sets the stage for the actual determination of the objective. The concern at this stage is with the adequacy of the study effort upon which that determination will be based. Is the determination in effect pulled out of the air, and hence more wishful thinking than cold reality? Or is the objective based on a reasonable examination of the pertinent factors involved. It is quite evident that unless the objectives are properly determined, there can be no meaningful ongoing control effort. In making this determination there are certain types of input which need to be provided and given proper consideration. These inputs include the following:

Key inputs for establishing objectives

1. *Historical Data*. One useful type of guide is what has happened in the past. From that experience we know how successful certain efforts have been, what problems have been encountered, and what costs have been incurred.

2. *New Factors in the Current Situation*. Historical data are, however, based on previously existing conditions. The situation now may involve different people capabilities, new types of equipment, and better techniques. Hence adjustments must be made to give considerations to all things that are different from the previously existing situation.

3. *Future Projections*. We need also to give consideration to further changes which may be expected in the future. Perhaps new types of equipment will be available. Or perhaps there is an environmental development that can reasonably be predicted. We need, therefore, to project these expected changes and build them into our future objectives.

4. *Extent of Task*. Finally, there is the factor of improvement which should be built into the objective. This is a highly judgmental question and is directly dependent on the relations of the higher and lower levels of supervision. The task factor can, on the one hand, be set so low that it fails to induce the full potential. On the other hand, however, it can be so high that it unduly discourages and alienates the parties whose performance is to be measured. The challenge here is to find the proper intermediate balance.

Rule of Reason. The discussion of the particular features of developing objectives has emphasized the need to select the right things to be controlled, to define them in specific terms, and to have an adequate basis for their actual determination. It is, indeed, right and proper that we should push in those directions. However, it is also important to apply a rule of reason in each case. We can, for example, extend the scope of our control to detailed activities which result both directly in excessive cost and conflict with other important management needs. We can also push the quantification effort to a point where important qualitative dimensions are ignored. Illustrative here would be measuring the effectiveness of a public relations program by the *number* of accepted news releases, without consideration of the size of the individual news stories or the substance of them. Such undue reliance on quantification provides an appearance of effective control that is both fallacious and full of risk. Finally in the area of actual determination, there can be an excessive concentration on underlying facts and details which is both too costly and too time consuming. The establishment of objectives, therefore, requires at all times a great deal of judgment and good sense.

Establishing control objectives requires judgment and common sense

Challenge of Establishing Objectives. We have endeavored in our discussion of objectives to show the needs and potential possibilities, and at the same time to point out the problems and pitfalls. The challenge that exists in all operational situations, at all levels, is to find the right kind of balance. The job of the control specialist is to push the control function into new areas by a more capable analysis of the pertinent factors, and by a more perceptive determination of proper objectives. At the same time adequate consideration must be given to the feasibility of subsequent implementation, the costs involved—both in terms of direct operational costs and in its other types of operational impact such as the human responses discussed earlier. To a considerable extent this is a part of the basic responsibility of every manager at each operational level. But it is the role of the control specialist to provide direct assistance in this area. What is increasingly clear is that the proper identification and development of meaningful control objectives is at the heart of the effectiveness of the total control effort. The challenge is to carry out this part of the total process in a way that will best provide a sound foundation for productive operational activities.

Proper identification of objectives is challenging

Problems of Measurement

The objectives that have been established now set the stage for the measurement of performance in terms of those objectives. The establishment of those objectives has, as we have seen, necessarily considered the supporting need for measurement. Presumably then the practicability of measuring the particular kind of performance involved has already been anticipated. However, it will still be necessary to provide for any special procedures that go beyond the regular reporting program. At this stage also there are certain

Measurement may require procedures beyond regular reporting system

features of the reporting which need to be given proper recognition. These include:

1. *Consistency with Structure of Objectives.* Performance data need to be reported in exactly the same terms as the objectives. This means that the structure of the objectives should be followed also in the reporting of performance data. This requirement has special application in relation to a budget or profit plan.

2. *Accuracy.* A second basic requirement is that performance data be accurately stated. Errors can never be completely avoided, but excessive errors destroy the credibility of the data, and to that extent undermine the effectiveness of the remainder of tbe control system. This does not preclude the use of sampling as a basis for the development of certain kinds of performance data, since this method frequently provides the basis for more effective management action. However, the manner in which the samples are used needs to be clearly disclosed.

3. *Timing.* Effective control depends directly on performance data being made available promptly. Every possible means should therefore be taken to streamline the processing and reporting of performance data. The importance of the managerial needs in many situations makes it desirable to use estimates.

Guides for adequacy of reporting

4. *Use of Preliminary Measures.* In many situations, as previously discussed, it is possible to develop preliminary measures that serve as warning signals. Illustrative would be the case where a periodic check of stocks of independent dealers can provide a basis for anticipating the volume of sales by a manufacturer to those dealers. The trend of incoming applications can similarly provide a good basis of judging how registrations for colleges will subsequently become actuality.

5. *Distribution.* In an effective control system performance data flow first to the supervisory level which has direct responsibility. The data are then summarized in an appropriate manner and made available to the next supervisory level. The sequence is important because normally the lower supervisory level needs to be alerted first as a basis for promptness in taking needed action. Also that supervisory level can then prepare itself for questions and discussions with the next-level supervisors. The further summarization at each operational level is important because higher-level supervisors have a range of larger responsibilities and must keep their work loads within the limits of effective use of time.

Problems of Comparing Performance with Objectives

The problems that arise in the comparison of actual performance with objectives involve all the problems previously cited in connection with measurement. This is because the two stages overlap and are normally combined in some way. However, several additional problems need to be properly dealt with:

1. *Presentation*. If control reports are to be used in an effective manner, it is first necessary that they be clear and understandable. Actual data and objectives are usually best put in separate columns and favorable and unfavorable variances clearly identified. In the case of interim reporting—as, for example, in the case of budgets—the comparisons are usually made both for the current period and the cumulative performance to date.

2. *Adjustments in Standards*. When conditions have changed and standards previously developed are to that extent obsolete, there is always the question of whether the basic standards should be adjusted for the known changes, or whether the fact of the change should continue to be a part of the later analysis of causes of deviations. There is no single answer to this question, but if standards are changed, the adjustment of the standards should be clearly disclosed.

3. *Use of Future Projections*. In many situations, especially in the case of budgets and profit plans, the best control is made possible by currently translating actual experience into revised future projections. As we move through the total period, new developments take place. The revised future projections then can be made to reflect the impact of these new developments. The revised projections then better alert management to the need to take all possible action to deal with new problems so that future results can be as close as possible to wanted objectives.

Measurement and comparison involve further problems

Problems of Analysis

At this stage we are probing for the explanations of why the actual performance is what it is when compared to the established objectives. What are the causal factors and what is their individual impact? The special problems here will include:

1. *Extent of the Analysis Effort*. The analytical effort is carried on in part by the responsible supervisor since he is the person best informed about the operations involved. To some extent, however, use is normally made of staff personnel. In all cases there is the judgmental question of how much effort is justified. Involved in this question is also how far one should go backward in examining causes of causes. We have here again the necessity for the rule of reason.

2. *Timing of the Analysis*. Since management action depends on identification of causes, the timing of the analysis again becomes a critical dimension of a good control effort. The extent of the analysis must,

Analysis provides explanation of causes

therefore, be balanced against the loss of value of the findings when unduly delayed.

3. *Identification of Controllable Causes*. The heart of the analysis effort is the extent to which controllable causes are identified and evaluated in relation to noncontrollable causes. We need to know which causes are those that we can do something about. The problems of separation is, however, often very difficult and there is need both for good techniques and good judgment. It is also necessary to recognize that the degree of controllability varies over time. For example, investment in equipment is fixed for the short run but *is* controllable in the longer run. But something like political action is always relatively uncontrollable.

Problems of Determining Constructive Action

Analysis provides the explanation of causes, but there still must be the determination of appropriate action which will best serve the company's interest. It is clearly crucial that this determination be made efficiently. The special problems at this stage will include:

1. *Supplementing the Analysis*. The determination of what should be done requires to a considerable extent the further and more definitive testing of the adequacy of the analysis. This further testing is especially important if the analytical effort has been delegated to staff personnel. It includes direct contacts and discussions with the people who have been involved in the actual performance, and with other people who either have provided various types of input or who have particular types of expertise. All of this supplementary analysis is directed to finding answers that are sufficiently reliable to become a sound basis for action.

Action decisions must include special considerations

2. *Timing*. When decisions for action are being made there is always the human tendency to stop short of the final determination. Although decisions should not be made hastily in relation to the seriousness of the issue involved, there is a time when decisions are necessary. We need, therefore, to discipline ourselves to do what on balance is needed.

3. *Evaluating Conflicting Factors*. Determining appropriate action, like all decision making, involves a balancing of conflicting factors. Short-run considerations need, for example, to be weighed against long-run impacts. In other cases the gains in one operational feature have to be weighed against the restrictions which are generated for another operational feature. Relative risks also need to be considered in the light of the capacity and willingness to assume risk. And the impact on people and people relationships must always be carefully evaluated. All of these conflicting factors, therefore, have to be evaluated and viewed incrementally as to their net addition to company interests.

4. *Need for Flexibility*. Finally, the determination of appropriate action

requires a flexible approach. Stereotyped determinations lose touch with the real world of change and frequently lead to undesirable types of actions. In addition, they undermine effective human relationships. Hence there must be a sensitive and flexible approach to these important determinations.

Problems of Taking Action

The decision to take particular types of action now having been made, the next step is to actually take that action. The concern now is with how effectively that action phase is carried out. The special problems here include:

1. *Who should take the action?* It would seem to be obvious that the best person to take the action is the responsible supervisor and therefore every possible effort should be made to see that the matter is handled in just that way. However, there may be cases where the action must actually be taken in some other way. In such a situation the responsible supervisor will normally alert the lower-level supervisor of what is to be done. In other cases the pressures of time and managerial responsibilities will make it necessary to work through staff personnel. The need in this type of situation is that the staff person carry out his role as the *agent* of the responsible supervisor. What needs to be avoided is that actions are taken by persons who are not viewed as legitimate sources of authority.

   How action is taken is very important

2. *How should the action be taken?* What is even more important perhaps is how the action is taken. First, it is necessary that recipients are given proper understanding of why the action is being taken, thus avoiding the undesirable interpretation that the action is arbitrary in nature. Second, the action needs to be free of emotional characteristics or personal indictments that will generate hostility and resistance. Wherever possible the facts should speak for themselves and action instructions presented in a purely objective and professional manner. We have here again the earlier mentioned problem of human responses to control and the need to deal with them in a capable manner. It is useful to remember that good managers are interested in results rather than proving they were right or demonstrating personal power.

Problems of Continuing Appraisal

We know that the operations of a business continue on into the future. The problems of control are therefore also never ending. The previously taken control actions therefore blend into the subsequent recurring control cycles. The further appraisal of the actions taken provides another important input for the effectiveness of the next control cycle. The special problems at this stage include:

1. *Need for a Learning Attitude.* The starting point for effective continuing appraisal is that the various responsible personnel have an attitude of wanting to improve operations and to learn how improvement can best be achieved. This approach emphasizes the fact that control actions are never perfect and can always be subject to further improvement.

2. *Providing for Feedback.* Coupled with the right attitude for learning and improvement is the importance of providing adequate means for feedback. This feedback provides information as to how effective the control action was and what we might have done to improve it. The feedback is made possible in part by establishing the proper climate for free expression. It is also made more effective by specific programs of inquiry and evaluation. In some cases, also, special types of reporting need to be utilized.

*Action tied to continuing
control process*

Impact of Computers

Any discussion of the control process must necessarily recognize the major impact that computers have had on all parts of that process. We will look at computer developments in more detail in Chapters 8 and 15. We should, however, at this point briefly identify the special types of impact on the control process.

*Computers have had major
impact on control process*

1. *Better Availability of Information.* An important contribution that computers make to the control process is in providing more complete information at all stages of the control process. This has a number of important features—more complete information, better analysis and dissemination of that information, and availability on a more timely basis. In all cases a better basis for effective control action can thus be provided.

2. *Programmed Controls.* The computer has a special capability to program the handling of sequences of transactions and operations so that they can be executed in a prescribed manner. It is also possible to build into those programs various types of controls. Thus to a considerable extent the objectives of control can be accomplished in a planned manner, and with intervention by individuals only in accordance with previously established rules and criteria. Control objectives are thus again more efficiently achieved.

3. *Direct-Access Capability Dangers.* A particular capability of computers is that they can establish memory banks of operational data which can be tapped by available technical means. In many respects this provides greater assistance to all persons charged with control responsibilities. It does, however, pose some special problems. These problems are that higher-level supervisors can have access to operational data relating to lower organizational levels before data flow up to them in accordance with the regular system. This availability does

not necessarily mean that the data should be or will be utilized in violation of normal organizational sequences, but it does provide a new possibility that it can and might be done. These possibilities can have a significant impact on the total control system and need to be covered carefully.

4. *Types of Risks.* The use of EDP by its very nature involves a concentration of data and processing that on the one hand eliminates segregation of duties and related safeguards that are part of manually operated systems. This concentration then brings with it increased security risks pertaining both to improper entry of data and the later protection of it from physical loss. These risks in part pertain to individual programs and need to be dealt with through individual application controls. Other risks pertain to the facilities as a whole and to all applications. The potentials of computer-based crime have become of major magnitude—as discussed further in Chapters 15 and 16.

5. *Built-In Controls.* A final aspect of the control problem generated by EDP usage is that needed system controls should to a major extent be built into the system during the design and development stage. If this is not done, it may be too costly or even impossible in any reasonable sense to remedy the deficiencies. The unique nature of this problem indeed poses special problems to internal auditors who typically review operational developments on an "after-the-fact" basis.

EVALUATION OF THE CONTROL PROCESS

Control System In Perspective

In concluding our discussion of the control process it may be useful to view the control system in summary perspective. Building on the total discussion of the chapter, five key aspects seem to stand out:

1. *Importance of Achieving Effective Control.* Before there can be control there must be operational activities to control. Hence we cannot say that control is the most important management need. We can say, however, that wanted results are not achieved unless operations are subjected to proper control. Operational progress must be measured and evaluated, and determinations made as to the best supplementary action to take to achieve objectives. Control therefore becomes a critical part of the total management effort. The challenge here is to provide the needed control in a manner that is most compatible with the total management effort.

Wanted results depend on properly controlling operations

2. *Recognition of the Interrelated Scope.* In devising effective control we need to understand the manner in which the control system rep-

resents a wide range of interrelationships. These interrelationships are on the one hand the inevitable result of the interrelationships of managerial objectives and subobjectives at all operational levels. All controls necessarily relate to other operational controls at higher levels, at lower levels, and in related operational areas. The interrelationships in a second important way also involve all other dimensions of the management effort—planning, organizing, providing resources, and administering.

3. *Need to Achieve Balance under Changing Conditions.* The problem of determining how much and what kind of control is needed requires a sensitive evaluation of different kinds of operational objectives and needs, and the application of controls must take cognizance of the existing differences. What this means is that we must provide control in a manner that appropriately balances conflicting operational objectives both as between the individual objectives themselves and with the control system itself. Moreover, conditions are continuously changing over time, and hence that balance must be continuously reappraised and adjusted.

4. *Eternal Problem of Cost.* This problem of balance between operational objectives and the control system unavoidably presents the problem of cost. There is, first, the necessity to understand all of the costs that are involved when controls are established so that we can endeavor to minimize them. Costs here include both the direct costs of providing the control and the costs in the form of undesirable operational responses. The second requirement is then to evaluate these costs in relation to the benefits actually expected to be achieved—better protection and utilization of resources in various ways. All aspects of the control system here must meet the important profitability test.

Control system must meet profitability test

Control a means and not an end in itself

5. *Control as a Means to an End.* Finally, it is important to remember that control is a means to an end, not an end in itself. This in effect is restating the profitability test in another form, but it serves to help us avoid the temptation to become so enamoured with the trappings of control that we overlook the greater effectiveness of achieving control through the other types of management effort. To a major extent good control is good management and we take supplementary measures only as justified to achieve the central objectives.

Summary Control Specifications

While effective control involves many substantive dimensions that are closely interrelated, it may be useful to have a summary checklist of the desirable specifications, to be achieved to the extent practicable, with unavoidable overlapping.

1. As to soundness of design:
   a. Maximum integration with regular operational procedures
   b. Objectives soundly established and quantitatively based
   c. Consistency with regular reporting system
   d. Maximum simplicity for ease of understanding
   e. Consistency of control procedures with legitimacy of authority
   f. Consideration of normal human resistance
   g. Reasonable balance of cost and potential benefit
   h. Consideration of conflict with other managerial objectives
   i. Participation by affected individuals in design
   j. Use of early warning signals
   k. Involvement and understanding at all management levels
   l. Adequacy of development effort for total control plan

   Checklist for reviewing individual controls

2. As to effectiveness of implementation:
   a. Timely reporting and analysis
   b. Maximum consistency with recognized authority
   c. Minimization of emotional and personal involvement
   d. Fairness of administration
   e. Understanding of noncontrollable problems
   f. Continuing managerial interest and support
   g. Timely corrective action
   h. Continuing reevaluation of soundness of objectives
   i. Maximum integration with regular operational actions
   j. Sound reconciliation of consistency with needed flexibility
   k. Continuing reevaluation of all control procedures
   l. Reasonable sensibility to human impact

Internal Auditor's Role in Control

In the earlier chapters we recognized the major concern of the internal auditor with the control process. The logical basis of that interest now becomes all the more apparent, and can be summarized as follows:

1. As we have seen, a major part of the management process has to do with control. Thus every manager has an important responsibility to develop a program of control that will most effectively contribute to the kinds of performance of which he is in charge. This control program consists of the overall control effort covering the activities for which he is responsible, and the individual control efforts which together comprise the total control effort.

   Control is basic core of internal auditor's role

2. The internal auditor is committed to organizational service and in turn to management service. Therefore, he is interested in the control effort as an essential part of his objective of management service.

3. The internal auditor is especially able to provide the board and man-

agement with assistance in the control area. The basis for this special capability to a major extent comes from the fact that he is independent of all operational activities but at the same time exposed to them. This provides both the necessary objectivity and the overview of all operational activities, their interrelationships, and the related controls. The internal auditor also possesses the capabilities for analysis and good business sense which are necessary in order to appraise the effectiveness of control.

4. The internal auditor additionally has the distinct advantage of being able to approach the various problems through the basic financial records. From those financial records it is possible to move effectively first to financial activities (with their related financial controls) to other operating activities with their related financial and operational controls. This does not mean that the control problems cannot be focused on directly and independently of financial records. However, most control problems to some extent involve financial records, all of which adds to the internal auditor's capabilities.

5. The special capability in the control area provides an essential entry to the various operational activities, which then in turn opens up the opportunity to observe and appraise all aspects of those operational activities. The foundation is thus laid for a range of greater service at all management levels.

The concern with the control process on the part of the internal auditor is thus both of major immediate and long-run interest. He should respond to that interest by focusing his efforts on a greater understanding of the control process and the means by which control can be made most effective in every type of operational situation.

Achieving Control in Operational Areas

In actual practice controls are developed and administered in terms of individual operational situations. In Part Two certain individual operational areas are reviewed and appropriate controls identified and evaluated. In all cases, however, the general principles and basic processes discussed in this chapter are applicable. Indeed, the foundations dealt with in this chapter should be continuously reexamined as individual operational areas are dealt with in more specific terms.

REVIEW QUESTIONS

1. Define the control function. How does it interrelate with the other key functions (subprocesses) of management?

2. Who has the basic responsibility for control? To what extent is the internal auditor responsible?

3. What is the range of the "control" concern in terms of type of operational activity and level of responsibility? Give illustrative examples.

4. How does the search for more effective control involve the past, present, and future operations of an organization?

5. Compare the external and internal auditor's interest in control.

6. Briefly describe the key phases of the control process.

7. What is meant by protective and constructive dimensions of controls? In which is the internal auditor more interested? Why?

8. Why are the human relations aspects of special importance in achieving effective control?

9. How can the control system be adapted to changing conditions that cannot be foreseen at the time the objectives are established?

10. To what extent does the internal auditor need to understand operational processes in order to be able to understand what control measures are appropriate?

CASE PROBLEMS

Problem 4-1

The social committee of the Chamber of Commerce had decided to sponsor a community picnic on the 4th of July. It is now April 1st, the Committee has asked you to lay out a suggested plan for carrying out this decision from the present stage and on through the picnic, and to finalize the disposition of all related items. You have been requested to submit the plan to the committee for review and approval on April 10.

Required. Prepare the plan as requested.

Problem 4-2

You have been assigned the responsibility of conducting an audit of one of your company's retail stores. You have two years experience in internal auditing but have never been involved in the audit of a retail operation. Upon arrival at the audit location your first action was to request an interview with the store manager. During the interview with the manager he asked you how much retail experience you have. When you advised him that you had none he responded, "How can you possible audit our store, when you know nothing about our operations?"

Required. Prepare an appropriate response to the store manager's question.

CHAPTER FIVE

Organizational Control

After studying this chapter you should be able to:

☐ *Describe in general terms, the nature and scope of organizational control*

☐ *Explain the organizational concepts of decentralization, line and staff, authority and responsibility, and span of control*

☐ *Identify organizational control as a part of the larger process of internal control*

☐ *Determine how the internal auditor can contribute to improving the effectiveness of organizational control*

NATURE OF ORGANIZATIONAL CONTROL

The problem of control has been dealt with on an overall basis in the preceding chapter and has been continuously identified as a major concern of the internal auditor. Organizing has also been dealt with in Chapter 3 as a major part of the total management function which the internal auditor seeks to support. Organizational control is a part of the larger control process and has to do with the more detailed coverage of the organizing activity. It will be the purpose of this chapter to develop a better understanding of the nature and scope of this important type of control and to determine how the internal auditor can contribute more effectively in this very important area.

Organizational control is part of a larger control process

A discussion of organizational control should most logically begin with a consideration of what is meant by the term "organization." This term is used interchangeably with the term "organizing" and to most people means about the same thing, that is, that organizing is the action process which results in organization. There is, however, a tendency for some individuals, both educators and practitioners, to use organization as a broader term. In some instances, indeed, the term "organization" is used so broadly that it includes all of the problems of management, and the latter two terms then become interchangeable. The situation is further confused by the fact that almost everyone uses "organization" as a general term to refer to an organizational entity, like a company, a corporation, or any organized group. We use "organization" in this chapter as the set of *organizational arrangements* which is developed as a result of the organizing process.

The concept of organization can be described as the way individual work efforts in any company or other organizational entity are both assigned and subsequently integrated for achievement of the larger organizational goals. In a sense this is a concept that could be applied to the way in which a single individual organizes his own individual effort. But in a more meaningful sense it becomes applicable when a number of people are involved in a group effort. In the case of the large modern business corporation it becomes increasingly a major problem. The organization of the total is clearly a necessity if the individual persons and subgroups of persons are to know what to do. Employees must have direction in terms of meaningful relationships to the total goals and objectives of the group or entity of which they are a part. Without such organization there could only be confusion and waste.

As we have also seen previously, the need for an effective organizational effort exists for every type of entity. There is an organizational problem in every kind of enterprise, whether the enterprise be business, governmental, philanthropic, or of any other type. It is a problem that exists at every organizational level in an enterprise as any subgroup looks at its own organizational needs within the framework of its own organizational setting. This situation is of course to be expected in view of the similar applicability of the total management problem.

Breakdown and Integration Aspects

Since the concept of organization has to do with both the assignment and integration of the total work effort, it will be useful to look at these two aspects of the organizing process more closely. The first aspect is essentially the way responsibilities are defined in terms of job descriptions and then structured in terms of organization charts. Although such assignments can never fully escape some overlapping or joint responsibilities, the more definitely and precisely these responsibilities can be stated, the better it will be. The decisions as to how the responsibilities will be assigned are primarily concerned with avoiding confusion and conflict as between individual and group work efforts, but they must also be concerned with the later feasibility of relating these efforts in the subsequent integration stage. The second aspect of the organizational process is now to bring back together the previously designed job responsibilities into an integrated total work effort. This integration also has its own special problems. Here there will normally be

Organization deals with assignment and integration of total work effort

the need for specific organizational arrangements to best assure the needed integration. Illustrative of this would be the creation of various types of coordinating committees, requirements for review and approval, and specific assignments of the responsibility for relating and integrating the results of different types of activities.

Design and Implementation Aspects

Another useful way to look at organizational arrangements, for a better understanding of them, is in terms of the design and implementation aspects. In the design phase the primary concern is with laying out the organizational arrangements as we think they should be carried out. At this point there should be, and there normally is, consideration given to the problems of implementation. But the primary focus is on the design of what *ought* to be. Now the stage is set for the implementation itself—how people actually operate under the previously designed organizational arrangements and under the actuality of the particular operational conditions. Here then is the testing of how sound the organizational design turns out to be and what unforeseen problems may now have to be contended with. The effectiveness of the organizational arrangements will be judged in large part on the basis of whether results are being achieved in terms of organizational goals and objectives. The difficulty is always to determine the extent to which the organizational arrangements are a causal factor. But if and when that determination is made, the stage is set for either different approaches to the various kinds of implementation or the modification of the underlying design of the organizational arrangements.

Tie Between People and Organizational Arrangements

Organizational arrangements depend on people at all stages

The development of effective organizational arrangements will very properly utilize the contributions which result from rational thought and analysis. This rational contribution consists of the logical expectations which come as a result of factual analysis, nonhuman forces, and views as to the way things ought to be. But at the same time, and even more important, is the basic dependence at all stages on people. The dependence exists in a number of ways. The design of the organizational arrangements first identifies the needs for people—what kinds, how many, and of what quality. The design must also necessarily take into consideration the people who are available within the company and the recognition of the fact that in most cases we will, for various reasons, have those same people with us for some time. What normally happens here is that we organize differently at this time because of the people who are available to be assigned the particular responsibilities—keeping in mind changes in those organizational arrangements which we can make later with new people. Also the design phase, to the extent that it deals with the later feasibility of implementation, must take into consideration how people will actually operate during that implementation phase.

In the implementation phase itself there is a still more important link to people. Here it is the people that make the organizational arrangements work. Are we recruiting the right kind of people? Have we too many or too few of the right type? Are we fully utilizing the people we have? These are problems that must be solved if the organizational arrangements are to be administered effectively. It is also these people relationships which generate the need for modification of the design of those arrangements. We deal with some of the more detailed problems of people utilization later in the chapter.

Approach to an Understanding of Effective Organization

Competence in the area of organizational control assumes a general familiarity with a number of basic organizational concepts. These concepts are sometimes referred to as organizational principles. At times also this approach is extended to take the form of a listing of do's and don't's. Such an approach does, however, have distinct limitations because of the extent to which individual operational situations vary, and that approach may actually be harmful. We prefer, therefore, to think of there being certain basic concepts with which anyone dealing with management and organizational problems needs to be familiar. It is also necessary to recognize that the important objective is to apply the various concepts to a variety of operational situations in a manner which will be most supportive to management. The applications to these varying situations to a major extent almost always involves controversial factors for which there must be a trade-off. This trade-off is a highly judgmental process. All this means that the greatest need for internal auditors is to understand the kinds of problems that are related to the various organizational concepts as they are applied in actual situations.

Objective to apply principles to varying situations

The individual organizational concepts can be identified and grouped in various ways. There is no really satisfactory solution to that problem because of the high degree of interrelationship between the various concepts. There is also an ever-present design and implementation aspect. For the present purpose we deal first with the concepts relating primarily to design, and then move to the concepts that relate more to implementation.

Alternative Ways to Group Activities

Perhaps the most far-reaching decision which must first be made in developing organizational arrangements is to which way and to what extent the activities shall be grouped. The major approaches normally utilized in practice are functional, product, and geographical. In the functional approach the company organizes along the lines of the major functions such as production, marketing, personnel, and finance. The control over these individual functions is centralized at the vice-president or divisional level, and while there may be some lateral coordination between the functions at lower levels, the major coordination comes at the highest level. The benefits exist in the specialized concentration of authority which flows down through the various

Activities usually grouped by product, function, or geographical areas

organizational levels. For example, production people report upward from the lowest operational level to other production people, and finally to the vice-president–production. The major disadvantages are that key decisions must be coordinated and made at the top, all of which is a very long and time-consuming process—restricting the possibility of more urgently needed response at field levels.

The product approach comes at the problem in terms of grouping the various functional responsibilities which pertain to a given product or group of products and fixing the responsibility for the results, normally the profit results, in terms of that product. Illustrative of this would be the Chevrolet Division of General Motors. The advantages here lie in the possibilities of more effective coordination of the activities pertaining to a major product or product line.

The geographical approach in turn is the grouping of activities in terms of geographical areas. The managerial responsibility will now be for all products, and all functions relating to those products, in a given geographical area. Illustrative of this would be the regional operations of a national grocery chain. The benefits here lie in the better coordination of all operations in the specified geographical area.

The choice of approaches depends of course on the kind of operational activities involved and what particular types of activities require or appear to need centrally controlled direction. In this respect the geographical approach would not fit General Motors, but it does fit the Great Atlantic and Pacific Tea Company. In all situations, however, there is bound to be some special adaptation. That is, some functions will be organized on one basis and some on another. Also there will normally be variations in the approach at different organizational levels. The sales effort, for example, may be set up at the top on a functional basis, but at the field level it may be organized on a geographical basis (with district and regional offices), and perhaps even on a customer basis at some level (retail users, industrial users, etc). The organizational problem in practice is to find what seems to be the best combination of approaches.

Decentralization

Authority and responsibility need to move downward in organizational hierarchy

Common to all of the previously considered approaches to the grouping of activities is the issue of the extent to which the authority and responsibility for various types of operations shall be decentralized downward in the organizational hierarchy. The scope of this decentralization will normally be greatest under the product approach but even in the functional approach—and again using the production example—the responsibility for the operation of a particular plant can be either narrowly or liberally construed. In some situations this decentralization becomes a practical necessity, as in the case of foreign operations. In other situations the benefits versus the risks will be harder to evaluate. The controlling factors include the importance of coordinating various operational factors at the field level, the urgency of decisions in response to changing conditions, the qualifications of the people who will make the lower-level decisions, and the significance of the particular decisions in terms of overall company welfare.

Profit decentralization is one of the more advanced types of decentralization. Here the responsibility for operational activities is defined in terms of profit results and all management activities can be coordinated and administered in terms of those profit results. Whether this is the best approach again depends on a number of factors. It may not be feasible to decentralize enough of the activities to make the profit responsibility meaningful—as where, for example, the design and production of products may need to be centralized. Or there may be certain interdivisional relationships which cannot be measured with sufficient accuracy. In addition, there are unavoidable extra costs for needed staff assistance. There may also be possible costs from dividing up operations which could otherwise be handled centrally with more efficiency. To offset these costs must be the better coordination of lower-level operational factors, greater managerial motivation, and perhaps management development. The net evaluation of all these factors has always been controversial and dependent to a major extent on managerial judgment.

Line and Staff

Traditionally, particular assignments of managerial responsibility have been viewed as either line or staff in basic character. The former type of assignment is considered to fix the responsibility for the final achievement of the company's goals and objectives. The staff group, on the other hand, is viewed as helping the line group to do its job. It provides this help through advice and counsel at various levels, through providing service, or by providing needed control for line executives at higher levels over both line and staff operations at lower levels. In more recent times the distinction between the two types of activities has become somewhat blurred, and many students of organization feel that the two types of activity are now so closely interrelated as to make the distinctions relatively meaningless. The development of modern computerized systems has been one important development which leads to this particular conclusion. Nevertheless, in most situations the line responsibility continues to exist in a meaningful sense as identifying the persons who must ultimately integrate all dimensions of operational activities and take the responsibility for the final results. It is also usually desirable that the responsibility for the success or failure of particular managerial policies and actions can be reasonably identified.

Staff needs to be viewed as helping line personnel to do job

A major type of design problem in connection with line and staff is how much staff support needs to be provided, and where in the organizational hierarchy it should be placed. In the area of advice and counsel, for example, it is never easy to know how much of that counsel is justified. Staff personnel in all the various areas can usually build a good case for the extent of their potential service to management. Also in many cases staffs can become empires in themselves and in addition to being unduly costly may dilute basic line responsibilities. It is also always difficult to know whether it is best to concentrate these staff efforts at particular organizational levels, or to diffuse them to line managers at other organizational levels. The latter type of problem is also present in the area of manufacturing service activities. The establishment of one service group at the headquarters level may appear to be very desirable because of the economy of scale resulting from the greater volume of activity, but it may not serve the current operational needs of lower-level managers as effectively. If the staff operations are essentially for control purposes over lower-level operations, we also again have our eternal question of whether the benefits outweigh the costs.

Scope of Assignment of Responsibility

Authority must be tied to responsibility and lines of responsibility must be clear

In developing organizational design a number of problems revolve around the matter of the scope of the defined responsibility. There is first the general desirability of matching properly the two dimensions of authority and responsibility. Authority without responsibility is certainly undesirable. Similarly, responsibility without authority is not realistic. A second desirable feature is that the lines of responsibility be as clear as possible. This is important both for the person directly involved to know to whom he is responsible and also to the superior who needs to know how much he can utilize the subordinate. At the same time other individuals need to know this to best get their own jobs done. A related consideration is that the responsibility should not be dual—that is, run to two superiors—again as far as it is possible to avoid such a situation. If for necessary reasons there is a dual reporting responsibility, the nature of the individual responsibilities needs to be defined, including the designation of which one has the central or controlling responsibility. All of this also needs to be supported by proper documentation, usually in the form of published job descriptions.

Responsibility can be arranged to achieve needed internal control

Relation to Internal Control. The assignments of responsibility are especially important to the internal auditor because it is here that responsibilities for different types of activities can be so arranged that adequate internal control can be achieved. At lower levels this often takes the form of separating the responsibility for performing the actual activity from the record covering that performance. Illustrative of this would be the separation of the responsibility for the accounts receivable ledgers from the creation of paper affecting the individual accounts. At higher levels one type of responsibility can serve as a control against another type of responsibility, as, for example, where customer complaints serve as a control against other groups who design, produce, or service the product. The merging of responsibilities must of course take place at some organizational level, as for example, in the case of a profit center, but the objective is that responsibilities at some lower-level point become as clear as possible and that to the maximum extent practicable we reap the benefits of the cross controls that these assignments can make possible.

Overlapping and Joint Responsibilities. Having described the benefits of clearly defined organizational responsibilities it is necessary to recognize at the same time that there are definite limitations to how far one can go in this direction, especially at higher organizational levels. There is in many cases the very real problem of properly defining the scope of the individual responsibility. There is here on the one hand the danger of making it so limited that the recipient will not be sufficiently motivated to extend his role in ways that might be very beneficial to the company. But there is also the danger that the assignment may be so broad that it becomes both un-realistic and unduly impinging on other responsibilities. A good illustration of this type of problem is where a vice-president–finance has a given as-signment of corporate-wide responsibility in the finance area, and the vice-president and general manager of an operating division has a line respon-sibility for profits for his division. The vice-president–finance responsibility for accounting procedures may be clear enough, but in the area of operational questions which also have major financial implications, the balance of au-thority and responsibility may not be that clear. The president, on the other hand, does not want the vice-president–finance to overrule directly the operational vice-president. Nor does he want the operational vice-president to ignore unduly the expertise of the vice-president–finance. The result is that there are unavoidable areas of overlap which the president hopes will be resolved on a mutually agreed-upon basis between the two officers. If necessary, the president can and will arbitrate a difference between the two officers, but this approach has its own longer-run problems and will normally be avoided as much as possible by all the parties.

Some overlapping and joint responsibility may be necessary

Span of Control and Levels of Organization

A frequently occurring problem concerns the number of persons any man-ager should have who report directly to him. This is referred to as the span of control. The problem also involves the number of organizational levels because action, for example, to reduce the span of control normally leads to the injection of additional managers, which thereby adds another level of organization. Although attempts have been made to fix limits as to what the span of control should be, such efforts have not been very productive. The best answer seems to be that it all depends on the particular situation. Pertinent are such factors as the type of work effort involved, the related need for interaction, the competence of the incumbents at both organiza-tional levels, and the overall climate of the company. However, a span of control with only one subordinate has very real problems. If it does exist at all it will probably be best justified on the basis of the need for two persons

Number of people reporting to one manager (span of control) needs evaluation

who would then function in a co-partnership role, although even in that case there can still be problems. We can also say that the adding of too many organizational levels may solve a span of control problem, but may at the same time result in undesirable delay as decisions move up and down the organizational hierarchy. As a normal objective it is desirable to keep the number of organizational levels to a minimum, thus making it important to justify carefully any increases.

Design of Coordinative Efforts

The design of all organizational arrangements must necessarily give consideration to how the various work assignments and related possibilities will subsequently be coordinated and integrated. The concept of organizational structure as a kind of a pyramid implicitly recognizes that individual responsibilities are merged increasingly at each higher organizational level, coming in the last stage to the overall responsibility of the chief executive officer. In addition there may be other types of organizational arrangements which focus directly on this integrative need. One of these efforts is illustrated by the stated requirements for various types of review and approval and/or concurrence by parties not directly in the line of primary responsibility.

Committees.   Another common approach is to provide for creation of various types of committees which will meet periodically to coordinate activities in which there is a wider range of interest. Illustrative of this would be scheduling committees, product planning committees, and capital projects committees. The use of committees is viewed more favorably by some managers than others. In some instances there can be undue reliance on committees, to the extent that basic managerial responsibilities are undermined. Moreover, committees may be unduly time consuming. There is no doubt that in many situations the committee approach is not used in an effective manner. However, such instances should not deny the fact that there is a proper and productive use of this particular organizational arrangement. The correct answer is to use this device, but to use it with care and judgment.

Project Teams.   Another commonly used coordinative effort is that of the project team. This is an approach that is used to study a particular type of problem or to carry out a special nonrecurring type of operational venture. Through this project team approach the representatives of all of the organizational components which have an important interest are brought together. It is usually not a permanent part of the organizational design in the usual sense, but is brought into being in response to special temporary needs. A good example is a project group that would be formed to study a proposed computerized system which cuts across a number of operational areas and which also usually involves a number of staff interests. This type of approach has demonstrated its usefulness in many situations and is increasingly used.

Benefits and costs of committees must be weighed

Implementation of Assignments of Responsibility

As we turn more to the phase of the organizational problem that involves the implementational arrangements, we need to understand a number of important concepts. The first group of these implementation concepts has to do with the earlier discussed assignments of organizational responsibilities.

Delegation. As previously noted, the design of the organizational arrangements necessarily involves the delegation of authority in combination with a resulting responsibility. Now at the implementation stage there is a further delegation process which goes on between every manager and his subordinate. This is when the particular person-to-person relationship is actually established. On the one hand the manager can go to the extreme of giving such freedom of action to his subordinate that he will improperly abdicate his own responsibility, something that he has no right to do. At the other extreme the delegation can be so restrictive that the subordinate is unable to do his job effectively. For effective implementation we seek the proper intermediate balance, recognizing that this must vary as between individual situations and over time in the same situation.

Proper delegation balances freedom with restrictions

Supervision. Closely related to the delegation problem is the nature and scope of the related supervision. Again there can be an extreme where the subordinate is not given adequate guidance and is left too vulnerable to operational problems. The result is then more often a less than required level of performance both in terms of quality and direction. The other extreme is where the manager is monitoring the performance so closely that both parties suffer—the manager because he is diverting his available time from other important matters, and the subordinate because he can neither make his own possible contribution or experience the management development which is possible. Again there is need for the more intermediate type of approach.

Supervision must support delegation approach

Accountability. We speak generally of accountability as an automatic expectation of assignment of responsibility. Actually the achievement of this desired end is somewhat more complicated. In more precise terms there are three necessary types of action:

1. An assignment of duties to be performed
2. A grant of authority to carry out those assigned duties
3. An acceptance of the obligation by the person involved

In this way responsibility in the very real sense of accountability is established. The important point here is that the relationship is bilateral, rather than being just unilateral, and that achieving the relationship requires both an understanding of what needs to be done and a certain managerial skill in carrying it out.

*Participation has great
potential benefit*

Participation.   Another important aspect of the implementation of assignments of responsibility is the extent to which the benefits of the participative process are fully realized. Participation means that the recipient of responsibility participates both in the assignment of the responsibility and in the subsequent major decision making which comes along pursuant to that responsibility. Participation has two major benefits. The first is that the extra input on the part of the subordinate can usually be an important contribution to what is being decided. An area is frequently involved where the subordinate has knowledge and experience over and above that possessed by the higher-level manager. The second benefit is that the subordinate will as a result of the participation more likely feel a sense of commitment—the very opposite of hostility which might otherwise be the case. Again there is the need for special managerial skill if the participative process is to achieve its proper potential. It is also important that it not be carried to such extremes as to either be an undue delaying factor or to create unrealistic expectations.

Good coordination essential

Coordination.   Finally, the effective implementation of the assignment of responsibility depends on adequate coordination. This desirable coordination needs to be generated both at the subordinate and higher managerial level. In the case of the subordinate it means keeping in touch with other organizational counterparts to be informed of developments which might in some way bear on the assigned responsibility. The subordinate should also keep his superior properly informed of progress and any new developments bearing on the assigned responsibility. In the case of the higher-level manager it means a similar type of alertness in counterpart areas to which he has access and then passing on what is appropriate to the subordinate.

Implementation of Line and Staff Relationships

In our discussion of the design phase the difficulties of the assignment of line and staff responsibilities were described. Now at the implementation stage more needs to be said of how this latter phase can be made most effective. We have here one of the most delicate of relationships and one that requires both a proper attitude and special skill on the part of both the staff advisor and the line operator.

Perhaps the greatest burden is with the staff advisor because that role can so easily be misunderstood and the potential power misused. The staff advisor in the first place is frequently younger, more aggressive, intellectually better equipped than the line manager, and usually possesses special expertise. Normally also he is in closer touch with top-management echelons and has a certain standing with them. Under these circumstances he is tempted to feel overzealous and overconfident in the rightness of his recommendations, and impatient with any obstacles to putting them to work. Finally he may be tempted to look good in the eyes of the superiors on which his advancement and level of compensation so much depend. The problem, therefore, is for him to recognize that the line manager has both the final responsibility for results and normally both ability and valuable experience. The need, then, is to see the total problem objectively and to accept a partnership relationship with the line manager from which the line manager will normally and properly receive the major credit.

Line management has final responsibility for results

The line manager at the same time has his responsibilities. He must recognize that he needs all possible help in doing his job and that the staff can have important contributions to make to the solution of the operational problems. He therefore needs to have an open and receptive attitude toward the studies and recommendations of the staff counselor. This does not mean that he is bound to accept those recommendations. But it does mean that he ought to have good reasons for rejecting them. In all cases he must be looking for the best possible answers and then it is his right and responsibility to make the final choice. He has that right because he and only he has final responsibility for the results.

Problem of Organizational Rigidity

The design of organizational arrangements normally includes the development of a structure of organizational responsibilities of the type portrayed in an organization chart. In the implementation phase the problem then becomes one of how rigid that structure should be. It may at the one extreme be a straitjacket by being interpreted as a requirement that all flows of information be only through the channels as formally reflected in the organization chart. Critics of formal organization have at times condemned this possible state of affairs as oppressive, and at other times have taken the view that it is both unrealistic and counterproductive. In any event the effective implementation of organizational design needs to recognize that there must be a great deal of interaction not directly in line with formal organizational design. Under these circumstances the organization chart becomes only a guide to basic organizational responsibilities and not as a requirement for burdensome intraorganizational interaction. It needs to be recognized also that organizational relationships evolve over time through informal relationships, and that these informal relationships set the stage for changes which ultimately need to be recognized and confirmed in formal organizational structure.

Proper management climate can help provide needed organizational flexibility

How do we avoid organizational rigidity? One major way is to disseminate information in a manner in which it can be immediately available and useful for the discharge of individual organizational responsibilities. Modern information systems are in fact contributing more and more to that need. A second major way to provide organizational flexibility is to create the right kind of managerial climate. The responsibility for this latter kind of climate is directly with the top management of the enterprise. It starts with the encouragement of a free interchange of information and organizational freedom. It also encourages creative thinking without premature judgment of the worth of that creative thinking. In addition, it also has a high tolerance for error. On balance it can produce a dynamic and creative organization with excellent motivation and a high degree of cohesiveness.

People Utilization

People utilization is basic to company welfare

The design of organizational arrangements should be and is concerned with people needs. In fact, unduly elaborate organizational design will automatically generate excessive manpower. But over and above this aspect is the fact that the implementation of organizational arrangements is the phase when an enterprise does or does not properly utilize people. This is to say that as the current operations go forward, judgments are continuously made about people utilization, and these judgments can have a varying quality level in terms of the total company interest. People utilization covers a wide range of managerial actions. How are the organizational requirements interpreted as to numbers of people? Similarly, how is the determination made as to the kinds of people required and as to what their particular qualifications should be? Is talent that is either very costly or very scarce wasted through assignment to jobs that do not fully utilize those talents, and are the people involved being supported and coordinated in a manner that makes possible the full utilization of their potentials? People as people are clearly both the most expensive and the most volatile resource. The proper utilization of people, therefore, becomes a major dimension of the effectiveness of organizational arrangements.

Leadership

Leadership is the lubricant that makes organizational arrangements work effectively

All of the foregoing leads to a final conclusion that the effective implementation of organizational arrangements depends to a major extent on the quality of leadership at all managerial levels, beginning at the top management level. Especially it is true that the chief executive officer sets the tone for both the development and implementation for effective organizational arrangements. Admittedly at this point we are in danger of taking over another previously assigned part of the total management process. At each level, however, it depends on recognized competence, basic integrity, and a clearly demonstrated consideration of other people. In all situations leadership is the lubricating force that makes even poor organizational arrangements work satisfactorily and makes *all* organizational arrangements work more effectively.

Concluding Observations as to Organization

As we look at the various factors that have played a part in the design and implementation of effective organizational arrangements we come to certain overall conclusions as to the nature and scope of the organizational process. These conclusions can be briefly outlined, as follows:

1. Organizational arrangements are and must always be viewed as supportive to management in the larger effort to achieve the stated goals and objectives of management. There is no one general answer as to what are good organizational arrangements. Rather, good organizational arrangements are those which in the particular situation enable the particular management to best do its job. They are a means and not an end.

2. Organizational arrangements need to be flexible and responsive to changing management needs. These changing needs are a result of changing internal and external factors. There is, therefore, a necessary dynamic and evolving character to all organizational arrangements. These dynamic requirements overshadow the stability that is normally sought through the development of organizational arrangements.

3. Organizational judgments require a consideration and evaluation of a variety of complex and conflicting considerations. The decisions regarding organizational arrangements are, therefore, often necessarily inexact and always highly judgmental in character. This is especially true because the organizational arrangements combine rational analysis with the unavoidable problems of human behavior. In all cases the major component is good sense.

Organizational arrangements must support management in achieving goals and objectives

The Nature and Scope of Organizational Control

We have devoted the greater part of this chapter to a consideration of the nature and scope of the organizational process. This can be defended only by the fact that the basis of organizational control depends primarily on an adequate understanding of what we are trying to control. This is all the more true when we describe organizational control as the means by which we best provide assurance of the most effective possible use of organizational arrangements. Put in other words, *organizational control is what we do to best achieve effective organizational arrangements*.

In Chapter 4 we also discussed in some detail the nature of the control process. All of this is generally applicable since organizational control is part of the total control process. The special character of organizational arrangements, however, as compared to the normal type of operational activity, suggests a special structure for our approach to the control of organizatonal arrangements. This modified approach is as follows:

Special structural aspects of organizational control

1. There needs first to be the careful development and establishment of a program of organizational arrangements. This problem should be a best effort to apply the kinds of considerations previously outlined to the needs of the particular enterprise. It is the equivalent of objectives which are basic to any type of control.

2. The second need is that there be policies and procedures for monitoring significant changes in the established organizational arrange-

ments. The types of changes and the organizational levels to which they apply must be identified. The procedures should be clear as to how those changes are to be proposed and approved. At the same time an official organization manual would normally be maintained.

3. Finally there is the need for a continuing program of reappraisal of all organizational arrangements. The study of the various aspects of those arrangements can originate through proposals under the procedures outlined above, or they might be initiated by the staff group that administers those procedures. In all cases there is the recognition that further experience, new developments, and new knowledge can set the need for improvements of various kinds in the organizational arrangements.

Thus we see that with an initial starting point the organizational control activity is administered in an orderly manner and that there is provision for its continuous self-renewal.

ACHIEVING ORGANIZATIONAL CONTROL

Assuring Reappraisal of Organizational Control[1]

Continuing reappraisal is basic to best organizational control process

As we have seen, the continuing reappraisal of the effectiveness of all organizational arrangements is a basic part of the organizational control process. The question then becomes one of how we best assure that continuing reappraisal at the proper level of professional competence. We will look first at what the company should be doing, apart from the internal auditing effort, and then consider what the role of the internal auditor should be.

Every manager must recognize his own responsibility for organizing

Basic Managerial Responsibility for Organizational Control. The clear responsibility of all managers for both the organizing and the control functions has previously been emphasized. It logically follows that each manager has a basic responsibility for organizational control as it pertains to his particular area of operational responsibility. He therefore should be continuously initiating such actions as he deems appropriate, putting them into effect insofar as he has the authority, or channeling his proposals to those individuals who have been charged with the responsibility of monitoring changes in the organizational arrangements. The initial ideas may originate from his own independent thinking. They can develop out of interactions with subordinates and superiors, or they may come from other managers in the company who frequently have an opportunity to see the problems with greater per-

---

[1]Additional material relating to the way individual companies and their internal auditors are responding to the need for organizational control is contained in *Research Report No. 18,* "The Internal Auditor's Review of Organizational Control," issued by The Institute of Internal Auditors.

spective and objectivity. In all cases the individual manager gives such consideration to the various ideas as he thinks appropriate.

In many situations the approach to organizational control is along these lines of primary dependence on the managers themselves. At the same time, however, there are certain paper and procedural problems which have to be handled by someone. Employees have to get on payrolls, raises have to be processed somehow, titles must be designated, and the like. These procedural matters are necessarily handled in some way by individuals in the personnel department and the accounting department. As an enterprise expands, the consistent and desired handling of these matters presents increasing difficulties. As gaps or problems develop, there is more and more likely to be confusion and an excessive diversion of valuable managerial time.

Special Staff for Organizational Control.   The kinds of problems just outlined tend gradually to move the enterprise toward a greater centralization of control over these various matters, which are on the fringe of basic organizational control. Combined with this pressure is one that comes out of the greater trend for forward planning at all levels. As a part of such planning there is the related need to project organizational changes and to consider further management personnel needs. All of the foregoing leads more and more to the creation of posts or units which are charged with the overall role of both coordinating current organizational changes and in studying ongoing organizational needs. In the first instance these new staff units have most often been set up within the personnel function, thus recognizing the important tie to people and to the related personnel services. In its more advanced stage, however, the organizational group is removed from the personnel function and made directly responsible to a more senior officer, in some cases to the chief executive officer himself. Under any of these arrangements there is no denial of the basic responsibility for organization control on the part of individual managers. Rather, the organizational department is set up to assist managers at all levels. There is also the need of providing necessary control company-wide over all organizational arrangements. This is necessary to provide assurance that all changes in organization arrangements are sound in terms of company interests and that they conform to established company policies. Also job ratings, titles, and levels of compensation need to be applied uniformly. The special staff group thus works in a close partnership relationship with the managers, at times initiating studies, but in the last analysis responding to management needs in the most effective fashion possible.

Special staff can provide further benefits for organizational control

Role of Internal Auditor in Organizational Control

The interest of the internal auditor in organizational control is a logical extension of his concern for the total control process as part of his overall objective of service to management. The practical question then becomes one of how he can best make his contribution in this very important special control area.

*Internal auditor can initiate
need for more organizational
control*

Interest in an Effective Setup for Organizational Control.   The point needs to be emphasized that the internal auditor's first interest is that the company have an adequate program for organizational control, as detailed in the previous discussion of the nature and scope of organizational control. This is to say that the internal auditor's role is the same as with any part of the control system—to assist in, but not to take direct responsibility for, providing organizational control. This is to say also that the internal auditor welcomes and supports the creation of a properly qualified organization department which will monitor current organizational changes and provide assistance to managers in the study of the changing needs for all types of organizational arrangements. When that organizational department is set up, the internal auditor will want to work with that group in every practical way possible.

Direct Focus on Organizational Control.   It follows also that there should be no more restrictions on the internal auditor's authority and responsibility to review the program of organizational control at any level than there would be with any other type of operational activity. The practical restrictions here would of course be the same as in any operational area, that is, the level of competence and the extent of genuine backing from top management. Admittedly, organizational arrangements involve some of the most sensitive management issues because they have to do with people—especially when those people are at high management levels. But there is, nevertheless, an even stronger basis here for concern on the part of the internal auditor. This stronger basis is that organizational arrangements are the key building blocks of effective management performance.

*Regular internal audit
reviews can cover related
organizational aspects*

Familiarization with Organizational Arrangements of Operations Audited.   The interest of the internal auditor in the field of organizational control can also be expressed in an important way through his regular internal audit reviews of all operational activities. The first application here comes when the internal auditor is doing his preparatory work for any one of his audit reviews. At that time the internal auditor will want to review the scope of the existing organizational arrangements. This review can take place in part at the headquarters office, and would properly include discussions with the organization department. It would take place also at the field level. The major purpose at this stage is to understand the nature of the particular operations to be reviewed, together with the related organizational arrangements, and at the same time to have a reference point to be used as he later determines how the organizational arrangements are operating in actual practice.

Relating Organizational Arrangements to Operational Deficiencies. It is possible that the audit review will lead directly to a deficiency in the organizational arrangements. Illustrative of this would be the case where the internal auditor found in his preparation phase that there was no up-to-date organization chart. Or the review could lead directly to an identification of a significant difference between the organizational arrangement in practice and those originally represented to be in force. Such deficiencies should of course be handled on their merits in the customary manner.

Organizational arrangements are frequent sources of deficiencies

There is, however, another type of development that can yield very important results. This is the situation when a significant deficiency of any kind is found to exist and when the internal auditor is then probing for the causal factors which relate to that deficiency. At that time the internal auditor is in an excellent position to consider the extent to which existing organizational arrangements in some way may be a cause of the problem. It is here that an understanding of basic organizational concepts provides the foundation for appraising the soundness of the particular organizational arrangements that have been developed. The identification of such problems, and such appraisal and recommendations reasonably warranted can, indeed, be one of the most valuable types of contribution made by the internal auditor.

Application of Organizational Control to the Internal Auditing Department. Finally there is the concern for organizational control which the internal auditor should have as it pertains to his own internal auditing group. The head of the internal auditing department is himself a manager of his own operations and he too must recognize his basic organizational responsibilities. As always the internal auditor also has a special responsibility to provide a kind of showcase example of what he is recommending to other operational units. Like any other manager, the internal auditor has the problem of balancing conflicting considerations and making judgments as to particular organizational arrangements. He must also be sure that he is alert to changing developments which may suggest the desirability of modifications in the existing organizational arrangements.

Internal audit department organization also needs appraisal

REVIEW QUESTIONS

1. Describe the breakdown and integration aspects of the organizing process.
2. Describe the design and implementation aspects of the organizing process.
3. What kinds of conditions bear upon the choice of a functional approach to organizing versus a product approach?
4. What are the advantages of profit decentralization? What are the limitations?
5. "The distinction between line and staff organizational assignments is obsolete." Do you agree or disagree? Why?

6. Why is it desirable that authority and responsibility be tied to each other in organizational assignments? What are the practical limitations?

7. Is there a proper size for span of control? Explain.

8. In what ways can a committee be useful? To what extent are they undesirable?

9. How can one determine the kind and intensity of supervision that a particular manager or supervisor should exercise over his subordinates?

10. Where do you think the responsibility for the organization control activity should be placed within an organization? Why?

11. What is the role of the internal auditor in organizational control?

CASE PROBLEMS

Problem 5-1

You are a senior internal auditor with the Abbott Manufacturing Company. During the course of an internal audit, the director of purchasing complained to you that some line managers circumvent the purchasing process by going directly to vendors to procure needed materials. In addition these same managers have, in some instances, had the goods which they ordered delivered directly to the work area without being processed through the receiving department. Your audit tests verified the allegations made by the director of purchasing.

Required. Identify the organizational controls which some of the line managers at Abbott are violating.

Problem 5-2

George Wilson had just completed an internal audit of the metal parts division of the Better Products Corporation. In that audit Wilson found that the metal parts division was capitalizing its very substantial research program expenditures in spite of the clearly stated corporate policy that all research be charged to expenses as incurred. Wilson has discussed the problem with Russell Bonner, vice-president and general manager of the division, but has been unable to convince Bonner of the necessity of complying with the corporate policy. Bonner said, "President Peters has told me that he wants results here at Metal Parts and that he will leave it to my judgment as to how the job is done. We are spending a lot of money researching a new metal cutting approach. The project is proceeding very satisfactorily and I am confident that when we eventually get into production we can amortize the cost of research against the new sales generated. That approach makes a lot of sense to me and I am going to follow it until Peters directs me to do otherwise. I have no hesitation in arguing my case with him." Said Barney

Huff, the division controller, "I agree with Russ Bonner. Perhaps I should have gotten corporate finance approval, but after all, this is Bonner's show. Moreover, Ben Dart, the vice-president–finance only wants to follow the rules regardless of the local merits." Wilson felt that he had no choice but to report the situation, but was uncertain as to what his recommendation, if any, should be.

Required. Analyze the conflicting aspects of the situation and determine what Wilson should do—including the making of any final recommendation.

CHAPTER SIX

The Operational Approach of the Internal Auditor

Upon completing this chapter you should be able to:

☐ *Differentiate between the approach to auditing of the internal auditor and the external auditor*

☐ *Describe the ways an internal auditor integrates financial and operational auditing*

☐ *Identify the phases of an individual audit project and explain the activities which take place during each phase*

☐ *Describe the internal auditor's involvement in internal accounting controls*

NATURE OF THE OPERATIONAL APPROACH

In the preceding chapters we considered at some length the nature and scope of the internal auditing function. In this chapter we focus on the internal auditor as an individual and how he views his internal auditing job. Our consideration of the operational approach of the internal auditor will include his attitude toward his work, how he defines the scope of his review, the needed qualifications, the key phases of his review, and certain problems he encounters which are common to all of his reviews. We also discuss the needs for satisfying the requirements of the Foreign Corrupt Practices Act of 1977, including the related regulations of the Securities and Exchange Commission. These requirements pertain to the now clearly established responsibilities of management for the adequacy of the system of internal accounting control. Although, as previously stated, the internal auditor's interests go beyond the system of internal accounting control, the internal auditor recognizes the expanded nature and scope of the greater concerns of the organization in that area. Additionally, the internal accounting control is an integral part of the total internal control, and the evaluation of the part is therefore a major portion of the evaluation of the whole.

Comparison with the Approach of the External Auditor

One way to help understand the operational approach of the internal auditor is to compare it with the way the external auditor views his work. It has often been said that the external auditor starts with the end result and works backward, whereas the internal auditor starts with the basic activities and works forward to his organizational service objectives. Although such a statement is an oversimplification of the comparative types of approach, it does have a certain amount of substance. In the case of the external auditor, his primary interest is to be able to express an opinion as to whether the financial statements fairly present the current financial condition and the results of the operations over the preceding year. He is therefore more concerned with final financial statement balances, and he works backward from them for the evidence to support the validity of those balances. The internal auditor, on the other hand, is more concerned with the effectiveness of basic operational activities, and how those operational activities contribute to the total company profitability and economic welfare of the company. All of this means that the two auditing groups will approach information sources with different priorities, in somewhat different sequences, and with quite different end objectives.

External auditor goes backward from results while internal auditor goes forward from basic activities

Operational-Financial Linkage

The work of the external auditor has sometimes been described as financial auditing, and this tie has perhaps partially contributed to the movement of the modern internal auditor away from so-called financial auditing toward operational or management auditing. As indicated in Chapter 1, however, the separation of the two types of auditing is not that simple. There is, in fact, some linkage at several different levels and in certain situations. The first of these is where the internal auditor is asked by management to make a standard financial audit of a division subsidiary or other operational entity. In this situation the internal auditor is doing regular financial auditing and at the same time extending his work into promising operational areas. At another level the internal auditor may be reviewing operating activities that relate primarily to the financial or accounting function. But in such situations the internal auditor may also extend his review into other operational activities which go beyond the normal financial or accounting jurisdiction. Finally, there is the situation where the review focuses directly upon a regular operating activity as, for example, the receiving operations, or perhaps the custody and control of mobile equipment. Here the review activities may properly extend into matters of expense and revenue control which become more financial in character. Although in some cases the operational auditing

Separating operational from financial auditing is often impossible

may deal almost entirely with nonaccounting activities, in most situations there are many important linkages which argue against the sometimes asserted noninvolvement in so-called financial auditing.

Going Behind Financial Statements.   The foregoing comments can now become a basis for a further statement of the integration of so-called financial and operational auditing into totally effective modern internal auditing. Financial auditing in its most fundamental sense focuses on the reliability of financial statement balances—including such aspects as accuracy, reliability, and compliance with authoritative rules and standards. But these financial auditing objectives are only a component and starting point for covering other objectives of organizational concern. Now we can go behind those financial results to examine all aspects of the processes whereby those balances were created, sustained, and finalized—with full recognition of the ever-present overlapping relationships between various assets and liabilities in the balance sheet and the different types of income and expense that comprise the income statement. In all cases we are concerned with the policies, decisions, procedures, and performance that affect those changing financial statement balances. In this sense financial auditing can be, to some extent, unavoidably a component of the total internal auditing mission—but a limited component only—that is expanded through operational auditing to cover the total objective of maximizing organizational welfare. Admittedly, the degree of emphasis on final balances and related operational issues can vary significantly in individual audit assignments, but the fact remains that so-called financial and operational auditing can be fully integrated in good internal auditing. The audit programs and audit activities must continuously focus on the broader total internal auditing mission.

Organizational Service Approach

As we saw in Chapters 1 and 2, the mission of the internal auditor is to serve the organization. The range of this service extends from the board of directors (including the audit committee of that board) to the various levels of management in the corporation itself. The practical effect of the foregoing extended range is that the different recipients of the services have needs that have major similarities but at the same time with varying degrees of emphasis. All recipients have some interest in operational effectiveness (including profitability) but in differing degrees of intensity and detail. All recipients also have need for protective service but in varying degrees and emphasis, depending on the nature of their particular responsibilities. For example, boards of directors are relatively more concerned with legality, public relations, and personal liability. Because of these varying needs, the approach of the internal auditor must be broad enough to properly serve *all* recipients. Our approach in this book, however, is to emphasize the operational needs. This does not mean that protective needs can or will be neglected. It does, however, reflect the belief that the organization's highest-level need is for operational effectiveness and that at the same time protective needs can be adequately provided. Thus we are concerned with internal accounting controls but not as the end or highest-level objective of the internal auditor. We thus focus first on the management service objectives of the internal auditor.

Management Service Focus

The wide range of management service that can be provided by the internal auditor was outlined in some detail in the preceding chapters. The tie to the operational approach of the internal auditor is that all aspects of the internal auditor's initial direction, the actual execution of his review effort, and the subsequent reporting of conclusions and recommendations are conditioned by the overall objective of helping management at all levels to do the managerial job most effectively. A good way to describe this management-oriented approach is that the internal auditor tries to look at things as if he were the owner himself, and thus directly seeks to get the needed facts for the solution of managerial problems. The focus here is on maximum company welfare. The internal auditor is trying to represent the owners in situations where the limitations of time and energy preclude both owners and the responsible managers from being directly exposed to particular aspects of the operations. The internal auditor in such a role has often properly been called the "eyes and ears" of management.

Internal auditor is the eyes and ears of management

Profitability Focus

Still another good way to understand the operational approach of the internal auditor is to recognize the primary focus on profitability. This has sometimes been called the business approach, to emphasize the continuing emphasis on doing what is good business: that is, finding the ways and sponsoring the types of action that enhance the long-run profitability of a particular enterprise. Long-run profitability here merges into the total management objective of achieving the most productive utilization of organizational resources, thus providing a focus that is equally applicable to all types of organizations, whether of a business or nonbusiness character.

Profitability is primary focus of operational approach of internal auditor

Profitability as a term itself is much more complicated than it first appears and needs further clarification. There is first the fact that profitability is the net result of cost and revenue factors which in some cases are independent, but more often very closely interrelated. We know, for example, that reducing costs will increase profitability, but we also need to recognize that additional costs might be the basis of generating revenue greater in amount than the amount of the additional costs. Illustrative of this could be increased advertising expenditures. Conversely, reduced costs could in some cases lead to a still greater reduction in revenue. Illustrative of this could be an excessive cutback in service, which would generate customer complaints and ultimately reduce sales. Because of this major interrelationship we more properly speak of effective cost performance, that is, of the level of costs (whether higher or lower) which, after taking into consideration the impact on revenue, yields the greatest profit.

Profitability also has the complication of encompassing a time dimension which must be evaluated over a sufficiently long-term period. This is to say that management action does not usually have its major impact until some time in the future. As a result we have two types of problems. One of these is that we must extend our time dimensions far enough into the future so that the cost and revenue effects are properly matched for sound evaluation. The second problem is that the longer the period necessary for that type of evaluation, the more speculative becomes the estimate of the longer-run benefit. All in all it is difficult, therefore, to evaluate properly the effectiveness of cost–revenue relationships, and to determine whether present actions are really in the long-term interests of the enterprise. But this is just what the business manager and owner must do, and in turn what the internal auditor must do if he is to provide useful help and counsel.

Coverage of the Review

An examination of the operational approach leads us directly to the problem of the various ways in which the internal auditor can define the coverage of his review. The major issue here is whether the review should deal with a given function or with the total operational responsibilities of a given organizational entity. The function being reviewed will be something like purchasing or receiving, and can involve a single operational entity or extend

Internal auditor can use either functional or organizational type approach

through all or particular organization levels, as desired. In the entity approach the review covers all of the activities carried on by a particular entity, regardless of how many functions are involved. The entity involved can be an entire company, division, or other operational unit. If a particular operational entity is responsible only for a single function, the two approaches of course become the same thing. Both functional- and organizational-type reviews can vary greatly in complexity, depending on the volume of operations and the number of people involved.

Although most internal auditing reviews have the character of either a functional or organizational type, many reviews will also have a defined scope which is determined by the specific request of management. Such requests can have to do with the verification of a particular fact or set of facts, the determination of the cause for a particular development, the correction of a specific deficiency, or for further information about any managerial question. Thus operational activities can be broken down in any way desired as a basis for establishing what is wanted in the way of the work of the internal auditor. In the last analysis the scope of a particular review is determined by a combination of what management wants and what the internal auditor sees professionally as being the needs of management.

IIA Standards Approach

In Chapter 2 we discussed the "Standards for the Professional Practice of Internal Auditing." We refer to them again at this point because the treatment of scope of work also provides an excellent framework for the operational approach of the internal auditor. That framework is: (1) Reliability and Integrity of Information; (2) Compliance with Policies, Plans, Procedures, Laws, and Regulations; (3) Safeguarding of Assets; (4) Economical and Efficient Use of Resources; and (5) Accomplishment of Established Objectives and Goals for Operations or Programs. Our own analysis was also stated in some detail in Chapter 2. That analysis, together with the earlier comments in the chapter, of the operational approach of the internal auditor are in most respects very similar to the aforementioned framework in the Standards. What is most significant, however, is our own greater emphasis on helping management *better utilize* its resources in terms of profitability and related management welfare. That better utilization also includes possibly still higher goals and objectives. Assistance to management in maximizing the achievement of managerial effectiveness is indeed the central core of modern internal auditing. It is in every respect the most rewarding level of service to the organization by the internal auditor.

TECHNICAL APPROACH OF THE INTERNAL AUDITOR

Up to this point we have dealt with the various kinds of attitudes which the internal auditor should possess and the problems of determining the scope of the review. We turn now to the way in which the internal auditor proceeds to carry out his internal auditing activities. Here we are concerned with the particular technical approaches which have general application to all types of internal auditing reviews.

Planning the Audit

The first and perhaps the most basic activity on the part of the internal auditor is to inform himself about the operational entity that is to be reviewed. This is done during the planning (or familiarization) phase. There are two broad levels of planning for an individual review. One level includes everything that is done prior to arriving at the audit location and the other includes the on-site survey which, as the name implies, is done on location. Before going to the field location the following types of activities will typically be carried out:

Information about organizational entity needed

Determining Audit Objectives. The most important aspect of internal audit planning of an indivdual assignment is establishing the objectives of the particular audit. The scope of an operational audit may be as broad as the management process itself. Considering such factors as management's higher-

Specific objectives need to be established

level objectives and desires, the various audit approaches available, audit staff capabilities, the nature of prior audit work, and available resources and time, the specific objectives and limitations of the audit must be established at the outset of each assignment.

Have preliminary discussions with affected personnel

Discussions with Other Interested Personnel.   Discussions with other company personnel should include any levels of responsibility between the level which may have requested the audit and the level of management at the field location. It should also include staff managers and key personnel to the extent that they are involved through the definition of the assignment. These discussions serve a number of purposes, but are primarily to alert these individuals to the fact that a review is to be made and to get from them either questions requiring special attention or information that may be useful in connection with the review.

Accumulation of All Pertinent Data.   The internal auditor should obtain and review any kind of information which he believes could be applicable to the field review. This information is normally available in the files of the internal auditing department. Generally the following items should be considered during this phase:

Use previous audit

1. *Prior Working Papers.* Permanent working paper files should be reviewed to gain some knowledge on the background of the organization or function being reviewed, gain some understanding of applicable internal controls, and determine the types of statistical data which were available during the previous audit. The scope of the prior internal audit should be ascertained and the internal audit working papers and audit programs should be reviewed to familiarize the internal auditor with approaches used and results of the audit. Special attention should be given to prior audit problems and methods used to solve them.

2. *Review of Prior Reports.* All prior internal audit reports issued for the entity being audited should be reviewed. Patterns in findings, their significance, and the extent of corrective action should be analyzed. To obtain leads about sensitive areas, reports on similar entities or functions in the company can also be studied. Similar findings in other

Get ideas from professional literature

areas may also provide some useful insight. In some instances it can be beneficial to review articles in professional literature which discuss successful approaches used by other internal auditors in developing findings in certain areas.

Use results of other audits

3. *Other Reviews.* Related reviews or audits completed, planned, or in progress should also be studied. This includes audits by the outside public accountant, including management letters and reviews by federal, state, and local governmental organizations. This may also include the results of reviews made by departmental or other company officials,

trip reports, and reports of accomplishments. Any indication of problem areas should be noted.

4. *Contacts with Appropriate Personnel.* At this point the internal auditor should have obtained sufficient knowledge about the audit to discuss it intelligently. He should be prepared to discuss the proposed objectives of the audit, work to be done, and steps to be taken with his audit supervisor and manager. Officials of the entity to be audited should be contacted to set up the time and date for an entrance conference. When setting up an entrance conference, the internal auditor may also request that statistical data and other reports be available for the audit team upon its arrival at the audit location.

Talk to other informed people

The On-Site Survey

The internal auditor is now ready to go to the field location. The field location of course can be a distant site or an activity of some kind at the home office where the internal auditing staff is usually located.

The survey is critically important in determining the direction, scope, and extent of the audit effort. The internal auditor cannot rush in and begin examining documents and other test data. He must first become familiar with the current system of internal control prior to developing an audit program and starting the actual fieldwork. He must determine the reliance that can be placed on the system and various subsystems of internal control before proceeding.

Use survey to determine direction, scope, and extent of work

The initial activities at the field location are of the following types:

1. *Discussion with the Responsible Manager.* This discussion will be with the manager to whom the final report will normally be directed. The discussion should include such matters as the overall purpose of the review, timing plans, and other special arrangements. The internal auditor will get a firsthand description of the operational activities, organizational relationships, problem areas, and other matters of audit interest from this manager.

2. *Discussion with Other Key Personnel.* The discussions with the responsible managers will then be supplemented with discussions with other key personnel. These discussions will normally provide additional detail about the various subactivities and at the same time serve as a cross check against the information previously obtained.

Carry out important related field activities

3. *Review of Policies and Procedures.* Discussions with personnel at all levels will necessarily be supplemented by a review of written policies and procedures of all kinds which bear on the administration and control of the various types of operational activities carried on by the total organizational group.

4. *Continuing Familiarization.* The familiarization phase now extends into the actual internal audit review. This is to say that the carrying

out of the regular review program involves a further familiarization with detailed activities which were not completely covered in discussions or through actual observations.

The survey serves as a means of identifying new and innovative approaches to the audit. The results of prior audits and related audit procedures used should have been studied earlier. New techniques are considered in light of changed operating conditions. All internal auditors involved in the review should be encouraged to make suggestions for improving the audit process in the interest of obtaining better results.

Usually the following approaches are used in conducting an on-site survey.

1. *Organization of the Entity.* The internal auditor should obtain and study organization charts of the activity to be audited. The charts should be reviewed to gain an understanding of the organizational structure and the responsibilities of the various positions. A mission or function statement should also be obtained and reviewed to determine the activity's purpose.

Mission or functional statements can provide valuable information

2. *Manuals and Directives.* During this level of planning the internal auditor reviews applicable policy and procedure manuals, extracting data of interest to the audit. Federal and state laws and regulations as well as planned operating controls should also be reviewed. Correspondence files should be screened for applicable material.

3. *Reports.* The internal auditor should study relevant management reports and minutes of meetings covering such areas as budgeting, operations, cost studies, and personnel. He should also analyze the results of inspections or management reviews, and actions taken. These reports may provide leads which can be helpful during the audit, and offer a summary of problems faced and progress made in their resolution.

Management reports and related material provide useful survey information

4. *Flowcharts.* The use of flowcharts is of major assistance to the internal auditor in the review of internal control. By providing a graphic summary of the documentation and flow of data, flowcharts enable the auditor to follow the complexities of a system more clearly. Also weaknesses may be more easily detected by looking at a well-designed flowchart.

Based on the survey, the auditor prepares the audit program and outlines the nature and extent of audit work to be performed.

The Audit Program

Audit program is the culmination of planning and survey

The audit program is a tool for planning, directing, and controlling audit work. It is a blueprint for action, specifying the procedures to be followed and delineating steps to be performed to meet audit objectives. The audit program is the culmination of the planning and survey processes. It represents the internal auditor's selection of the best methods for getting the job done.

Program Criteria.   Preparing an audit program requires planning, judgment, and experience. The internal auditor has obtained and evaluated preliminary information in his survey—now he has to use it.

The most important criterion is of course the system of internal controls. Based on the survey, the internal auditor determines, on a preliminary basis, the reliance that can be placed on the system. He also selects the aspects to be further examined and the sensitive areas that require audit emphasis.

Materiality and relative risk are also criteria for developing the audit program. Materiality is based on the significance of an item compared to other items. In preparing the program the internal auditor may extend or limit his work in light of materiality. Although an area may not be material, it may be essential because of relative risk. Under relative risk the internal auditor reviews those items that require increased attention because of possible adverse circumstances. For example, property leased from officers or employees of the company would be scheduled for review.

Materiality and risk are criteria for program development

The reliability of evidence and types of information available should also be considered. The internal auditor will try to select audit steps that will produce reliable evidence as discussed later in this chapter.

Advanced auditing techniques will also be used wherever practicable. Computer software packages are available for the internal auditor to carry out particular audit steps. Statistical sampling procedures, combined with computer techniques, enable him to obtain data quickly from large populations. These and other techniques should be considered in preparing the program and are discussed in Chapters 8 and 9.

Detail in the Program.   An audit program usually includes a statement of objectives, audit steps—with a space provided to indicate the auditor responsible for each step, a space for the auditor to initial upon completion of the step, working paper reference, budget by audit steps, and estimated start and completion dates.

Audit program may be general or detailed

Audit guides, such as those included at the end of the chapters in Part Two of this book, and preliminary programs may be available in a given area. These should be used as guides only, with changes made as needed, based on the circumstances. Audit programs may be written in general form or may contain detailed steps, depending on the area to be reviewed and the level of experience of the internal auditor performing the work.

Program Modification.   The audit program should be considered a model of the assignment in discussions with management and the audit staff. The internal auditors must, however, be responsive to new evidence, changes in staff assignments, and other changes in conditions. In the early stages of

Modify objectives if assignment is redirected

the audit it may be necessary to redirect the assignment as well as modify objectives.

Performing the Audit

Internal auditor confirms actuality to assertions

From the base of planning, the internal auditor moves to the verification phase—the fieldwork. We need to recognize that the two types of activity, familiarization and verification, are interwoven as one moves downward through the organizational levels. But conceptually, fieldwork is the independent determination of the extent to which actuality conforms to what was asserted to be during the planning phase.

Auditing Procedures. Auditing procedures are the specific acts performed or methods used to obtain the necessary data to achieve the objectives of the audit and prepare the audit report. In internal auditing, procedures are related to various sources of information because of the emphasis placed on processes by the internal auditor. These procedures typically involve the following types of actions:

COMPARING. The internal auditor frequently compares related information and analyzes differences. For example, he compares actual costs with budgeted and standard costs, and reviews explanations for significant variations.

VOUCHING. In addition to tracing items to subsidiary records, the internal auditor reviews support for entries and for amounts in reports. This involves the inspection of documents on a test basis. Judgment sampling or statistical sampling may be used as appropriate to arrive at conclusions as to the validity of information.

CONFIRMING. If documents prepared by third parties are sent to the internal auditor, they are considered especially reliable. In recent years internal auditors have extended their use of confirmations, especially in instances where internal control is weak or documents are missing from the file. An example is confirming payables to disclose unrecorded liabilities and the validity of account balances.

SCANNING. In some cases the internal auditor may wish to scan or examine the records and reports visually to determine if there are sensitive items requiring further attention. This procedure does not substitute for testing; it enables the auditor to become familiar with the system and pinpoint areas for inquiry.

ANALYZING. It is through analysis that the internal auditor breaks down a process or an item into its component parts. This breakdown facilitates the review through highlighting essential elements. It also serves to identify major causes for conditions.

An example is the review of increases in maintenance costs. The internal auditor prepares a matrix of maintenance costs by departments, equipment, and period, breaking costs down by labor, materials, and overhead. He then uses this analysis to determine trends, review differences, and determine causes for the increases.

INQUIRING.   Information obtained orally is an important means of explaining the facts that are in the records or developed from other sources. It also enables the internal auditor to visualize the activities and processes that are in operation, and provides him leads for further review. The internal auditor can secure such explanations from individuals involved in the particular area being reviewed, as well as from individuals in other departments.

Internal auditor procedures involve different types of action

OBSERVING.   There may be listed under this procedure all the impressions and observations that the internal auditor has experienced during the audit assignment. The internal auditor observes the physical layout of plant, storage of equipment and inventories, physical inventory procedures, coordination and utilization of personnel, and other operations of all kinds. These observations give additional meaning to reviews made of the underlying data. The importance of planned observations makes it desirable for the internal auditor to carry out his assignment in such a manner that he can move about and observe the various phases of the company's operating activities.

RECOMPUTING.   The internal auditor is called on to check selected footings, extensions, and other calculations as part of his audit. His review of controls, including computer controls, will determine the nature and extent of testing to be performed. An example is in the use of dollar-unit sampling, in which it is necessary to check the footing of the total dollars in the universe prior to selecting the sample.

As can be seen, verification can be accomplished in a number of ways, but the essence of that accomplishment is that there is evidence of some kind which is sufficiently credible.

Audit Evidence.   The "Standards for the Professional Practice of Internal Auditing" state that the internal auditor should examine and evaluate information on all matters related to the audit objective. This information, or evidence, should be sufficient, competent, relevant, and useful.

Audit evidence should be sufficient, relevant, and useful

The internal auditor must gather evidence to support both the positive and negative conclusions resulting from the examination. He must be assured that all information in the working papers has been checked for possible findings. He must also determine that there is sufficient evidence to support his conclusions. In carrying out the review he must always evaluate the different types of evidence, discuss that evidence with the auditee, and obtain feedback to test his observations. The final conclusions are then based on a multitude of auditing procedures selected by the internal auditor as needed to distinguish between fact and fiction.

ANALYTICAL EVIDENCE.   The internal audit often includes extensive analysis of business operations, with emphasis on internal controls. This evidence is considered circumstantial, since it involves circumstances from which inferences can be drawn. By examining relationships in the system and determining whether internal controls are operative, the internal auditor arrives at conclusions with respect to the system and determines the extent of testing that needs to be done.

Gathering evidence highly judgmental

SUPPORTING EVIDENCE.   The internal auditor must decide on the specific type of corroborative evidence needed in the review. This may take the form of documentary evidence, testimonial evidence, or a combination of the two. For example, in determining why competitive bids were not obtained in acquiring equipment, the internal auditor reviews the purchase files for justification for sole-source procurement. In addition he may discuss the problem with the purchasing agent and with the requisitioner to obtain additional information.

STRUCTURE OF BEST EVIDENCE.   In obtaining and evaluating information, the internal auditor must select the strongest evidence available. He realizes that if an employee tells him something, it is not as strong as obtaining a written statement. He also recognizes that oral or written statements have to be tested and verified. The following is a structure of best evidence which is useful to the auditor.[1]

Classifications	Strongest	Weakest
Relationship to agency	External	Internal
Techniques	Observation–confirmation	Inquiry
Origin	Corroborative	Underlying accounting data
Form	Written	Oral
Sophistication	Formal	Informal
Reality	Actual system	Designed system
Auditor	Self	Others

The quality of the evidence will vary, not only with the type of evidence, but with the diligence with which the individual collection effort is carried out. The gathering of evidence is highly judgmental in character, both as to the quality of the particular evidence and as to how much effort should be expended in obtaining additional evidence. The application of the necessary judgment in turn, depends on the particular level of competence possessed by the internal auditor.

[1]Alan Johnson. "A Structured Theory of Management, Footnote (5). *Journal of the HEW Audit Agency*, Winter 1971–1972, p. 17.

Analysis

A related phase of the internal auditor's approach concerns analysis. This is *Detailed examination of* the more detailed examination of information in terms of its component *information needed* elements. It is very frequently carried out as part of the verification process, as where, for example, the detailed analysis of an account balance might also serve to help verify the correctness of the account. On the other hand, in an operational situation the detailed breakdown of performance under different types of operating conditions can provide the basis for determining better ways to control the particular type of performance. In all types of analysis there is a highly judgmental aspect both in making the decision as to *how* a particular type of information or operational activity shall be analyzed and subsequently in obtaining the potential benefits as the analysis is carried out. In the latter case there is an especially fine opportunity to observe the evolving elements and to perceive relationships or other matters of managerial interest. Analysis is, indeed, the major route to effective internal auditing service.

Evaluation

Familiarization, verification, and analysis have now set the stage for evaluation. This is the critical phase of the internal auditor's work when he seeks to draw conclusions that may provide a basis for definitive management service. Its scope can best be understood by viewing it as being carried out at three levels:

1. *How Good Is the Result Presently Being Achieved?* This may be a *Drawing conclusions critical* fairly narrow question such as how well a particular procedure has *phase of audit* been complied with, or it may be a more serious question as to how efficiently a given operational activity is being carried out. It may also be the overall judgment as to the effectiveness of the total performance of the operational activity under review.

2. *Why Is the Result What It Is?* At the next higher level, and interwoven with the first evaluation, is the evaluation of why the results are as they are. Why is the performance as good or bad as it is? Why it is not better? This now involves the evaluation of causal factors, especially, the evaluation of the extent to which those causal factors might have been more effectively controlled.

3. *What Could Be Done Better?* And now at the highest level, and again unavoidably interwoven with the former types of evaluation, are the judgments as to what could be done to achieve better results in the future. Can the procedures be made more effective? Should a particular policy be changed in some respect, or even abandoned? Are the right type of people involved and are they properly trained and administered? Some of these conclusions may be reasonably clear and can become the basis for specific recommendations. In other cases

more information may be needed. In the latter cases it may be feasible for the internal auditor to develop the further information. Or in other cases this may not be practicable and the recommendation may simply be that further study be made. These determinations as to the scope of the recommendation are, of course, highly dependent on the situation and the capability of the internal auditor.

Continuing Search for Effectiveness

The internal auditor must be alert, and not be routine or mechanical

During all phases of the internal auditor's work there is always the continuing need for maximum effectiveness. Nothing the internal auditor does can ever be done in a routine or mechanical manner. Whether the internal auditor is examining documents, talking with individuals, or observing various operational activities, he is always thinking of the underlying conditions pertaining to that part of the review. What is right? How responsible was the particular action carried out? How valid are the results? What else could be done? These are typical questions that are always in the internal auditor's mind. The internal auditor does not have a distorted belief that everything is wrong or that disaster is imminent. But on the other hand he is not a naive optimist. In short he has an inquiring and challenging approach and a relatively greater need than an ordinary person to be convinced. Hopefully, the internal auditor is always open-minded and fair. But there is more natural skepticism and a need that there be a reasonable showing of relevant facts. All of these qualities come together in the constant alertness of the internal auditor as he continuously seeks to utilize all relevant information bearing on the objectives of his review and related conclusions. It is an alertness that helps to provide protective service. But it also always goes further in the continuing search for improvement.

Maximizing Completed Action

Company interest best served by earliest possible completed corrective action

The work of the internal auditor has now come to the stage of the conclusion and recommendation. There is now a range of possibilities as to what might be done in the way of completed action. At the one extreme there will be no action now and we will proceed directly to the reporting phase, leaving the determination of exactly what action will be taken, and when, to a later time. At the other extreme is the completion of the recommended action in the field while the internal auditor is still there. The real issue is the extent to which it is possible to move individual matters toward completed action. In many cases the particular matter will clearly be something that should be handled immediately. This could be the correction of an error, or perhaps a more informed interpretation of a company policy. Other cases may be more controversial and may require decision review at higher organizational levels. The important thing, however, is that all parties are committed to the concept of maximum completed action. The reasons for this approach quite obviously reflect the truth that the earlier action accelerates the timing of the achievement of the expected benefits. A further important reason is that the partnership relationship of the internal auditor and the responsible management is thus more effectively implemented. Now the internal auditor and the management work more closely and agree together as what needs to be done. It can also be more realistically demonstrated that the internal auditor is there to *help* local management—and not to police them—and that they can work together in the overall company interest.

Reporting

The reporting phase is now the means by which the internal auditor summarizes what has been accomplished and makes this information available to higher-level management and other interested parties. The content of the reports will of course be determined directly by the extent of the completed action and what matters still require further consideration and possible action. In Chapter 10 we deal in greater detail with the various ways in which reports can be developed. But it can be said at this point that it is a major means by which the internal auditor relates to all interested company personnel, especially to the officers to whom he is directly responsible. Reporting therefore needs to be handled with special care. However, it needs to be said that the modern internal auditor is more and more concentrating on what can be accomplished at the field level and less on what goes into reports. This is to say that the internal auditor is serving company interests better in most situations by helping responsible management at the field level. Under these circumstances the reporting of completed action does not need to be as elaborate as when the basis for a recommended action is being presented. At the same time the higher-level management needs to understand this newer approach and to be supportive of it.

Scope of reporting depends on need to inform higher level management.

Report Follow-Up

Reference has previously been made to the internal auditor's possible role in connection with the follow-up of reports. It sometimes happens that top management requests this follow-up role as the best means in its opinion to ensure that needed actions based on the audit are actually taken. In some cases also a particularly zealous general auditor will propose this procedure. The desirability of follow-up action in itself is very clear. The problem however is whether this is a proper responsibility of the internal auditor, and whether such action by the internal auditor will undermine the basic responsibilities of the managers who are in charge of the particular activities. It also puts the internal auditor more in the role of a policeman, and this tends to conflict with his ongoing partnership relationship with the auditee. In many companies, therefore, the internal auditor plays no specific role after his report is released, other than to respond to questions and again

Standards require follow-up by internal auditor

review the situation at the time of the next audit assignment. Many companies, however, have adopted some intermediate type of approach.

A typical intermediate approach is that the coordination of the total follow-up effort is placed in the hands of another office, usually the Finance Department or some more neutral administrative services group. The corrective action is then initiated by the responsible line or staff manager, but responses are made to the coordinating officer. If there are undue delays in dealing with the recommendation, the coordinating office issues follow-up inquiries. Under this approach copies of responses can also be supplied to the internal auditor group for information, or the internal auditor can maintain other liaison with the coordinating group. There is no final answer as to how this total follow-up effort should be handled, but on balance it seems best to subordinate the internal auditor's formal role in it. The help of the internal auditor can always be asked for on a special basis, either by the coordinating office or by individual managers. In addition the lack of action can be highlighted at the time of the next review.[2]

Internal Auditor's Credentials

A continuing issue is the extent to which the other members of the organization understand and accept the role of the internal auditor. The range here extends from the lowest-level employee in the operational area being reviewed to the highest-level responsible managerial executive. Especially important is the manager who is responsible for the operational area to be reviewed. The question can arise in such circumstances as to whether the effort required to accommodate an internal audit is justified in relation to the benefits to be received. That is, the manager may resent the making of the internal audit activity as counterproductive to the achievement of his own operational objectives. Our interest at this point is to identify more clearly the fact that this problem often does exist and what the rationale is for overcoming the obstacles. We assume of course that the manager wants to maximize his own interests in terms of greater achievement of his objectives but that he does not see the internal auditor as being able to contribute to that end in a worthwhile manner.

Internal auditor cannot claim technical expertise of operational managers, but can advise on controls

The reconciliation of the dilemma described above is that the internal auditor must make it clear that he does not claim to have the technical knowledge or experience to tell the manager what his operational objectives should be or how those objectives should be achieved in an operational sense. Instead the truth that needs to be conveyed is that all operational activities have common needs in the *manner* in which they establish objectives and the *manner* in which implementing actions are planned and controlled. The internal auditor's major competence is in understanding how the planning and operational activities can utilize the best possible controls

[2]See also the comments in Chapter 2 relative to Section 440 of The Institute's Standards.

as proven to be effective in other operational situations. These approaches include both underlying management concepts and more detailed procedures that assure desired levels of performance and final results. Once the internal auditor has been given the opportunity to demonstrate what he can do in providing such assistance, the credentials and related acceptability of the internal auditor rise steadily. Hopefully, however, better communication to such a manager of the rationale of potential service can help to provide the initial acceptance. If, additionally, the particular internal audit review is mandated by higher-level management, the same kind of communication can help break down otherwise existing barriers.

QUALIFICATIONS OF THE INTERNAL AUDITOR

Technical Qualifications

If the internal auditor is to be effective in carrying out the technical approaches just described, he must necessarily have a certain professional competence. This leads us to a consideration of the various technical and personal qualifications which are important. In the technical group a number of questions are involved which deserve consideration.

1. *What Basic Technical Qualifications Are Needed?* We know that the individual internal auditor must be prepared to deal with a wide range of operational situations. For that reason he will need to have technical qualifications of the broadest possible application. These technical qualifications pertain to both education and experience. For education the current trend is for a college degree in an established school of business. For experience there needs to be previous involvement in operational activities or at least reasonable exposure to them. The activities most useful would vary with the individual company but they will preferably have been in situations where a number of people were involved and where there were problems of administrative direction and control. Second, a generally useful qualification would be some experience in or understanding of the accounting and financial control processes. This type of qualification does not necessarily involve direct work of an accounting nature but it does at least involve the kind of exposure that provides a reasonable understanding of this area. This is consistent with the view that the financial control dimension can be an effective starting point for the examination of the broader types of operational control.

2. *To What Extent Are Special Types of Technical Qualifications Needed?* In reviewing many operational activities it will be helpful to have some special expertise with respect to those particular operational areas. Illustrative of this would be computer activities, various kinds of engineering activities, and different kinds of production processes. Again

Need for technical qualifications can be satisfied in different ways

depending on the company, the need for this special expertise may be of different degrees. The answer here would then seem to be to look for these special skills as staff members are recruited and developed. At the same time, however, it must be recognized that there are some very real practical limitations. In the first place it will clearly be impossible and impracticable for all personnel to have all of the types of technical skill that might be needed at one time or the other. At best we should seek to have a balanced staff with some personnel having certain skills and others having different ones. In the second place, at some level of excellence in the particular skill, the question might be raised as to whether a particular individual could not be more useful to the company if he were assigned directly to those operations.

3. *When Are the Skills Needed?* In addition to the problem of agreeing on what kinds of general and special technical skills are needed, there is the question of when they need to be available. The answer here is of course that everything is relative. To some extent we need to have personnel who do already meet certain standards with respect to these skills. In other cases we can acquire individuals who fall below those standards but who have the potential to acquire them. We might, for example, start with a college graduate, or perhaps with an employee who has been working in some part of the company operations. Through experience and perhaps some special training we can then expand the area of competence. What is important is that the personnel capabilities in total meet the needs of actual internal audit assignments. In addition, there is always the possibility of going outside the department to obtain special expertise. The latter may be available in the company, but it may at times be necessary to go outside the organization.

Personal Qualifications

While the technical qualifications just discussed are an important foundation for the internal auditor's level of effectiveness, the personal qualifications of each individual also play a major role. Here we are confronted with a long list of personal qualifications which are normally deemed to be desirable. The problem is further complicated by the fact that the identification and evaluation of these individual qualifications is at best very subjective. Yet the area is important and we must try to cope with it. Perhaps the most useful approach is to look at these personal qualifications in terms of the major end objectives. Under this approach we can identify three types of end objectives:

End objectives determine needed personal qualifications

1. To achieve a good first impression
2. To develop a more enduring relationship over a longer period of time
3. To provide an additional basis for sound professional results

These three end objectives are, of course, closely related, but they do emphasize particular types of personal qualifications.

Achieving a Good First Impression.   First impressions can be, as we know, both good and bad. When there is to be a longer relationship the importance of the first impression may not be so great, although even then it may help to get things off to a good start and avoid handicaps which later have to be eliminated. But in many situations the contact is by its very nature a limited one. Illustrative of this would be a particular inquiry made in connection with any audit review, especially when that inquiry involves an outside party or where there are limitations as to being able to go back again. Also illustrative of this would be the case of conferences where matters are going to be discussed with new people and decisions of one kind or another reached. Under these circumstances the emphasis must necessarily be on making a good impression in a very short time. It leads us to the question of what can be done to contribute to a successful first impression. The answer is: a combination of personal appearance and the ability to capitalize quickly on limited opportunities. With respect to personal appearance, standards of dress and grooming should be in the middle range between extreme conservatism and high style. With respect to the capitalizing of opportunities, one should be able to respond effectively to questions and inject himself in the discussion in a manner that demonstrates courtesy and professional competence. In total the objective sought is to engender respect and confidence as a basis for a proper degree of receptivity for the technical contribution that the internal auditor is prepared to make.

A good first impression is important

Building Longer-Run Relationships.   In the longer run there is the greater opportunity to develop effective personal relationships. The major difference here is that there is a more ample period for the demonstration of good qualities through ongoing actions and the testing of those actions. The relationships here can be with personnel in the operational activities being reviewed and with managerial personnel at all levels. In these kinds of situations what are the types of personal qualifications that become especially important? In other words, what personal qualifications most contribute to achieving a relationship in which the internal auditor will earn respect and cooperation? We suggest that the following are especially important:

1. *Basic Fairness and Integrity.* The kind of response that anyone will make to the internal auditor is first conditioned by a judgment as to whether he can reasonably expect fair treatment. At lower levels the concern will be whether the internal auditor will take advantage of his position in any manner, and whether he can be trusted to deal fairly with information made available to him. At higher levels there will be a similar judgment—even though in a more sophisticated manner—which then determines how candid that higher-level manager will be in his relations with the internal auditor.

Effective long-run relationship with auditor is vital

2. *Dedication to Company Interest.* Closely related is the concern as to whether the internal auditor is primarily motivated by what is good for the company. The internal auditor must demonstrate that he will

not be putting special or personal interests ahead of the company welfare.

3. *Reasonable Humility*. All of us tend to react in a hostile manner to someone who gives the impression of being too egotistical. More often no one individual can be that sure of having all of the right answers, and a reasonable recognition of those limitations is both more realistic and more likely to impress the people one is coming into contact with.

4. *Professional Poise*. People respect a person who appears to be competent and who conducts himself in a professional manner. This also combines a lack of aloofness with the avoidance of being too forward or excessively friendly.

5. *Empathy*. This is the ability to project oneself to an understanding of how the other person feels. It involves courtesy and consideration for how what one is saying or doing is affecting the other person. It reflects a proper degree of general interest in people, to which all of us respond favorably. On the other hand it can stop short of being overly solicitous or insincere.

6. *Role Consistency*. The persons with whom the internal auditor has contact have a set of expectations as to what the role of the internal auditor should be. To the extent that those expectations are appropriate, they need to be confirmed, and to the extent that they are inappropriate, they have to be modified carefully by the actions of the internal auditor. In all cases, however, the role played by the internal auditor must be stable and consistent. We need to build a feeling of confidence in the eyes of the people with whom we associate.

Building a Basis for Professional Results.   All of the foregoing are important in establishing an effective relationship with the people with whom the internal auditor associates. There are in addition, however, a group of personal qualifications that bear more directly on his competence in a strictly professional sense. These personal qualifications relate particularly to the way he goes about his actual internal auditing activities. We suggest the following:

Personal qualifications contribute to professional excellence

1. *Curiosity*. The internal auditor should have a natural curiosity to probe for possible underlying explanations. He should not be satisfied with generalizations or types of explanations that ignore important considerations.

2. *Critical Attitude*. The quality here is not to be critical in the sense of giving criticism, but critical in the sense of making careful judgments about the various matters with which the internal auditor is involved. It is an extension of the previously mentioned curiosity with a high standard for the adequacy of information.

3. *Alertness*. The internal auditor needs to be alert to all possible sources

of information that may in some way bear on the issues under consideration. He utilizes the innumerable interrelationships which always come with individual types of developments.

4. *Persistence.* The internal auditor does not give up easily when he is blocked in some way in his pursuit of needed information or for possible solutions of problems that need answers. He needs to have a genuine motivation to get good answers.

5. *Energy.* Energy is in a sense the backup quality for persistence. It is the force that keeps us going when others would give up and settle for whatever has already been found. It is a combination of temperament, dedication, and good health.

Guides for needed personal qualifications

6. *Self-Confidence.* Self-confidence generates confidence in others. It is the inward conviction that one knows what one is doing and that it is the right thing to do. It is backed up both by knowledge and the belief that one is doing the best thing possible.

7. *Courage.* Closely related to self-confidence is courage. The quality of courage, however, goes further and involves the willingness to stand one's ground in the face of pressures and risks. It is a personal qualification that indeed adds status to the internal auditor and to his effectiveness, especially when that courage has been demonstrated. All internal auditors will face this problem at one time or another.

8. *Ability to Make Sound Judgments.* All of us are beset with conflicting factors of all types as we deal with individual questions. Judgment is the ability to weigh these conflicting factors calmly, including the impact of the varying time dimensions, and to come out with sound judgments. Here the requirement is not for a perfect record but rather how many more correct judgments there are versus the ones that were in error.

9. *Integrity.* We repeat integrity here because of its basic importance. It is the quality that leads others to rely on the findings and conclusions of the internal auditor. This reliance includes the belief in the professional competence and fairness and honesty with which the material has been presented. It is, indeed, a major basis for any continuing good professional relationship.

10. *Independence.* Closely interrelated with all of the foregoing is the capacity to be independent and not to compromise unduly in the face of pressures of various kinds. It builds especially upon courage and integrity.

Professional Standards

The desire on the part of the internal auditing profession to maximize its effectiveness in serving management leads naturally to the desire to develop standards by which there can be some better measure as to how well the internal auditor is carrying out his function. Moreover, the basic interest of the internal auditor in achieving effective control and the customary use of standards in that effort would logically suggest that he can better control his own internal auditing activity through the development of standards. In response to these needs The Institute of Internal Auditors authorized a major study effort and in 1978 published its new "Standards for the Professional Practice of Internal Auditing." These Standards were reviewed in considerable detail in Chapter 2.

Standards provide information about expectations from internal auditors

The new Standards have been accepted with real enthusiasm by all interested parties. For internal auditors they have provided an important base of reference in their practice of modern internal auditing. For all others—including management, boards of directors, public accountants, government, businessmen, and educators—there is more definitive information about what they should expect from internal auditors. Admittedly, the Standards have limitations—as discussed in more detail in Chapter 2—but they do constitute a major step forward. It is also to be expected that there will be further refinements and elaboration as necessary based on experience and changing conditions. As discussed in Chapter 2, The Institute of Internal Auditors has initiated a program to issue "Statements on Internal Auditing Standards," which elaborate on the general standards.

Certification Program of The Institute of Internal Auditors

Institute's certification program is important step toward professionalism

Another important accomplishment of The Institute of Internal Auditors has been the development of a certification program in 1972 utilizing the designation Certified Internal Auditor (CIA). The foundation for this program was a major study of what constituted a needed "common body of knowledge for the internal auditor." Subsequently, an examination program was established that has been administered by The Institute on a regular basis. While a large number of qualified practicing internal auditors were given certificates on the basis of previous experience—the so-called grandfather clause—the number of persons sitting for the examination has steadily increased. In combination, an increasingly large number of internal auditors now have the certificate.

A continuing problem of the certification program is the difficulty of defining and evaluating the knowledge that internal auditors should have. This is because the operational activities covered by internal auditors in actual practice are so broad. However, that problem has been dealt with in a most commendable manner and the major benefits of the total certification program have been amply demonstrated.

One unfortunate coincidence of the CIA designation has been the possible confusion of the letters CIA with an existing governmental organization—especially in worldwide usage. In retrospect, a word such as "Registered" or "Approved" would have eliminated that problem, but thus far it has been considered even less desirable at this late time to change the name of the program.

Still another problem pertaining to the certification program is the fact that the greater number of Institute members are still not certified. This is in contrast to the approach taken by the American Institute of Certified Public Accountants, where the holding of a CPA certificate is a requirement of membership. One contributing factor to the existing problem is that movement of individuals in and out of internal auditing practice is often very great—thus reducing the incentive to make the effort needed to achieve certification. Although we strongly support the increased professionalism of the internal auditor, the related greater career commitment, and the resulting longer tenure in internal auditing practice, we do at the same time recognize that management's interests can often be best served by moving individuals in and out of the internal auditing department. We therefore see no presently foreseeable basis for changing the now existing restrictions. However, we should at the same time encourage all internal auditors to qualify for the CIA certificate.

Relationships with People

In carrying out his internal auditing activities, the internal auditor interfaces with other individuals in and outside the organization. These relationships extend from the level of the board of directors to all levels of management and other organizational personnel. There are also the relationships within the internal auditing department itself. The relations with auditees present a special challenge to induce their cooperation in achieving the audit objectives to which internal auditors aspire. In addition, there are the critical relationships with higher-level management personnel whose support for the internal audit effort is so essential. In total the relations with people are so important that all of Chapter 7 is devoted to the many human problems always involved. At this point we say only that these relations with all individuals are critical to any successful internal auditing effort.

Good relations with individuals are critical to successful audit effort

REVIEW OF INTERNAL ACCOUNTING CONTROL

Internal Control and Internal Accounting Control

We have previously defined the major mission of the internal auditor as assisting the organization in achieving the most effective use of its resources. We have also recognized that this mission is achieved primarily through the review of all types of internal control. We further recognized that this broader range of internal control included the narrower internal accounting controls that focuses more directly on protection, reliable financial statements, and compliance with the Foreign Corrupt Practices Act of 1977. The latter sta-

Internal auditor has shared interests in internal accounting control

tutory development has also sparked a major effort on the part of the larger public accounting firms to propose systematic approaches to the review and evaluation of internal accounting control. This new material is clearly helpful to corporate financial and accounting personnel directly responsible and to internal auditors discharging their own related review responsibilities. However, the question is how the internal auditor can use that material and at the same time carry out his previously described broader objectives. Put in other words, how can the internal auditor best shape his own review in terms of blending the narrower interests of internal accounting control with his broader interests in the entire system of internal control? Also how can internal auditors best utilize the total review as a means of achieving the full range of service to the organization?

Recommended Framework for the Review of Internal Accounting Control

It is neither feasible nor appropriate in this book to develop still another set of guidance material reflecting our own views for developing and completing an effective review of internal accounting control. We do think, however, that it would be useful to suggest an overall framework for the review of the adequacy of individual systems and then to supplement that framework through further brief comments. We therefore propose the following overall framework:

1. *Review and Evaluate the Background Environment.* This includes an understanding of the kind of business (or businesses) carried on by the particular organization, the goals and objectives, and the current status of the operations. It includes also a reasonable understanding of the major internal activities, policies, and organizational arrangements. The focus is consistently on the extent of risk thereby generated.

An overall framework is needed to review internal accounting control

2. *Acquire an Understanding of the Existing System of Internal Accounting Control.* This includes whatever is required in the way of observations, inquiries, and transaction analysis. It also includes proper documentation of those findings. The focus continues to be on the extent of risk.

3. *Undertake a Preliminary Evaluation of the Adequacy of Design of the Existing System.* This includes the extent to which the organization has defined its internal accounting control objectives and the manner in which it perceives the achievement of those objectives. Cost/benefit analysis is utilized in a preliminary manner based on professional judgment and experience.

4. *Test Compliance with the Aforementioned Existing System.* This is the more precise determination of whether the system is functioning in the manner intended. This includes both observation, interrogation,

and scientific sampling. The focus is on the nature and scope of errors being made.

5. *Reevaluate the Entire System in Depth in Terms of Both Current Design and Actual Implementation.* This includes more definitive evaluation of all significant controls—both individually and in combination. It uses cost/benefit analysis extensively. The evaluation covers both the goodness of the design and the quality of implementation singly and in all combinations.

6. *Summarize and Report on Deficiencies and Present Appropriate Recommendations.* In this final phase judgments are made as to significance and materiality. These conclusions and recommendations do recognize the prerogatives of management to make final decisions as to the extent they wish to incur costs to control risk. However, management should have the views and recommendations of the reviewer.

Collateral Considerations

The framework just outlined is subject to certain important collateral considerations, as follows:

Framework is subject to certain other considerations

1. *Recognition of Direct and Indirect Factors.* All evaluations involve a range of factors from those very direct and immediate to those that are more indirect—and hence more difficult to perceive. For example, in evaluating the environmental factors it is as much what responsible people do, and how they do it, as what it is that those people assert. Thus top management can assert the desire for control but not respond vigorously or decisively to disclosed deficiencies. A further example involves the causes of faulty compliance with a procedural control. Is the deficiency caused by such direct factors as inadequate design of the control, unusual operating conditions, or inadequate training of personnel? Or is the deficiency due indirectly to the more basic environmental factors?

2. *Documentation of Findings.* The impact of the Foreign Corrupt Practices Act has been to put increased emphasis on adequate documentation. Such documentation is desirable both to assure a more systematic and thorough review and to provide backup evidence if the adequacy of the review is later challenged. However, documentation can become too elaborate and too costly to prepare. There is also continuing cost to maintain such documentation to reflect changing conditions accurately. An example here could be overly elaborate transaction analysis and related flowcharts. Clearly, good judgment is very much needed as to where to strike a practical balance.

3. *Choice of Transactions.* The fact that the different review guides prepared by the various CPA firms have used different transaction group-

ings, with varying degrees of overlap, demonstrates that there is no single best grouping. Moreover, the varying operational practices in different kinds of organizations require different types of classifications. The more important thing quite clearly is to define properly the terms actually used and to provide enough flexibility so that they can be adjusted to the needs of the particular organization.

4. *Structuring of Review Approach.* The different approaches by the CPA firms to the sequencing and combining of the review steps again demonstrates that there is no single best approach. The problems stem from the fact that evaluation proceeds at various levels and that it is unavoidably interwoven to some extent with the checking of compliance. Our own recommendations are of course subject to these same limitations, but we believe that our proposal presents a sound and practical approach.

5. *Need to Distinguish Between Design and Implementation.* It is inevitable that design considerations overlap with considerations of implementation. It is important, however, to try to draw the line between design and implementation in the several review steps as a basis for focusing more sharply on the source of existing significant strengths and weaknesses. In most situations the remedial action is significantly different for correcting design as compared to implementation.

6. *Need to Adapt to Established Responsibilities.* Responsibilities for the environmental conditions, the design of controls, and the implementation of those controls exist at various levels in the organization. At the same time the basic responsibility varies—as for example among the accounting department, operational personnel, the internal auditor, and the external auditor. It is important at all times therefore that the review and evaluation procedures be compatible with the underlying responsibilities as defined for particular individuals and groups of individuals.

Cost of reducing risk must be evaluated

7. *Continuing Focus on Risk.* In all phases of the review and in evaluating each activity level the central focus of the review and evaluation of internal accounting control must necessarily be on risk and related cost benefit. This is simply to say that risk is what we are trying to minimize but that the desired minimization must be in balance with the costs thereby incurred. Here we must also recognize that all kinds of costs must be considered to the extent significant. There is also always the question of how accurately we can measure the current and future impact of alternative procedural approaches on risk. There is also the question of the level of risk acceptable to management.

We outline these related considerations, not to emphasize the inherent limitations of every review of internal accounting control, but rather to help reviewers better understand the problems and thus induce the level of competence and care that is necessary. Certainly all participants in the total review process—including the internal auditor—can make important contributions in helping to generate the needed capabilities.

Operational Approach in Perspective

Having the proper operational approach is a necessary basis for effective internal auditing. As we have seen, the starting point is the development of professional competence. Here the important ingredients are personal and technical qualifications, combined with a reasonable understanding of human relations issues and problems. The major thrust of the operational approach of the internal auditor is to see the operations of the company through the eyes of management, and to seek to appraise all operational situations as the responsible manager would do it if he himself were actually there. In doing this the internal auditor does not take the place of management or relieve individual managers of their own responsibilities. But he does everything possible to provide the means by which management can have both the backup it desires and the basis for ongoing management determinations. This is the management service focus of the internal auditor, which properly envelops and conditions his total internal auditing effort. It is the hallmark of the operational approach of the internal auditor.

Professional competence requires personal and technical qualifications plus human relations skills

Historically, the narrower internal accounting control has also always been part of the internal auditor's concern but in many cases being increasingly a smaller proportion of the total internal auditing effort. This changing proportion was a natural result of the expanded operational auditing role in terms of both scope and management level. At the present time the special concern for the more protective internal accounting control, as reinforced by the Foreign Corrupt Practices Act, has reversed to some extent the aforementioned trend. In the light of the presently perceived needs of management this is a needed and proper special concern by internal auditors for internal accounting control. At the same time, however, it is important that the special current interests in internal accounting control do not limit the broader service role. Ideally internal auditing staffs will be increased to take care of the special current needs for achieving sound internal accounting control, so that there will be no diminution of broader management services. This is consistent with our own belief that the greater service potential of the higher-level contribution is achieved through modern operational auditing. Our continuing structure of the areas of operational auditing in Part Two are again also consistent with that view.

REVIEW QUESTIONS

1. How do the approaches of the internal auditor and external auditor differ, and why?
2. How does the internal auditor integrate financial and operational auditing?

3. Explain how the approach of "Modern Internal Auditing" differs from that of the IIA Standards.

4. Describe the way the internal auditor proceeds to carry out his internal auditing activities?

5. Describe the difference between analytical evidence and supporting evidence.

6. Discuss the potential benefits that can come through the certification program of The Institute of Internal Auditors.

7. What is the difference, if any, between the system of internal accounting control and the system of internal control? To what extent is the internal auditor responsible for each?

8. What items are considered in the on-site survey and why are they important?

9. Explain the problems of internal auditors in achieving acceptance by auditees. How can the internal auditor best achieve the needed acceptance?

10. Why is it important for the internal auditor to study prior audit reports?

CASE PROBLEMS

Problem 6-1

Two speakers at a recent internal auditing seminar expressed quite different views as to the impact of the Foreign Corrupt Practices Act on internal auditing. Willard Butz, an ex-internal auditor turned consultant, said, "The Foreign Corrupt Practices Act has been a major tragedy for internal auditors and has set the profession back at least five years. The tragedy is the diversion of internal auditing resources from helping management become more productive to checking procedures and managerial actions for fraud and asserted questionable ethical standards." But Gerald Thompson, a practicing lawyer said, "The Foreign Corrupt Practices Act has gotten the internal auditor back on the track. Now he is less a frustrated self-viewed management expert. Instead he once again focuses on having business transactions properly recorded, avoiding fraud and other avoidable physical losses."

Required. Who do you think is right? How does your conclusion affect the "operational approach" of the internal auditor? How does it affect the relationship of the internal auditor with the external auditor?

Problem 6-2

Tom Davis, senior auditor, is a capable technician and often comes up with good findings. However, he does not use a survey approach, believing that auditors should "examine documents as soon as possible." The supervisor, James White, reviewed Tom's working papers and found an excessive amount of detailed checking.

Required. Advise James White on how he should explain to Tom Davis the need for a changed approach.

CHAPTER SEVEN

Understanding People in Internal Auditing

Upon completing this chapter you should be able to:

☐ *Explain the need for good human relations skills on the part of the internal auditor*

☐ *List the necessary points to be made during the opening conference*

☐ *Recognize the reasons why operating people may not cooperate with the internal auditor during an internal audit*

☐ *Identify what can be done to help assure a successful audit and closing conference*

☐ *Describe which groups, other than auditees, with whom internal auditors must maintain good relationships*

Importance of People

All internal auditing is done by people and affects people

We have emphasized the importance of people in every kind of operational activity that directly or indirectly concerns management and in turn the internal auditor. People are resources that need to be properly used. Further, all managerial activities are carried out by and through people. Whether those managerial activities involve planning, organizing, providing resources, administering, or controlling, we do things through people. It is therefore quite clear that we need to do everything practicable to understand people and thus to be better able to deal with the especially difficult problems of using them. in this way we can obtain the rewarding benefits and better achieve maximum organizational welfare.

The importance of people in the practice of internal auditing can be identified in three major areas:

1. All operational activities reviewed by internal auditors involve people. Therefore, in every major issue dealt with and every conclusion reached

we need to consider the impact on people. In most operational judgments the way people are used and the way they perform become a critical element.

2. As the internal auditor carries out his audit work, he interfaces with people at all levels of responsibility. His effectiveness directly depends on how successful he is in influencing those people to take action and in receiving the information and other assistance from them that he must have to be productive. Here an understanding of people enables internal auditors to get the responses and support that help them best achieve their professional objectives.

3. The internal audit manager, like every operational manager, selects and supervises people. An understanding of people enables the internal audit manager to work with his staff effectively and to promote the professional interests of the internal auditing group.

Overall Image Problem of the Internal Auditor

An overall burden of the internal auditor is that he has an image problem. To some extent the problem is caused by the use of the term "auditor" in his title. An "auditor" is often thought of as an individual who focuses excessively on detail and compliance and represents a threat to the careers of the individuals working in the audited entity. In many instances the image has been earned because of the manner in which internal auditors were first used in organizations. In some instances the image is perpetuated by internal auditors today who do not build a better image through their audit work and mode of personal relations.

Internal auditors have an image problem

But in fairness to the internal auditor we must recognize that there are also some serious problems in changing the existing image. This is because the internal auditor is typically charged with some protective-type responsibilities that tend to make others see him in the role of an antagonist. But the internal auditor's total role, as we have seen in preceding chapters, goes far beyond the narrow protective service. The modern internal auditor is no longer the "policeman" as such or the person with the green eyeshade who buries himself in detail. Instead the internal auditor is concerned with total organizational welfare at all levels and in relation to all organizational activities. The internal auditor is a specialist in internal controls. The challenge is to enhance the image of the internal auditor as a professional serving total organizational welfare.

Modern internal auditor is concerned with total organizational welfare

With this background we propose to focus more directly on the typical relationships of the internal auditor with people outside his own department and try to identify the best available opportunities for the auditor to work with people in achieving his broader organizational objectives. We will sequence our coverage to follow the announcement, conduct, and completion of an internal audit. We will also consider relationships with certain higher-level groups.

Early Contacts Relating to the Audit

Particular audits can be initiated in various ways

The decision to conduct a particular internal audit is made in a variety of ways. It can be requested by the individual who has the responsibility for the operational area to be reviewed; it can be requested by still higher authority, or it may be initiated by the director of internal auditing as a part of the broader program of needed audit coverage. The significance here is that in the first instance the receptivity for the audit has been at least partially established. However, there is still a need for a face-to-face discussion (usually referred to as an opening conference) with the responsible officer to ensure he understands that:

1. The internal audit to be conducted is part of an overall program mandated by top-level authority to meet organizational needs for both protection and maximum constructive benefit.
2. The objective of the review is to provide maximum service in all feasible managerial dimensions.
3. The review will be conducted with minimum interference with regular operations and with few demands on operating personnel.
4. The responsible officer will be kept fully informed and have an opportunity to review findings and recommendations before the audit report is formally released.

At this early point in the internal audit major benefits can be achieved or, contrariwise, a hostile image can be established. The principles expressed also apply to any other individuals who need to be informed prior to the time the audit actually begins. The benefits derived include a better understanding of the internal auditor's role, avoiding the undesirable reactions of those individuals who might otherwise be caught by surprise, and the personal gratification given such individuals that the internal auditor is concerned about their feelings. Virtually everyone has apprehensions about the impact of an audit and needs to be put at ease to the degree possible. The internal auditor needs to go out of his way to establish good interpersonal relationships.

Internal auditor should go out of his way to establish good relationships

Relations with Auditees

Assuming at this point that the audit is in progress, the next group with whom relationships must be considered are all of the personnel whose work and records are being examined or to whom various inquiries are made. In these cases, the aforementioned principles are also generally applicable. However, now there is the more definitive problem of obtaining the desired cooperation of the individuals directly involved in the particular operations being reviewed. The problem can be substantial because a number of possible factors may generate resistance. Such factors include:

1. A bad experience with an internal auditor in the past
2. The general image of the internal auditor as a policeman against whom all manner of resistance is appropriate
3. The fear that errors or faulty performance will be discovered and used against them by their superiors
4. The fear that the internal auditor will go out of his way to find things that can be used for personal advancement of the auditor
5. A resentment at the presence of the auditor with its related potential of siphoning off the workers' time and effort, and generally interfering with necessary work performance
6. Some lack of confidence in the quality of their own work, and the fear that it will not stand up under close scrutiny

Cooperation of auditee is critical

The problem the internal auditor faces is trying to alleviate those fears but at the same time not providing assurances that cannot fully be delivered. In other words, the internal auditor does wish to help the auditee in every way practicable, but he does have a responsibility to other affected organizational personnel. At this point in the audit the internal auditor does not know what problems he may find. He should try to convince the auditee that he is fully motivated by total organizational welfare and that he intends to be honest and fair. Typically, the internal auditor can only be partially successful in achieving these objectives at the outset of this particular part of the audit (unless his relationship has already been established through a previous audit) and further time will be required before the auditee will have any degree of confidence. The internal auditor must therefore be patient, making as much progress as possible during the current audit but also looking ahead to future audits.

Need to demonstrate commitment to total organizational welfare

Finding the Best Balance. The internal auditor's problem of having effective relationships with auditees comes down to finding the best possible balance between two inherently conflicting forces. On the one hand there is the unavoidable truth that the auditee to some extent feels threatened by the internal auditor, and on the other hand the unavoidable truth that the internal auditor has a responsibility to determine and report on the existing facts. Therefore, there is some unavoidable conflict. Under such circumstances the internal auditor can go to the one extreme and give the first priority to appeasing the auditee—the so-called be nice approach—or the internal auditor can go to the other extreme and focus only on his need to get the facts and to report them to his superiors. The higher-level truth, however, is that organizational welfare is best served by everyone working together to get the operational job done better. The internal auditor needs to find the proper balance between the two extremes and to find the com-

Auditee may feel threatened by internal auditor

Internal auditor has responsibility to report existing facts

posite approach that will minimize existing conflict and best assure long-term benefits. This is an approach that requires understanding, continuing education, patience, sincerity, and sound judgment. As with everything one does, this is the eternal problem of finding the best possible balance between a number of divergent forces.

Partnership Approach. In its most successful form the internal auditor induces a problem-solving relationship with the auditee. The essence of such a relationship was especially well-stated in Research Report No. 17, "Behavioral Patterns in Internal Audit Relationships," published in 1972 by The Institute of Internal Auditors, as follows:

Internal auditor and auditee should work together to improve conditions

> The participative approach—the teamwork approach—the problem solving partnership may well be the light at the end of a dreary tunnel. Our goals should be the auditor and auditee working together to improve conditions; and not the critic telling the doer how to do his job better.

This partnership approach at its most effective level is a cooperative effort between two mutually respected persons with full understanding of their respective responsibilities, but with clear recognition of their very real long-term common interests. It is the internal auditor's special challenge to generate that type of constructive relationship.

Closing Conferences

Closing conference should confirm findings

To a considerable extent the closing conference is an extension of the human relationships described previously and is guided by the same previously stated principles. It is a key stage in finalizing an internal audit because it is a systematic exposure of the audit findings and draft conclusions, a confirmatory check on the content of the findings and the soundness of the conclusions, and a means of generating commitment for appropriate managerial action. Selection of the operating personnel who will attend the closing conference is made by the operating official responsible for the audited entity. The size of the conference will vary depending on the nature and scope of the particular internal audit. Typically, however, the group will include (1) higher-level staff and line-operational personnel not previously directly involved in the audit, (2) key operating personnel already involved in the audit work, (3) all or key audit personnel who participated in the audit, and (4) in some instances a higher-level internal audit official. The closing conference is usually the final and most decisive event just before the departure of the internal audit staff from the audit location.

Closing conference involves critical interface of participants

Preceding the closing conference there have already been considerable interfaces between members of the audit staff and operating personnel. However, from a human relations standpoint, the closing conference now takes on a new sensitivity. This is because the large number of people involved are to a major extent reviewing each other—both the internal auditors themselves and operational personnel as individuals and groups directly or indirectly involved. At this point there is the normal desire on the part of each person to "look good" to the others present. There is also the deeper knowledge that individual and group interests can be significantly affected by what actually goes into the final report.

What can be done by the internal auditor to assure the success of the closing conference in terms of effective human relationships? We suggest the following:

1. Careful preparation for the actual conference. If the time budget allows, advance dissemination of the draft material is helpful. Early dissemination projects fairness to the recipients and at the same time assures the adequacy of the internal auditor's preparation.

   The internal auditor's professionalism in conducting the conference can be enhanced by holding a "mock" closing conference with a member of the internal audit staff who was not actively involved in the audit assuming the role of the highest-level operating official.

2. Courteous but firm direction of the conference by the internal auditor chairing the meeting minimizes disruptive diversion of the discussion. Openmindedness and company welfare interest must be continuously demonstrated with full consideration given to information and viewpoints of operating personnel.

3. Conclusions reached must be as definite as possible. However, the internal auditor needs to retain the right for such later editing as may be required to comply with standards of good presentation and higher-level views. Continuing good relations require that the auditees later receive no unreasonable surprises when the final report is released.

   Auditees should not be unreasonably surprised when report is released

4. Expression of appreciation by the internal auditor for the cooperation extended by operating personnel builds goodwill. The objective is to retain the continuing cooperation and support of all company personnel.

Follow-up Activities

Finally, good relations must be maintained with people during follow-up activities after an audit report is released. These activities may pertain to the further explanation of findings and related recommendations or the adequacy of operational actions being taken as a result of the audit recommendations. The importance in terms of people relations is that the extent of the internal auditor's competence and overall assistance to management is being tested continuously. The follow-up contacts are also important in that they provide a major setting out of which further internal audits can be made more responsive to managerial needs. It is most important that these follow-up contacts be carefully nurtured and effectively serviced.

Postaudit contacts with auditee should protect future relationships

Follow-up activities in a broad sense also include other contacts with managerial personnel that apply to other possible internal audits. In those circumstances the nature of the people relationships is similar to those discussed above in connection with early contacts.

Relations with Audit Committees

Audit activities may be mandated by audit committee

In some instances the significance of a particular internal audit will lead to involvement of the audit committee of the board of directors, usually via the chairman of that committee. In other cases internal audit action of various kinds will be mandated directly by the audit committee. In still other cases the contacts with the audit committee will be in connection with required summary reports of prior audit activities. Greater legal and public concerns are generating expanded responsibilities for audit committees and a more active participation in the activities of the organization—including a more active interface with the internal auditing department. This interface is especially important to the internal auditor because of the authority of the audit committee and the related effect on the nature and scope of the internal auditor's work. Audit committee members are also typically people of considerable stature and ability. All of this means that the internal auditor needs to handle his relations with them with special care. What can the internal auditor do to make these relationships effective? We suggest the following:

1. Although the internal auditor cannot by himself establish proper reporting arrangements with the audit committee, he should be alert to every opportunity to do so. He should then respond promptly and fully to needs thus initiated.

2. The internal auditor should study the nature and scope of the audit committee needs thoroughly and do all possible to demonstrate an understanding of those needs—thus enabling the internal auditor to respond properly to all needs expressed to him by the audit committee and at the same time help guide that committee. If guidance is ever requested of the internal auditor as to the role and responsibilities of the audit committee, The Institute of Internal Auditors is an excellent source of information in this area.

Audit committee contacts should avoid adversary posture toward management

3. The internal auditor needs to be continuously aware of the possible apprehension of top management about the impact of direct relationships with the audit committee. The internal auditor needs to keep top management fully informed about those relationships. At the same time the internal auditor needs to avoid being put into an adversary posture toward management by the audit committee. Again the demonstration of total company welfare is the greatest strength of the internal auditor in preserving good relationships with both management and the audit committee.

Relations with the External Auditor

As we have seen in previous chapters, the internal auditor and external auditor have different primary missions but at the same time certain common interests. Some factors to keep in mind which will make these relationships effective are the following:

1. Because the external auditors have a great deal in common with the internal auditors, there is a better basis of understanding each other and thus relating to each other effectively. However, there is at the same time a certain amount of professional pride and different self-interest that often makes the relationships extremely sensitive.

2. Both audit groups have certain power capabilities that generate caution in the various face-to-face relationships. The internal auditor is in a position to press for greater company welfare through more effective coordination (usually resulting in reduced external audit costs) while the external auditor usually has special access and influence with the audit committee and top management, and hence can importantly influence those parties in their attitudes toward the internal auditor.

3. Joint appearances of the internal and external auditors before both management and the audit committee involve especially sensitive considerations and therefore need to be carefully planned and executed.

4. The internal auditor again needs to demonstrate his dedication to total organizational welfare, and his interest in the partnership efforts of the two audit groups to further that organizational welfare.

Common interests with external auditor need emphasis

Partnership effort needed between internal and external auditors

Relations within the Internal Auditing Department

As we know, internal audit managers like all other managers must manage their people resources in an effective manner. At the same time each member of the internal auditing staff has common human needs. Consequently, the following should be observed:

1. Internal auditors are professionals and there is therefore the special need to relate to them as professionals. This means less direct supervision and more coaching and dependence on established objectives.

2. Internal auditors have above-average visibility in the organization and therefore need to recognize that they have special responsibilities to serve as a model and set standards in their relationships with others in the organization.

3. Internal auditors in their own departmental relationships need to develop the kind of high-level image that builds a better foundation for projecting the same image to other organizational personnel.

Internal auditors' internal relationships should be a model

4. Staff personnel need to be indoctrinated continuously as to their opportunities to help build the proper internal auditor image with all organizational personnel with whom they are involved. At the same time they need to be fully assured that they have proper backing when they take needed positions with auditees.

Understanding People in Perspective

Internal auditor must always be alert to people impact

Understanding people is essential if an internal auditor is to accomplish his objectives effectively. As we have seen every major audit issue and conclusion has an impact on people. Furthermore, in performing his audit tasks, the internal auditor interfaces with people at all levels of responsibility and must have their assistance and support to complete the tasks efficiently and effectively. Additionally, as the internal auditor moves up within the internal auditing department he must understand people in order to manage his own staff effectively. We believe, therefore, that it will be useful to summarize the key factors of a proper approach to an internal auditor dealing effectively with people:

1. An effective opening conference should be held with the responsible official of the organization to be audited. The internal auditor should explain his authority to audit and the objectives of the review, that interference with operating personnel will be held to a minimum, and that the responsible official will be able to review the audit report before it is issued.

Key guides to people relationships

2. The internal auditor must continuously balance the need to attempt to alleviate the fears of the auditee and his responsibility to determine and report on the existing facts.

3. The closing conference should be carefully planned, chaired by an internal auditor, result in conclusions which are as definitive as possible, and end on a good note, such as thanking all involved for their cooperation.

4. Follow-up activities should be made with the same human relationship approach as used during the internal audit.

5. Good human relationship skills are extremely important when dealing with the audit committee of the board of directors and with the external auditors.

REVIEW QUESTIONS

1. How does a knowledge of human relations and the ability to work well with people make one a more effective internal auditor?

2. Explain the problem of internal auditors in achieving acceptance by auditees. How can the internal auditor best achieve the needed acceptance?

3. To what extent does the internal auditor have an image problem? If so, why? What can be done about it?

4. In what areas in your own business or private life do you think you can improve the effectiveness of your human relations?

5. Auditees are likely to resist internal auditors and not provide needed cooperation during an audit? Do you agree or disagree? Why?

6. The opening conference can either be of major benefit to an internal audit or create a hostile image. What principles can be applied to help make it a positive meeting?

7. A key stage in finalizing an internal audit is the closing conference. What can be done to help assure its success?

8. Follow-up activities also involve people relations. Why are people relations important in this instance?

9. The relationships between the internal auditor and external auditor are often very sensitive. Why? What can the internal auditor do to improve the relationships?

10. What can the internal auditor do to reduce the apprehension of top management about his direct relationships with the audit committee?

CASE PROBLEMS

Problem 7-1

The day had been going well for John Flood, the general auditor of EZ Manufacturing, until he had answered a call from Bruce Ward, the eastern division manager. "John," bellowed Ward, "I have just told your man Wesley Simon to get off the eastern division premises and never come back. I tried to put up with him, but he has now exhausted my patience. I know you have a job to do and we want to cooperate but my people are busy and have jobs to do. Also they resent the implication that they are defrauding the company and that the auditor seems mostly interested in proving that they are thieves or incompetents. Sorry John, but that's my position." As it happened, Simon was a new recruit but had a good record of 10 years in public accounting and five years with the CIA. Flood had therefore thought him well qualified to take on a major internal audit review of the eastern division. The phone rang again—this time the call coming from Wesley Simon. Said Simon, "You have a real problem in that man Ward. It's impossible to get along with him. Anyway, I have just had a 'run-in' with him and he has ordered me off the premises. What do you want me to do now?" "Well, Wes," replied Ward, "Let's cool it for the moment. Come on in this afternoon and we will talk about it further in my office tomorrow morning."

Required. Help Flood formulate a plan for the discussion with Simon.

Problem 7-2

"Bernie," said Ron Clark, the divisional manager of the Heating Controls Division of Bright, Inc., "You said this was a partnership and so we worked together to identify the purchasing control problem and then develop the program for solving the problem. But why do you insist on spelling it all out in your report. That's not going to help anybody or anything except raise questions in the big boss's mind as to why I let the trouble ever develop initially. Frankly I resent your using my reputation as a way to impress your boss as to the work you are doing."

Bernie Huff, the auditor in charge, sensed he had a real problem. He appeared to be caught in between Clark's strong views and his own boss's decision that the particular problem be covered in the report. While he felt honestly that his boss, the General Auditor, was correct in his decision, he had a great deal of empathy for Clark's view and he felt that to override it would seriously handicap later internal auditing relationships. But the time had come for a closing conference and somehow a decision had to be made.

Required.   Help Bernie Huff decide how to handle this matter?

CHAPTER EIGHT

Using Computers in Internal Auditing

Upon completing this chapter you should be able to:

- ☐ *Differentiate between the two levels of computer auditing*
- ☐ *Explain the evolving role of the internal auditor in computer audits*
- ☐ *Understand the purpose and use of generalized audit software*
- ☐ *Identify the characteristics of an effective computer audit program system*

The continuous expansion of the range of internal auditing services, together with the limited human resources available, has made it necessary for internal auditors to find new and efficient ways in which to increase auditor productivity while achieving audit objectives. It is only natural then for the internal auditing profession to turn increasingly to electronic data processing (EDP) where the hardware and, to a considerable extent, the software program packages are readily available. This chapter is designed as an overview of computer-assisted auditing and use of computer aids in internal auditing. In Chapter 15, we discuss in more detail both computer operations and the audit implications.

Computers can increase internal auditor's productivity

COMPUTER-ASSISTED AUDIT TECHNIQUES

The extended use of computers by companies of all sizes has stimulated changes in the internal auditor's approach. The internal auditor can no longer be satisfied with manual auditing procedures to fulfill audit objectives. In many organizations the entire internal control environment is rapidly changing from a manual setting to one which is automated. Of particular significance to internal auditing is the fact that the nature of audit evidence changes

Internal control environment changing from manual to automated

when information is readable only by electronic means. The use of computer-assisted audit techniques can result in the performance of audit tests by the computer which were previously done manually. In addition, these techniques enable internal auditors to carry out audit procedures that were previously impracticable. As new systems are acquired or developed, the internal auditor can determine whether data can be accumulated and stored in a manner that will facilitate later audits. Through maximum use of computer-assisted audit techniques, the internal auditor can not only improve the quality of audits, but also extend his capabilities to perform special reviews for management and thus provide better service.

The earliest business applications for computers were little more than a replacement of the existing manual systems with identical automated systems, while maintaining redundant controls which were external to the computer. Consequently, internal auditors felt little effect from this rather simple transition. However, as automated systems became more advanced, traditional audit approaches were no longer adequate. Despite the risks inherent in complex computerized systems, some organizations continue to audit "around" the computer, testing only the controls over data put into

Auditing around computer ignores program controls

(input) and information put out (output) by the computer. However, most internal auditors have recognized that auditing "around" the computer ignores the important fact that computer programs, themselves, may not be properly controlled. Adequate testing of these critical program controls necessitates the use of computer-assisted auditing techniques under actual operating conditions.

Levels of Computer Expertise Needed

Specialists needed on internal audit staff

Computer audits may be considered as being performed at two levels. One level includes that portion of the audit which must be done by an auditor with considerable knowledge of data processing. For these audit procedures he must understand computer hardware, operations, systems design and systems analysis. His audit activities extend to operating systems, storage device management, physical security, hardware and data security, and job accounting—as discussed in Chapter 15. The individuals assigned to these technical audits are usually specialists on the internal audit staff who are designated as EDP auditors.

In addition to the technical audits described in the previous paragraph, comparably skilled auditors are also needed to review application systems[1] while the systems are under development. The auditor's involvement in developmental activities is commonly referred to as a design-phase or preim-

Preimplementation reviews help avoid design errors

plementation review. The purpose of the review is to help ensure that adequate controls and audit trails are included in order to avoid design errors

---

[1]Application systems are specific processing functions performed by a set of computer programs. Examples of applications are billing, payroll, and inventory recordkeeping.

and thus costly changes after the system has been installed. A review to determine the effectiveness, auditability and controllability of a new billing application is an example of a preimplementation review.

The second level of computer auditing involves the postimplementation audit of systems applications. With increasing frequency we find that the auditors responsible for auditing the controls within actively operating application systems (postimplementation audits) are the internal auditors who are also responsible for performing operational or financial audits. This is due to the fact that application systems are an integral part of the financial and operational systems which they support. It has been projected that in the 1990s application systems audits will be performed by internal auditors and that EDP auditors will serve in the capacity of consultants to their organizations on the increasingly complex information systems which will be in use at that time.[2]

Review of controls in application packages increasingly done by internal auditors

Use of Audit Software Packages

The use of the computer in internal auditing is especially desirable when there is a large volume of data and those data are readily available from the computer files. If data of audit interest are processed on a computer, the internal auditor should be constantly searching for methods of using the computer to audit such data.

As discussed in Chapter 6, an internal audit project begins with detailed planning, the end result of which is an audit program. In this respect computer auditing is no different. Detailed planning and a well-conceived audit program are essential to the successful conclusion of a computer audit project. Invariably the computer audit program will require manual tests as well as computer-assisted tests. This is primarily because the computer audit extends beyond the computerized system itself and includes the entire data processing environment as previously described.

Computer auditing includes entire data base environment

Generalized Audit Software. By using a generalized audit software (retrieval) package the internal auditor can access, extract, manipulate, and present data and test results in a format appropriate to his audit objectives. It permits the internal auditor to manipulate computer masterfiles without writing a special computer program. Generalized audit software is the tool most frequently used by internal auditors and is one of the more important, even though not the only tool available, for the computer-assisted audit testing. Exhibit 8.1 reflects the computer application tools and techniques most commonly used by auditors.

Generalized software is commercially available or it may be developed in-house. Due to the time and skill required to develop and maintain such

Generalized computer software permits manipulating master files without special programs

---

[2]The Institute of Internal Auditors, *Proceedings from "The EDP Audit Forum," New York City, February 1983.*

EXHIBIT 8.1. Frequently Used Computer-Assisted Audit Techniques[a]

Audit Technique	
Test deck	Uses simulated transactions processed by applications program. Compares test data with predetermined results calculated independently.
Integrated test facility (ITF)	Simultaneous processing of real data and test data during regular runs. Compares results of test data with predetermined amounts.
Generalized audit software package	Uses computer itself. Prewritten program permits: search and retrieve; select samples; perform basic calculations; prepare subtotals; compare, sort and merge; copy data; user exits; summaries; printout.
Tagging and tracing	Permits close examination of selected transactions as processed according to programmed logic system.
Parallel test facility (PTF)	Used for parallel processing for compliance testing and parallel simulation for substantive testing.

[a]Adapted from Sardinas, Joseph, Burch, J. G., and Asebrook, Richard. *EDP Auditing: A Primer* (New York: Wiley, 1981), pp. 124–133.

a program, except for the larger internal audit organizations, most have chosen to acquire a package from one of the many vendors selling such products. As can be seen in Exhibit 8.2, many different packages are available and currently being used.

The capabilities of most generalized computer audit packages open up new opportunities to use the computer to fulfill audit responsibilities. The generalized audit software package, however, will only do what the original computer programmer instructed it to do. It is incumbent upon the auditor to decide on what data to retrieve, process, and display for audit evaluation.

Mechanics of Use.   Once the internal auditor has recognized the availability of computer files of interest in the audit, he considers methods for using a computer audit package. Consequently, it is important to understand how the computer audit package works. Basically the package has the capability of listing those records (a collection of data fields treated as a unit) which match other records in the same file (a collection of related records) or in different files. One or more data fields (subdivisions of a record) designated by the auditor are compared. Record layouts of the two files can be different, except for the fields to be matched. The computer audit package can also print account details and totals for records defined by the auditor.

Computer audit packages permit direct operational cross checks

EXHIBIT 8.2. Use of Generalized Audit Software Systems[a,b]

Audit Software	Banking	Government	Insurance	Utilities	General Manufacturing	Education	Heavy Industry	Trade	Service	Total
None	25.3	51.0	22.3	24.2	49.4	42.3	33.5	34.7	48.2	36.6
ASI-ST	0.0	2.7	2.5	3.3	0.0	0.0	1.4	1.0	1.0	1.2
AUDEX 100	0.8	0.0	0.0	3.3	2.4	0.0	1.4	1.6	1.0	1.1
AUDIPAC	0.0	0.7	2.5	2.2	0.0	3.8	2.8	1.0	1.3	1.5
AUDIT (or DATA) ANALYZER	2.6	3.4	5.0	11.0	3.6	1.3	8.2	4.7	3.3	4.7
AUDITAPE	0.4	2.7	4.1	7.7	3.6	12.8	5.3	3.6	5.7	4.4
AUDITEC	0.4	0.7	5.8	3.3	2.4	0.0	2.1	1.0	1.3	1.7
AUDITRONIC	2.6	0.0	1.7	1.1	2.4	0.0	1.8	2.6	2.7	1.9
AUDIT REPORTED	3.0	2.0	1.7	1.1	1.2	1.3	0.4	1.0	1.0	1.4
BASE	4.9	0.7	0.0	0.0	0.0	0.0	0.0	0.0	1.3	1.2
CARS	9.4	6.7	4.1	2.2	8.4	1.3	4.3	3.6	4.3	5.3
EDP AUDITOR (or CULPRIT)	15.1	8.1	19.1	11.0	10.8	7.7	11.0	13.0	9.7	11.9
DYL-AUDIT (or DYL-280)	5.7	2.0	9.9	8.8	3.6	0.0	10.3	6.2	7.0	6.6
EASY AUDIT	0.8	1.3	3.3	1.1	1.2	1.3	0.7	0.5	0.7	1.0
IBM utilities	9.4	13.4	30.6	23.1	18.1	9.0	18.1	19.7	13.4	16.3
MARK IV AUDITOR	2.3	3.4	11.6	4.4	3.6	6.4	4.6	5.2	2.3	4.3
PANAUDIT (or EASYTRIEVE)	13.2	14.8	20.7	15.4	3.4	12.8	16.4	21.8	16.1	16.0
PROBE 5	3.4	0.0	0.0	0.0	0.0	0.0	1.1	0.0	0.7	0.9
QUEST	5.7	0.7	0.0	0.0	0.0	0.0	0.7	0.5	1.0	1.4
SAS	1.9	7.4	10.7	19.8	3.6	3.8	8.9	9.8	5.7	7.3
STRATA	3.4	2.0	3.3	3.3	1.2	5.1	6.0	3.6	3.7	3.8
SYSTEM 2190	6.0	2.0	5.8	1.1	1.2	6.4	2.1	3.6	6.0	4.2
Other	8.3	12.1	8.3	11.0	12.0	10.3	8.5	11.9	9.4	9.8
Sample size	265	149	129	91	83	78	281	193	299	1560

[a]Percentages (all entries except sample size) are the percent of respondents checking the indicated items.
[b]Various software systems are used by the audit organizations which responded. Of particular note is the result that 36.6% indicated that they did not use any software systems, with more than 60% of the small audit staffs in the United States, Canada, and Puerto Rico not using any audit software.
Adapted from The Institute of Internal Auditors, Inc., *1983 Survey of Internal Auditing* (Altamonte Springs, Fla.: The Institute of Internal Auditors, Inc., 1984), p. 92.

The audit package is also capable of performing various calculations and applying programmed formulas. Special programs can be used for any computational task required. For example, sampling plans can be developed, and the results of sampling tests then evaluated and projected. In addition, the computer, using its comparison capability, can select all or a sample of records having the characteristics stated by the auditor.

Software packages limited only by internal auditor imagination

Applications. There are various areas in internal auditing for use of audit software packages. Once the techniques are mastered, the applications to computer files are limited only by the auditor's imagination. One approach is to review prior audit procedures performed manually and determine the feasibility of applying computer techniques. Another approach is to include special computer routines in normal, everyday processing. An example is in the review of check disbursements. As transactions are processed, the computer can automatically select a sample or print out expenditures in excess of a specified dollar amount by classification. The following are some applications for potential use by internal auditors:

Computer software packages save audit hours

1. *Inventories.* The use of computer software packages in reviews of inventories results in significant savings of internal audit staff time and elimination of detailed manual checking of voluminous data manually. In testing a perpetual inventory, a computer statistical sample can be taken of inventory parts, stratified as to high- and low-dollar amounts. Counts made by the internal auditor can then be compared with the inventory record on tapes and the differences summarized and tabulated by quantity, dollar amounts, and percentages. In addition, tests of pricing can be made by comparison of perpetual inventory records with a master cost tape showing the costs of all parts. Other applications include tests for meeting standards for filling requisitions, printouts of stock with recurring shortages or overages, and summaries of trends in losses through pilferage.

2. *Payrolls.* There are various operational as well as financial areas relating to payrolls which lend themselves to the use of audit software packages. Printouts can be made to review labor utilization—amount of overtime, labor charged to jobs in excess of standards, and downtime. Comparisons can also be made with prior performance as well as with standards to indicate performances needing improvement. In addition, the programs can identify new and terminated employees, as well as changes, for checking against payroll authorization files in the personnel department.

3. *Production.* Overruns in excess of specified percentages can be pinpointed for analysis of causes. Backlogs of maintenance requests can be aged and printed out for review.

4. *Energy.* Plants or departments with excessive use of gas and electricity can be identified for closer monitoring for compliance with an energy conservation program.

5. *Travel and Telephone Expenses.* Excessive charges by employee or department can be identified for follow-up and possible cost savings.

6. *Sales.* Data can be accumulated as to sales by individual, territory, or product in relation to quotas and performance by others.

Special-Purpose Programs

Special-purpose audit retrieval programs may also be developed. However, the cost and high level of computer programming knowledge necessary to develop these programs, makes them much less practicable. Generalized software is also, unfortunately, not compatible with some systems and smaller equipment, and is not adaptable to nongeneralized audit tasks. In these instances special-purpose or special-interface programs must be especially designed, if computer-assisted tests are to be made.

Requirements for a Computer Audit Program System

Before a computer audit package is selected, a review should be made of the generalized computer audit program systems available through a number of organizations. No single software package may satisfy all the requirements of every audit group or assignment. The following are some characteristics of an effective system.

No single software package can satisfy all requirements

1. *Simplicity.* The system should be simple to use and eliminate the need for remembering countless details normally required in writing or revising computer programs.

2. *Understandability.* The system should be readily understandable by members of the internal audit staff—even those with little computer expertise. The capabilities of the system should be known, and it should be easy to use. Coding forms provided should not be difficult to complete.

3. *Adaptability.* The system should be capable of writing computer audit programs for the various types of computers presently used or under consideration by the company.

4. *Vendor Technical Support.* In considering the type of package to be acquired, it is important that the vendor provide adequate support. This includes providing adequate documentation and assisting in the initial installation of the program. In addition, training should be available for the internal audit staff. The maintenance service offered and provisions for future revisions in the programs are also important considerations.

5. *Statistical Sampling Capability.* Since statistical sampling is an important tool in auditing, the package should be able to perform the various statistical routines. The selection of items on a random basis, determination of sample size, and evaluation of results at different confidence levels should be included. In addition to simple random

Software packages can be used for statistical sampling

sampling and stratification of a population, the package should have routines for more complex sampling such as cluster and multistage sampling. Statistical sampling is discussed further in this chapter and in Chapter 9.

6. *Acceptability.* The system should be acceptable to both the internal auditors and computer center. For the internal auditors the programs should be easily carried to the site and practical to use. The computer center programs should be compatible with the system and be capable of minimum interference with normal routines.

7. *Processing Capabilities.* The package should be capable of processing many different types of applications. For example, it should accept all common file media and process multiple file input. It should have the capability for extended data selection and stratification. It should also have the ability to operate under multiprogramming situations and have powerful, generalized audit commands.

8. *Report Writing.* The package should include a strong report writing function. The ability of the package to prepare multiple reports in a single program run and to generate flexible output report formats is an important consideration.

Computer Aids for Internal Auditing

Microcomputers new tool for internal auditors

Numerous innovative uses of computers, and particularly microcomputers, and state-of-the-art software packages are being introduced into internal auditing. Internal audit organizations are increasingly using computers for office management, audit research, and audit work stations. In some instances microcomputers are used alone. In others they are used as terminals to access mainframe computers or other microcomputers.

Computers facilitate preparation of reports

Office Management.   One significant use of computers in office management is in preparing internal audit reports. When the text of the report has been entered by the internal auditor, it is then readily available to audit supervision and audit management to review and edit. Additions, deletions, and changes are easily accomplished by using any one of the several word processing packages which are available commercially. Most word processing packages have the capability of checking the spelling and mathematics, paginating, and formatting the report. In addition to using the computer to prepare internal audit reports, among its other administrative uses are audit planning, budgeting, maintaining time and training records, and preparing various administrative reports.

Automated audit research system now available

Audit Research.   An automated audit research system may be used by internal auditors in preparing for an audit project. The amount of assistance such a system can be to an internal auditor is limited only by his knowledge and skills as an internal auditor and by his imagination. One company[3] maintains a computerized catalog of information about various subjects. The catalog is available for the internal auditor to "computer browse" the information and to print out the portion which will be useful in planning for an audit. For each subject, the catalog contains information on the results of limited risk-analyses, documentation of existing controls, plans and programs, plus findings and recommendations from prior audits. Another resource is computerized data bases available commercially and in libraries which can be accessed for information on special subjects.

Audit Work Station. The company mentioned in the preceding paragraph[4] is also designing an audit work station through which the internal audit staff will be able to locate specific records, sort the data in these records, prepare field-review schedules, store completed checklists, select audit samples, and perform statistical analyses. Data entered into the system while the audit is in progress will be retrievable for use in preparing the final working papers and the audit report.

Automated Working Papers. Through the use of an electronic worksheet program and a word processing package, virtually all of the internal auditors original work on an audit project can be stored on diskettes. This not only increases internal auditor productivity by facilitating the creating of working papers, but also simplifies maintaining and using the working paper files.

Electronic worksheet programs provide new backup

Spreadsheets. Electronic worksheet programs, which are available commercially, are becoming popular as a convenient means of recording data on worksheets which are necessary to arrive at and then support internal audit conclusions and findings. These electronic worksheets are particularly helpful for lengthy and detailed worksheets and those requiring a large number of calculations. These spreadsheets also have several applications in internal audit management. The spreadsheet can also facilitate analytical reviews, such as using linear regression and trend analyses in determining the relationship between groups of numbers.

Word Processing. A word processing package not only can facilitate the documentation of audit observations and interviews in the field but also, as previously mentioned, can be used to prepare the draft report and produce the final report.

---

[3]Lester B. Johnson, "Micros: Today's Audit Management Tools," *The Internal Auditor*, October 1984, p. 41.
[4]Ibid., pp. 41–42.

USE OF COMPUTERS IN SAMPLING

Advantages of Use

Computers provide major capabilities for statistical sampling

The computer has proved to be an invaluable tool to internal auditors in applying statistical sampling. It simplifies the calculations necessary, eliminating the need for reference to formulas or tables. In addition, it facilitates the use of sophisticated techniques, thus enabling the auditor to obtain more precise and unbiased results. The internal auditor can of course use calculations in some instances to solve formulas when a computer is not available, but this is more time consuming. Internal auditors can sometimes take a portable terminal or microcomputer to the site when needed for statistical applications. The auditee may have a computer available. In other cases the data may be sent to a central location for input to the computer.

Programs Available

There are various statistical programs available in software packages. Some commonly used ones are as follows:

1. *Random Number Generators.* Numbers can be obtained in generated order or arranged in sequence. Single numbers or numbers in pairs can be obtained, such as for selecting a random page number and item on the page. Also, random numbers can be developed for more than one strata using different frames, or numbering sequences, and strata limits can be determined.
2. *Determining Sample Size.* These programs give the sample size required for various types of statistical samples, such as attributes, variables, and stratified.
3. *Appraisal of Results.* These programs give appraisals of various types of samples: unstratified, stratified, multistage, and dollar unit. Included in these are special programs for mean unit estimates, difference estimates, and ratio estimates.

Exhibit 8.3 is an example of a computer printout used for evaluating the results of a statistical sample using difference estimates. Data are stated for confidence levels at 90% and 95%.

Using Computers in Perspective

Internal auditors need greater knowledge of computers

In addition to making the internal auditors responsible for the postimplementation audit, as discussed earlier in this chapter, some internal audit organizations are now requiring that the internal auditors, not the EDP auditors, conduct the preimplementation reviews. We believe that this trend will continue. As a consequence it behooves every internal auditor to seriously pursue a study of computer sciences and take every opportunity to become involved in the use of computers in his organization, lest he become obsolete in his profession.

EXHIBIT 8.3. Evaluation of a Statistical Sample Using Difference Estimates

THIS PROGRAM COMPUTES CONFIDENCE LIMITS OF POPN MEAN FOR 90 AND 95 PCT CONFIDENCE LEVELS BASED ON STATISTICAL SAMPLING DATA. TO USE, ENTER THE DATA STARTING W/LINE 200, PER BELOW:

200 DATA x(1),x(2),x(3),x(4)...x(N)
(CONTINUE W/SUBSEQUENT LINE NOS. AS NEEDED)

WHERE THE X(1) ARE VALUES, OTHER THAN ZERO, OF SAMPLE OBSERVATIONS.

AFTER ALL SAMPLE OBSERVATIONS HAVE BEEN INPUT, ENTER 'RUN' AND PRESS THE 'RETURN' KEY.
NOW AT 3810
SRU'S:0.8
READY
200 DATA 120,65,57,121,235,146,67,82,51,74,25,70,5,240,196
RUN

*VARIAB   15:42   10/03/80

ENTER '1' FOR ADDITIONAL ANALYSIS, ELSE '2'?1

SIZE OF POPULATION	?1297
SIZE OF STATISTICAL SAMPLE	?200
NO. OF ZERO VALUE OBSERVATIONS	?185

VARIABLES

VALUES OF SAMPLE STATISTICS

SIZE OF POPULATION	1297
SIZE OF STATISTICAL SAMPLE	200
MEAN VALUE-SAMPLING UNIT	7.77
EST OF STD DEVIATION	33.3752
EST OF STD ERROR OF MEAN	2.17125

PRECISION OF MEAN VALUE, AT
CONFIDENCE

LEVELS	90%	95%
LOWER LIMIT	4.18093	3.4883
UPPER LIMIT	11.3591	12.0517

POINT ESTIMATE FOR POPN	10077.7

PRECISION OF POINT ESTIMATE, AT
CONFIDENCE

LEVELS	90%	95%
LOWER LIMIT	5422.67	4524.33
UPPER LIMIT	14732.7	15631.1

REVIEW QUESTIONS

1. What is the risk of auditing "around" the computer?
2. Describe the two levels of computer auditing.
3. What is the purpose of a generalized audit (retrieval) software package?
4. What are the characteristics of an effective computer audit program system?
5. Every internal auditor should be capable of using a generalized audit software package. Do you agree or disagree with this statement? Why?

CASE PROBLEMS

Problem 8-1

A new internal auditor on the staff has just returned from an out-of-town seminar. As his audit supervisor he reports to you to discuss his reaction to the program. He advises you that in reviewing the *Standards for the Professional Practice of Internal Auditing,* the seminar instructor stated that to be objective in his audit work, an internal auditor should not design or install systems. This now puzzles him because just before going to the seminar he learned from one of the EDP auditors that she participates in the design phase for computer application systems. He tells you that, to him, this appears to be in direct conflict with the standards and asks you for clarification.

Required. How would you explain this seeming contradiction to the new auditor?

Problem 8-2

At a meeting between the vice-president–finance, the general auditor, and the corporate pension fund manager, the problem of determining when retired employees die was discussed. It was believed that the fund was losing thousands of dollars because of erroneous payments and that other companies have methods of getting deceased retired employees off the pension rolls. Surviving relatives are requested to disclose deaths, but some do not because they think they are entitled to a continuation of benefits. Vital statistics are available from the state but 25% of the retired employees reside outside the state.

The vice-president–finance requested that the internal auditing department look into using the computer to check on retiree deaths.

Required. How should the general auditor respond, and is the assignment the type that the internal auditing department should perform?

CHAPTER NINE

Using Statistical Sampling

Upon completing this chapter you should be able to:

☐ *Explain the advantages of using statistical sampling in modern internal auditing*

☐ *Describe the purpose of attributes sampling and sampling for variables*

☐ *Determine the appropriate selection technique for a given population*

☐ *List some of the statistical applications used by operating management*

☐ *Evaluate the results of sampling tests where a significant number of errors were found*

NATURE OF STATISTICAL SAMPLING

The responsibilities of the modern internal auditor are often extensive and require the use of many different audit approaches. In a particular assignment the internal auditor may review policies and procedures of the company to determine if they are adequate. He may perform surveys and overall comparisons of information to determine trends. He may perform a study and evaluation of the existing internal control system of the company to determine its reliability.

When the internal auditor finds the internal control system satisfactory in principle, he still must determine whether the system is operative. He thus must examine documents and other records to determine the effectiveness of the system in practice. For example, the review of a purchasing system may indicate that effective controls exist on paper to assure that the company's interests are protected. It is only by testing actual documents of

Statistical sampling is learning about many items by looking at a selected few

purchasing transactions, however, that the internal auditor has assurance that the system is working and employees are not evading the requirements of the system.

It is when the internal auditor decides to test (invoices, reports, inventory items, etc.) that he considers using statistical sampling as an audit tool. Statistical sampling is basically a method of learning about many items by looking at a selected few. In the early stages of internal audit it was not uncommon to perform a 100% examination of entries or documents. As companies grew larger it was no longer feasible to examine items on a 100% basis. Thus the internal auditor examined a portion of the entries, using what was called the test approach. As illustrated in Exhibit 9.4, statistical sampling developed as one method that could be used in testing.

Use of statistical sampling involves judgment

The internal auditor faced with performing a variety of tests in a review must answer the question: "Should I use statistical sampling?" The decision may be complicated because of such factors as small population size, lack of technical expertise or computer availability, nonacceptance by management, and shortage of audit resources available for reviewing any areas other than those with known problems. Since the decision as to what audit procedures are to be used is a matter of judgment, the internal auditor must carefully weigh the advantages of the various procedures in a particular situation, with statistical sampling as one option.

Reasons for Using Statistical Sampling

We are all familiar with the use of statistical sampling, whether in public opinion polls or in quality control testing in a production plant. The transition to an approach of considering the use of statistical sampling in each test an internal auditor performs, however, may be difficult. Some of the reasons for using statistical sampling are as follows:

Statistical sampling can save time and money

1. *Conclusions about Entire Field.* If a statistical sampling method is used, information can be obtained about the entire field (commonly referred to as the population or universe), within certain statistical limits as explained later. The internal auditor can thus arrive at conclusions about the field without performing a 100% check, resulting in considerable savings in both time and money.

2. *Sample Result Objective and Defensible.* Since, in using statistical sampling, test items must be randomly selected from the field, each item in the field has an equal opportunity of being selected. The audit test is thus objective, and is defensible in a court of law, since it is based on mathematical theory. A judgment sample, however, may be distorted (only large or sensitive items may be examined, for example).

3. *Less Sampling May Be Required.* The amount of testing does not increase in proportion to the increase in the size of the field being

tested. Frequently, large fields are oversampled because of the belief that larger fields require proportionately larger samples.

4. *May Increase Accuracy Over 100% Test*. When voluminous data are counted in their entirety, there is often the chance of clerical errors. However, when a small sample is taken, there may be fewer errors made. Consequently, the sample would be subject, primarily, to sampling error resulting from the statistical projection and not clerical errors.

5. *Coverage of Different Locations*. Since under statistical sampling internal auditors can work independently and their work combined, audits can be performed at different locations. Small samples may thus be possible at individual sites under an overall sampling plan. Audits started by one internal auditor may also be continued by another.

6. *Simple to Apply*. With the availability of computer software packages, the application of statistical sampling has become simplified. Recently, professional books and manuals have become available that show how to apply statistical sampling.[1] Also training courses have been increased by professional organizations to facilitate learning sampling techniques.

The internal auditor must keep in mind, however, that exact information cannot be obtained about a population of items based on a sample, whether it be judgmental or statistical. It is only through making a 100% test that the internal auditor can obtain the exact information. If the internal auditor uses judgmental sampling, however, he obtains information only about those items he examines. If he uses statistical sampling, he obtains positive information about all of the items in the population (a range at a given confidence level). Regardless of the number of items examined, if the internal auditor makes a random selection, he can project the results of the sample to the entire account or transactions.

Exact information not possible from sampling

Judgment Sampling

Although the merits of statistical sampling are generally accepted, internal auditors frequently use judgment, or nonstatistical, sampling to perform tests. Statistical sampling is not mandatory in the public accounting profession, as borne out by the American Institute of Certified Public Accountants Statement on Auditing Standards 1, paragraph 320A.04, which states that

---

[1]Especially recommended are the *Handbook of Sampling for Auditing and Accounting* by Herbert Arkin (New York: McGraw-Hill, 1984), and *Sampling in Auditing* by Henry P. Hill, Joseph L. Roth, and Herbert Arkin (New York: The Ronald Press, 1962). These references provide more detailed material covering the various statistical concepts and methods, examples of statistical applications, and useful statistical tables.

the use of statistical sampling "is permissive rather than mandatory under generally accepted auditing standards."

Internal auditors generally justify the use of judgment sampling by the following:

Auditing is a matter of judgment rather than mathematical analyses.

Judgment sampling is easier to apply.

The internal auditor's general reviews and analyses identify the sensitive items that need to be examined.

Management is interested in information as to specific deficiencies found, not projections based on statistical sampling.

There is thus a tendency on the part of some internal auditors to use judgment sampling despite its disadvantages. Judgment sampling may take many forms: (1) examination of fixed percentage, such as 10%, of the items or dollars, often selected haphazardly; (2) selection of all or part of items in a period, such as a month, or of a particular letter of the alphabet; (3) selection of items for audit with a large dollar amount; (4) examination of items readily available, as in a particular file drawer; (5) review of sensitive items only; and (6) selection of one or a few transactions for audit to determine if a system is working. Although useful data may be obtained by these samples, the results may be misleading and cannot be used to arrive at conclusions about the whole.

Judgmental sampling has major limitations for conclusions about whole

In using a judgment sample the internal auditor is making a threefold judgment: size of sample, method of selection, and interpretation of results. Without the use of statistical sampling, there can be no scientific way of measuring the effect of errors or determining other information about the whole based on a test check. The internal auditor's reliance on judgment may thus often be the use of intuition. As knowledge of statistical sampling in auditing expands and internal auditors become more proficient in the techniques, it is expected that the use of statistical sampling will grow.

Exhibit 9.1 illustrates statistical sampling applications used in one company. Applications were selected based on review of prior tests performed, errors found, and volume and accessibility of data.

Statistical Probability

When a sample is selected on a random basis from a group of transactions, it is one of many samples that can be selected. The characteristics of the sample drawn by one internal auditor may be different from the characteristics of the sample drawn by another internal auditor, and both may be different from the results of an examination of all the transactions. To determine how far a sample result differs from that of a 100% test, the internal auditor must have knowledge of the behavior of all possible results of samples that might be drawn from the population.

EXHIBIT 9.1.   Selected Statistical Sampling Applications

Maintenance orders (cost overruns, warranties)

Customer accounts (circularization, write-offs)

Consultants (need, effectiveness)

Equipment rentals (lease versus buy, options exercised)

Purchase orders (need, competition, timeliness)

Inventories (physical observation, pricing, quantities, obsolescence)

Payroll (rates, hours, classification, utilization)

Expenditures per voucher register (need, discounts, distribution, double endorsements)

Research projects (cost transfers, overruns)

Travel (entertainment, need, personal)

Reports (need, accuracy, use)

Service centers (billing rates, surpluses or deficits)

Fixed assets (need, acquisition, utilization, disposal)

Depreciation (accuracy, life, capitalization)

Sales (prices, discounts, warranties)

Quality control (tolerances, corrective action, timeliness of reports)

Investment portfolio (rate of return, safety)

Bills of materials (quantities, prices)

Production orders (timeliness, overruns, validity of costs)

If the sample means of all possible samples were determined and plotted, the distribution would approximate the normal curve, or normal distribution. The properties of this normal distribution have been scientifically determined, and are that 68% of the individual members of the distribution lie within plus or minus one standard deviation of the arithmetic mean of the total distribution, and 95.5% lie within plus or minus two standard deviations. Expressed another way, 90% of the members lie within plus or minus 1.65 standard deviations and 95% within plus or minus 1.96 standard deviations. Based on this, if one sample were drawn at random, the internal auditor can calculate the probability that the sample mean would fall within a certain range. For example, with a mean of $100 and a standard deviation of $10, 95% of the observations would fall within plus or minus 1.96 standard deviations, or plus or minus $19.60. Thus there is a 95% probability that the mean of a sample drawn at random would be within the range $80.40 to $119.60. If there are 1000 items in the population, the point estimate (or estimated parameter of the population) would be $100,000, and the range at the 95% probability would be between $80,400 and $119,600.

The term "confidence level" is used to express the probability that the value obtained from the sample will not depart from the true value of the

Normal distribution a useful basis for estimates

population by more than the precision. The term "precision" refers to the measure of closeness between a sample estimate and the characteristics of the population.

SAMPLING PLANS

Sampling plan supports audit objective

Statistical sampling activities of internal auditors are carried out under a number of different types of sampling plans. These sampling plans are applicable to special types of conditions and reflect the different audit objectives that exist in each case. We discuss three of these plans that are most often used by internal auditors. These are attributes sampling, variables sampling, and discovery sampling.

Attributes Sampling

A type of sampling plan commonly used by internal auditors has to do with the measurement and evaluation of attributes. This is a qualitative evaluation of a particular group of items or transactions based on how many times a particular attribute is occurring. Normally the attribute being measured is an error or other type of deficiency. The extent of the existence of the particular deficiency determines the seriousness of the situation and what the internal auditor will report in terms of conclusions and recommendations. The attributes or characteristics can have to do with any physical item, any financial record, any internal procedure, or operational activity. Its focus will normally be on compliance with a designated policy, procedure, or established standard.

Attributes sampling focuses on "How Many"

The use of the attributes sampling plan can be illustrated by the concern that might exist for the correct coding of accounts payable disbursement vouchers. The starting point will be the determination of an expected error rate. At the same time a judgment must also be made as to the acceptable precision limits and the degree of wanted confidence. It is now possible to determine the size of the sample that will provide the basis for a reliable conclusion as to the total condition of the population of the size being dealt with. This determination is made for us through statistical methods and can be obtained from available tables or by computer runs. This provides the *initial* basis to the internal auditor for the size of the sample to be reviewed. The internal auditor now selects his sample in a proper manner and examines it to determine the number of errors that exist in the sample. As can be expected, that error rate in the sample will normally be higher or lower than the previously designated acceptable error rate. If it is lower, the internal auditor has of course established that he is safely within the limits he selected. If, on the other hand, the sample shows a higher error rate, tables are available to tell him what degree of reliability he now has. The internal auditor will now have to determine whether the results are satisfactory and what further he should do. Conceivably the sample can be expanded or the internal auditor may feel that he has an adequate basis for arriving at a conclusion.

Variables Sampling

A second type of sampling plan, referred to as variables sampling, has to do with the size of a specified population. Here the focus is on "how much" as opposed to the "how many" of attributes sampling. The objective served is to be able to project aggregate quantities on the basis of a sample. Illustrative would be the desire to estimate the total value of an inventory, or perhaps to estimate the amount of obsolescence in that inventory. Still another practical application would be the determination of the estimated aggregate dollar amount of excessive items in a group of expense reports. Variables sampling is thus concerned with absolute amounts as opposed to the number of a particular type of error.

Variables sampling focuses on "How Much"

The statistical problems involved in this type of sampling are closely related to attributes sampling, but include certain additional concepts and calculations. One of these additional complexities is the necessity to compute the standard deviation of the sample as a measure of the range of variability of the sample. Because of the more complicated nature of this approach, a step-by-step analysis of the method of application is given below for single-stage variables sampling. The example is based on a simplified manual method for estimating the standard deviation when computer-developed or other information on the standard deviation is not available.

Steps in Application. The total application of variables sampling can be understood best by listing and discussing the sequential steps that must be carried out. These are:

1. *Determination of Audit Objective.* Assuming that the internal auditor has an assignment to determine the validity of a given population— as, for example, an inventory—the first step is to decide the desired level of confidence and the desired degree of precision. The latter is normally first expressed as a percentage, but is then converted into a dollar amount. This dollar amount can then be translated into the average amount per inventory item. This degree of precision can be called the sampling error.

   Variables sampling has eleven steps

2. *Selection of Preliminary Sample.* Through a proper selection process, discussed later in the chapter, a preliminary sample of about 50 items is selected.

3. *Arrangement of Preliminary Sample.* The preliminary sample is now arranged in the order selected, in groups of six, seven, or eight items, but subject to the requirement that the number of groups, as a multiple of the item content, equals the total of the items in the prelim-

inary sample. For example, a preliminary sample of 48 items would be composed of eight groups of six each.

4. *Determine the Average Range.* In each group the difference between the highest and lowest item constitutes the range. The ranges of all groups are then added and an average computed.

5. *Calculate Estimated Standard Deviation of Population.* The estimated standard deviation of the total population can now be calculated through a simplified method by dividing the average range, just computed, by an amount which is known in statistics as the d_2 factor. For a group content of 6, 7, and 8, the d_2 factor is respectively, 2.534, 2.704, and 2.847.

6. *Computation of Stipulated Sampling Error.* The sampling error per average inventory item, as expressed in dollars, is now divided by the previously calculated estimated standard deviation. This will yield a new ratio called the *stipulated sampling error*.

7. *Determination of Complete Sample.* Using the previously established level of confidence and the just computed ratio of sampling error, tables are available to show the size of the complete sample to be used.

8. *Evaluation of Sample Size.* At this point the internal auditor has an opportunity to reevaluate his audit objective. It may be that the sample indicated is so large that he may wish to reevaluate the confidence level and level of precision (the amount of the sampling error). It is possible by decreasing the former and/or increasing the latter to decrease the size of the needed sample.

9. *Examination of Sample.* The indicated sample, based on the criteria just discussed, will now be examined in complete detail and the sampling error determined for this now more complete sample.

10. *Reevaluation of Sampling Error.* The reliability of the complete sample can be further established by recomputing the stipulated sampling error for the complete sample in the same manner as was done for the preliminary sample. Again tables are available to measure the significance of the variance from the error shown by the preliminary sample, and a reevaluation of the audit objectives may be necessary.

11. *Projection to Total Population.* The results obtained from the complete sample can now be projected to the total population. In some cases the conclusion or recommendation developed may be of a general nature. In other cases the final action may be a definitive adjustment of the inventory by operating management.

Difference Estimates. The preceding application has been based upon the dollar amounts of the individual inventory items. Frequently, it is practicable instead to deal with the differences between the book and actual value (as determined by the internal auditor). Under this approach a similar procedure is followed but all of the samples and computations pertain to the differences data. The advantage to be achieved is that the internal auditor is dealing with smaller amounts (and thus smaller standard deviations) and that, therefore, normally a smaller sample will be required to achieve the same levels of confidence and precision. It is of course possible that the differences will be as great or almost as great as the absolute values and, therefore, the advantages may disappear. However, the use of differences is a good technique in the appropriate situations, and can often be used as a first approach.

Ratio Estimates.   A similar type of special efficiency is often achieved through working with ratios instead of absolute values. Computations of the standard deviations under this method are more complicated. But where these computations can be made by computers there can be significant time savings. The ratio estimates method is preferable to the use of the difference estimates method when the errors found are related in size to the value of individual items being tested.

Discovery Sampling

In certain situations the concern of the internal auditor may be as to whether a particular type of deficiency exists. The deficiency involved is normally a serious one and would be expected to have a very low occurrence rate. Illustrative of this kind of situation would be the possibility that there are fictitious employees on the payroll, or perhaps the failure to obtain collateral for loans which, under company policy, are supposed to be secured. In this case we are concerned with a type of occurrence, and to that extent it is like attribute sampling. However, in this situation we know the size of the population, and we are endeavoring on the basis of a given sample to determine the probabilities that the particular kind of deficiency does or does not exist. Discovery sampling is used for a more limited or special purpose, but again is part of the kit provided by the statistical approach.

Discovery sampling used for limited or special purpose

Application of Discovery Sampling.   In applying the discovery sampling plan we first determine the population, decide what is an acceptable occurrence rate, establish the desired confidence level, determine the sample size required, examine the sample, and evaluate the results. Tables are available that will provide the size of the appropriate sample when the population is known and the confidence level established. If in the examination of this indicated sample no instances of the deficiency are found, the internal auditor can safely conclude that he is within the boundaries of the previously established confidence level and occurrence rate. If one or more deficiencies are discovered, the procedure can be changed to attributes or variables sampling to estimate the rate of occurrence or number of deficiencies in the population. At the same time, of course, the internal auditor

Discovery sampling facilitates audit exploration

would focus on the causes of the deficiency or deficiencies actually encountered and appraise the scope and timing of various types of corrective action.

Minimum Sample Sizes

In practice there are various sample sizes used by internal auditors as minimum samples in an audit. On the one hand, an internal auditor may conservatively select a large sample, say 1000, on the basis that he will get better results and management will be more apt to accept the results if a large sample is selected. On the other hand, an internal auditor may choose a sample size of 50 on the basis that he may be able to arrive at adequate conclusions based on a limited amount of work. These decisions are sometimes made without regard to scientific statistical analysis as to required sample size.

Objectives determine extent of sample

The objectives of the audit of course determine the extent of sampling. If survey work is being performed, tests to determine acceptability of the system may be minimal. If significant weaknesses are found, however, and the test is to determine the extent and magnitude of the deficiency, then the internal auditor should perform appropriate statistical analysis to determine the number to be tested. Under conditions such as this, some audit organizations have adopted a minimum size for sampling, such as 200, with the use of a larger sample as considered necessary. This provides internal auditors and management with a minimum assurance that conclusions reached are valid.

Reporting a Specific Amount

In variables sampling the internal auditor must decide how he will report the projection of dollar amounts, whether it be for adjustments or for estimates of the effect of a particular deficiency. Under statistical sampling the projection would normally be stated at a range of values for a given confidence level. From the viewpoint of management, however, the use of a specific dollar amount may be preferable.

Point Estimate or Midpoint. The point estimate is the best single estimate of the value of a universe, being the point of maximum likelihood. It is calculated by multiplying the sample mean times the number of items in the universe. This estimate is generally used when the range of values, or confidence interval, around the point estimate is small. For example, the point estimate based on a statistical projection of the results of audit was $100,000. The precision at the 95% confidence level was $\pm$ $4000, for a range between $96,000 and $104,000. Under these circumstances the use of the point estimate would generally be warranted. However, if the range were between $60,000 and $140,000, the auditor would have to either increase the sample size or use a different method of reporting. One method of reporting is to state: "We estimate with a probability of 95% that the recorded inventory value of $2.5 million is overstated between $60,000 and $140,000, and is most likely $100,000."

Upper Limit. By stating the projection in terms of the upper limit, the auditor can determine the assurance that the amount of error or deficiency is not greater than this amount. For example, in a statistical review of equipment on hand the internal auditor projected at the 95% confidence level that the maximum overstatement of the equipment was $30,000. Since this amount was not material in relation to the $5 million of equipment owned by the company, the internal auditor concluded that the amount of error was not significant. He also analyzed, however, the causes of errors found in his sample to determine procedural weaknesses that required correction.

Confidence level provides measure of reliability of an estimate

The upper limit is frequently used by the internal auditor to determine the validity of account balances for financial statement purposes. A tolerable error rate is first determined for the population. If the projected error rate using the upper limit does not exceed the tolerable error rate, the account is considered reasonably stated for financial statement purposes.

Lower Limit. A one-sided confidence limit can be used to demonstrate that the total universe value is not less than some amount at a given confidence level. For example, in a statistical sample of fixed asset acquisitions it was found that equipment costing over $1000 was being expensed rather than capitalized. The internal auditor's projection showed that there was 95% confidence that the amount expensed in error was at least $150,000. The lower limit is used sometimes in government auditing for recommending refunds, as discussed previously, especially when the precision is not sufficiently narrow. Appendix G shows this treatment in the policy statement of the Internal Revenue Service.

Use of Standard Confidence Level

Some audit organizations have adopted a fixed confidence level, such as 95%, for performing and evaluating statistical tests. This is justified on the basis that the confidence level should be sufficiently high in all instances, and should be a consistent reference for projections. See Appendix G for the use of a fixed confidence level by the Internal Revenue Service.

Other audit organizations use flexible confidence levels based on individual circumstances. For a particular audit test an 80 or 90% confidence limit may be used; in another test a 95 or 99.9% confidence level might be preferred. In some cases the internal auditor will restate the precision at two or more confidence levels as a basis for making judgments.

SELECTION TECHNIQUES

Sample must be representative of population

To obtain the advantages of statistical sampling, a probability sample must be drawn. This involves a more precise approach than is used in judgment sampling in order to be able to evaluate the results scientifically. The auditor must remove bias in his selection once the sampling plan has been developed. Through this method a sample can be obtained that is representative of the population, and the results become defensible. Exhibit 9.2 is a listing from a form for outlining the sampling plan as well as a method of selection and evaluation. These more precise requirements can be stated, as follows:

1. The population (or universe or field) that is to be sampled must be clearly defined. The population is made up of sampling units, which are the individual items from which the sample is drawn. This definition must include scope (for example, the accounts payable vouchers for a year) and the specific characteristic of audit interest (for example, the fact of a specific type of approval).

2. The population should not cover such a range of characteristics (for example, such very large and small amounts) that the statistical conclusions will not be sufficiently precise.

3. Every item in the particular population must have an equal chance of being selected in the sample. Thus there must be no bias created

---

EXHIBIT 9.2.   Statistical Sampling Plan

1. Statement of objectives
2. List of characteristics to be tested
3. Sampling unit
4. Type of sampling plan used (attributes, variables, etc.) (If stratified sampling not used, explain why.)
5. Size of universe and strata
6. Expected error rate
7. Desired precision
8. Desired confidence level
9. Selection of sample size (Indicate if probe sample.)
10. Random number table used—include start and end point (If computer was used, attach documentation.)
11. If using systematic sampling—starting point and method of selecting random start and interval between sample units
12. Evaluation of results and conclusions

Prepared by: Date   Approval   Date

_____   _____   Supervisor: _____   _____

through the poorer availability (or even lack of availability) of particular items.

4. The person selecting the sample should have no bias in that selection. This includes also the avoiding of any method of selection that could involve such a bias.

Four common types or techniques involved in the selection process are: random number selection, interval selection, stratified selection, and cluster selection, including multistage. The latter two techniques are also often referred to as kinds of sampling, but they are more properly identified as selection techniques. Next we discuss very briefly each of these techniques.

Random Number Selection

The random number technique by its name emphasizes the basic requirement of the sample that it should be selected at random, with each item in the particular population having an equal chance to be selected as a part of the sample. If it were practicable, we would place all the items (or numbers that would identify particular items) in a container, mix the items thoroughly, and then draw the individual items for the sample from the container in a blindfolded manner. Since this may not be feasible, we must seek other means. One of these means is the use of random number tables. This type of table is illustrated by Exhibit 9.3. Random number tables can be utilized as a basis for determining the sample of items actually to be reviewed by the internal auditor. Random numbers can also be generated by computers, but our discussion will at this point pertain to the way in which the tables are used in typical audit situations. The problems here center chiefly around the way in which items in the population are related to numbers in the tables, the starting point in using the tables, and then the route to take after the determination of the starting point.

Use of random number tables

Relating Audit Items.   Where the audit items in the population to be evaluated are already numbered, the numbers provide a ready basis for use of the table. It will be necessary, however, to work with the table in a way that will provide random numbers with the same number of digits. The columnar data can be used in any manner desired, provided that the particular approach is used consistently. Numbers encountered that are outside the limits of the audit sequence must be ignored. If the audit items are in a broken series, the internal auditor will have to ignore the random numbers encountered that do not apply to the actual audit sequences. Where the audit items are lettered, the letters need to be converted to a number equivalent before the random number tables can be used. Similarly, audit items lacking any formal sequencing designation must be provided with some kind of a numerical equivalent. If by chance the same random number comes

EXHIBIT 9.3. Table of Random Numbers

10480	15011	01536	02011	81647	91646	69179	14194	62590
22368	46573	25595	85393	30995	89198	27982	53402	93965
24130	48360	22527	97265	76393	64809	15179	24830	49340
42167	93093	06243	61680	07856	16376	39440	53537	71341
37570	39975	81837	16656	06121	91782	60468	81305	49684
77921	06907	11008	42751	27756	53498	18602	70659	90655
99562	72905	56420	69994	98872	31016	71194	18738	44013
96301	91977	05463	07972	18876	20922	94595	56869	69014
89579	14342	63661	10281	17453	18103	57740	84378	25331
85475	36857	53342	53988	53060	59533	38867	62300	08158
28918	69578	88231	33276	70997	79936	56865	05859	90106
63553	40961	48235	03427	49626	69445	18663	72695	52180
09429	93969	52636	92737	88974	33488	36320	17617	30015
10365	61129	87529	85689	48237	52267	67689	93394	01511
07119	97336	71048	08178	77233	13916	47564	81056	97735
51085	12765	51821	51259	77452	16308	60756	92144	49442
02368	21382	52404	60268	89368	19885	55322	44819	01188
01011	54092	33362	94904	31273	04146	18594	29852	71585
52162	53916	46369	58586	23216	14513	83149	98736	23495
07056	97628	33787	09998	42698	06691	76988	13602	51851
48663	91245	85828	14346	09172	30168	90229	04734	59193
54164	58492	22421	74103	47070	25306	76468	26384	58151
32639	32363	05597	24200	13363	38005	94342	28728	35806
29334	27001	87637	87308	58731	00256	45834	15398	46557
02488	33062	28834	07351	19731	92420	60952	61280	50001
81525	72295	04839	96423	24878	82651	66566	14778	76797
29676	20591	68086	26432	46901	20849	89768	81536	86645
00742	57392	39064	66432	84673	40027	32832	61362	98947
05366	04213	25669	26422	44407	44048	37937	63904	45766
91921	26418	64117	94305	26766	25940	39972	22209	71500
00582	04711	87917	77341	42206	35126	74087	99547	81817
00725	69884	62797	56170	86324	88072	76222	36086	84637
69011	65795	95876	55293	18988	27354	26575	08625	40801
25976	57948	29888	88604	67917	48708	18912	82271	65424
09763	83473	73577	12908	30883	18317	28290	35797	05998
91567	42595	27958	30134	04024	86385	29880	99730	55536
17955	56349	90999	49127	20044	59931	06115	20542	18059
46503	18584	18845	49618	02304	51038	20655	58727	28168
92157	89634	94824	78171	84610	82834	09922	25417	44137
14577	62765	35605	81263	39667	47358	56873	56307	61607
98427	07523	33362	64270	01638	92477	66969	98420	04880
34914	63976	88720	82765	34476	17032	87589	40836	32427
70060	28277	39475	46473	23219	53416	94970	25832	69975
53976	54914	06990	67245	68350	82948	11398	42878	80287
76072	29515	40980	07391	58745	25774	22987	80059	39911
90725	52210	83974	29992	65831	38857	50490	83765	55657
64364	67412	33339	31926	14883	24413	59744	92351	97473
08962	00358	31662	25388	61642	34072	81249	35648	56891
95012	68379	93526	70765	10592	04542	76463	54328	02349
15664	10493	20492	38391	91132	21999	59516	81652	27195

up again, thus repeating the identification of a particular audit item, the duplicate number should be ignored, and the next applicable number used. There is clearly no point in testing the same item twice.

Starting Point. The objective is that all starting points be established on a random basis. One danger here is that many of us tend to start at the top left position. However, this will technically introduce bias in the results. A practical method is not to look at the table and simply let one's finger find a starting point on a blind-thrust basis.

Route. Once the starting point has been established and the number of digits related to the table in some way, the identification of the random numbers to be used can proceed in any direction. The only condition is that the use of the columns and the selected direction be maintained on a consistent basis.

Other Problems. Frequently the size of the sample as originally selected may have to be increased or decreased. In the first situation the internal auditor should go back to his previous stopping point and then again continue. If the sample needs to be reduced, the random numbers last selected should be eliminated in reverse sequence. Normally, it is more convenient to err on the overselection side.

A second problem has to do with putting the random numbers in a sequence that will make it convenient to proceed sequentially to locate the actual test items. In some cases the simplest solution is to rearrange the random numbers sequentially after they have been selected. In other cases it may be easier to use a work schedule to line up the selected numbers on a sequential basis during the actual process of selection. Random numbers may be arranged sequentially by use of a special program, if a computer is available.

Finally it is important to document the manner in which the random selection process was actually carried out. This documentation then serves to confirm the scientific basis for the sample selection, and can in fact be auditable, if such proof is ever necessary.

Interval Selection

Another way to select the items in the sample and still to provide a statistically sound sample is through interval selection (sometimes called systematic sampling). This approach consists of selecting the individual items of the sample based on a uniform interval in the series of items comprising the total population to be sampled. This technique is especially useful when the particular population does not have assigned numbers that make it practicable to work from random number tables. For example, we would be able to develop our sample by selecting every nth item in an inventory listing. It is of course necessary that we are dealing with a reasonably homogeneous population, in terms of type of item, and that there is no bias in the arrangement that would result in the interval approach coming up with a sample that is not statistically representative of the population.

Application of Interval Selection. The special requirements in the application of interval selection is that the interval to be used is properly related to the size of the sample (as determined in the usual manner) and the size of the total population. Where necessary the population can be estimated. The sample size divided into the population size then establishes the proper interval. Thus a population of 5000 and a needed sample of 200 would yield an interval requirement of 25. We would then examine every twenty-fifth item in the population series. The starting point in the first interval group must now be established on a random basis, preferably from a random numbers table. In the event that the actual population turns out to be larger than was estimated, a practical solution is to increase the sample by extending the interval selection on the same basis. If, on the other hand, the actual population is less than estimated, it will be necessary to complete the sample through a new interval selection based on the number of items short in relation to the total population size. The latter more complicated problem can be avoided by having a safety margin through selecting a larger sample.

Stratified Selection

Stratification reduces variability and thus size of sample

The nature of stratified selection is that the particular population is divided into two or more subgroups or classes (referred to as strata) and that each subgroup is dealt with independently in the statistical sampling processes. In its simplest terms two or more separate populations are established within the framework of a larger population of which they are a part. It is a supplement to the random and interval selection techniques because either of those selection techniques can be applied to the smaller population. In some cases one of the new populations may be examined in complete detail. The basic need for this stratification or subdivision is that the larger population combines a number of significantly different characteristics, and that the internal auditor wishes to evaluate the subgroup on a more individual and precise basis. Through reducing variability, stratification can decrease the standard deviation, and thus help to reduce sample sizes.

Use of Stratified Selection. One of the most common situations requiring stratification is one in which the particular population—such as inventories, accounts receivable, or invoices—has some items of very high value. Since these high-value items have much greater significance, the internal auditor may properly wish to subject them to higher standards of scrutiny. This may take the form of higher sampling standards or detailed examination. In other cases the need for stratification may arise from the fact that individual subgroups are processed in different ways, or by different groups. In other cases the nature of the items may call for different standards of audit scrutiny, as, for example, where some types of inventory are more subject to theft. Under these kinds of conditions the larger variability in the total population makes a single type of testing and evaluation inapplicable. Needless to say, these principles have long been recognized and applied by good internal auditors. The special importance in statistical sampling is, however, the contribution of stratification to more meaningful statistical measures (higher levels of confidence and lower precision limits), together with the possibility of using smaller samples.

Once the stratification selection technique has been adopted and the subgroups subjected to different standards of audit scrutiny, the results of each evaluation can be used in several ways. In some cases the results are used quite independently, based on the sampling of the separate populations. In other cases they may be brought back together to support a consolidated finding and conclusion relative to the total operational population, using a stratified sampling projection.

Cluster Selection

Another approach used by internal auditors is known as cluster selection. Under this approach the sample is made up by systematically selecting given subgroups or clusters from the particular total population. All items within each cluster, or a predetermined number in order, such as 5 or 10, are selected. It is used when items are filed on shelves or in drawers and it is physically more convenient to select subgroups based on shelf area or individual drawers. The rationale is that the items on particular portions of the shelf areas (or in designated drawers) are substantially similar, and that a sample thus selected will be representative of the total population. However, the reported experience is that the variability *within* the individual samples is frequently less than the variability *among* the samples. Hence it is customary to use a larger sample when using the cluster selection approach to offset this lesser reliability. A variation of the aforementioned approach, called multistage sampling, is to *sample* the individual clusters instead of examining the sample as a whole or a predetermined number within each cluster.

Storage facility arrangements favor cluster selection approach

Use of Cluster Selection. Assuming a population of 60,000 items filed on shelves that have a linear coverage of 2000 feet, and that a sample of 600 will provide the desired level of confidence and limits of precision, we might, perhaps, plan on 20 clusters. Then each cluster would need to have 30 items. Since the average number of items is 30 per linear foot (60,000 ÷ 2000), each cluster will cover an area of one foot (30 ÷ 30). These individual clusters would then be selected at intervals of 100 feet (2000 ÷ 20) and with a random start. It should be recognized that the scientific basis of the total sample is more dependent on a consistency of the population. That is, random number selection or regular interval selection would presumably assure a better representative sample. Hence cluster sampling must be used with special care.

STRATIFIED SAMPLING APPLICATIONS

The trend in statistical sampling is to use stratified sampling in most auditing applications of variable methods.[2] Although in some cases it may not be practicable to stratify the population, or it may not be possible to identify the items for which differences will occur, these situations are rare.

Changes in Approach

When judgment sampling was the method primarily used in testing, the internal auditor often performed preliminary analysis before deciding which items to select. This analysis was based on review of correspondence in the files, discussions with auditee's staff to obtain explanations and leads, review of prior audit findings, comparison of operations and data, and study of the universe to determine the larger or sensitive items for test.

When statistical sampling was first introduced into auditing, simple random sampling was generally used. This method was relatively easy to learn and apply, especially under manual methods. Thus, when there was an area to test, the internal auditor immediately took a random sample of the universe. In some cases this was justified as a probe sample, or test of the universe, to find out more about the items before developing a sampling plan. The results of the probe sample, however, were often used to arrive at final conclusions as to the acceptability of the area being tested. Thus, in the process of switching to the new statistical sampling technique, the internal auditor may have used relatively simple statistical approaches.

With the advent of the computer to simplify sample selection and projection of results, the use of stratified sampling has grown. Often the only practical method for selecting a stratified sample is by use of a computer. Also as internal auditors gained in sophistication in applying statistical sampling, they experimented with more advanced techniques to get greater precision.

[2]Donald M. Roberts, *Statistical Auditing* (New York: American Institute of Certified Public Accountants, 1978), p. 65.

Advantages of Stratified Sampling

Stratified sampling provides greater representation of the larger recorded amounts if they are included as separate strata. In this respect the method resembles dollar-unit sampling, in which each dollar is the sampling unit.

A major advantage of stratification is that it improves the efficiency of the testing. When the population variability (standard deviation) is high, sample sizes may be reduced for the desired levels of precision and reliability by using stratified random sampling. If a sufficient number of strata are selected, often the sampling error can be reduced substantially. With the use of computers, this becomes more feasible as an approach to be used by internal auditors.

Stratification improves testing efficiency

Another advantage is that emphasis can be given to sensitive areas that require audit. Often the internal auditor's preliminary analysis will disclose areas with potential errors or problems. These can be classified in separate strata and audited 100% or on a sampling basis, as warranted.

Methods of Stratification

As described above, the use of stratification provides the internal auditor with a tool for reviewing sensitive areas on a scientific basis. He must, however, use the utmost judgment in selecting strata for audit. The information available on computer tapes will, of course, be important in selecting a method. The following are some factors to consider in determining methods of stratifying.

Type of item

Dollar amount

Storage location

Volume of activity

Prior problems or deficiencies

Items handled by certain employees

Items involving weak controls

Post-Stratification

An internal auditor may take a random sample of units, expecting to project by using difference estimates. In some instances where the results are imprecise, the internal auditor can stratify after the simple random sample is selected. This is referred to as post-stratification.

If the internal auditor knows the number of units in the population for each strata, he can take the results of the original sample, eliminate the sensitive (or special strata) units, and put them in a separate stratum. If the auditor does not know the total number of items for the separate strata, he can assign a zero value to the sensitive (or separate strata) items without decreasing the sample size. He then examines the separate strata, with an estimate made of the strata universe based on the incidence in the original sample.

DOLLAR-UNIT-SAMPLING APPLICATIONS

Method of Application

Dollar-unit sampling is a method of statistical sampling in which every dollar, or other monetary unit, in a population has an equal chance of selection. The sampling unit is thus each dollar rather than a physical unit such as an invoice or payroll check. For example, if purchases are being tested for a year, the population consists of the total dollar value of purchases made, and the sampling unit is each dollar of purchases.

Dollar units replace physical units in certain situations

When errors are found in the invoice, they are related to individual dollars in the invoice by various methods. One method, called tainting, determines the ratio of dollar errors to the amount of the invoice. This ratio is then applied to the dollar sampling unit. Another approach is the use of a fixed-decision rule in which an assumption is made as to which dollar units within the physical unit are in error. This assumption is then applied on a fixed, or consistent, basis whenever errors occur. Under this method, as one option if there is an error, the last dollar units within the physical unit, to the extent of the errors, may be considered wrong.

As a relatively new method used by auditors, dollar-unit sampling is currently being experimented with by various groups. Public accountants have been especially interested in this method for estimating the amount of overstatement of accounts. In evaluating the merits of the method, comparisons are often made with the more conventional probability methods, commonly described as the *classical approach*. The following are some advantages and disadvantages of dollar-unit sampling in relation to the classical approach.

Advantages of Dollar-Unit Sampling

Detection of Material Errors.   Dollar-unit sampling provides a probability of including a unit in the sample proportional to its dollar value. Thus there is less risk under this method of failing to detect a material error. Although stratification reduces the risk under usual probability sampling methods, there is less risk under dollar-unit sampling since all the large dollar units are divided into individual dollars.

Smaller Sample Size.   When no errors are found in the initial sample, relatively small sample sizes may be used. The internal auditor can readily determine the maximum possible overstatements and restrict his auditing in some circumstances. In addition the internal auditor obtains the benefits of unlimited stratification by use of unit dollar sampling.

Normal Sampling Distribution. The sampling distribution involved is the binomial distribution, for which exact confidence limits can be established. Thus normal approximations are not necessary as in the use of variables sampling.

Advantages and disadvantages of dollar unit sampling need evaluation

Low Error Rates. When few errors are found in classical sampling the confidence level may not be reliable.[3] Under these circumstances a larger sample may have to be drawn. A major advantage of dollar-unit sampling also is that it eliminates the problems of nonnormal distribution.

Disadvantages of Dollar-Unit Sampling

Overstatements. The dollar-unit method can be applied only to overstatements. Since the method results in the selection of dollars reported, any understatement of dollars results in units missing from the population. They thus cannot be sampled. Accordingly the auditor cannot project a value of the population using dollar-unit sampling.

Zero or Negative Values. Under this method, zero or negative values would have to be sampled using a physical unit approach. Since there are no dollar values included in these, there is no chance that zero or negative values would be sampled.

Total Population Value. Since the projection is made to a universe of dollars, a total book value must be known. The method cannot provide estimates of unknown population values. Also under dollar-unit sampling it is necessary to accumulate the dollars progressively in drawing the sample.

Training Availability. As a relatively new concept for use by internal auditors, there is currently little training provided in dollar-unit sampling. The method is now being subject to rigorous proof to determine its acceptability. The literature in the field is related primarily to classical sampling, and professional certification examinations are based on the classical approach. As the use of dollar-unit sampling becomes more widespread, and its benefits

[3]John Neter and James K. Loebbecke, *Behavior of Major Statistical Estimators in Sampling Accounting Populations* (New York: American Institute of Certified Public Accountants, Inc., 1975), p. 5.

and limitations better understood, it is expected that additional training will be developed.[4]

COMPANY USE OF STATISTICAL ANALYSIS

Most company operational activities make use of statistical methods and concepts to some extent. The key questions are first, whether they are being as fully utilized as they should be, and second, whether the uses actually being made are carried out in an effective fashion. The internal auditor will of course be very much interested in both of these questions. The answers to these questions may require special counsel from persons with adequate professional expertise, but much can be done in the way of a preliminary screening. Also, much can be done in the way of evaluating how operational managers are developing orderly procedures and good administration over these more technical activities. For our present purposes it will be useful to identify some of the more common applications of statistical methods in the various operational activities.

1. *Production Activities.* Production has always been one of the major areas for statistical applications. One of the most common of these is the use of statistical tests by quality control groups as to the extent to which individual manufacturing units are completing particular parts or processing operations in accordance with desired specifications. The same problem exists also in connection with purchased parts, materials, and partial assemblies. Other applications will include the forecasting of machine capacity needs and the continuing maintenance needs.

2. *Inventory Management.* A related important statistical application is in connection with the determination of needed inventory levels by individual types of items. This will involve production and other operational areas as well.

3. *Marketing.* In recent times statistical testing has come to be widely used to measure and evaluate consumer preferences. A related application has to do with the testing of new products before commitments are made to large-volume production. Other major applications relate to the evaluation of advertising approaches, promotional activities, sales techniques, and the like.

4. *Personnel.* Common statistical applications in the personnel area include the analysis and evaluation of staff needs, recruitment policies, training methods, employee turnover, compensation schemes, and so on.

Many operational uses of statistical sampling

[4]See Donald Leslie, Albert Teitlebaum, and Rodney Anderson, *Dollar-Unit Sampling* (Toronto: Copp Clark Pittman, 1979), for further discussion of theory and applications.

5. *Finance*. At a high level the statistical applications in the finance area will include pricing policy, capital project evaluation, and all types of cost and revenue projections. At the lower level they will be used in testing accuracy and compliance in connection with the various types of internal processing.

6. *General*. The ready availability of computer capabilities has provided a major impetus to the statistical measurement and evaluation of many new types of activities. Illustrative of the newer applications are leadership styles, organizational arrangements, types of work assignments, group incentives, and communication patterns.

GUIDELINES FOR APPLICATION

Audit Decisions

The internal auditor may or may not decide to test transactions in performing an audit. He may, for example, decide on the basis of overall comparisons and other auditing procedures that a test of transactions is unnecessary. Also, the amounts involved may not be sufficiently material to warrant testing.

However, in reviewing internal controls the internal auditor is often faced with situations that require sampling of transactions. The best of control systems cannot eliminate errors resulting from system breakdowns. Overall reviews or tests of a few transactions may not be sufficient to disclose whether internal controls are operating effectively. The company's procedures may appear to be adequate, but the internal auditor generally must test actual transactions to determine whether the procedures have been followed in practice. If tests are made, statistical sampling should be considered as a basis for arriving at more valid conclusions.

If the test of transactions indicates that the operations are acceptable, no further work is required. Where errors are found, however, the internal auditor is faced with the decisions described below in arriving at a conclusion.

Isolating Errors.   Through review of the types of errors and their causes, the auditor may be able to isolate the total number of errors. For example one vendor may be submitting erroneous invoices, and a review of all of the vendor's invoices may pinpoint all the errors. As another example, one accounting clerk may be causing the errors, and a special review of his work may be required. This type of analysis may enable the internal auditor to determine the amount of deficiency as well as the basic cause.

Sampling decisions when errors are found

Reporting on Items Examined.   When the internal auditor encounters significant errors, it may only be necessary to report the results of the tests to operating personnel. The nature of the errors may be such that it is the responsibility of operational managers to strengthen procedures and determine the magnitude of errors. As part of his review the internal auditor may determine the causes for the condition and make specific recommendations for corrective action. Unless the internal auditor projects the results of his statistical sample, however, management is provided only with errors or amounts pertaining to the items examined.

Performing 100% Audit.   Although the internal auditor is not expected to perform a detailed examination, in some instances he is called upon to do so when significant errors are found. An example is where recoveries are due from vendors, and the specific vendors and amounts have to be identified. In other instances the necessity to have exact information as to the extent and amount of errors may not be justified in terms of cost involved. Under such circumstances a projection of a statistical sample may suffice.

Projecting Results of Sample.   If the selection of items for the test is made on a random basis, the results can be evaluated. The number and dollar amount of errors can be projected to determine the range of errors in the entire field at a given confidence level. The projection can be used to make an adjustment, or as a basis for decisions of the kind described in the preceding paragraphs.

Audit Sampling Decision Model.   A decision model for assisting the auditor in the use of statistical sampling in audits is shown in Exhibit 9.4.

Extending the Use of Statistical Sampling

Internal auditors are continuously experimenting with the use of statistical sampling in operating areas. Examples are in the review of equipment to assure effective utilization and in tests of purchase requisitions to determine the timeliness of filling requests.

There are many other areas in which the internal auditor performs tests of transactions or items in connection with various auditing techniques or procedures. These procedures include inquiry, observation, vouching, confirmation, computation, and analysis. In performing these tests, statistical sampling should be considered as a useful method for improving audit results.

Use of statistical sampling needs continuing evaluation   As a basis for extending the use of statistical sampling, the internal auditor can review areas in which testing was performed on prior audits. An analysis is then made of the objective of each test, period covered, use of judgment or statistical sampling, number of items in both the field and sample, results of test, and feasibility of using statistical sampling in subsequent audits. A review of this nature has the following benefits:

   1. Pinpoints areas where internal auditors have been overauditing on the basis of judgment sampling

EXHIBIT 9.4.   Audit Sampling Decision Model.

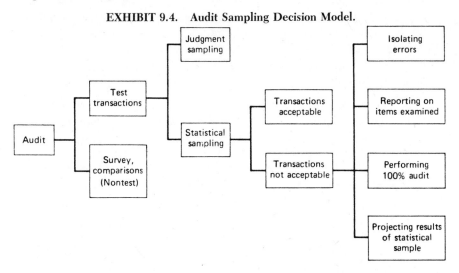

2. Indicates examples where testing has been performed for short periods (for example, one month, although the internal auditor reports for the entire year)

3. Indicates areas where internal auditors have not been testing other than sensitive or high-dollar items

4. Discloses areas where statistical sampling is practicable in light of objectives of the test, number of items in the field, and prior testing performed

Techniques for Efficient Use

The following techniques will facilitate the use of statistical sampling by internal auditors:

1. *Combining Audit Steps.* Savings in audit time can be achieved if various audit steps are performed as part of the same statistical sample. This can be done by testing for as many attributes or characteristics as possible in the sample. For instance, in a review of purchases the primary audit objective may be to determine whether there is adequate documentary support. In addition, the internal auditor may decide to include tests, as part of the statistical sample, to determine whether excess materials are being acquired.

2. *Using Preliminary Sample.* Internal auditors often devote considerable effort to developing a sampling plan based on a certain confidence level, precision, and expected error rate or standard deviation. However, in many cases there is insufficient information on which to develop the sampling plan, as, for example, in a first audit. By taking a

preliminary sample of from 50 to 100 items, the internal auditor is in a better position to make decisions on the extent of sampling required. The preliminary sample can then be included as part of the final sample. Also the results of the preliminary sample may lead the internal auditor to conclude that no additional testing is required.

3. *Performing Interim Audits.* When a sampling plan is prepared in advance for a year, the items can be examined on a monthly or other interim basis without waiting until the end of the year. Thus staff auditors can be utilized, when available, to perform the statistical sampling on an interim basis. For example, if the sample calls for examination of every hundredth voucher, these can be selected for examination as the transaction is processed.

4. *Enlarging the Field.* A basic consideration in statistical sampling is that the sample size does not vary to a great extent with an increase in field size. Thus savings can be obtained by sampling for longer periods of time, or from a field composed of more than one department or division. In some cases the internal auditor may decide to test a particular account for a two-year period, with selection of items during the first year on an interim basis as part of the two-year test.

Facilitating techniques should be evaluated

5. *Using Attributes and Variables Sampling.* In some cases the internal auditor does not know in advance whether variables sampling is required. Since variables sampling is more complex to apply, he may pick a random sample for attributes, evaluate the results, and decide at that point, on the basis of dollar errors, whether variables sampling is required. If it is, the sample can be projected at that point or incorporated in an extended sample selected for variables. The important point is that once a sample is taken on a random basis, it can be evaluated using different sampling methods.

6. *Applying Simple Methods.* Some internal auditors believe that they must use complex methods of sampling and spend considerable effort and study in arriving at the method to use. In most instances a simple estimation sample will provide adequate results, without the need for techniques that are difficult to understand, apply, and explain.

This does not mean that the internal auditor can overlook judgment in his tests. Sensitive items should be examined in addition to a random selection of items, if required. These can be examined on a 100% basis or sampled as part of a separate stratum.

7. *Determining Costs versus Benefits.* The internal auditor should consider the costs of examining each sampling unit when considering extending his sample. The costs of additional work should be compared with benefits from obtaining increased confidence or precision in the final results.

The manner in which statistical sampling techniques can be used in everyday practice can be illustrated by the following typical examples.

1. Computer Selection of Sample of Disbursements

The company's yearly disbursements, made on a centralized basis, are approximately $650 million. The number of checks written is about 420,000 per year, or 35,000 a month. All accounting records are maintained on a large-scale, third-generation computer.

Objectives. The internal auditor was interested in determining that disbursements were properly supported, reasonable, justified, and economical. In order to see that controls over disbursements are operative on a continuing basis, he performs interim checks of disbursements during the year. In addition to the review of high-dollar, sensitive items, he makes selective tests of low-dollar items (items under $5000). Although stratified sampling could have been used, the following illustrates the use of statistical sampling with the computer in testing the low-dollar items only.

Statistical Sampling Plan. With a universe to test of about 350,000 items under $5000, the internal auditor reviewed prior experience in the audit of disbursements and found that the maximum error in tests of any of the attributes examined was 5%. With an expected error rate of 5% and a desired precision of ±2% at the 90% confidence level, the sample size required was 321.[5] Using systematic sampling, every 1090th item would be selected (350,000 ÷ 321).

Computer Selection. A flowchart was prepared and given to the programmers for developing a program to select the items during normal processing of vouchers. The program was prepared at the time the system was being developed for the computer, thus minimizing changes required. An interval of 545 was used in order to select twice the number of items (642, or 2 × 321) in the sampling plan. This was done to provide additional items in case the auditor wished to increase his sample. By looking at every other item selected by the computer, he would be examining 321 and could extend his sample if required without an additional computer run. A printout of the items selected was furnished to the internal auditor.

Coordination with Other Auditors. The selection of the first items in January was made at random jointly with the outside public accountants and government auditors in residence. The purpose of the joint selection was to assure objectivity. The results of the internal auditor's review of the vouchers

---

[5]See Arkin, *Handbook of Sampling for Auditing and Accounting*, p. 297.

were made available to both the public accountants and the government auditors, thus limiting the cash auditing required. Since printouts were made available monthly, the internal auditors could review disbursements on a continuing basis, thus pinpointing weaknesses in controls as soon as they occurred.

2. Statistical Sample of Personnel Management

The internal auditor in a large research and development organization was interested in expanding the audit of payroll to include attributes related to personnel management. Once the statistical sample was selected, these attributes could be incorporated in the audit program applied to each payroll check (sampling unit) selected.

Objective.   The objective of the statistical sample was first, to determine the accuracy of the total company payroll for the year, and second, to determine whether controls over personnel administration were adequate for the period.

Attributes.   In accordance with the objectives, each item on the payroll selected for test was verified by checking hours and rates, as well as payroll deductions, to underlying documents and records. In addition, factors relating to the individual throughout the personnel program cycle were evaluated, such as the basis for hiring, assignment, training and advancement, and utilization.

Statistical Sampling Plan.   Based on the prior year's experience and staff projections for the coming year, it was estimated that there would be approximately 104,000 annual payroll payments made for the 4000 average number of employees. With an expected error rate of 2% and a desired precision of ±1.25% at the 90% confidence level, a sample of 339 was selected.[6]

Selection.   Since all payroll checks are serially numbered, random numbers were selected between one and 104,000. The selection of the random numbers and the rearrangement of the numbers in sequence were done by use of a computer. As the payroll checks with the preselected numbers were written, they were automatically selected for interim audit work (about 28 per month).

Evaluation.   The error rates for attributes related to payroll accuracy were minimal, resulting in general acceptability of payroll amounts. Review of attributes related to general personnel management also disclosed the ef-

[6]Ibid., p. 296.

fectiveness of controls, except in the area of utilization. It was found that 10% of the employees paid in the sample had excessive idle time. At the 90% confidence level this represents 7.3 to 13.3% of the total number of payments for the year.[7] Analysis indicated that the employees with excessive idle time were charging the idle time to various indirect cost categories. Because sample results showed that the idle time was extensive, the results could be disclosed to management without the need for further sampling.

Analysis as to Cause. Review of the sample results indicated that management was not separately identifying idle time. Analysis indicated that certain types of research work had decreased during the year, and researchers who ordinarily charged their time direct were idle for long periods and were charging time to various indirect categories. Summary information was not provided management as to the extent of this type of idle time. Based on recommendations of the internal auditor, a special computer report was prepared, showing direct project workers by department who were idle for more than one month. This report was then used to facilitate certain management decisions, such as action required on work-load scheduling, hiring and termination policies, and pricing under changing conditions.

3. Statistical Sample of Facilities Management

As part of the audit of facilities in a manufacturing company, the internal auditor wished to test selectively internal controls over fixed assets. There were 5470 items of fixed assets on hand according to the property records, with a book value of $22.5 million. Previous audits had covered only specific segments, such as accuracy of depreciation, accuracy of property records, and verification of acquisitions and disposals.

Objective. The purpose of the statistical procedure was to test management decisions, review internal controls, and verify the accuracy of fixed-asset records.

Attributes. For each item selected in the statistical sample, the approach was to:

1. Review controls over the determination of need, acquisition, utilization, maintenance, and disposal. When items were acquired in prior years, reliance is placed on previous audit work, with current emphasis on savings through buying equipment now leased, or examining present use of the equipment.
2. Verify the accuracy of recording purchase, depreciation, transfer, and disposal.

---

[7]Ibid., p. 400, noninterpolated table.

3. Make physical examination of items, determining that they are on hand, and observe or test that they are properly maintained and in use.

Sampling Plan. Based on an expected error rate of not over 5%, with a precision of ±2.5% at the 90% confidence level, a sample size of 199 was drawn.[8] The expected error rate was based on the results of previous audits as well as potential deficiencies in areas not audited before.

Selection. The sampling unit was each item of equipment on hand during the year, both owned and leased. Each item of equipment was recorded on a separate IBM card. Using systematic sampling, each twenty-seventh card was selected for testing (total universe of 5470 divided by sample size of 199). Since there are approximately 145 IBM cards to the inch, a card would be selected every 0.19 inch by measuring off with a ruler.

Results. Minor deficiencies were noted in recording fixed asset transactions and in calculating depreciation. In addition there were 12 deficiencies in providing adequate documentation to support lease versus buy decisions. These represented a 6% error rate and, when projected to the universe at the 90% confidence level, an error rate between 3.6 and 9.5%.[9] A recommendation was made to improve documentation in support of these decisions.

Further analysis indicated that there were four examples of office equipment being leased when the period of the lease justified purchase. These represented a 2% error rate and, when projected at the 90% confidence level, an error rate between 0.7 and 4.5%.

The annual savings per year through purchase were $1000. These savings were projected using variables sampling to provide an estimate of the total annual savings on leased equipment. With a confidence of 90% it was estimated that the annual savings through purchasing rather than leasing equipment were between $19,309 and $35,719, and were most likely to be $27,514.[10] Based on the potential dollar savings a review was made of all lease agreements. Annual savings of $25,500 were obtained in equipment costs by changing from lease to purchase agreements. This amount was within the confidence limits disclosed by the sample.

Conclusions. The review included tests of controls in management areas, as well as in accounting, for items selected in the statistical sample. The internal auditor was thus able to obtain information about the facilities as a whole (universe), for the use of both management and the public accountant.

---

[8]Ibid., p. 297.
[9]Ibid., p. 388.
[10]Ibid., p. 456. Calculated by multiplying the standard deviation of $13.16 by the multiple in the table of 0.1140 and then projecting it to determine the range.

REVIEW QUESTIONS

1. Explain the advantages of using statistical sampling.
2. What is wrong with the examination of 10% of the items or dollars in an area, selected haphazardly?
3. Under probability theory, what percentage of the individual members of a distribution lie within plus or minus two standard deviations of the arithmetic mean?
4. In what type of sampling is the focus on "how much?"
5. How does one establish a starting point for a random number selection?
6. What is the danger of using systematic sampling?
7. What are some methods of stratification?
8. List some areas of statistical analysis useful to management in operational activities.
9. What types of decisions are faced by an internal auditor if errors are found in items selected for testing in a statistical sample?
10. List five techniques for efficient use of statistical sampling by internal auditors.

CASE PROBLEMS

Problem 9-1

Ann Simpson, senior auditor, was developing a sampling plan for auditing travel expenditures at the 58 branches of the company located throughout the state. The president of the company, Bryon White, had asked for an audit of travel vouchers because of allegations that employees were charging costs of personal entertainment to the company. "I don't believe my employees would do this," he told the general auditor, Barbara Johnson. "However, I would like you to check some of the branches, and give me an estimate of how many employees are putting personal expenses on travel vouchers company-wide.

Required. Help Ann Simpson develop a sampling plan to provided the information requested. What statistical sampling plan and selection technique should Simpson use?

Problem 9-2

Tim Holt, senior internal auditor, was summoned to the office of Bob Norwich, general auditor. Upon Holt's arrival Norwich said, "Tim, we've got a terrible problem and I have been unable to resolve it as yet. I met with the executive vice-president this morning to discuss your finding in the eastern division, which indicates a serious inventory shortage. When I told the EVP the magnitude of the problem, he gulped and said, 'Are you sure of your numbers?' I explained to him that we had used statistical sampling in arriving at the figures, and that we are 95% confident that our test data are representative of all of the items in the population, plus or minus 1%. He then told me that if he is going forward with such a significant revelation, he wanted us to be 100% certain, not 95. I told him the only way we could be 100% certain would be to review every item, which would be prohibitive in light of the current manpower crunch."

Tim Holt responded, "as you may recall, there were over a million line items in the population and to do a 100% test would take me to retirement and I'm only 29 years old. Did the EVP give us an alternative?" Norwich smiled and said, "He gave us an appointment for nine in the morning, to explain how he can have confidence in the information we have given him. Now it's up to you Tim, to put together a pitch that will sell him on stat sampling."

Required. What went wrong in the discussion between Norwich and the EVP? Help Tim Holt prepare a short presentation that will convince the EVP that the results of statistical sampling are reliable.

CHAPTER TEN

Internal Audit Reporting

Upon completing this chapter you should be able to:

- [ ] *Describe the internal audit reporting process*
- [ ] *Identify and explain the purposes of the various types of internal audit reports*
- [ ] *Identify and define the elements of an audit finding*
- [ ] *Describe the organization of a formal internal audit report and explain the contents of the major subdivisions*
- [ ] *Explain internal auditing's role in report follow-up*

PRINCIPLES AND ALTERNATIVES

Developing and issuing audit reports is one of the most critical phases of the internal auditing process. The Institute of Internal Auditors has emphasized the criticality of reporting by making it the subject of one of the earliest Statements on Internal Auditing Standards (SIAS).[1]

Reports are the major means by which individuals, both inside and to a limited extent outside the company, are made aware of the internal auditor's work and evaluate his contributions toward achieving company objectives. Reports also constitute the most enduring type of evidence about the total professional character of the internal auditing function. Effective reporting obviously depends on the quality of the work that is being reported. However, good internal audit work can be negated by ineffective reporting. The quality of reporting is, therefore, one of the major concerns of internal auditors at all levels of responsibility.

Reports reflect professionalism of internal audit function

[1]Statement on Internal Auditing Standards No. 2, *Communicating Results*, issued in February 1984, will be found in Appendix E. This SIAS should be studied as an integral part of this chapter.

We especially need to recognize that good reporting is more than just issuing a report on the results of a particular audit. The reporting process reflects the basic philosophy and related concepts of the total audit approach. This total approach includes the underlying objectives of internal auditing, the supporting strategies and major policies, the procedures used in conducting the audit work, and the caliber and performance of the internal auditors themselves. The character of these basic components ultimately determines the contents of reports.

Purpose of Reports

The internal audit report serves four important functions which must be considered carefully in performing the audit work and in determining how to write the report.

1. *Conclusions Based on Audit.* The report summarizes the evidence obtained during the audit, with the presentation of findings and conclusions. It represents the end result of the internal auditor's work.

2. *Disclosure of Conditions.* A summary of areas needing improvement is provided the organization through the report. Thus it can be viewed as an information device for management concerning operations of the organization. It is also viewed by some as an evaluation of performance, showing those areas which are performing well or not so well and the extent to which improvement is needed.

3. *Framework for Managerial Action.* The recommendations in the report are the internal auditor's conclusions as to actions which should be taken by management. Based on the conditions disclosed and causes identified, the recommendations serve as a framework for action in correcting deficiencies and/or improving operations. The report is also used as a reference when reviewing other areas of the company and in following up to determine whether recommended actions have been taken.

4. *Clarification of Auditee's Views.* Every effort should be made to reach agreement between the auditee and the internal auditor on all points covered in the audit report. However, there may be instances in which the auditee wishes to cite mitigating circumstances, or provide clarification on issues of nonconcurrence. A clear statement of the auditee's viewpoint, with comments by the internal auditor, helps to pinpoint the issues for management and provides a basis for arriving at decisions as to actions needed.

For Whom Is the Report Prepared?

Audit report is prepared for all management

The answer to this question appears quite simple—the report is prepared for management. But there are many levels of management including managers of the audited entity and management at higher levels and elsewhere in the organization to whom those managers are directly or indirectly responsible. Each management group has special interests and needs, and the question becomes one of what relative recognition of these types of needs best serves the company interest. In more specific terms, the question comes down to what the internal auditor's respective responsibilities are to the auditee versus the auditee's superiors. As we look at this question more closely, it becomes increasingly complex. However, we must understand it as best we can and deal with it as effectively as possible.

From the Standpoint of the Auditee. The auditee—that is, the organizational staff or line component that is being reviewed, and the responsible management group—is motivated by a combination of company and local entity interests. The auditee management knows that its ultimate welfare is closely related to the total company welfare, but auditee management knows also that its own rewards are largely determined by its own performance. Performance is a combination of operational results achieved and upper-level management's perception as to the extent local management actually contributed to the overall welfare of the company. Local management strives to look good to upper-level management. What this means with regard to the internal auditor is that local managers want help, but on a basis whereby as little as possible will be said or done to discredit them in the eyes of upper-level management. Local management would, in fact, like to have internal auditors work for them on a private professional basis.

Needs of local management include both self and company interests

The internal auditor wants to help local managers to do a more effective job. He knows that if he is to do so he must have their full cooperation and, as discussed in Chapter 7, a partner relationship with them. The internal auditor is, therefore, strongly motivated to deal with the audited entity in the way local management wants, and thus to achieve best what really counts most—more effective operations.

From the Standpoint of Upper-Level Management. Upper-level management consists of both (1) managers to whom the local manager has line responsibility and (2) staff managers to whom the local staff managers have a functional responsibility. The upper-level managers have a practical type of control need. They want to be apprised of significant deviations from established company policies and procedures. They also want to know of major operational problems and of important alternatives to carrying out the particular operational activities more effectively and more profitably. This is in part a need for protecting the entire company and in part a desire to be of the greatest service to operating managers. It is only natural then, that to achieve the desired control, higher-level management looks to the internal auditing function. The internal auditor wishes to provide these managers with the services they seek. Moreover, it is these upper-level managers who pass final judgment on the worth of the services of the internal auditor and

Upper level managers depend on internal auditors

who influence and ultimately have an impact on his compensation, organizational status, and overall progress within the company.

Managing the Conflict.   The starting point for a solution to the conflicting demands is to help both management groups understand the concerns and needs of each other with regard to internal audit services, and demonstrate to them that internal audit understands these needs and makes every effort to serve both groups. That is, internal audit needs to increase the level of tolerance and flexibility on each side. A second way in which the conflict can be minimized is through raising the level of what is considered sufficiently significant to warrant report coverage. Minor matters, which can and should be handled at the local level, can be eliminated from the report, thereby removing the irritations that come from involving higher-level managers. Another way to minimize the conflict can come through a determined joint effort between local managers and the internal auditor to work out needed action during the course of the audit. The general effect of all of the above actions is to move the internal auditor in the direction of the "service to local management" concept. This concept stops short only of recognizing that there is still an important final reporting responsibility to upper-level management.

Conflicting needs of various managers need reconciliation

Types of Reports

Internal audit information may be presented orally or in writing depending on the circumstances and the nature of the information. To some extent there will always be oral reporting as a means of supplementing written reports, and particularly when the written report is being presented to individuals having a need for more detailed information or other special needs. Oral reporting, therefore, serves a useful and legitimate purpose. It is recognized that it has the major limitations in that there is no permanent record and can result in misunderstanding. What is important, therefore, is that oral reporting be used judiciously and, if significant matters are involved, be followed by a written report. The more significant forms of reports are as follows:

Written reports should follow oral reports when significant matters are involved

Interim Reports.   A major use of interim reports is to cause early corrective action to be initiated when an audit finding shows that a serious ongoing problem exists. Other uses include making progress reports to local management or advising local personnel of changes in audit activities which impact operations. Interim audit reports are a good device to improve the total reporting process. They are frequently given orally.

Final Audit Reports.   Developing and issuing the final audit report is an integral part of the internal auditing process. The form and content of these reports vary widely, both as between individual audit assignments and individual companies. In some organizations they are quite brief and in others they contain considerable detailed information. They may be presented in many different ways, including the extent to which quantitative or financial data are included. We discuss the problems and alternatives associated with this most common type of report later in this chapter.

Summary Written Reports.   Summary reports highlighting the results of an internal audit project are frequently prepared for higher-level management. When the final report is quite lengthy summary reports serve to keep top management informed of audit activities without being burdened with unnecessary detail. Summary reports may be issued separately or as a part of the final report.

Approaches to Written Reports

As has been stated, the form and content of regular written reports will vary widely. We can, however, identify certain common approaches, and briefly appraise their merits.

1. *Encyclopedic Coverage.* Some internal audit reports strive to present a great deal of information about the activity that has been reviewed. The objective seems to be to provide an in-depth reference source to the audit report user. The information can be of a historical nature or pertain to the current situation. It may cover operational practices and results or may deal with financial information. The latter is more commonly done in the case of audit assignments covering the review of financial statements. The major question here is whether providing such reference type information is really a proper function of the audit report. This is an especially valid question when one considers the time and cost required to provide such detailed information. On balance this type of approach is not recommended unless specifically requested by management. *Encyclopedic coverage in report undesirable*

2. *Description of Audit Work.* Another approach that is sometimes adopted is to provide a great deal of information about the audit work actually carried out. Audit steps may be described as well as the scope of actual verification and testing. To some extent this coverage overlaps with statements of procedures contained in audit manuals. The question here is primarily how interested a reader of the report is in this procedural detail, and what purpose it really serves. It is believed that most users of the reports are willing and eager to rely on the competence of the internal auditor for those technical dimensions. On balance, therefore, such detailed accounts of technical auditing coverage should be excluded, or at least minimized.

3. *Detailed Explanations of Audit Findings.* A closely related approach of some internal auditors is to go into fairly voluminous detail about

the results of the various audit efforts. Although the coverage here may in some respects be impressive, it is again doubtful whether the lower level of items dealt with and the greater amount of detail serve a sufficiently useful purpose. There is, indeed, a very real possibility that the reader may be turned off by such an approach, and thus miss things that are really important. We, therefore, recommend the maximum summarization of audit findings that is possible.

Summarize information to extent possible

4. *Focus on Significant Issues.* The more commonly used approach in written reports is to focus on the really significant issues. Significant as a term used here means types of issues that have an important bearing on policies, operational approaches, utilization of resources, worker performance, and results achieved (or achievable). Higher-level company managers are interested primarily in problems that are of such a nature and scope that they wish to be informed and have the opportunity to contribute to solutions. These significant issues sometimes also relate to completed action, but in this case the issue would have to be still more significant to merit the actual reporting. The special advantage of this focus on significant issues is that higher-level managers can get the information they need without wading through excessive detail. It is the type of approach that leaders in internal auditing try to follow.

Reader of report concerned with significant issues

Elements of a Finding

The internal auditor must analyze the evidence gathered during an audit to determine what should be included in the audit report as audit findings. To facilitate this analysis a systematic process is most helpful. SIAS No. 2 (see Appendix E) recognizes the "Attributes Approach" to making the analysis. While not specifically stated in the SIAS, this approach is based on the premise that all well-developed internal audit findings contain five common attributes, as follows:

What should be?

Criteria.   Internal auditing is basically measurement and evaluation. The criteria are the standards against which an internal auditor measures the facts which he has discovered during a review. Some common internal auditing criteria are published policies, procedures, rules, regulations, objectives of the entity, industry standards, good business practices, etc.

What is?

Statement of Condition.   The statement of condition reflects the evidence the internal auditor discovered during the course of a review. In a deficiency finding, it is the facts discovered when the internal auditor observed that something is not as it should be. It is a brief description of the deficiency which needs to be corrected or situation which could be improved.

So what?

Effect.   When the *condition* is measured against the *criteria*, the difference is a deviation from the standard. The effect is the risk or exposure the audited entity faces because a situation exists which is not in agreement with the criteria. Some examples of the *effect* in an operational audit are uneconomical or inefficient use of resources, violation of law, funds being spent improperly, loss of potential income, not achieving objectives, and so forth.

Cause.   The cause is the reaon why the *condition* does not agree with the criteria. It is the underlying reason why the questionable action, lack of action, weakness, deficiency, or inadequacy occurred. The cause may be the result of inadequate communications, noncompliance with procedures, negligence or carelessness, lack of training, dishonesty, inadequate resources, unfamiliarity with requirements, and so forth.

Why did it happen?

Recommendation.   The recommendation flows from the previously identified cause. It is the internal auditor's opinion as to what action or actions should be carried out to correct or improve the *condition*. Workable solutions are often arrived at in conjunction with personnel of the audited entity.

What should be done?

The attributes can also be thought of as questions, as follows:

Attribute	In Question Form
Statement of Condition	What is?
Criteria	What should be?
Effect	So what?
Cause	Why?
Recommendation	What should be done?

An example of an internal audit finding with each attribute identified is shown in Exhibit 10-1.

Balanced Report Presentation

A significant amount of the internal audit effort is devoted to evaluating the efficiency, economy, and effectiveness with which management is accomplishing its objectives. This involves weighing both satisfactory and unsatisfactory conditions disclosed during the audit. When conditions are noted which need improvement, the finding should be stated with as few negative terms as possible, while encouraging management to take the needed action. The audit cannot be completely successful if the auditee is not receptive to the internal auditor and his ideas. Consequently, the internal auditor should adopt a positive reporting style that includes favorable as well as unfavorable comments and presents matters in perspective.

Reporting style should be positive

In providing balance in internal audit reports, the question is frequently asked: "How does one decide on the favorable comments to be included?" While the answer to this question cannot be laid down in precise terms, to

EXHIBIT 10.1.   Internal Audit Finding with Attributes Identified

Statement of Condition

A review of 210 purchase orders which had been sent to vendors in November 1985, revealed that in 96 instances neither freight nor discount terms were shown. A review of these 96 purchase orders indicated that in 10 instances discount and freight terms to which the company is entitled had not been granted by the vendors, resulting in additional costs of $3840.

Criteria

The Corporate Purchasing Manual, paragraph IIIA9c, specifies that buyers will complete each block on the purchase order form prior to issuing the purchase order to a vendor.

Effect

The absence of terms on a purchase order has two major disadvantages:

1. It fails to provide a reference for accounts payable personnel to insure that vendor terms are accurately reflected on invoices, and
2. It can easily indicate to those personnel subsequently involved in the handling of the transactions that the terms and conditions *not* displayed are not important.

Cause

The director of purchasing advised that in most instances the terms of the purchase are included in catalogs and on pricing contracts. Buyers, therefore, had been given permission to omit the terms from purchase orders. He was not aware whether the catalogs and contracts were readily available to accounts payable personnel. However, the internal audit disclosed that some vendors were not complying with catalog or contract terms or were not granting special concessions without a specific statement on the purchase order.

Recommendation

It is recommended that all information be included in every purchase order issued. This will provide a ready reference for accounts payable to verify that the company receives the terms of purchase agreed to between the vendor and buyer, and will demonstrate to clerical personnel the importance of terms to the company's financial welfare.

---

comment on improvements made since the last review and/or about a well-controlled operation, if deserved, would certainly be appropriate.

Providing Perspective.   Perspective is added by presenting the results of the audit accurately, completely, and professionally. The internal auditor should avoid the temptation to cite only those factors which support his conclusions and ignore those which distract from them. For example, perspective requires that when a deficiency is cited in terms of dollars, the total dollar amount involved in the records where the errors were discovered, also be included in the finding. The significance of the finding is made evident by this procedure. Also when deficiencies are disclosed in only part of an area examined, balance is added by reporting those areas examined in which no deficiencies were found.

Examples of the above where perspective has been added are:

Use perspective in reporting findings

Original	With Perspective
Inadequate screening procedures resulted in the payment of duplicate claims totaling $50,000.	Improved screening procedures could have helped reduce duplicate payments of $50,000 in processing claims totaling $10 million.
The policies and procedures used for estimating materials and computer costs were not adequate.	The policies and procedures used for determining salary, travel, equipment, and overhead costs were adequate to assure accurate estimates. However, procedural improvements were needed in order to develop sufficiently accurate estimates for materials and computer costs.

Reporting Accomplishments.   Reporting the auditee's accomplishments together with the noted deficiencies or areas with improvement potential can add much to the usefulness of the internal audit report as a management tool. Since the evaluation process involves the weighing of both satisfactory and unsatisfactory aspects of the operations reviewed, such information should be included in the report.

Showing Auditee Action.   In those instances where the auditee has taken or initiated corrective action while the review is in process, the audit report should reflect it.

Reporting Mitigating Circumstances.   Mitigating circumstances are usually factors relating to a problem or condition over which management has little or no control. Since these factors lessen management's responsibility for the condition, they should be reported as a part of the cause.

Including the Reply.   The auditee's reply to a finding may contain information which provides additional balance to the audit report. The auditee may indicate accomplishments and cite additional facts or mitigating circumstances. Also the auditee may indicate the action taken or in progress, to correct a deficiency. In instances where agreement has not been reached on a finding or recommendation the auditee should be given the opportunity to explain the basis for nonconcurrence.

Consider auditee comments

Improving Tonal Quality.   Good tonal quality is achieved by using positive and constructive words and ideas rather than negative and condemning language. Findings that begin with phrases such as "failed to accomplish," "did not perform," and "was inadequate" emphasize the negative rather than *Avoid negative statements*   the constructive aspects of the audit. The following examples illustrate how negative opening statements can be phrased in a positive, constructive manner:

Negative	Positive
The department failed in four of its training program operations.	Opportunities exist for strengthening controls in four training program operations.
The budgetary system was not adequate to assist management in the control of project funds.	Establishing a proper budgetary system would assist management in controlling project funds.

In addition, negative titles and captions should be avoided since they do not add to the finding and may misrepresent the actual situation. Thus a negative title such as "Inadequate Cash Controls" should be replaced by "Cash Controls" or "Need to Improve Cash Controls."

PREPARING AND FINALIZING THE AUDIT REPORT

Improving the Report Process

Skeleton Report.   During the early stages of the audit it is desirable to develop a framework for the report, filling in as much of it as possible. Information and statistics on the background of the area being audited can be gathered during the survey stage. This will assure that the needed information is obtained early in the audit and prevent delays in the final writing process. In addition the objectives and scope should be defined clearly at the start of the audit. These serve as useful guides for the audit staff in planning and carrying out the audit assignment.

As findings are developed and completed, they are inserted in the proper sections of the report, together with comments of the auditee.

Delegation of Writing.   Staff auditors should be given every opportunity to write the findings in areas in which they are auditing. This gives them the opportunity to obtain writing experience, which is so important to their *Report can evolve*   development. Also by using a report-oriented audit approach, the auditor *during audit*   obtains needed information for the report while he is performing the audit.

Supervisory Assistance.   The supervisor should become involved in the writing process early in the audit. He should review leads when developed to assure that there are sufficient criteria for a finding. He should check that the staff auditor prepares an outline of the finding in advance. He should discuss the possible causes and effects of the finding and obtain agreement as to how it will be developed. In some cases an approach of hypothesizing as to possible causes and then verifying them in the audit is useful.

The supervisor should also review working papers to determine whether there are any leads that have not been followed up by the auditor. This will prevent the need for developing findings late in the audit.

Discussion with Auditee. As findings are developed the auditor reviews them with company employees, soliciting ideas as to their validity. He also discusses possible causes with them and data needed to prove or disprove the condition. In some instances company personnel will assist in obtaining information to develop the findings. They will also provide useful feedback as to whether the auditor's facts are correct and whether he is on the right track. Areas of disagreement can be pinpointed and resolved.

Review findings with auditee as developed

Discussing findings with company personnel has another benefit—it helps to get agreement and implementing action. When agreement is reached, the auditor may be able to limit the amount of detail included in his finding, thus shortening the writing process.

Organizing the Written Report

An internal audit report may contain a wide range of information, however, as a minimum, it should reflect the purpose, scope, and results of the audit. The form and content of the report depend on the type of audit being reported and the preference of the internal audit organization. The internal audit organization's preference is often influenced by upper-level management. The report usually includes a number of sections the majority of which are discussed below. Exhibit 10.2. is an example of an internal audit report prepared in letter form.

Date of Report. The report should be dated at the time it is released. As a practical matter this is usually the date final approval has been given to the report by the general auditor and action is initiated to produce it in final form.

Addressee. Usually the report will be addressed to the manager who has direct responsibility for the company activity that was reviewed. In some instances, however, the review is made with the specific authorization and instruction of a higher-level manager, and the internal auditor may have been asked to report directly to that manager.

Opening Paragraph. It is standard practice to use the opening paragraph to state the nature and scope of the audit assignment as well as the period

EXHIBIT 10.2.   Illustrative Internal Audit Report

November 29, 1985

Mr. Bruce R. Weston
General Manager
Bright Products Division
The Wonder Corporation
Central City, Florida 33999

Dear Mr. Weston:

The scheduled operational review of the Brighton Products Division was conducted during the period October 14 to November 1, 1985. The review covered division operations during the fiscal year June 1, 1984 to May 31, 1985. It was conducted by Roger G. Wilson and Bruce A. White, of the internal auditing staff.

Scope

The review was made to determine whether internal controls within the division are adequate and operating as intended. Based on a survey at the outset of the review, we determined that the scope of this review should be limited to the supply function and related computer activities.

Summary of Major Issues

1. On May 31, 1985, inventories controlled by the supply department exceeded operating needs by $875,000.

2. User departments are being billed for computer time at a greater rate than necessary to support the operation of the computer department.

Findings and Recommendations

1. Supply Inventories.

Finding

Inventories on hand at May 31, 1985, exceeded established stock levels by $875,000. Further, during the year the stock overages averaged $650,000. This represents a $91,000 interest cost when computed at the current market rate of 14 percent. The excess inventory was caused by not recording unused stock returned from production and by ordering stock items in quantities which caused excessive stock levels. Although the records were adjusted at the end of the fiscal year to reflect physical counts, records used to establish quantities to be purchased during the year did not reflect the actual quantities on hand.

Recommendations

a. Procedures should be revised to provide for early recording of unused parts returned from production.
b. Supplies requisitioning should be monitored closely, to avoid purchasing overstocked items until the excess quantities have been depleted.

EXHIBIT 10.2.   Illustrative Internal Audit Report (*continued*)

2. Computer Billing Rates

Finding

At the end of the year the computer department had a reserve of $1,215,000, which represented overbilling of user departments. Had the billing rates been adjusted to reflect actual costs at the end of the fiscal year, income for the division would have increased by the amount of the reserve. The computer department manager advised that rates were not reduced in order to establish a reserve to cover potential increases in costs and to cover possible reduced usage in the future.

Recommendations

a. Procedures should be developed to adjust computer rates periodically to reflect actual operating costs.
b. The surplus should be credited to computer users and reflected in income.

Management Comments

Division personnel agreed with both findings and recommendations and initiated corrective action while the review was in progress. They stated, however, that with respect to excessive computer billing rates some reserve had to be maintained, but that they would reduce the balance to $75,000 for carryover to the next period.

Thank you for your support and the excellent cooperation received from division personnel during the review.
Respectfully submitted,

Charles W. Reiber
General Auditor

Distribution

R. C. Gulick	Group Vice-President
J. R. Whelan	Vice President, Finance
G. E. Bender	Vice President, Purchasing
W. R. Timms	Vice President, Production
J. R. Miller	Manager, Administrative Services
P. R. Thoms	Thoms, Thoms, and Company, Certified Public Accountants

covered in the review. In some organizations the names of the internal auditors who conducted the review will also be included. Finally, some organizations believe it necessary to include one or two additional sentences describing the major parts of the audit work, but any substantial detail of this nature should be avoided.

Background Paragraph.   This paragraph traditionally covers the general nature of the operational activity involved in the review. Such information as action taken on recommendations in previous audits and whether the review was a regular or special audit may also be included. This paragraph is background information for the reader and is not intended to be complete reference in any sense.

Summary of Key Issues.   When there are a substantial number of significant issues dealt with in the report it is sometimes desirable to list the individual issues early in the report. This enables the reader to inform himself quickly as to the nature and scope of the issues, without a detailed examination of the entire report.

Summary evaluations
usually desirable

Summary Evaluation.   It is also useful to provide a summary evaluation of the effectiveness of the operational performance of the particular company component or activity. This evaluation is usually expressed in general terms. Such comments as "the objectives and goals of the activity are being met" and/or "the activity is functioning as intended," are frequently used. In some organizations the evaluation becomes more specific. In three instances known to the authors, it takes the form of specific adjective ratings—excellent, good, marginal, and unsatisfactory. In these instances the audit report is being used primarily as an instrument of control by higher-level managers. Even in these organizations, however, there seem to be problems in applying this approach to all types of audit reviews, and in any event a considerable price is paid through the defensive posture that such an approach induces on the part of the auditees.

Presentation of Individual Issues.   The main body of the report is made up of a series of subsections dealing with individual issues of special significance. The manner recommended for the presentation of each issue is as follows:

Four key steps
for presenting each
selected issue

1. *Heading.* The heading is a thumbnail description of the issue that follows. It is much like a newspaper headline which is used to capture the reader's interest. Examples are "Quality Considerations in Production Process" or "Control over Personal Computers."
2. *Finding.* Under this heading the major finding of the internal auditor will be briefly described and interpreted. This will include the condition found to exist, the particular standard or standards not being met, the significance of the resulting deficiency or area needing improvement, and judgment as to the cause of the out of tolerance condition. The section may be relatively brief or expanded, depending on the complexity of the particular issue. The objective should be to include only such information as will be directly pertinent to the conclusion or recommendation which follows, and to be as brief as possible.
3. *Conclusion or Recommendation.* The previous description of the finding will now provide the basis for a conclusion or recommendation.

Conclusion as used here is a final statement that is important even though it does not involve a further recommended action. The most sought-after type of conclusion is that local management has already taken, or has agreed to take, certain corrective or improvement type action. Such a conclusion is then only to keep higher-level managers informed of the problem and its solution. A conclusion may be limited to a statement that management recognizes the existence of the problem and is continuing its study of what should be done.

Conclusion or recommendation is key judgment

In most cases there will be a specific recommendation made by the internal auditor, and preferably in conjunction with local management, to resolve the issue. If a recommendation is made and the internal auditor and local management are not in agreement, a decision must then be made by higher-level authority. This places higher-level authority in the awkward position of having to overrule either the local management or the internal auditor. The internal auditor should make every effort to resolve such matters at the local level, using higher-level authority only as an extreme last resort. If, in the unfortunate event, a meeting of the minds cannot be reached, the local management position should be included in the audit report.

Resolve disagreements to maximum extent possible

4. *Auditee Comments.* This section covers the reaction of the auditee to the audit findings. As indicated previously, where there are differences of opinion or mitigating circumstances, the report should include the auditee's comments with additional comments by the auditor as needed.

Closing Paragraph and Signature. Finally, there should be a closing paragraph in which the internal auditor expresses his appreciation of the cooperation and assistance received during the course of the audit. The report should be signed by the director of internal audit or his designee. If the report is *not* forwarded with cover letter or memorandum, it should also contain a phrase such as, "Respectfully submitted," followed by the appropriate signature.

Distribution

The director of internal audit or his designee decides who should receive the final audit report. Usually it is sent to the head of each of the units audited and to those officials in the organization who are able to ensure that audit results are given proper consideration. Higher-level individuals may be sent only summary reports as mentioned earlier in this chapter. Reports may also be distributed to other parties such as the external auditors and the audit committee of the board of directors. These decisions should be made with great care, giving consideration to the nature and scope of the particular report.

Use care in distribution of report

Validation of Findings and Conclusions

Among the important aspects of the internal audit reporting process are the steps taken to validate the adequacy and accuracy of the reported findings, as well as the soundness of the related recommendations, prior to the finalization of the report. The basic foundation for this validation is the audit work and the reviews that are made by the internal auditing staff. But this foundation needs to be supplemented by certain types of review and confirmation with auditee personnel, ultimately including auditee top management. The benefits of this supplemental validation are twofold. First it provides a crosscheck on the accuracy, completeness, and quality of the audit work performed. Important facts may have been overlooked or erroneously interpreted. There may also be other factors affecting the particular matter that are known only to certain people. The exposure to the auditee thus provides an important check on whether the findings and recommendation will stand up under subsequent scrutiny. The second benefit of the review is to induce a partner relationship with local management. The opportunity for this kind of participation creates both a cooperative spirit and a more likely commitment to working out the best solutions to problems. If such a review is not made with local management, there is a real possibility that they may be embarrassed and embittered by having their bosses informed of audit results at the same time as they are, through the medium of the final report. In this event, the internal auditor is likely to find an uncooperative auditee when he returns for the next audit.

Closing Conference. While the previously mentioned type of validation goes on to a major extent at all stages of the review, one of the most important ways in which this is effected is through the closing conference. This closing conference takes place at the close of the field work and just preceding the planned departure of the field audit personnel. It includes the top members of the audit group and the top members of local management. At the conference major findings and proposed recommendations are reviewed. Frequently also the next-higher-level audit manager will travel from headquarters to the field location to participate in this conference. To the extent that agreement has already been reached between audit personnel and local company personnel on particular matters, an opportunity is now provided to inform the top manager and to secure his further agreement. At the same time any question still open can be resolved. Sometimes the participants will have drafts of report coverage for review, but in most cases the discussion will be based on preliminary memoranda or point listings. It is possible that the discussions here may require additional audit work, but only in unusual circumstances.

The closing conference is an excellent opportunity for the internal auditor to confirm the soundness of the audit results and to make such modifications as seem to be justified. It is also an opportunity to demonstrate the constructive and professional type of service the internal auditor is seeking to provide. It can also be a major means for building sound partnership relations with the auditee. The objective should be to get as much agreement as possible so that more can be reported as completed action, and less as recommendations for necessary later follow-up. Other aspects relating primarily to the relations with people were discussed in Chapter 7 and should be reviewed to achieve the maximum benefits from this major auditee contact.

Reviewing of Draft Reports.   As previously noted, the closing conference may in some cases be based on drafts of text that will be included in the final reports. In some companies also there may be a further phase where draft reports are forwarded to the local management for their review and comment, prior to the finalization of the report. The use of draft reports in closing conferences has certain major disadvantages. These disadvantages are primarily the danger that the discussion will center unduly on words rather than on the substantive issues. In addition, the later independence to make modifications, including the usually necessary editing, is importantly restricted. On balance, therefore, it would seem best to avoid the use of draft material at the closing conference stage.

The submission of draft reports to the auditee management at a later stage has merit through the demonstration of genuine consideration for the auditee. However, there are again certain significant disadvantages. The first one is that the internal auditor tends too much to become the captive of the auditee as to the way thoughts are expressed and particular words used. The finalization of reports is then more likely to become a special kind of game. This leads to the second disadvantage, which is that there is excessive delay in finalizing the report. A major part of the effectiveness of the report is the extent to which it is issued promptly. Again on balance, therefore, it is believed that the closing conference provides an adequate basis for the finalization of the report at the headquarters office. This would not of course preclude telephone conversations during the finalization stage to confirm particular facts and interpretations.

Review of draft reports by auditee can pose problems

Following Up

The "Standards for the Professional Practice of Internal Auditing", general Standard 440, "Follow-up" states that "Internal auditors should follow up to ascertain that appropriate action is taken on reported audit findings." The guideline for this standard (.01) indicates that "Internal auditing should determine that corrective action was taken and is achieving the desired results, or that management or the board has assumed the risk of not taking corrective action on reported findings."

In the past there was general concern that for the internal auditor to follow up on audit findings placed him in the role of policeman and tended to conflict with his ongoing partner relationship with the auditee. In many

Internal auditor shares follow-up responsibility with management

companies, therefore, the internal auditor played no specific role after the report was released other than to respond to questions and to review again the situation at the time of the next audit assignment. In other organizations the responsibility to follow up was placed in another office, usually the finance department or some neutral administrative service group. In these instances the internal auditing department was, in fact, the reviewing authority, but an effort was made to mask internal auditing's participation.

Today many modern internal audit organizations have assumed the responsibility for following up as set forth in the Standards, and make this activity a part of the internal auditing process. Local management should be advised at the outset of the review that to follow up is a responsibility of internal auditing as a function of completed staff work. If proper relationships are established with operating personnel during the course of the audit and audit reporting is in a professional and positive tone, following up can then be accepted by operating people as a natural extension of the internal audit work itself. At the same time management should recognize its own basic organizational responsibilities.

Criteria for Effective Report Presentation

It is the internal auditor's responsibility to produce a report that is readable, understandable, and persuasive. The objective is to have a report that will command the attention of the managers who have the responsibilities for the various operational activities, and to induce them to press for appropriate action. The objective also is for a report that will build respect for the internal auditing effort. These professional criteria include the following:

Checklist to assure effective report presentation

1. *Professional Tone*. Professional tone avoids excessive casualness on the one hand and stilted formality on the other. It reflects dignity, perspective, and objectivity. It denotes the professional level and stature of the internal auditor.

2. *Accuracy*. Individual statements and related data must be accurate. Moreover, they must meet the standards of reasonableness, considering the complexity of what is being covered. There is probably nothing that can be so damaging to the internal auditor's image as the later discovery of an erroneous statement of fact, the inclusion of erroneous data, or unreliable estimates.

3. *Courtesy and Tact*. We need to remember that people involved in the findings and recommendations will be sensitive as to any reflection on their performance. By being courteous and tactful one can do much to neutralize this sensitivity.

4. *Consideration*. Closely related is the ability to show proper consideration for the people involved. Where people have tried hard they appreciate having this recognized, even if they have failed.

5. *Persuasiveness*. Everything that is said should be handled in a way that will provide the proper setting and subsequent motivation to

take the needed types of action. The key ingredients here are logic and fairness.

6. *Sentence Structure*. We need to avoid long and dangling sentences. Simple and shorter sentences are more easily understood, and hence are more effective.

7. *Paragraphing*. The thoughts expressed need to be arranged in paragraphs that deal with designated segments of that thought. Paragraphs that are too long are discouraging and hence resisted.

8. *Choice of Words*. Care in selection of the right words will be rewarding. We want words that reflect the particular shades of meaning desired, that do not have special emotional content, and that are not stereotyped.

9. *Good Grammar and Spelling*. Mistakes in grammar and spelling both distract and annoy the reader. There is then the risk that the force of the impact of the message on the reader will be undermined.

10. *Physical Processing and Binding*. The needed physical standards of a good report include accuracy and attractive physical arrangement of text material, quality reproduction, and accuracy of report page assembly. There is also a need for a quality cover of a uniform character, with an adequate label describing the audit assignment and the time period or date involved. A distinctive color for the binders also makes for easier identification when used in connection with other company reports.

Reporting in Perspective

While the final payoff of the internal auditing process is the action taken by company personnel to increase the overall effectiveness and profitability of the company operations, a major means by which that action is achieved is the background, development, and execution of good reports. Reporting is a combination of technical skills and the ability to communicate audit results to people in a way that will best assure their acceptance and active support. The importance of this part of the internal auditor's work in terms of service potential underlines the desirability of the general auditor and his associates of giving it the most careful attention. It means especially that the general auditor should himself be actively involved. It means also that all levels of the internal auditing staff should think in terms of ultimate report needs. In this connection the problems of report development should also be given proper attention in training programs.

Reports show character of internal auditor

The written report thus is a major tool of the internal auditor for greater management service. It is at the same time his credential when the report is subsequently circulated, referred to, and implemented. It is usually one of the most important ways in which the reputation of the internal auditing department is established. It follows, therefore, that reports should be prepared with special care. It follows also that the department's influence will be better served by issuing better reports, even though this may mean that fewer reports will be released.

Concluding Statement to Part One

With this chapter we complete our discussion of the basic foundation aspects of internal auditing. These ten chapters are applicable to the actual operating work of the internal auditor to be discussed in the chapters that follow. The sections in Part One should be reviewed from time to time in connection with the considerations of the new material.

REVIEW QUESTIONS

1. Why is good reporting more than just the preparation of the reports themselves?
2. Discuss the use of oral reports in internal auditing. What are the disadvantages of oral reports?
3. What are some of the criteria of an audit finding? What can be used if there are no definitive criteria?
4. Summarize your understanding of the use of the common attributes approach to developing internal audit findings.
5. Should the internal auditor include recommendations in a finding or should he let management decide what should be done?
6. Why is it important to provide positive comments in an internal audit report when a department is found to be operating well?
7. What are the special techniques which can be used to provide balance in the report presentation?
8. Discuss the advantages of starting to write the report during the course of the audit.
9. How should the internal audit report be organized?
10. What responsibility does the internal auditor have for following up to see that action has been taken on findings?

CASE PROBLEMS

Problem 10-1

Joanne Thompson, head of the marketing department, asked Bill Jansen, internal auditor, if he would eliminate a finding on the basis that Thompson had become aware of the problem six months ago and was planning to do something about it. She said, "I always thought that internal auditors should write up only new items that we are not aware of."

Required. How should Jansen respond to Thompson?

Problem 10-2

Sandra Johnson, internal auditor at the Whitter plant, was reluctant to develop findings unless there was a dollar cost savings. Although her reports had excellent findings, she often disregarded leads of a procedural nature. In addition she did not develop the cause of deficiencies. On the other hand Robert Bates, internal auditor at the Murietta plant, reported detailed procedural findings as well as incidents of noncompliance of a minor nature. He believed that cost savings were incidental to having effective controls and complying with company policies.

Required.   Do you approve of either of these approaches, and if not, why?

PART TWO

Operational Areas

CHAPTER ELEVEN

Introduction and Basic Financial Control

Upon completing this chapter you should be able to:

☐ *Describe the controls necessary for properly receiving, handling, and maintaining custody of cash*

☐ *List the special control aspects of cash disbursements*

☐ *Explain the major control considerations in generating, administering, and disposing of receivables*

☐ *Explain payables controls as they relate to generation, administration and payment*

☐ *Describe basic internal control for payrolls*

☐ *Explain the internal auditor's interest in basic accounting activities*

AUDIT APPROACH FOR OPERATIONAL AREAS

Nature and Scope of Operational Areas

The modern internal auditor is primarily concerned with the operational areas in the organization of which he is a part. These operational areas will vary among individual organizations, depending on the kinds of products produced and services offered. These areas will also vary, depending on the way the particular organization chooses to conduct its operations. There are, however, a range of types of activities that are carried out in the typical business organization, and to a considerable extent in all kinds of organizations. The need therefore, is to understand these various types of operational activities and then to utilize that understanding as a basis for developing a program for effective review. The chapters in Part Two deal with these commonly encountered types of activities and provide guidance for the related operational reviews.

Operational areas are primary concerns of internal auditors

General Approach to Be Followed

The development of any audit program and the carrying through of the related internal audit review must, if it is to be truly effective, be based on an adequate and effective thought process. We believe that we can contribute best to that thought process by raising the right kind of questions. This means that while some descriptive and directive material is always necessary, the major emphasis will be on the nature of the more significant types of problems that are likely to be encountered. In that sense the material is intended to be provocative rather than prescriptive.

Manner of Treatment for Each Type of Operational Activity

Each operational activity has special character

Each type of operational activity that is reviewed by the internal auditor will have its own special character and unique aspects and these differences will necessarily have to be recognized. However, as far as possible, we plan to deal with each operational activity in the same manner in terms of general approach. We first describe the general nature of the particular activity, with emphasis on the function served and the objectives to be achieved. To the extent possible we also look at each activity in terms of the major stages of the operational cycle. Second, we look at the activity in terms of its major control points. As we will see, the identification of these major control points—linked as they necessarily are to the way we structure the various subobjectives—can usually be approached in alternative ways. There is also the further problem of controls within controls. As a third step we cover any special types of problems which exist in the case of that particular operational activity but which have not previously been discussed. Finally, as a fourth step we move to an examination of the internal auditor's specific role in connection with the activity. The purpose of the uniform approach is, on the one hand, to induce a consistent effort as respects each operational area, and on the other, to provide greater ease of reference for the reader. In all cases there is the common objective to find all possible means of extending the range of management service on the part of internal auditors.

Audit Guides

While the detailed discussions of the various operational areas are intended to provide substantial assistance to the practitioner in developing audit programs for specific situations, there can be some additional benefit in restating some of this material in the form of specific audit guides. Such audit guides cannot provide the depth coverage of the detailed discussions, but they can serve as a convenient summary-type reference.

Use audit guides as summary references

The audit guides will generally be of two types:

1. Specific kinds of audit actions to be taken
2. Questions regarding individual aspects of the operational process being reviewed

The first type will necessarily be quite general and will especially need to be adapted in the individual situation, both for the way the particular activity is actually being operated and to reflect the auditor's judgment as to the extent of the particular test or other audit action. The second is a useful type of approach to open up a line of inquiry that is appropriate in the individual area or subarea involved. Needless to say, it is not intended that there just be a "yes" or "no" answer. The result desired is careful investigation and critical appraisal, with the subsequent determination of any significant deficiencies, and the opportunities for bettering the operation in some worthwhile manner.

It needs to be recognized also that audit guides can be expanded to almost any level of detail and that the extent of detail actually presented represents an unavoidable compromise between possibilities and practicabilities. Additionally there is unavoidably some overlap between the various items.

Relation of Audit Guides to Scope of Review. As we have seen previously, an operational activity can usually be reviewed as a single functional activity or can be made a part of a broader review of an integrated operational location. For example, purchasing is an activity that can be approached on a company basis or as part of a broader field operation, or in some combination of the two. If undertaken on a company or total functional basis, the emphasis will most likely be on the broader company-wide policies, and on the type of approach being made to the more important purchasing management problems. Another variation of this functional approach may also take place at a subsidiary or divisional level. In either case there may be some review of the actual purchasing activities at a number of individual field locations.

Adapt audit guides to selected audit scope

The other type of approach will be that of examining the purchasing activity at a particular field location as a part of the total operations carried on at that particular field location. This situation is good from the standpoint that all the various types of operational activities are seen in an actual working relationship.

An intermediate type of approach will be the examination of the purchasing activities only at a particular field location. The size of the overall operations at that field location may make this a practical necessity. The audit guides presented cut across all of the three approaches and will necessarily have to be drawn on in a manner appropriate to the scope of the particular review being made.

Types of Audit Guides Applicable to All Operational Areas. In developing audit guides for the various types of operational activity there are many specific guides that cover similar types of inquiry, even though the individuals and organizational units are different. To avoid significant duplication we are including certain standard audit guides at this point. This will make it possible to refer to these standard guides as we deal with the audit guides for individual operational areas, and then to supplement them as necessary.

AUDIT GUIDES

Common to All Operational Areas

I. Introductory
  A. The nature of audit guides as broad guidelines to the development of definitive audit programs should be recognized.
  B. The entire audit program needs to be adapted to the functional or organizational scope of the review.
    (*Note:* The audit guides will usually refer to the activity reviewed as a department regardless of whether the activity being reviewed is a functional activity or an integrated operational entity.)

II. Preparatory Activities
  A. At Headquarters
    1. Discuss timing and scope of planned review with the officer to whom the manager of the department reports. Determine if there are any questions or suggestions.
    2. Review reports, working papers, and subsequent development aspects in audit files covering last review.
    3. Determine what other individuals should be contacted before beginning the actual review, and arrange and complete such contacts. Determine if there are any questions or suggestions.
    4. Make such advance arrangements with the department as are appropriate—living accommodations, work space, needed supporting actions, etc.—depending on the site location.
  B. At the Office of the Manager of the Department
    1. Explanation of scope of planned review.
    2. Determination of manager's concept of his operations, its role, objectives, and special problems.
    3. Determine if there are any questions or suggestions.

III. Organizational Factors
  A. Organizational Relationships of the Department with Other Company Activities
    1. To whom does the head of the department report?
      a. Is this reporting satisfactory in terms of that individual's other responsibilities?
      b. Is the organizational level sufficiently high?
    2. Establish that the department is independent of the other company activities from which it receives input and to which it provides output.

3. Obtain and appraise for adequacy all statements of mission, organizational purpose, and major policy relating to the department.
4. To what extent is the responsibility for various types of activities by the department made clear?
5. To what extent do committees or other organizational components participate in the control over policy?
6. To what extent is the function decentralized to other operational components, with only a functional reporting responsibility to the central department? Are the responsibilities clearly stated? Is necessary coordination adequately specified?

B. Organizational Relationships within the Department
1. Obtain and review a copy of the organization chart for the department. Are the assignments of responsibility clear and reasonable for effective internal control?
2. If the department is decentralized on a line basis, review and appraise the manner in which responsibilities are assigned and coordinated.
3. Review and appraise the adequacy of supporting job descriptions.
4. Review and appraise the adequacy of manuals covering policy and procedures.

IV–IX.   Operational Activities
To be developed, as required, for each operational activity.

X. Overall Appraisal of Departmental Effectiveness
A. Examination of Reports Rendered
1. To appraise adequacy of scope.
2. To confirm accuracy of data being reported.
3. Adequacy of backup for reported results.
B. Program of Goal Achievement
1. Adequacy of program for establishing and updating operational goals.
2. Extent of achievement of projected goals.
3. Extent of best utilization of available resources.
C. Relations with Other Company Activities
1. Adequacy of coordination with other company activities to achieve operational effectiveness and maximum company profitability.
2. Evidence of close relationships with higher-level management for maximum contribution to overall planning and performance.
D. Relations with Outside Parties
1. Evidence of efforts to relate effectively to outside parties in current operations.
2. Adequacy of effort to exploit longer-term dimensions of achieving greater mutual profitability.

    E. Appraisal of People Utilization
1. Levels of turnover.
2. State of morale.
3. Order and efficiency.
4. Cost performance.
5. Proper use of qualifications of personnel.
6. Effectiveness of key personnel.

    F. Appraisal of Fraud Control Efforts
1. Are fraud potentials adequately considered by the company, both as respects fraud prevention and to minimize temptations to individuals?
2. Have particular cases of fraud detection been properly handled in accordance with company policies and procedures and general sound business practice? Has proper consideration also been given to the need for modified procedures to avoid similar future developments?
3. Did the internal auditing department provide all possible assistance to other individuals in the handling of fraud investigations currently in progress?

    G. Extent of Major Problem and Opportunities
1. What, if any, are the major areas of difficulty? What are the causes and possible remedies?
2. What are the major areas of improvement? What action is needed?

BASIC FINANCIAL CONTROL

Nature of the Financial Process

This chapter and Chapter 14 will deal with the financial operations that normally are the responsibility of the finance department in a modern business organization. In this chapter we are concerned with the basic operational processes that are in a very real sense part of the total concerns of operational auditing. In the later chapter we will be concerned with a higher-level type of financial policy that is linked more closely to major management decisions and related management policy. We see these financial operations at both levels as part of the continuing concern of the modern operationally oriented internal auditor.

Rule of Reason for Financial Controls

A general word needs to be said about the application of controls in the basic financially oriented operations of the company. We begin always with stating the kind of control we would ideally have in every individual situation.

Whether that kind of control is actually practicable in terms of balancing costs and benefits is, however, a further question. In some situations geographical factors may make it necessary that a single individual carry out combined activities which under normal circumstances should be separated. In other situations the volume of a particular activity may be so small that it is simply not realistic in a practical business sense to hire additional personnel to achieve an otherwise desirable distribution of responsibilities. It is important not only that we understand the bases of the most effective control and use them as guides, but also that we evaluate the degree of implementation in terms of the practical aspects of the individual situation. What we actually do is to get as close to proper principles as we can within the limitations of each situation. The philosophy needs to be kept in mind especially as one reads this chapter.

Ideal guides not practicable in all situations

CASH PROCESSES

From a financial control standpoint cash is of special interest and concern because of the fact that in its most basic form it is the most transferable, and from a risk standpoint the most vulnerable type of item. Because of the greater risks involved there is the greater need for protection and control. There is also the ever-continuing objective to minimize the extent of the problem by eliminating the use of cash to the extent practicable. At the same time there are important managerial dimensions of using cash in the most effective manner. For all these reasons the various cash processes are of major concern to the management-minded internal auditor.

Cash is the most vulnerable area

Sources of Cash

A discussion of the cash processes starts most logically with an identification of where and why cash is received in a particular company situation. In each case we can properly ask ourselves the question of whether this is necessarily so or whether it might be done differently. For example, is it really necessary that salesmen accept cash from customers? Or if there must be collections, do they have to be in cash? Perhaps, however, cash is best in terms of accelerating and maximizing collections. On the other hand, we might either urge (but not require) a different procedure, and in certain cases actually require it. The important thing is that the reviewer critically appraise each situation and determine what degree of compromise from a control standpoint is justified because of other operational considerations.

In most situations the sources of cash also lend themselves to another type of control. This control is the extent to which estimates can be made of the amount of cash that should be received from the different sources. This does not take the place of regular records of claims which must be ultimately liquidated by cash received—as, for example, accounts receivable—but it supplements such records. Thus we might have initial expectations as to the amount of the cash collections to originate at a certain point at particular times. In cases where there are lesser degrees of control, the estimate of what ought to be becomes all the more important. An example of the latter would be miscellaneous cash sales, or perhaps service fees.

Receiving of Cash

The receiving of cash as a phase of the total cash process can be defined in various ways. As a minimum it covers the *first* receival of the cash from any party outside the company. Thereafter it blends with the handling of cash, as the cash received moves internally toward the centralized control which is normally exercised by a company. There is thus some unavoidable overlap, requiring a consideration of the total span of the cash process. It will be useful, however, to describe first the key principles of control which apply partially or completely to cash receipts. These controls focus both on the outside party, to be sure that we receive cash which should be received, and on the employee, to be sure that cash received is not improperly diverted.

Controls over cash receipts
focus on accountabilities

1. *Accountability should be established at the earliest possible time.* The sooner we can bring cash received under control the better. This is accomplished by establishing the best possible kind of record of initial accountability. A common example would be the issuance of a serially numbered cash receipt, with one copy to the outside party. Another example would be the ringing up of the transaction on a cash register. Or a serially numbered ticket of some kind might be issued in exchange for the cash received.

2. *Relief of internal accountabilities should be tied to the cash receipts to the extent practicable.* Ideally, the receipt of the cash, which establishes a new accountability, will be linked to the relief of a previously existing accountability. Illustrative would be the collection of an account receivable. Another illustration would be the sale of merchandise controlled on an item-by-item inventory basis, where the company employee must account for inventory or cash.

3. *Controls should be instituted to assure collection for services provided.* The first requirement here is that the customer pays for a service he is receiving. In some cases this might be a cash sale slip or a ticket, without which the customer could not receive a service. This might also need to be supplemented by physical protection over merchandise or restricted entry to areas where services are rendered, as in the case of a theatre. Internally the control might require the segregation of responsibilities, as where one person sells the tickets or issues the particular authorization, and another person collects the ticket or authorization.

4. *The outside party should be utilized where possible as a further control.* In some situations the presence of the customer can serve to some extent to check on the action of the employee. For example, the customer's presence will help provide assurance that the employee rings up a cash receipt on a cash register.

5. *Consolidation of cash receiving points.* From a control standpoint the fewer the number of cash receiving points, the more effective the control will be. Also the consolidation of the cash receiving, with the greater volume at the fewer points, makes it possible to separate responsibilities to a greater extent between different individuals. Obviously these benefits must be weighed against the needs of properly servicing customers or other parties involved.

Fewer cash receiving points provide better controls

6. *Cash receipts should be separated from cash disbursements.* There is frequently the pressure to utilize portions of the cash received to cover current expenditures of one kind or another. Under normal circumstances this pressure should be resisted. More effective control and cleaner accountabilities are possible if the cash receipts and cash disbursement processes are completely separated and each is controlled by different means.

7. *Cash receipts to be channeled intact and promptly to the central cash depositories.* Closely related to the preceding principle is the desirability of depositing, or otherwise transferring, the cash received intact for the specified day or other period, and as promptly as is practicable. For example, a day's receipts should normally be deposited intact as soon as possible after the cutoff for the day. This is important for several reasons. First, a delay in deposit results in a greater risk of theft or diversion. Second, checks might be good now but not at a later point of time. Third, it is important to be able to identify a particular deposit with a given period of time. Finally, as we shall discuss later at greater length, undeposited cash is idle cash and is not contributing to the best possible utilization of corporate resources.

Cash received should be deposited intact

8. *Accountabilities should be properly established for all transfers.* Since the accountability for cash should be fixed at all times, it is important when cash is transferred that the accountability of the transferor be properly relieved and that the new accountability of the transferee be clearly established. This is normally accomplished by some type of a cash receipt or transfer record.

9. *Records covering accountabilities should be independently operated.* The records by which the accountabilities for cash are established and controlled should be maintained by persons who are independent of the persons charged with the direct accountability. The latter persons should not have access to the records and hence not be able to improperly relieve their own accountabilities. Checks should

Records should be separate from handling

be made periodically by an independent person to assure that cash has been properly handled and accounted for.

Cash Handling and Custody

The handling of cash, as has previously been noted, is interwoven to some extent with both the receiving and disbursement phases. There are, however, certain additional control aspects which can be best considered under the heading of cash handling and custody.

1. *Physical safeguards should be adequate.* The types of physical safeguards needed in individual situations will depend on the amounts of cash normally on hand and the extent of the risks that exist. In certain cases locked cabinets may be adequate; in other cases small safes are needed; and in still other cases the most elaborate type of burglar proof vaults will be needed. These facilities then must be actually used. The access to these facilities must also be controlled through the care with which keys and combinations are made available. During operational periods the area used by the cashier needs to be adequately sealed off by cages or separately partitioned portions of office quarters. Finally, when cash is transferred there must be suitable protection, depending on the scope of the exposure.

2. *Adequacy of insurance coverage.* Cash on hand is subject to the risks of fire and burglary. Normal business prudence requires that these risks be covered by insurance at adequate levels.

Protect custody exposure if at all possible

3. *Cash on hand should be kept at minimum levels.* The greater the amount of cash on hand at any given location, the greater is the risk of loss in a physical sense. At the same time, having cash on hand which is in excess of actual needs means a loss of potential earnings through the lesser utilization of that cash. Keeping cash at minimum levels is therefore important for the company's interests. This holds true at any level in the organization, including the central depository itself.

Seek all possible earnings

4. *Earning potentials should be realized to the extent practicable.* Since "cash" is a broad term that goes beyond physical cash on hand to include all types of bank accounts, we need to recognize the earning potentials that can be realized, where practicable, through the placement of funds in interest-bearing accounts or instruments. In some cases, however, the maintenance of given bank balances may be the basis for credit lines or other services rendered by the banks involved. The objective is to exploit these potentials to the maximum extent possible. For other cases it may be possible to maintain balances only sufficient to meet checks as they clear the account.

Cash Disbursements

Cash received and available in various forms is now ready for use by the company—for the purchase of operating facilities, payment of expenses, and for investments. The general objective is that these disbursements be for valid and proper purposes, that fair value has been received, and that they are in the correct amounts. The special control aspects can be summarized as follows:

1. *Separation of the Disbursement Function.* As previously noted, the cash receipts and cash disbursement phases of the total cash process need to be as separate as possible. Cash received has been channeled to the central cash depository and now the disbursement phase can be separately handled and controlled.

2. *Adequacy of Documentation for Liquidation of Payables.* In the normal financial operations the major types of expenditures are processed through the creation of a payable, which is subsequently liquidated by the cash disbursement. At the same time, however, the disbursement is normally reviewed in terms of the validity of the underlying payable, plus the propriety of the timing of the liquidation of that payable. The nature and scope of this documentation will be discussed further under accounts payable.

3. *Use of Petty Cash Funds.* A number of situations will arise when small cash expenditures must be made without delay. In other situations the amounts may be too small to justify the application of the formal disbursement procedures. In these circumstances cash must be advanced and be available to service those needs. Normally this can be best accomplished when the funds are handled on an "imprest" basis. *Imprest fund approach for small expenditures* Under this procedure a designated amount is advanced and then reimbursements are made to the fund from time to time covering exactly the total amount of expenditures, thus bringing the fund back to its original level. The receipts or other documentation supporting the individual expenditures provide the documentary backup for the reimbursement of the fund. The size of the fund should be large enough to sustain expenditures of the amounts reasonably expected, but with allowance for the time required to process the previously described reimbursements. On the other hand, as previously noted under cash handling, the size of the fund should be no larger than necessary. The level of the fund can be changed at any time, and from time to time the need for such change should be reappraised in the light of experience and new conditions.

    Several other important matters relating to petty cash funds need to be mentioned. Since the individual expenditures involve cash it is *Require adequate backup evidence* extremely important that satisfactory evidence be obtained to support the expenditure. If such evidence is not directly available in the form of an invoice, cash register slip, or receipt, it will be necessary that a special receipt be prepared and signed, preferably by the recipient of the cash, but at least by the person making the expenditure. These supporting documents should be canceled at the time of reimbursement to prevent their reuse. There is the continuous temptation to relax on obtaining adequate documentation. There is also the temptation to use the cash for improper purposes, as, for example, personal employee needs. The matter of documentation can be monitored via the review at the time of reimbursement. The improper use, however, cannot be detected except by an actual examination and count of the fund. Both of these protective efforts need to be carried out on a continuing basis.

4. *Use of Branch Imprest Funds.* In other higher-level situations it becomes useful or necessary for a branch location to issue checks for local expenditures. Here again the imprest approach can be effectively utilized. Again also the same principles apply as to the handling of the documentation, the usage of the fund, and as to the level of the fund itself.

Two signatures on checks aid in controlling

5. *Control over Check Signatures.* In most situations it is useful to require two signatures on checks. This serves as a cross check of one person against another, both for the prevention of fraud and error and as to the care and judgment being exercised. In some situations, however, signature plates may be used, and here the important point of control becomes that of access to the plates and the condition of the usage of them.

6. *Designation of Payee of Checks.* It is important that all checks issued should be made payable to the specific individual or firm from which the products or services are obtained. The writing of checks to cash or to bearer should be strictly avoided since cash can then more easily be used for unauthorized purposes.

7. *Maximum Separation of Duties and Responsibilities.* The cash disbursement process particularly highlights the desirability of breaking down the various aspects of the activities and assigning them to different individuals. Thus one person might review the documentation, another prepare the check, a third review the propriety of the combined set of documents, a fourth provide the primary signature, and a fifth the secondary signature. Each activity then serves as a cross check on the other.

Other General Aspects of Cash Process

A number of matters pertaining to effective control cut across the receival, handling, and disbursement aspects of the cash process. These are as follows:

1. *Bonding of Employees.* Normal business prudence requires that all employees participating in any part of the cash processes be bonded. The benefits to be derived are twofold. First, there is the actual protection to the company in the case of any defalcation or other improper diversion of company funds. Second, the fact of the bonding is more likely to motivate the individual employee to exercise a higher standard of care and integrity. To accomplish the latter there is the need that the bonding action be properly publicized.

2. *Maximum Exploitation of Mechanical Aids.* A considerable range of mechanical aids has been developed covering various phases of the cash processes. The types of assistance rendered include record keeping, physical protection, better control, and labor efficiency. The modern cash register is illustrative of a device that protects cash by restricting access, establishes a record of accountability, and motivates good control through its visible record of a transaction. The special benefits of most mechanical aids is that they better assure a uniform handling of designated matters at the desired level of control. All of these opportunities need to be considered and adequately exploited.

3. *Keeping Records Up to Date and Prompt Reporting.* In all parts of the cash processes it is especially important that all records be kept up to date as a basis for both efficient current reference and prompt periodic reporting. There is at the same time the important psychological motivation to the people participating in the cash process as to the need for special care. Delays in carrying out various parts of the cash processes can generate greater physical risk and at the same time restrict the efficient utilization of cash resources.

Up to date records and prompt reporting critical

4. *Control of Blank Checks and Other Supplies.* The proper control of papers and forms is always important in terms of physical protection and efficient usage. In the case of the cash processes this control becomes especially important since certain forms, as in the case of blank checks, might somehow be used for improper purposes.

5. *Independent Reconciliation of Bank Accounts.* The periodic reconciliation of bank accounts represents an important point of control over both the cash receipts and disbursement activities. It is important therefore that these reconciliations be made by persons who are independent of the regular receiving and disbursing operations. Bank statements and canceled checks should also be obtained or received directly from the depositories to assure that they have not been tampered with in any manner by any intermediary. Bank reconciliations also provide the opportunity to review various aspects of how receipts and disbursements are handled, and additionally to identify unusual actions.

RECEIVABLE PROCESSES

Nature of Receivable Processes

The receivable processes cover any type of company action that generates claims against individuals or companies. The claims are usually against parties outside the company, but at times can also involve employees and officers. The claims are brought into existence as an intermediary phase pending the ultimate collection of them in the form of cash or other types of consideration. Although these claims can originate in a variety of ways, the major category has to do with the sale of products produced, or services rendered by the company. We will therefore deal first with this category and then later touch on some of the other types.

Complete credit policy essential

The receivable processes that relate primarily to sales have a number of important relationships. There is the immediate necessity for policies covering the extent to which credit is first granted and then subsequently administered. Who should be extended credit? In what amounts? How aggressive should the company be in pressing for subsequent collection? A second type of consideration has to do with how these receivable activities bear on customer satisfaction and continuing customer goodwill. The company is unavoidably interested in how customers react to the modes of credit authorization, billing, and collection. The company is also interested in what it can learn through the receivable relationships about how the customers are reacting to company products and policies in a broader sense. Finally, there is the specific interest of the company in the efficiency of its various receivable activities and the effectiveness of the control.

The processes relating to receivables group themselves into three phases. The first phase has to do with the conditions under which the receivable comes into existence. The second phase covers the administration of the receivables thus created. The third phase consists of the means by which the receivable is finally liquidated. Our objective in each case will be to understand the general range of matters involved and to identify the major problems of control.

Generating Receivables

Receivables should be evaluated through knowledge about sources

Since the account receivable normally arises out of the sale of company products or the rendering of some kind of service, the first interest has to do with establishing a direct linkage with that underlying basis. There is the objective of being certain that the receivable being created is backed up by the shipment of the product or the performing of the service. At the same time we want to be sure that all receivables are brought on to the record that should have been. Both objectives are more likely to be satisfied when the creation of the receivable can be directly linked with the relief of an inventory accountability or with the record of the performance of the service. We therefore strive to establish this linkage in a specific procedural sense.

As we have previously noted also, the generating of the receivable immediately involves the question of whether the company wishes to extend the required credit to the customer to cover the sale. Underlying this determination is the general credit policy of the company, but now the general policy must be applied to the particular customer in the light of that customer's credit standing and our own experience with him. When that credit acceptability has been determined the regular sales and billing procedures are initiated. As a part of those procedures an invoice is prepared and the account of the customer charged.

The major control considerations that apply to the generating of the receivables are as follows:

1. *Independent Review and Approval of Credit.* When an order is received the credit approval must be obtained. This approval should be provided by an independent department or person within the framework of established company policy and appropriate information about the particular customer. This latter information covers the financial standing of the customer and his general credit standing. It also includes up-to-date facts as to the company's own experience with the party, including his present receivable position. The approval itself is made by properly authorized individuals, depending on the amount involved.

   Creation of receivables should follow prescribed steps

2. *Determination of Product Availability.* All items ordered by the customer may not be available for shipment at this time, and hence cannot be included in current billings. The goods actually available must be identified on appropriate assembly and packing papers, which then establish the specific basis for shipment and billing. Other items not now available must be covered by backorder procedures for later shipments.

3. *Authorization of Prices and Terms.* Prices and terms may be completely standardized for all customers. In some cases, however, these will vary for different groups of customers and for different quantities being sold to those customers. For billing purposes the applicable prices and terms must be provided based on established company policy. Interpretations or special deviations must additionally be approved by properly authorized individuals.

4. *Multicopy Papers for Related Purposes.* Invoices need to be prepared in enough copies so that the same identical information can be used for a number of operational purposes. Thus one copy authorizes the shipment, another goes to the customer, another is used for the compilation of sales data, and still another goes to the accounts receivable department for posting. Controls can also be established covering the total of the individual invoices for a given period, usually one business day.

Administration of Receivables

The administration phase of the receivable process picks up where the generating phase ends and goes on to handle the receivable until it is paid or otherwise liquidated. The major control considerations during this new phase include:

1. *Independent and Controlled Accounts Receivable Records.* The actual accounts receivable records in some situations may be maintained manually and in others on various types of bookkeeping machines. In others they will be handled on a computer. The principles, however, in all cases are that the records be independently maintained and not subject to access by outside parties, especially by those who might have access to cash or to the customers themselves. In all cases also there must be control accounts, and possibly subcontrol accounts, which are supported by the individual detailed accounts.

No outside access to receivable records

2. *Current Posting and Control.* Ideally, newly generated charges, credits from cash collections, and all other miscellaneous charges and credits will be posted on a daily basis so that up-to-date information is currently available to serve the various operational needs in the company. At the same time accuracy is maintained through the current check on the agreement of detailed accounts with the control accounts.

3. *Prompt and Adequate Reporting.* In addition to information furnished currently, there should be periodic reports of current balances, together with an aging analysis. The latter analysis shows the portions of the account balance which have been unpaid for different time periods—for example, current, one month overdue, two months overdue, three months overdue, and so on. This analysis is an important basis for the administration of the ongoing credit and collection efforts.

4. *Direct and Independent Mailing of Statements.* A basic feature from a control standpoint is that statements are mailed directly to the individual customers without any opportunity for diversion or modification by any other company personnel. This makes it possible for the statements to serve as a reliable cross check upon the accuracy of the individual accounts. It is also an important means of disclosing the delayed reporting of collections.

Disposition of Receivables

Types of relief of receivables should be separately controlled

The receivables represent an asset claim against the particular parties involved. It is therefore important that this claim not be relieved except in a properly authorized manner. The four normal modes of relief can be listed together with the major control considerations, as follows:

1. *Cash Collections.* The most usual development is that cash collections from customers will liquidate the previously generated receivables.

Summary controls cover the relief of receivables and a corresponding charge to cash accountabilities. This is our previously discussed problem of achieving adequate control over cash receipts. At the same time assurance must be provided that discounts deducted are properly earned and accounted for.

2. *Merchandise Returns.* When products sold are returned for one reason or another, we have the reverse process of the original sale. First, there is the requirement that the actual return be authorized. Second, there is the requirement that the products actually be received and that they are in proper condition. Finally, there is the need to be certain that the credit is in the proper amount. These three assurances when properly documented provide the basis for a sales return credit.

3. *Adjustments and Allowances.* Still harder to control are the many situations where a customer is granted some kind of a special allowance or credit. This may be for volume purchases, for the sale of particular types of products by the customer, or to adjust for product deficiencies. Where the allowance is pursuant to a specific arrangement the control is to confirm compliance with the arrangement. In many cases, however, the authenticity of the credit is based on judgmental factors as evaluated by an executive who then approves the credit within the limits of his own authority.

4. *Write-off to Bad Debts.* To some extent there are normally some customers who simply fail to pay. Although every possible effort should be made to enforce payment, there may be bankruptcy situations, disappearance of the debtor, or other causes which leave no other alternative but for a write-off. Usually provision has previously been made for such losses through the creation of reserves for doubtful accounts, and now the actual write-off is charged to that reserve. One specific interest at this point is that the write-off has been properly authorized by a sufficiently high-level company officer. The other interest is that the accounts written off are covered by new controls and given adequate continuing attention in the way of such further collection effort as is practicable and reasonable.

Policy Aspects of Accounts Receivable

Having considered the operational framework of the receivable process, we need to look more carefully at several key policy areas relating to the handling of receivables.

Economics of Credit Levels. A continuing policy question is how liberal a company should be in its extension of credit. It is of course clear that the tighter the credit granting the lower will be the ultimate bad debt losses. But the judgment of what credit policy best serves the company's total interests cannot stop there. The sales made pursuant to the more liberal

Low bad debt losses not necessarily good

credit policy may be additional sales which otherwise would not have been made. But these sales will yield extra profits. Hence it may well be in the company's interests to generate these higher sales. Also higher sales may generate additional production economies. It may be very difficult to measure the incremental benefits accurately but it is important to recognize the several dimensions of the problem. What it means is that a low record of bad-debt losses is not necessarily in the company's overall interests, and that hence we must examine the entire situation in greater depth.

Customer Relations Impact of the Receivables Process. A related important aspect of both the operation of the credit department and the total receivable process is the major impact that all activities have on good customer relations. We know on the one hand that it is in the company's interests to develop efficient internal procedures and operations. In this endeavor it is frequently desirable to streamline procedures and to reduce the degree of personal contacts and treatment in the handling of the various relationships. On the other hand the receivable processes unavoidably involve customer relationships. We need therefore to handle these customer contacts in a way which minimizes customer irritation and builds positive customer good will. Examples of these contacts would include the handling of credit applications, clarity of billings, processing of credits and adjustments, and the various collection efforts. Real effectiveness here is to combine internal efficiency with courteous and reasonably cooperative customer relationships. Very often also customer dissatisfaction due to many different causes (and quite independent of the receivable process) may surface through the receivable contacts. Here the receivable personnel have a further opportunity to help channel these problems to company personnel who will solve them, and to thus build greater customer goodwill.

Other Accounts Receivable Processes

Although regular company sales activities provide the major source of accounts receivable, there are various other activities and developments that may lead to some special types of accounts receivable. Illustrative of this group would be:

Different types of receivables need special analysis

1. *Advances to Employees.* Sales of regular company products or services would be normally included in the regular accounts receivable. However, there may also be advances of one kind or another—for travel, special business purposes, or possibly for personal reasons. While there is the special security of salaries and wages which are currently being earned, the extent of such advances is normally very closely controlled. Advances for personal purposes would especially require approval by properly authorized officers.

2. *Deposits with Outsiders.* In many situations deposits are required in connection with establishment of utility services or for other reasons.

These deposits may be of a temporary nature or may be permanent as long as the service is being utilized. The record is important so that recovery of the deposit is made when the original need no longer exists.

3. *Claims*. Relations with vendors, carriers, or any outside service group can lead to claims asserted which need to be recorded pending actual reimbursement. Insurance claims will provide still another source of such receivables. Although an alternative approach is to forgo setting the claim up on the books, and recording the proceeds when received, more effective control is provided by the actual recording of the claim as a receivable.

4. *Accruals of Income*. A special type of receivable in a very loose sense exists when earned income is accrued prior to being due and collectible. The objective here in an operational sense is to recognize income in the periods actually earned and to thus provide a better evaluation of current operational performance.

Special Aspects of Other Receivable Processes.   While the nature and scope of the transactions and activities that generate these miscellaneous types of receivables can vary greatly, there are certain control aspects which are generally applicable to all. The first of these is that the conditions under which the particular type of receivable is created is clearly defined in both a policy and procedural sense. A special objective is to provide adequate safeguards that the receivable is actually brought on to the books at the earliest possible time, and in the proper amount, as far as it can be determined. The second control aspect is that procedures need to be established for the periodic review of the status of all of these miscellaneous receivables. What frequently happens is that these miscellaneous receivables get overlooked in a regular operational sense, and are not given adequate attention. It is necessary therefore to take specific precautions that will combat such tendencies.

Notes Receivable Processes

In some situations it may be that practice of a particular company to make sales for its products and services on a deferred payment basis. In such cases contracts may be executed which specify the timing of the payments. In other cases notes receivable may be obtained. Notes receivable can, however, also originate as an outgrowth of the collection problems with regular accounts receivable. It may be that circumstances have developed where the regular account cannot be liquidated in accordance with the intended plan. It may be in such a situation that the company wishes to obtain what it regards as a more precise recognition of the receivable through the use of notes receivable. Also it may be that interest can now be charged. In all these situations the circumstances need to be defined and properly author-

Special evalation of notes receivable

ized under which the notes receivable come into existence. Subsequently there is the need for a regular monitoring of the collection of the notes on the dates specified, including the collection of such interest as has been agreed upon. Notes receivable also pose a further problem of custody, since the notes exist as separate documents. There is the possibility that since the use of notes receivable is a more unusual type of transaction, regular and systematic attention will not be given to them. Hence specific procedures may be needed to assure periodic review and possible action.

PAYABLE PROCESSES

Nature of Payable Processes

The operation of any company necessarily requires that there be expenditures. These expenditures are for materials, products, equipment, salaries and wages, and services of various kinds. All of these expenditures involve the creation of company obligations which are then either immediately liquidated, as in the case of a cash expenditure, or are liquidated at some future time. The payable processes have to do with the recognition of all of these obligations and the subsequent control and handling of them. When these obligations are liquidated the payable processes merge with the cash disbursement procedures discussed earlier in this chapter. The payable processes are thus generated by the underlying operating activities of the com-

Legitimacy and timing key considerations with payables

pany but focus on the financial control of the total process. This financial control is concerned with the promptness and accuracy with which such obligations are formally recognized, the legitimacy and propriety of those obligations, and the procedures by which the stage is set for the final liquidation.

The payable processes involve activities that fit into fairly well-defined groups. There is first, the activities which have to do with the creation of the payables. How do we control the amount of the payable and how do we determine the validity? Second, there are the various activities in administering the existing payables. What kinds of special problems are encountered in terms of current recording and control? Finally there are the procedures by which the individual payables are prepared for actual payment, thus leading to the issuance of a check covering the actual liquidation. We will briefly discuss the payment processes under these headings.

Generating Payables

Payables can originate from a variety of sources. The normal and most voluminous source will be as a result of the purchase of products and services by the regularly established purchasing department, as discussed in Chapter 12. These products and services will relate largely to items purchased for resale or for use in the production of products and services to be sold by the company. But as we will see, they can also be for any operational need

of the company. Additionally, many purchases of products and services are
for various reasons procured directly by company personnel directly involved
in other line and staff activities. In terms of value importance the item can
range from the smallest type of purchase to the purchase of major capital
items. In all cases the basic control issue is that obligations are incurred only
within authorized limits. These authorized limits cover the kind of expenditure, dollar amount of that expenditure, and individual incurring the particular obligation. What we have here are delegations of authority from the
basic source of authority—the board of directors—plus authorized redele-
gations. Needless to say, emergencies may develop when these authorized
limits are violated, in which case the unauthorized action must be ratified
to give it proper standing. However, such emergencies should be carefully
evaluated to be sure that emergencies are real emergencies and not just a
device to get around established limits of authority.

*Emergency purchases
need justification*

What Constitutes a Valid Payable?   Regardless of the source of the payable
there are certain common objectives which exist from a financial control
standpoint over all types of payables. These objectives can be described as
follows:

*Key steps in validation of
payables*

1. *Is the Type of Expenditure Reasonable?* The objective here is that the
   expenditure bears a reasonable relationship to the operations of the
   business. Normally this relationship is self-evident, but in other cases
   it may be partially or completely obscure. In that case a question is
   raised that needs to be probed for a reasonable explanation. To the
   extent that such a reasonable explanation is not available, there is the
   greater dependence on the approvals recorded by individual company
   officers.

2. *Are Quantities Excessive?* A related question is whether the expenditure is of a reasonable magnitude in terms of the quantities or volume
   purchased. The pressures for higher levels may be to obtain lower
   prices or simply to provide higher reserves for operational needs. In
   either case there is a level of judgment involved, which is subject to
   reasonable evaluation. Again the more excessive the deviation from
   normal levels, the greater dependence that must be placed on the
   judgment and approval of the officers who authorize the particular
   expenditure.

3. *Are Prices and Terms Correct?* The concern with prices and terms is
   twofold. One question has to do with their correctness in terms of
   previous agreements covering expenditures of which the present payable is one portion. The second concern is that the prices and terms
   are the best obtainable. In the latter case it may be that nothing can
   be done about the particular payable, but there may be the possibility
   of affecting future expenditures. Prices and terms as used here will

include list prices, discounts, time of payment, freight basis, warranties, guarantees, and the like.

4. *Was Proper Value Received?* There is always concern that the proper value has been received. One aspect of this concern is that the services invoiced have actually been rendered, or that the products invoiced have actually been received. The second aspect is that the goods or services were of the proper specifications, condition, and quality. There is the need for proper evidence to cover both of these aspects. If payables are to be validated prior to the receipt of value as described previously, there will again be the need for adequate approval by authorized officers. There will also be the further need for supplementary controls to check on the later compliance with the temporarily waived requirements.

5. *Are Approvals and Supporting Evidence Adequate?* The validation of payables requires that there be proper documentary evidence to back up the concerns of the type previously described. This evidence will consist of basic papers such as purchase orders and receiving reports. It will also include the specific approvals of properly authorized and qualified officers. These specific approvals cover various aspects of the validity and in each case the question needs to be asked both as to whether the person approving has the authority to make that approval and whether the level of that authorization is adequate.

Intermediate Administration of Payables

In some cases the validation of the payable leads immediately to the cash disbursement phase. In other cases the validated payables are held for later liquidation. From a control standpoint it is desirable to recognize the payable formally at the earliest possible time. However, it may be more efficient to achieve this control through filing procedures and to defer the formal accounting recognition until either the time of payment or the end of an accounting period, whichever comes first. Under such an approach, however, there are certain matters that have to be handled, as follows:

Handling validated payables

1. *Coordination and Control of Incoming Papers.* Under a system of proper internal control the various papers relating to the individual payables will be flowing directly to the accounts payable department. These will include a copy of the purchase order from the purchasing department, the receiving report from the receiving department, claim forms from shortages or quality deficiencies, charges for transportation paid for our account, and original copies of invoices and statements received from vendors. All of these papers need to be filed in a manner that will facilitate later assembly to support final payments.

2. *Making Accounting Distributions.* All expenditures must ultimately be charged to the proper expense or asset accounts, as determined by

the existing accounting policies and procedures. In some cases also, supplementary budgetary charges must be made. The analysis of the correct distributions requires an adequate knowledge of the total account structure. The actual distribution may also require special supplementary work sheets.

3. *Subsidiary Ledger Control.* Once the payables are formally recognized, the overall control of payables is achieved through one or more control accounts backed up by subsidiary ledgers. The latter must be periodically checked to determine that they are in agreement with the controls. Offsetting errors in individual accounts will be checked and reconciled when vendor statements are received. These detailed ledgers are commonly maintained on computers.

4. *Planning for Payment Dates.* Where the eligibility exists for the application of various discounts through timely payments, the controls must be provided to exploit these benefits. Normally the loss of discounts represents a severe financial penalty in terms of current interest costs. In other cases the terms of the payables will require payment by specific dates. Good relations with vendors depend in part on making payments at the proper times. Late payments and deduction of unearned discounts are especially irritating. All of this means that controls must be set up to assure completion of the final processing and payment in the manner and at the time intended.

Final Review and Payment

The final phase of the payable process is to prepare the payable for payment. The key control points at this stage are:

1. *Final Assembly and Matching of Supporting Documents.* Now the pertinent supporting papers—purchase order, receiving report, and invoice—must be brought together and checked for clerical accuracy and agreement. The total set is assembled in a physical sense and a request for a check then prepared.

Key steps in final review and payment

2. *Deduction of Counter Claims.* Control procedures are now necessary to identify all outstanding claims against the particular creditor that should be deducted from the payment. In some cases amounts are to be withheld pending final inspection or usage. The request for a check is appropriately modified to reflect these deductions.

3. *Preparation of Check.* The request for check, supported by the previously described set of documents, is now subjected to independent review, and, when approved by a properly authorized individual, is routed to individuals who will prepare the actual disbursement check.

4. *Final Review and Release.* The check and supporting payable package is now ready for final review by independent reviewers. These independent reviewers will either provide one of the check signatures or

will initial the authorization for an officer to sign. If a check has been mechanically signed the approval validates that action. At this stage the reviewers and signers are concerned both with the completeness of the supporting papers and the kinds of questions discussed earlier under general validation. When this phase has been completed, the check is referenced on the supporting documents, supporting papers are canceled in some way to prevent reuse, and the check is mailed directly to the vendors.

Separation of Processing Responsibilities

Processing responsibility for payables needs to be separated

The payable process as just described is one that can vary in many respects in individual situations. Especially in the case of computerized systems there will be many different kinds of procedures. In any of these procedural arrangements the most critical aspect from a financial control standpoint is that the various processing activities are separately assigned to different individuals. The resulting separation and independence is important for purposes of clerical cross check, thus assuring greater accuracy. It also prevents manipulation by any one individual to create disbursements or relief of payable obligations where somehow he could personally profit. In such a separation the accountabilities of the individual persons can be more precisely fixed.

Other Payable Processes

While the greater part of the payable process will normally be concerned with the types of accounts payable just described, there are a number of other operating activities which generate various types of other payables. Although some of these focus more directly on the correctness of the periodic financial statements, there is a significant operational aspect. We will consider several of the more common supplementary payable processes.

Travel expenses handling touches on sensitive areas

Travel Expenses. A type of payable that has some very special characteristics is that of obligations incurred for travel expenses. Although the usual sequence is to advance funds to the individual travelers and to then credit those advances at the time properly approved expense reports are submitted, the basic nature is that of a company expenditure within the framework of the payables group. However, the fact of the cash advance does often create a supplemental operating problem in that such advances may be misused by the recipient. This misuse is commonly the use of the funds for personal purposes or the comingling of such advances with personal funds. In other cases the money may be legitimately used, but there is an undue procrastination in preparing the expense accounts which relieve the existing accountabilities. Systematic follow-up is, therefore, required on keeping the submission of expense reports up to date.

When the expense accounts are actually submitted, the need becomes one of validating the propriety of the expenditures claimed. A number of problems are involved of which the following are the most common:

1. The traveler may have incurred expenses beyond levels established by the company, or in the absence of such established levels, in excess of prudent levels
2. Items may be claimed which are not allowable as expenses
3. Amounts claimed may not be properly documented, leaving open the possibility that the items have been overstated
4. Entertainment expenditures may be for persons not in the regular line of company business, and where the legitimacy of the expenditures may be very doubtful
5. Approvals of responsible supervisors may not be obtained

The handling of expense accounts is a very difficult one, especially where individual expenditures are a matter of judgment. Normally it is desirable to have established policies covering the various types of expense. Also the entire procedure should be continuously monitored. This means that questions must be raised when established policies are unduly violated or where the evidence is not sufficiently clear. Receipts and hotel bills should also be required to the extent practicable. These controls are necessary both to provide needed support for company expenditures, but also to minimize the always existing temptation of a traveler to use expense accounts for personal advantage.

Comprehensive policies are critical

Financing Activities. The financing activities will be discussed in greater detail in Chapter 14 as a part of the financial policy area. We take note here, however, that they do lead to the creation of some very important payables and related financial control processes. The financing activities pertain to two quite different, although obviously related, types of needs. One of these is for short-term purposes and includes principally loans obtained from banks and other short-term creditors. The other kind of financing activities has to do with long-term needs. The latter needs are satisfied either by equity financing or through bonds or long-term payables. In the case of the bonds payable the detailed procedures are normally carried out by banks which act as agents. Procedural controls maintained by the company would, therefore, not be elaborate in most of these situations. However, they will need to be sufficient to assure timely payments of both principal and interest.

Expense Accruals. The desire from an operational standpoint to determine financial performance again leads us to recognize expenses applicable to current periods which have not yet been processed as regular payables. These accruals are in effect a preliminary recognition of obligations which will later be fully recognized and then liquidated. Illustrative would be interest on notes and bonds payable, taxes, and salaries and wages. The

Expense accruals very judgmental

control objective is to recognize all pertinent accruals and to measure them in as accurate manner as is practicable.

Notes Payable. In many situations the payable process may by agreement result directly in the creation of notes payable. This treatment is adopted usually when longer payment periods are envisioned and where interest may be involved. The vendor also may wish to be able to discount the notes with financial institutions or to use them as collateral for loans. In other situations the notes payable may come as a later development when accounts payable cannot be liquidated on a timely basis. From a control standpoint the interest would be in the conditions for the creation of the notes payable and in the procedures which will adequately assure the meeting of future payment dates for both interest and principal. Adequate detailed supporting records will also be necessary for current reference and control.

PAYROLLS

Nature of the Payroll Process

Salaries and wages trigger major control needs

The payable process includes expenditures for salaries and wages of company personnel. The expenditures of this latter type, however, require special consideration for a number of reasons. One of the reasons is the fact that salaries and wages usually represent the largest segment of the company's operating costs. A second reason is that these expenditures involve people and consequently the inevitable people problems. Payrolls are also of special interest because they relate so closely to the operational problems of all company activities and the efforts to achieve effective labor utilization. A final special aspect concerns the many interrelated legal considerations which come about through minimum wage legislation, unemployment insurance, and social security. Payroll costs are thus at the heart of the total company operations. Our interest at this point, however, is with the way payroll data are initially developed and subsequently processed. We are especially interested also in the way adequate control is achieved. The latter is of special importance because of the frequent cases of fraud which arise in connection with the payroll activities.

Tie to the Personnel Department. As we saw previously, the personnel department is engaged in a wide range of activities that pertain to the administration of people relationships. At the same time the personnel records maintained constitute a major independent source of authority for the payroll operations. It is here in the first instance that the record of hires exists and the conditions of such hiring actions. Subsequently, changes in status and compensation are recorded. Administered here, partially or completely, are the various programs that generate special charges or credits.

Finally, the record here covers termination from the company. From a control standpoint all of these records become a major source of reference and authority. Needless to say, it is extremely important to protect that independence in all the operations relating to the processing of payrolls. The actual processing itself is done by an operational group which is normally a part of the accounting group.

Tie to Computerization.   The preparation of payrolls in the typical situation involves a great deal of detail and clerical activity. It has, therefore, been an area where computers have had their earliest advantageous applications. Computers have the capacity to handle the many detailed calculations and summarizations required. These computer operations in their broader sense are dealt with more fully in Chapter 15. At this point we will be concerned with the basic problems and issues that relate to payrolls irrespective of the means by which the payrolls are actually processed.

Automation needs and policy aspects need integration

Source of Payroll Data

Since payrolls have to do with employees and their compensation for work performed, the starting point is the requirement that the individual be a properly authorized employee. The individual must have been officially hired and not subsequently terminated prior to the starting date of the current payroll period. This fact is of course subject to independent verification through the personnel department. The second requirement is the evidence of work performed. In the case of salaried employees the documentary activities will vary depending on the policies of the particular company and the organizational level of the particular employee. At lower levels there will normally be time cards generated by the individuals under established time-clock procedures. In other cases there may be records maintained by supervisors at the various levels. But at higher levels the control is usually of a less formal type, depending more on general observation and the integrity of the individual. As to rates the records of the personnel department will again provide the most reliable independent authority for the presently existing salaries. Where overtime compensation is involved there is the further need for records maintained by supervisors and for adequate higher-level approval.

The situation in the case of hourly employees is normally handled in a more systematic manner. This will include at least time-clock cards covering time actually spent in the plant. In many situations also there is the need for information as to how much time is spent on individual projects, job orders, or other specific work assignments. Such records may be prepared by the employees themselves, and then subsequently reviewed and approved by supervisors, or be prepared directly by the supervisors themselves. When such supplementary records are maintained there is the opportunity for a cross check between the two sets of records for accuracy of

Authorization of responsible supervisor is key payroll control

the total time, including also the accuracy of the allocations of a cost accounting nature. The accuracy of rates used is again subject to independent confirmation with personnel department records. There is also the problem of individuals working on different jobs which carry different job classifications, and which therefore call for different bases of compensation. Here there is the special problem of possible manipulation plus the managerial question of whether labor was effectively utilized. For payroll purposes, however, the authorization of the responsible supervisor is a key control.

Preparing the Payroll

Employees of the several categories are paid on different time period bases. Hourly labor will normally be paid on a weekly basis, certain salary personnel on a semi-monthly basis, and other salary personnel on a monthly basis. At the end of the designated payroll period the payroll department is now charged with the responsibility of preparing the payroll. This action has to do with the determination of what is owed and payable to each employee for work performed during the given payroll period. The key aspects of this preparation of the payroll can be briefly listed, as follows:

Individual aspects of preparation of payrolls need validation

1. *Accumulation of Work Evidence.* Time cards and other basic records of work activity must be accumulated. This requires first that the source data are clerically accurate and properly approved by responsible supervisors. Where inaccuracies are found the correction to be made must be determined and carried out. Required also is the summarization by individuals and organizational components. The clerical accuracy of this summarization must be assured by internal controls of various kinds, including segregation of clerical work and responsibility. The fact of whether individuals are bona fide employees is determined by cross reference to personnel department records and reports to the extent needed.

2. *Application of Rates.* Work performed must be compensated at proper rates. These rates are established by existing union contracts and by other company actions reflected in the records of the personnel department. When the authenticity of the rates has been adequately established the necessary calculations must then be made and the resulting amounts summarized.

3. *Accounting Distributions.* The amounts payable for services performed must be allocated to the proper operational activities in conformance with the established accounting requirements of the company, including those of a cost accounting nature. Although it is possible, and sometimes necessary, to defer the determinations of these distributions, the actions here should be accomplished as soon as is practicable because of their value as a cross check on the accuracy of the payroll itself.

4. *Application of Deductions*. Deductions will be required for a number of reasons. Illustrative will be those for social security, union dues, pension plans, and personal purchases. The charges for these different purposes must then under proper control be applied to the individuals affected.

5. *Determination of Net Pay*. Finally, the difference between the basic compensation earned and the deductions provides the net pay that is due to the individual employees. Again also there must be summarization and proof against the detailed data.

Payment of Salaries and Wages

The preparation of the payroll as just described leads directly into the question of how payment shall be made and the preparation of the various checks and other papers that will implement the payment mode. The preferable mode of payment to each individual is by check. This reduces the risk of handling cash and of course also provides an automatic record of receipt by the employee. In some situations, however, it may be necessary to pay in cash. In still other cases checks can be used but special check-cashing facilities must be provided. The payroll preparation procedures will normally tie into the policies and requirements that exist and provide for the preparation of the individual checks. Where cash must be made available a check will usually be prepared covering the aggregate amount. The summary journal entry will provide for the credits to the accounts for which deductions were made. These credits will then provide controls for the later preparation of governmental reports covering social security and unemployment insurance.

Direct delivery to individuals very important

The checks or cash for the individuals covered by the particular payroll will now be distributed to them. It is important that this delivery be made directly to the various individuals so that there is no opportunity for any diversion or manipulation to take place on the part of any intermediary. Identification of the recipient is also important for the same reasons. Receipts should be obtained where payment is made in cash. Where cash is paid, or where check-cashing facilities are made available, there is the additional requirement of adequate physical protection. In the event that individuals are not available at the time of the regular distribution, the cash or checks should be taken back to a designated cashier location, and the individuals affected should then be required to present themselves in person to receive payment.

Basis of Internal Control for Payrolls

While extremely voluminous and extensively involved with the detailed complexities of varying rates, calculations, and deductions, the payroll process in principle is straightforward and subject to basic internal control considerations. First and foremost is the necessity that the handling of or

Payroll process involves all basic internal controls

access to cash be entirely separate from the creation of any part of the record that supports the cash payment. There is also the essential requirement that all parts of the process be broken down as between departments and individuals within individual departments so that the maximum cross check exists. The use of control totals at the various stages provides necessary control over voluminous detail. The latter is especially important in the payroll department itself where the payroll itself is prepared. A reviewer such as the internal auditor will in turn appraise both the adequacy of the existing cross checks as provided for in the basic design of the payroll procedures and also the care with which the procedures are actually executed. Constant effort is required to enforce the proper level of care and also to reappraise the need for procedural modification to meet the needs of changing situations.

FINANCIAL CONTROL OVER SECURITIES

The handling of securities represents a special problem of financial control that has great importance, especially for a financial institution like a bank or investment company. In the case of a typical company the handling of securities may be delegated to a financial institution. Back of the handling problem are of course the broader questions of why securities are acquired, and if so of what type and of what amount. These broader questions pertain to the company financial policies and will be touched on in Chapter 14. In this chapter we are concerned with the problems of basic financial control. The problem that exists is how procedures can be established that will provide adequate accountability and protection for securities. The operational requirements here include the receipt of securities, current access to them as required, and release of them at the proper time for sale or other authorized purposes.

Receiving Securities

Securities purchased may be registered in the company name or be payable to bearer. While the latter have the advantage of greater convenience in the event of transfer, the risk of theft is much greater. However, in the case of securities left as collateral or for other special purposes by customers or other outside parties, the company may have had no election as to the form of the securities. In any event the receival of the securities by a company officer or employee marks the assumption of responsibility and accountability on the part of the company. What is then needed are records that properly establish accountability and physical facilities that will provide adequate protection. Where this custody is a significant activity of the company these facilities will be burglar-proof vaults. In all cases the accountability of those individuals accepting custodial responsibility should be clearly established

Initial receival of securities need good control

through the issuance of formal receipts. At the same time records of the accountability should be established both by the custodian and by an operational group independent of the custodian. These records should cover both the basic securities and the interest coupons that are attached to bearer bonds. The latter coverage is important both for the custodial responsibility and for the scheduling of clipping coupons as they become due.

Handling and Release of Securities

As time goes on there will be instances when parties other than the custodian will require access to the securities. Effective control in these circumstances first of all requires that the party to be granted access is properly authorized. A second requirement is that the inspection of securities be carried out jointly by the custodian and the second party. In the case of interest coupons the procedure in a banking institution will normally be to clip and transfer coupons that are due to a collection department for collection and credit to the customer's account, with the relief of the custodian's responsibility being thereby formally established. When securities in a bond category become due the procedure would be similar. Securities may also be withdrawn for other reasons when properly authorized. In a company situation coupons and bonds that are due will necessarily be removed and transferred to a bank for collection. In summary, the important considerations from a control standpoint are adequate physical protection, plus clearly established accountabilities, with access to the securities being always on a dual basis. Adequate insurance and the bonding of all employees who participate in the handling of securities is also a basic requirement.

Protection needed against access of outside parties

Review of Control Adequacy

As always the first requirement is that the procedures and facilities be adequate in terms of basic design. An outside reviewer like the internal auditor will wish to reappraise that aspect periodically because of changing conditions. Especially does the changing volume of security holdings and related transactions require changes both of facilities and operational procedures. Additionally, changing environmental factors may result in greater risk exposure. But good procedures and adequate facilities are not enough. The procedures themselves must be carried out with proper precision and care. The appraisal of these procedural operations is accomplished both by careful observation and by testing the record of previously executed transactions. In this connection the verification of securities and coupons on hand against the records of accountability as independently established provides basic assurance that securities have not been improperly diverted. An important aspect of the foregoing also is the appraisal of the trustworthiness and competence of the personnel carrying out the custodial activities. One is also interested in the efficiency of personnel utilization.

Accountability for all aspects of handling need evaluation

BASIC ACCOUNTING ACTIVITIES

Scope of the Accounting Process

The accounting function covers a wide range of levels. At its highest level it involves the development of major policies that are part of the broader financial and management policies. Illustrative would be the handling of the investment credit or the policies for taking up profits on installment sales. At its lowest level the accounting activity is a primary paper—as, for example, a cash receipt form—and the procedures for its use. In Chapter 14 we deal with the higher-level financial management policies which determine the directions of the supporting accounting activity. In the present chapter our concern is with the more operational aspects of the accounting system on a day-to-day basis. This system has both a design aspect and an implementation aspect. Although the two aspects are closely interrelated, there is the question of whether forms, records, and procedures are adequate as designed to deal with the various operational requirements. There is also the question of whether we have the right kind of people and whether they are applying themselves in the proper manner.

General Character of Accounting Activities

All company activities have accounting and financial dimensions

The basic accounting activities do not exist as an end in themselves but for the support of the total operating activities of the company. They are thus interwoven with all of the operational activities discussed in other chapters. This interrelationship emphasizes the point that all company activities have a financial dimension that ties them in some manner to the overall accounting activities. Accountabilities must be established in various ways, information must be provided, and the basis provided for necessary control. Because these situations and the related requirements vary so greatly, as well as the views as to how the individual situations can be best administered, the accounting applications will also vary widely. This is especially true as more and more of the basic accounting activities are computerized and blended with broader operational needs. We will, therefore, be more concerned with principles and common characteristics, rather than with specific forms, records, or procedures.

General and Cost Accounting

The basic accounting activities include both those termed as "general" and those termed "cost." The former area has traditionally been concerned with the general aspects of assets and liabilities, and similarly with expense and revenue, whereas the latter has focused more on the cost of individual products and services. Actually the distinction becomes increasingly artificial since the latter is an extension of the other and to a considerable extent is motivated by common objectives. What we are really trying to do is to establish a total accounting framework that is sufficiently flexible to provide the types of data that can be useful for the total range of management needs. At the same time all of the special data need to stem from common sources and in some manner be generally reconcilable.

Internal Auditor's Interest in Basic Accounting Activities

The interest of the modern internal auditor in the basic accounting activities comes about in two rather different ways. The first of these lies in the recognition that the accounting activity is a part of the operations which must be reviewed just like any other operational area. There is an accounting job to be done to meet the needs of the total organization. At the same time the accounting activity costs money and we wish to achieve its proper service role in as economical and efficient manner as possible. Thus this operational aspect of the accounting activity confirms the need that the internal auditor continue to be concerned with it.

Accounting activities need review like any other operational activity

There is also, however, a second way in which the interest of the internal auditor in the basic accounting activities arises. In his review of the various operating areas one of the sources of input as to what is going on is the review of the basic accounting activities as they pertain to those operations. At the same time there is the question as to whether the accounting activity is servicing the particular operational area in the most effective manner. For these reasons the basic accounting activities become of great importance to the internal auditor in carrying out his new broader operational role.

Areas of Concern in Review of Accounting Activities

It will be useful in planning the review of the basic accounting activities to identify the major areas of concern. These concerns fall into two broad categories: (1) the component parts of the typical accounting system, and (2) the major operational dimensions. Admittedly the lines between these component parts and the related operational dimensions comes to be blurred somewhat as various activities are integrated in modern computerized systems. However, it is still useful to know the subfunctions which are being integrated. Also in smaller divisional and subsidiary operations the accounting system still tends to retain the more traditional approach.

Components of the Accounting System. The individual components that exist to some extent separately, or that represent the functions that are combined, are as follows:

1. *Primary Papers.* The accounting system begins in an operational sense through the creation, completion, and initial processing of primary papers. Illustrative is the preparation of a purchase requisition, or the execution of a cash receipt form. These primary papers need to be designed such that essential information and approvals will be picked

up and recorded. They need also to be as simple as possible so that there will be minimum misunderstanding and error. Finally, the procedures for their use, including their routing and ultimate disposition, must be properly designated.

2. *Journals.* The journal function is to provide a chronological record to the extent that such a record is needed. Illustrative would be a chronological register of purchases. The nature of this chronological record will vary widely and in many cases can be a file of primary papers under proper batch control. The test is whether later reference to the sequence of given transactions for a given time period satisfies operational needs.

Individual accounting system elements need identification and evaluation

3. *Ledgers.* The data accumulated at the journal stage provide the source information for classification in the various accounts of the company—that is, for the various assets, liabilities, equities, and types of expense and income. General ledgers deal with the aggregate-type accounts and where needed these aggregate accounts are supported by detailed accounts in subsidiary ledgers. The general ledger account "accounts receivable" thus would be supported directly or through intermediate controls, by detailed accounts with customers. The key questions involve the adequacy of the tie-in with the source date and the controls to keep detailed subsidiary ledgers in agreement with the aggregate accounts.

4. *Auxiliary Records.* An accounting system will also include a number of auxiliary records, which are related to the basic ledger accounts but which perform auxiliary functions. Illustrative would be an insurance policy register describing the coverage of the various insurance policies and perhaps developing basic expense allocations. The key questions here will be whether the auxiliary records properly support the required operational needs and whether they are efficiently maintained. In some cases the auxiliary records also include a subsidiary ledger function.

5. *Manuals.* The accounting manuals describe the total account structure and the policies and major procedures for the operation of these accounts. The issues involved have to do with the highest-level type of policy and ranging down to lower-level procedures. The key questions are the logic and practicality of the basic determination and then the clarity with which the required implementation is described.

6. *Reports.* Information developed by the accounting system is in part made available on an informal or individual request basis. In the main, however, it is through formal reports that information is provided to the various interested parties in the company. These reports cover a wide range of matters and levels of summarization. The problem is extremely complex but centers mostly around the adequacy of the information provided, manner in which it is presented for effective

use, extent to which the information is provided on a timely basis, and finally whether it is being distributed to the right people.

Operational Dimensions of the Accounting System. Having looked at the accounting system in terms of its major components, we now come at the total system from the standpoint of its operational dimensions. These dimensions are not as well standardized as the components, but will typically include the following:

1. *Distribution of Work Assignments.* As in the case of every operational activity, the starting point is the manner in which work assignments are made to the individuals involved. Through these work assignments we can achieve the benefits of specialization, and at the same time the cross check between individuals that minimizes both error and fraud. In each operational situation and at various levels of organizational responsibility the challenge is to exploit these advantages fully.

   Key operational dimensions need coverage

2. *Competence of Personnel.* Different work assignments require different types and levels of technical competence. The extent to which individuals interface with other personnel calls for varying levels of professional qualifications. The objective is to obtain the kind of personnel in each instance that fits the need, avoiding a serious lack of competence, and at the same time a level of competence that is not significantly in excess of the particular requirements.

3. *Utilization of Personnel.* Closely related to the proper level of competence is the need to supervise and manage existing personnel in a manner that properly utilizes the existing productive potential. Included also is the need to avoid both significant under- and overstaffing. At the same time there is the need to avoid excessive overtime. All of these often conflicting factors need to be evaluated and combined with reasonable competence.

4. *Coordination and Support.* An effective accounting department operates as a partner and counselor to all other operational activities. The opposite extreme is to make the accounting product an end in itself and to function more restrictively than constructively. This means that the accounting group needs to reach out to the other operational activities to render help and support, and to join with them in the solution of problems.

5. *Extent of Decentralization.* A final important operational dimension is that of finding the right balance of decentralization. What this consists of is determining where and by whom the accounting work can be best accomplished. An illustration at a low level would be the extent to which a salesperson is charged with preparing forms and summaries that might better be done by the central accounting group. At a higher level there is the question of how much accounting work should be

done at field locations versus centralization at the headquarters or other central location. Illustrative would be the handling of billing operations. The key factors for these decisions are the operating economies to be achieved versus the need to support local operations.

Operational Criteria for Appraising the Accounting System

Operational effectiveness of accounting system tied to key criteria

To a considerable extent the review of the major areas of concern above have already provided essential criteria for the evaluation of the effectiveness of the accounting system. There are, however, some additional ways in which the accounting activity can be appraised. These are as follows:

1. *Cost of Operation.* One important criterion for evaluation is always the degree of economy achieved in carrying out the various parts of the accounting operation. One standard that can be used are comparisons with other companies, either through the direct exchange of data or through industry associations. However, such comparisons must be used with care because of different operational conditions. Another standard is the company's own past performance. Still another approach is the study of what costs would be under alternative types of approach, including various types of automation.

2. *Error Experience.* Some errors are unavoidable as a practical manner. In the last analysis we are dealing with human beings, and human beings are never perfect. Moreoever, the greater the control structure the greater the cost. Nevertheless, excessive error experience indicates levels of weakness of some kind that need to be studied. The cause may be improper design, ineffective operation, or a combination of both. The objective is to strike the right balance between cost and the degree of error.

3. *Fraud.* Similarly, the extent to which fraud has developed will provide another rough measure of whether basic accounting controls in combination with other operating controls are adequate. We look more closely at the fraud question later in Chapter 16.

4. *Orderliness of Accounting Operations.* An important measure of the effectiveness of the accounting operations is the order and efficiency with which they are carried on. Order and efficiency is the result of having good people, properly trained and supervised. It reflects also the soundness of the accounting procedures. Additionally, it normally reflects the existence of adequate facilities and modern mechanical equipment. A qualified observer can recognize the absence of confusion, the businesslike execution of the various tasks, and the capacity for ready response to daily operational needs.

5. *Company Service.* The most basic test, however, of the effectiveness of the accounting group is whether the needs of the various operational activities are being adequately and properly serviced. The needs to

be served cover a wide range. They include obtaining reference information being accumulated by the accounting system. They include also getting comprehensive and useful reports on a timely basis. Last but not least they include the receiving of help and counsel in dealing with the accounting dimension as it pertains to their own operational problems. The measure of this service can best be evaluated from the user's standpoint. Is the needed assistance available and how easily can it be obtained? Frequently the development of supplementary records by a user group also provides the clue to a less-than-satisfactory degree of cooperation. A reviewer approaches this problem by getting the user's viewpoint and by critically appraising the existing needs for accounting information and controls.

AUDIT GUIDES
BASIC FINANCIAL CONTROL ACTIVITIES

I. Introductory
  A. Reference should be made to the general discussion of audit guides, as discussed earlier in this chapter.

II. Preparatory Activities
  A. See standard Audit Guides.
  B. The organizational group involved will be the accounting department or that part of the finance group which has the responsibility for basic financial control activities.

III. Organizational Factors
  A. See standard Audit Guides.
  B. Matter of special interest in the review of manuals will include:
    1. Scope of chart of accounts and description of individual accounts.
    2. Policies and procedures relating to the areas dealt with in this chapter.
      a. Cash processes: receipts, disbursements, custody, petty cash funds, branch funds, and administration of bank accounts.
      b. Receivable processes: credit sales, maintenance of accounts, adjustments, bad debts, special receivables activities, and notes receivable.
      c. Payable processes: vouchering, internal review procedures, records, special payables, travel expenses, accruals, and notes payable.
      d. Payrolls: preparation, review, and payment.
      e. Handling of securities: receiving, custody, and release.
      f. General procedures: types of records, reports, and operational aspects (both general and cost accounting).

      3. Coordinative arrangements with other company activities.

      4. Handling of deviations.

IV. Internal Operations

  A. Cash Processes

    1. Cash receipts

      a. Review the sources of cash and appraise both the possibilities of reducing or eliminating difficult-to-control conditions and for better assuring effective establishment of accountabilities.

      b. Determine that cash flows promptly and intact—without diversion for cash disbursements—directly to central depository control. Appraise the necessity of all deviations.

    2. Cash handling

      a. Are physical safeguards adequate at all stages?

      b. Is insurance coverage adequate?

      c. Is cash on hand—in all forms, at all levels, and for all purposes—at lowest possible level?

    3. Cash disbursements

      a. Are petty cash and branch funds utilized and operated on an imprest basis?

      b. Are standards adequate for documentary support? If not, why not? Appraise also the standards of review at the time of disbursement.

      c. Are credit cards adequately controlled and payments properly documented?

    4. General

      a. Are all employees who handle or have any direct or indirect access to cash adequately bonded?

      b. Are independent work assignments in effect to the extent practicable, including the reconciliation of bank accounts?

      c. Are records of accountability separately maintained?

      d. Are cash funds periodically verified by independent parties?

  B. Receivable Processes

    1. Regular accounts receivable

      a. Appraise the adequacy of procedures for credit authorization.

      b. Review sources and control of data used in billing.

      c. Are customer records independent and accurately maintained on an up-to-date basis?

      d. Are monthly statements mailed directly to customers?

      e. Are cash credits adequately linked to cash receipts processes?

      f. Are other types of charges and credits properly authorized and controlled—special charges and credits, merchandise returns, bad-debt write-offs, and the like?

      g. Are credit policies periodically reappraised for level of bad-debt losses versus sales revenues generated?

      h. Appraise in all possible ways the impact of receivable procedures on customer relations.

  2. Other receivable processes

      a. Review all special types of procedures—for example, advances to employees, deposits with outsiders, claims, and income accruals—to assure adequacy of conditions of their creation and the control thereafter exercised.

      b. Review and appraise the circumstances for accepting notes receivable and the adequacy of subsequent control, including interest due.

C. Payable Processes

  1. General

      a. Review and appraise the adequacy of the controls over the creation of all types of company obligations. Is reasonable provision made for contingencies?

      b. What procedures exist for the subsequent administration and liquidation of these obligations? Are they adequate?

  2. Regular accounts payable

      a. Review and appraise the procedures for the receipt, coordination, and ultimate matching of supporting documentary papers.

      b. Are adequate control records maintained?

      c. Review and appraise the procedures by which the payables are ultimately approved and linked with the check payments. Is proper provision made for the deduction of all existing counterclaims?

  3. Other payables

      a. How are obligations covering financing authorized and subsequently controlled? Are supplementary controls adequate where interest is payable?

      b. How adequate are the policies and procedures for the handling of expense accounts? How carefully are these policies and procedures subsequently administered?

      c. Review the policies and procedures covering expense accruals.

      d. Review and appraise the conditions by which notes payable come into existence and the control exercised over them, including interest obligations.

D. Payrolls

  1. Are independently prepared personnel department records used properly as cross controls for the preparation of payrolls?

  2. Review and appraise the effectiveness of the primary procedures and records by which the record of work is accumulated and validated.

3. Review and appraise the procedures by which payroll data are processed, authorized deductions made, payrolls finalized, and checks (or checks for cash) prepared.

4. Are the procedures for payment adequate to assure the release of checks (or cash) to the proper individuals without the opportunity for diversion or modification?

E. Securities

1. Are securities adequately safeguarded from theft and burglarization?

2. Review the adequacy of records established which are independent of those responsible for physical custody of the securities.

3. Is the receipt and release of securities properly documented?

4. Is access to securities restricted, and when necessary adequately controlled through witnesses?

F. Basic Accounting Activities

1. Are primary papers, journals, ledgers, auxiliary records, and reports adequately structured and administered in connection with the various accounting activities, and in a collective sense?

2. Review and appraise the operational effectiveness of the basic accounting activities—again in connection with particular financial processes and in total—as to:
    a. Distribution of work assignments.
    b. Competence of personnel.
    c. Utilization of personnel.
    d. Effectiveness of coordination and support of other company activities.
    e. Reasonableness of decentralization.

3. Review and appraise extent of automation of accounting activities, especially with respect to use of computers.

4. Evaluate the basic accounting activities, as to:
    a. Cost of operation.
    b. Error experience.
    c. Fraud experience.
    d. Orderliness of operations.
    e. Recipients' views as to service received.

V. Special Audit Tests

Audit tests of policies and procedures may also include a certain amount of test verification of cash funds, receivable balances, securities, payable balances, payroll authenticity, and the like. In addition, more extensive verification is frequently made of complete sectors of these assets and liabilities. As previously stated, these verification activities overlap to some extent with the financial auditing carried out for the purpose of the review of financial statements.

VI–IX. Not used.

X. Overall Appraisal of Basic Financial Control Activities
    A. See standard Audit Guides.

ILLUSTRATIVE AUDIT FINDINGS:
BASIC FINANCIAL CONTROL

Overly Large Cash Balances

A review of cash operations at the Dallas plant indicated that cash balances were in excess of needs. An analysis of receipts and disbursements showed that the plant controller was maintaining a cash balance large enough to meet all planned expenditures for the month. Since the major expenditures were made on the 15th and 31st of the month, cash was needed for only half a month's expenditures. By reducing cash on hand, interest savings of $25,000 a year could be earned on the excess.

Reducing Bank Balances Based on Float

A comparison of cash balances per books and per bank statements showed that excess cash was being kept in the bank. This resulted from float or delays in cashing checks and presenting them to the bank for payment. It was recommended that the bank balances be restricted to need based on estimates of checks that will be presented for payment. This would result in net interest earnings of $150,000 a year after deducting additional bank costs for services.

Excessive Bad Debts

Write-offs of bad debts in the Chicago division were 10% of divisional sales during the year, significantly in excess of other divisions. Divisional management had authorized the excessive write-offs without determining the causes and taking corrective action. It was found that the division granted credit to customers without sufficient study of their financial capability. The division also continued to extend credit to customers for long periods even though payments on account were not being made.

Unreasonable Payables

In performing an audit of material and equipment acquisitions it was noted that significant overruns in expenditures occurred from budget. An analysis of the payables function indicated that although purchases were properly authorized and approved, insufficient attention was being placed on the type of item acquired. Automobile fleet specifications were exceeded, both in size and cost of vehicles acquired. Unique types of equipment were purchased when standardized equipment was available. In addition, items with defects were accepted for payment without return to the manufacturer. Closer control was recommended over the generation and approval of payables.

Elimination of Manual Accounting Reports

Manual accounting reports continued to be prepared even though a new computerized system had the capability of producing the same reports. In some cases there was a duplication, primarily because personnel wanted information presented in a different form. By summarizing all accounting reports prepared, reviewing needs, and changing report formats, management was able to discontinue four reports prepared manually.

REVIEW QUESTIONS

1. What is meant by the "rule of reason" for financial controls? Why do we need it?
2. Why is it desirable to separate the processes pertaining to cash receipts from those pertaining to cash disbursements?
3. Explain the "imprest" basis for handling a petty cash fund. What are the benefits of the "imprest" approach?
4. Discuss the advantages of bonding employees who are involved in the handling of cash.
5. To what extent are controls over cash and accounts receivable similar? To what extent are they interrelated?
6. Discuss the range of levels of significance that can be involved in the case of controls pertaining to payables.
7. What special problems exist in connection with administering travel expenses?
8. What special problems exist in the case of payrolls as compared to other types of payables?
9. Explain the role of the personnel department in the payroll process.
10. To what extent is the internal auditor concerned with basic accounting activities?

CASE PROBLEMS

Problem 11-1

The Burner Oil Company is a wholesaler of petroleum products serving over fifty retail dealers via a fleet of modern delivery tank trucks. Most of the dealers are served on a credit basis and are billed monthly. However, in certain cases dealers are restricted to a "cash on delivery" basis. In some cases dealers also make total or partial payments on account by check or cash directly to the drivers. Dealers buying on credit make their payments by mailing their checks or bringing cash directly to the Burner Oil Company office.

It came to light recently that one of the delivery men had delayed the reporting of cash received on account from credit customers. On investigation it was disclosed that this had been done frequently by this particular driver, but it had not attracted attention until one of the delayed reportings of cash had extended over the date of sending monthly statements. Tom Brunner, the president of Burner Oil, is now considering a new instruction to prohibit the receiving of cash payments by delivery men from credit customers. Before doing this, however, he asks you as general auditor to give him your views as to the merits of the new instruction and as to the overall problem of controlling delivery men.

Required.   Respond to Tom Brunner's request.

Problem 11-2

You are a staff auditor with a reputation for being an outstanding operational auditor. Your audit supervisor calls you to her office and announces that you have been assigned a project to conduct an operational audit of the corporate accounts payables department. You advise her that you can certainly audit accounts payable, but you would never considered the audit to be operational. You leave the office with the comment, "I'll do my best."

Required.   Develop an outline which can be used to explain to the staff auditor that an operational audit can be made in accounts payable as well as in other operating areas.

CHAPTER TWELVE

Purchasing and Transportation

Upon completing this chapter you should be able to:

☐ *Describe the purchasing function's role in procurement*
☐ *Explain the normal cycle of the purchasing function*
☐ *Explain how the effectiveness of the purchasing function can be evaluated*
☐ *Understand the control problems of actions involving outside vendors*
☐ *Explain the normal cycle for a transportation function*

PURCHASING

Purchasing as a Major Part of the Procurement Function

The starting point in the total operational cycle of a company is the procurement of the materials and services which are to be marketed either in their existing form, or used, processed, or combined in some other fashion to provide the products and services actually offered for sale. This procurement can involve raw material, processed materials, parts, subassemblies, services, supplies, facilities, people, and money itself. In many of these areas of procurement there are special problems which require special skills. Illustrative would be the recruitment of people—which would be handled by a personnel staff, or obtaining capital funds—which would be handled by a treasurer's office. A large portion of the procurement, however, is normally handled by a group specifically established for this purpose. Although, as we shall see, the scope of this group's procurement activities will vary, the items handled usually include most of the materials, parts, and supplies used by the company.

The importance of the purchasing activity is usually very great, with its purchases running typically a large part of the costs incurred by the company for the products and services marketed. It is, therefore, an activity that deserves a great deal of attention on the part of management. It is an important activity also because it interrelates in such a significant manner with other management activities. What is purchased is directly related to production efficiency. The volume of the purchases is also a determinant of inventory levels. The investment in inventories is a major factor in the achievement of a favorable return on capital employed. In addition, the purchasing function has direct operational relationships with such activities as receiving, warehouse operations, scrap sales, and accounts payable. For all of these reasons the purchasing area is also an important area for review by the internal auditor.

Purchasing is important area for review

Basic Purchasing Role

For those areas of procurement where the responsibility has been assigned to the purchasing department,[1] the basic role is, like any area of procurement, to provide the right products (or services) at the right price, at the right time, and at the right place. "Right" is used here to signify the "best possible," all things considered, as judged by the long-term interests of the company.[2] It is of course a determination that often cannot be precisely evaluated, and hence one that involves a great deal of judgment. This is especially true because of the major interrelationship with other operational activities and the long time often required to appraise particular types of benefits or penalties. These key dimensions of the basic role are at the same time the objectives of the purchasing activity. It is these objectives in which we are interested in our discussion of the purchasing activity. Our interest in this basic purchasing role exists at several levels. At the lowest level is the clerical efficiency with which the procedural part of the operations is carried out. At the next higher level we are interested in the effectiveness with which individual activities cover more substantive matters such as the selection of vendors and the negotiation of prices. At the highest level our concern is with the extent to which opportunities are perceived for better relating the purchasing function to the other major management functions.

Normal Cycle of the Purchasing Function

The purchasing function can be viewed as a cycle that includes a number of fairly well-defined steps. These are:

---

[1]Department is used as a general term to refer to the organizational component charged with purchasing responsibilities.
[2]Company is used to cover any type of business or nonbusiness organization involved in any kind of an operational activity.

*Normal cycle has six
key steps*

1. *Determination of Needs.* We must first determine what the specific need is that must be satisfied through the procurement action. This would include the identification of the product and its specifications, quantities, delivery requirements, and any other pertinent information.

2. *Authorization of the Purchase.* As a second step there must be an authorization to proceed with the purchase. Something is needed and now we decide we will actually get it.

3. *Making the Purchase.* The purchasing group then carries out its search for the vendor which it is believed will provide the goods sought, on the basis which is most advantageous to the company. The selection of the vendor then leads to the decision to enter into a definitive purchase agreement.

4. *Follow-Up.* To the extent necessary there must now be such follow-up action on the part of the purchasing group as will best assure the delivery of the needed goods in the manner that will satisfy management requirements.

5. *Completion of Delivery.* Actual deliveries are now made and a determination is made as to whether there has been proper compliance with the purchase agreement, or if not, what offsetting claims exist.

6. *Financial Settlement.* Finally, the settlement is made with the vendor on the proper basis, and the purchase transaction is complete—subject only to such continuing warranties by the vendor as may have been part of the basic agreement.

Major Control Structure

We discuss next the control problems around the previously listed operational steps in the normal cycle of the purchasing function.

Determination of Needs

The basic control issue in the determination of needs is the extent to which that determination is made on a sound basis and then accurately communicated to the purchasing group. Typical sources of these determinations include:

*Evaluate how well needs
being determined*

1. A production schedule which, when exploded as a bill of materials, identifies the specific requirements in terms of individual product items, pertinent specifications, and conditions of delivery.

2. An inventory system with predetermined stock levels for individual products, which then generates order requirements for individual items as the stock level reaches a given minimal point.

3. Special projects of either a capital or operational nature which carry with them particular kinds of requirements for goods and services.

4. Other operational needs which are evaluated in some way and translated into purchase requirements.

In any one of these situations a number of different types of questions arise,
which have to be considered in a manner dependent on the significance of
the particular item. There is, first, the question as to the general validity of
the underlying need. This would include both the purpose for which the
particular items are to be used and the soundness of the way in which the
basic need is translated into the definite requirements. Illustrative of this
would be the need for a particular item for warehouse stocks and the kind
of decision formula applied for the determination of the stocking requirement. Second, there is the further question of whether the system as designed is actually being operated efficiently. Finally, there is the question
of whether the determined need is properly transmitted to the purchasing
group in the form of an approved requisition or by other proper documentation.

Responsibility for Determination of Needs. How needs are determined is
normally the responsibility of other company personnel. While these determinations initiate the purchasing process, the purchasing group does more
than just process them. The purchasing department is very often in a good
position to know what is sound in the way of an underlying method or policy
for determining needs. It is also well qualified to serve as a kind of a check
on unusual and abnormally high supply requirements. The role of the purchasing group also extends to the determination of needs in a different way.
The purchasing group through its purchasing activities is in touch with
market conditions and should be able to appraise new developments and
trends in the way of shortages or oversupply. The individual buyer also
knows more intimately the situations of the various vendors, especially the
more important vendors. Thus purchasing personnel should be able to make
an important contribution in advising other company personnel of the changing developments, and as to what bearing these developments might have
on the current ordering actions. The purchasing group thus does in part
share the responsibility for the proper determination of needs and should
be as helpful as possible.

*Purchasing should monitor
needs and not just process
paper*

Procedural Aspects of Determination of Needs. The needs as determined
must now be put into proper documentary form. Normally there will be
requisition forms or other types of advice which list the specific needs with
the pertinent specifications, required approvals, and any other information
needed for other company purposes. Specifications should be used to develop standardized parts wherever practicable. Although a substantial part
of this procedure may be automated in individual situations, there is still
the question of the propriety of the basic input to the automated process.
In some cases standard and so-called "traveling requisitions" are used in
repetitive situations to minimize excessive clerical effort and human error.

The important aspects in all of the situations are:

1. Propriety of approvals
2. Completeness of all information needed
3. Accuracy of the clerical and processing effort

Authorization of the Purchase

Authorization procedures need evaluation

In some cases the determination of the need will at the same time become the authorization to purchase. But this is not necessarily so, because the authorization to purchase involves some further questions which are not normally the final responsibility of the people who determine the need. Typical of these questions would be:

1. *Is the Item Available Within the Company?* The purchasing group may have knowledge of the availability of the item elsewhere in the company. In other cases there may be enough question to justify making a specific search as to that possibility.
2. *Should the Item Be Made Rather Than Purchased?* This is a question that is normally under continuing scrutiny. Changing conditions such as increasing difficulties of procurement, increased volume, or increased cost will sharpen the interest in the make possibility and be the basis of initiating more depth studies. The impetus for the make-or-buy investigation can come from a number of sources, but possibilities here are part of the overall concern of an effective purchasing group.
3. *Can the Purchase Be Made?* Conditions may have arisen where the items specified cannot be purchased, or perhaps only in a modified form. In such a situation there must be further discussions with the using organizational component.
4. *Are Budgetary Requirements Complied With?* If not previously covered at the requisition stage, there will normally be the necessity for budgetary approval. This would be true especially if the purchase would result in an overbudget condition for the requisitioning activity.
5. *Are There Financing Problems?* Since the purchase will establish a definitive financial obligation, the question may arise as to whether the purchase at this time is within the company's financial capabilities. In some cases it might be necessary either to defer the purchase or to reduce the quantities.

Procedural Aspects of Authorization of Purchase. The actual authorization of the purchase can be handled either as a part of the requisition form or as a supplemental or separate form. The important thing is that the designated approvals have been secured and that the purchasing group has raised any questions that would be in the company interest before proceeding with the operational execution of the actual purchase. In most cases this would be handled as a supplementary set of approvals to the basic requisition.

Making the Purchase

We come now to the heart of the purchasing activity—the search for the vendor and the making of the definitive arrangement for providing the items needed. In selecting the vendor the important considerations include at least the following:

1. The diligence of the search which has been made for all vendors who would reasonably seem to be a possible qualified source, including both new vendors and vendors who have supplied other items.

2. The extent of field contact which has been made to look over facilities and to discuss operational capabilities and related problems with existing and potential vendors.

3. The individual vendor's reliability in terms of past procurements, general reputation, and financial standing.

4. The weighing of the various factors that comprise the determination of the value to be received, including price, terms, absorption of delivery costs, treatment of tooling charges, maintenance of reserve inventories, capacity to satisfy delivery requirements, quality, service backup, product development activities, and the like.

5. The extent to which there are supplementary considerations such as community relations, support of small business, competitor disclosure risks, sales reciprocity, or government direction.

6. The extent to which the company desires protection for supply through dual or multiple sourcing.

Vendor selection involves range of considerations

Exploiting Competition. Except in the case where the price with a single vendor is to be determined later, the selection of the vendor is at the same time the fixing of the terms of the purchase arrangement with that vendor. The basic control factor is, therefore, the extent to which the purchasing group has fully exploited market opportunities through competitive bidding. Has every legitimate competitive pressure been used to get the maximum value for the company? Here it must be recognized that this normally desirable objective could conceivably be carried too far. This could be where the vendor so much needs the business that the purchaser is in a position to exploit that power by forcing the price down to an unfair level. The more enlightened company, however, recognizes that it is in the company's long-run interest to have a solvent and reasonably prosperous vendor. These conditions are in fact the basis for securing quality products and in being able to rely on the vendor. But the company must at the same time recognize its own problem of competitive survival and find that proper balance of

Balance between toughness and fairness needed

toughness and fairness. To achieve these ends it must seek continuously to have a strong and healthy competition among its vendors.

Soliciting competitive bids
should be standard
procedure

What this means is that the solicitation of competitive bids must be standard procedure to the maximum extent practicable. The only exception is for the special situation where there is no satisfactory second source, or where emergency pressures do not allow adequate time to get the competitive bids. But such situations should be minimized in every way possible by better planning and by a deliberate effort to develop alternative sources. It is also important that the solicitation of competitive bids be done often enough for the same item to take advantage of new developments in the field. In addition, the bid solicitation must be in good faith and the basis for the actual award, as opposed to the possible situation when it might be a cover-up or be manipulated to support an already determined selection. A good purchasing group will, therefore, continually strive to expand and to make more effective its effort to seek competitive bids, and it should be prepared to justify the extent to which that approach is not in fact followed.

Negotiated Fixed-Price Contracts. Despite the objective to seek competitive bidding to the maximum extent possible, the fact must be faced that in some situations the vendor choice will be dictated by other factors. It may be, for example, that a particular vendor alone has the know-how, experience, or patent position. Or the choice may be dictated by our customer, as is often true in the case of government work. Under such circumstances the vendor may have an established price and that will be the price if we want the product. In other situations there will be a negotiation of the pricing arrangements. The approach here is normally a more detailed showing of costs which it is estimated will be incurred, plus a factor for profit. In some cases these costs estimates are subject to field review, especially if there is to be any later incentive-type price redetermination based upon actual cost experience. Cost estimates prepared by company personnel should also be used to the extent possible. It is also frequently possible for finance personnel to assist purchasing personnel in the various stages of the price negotiations.

Problems with
cost-reimbursement type
procurement

Cost-Reimbursement Types of Procurement. In certain situations the experience with a product may be so limited that it is not even possible to negotiate intelligently any kind of a fixed-price type of contract. In that case resort must be made to an arrangement where the payment is determined by actual costs plus an agreed-upon profit factor. Several important cost control problems exist with this type of procurement. First, there is the difficulty of defining which types of cost are to be reimbursed. This includes the problem of defining what costs are to be considered as direct charges and what kinds of overhead items will be proper. In the case of overhead there is the further problem of how they will be allocated to the particular products. A second major type of difficulty lies in the lack of sufficient motivation to reduce costs as compared to the fixed-price type of contract. In fact there can often be a reverse type of motivation. The third major difficulty is with the determination of the profit factor. Especially to be avoided are percentage approaches that result in higher profit when costs increase, again providing the wrong kind of motivation. All of this means that cost-type contracts are to be avoided to the maximum extent possible, and that, if we have no other alternative, they be handled with extreme care. Again, finance people are normally brought in to help define cost relationships and to review the propriety of claimed costs. The monitoring of work and costs in progress is especially important in cost-type contracts.

Procedures for Making the Purchase. The procedure for the handling of this phase of the purchase transaction can vary, but in a typical situation include:

1. "Logging in" the authorization to purchase and assigning it to a member of the purchasing group, usually called the buyer, depending on the size of the proposed purchase and the type of item. Specialization of buyers is normally the practice but the extent of it will, of course, depend on the size of the purchasing operation. *Defined procedures needed for making purchases*

2. Vendor records are normally cross-referenced for the various types of items and these will be consulted for possible sources.

3. The responsible buyer consults with his superior and with the company user to clarify any questions he might have about the procurement.

4. Bids are solicited by means of standard forms, but these may be supplemented by telephone contacts.

5. Bids are received and summarized on standard forms and the lowest bid, all things considered, will be determined. Factors in the selection of the bid are noted. If the recommendation is made without competitive bidding, the supporting reasons are attached.

6. The recommendation of the buyer is reviewed by the superior to the extent required.

7. The "authorization to purchase" record is completed and cross-referenced to the purchase order number as listed in the register of purchase orders issued.

8. The purchase order is mailed to the vendor with a copy provided on which he is to acknowledge acceptance and to return to the purchasing department.

The purchase order is normally a serially controlled document. It is prepared in multicopy form so that information copies can be forwarded to other interested company activities, such as the user, receiving department, and accounts payable. It contains the standard contractual terms plus any approved modifications. The purchase order normally states all warranties and may provide the alternative right of rejection or repair in case the goods do not meet the specifications. It also may provide a measure of damages in the event the goods are defective.

Whereas the transportation costs may be the responsibility of either the vendor or purchaser, the mode of transportation and, where applicable, the routing via a selected carrier are normally the prerogative of the purchaser. These directions will also be included as a part of the purchase order. We deal in greater length with the transportation problem later in this chapter.

Follow-Up

Expediting capabilities should be available

The continuing concern of the purchasing group is now that the products purchased are actually delivered in accordance with the purchase order agreement. In many situations the dependence of other company activities on agreed deliveries is so great that all possible steps must be taken to ensure the wanted result. Frequently, it is desirable for the buyer or his representative to visit the vendor facilities to check on progress. Other company personnel may also be brought into the picture to act in an advisory capacity or to verify quality performance. The emphasis here is on taking all preventive measures in any way which will best assure the wanted final result. In other cases the buyer will be in touch with regular company activities to review interim progress with repect to deliveries. If and when problems of delays or below-standard specifications develop, the buyer can act as a liaison with the vendor. Another term sometimes used for the follow-up activity is "expediting."

Procedural Aspects. The extent of the procedures will necessarily vary with the complexity of the delivery schedules and the length of the delivery period. Normally, some type of visible follow-up record will be utilized to keep the purchasing group apprised of key performance dates. Each buyer will be responsible for monitoring the progress of those purchase orders which he handled. Regular written reports are also useful in some situations.

Completion of Delivery

Receiving function to be separate from purchasing

Under best practice there will be a separate receiving activity which will establish the facts as to what has been received and in what condition. In the case of certain products there will also be necessary inspections for conformance to agreed-upon specifications and level of quality. In some cases more elaborate tests will be necessary, with approvals by responsible operating executives. In some cases also it may be necessary to hold the questioned items for later vendor inspection. Thus the determination is made for acceptance or rejection, or for various types of claims. There may also be claims against the transportation agencies that have acted as carriers. Now, subject to any continuing warranties, the basis is established for the expected financial settlement.

Procedural Aspects. The key procedural requirements are that the receiving and inspection activities are organizationally independent of the purchasing group and that the records of these activities are transmitted directly to the accounts payable activity. At the same time all records of claims of any kind should be clearly stated and also transmitted to the accounts payable group. To the extent that there are other types of proof of receipt—as, for example, the continuing operation of a particular manufacturing operation— it must be adequately demonstrated that the goods were received and in proper condition.

Financial Settlement

The financial settlement will actually be carried out by the separate accounts payable group. Here there will be the final matching of the original purchase order with the receiving data, and subject to the consideration of deductions or adjustments, the final approval for payment and subsequent disbursement. The negotiation of the adjustments is normally made by the affected buyer, but in certain cases it may be desirable to bring finance people into these negotiations. We covered the settlement procedures when we discussed the basis financial controls in Chapter 11. Our interest at this point is to recognize the financial settlement as the final step in the purchase transaction. Although the purchasing group is kept informed, as necessary, the important control aspect as it relates to purchasing is that financial settlement not be under purchasing control.

Financial settlement must be separate from purchasing

Other Matters of Special Interest

Our review of the major control points now needs to be supplemented by a consideration of some related matters that bear importantly on the effective control of the purchasing activity.

Organizational Status. One of these broader issues is the question of the organizational status of the purchasing function. Although it must be recognized that the volume and importance of the items purchased determine in the first place the importance of the purchasing function—and to that extent its organizational status—there is still the question of whether the purchasing group has been accorded the level of organizational status it really deserves. In the typical situation a vice-president ranking is warranted at the corporate headquarters level with counterpart organizational status in component operational units. What is needed is an organizational status that will best assure the ability to attract a person who will have sufficient stature, and which will provide the proper degree of independence and position for effectively relating with other staff and line members of the top management group. At the same time the responsibilities should not include collateral activities such as receiving, warehousing, and payment, which are needed as legitimate and constructive counter-controls.

Purchasing needs organizational status that assures adequate independence

Extent of decentralization
depends on many factors

Centralization versus Decentralization. A related organizational problem is the extent to which the purchasing function should be centralized at the corporate headquarters level versus the extent to which lower-level operating subsidiaries, divisions, and other profit centers should have their own purchasing activities. Another possibility is that purchasing personnel may be physically located at the lower levels but organizationally be directly responsible to the central purchasing group. To a considerable extent the answer here depends on the overall picture of the company with respect to decentralization. If this is a centralized company, it will be logical that purchasing will also be centralized; and if the company is strongly profit-center oriented, we would expect to find separate purchasing groups in the individual profit centers. Even in the latter situations there will normally be the need for some kind of a central purchasing group. In the first place, there will always be the need for some central group to develop and administer certain types of company-wide purchasing policy. Also such a central group can provide needed central research and special expertise in a staff capacity. Second, in many situations there is a need for the central coordination or central control of certain procurements on a company-wide basis. To the extent that there are local purchasing groups it would seem to be preferable to have them report to the local management group in a line sense and to the central purchasing group on a so-called dotted-line functional basis. The important thing is that the respective jurisdiction and related responsibilities of the central purchasing group versus the field purchasing groups be clearly stated. If this is done properly it is usually possible for the total company purchasing operations to operate effectively and to serve adequately the needs of both the operational component and the central headquarters. All of this assumes that the central purchasing group will exercise adequate control over the field units. Part of this control will be built in as a part of the day-to-day operational relationships, but will normally be supplemented by the review of reports and periodic field visits.

Purchasing Jurisdiction. Another type of organizational problem concerns defining and administering the jurisdiction of the purchasing group. This problem appears in a variety of forms but perhaps the most common one is determining what types of purchases will go through the purchasing department. In some cases the conclusion may be reached that it is more efficient for a particular operational group to satisfy certain types of procurement needs through its own direct efforts. The personnel department has already been referred to as such a case. Another illustration would be that of an advertising department obtaining media space directly or through an advertising agency. In making the official determination of jurisdiction the basic issue is whether the purchasing group can make a contribution, either as a result of its actual experience in a given area of procurement, or because a professional purchasing approach can be expected to yield special benefits.

Another type of problem exists when the official determination is clear enough but there is an evasion of some kind. One frequent type of evasion is when the user jumps the gun, so to speak, and in effect carries out his own investigation of the particular type of availability and then comes to the purchasing department only to legitimatize the effort through a perfunctory handling of the actual purchase through the purchasing department. Here the possibility of the contribution of the regular purchasing group is precluded. The best remedy in this kind of a situation is that the purchasing department turn back the request. The need to get the expenditure authorized properly to fit into regular accounts payable routines will then serve as a discipline to let the purchasing department do its proper job in the future.

A more commonplace type of problem is the avoidance of regular purchasing controls by effecting the procurement through petty cash, credit cards, or other types of operating funds. Such funds have presumably been set up for relatively limited purposes, usually for small expenditures and those of a special nature. The problem arises when those purposes are abused through a more extended use of them, and in this instance for the procurement of items which should go through regular purchasing channels. The result is a loss of control over these procurements and the loss of advantage that can come through the more consolidated procurement. The basic control here is that the ground rules be clearly stated and enforced through the procedures under which these established operating funds are reimbursed.

Emergency Purchases.   Another variation of the evasion problem is that of emergency purchases. This particular problem exists when the operational activity simply does not act on a timely basis. Because of the delay the purchasing group is then placed in the situation where it does not have enough time to do its job efficiently. The problem is usually confused by the fact that emergency needs are to some extent unavoidable, and that in those situations there is no choice but to compromise through completing the purchase on the best possible basis within the time constraints. As a result, prices will usually have to be accepted which might have been reduced through competitive bidding. It can lead also to the undesirable situation where purchase commitments are made without price agreement; that is, the vendor is asked to proceed with the production or shipment of the item and then to advise the company what the price will be. As we have seen, emergency needs are often unavoidable. There may be a breakdown of equipment, or perhaps an unexpected rush order from one of the company's customers. The issue here is for the need to make a fair determination of what volume of emergency needs is in fact reasonable and in taking steps to eliminate the portion that is due only to various kinds of inefficiency.

Purchasing for Employees.   It is inevitable that company personnel will seek help in one way or another from purchasing personnel in making their own

Purchasing by other than purchasing department needs clear justification

Emergency purchases needs should be continuously questioned

Purchasing for employees can often go too far

personal purchases. This is especially likely to be true if the items involved are the same as are being purchased for company use. It is a practice that is especially common in the case of company officers. Normally this is not too serious a problem, but it can get out of hand. The main concern is that such service be extended on an equitable basis—that is, to individuals at specified organizational levels—and that it not be permitted to affect the ability of the purchasing group to discharge their regular responsibilities in an effective manner. Consideration must be given not only to the dilution of buyers' efforts, but also to the nuisance to vendors, including the administrative difficulties of effecting delivery and payment. Normally the more this practice can be restricted the better it will be.

Effective purchasing dependent on good analysis of alternatives

Analytical Role in Purchasing. Although the effectiveness of the purchasing representative is determined to some extent by his so-called trader skills, there is perhaps no type of activity that depends so much on basic analytical ability. This analytical ability is a combination of a vigorous and imaginative search for facts and the related capacity to relate those facts to specific procurement situations. In his special product area the buyer needs to know what goes into the making of the product, the nature of the manufacturing processes, and the major operational problems that affect the completion and delivery of the product. He also needs to know what things should cost and what are good levels of cost performance. Related also is a knowledge of how the product will be used and what types of problems can arise in that utilization. His job is to put all of this knowledge together in the most advantageous manner possible in terms of ultimate company interest. Perhaps the most important aspect of this entire process is that he can be instrumental in finding better ways to accomplish the objectives as opposed to simply trying to squeeze profit out of a vendor. A good illustration of his work along these lines is the so-called "value analysis" of products where consideration is given to how different material and/or different processes might be used to take cost out of a product without impairing its usefulness. Under this kind of approach the buyer is also more likely to win the cooperation of vendors, and it should similarly provide attractive possibilities to other company personel. Fortunately this particular capacity on the part of the buyer also tends to increase over time as his knowledge is augmented by further experience and breadth of contacts.

Undue influence of vendors needs continuous alertness

Controlling Undue Influence. A particularly troublesome operational problem in the purchasing area exists in the temptation for purchasing personnel deliberately to favor particular vendors. Since the purchasing department's decision as to which vendor shall receive the order is one that has such a major impact on the financial interests of that vendor, it is to be expected that the vendor will exert a great deal of pressure on the person in the purchasing group who can control that decision to any significant extent. The types of pressure run from legitimate sales presentations and persistent follow-up to friendship factors, entertainment, gifts, and on to various types of actual bribery. Frequently, the line between the proper and improper is a hard one to draw—as, for example, in the case of a Christmas gift—and the standards of what is right and wrong often tend to deteriorate over time. Most well-managed companies recognize the danger that exists and endeavor to control it by strong policies prohibiting the acceptance of all favors, including the publicizing of those policies both to the purchasing personnel and vendors. The dangers here in any event increase the importance of good purchasing supervision and review, and continuous alertness to anything that appears to be an unwarranted favoritism to particular vendors.

Measuring the Effectiveness of the Purchasing Activity

A central problem that concerns both the management of the purchasing department and other company management is how to measure the effectiveness of the purchasing function. At the level of internal administration there can be the usual measures of the volume of purchasing handled, the number of purchase transactions effected, the length of time to handle the various types of operations, and the costs of these activities. These measures are of course most meaningful when they are compared with the performance at other purchasing operations where similar types of purchases are made. Useful comparisons can also be made with the performance of previous periods. It is important, therefore, that these measures be applied through a series of monthly and quarterly reports.

Measuring purchasing effectiveness requires well-defined goals and objectives

But the real problem in measuring the effectiveness of the purchasing activity is that each purchase transaction involves judgment, and that it is difficult to measure the quality of that judgment. Savings here are also passed on to the user groups in the way of lower procurement costs and are reflected in the operational results of those other groups. Still another difficulty is that the contribution of the purchasing department in many cases is a joint effort with other company personnel. Yet despite the difficulties involved, there is the clear necessity to do something reasonably precise in measuring this larger and more important contribution of the purchasing group. The question is how to do it in a meaningful way.

The starting point of the measurement effort is, as we would expect, to establish meaningful objectives. The dollar volume of purchasing expected to be routed through the purchasing department is the gross base from which we must determine possibilities for savings through purchase price reductions. As we have seen previously, one type of possibility exists through the expansion of the competitive process, which in turn depends to a major extent on the development of additional vendor sources. Another possibility exists through working with individual vendors to develop new approaches that can provide the basis for lower costs. As we have seen also, the latter effort involves working with company personnel, and determining how their needs can be served in different ways. Throughout this entire effort the emphasis is on lower-cost approaches which will not reduce the value to the user. In all cases we are seeking to increase the number of options available. Finally there is the possibility of interpreting market conditions so that buying can be done at the most advantageous time possible.

Once having analyzed the foregoing types of possibilities, to the extent possible, the basis is provided for establishing meaningful objectives. Needless to say, all of the purchasing group needs to participate in this effort because it will largely be individual buyers who can speak to the real possibilities in particular product areas. It will also be these same individual buyers who will actually effect the savings. The objectives thus established now become the basis for a periodic reporting of results actually achieved against these objectives. The savings reported to be achieved then have to be supported as well as possible with credit to other parties as is appropriate. Although the entire sequence is to some extent unavoidably inexact, experience has demonstrated that more will be accomplished by the program of savings objectives than simply to proceed in the usual manner. Certainly other company personnel have better visibility of the nature of the purchasing effort and, therefore, have a better opportunity to support it.

Internal Auditor's Role

Purchasing needs same kind of review as other operational areas

The role of the internal auditor in relation to the purchasing function will follow generally the pattern that would exist for any operational activity, but we restate it with particular application to the purchasing activity.

1. To understand the nature and scope of the purchasing function
2. To check on the administrative efficiency of the purchasing activity in terms of presently designated policies and procedures—at the same time determining the extent of actual compliance with those policies and procedures
3. To appraise those policies and procedures in terms of possible improvement
4. To seek to identify the management service potential as purchasing works in a collaborative partnership fashion with both vendors and operational managers of the company
5. To seek to contribute to increased company welfare through identifying any other means by which the purchasing effort can be made more effective.

To summarize, it is the role of the internal auditor to see the purchasing department through the eyes of top management, but with an understanding of the problems of the purchasing department, the company users, and the vendors. He seeks to appraise efficiency and control in a basic operational sense, but at the same time to determine whether its full potential for contribution to company interests is being adequately exploited.

AUDIT GUIDES

REVIEW OF PURCHASING

I. Introductory

   A. Reference should be made to the general discussion of audit guides, Chapter 11.

II. Preparatory Activities

   A. See standard Audit Guides, Chapter 11.

III. Organizational Factors

   A. See standard Audit Guides, Chapter 11.

   B. Establish that the purchasing department is independent of receiving, inspection, stores, and accounts payable activities.

   C. Matters of special interest in the review of purchasing manuals will include:

      1. Standards of vendor relationships.

      2. Competitive bidding requirements.

      3. Extent of multiple sourcing.

      4. Reciprocity.

      5. Extent of local purchases.

      6. Coordination with user organizational components.

      7. Authorized levels of approval.

      8. Conflict of interest and acceptance of gifts.

      9. Follow-up responsibilities.

     10. Special types of purchase orders for applications that are more extended —over long time periods, or covering usage at a number of locations.

     11. Handling of employee purchases.

     12. Handling of deviations from established procedures.

IV. Authorization for Purchase

   A. Review the procedures for authorizing purchases. Points of special interest include:

      1. Who initiates?

      2. What approvals are necessary for particular types of items and amounts in terms of either quantities or dollar value?

      3. What forms are to be used?

      4. How are supplementary approvals handled when actual purchase cost exceeds original estimates?

      5. What provision for changes in specifications or quantities?

   B. On the basis of actual tests, verify and appraise:

      1. The extent to which the procedures are complied with. (Where they were not complied with to any significant degree, what were the causes?)

2. Do the procedures appear to be adequate?
3. Where there are unusual authorizations in terms of types of products, quantities, source restrictions, and the like, does it appear that these are questioned and discussed?

V. Internal Operations

A. General

1. Are the facilities adequate:
   a. For reception and interviews with vendor representatives?
   b. For internal operations?
2. Are the internal operations being carried out in a manner consistent with established organizational responsibilities, policies, and procedures? If not, what are the causes, and what kind of corrective action seems to be warranted? This part of the review would include such questions as:
   a. Should the organizational responsibilities be modified?
   b. Should operational policies be reappraised?
   c. Should operational procedures be revised?
   d. Do we need different people?
3. To what extent do the operations reflect a high degree of efficiency and morale? Factors of special interest are similar to question 2 above.
4. Are internal records and files of various types adequate in terms of special purpose and relation to other records and procedures? Are they being maintained efficiently?
5. Is the total purchase cycle adequately controlled as to receipt of authorization, assignment to buyer, making of purchase, follow-up, and completion—so that the status of individual procurements can be easily determined?
6. Are purchasing forms properly safeguarded and controlled?
7. Are purchasing actions being processed on a timely basis?
8. Is the computer used for controlling orders, expediting, and reporting?

B. Relating to Vendors

1. Are adequate vendor records maintained showing supply capabilities and continuing purchasing relationships?
2. How adequate is the effort to develop new vendor sources?
3. How adequate are the field contacts with vendors to keep abreast of these vendor situations and to maintain cordial, high-level relationships?
4. Are vendor financial capabilities adequally investigated through banks and credit agencies?
5. What efforts are being made to evaluate vendor performance for price, delivery, and quality? And are adequate files pertaining to these factors maintained?

6. How adequate are the efforts to work with vendors to study cost reduction possibilities?
7. With respect to competitive bidding:
   a. Are competitive bids solicited in all cases possible?
   b. Are bids invited from at least three qualified vendors?
   c. In the case of recurring purchases are competitive bids solicited with needed frequency?
   d. Are all factors directly or indirectly related to price properly considered?
8. If price lists of vendors are used, are they updated with reasonable frequency?
9. With respect to negotiated purchase prices:
   a. Is the need to purchase on this basis adequately justified?
   b. Are adequate cost breakdowns made available as a basis for negotiation?
   c. Are all possible cross checks utilized in the way of comparison with products involving similar materials and processing, or via "in-house" estimates?
10. With respect to cost-type procurement:
   a. Is the need to purchase on this basis adequately justified?
   b. Are clearly defined and reasonable agreements reached as to recoverable costs prior to award of the purchase?
   c. Is profit reasonable and established in such a manner as to best motivate the lowest possible level of cost?
   d. Is cost performance adequately audited for compliance with established agreements?
11. Is the selection of the vendor and the basis of the proposed procurement reviewed and approved by a higher-ranking member of the purchasing group?

VI. Special Audit Tests
A. In addition to such observations and queries as have been made relative to specific aspects, it is desirable to test a representative number of purchase transactions by following them through all steps in the purchasing cycle. The sample should be picked at random from the original input of authorizations to purchase. Points of special interest at all stages would include:
   1. Compliance with all policies and procedures.
   2. Reasonableness of timing at the various stages.
   3. Evidence of care and maximum protection of company interest.
   4. Evidence of good team work in the total purchasing group.
   5. All possible evidence of good value received.
   6. Excessive rush or emergency orders.
   7. Possibilities for combining separate purchases.

8. Orders for unauthorized items—as, for example, capital equipment.
9. Necessity of commitments in advance of price agreements.
10. Effectiveness of internal records and related procedures.
11. Leads for matters to be investigated in the review of other operational activities.
12. Any evidence of vendor favoritism.
13. Overall evaluation of the competence of the management of the purchasing activity.

VII–IX. Not used.

X. Overall Appraisal of Purchasing Effectiveness
   A. See standard Audit Guides, Chapter 11.
   B. Appraisal of relations with both vendors and company personnel should focus especially upon reduction of costs through substitution of materials, modifications of production processes, different delivery arrangements, and the like.

TRANSPORTATION

Transportation as a Part of the Procurement Activity

Transportation is part of procurement role

Transportation services are an important group of services which must be procured by the company. Although to some extent the company may elect to provide these services with its own facilities—as, for example, through the use of company-owned trucks—there is still normally a large volume of transportation services to be obtained from outside parties. Outside parties include principally railroads, ships, barges, truckers, express agencies, airlines, and the U.S. Postal Service. The procurement here may be associated with the procurement of purchased goods, company shipments to customers, or any type of internal transfer of materials. Its overall importance will depend on the range of operations of the particular company, but it will normally represent a very substantial type of operating cost. It is a type of procurement that has many special complexities, but which like any other operational activity presents opportunities for effective control.

Nature of the Transportation Process

Transportation in its most basic sense has to do with moving the various materials from the place of origin to a newly desired location in the most efficient manner. Materials include raw materials, processed materials, parts, facilities, products, or any other tangible item. Efficiency means the combination of price, other terms, timing, and physical conditions, which best serve the company's interests. We are concerned at this point only with the transportation services obtained from outside parties, although any company-provided transportation activity should always continually be reviewed as to the alternative of securing that service from an outside group. As managers, and in turn as internal auditors, we are interested that transportation activities are carried on in a manner that best serves the total company interest.

The functions of the transportation group, commonly designated in the company organization as the traffic department, fall into two general groups. The first of these groups has to do with the development of transportation policy and in carrying out the various studies and investigations that pertain to major decisions. What mode of transportation should be used in the various situations? What routings are best? What can be done in the way of new approaches to reduce transportation costs? The second group of activities on the other hand concerns the day-to-day operations which are carried on pursuant to the aforementioned policies and key decisions. These are the operational activities that have to do with daily carrier relations, shipments, follow-up, and the like—including the maintenance of current files and records. The latter activities also lend themselves to decentralization to field offices or to other lower-level operational organizational components.

The basic operational cycle is generally similar to that which we found in the case of purchasing:

Operational cycle similar to purchasing

1. The determination of the need
2. The determination of the specific arrangement for obtaining the transportation service.
3. The notification of the transportation arrangement to be used
4. Any necessary follow-up
5. The financial settlement
6. The handling of claims

These operational stages, and the particular objectives associated with them can also again become the basis for looking at the structure of control and the related control problems of major significance.

Determining the Need for Transportation Services

Like purchasing, the starting point of the transportation problem is the identification of the need. There is first the validity of the need itself. Here the main question is whether there are other operational approaches that would eliminate or modify the asserted transportation need. For example, could delivery be made at a closer location? Or could we establish a storage point to eliminate a larger number of small shipments? There is also the question of whether the need has been accurately defined. Is the asserted urgency realistic? In many of these situations the transportation representative can provide good advisory counsel. It is always necessary that he[3]

---

[3]The use of the personal pronouns he or him—here and throughout this book—is for convenience only. Excellence in the business community is not limited by sex, color, race, or nationality.

know the exact nature of the need if he is to satisfy that need in the most economical manner. From a control standpoint we are interested in everything that will best induce this careful determination. Although this determination of need may be the basic responsibility of other operating personnel, the transportation personnel have a professional interest in it and to some extent a share of the responsibility.

Determining the Specific Transportation Arrangement

Transportation features need continuous review for new conditions

The heart of the transportation function is the study and search that goes into the determination of the specific transportation arrangement that will best satisfy the properly defined need. Here the special expertise of the transportation professional is fully utilized. Typical features that might be applicable will include:

1. The savings to be achieved by using the proper commodity rate
2. The decreasing costs of shipping in carload or truckload quantities
3. Possibilities of pooling shipments with other shippers
4. In transit stopovers or in transit privileges that can be obtained at a small extra cost
5. Delivery schedules
6. Risk of damage or theft
7. Extra services for premium rates
8. Customer preferences in connection with outbound shipments
9. Reciprocity pressures
10. Availability of special equipment
11. The relative costs of different modes of transportation in relation to the existing operational need

In some cases costs can be saved by hauling for compensation for wholly-owned subsidiaries or for others, as allowed under the Motor Carrier Act of 1980. Before this Act, private fleets of trucks were restricted to hauling their own goods. Also, although it was permissible for a subsidiary to haul for another subsidiary, it had to be gratuitous. Under the new Act a company may become involved in for-hire transport for unrelated companies or obtain contract carrier authority to haul for its subsidiaries. In the past subsidiaries often approached freight movement methods independently, and the new regulatory changes have created opportunities for joint freight operations.

The transportation department weighs these various considerations to arrive at the final conclusion that seems on balance to be the best. There will also, where necessary, be continuing discussions with customers, vendors, and company personnel. For repetitive shipments the same decisions will apply until there is some indication that some significant dimension of the evaluation has changed. In all situations the importance of this step from a control standpoint is that this is where the decision is actually made and that, therefore, this decision should reflect the greatest possible degree of efficiency and good judgment. The focus is on all evidence which indicates that the various factors pertaining to the decision have been recognized and properly evaluated.

Making the Transportation Arrangement

The determination of the transportation arrangement may at the same time become the actual notification to all interested parties, or in other cases this notification may be handled separately. The parties to be notified in different situations may be vendors, customers, or our own company personnel. In the case of a purchase the selected routing will normally be included on the purchase order. In the case of outgoing shipments, the proper bills of ladings will be prepared, or other company personnel instructed to do so. The control objective is a clear and timely notification of the underlying decision. In the case of repetitive shipments this becomes the operational implementation of standard routing instructions.

Follow-Up of Specific Execution of Transportation Arrangements

The extent of follow-up efforts depends on the urgency of the need for the materials being transported. In some cases this requires the monitoring of actual loading operations and interim reports on the progress of the shipment up to the point of actual delivery at the final destination. In other cases the failure of the materials to arrive at destination at given points of time would initiate the follow-up effort. The control objective is that the follow-up effort is adequate in the circumstances.

Settlement of Completed Transportation

Review of freight costs requires special expertise

In certain situations the transportation cost may be paid by the vendor or the customer. If, according to the applicable agreements, this cost is to be absorbed by them, the problem of the validity of the settlement is theirs—subject only to claims that we may have against the carrier involved. In other situations the basis of purchase or sale may be that the cost of transportation is to be borne by us, and we will ultimately be billed that cost either by the carrier or by the vendor or customer who has paid it on our behalf. Although these costs will ultimately be paid through an accounts payable department—or in some cases through credits to customers who have paid them for us—the review and approval of these charges are normally made by the traffic department. One reason for this practice is that the accounts payable department does not have rate information on the purchase order. But the more important reason is that the review and approval of the freight costs require special expertise. In addition, a great deal of money is involved and special effort is warranted to be sure the company is not overcharged. The normal practice is, therefore, for the transportation department to make a general review of the billings prior to payment, covering the clerical and more obvious basis of the billing, and then to conduct an audit of the rates on a more thorough basis at a later time. This second review in many cases is subcontracted to an even more specialized outside service group.

Handling Claims

Control over claims is critical

Claims against carriers are of two broad types, those arising out of incorrect billings, and those for damage to goods while being transported. In both cases it is the usual practice for these claims to be handled by the transportation department. The control aspects here are that the operating group which originally identifies the claim promptly records it and transmits it to the department. Such operating groups would include receiving departments, inspection departments, and accounts receivable activities. The transportation department must then establish adequate controls over the filing of these claims and the subsequent follow-up of them. The key concerns are that we maintain our record of the claims and that we give them adequate follow-up attention. From an internal control standpoint it is preferable that claims be controlled through the regular financial accounts.

Organizational Aspects of the Transportation Activity

Organizational status for transportation needs careful evaluation

Like an operational activity, the effectiveness of the transportation activity is closely related to its organizational status. Certainly the importance of the transportation function would argue for a high-level status. In a great many cases the close relationship of the transportation activity to purchasing is recognized by making transportation a part of the purchasing department. There is no harm in this arrangement as long as the role of the transportation group is not restricted to serving the normal purchasing operations. The transportation activity as we have seen involves outbound shipments and intracompany shipments as well.

Quite commonly also, the transportation function is decentralized to a considerable extent. Normally the central group will cover the staff functions and such operational activities as involve the entire company. The operational activities pertaining to the operational components—subsidiaries, divisions, and other operational groups—will then be decentralized. Although these decentralized groups may report on a line basis to the local management, there is necessarily a strong functional tie to the central group. The objective is to centralize those aspects that need a total company approach and at the same time to give local operating management the direct support it needs.

Company Welfare Potentials

At many points we have seen the possibilities of significant contributions by the transportation group to the overall company welfare. Very often, these potentials are lost sight of in the actual company situation in the volume of day-to-day work that is carried out by the usual traffic department. It is important, however, that all parties recognize the wide range of potentials. These potentials come especially out of a close collaborative relationship between the transportation group and the other operating activities. We list some of these areas of company service as illustrative:

1. The decision regarding the building of a new plant, or the relocation of an existing plant, is significantly affected by available transportation alternatives and their related costs. Pertinent is the impact on vendor supply, transfers of partially processed materials from one plant to another, and customer service.

   Potential contributions of transportation linked to wide range of impact

2. The utilization of plant capacity and the location of particular types of production processes will involve the same types of considerations.

3. Similarly, the location of warehouses depends on proximity to plants, vendors, and customers.

4. New approaches to the use of existing transportation services might have important marketing implications—as, for example, the use of air freight. Also, the increased volume may be a basis for pressing for further rate reductions.

5. New types of shipment may materially reduce handling costs—as, for example, the use of containers for small parts.

6. It may be possible that costs can be reduced through the company acquiring its own facilities.

7. The more careful study of rate structures may indicate different ways in which the company can qualify for lower rates—as, for example, different-size shipments, the use of different commodity classifications, and the like.

There are of course the efficiencies of a well-administered operational activity, which are significant and should be fully exploited. Our purpose here is to demonstrate that there are additional potentials which also need to be studied and adequately explored.

Measuring the Effectiveness of the Transportation Activity

It may again seem that the nature of the transportation services is so interrelated with other company activities that it is not practicable to set up meaningful goals and objectives, and thus that it is not really practicable to measure the effectiveness of the transportation group. Again it needs to be emphasized that there is much to be done along these lines. At the lower operational level there are standards that can be established as to what can be done in the way of individual performance. These are the considerations covered by the usual personnel and expense budgets. But at the higher level also it is desirable to project plans for providing more value for transportation expenditures. These can be reductions of cost or other types of added value provided to company operating activities. Normally these plans are expressed in terms of specific projects to be studied and are then grouped in the best possible fashion. These plans then provide the basis for a periodic reporting of accomplishments with adequate backup to support the claimed savings.

Internal Auditor's Role

The role of the internal auditor should follow an approach similar to the one outlined at the close of the discussion of purchasing. In summary this should include:

1. Understanding the transportation process
2. Reviewing the efficiency of the administrative operations and related compliance with current policies and procedures
3. Appraising the effectiveness of existing policies and procedures
4. Endeavoring in all ways possible to determine how the transportation group can increase its contribution to the total company welfare

AUDIT GUIDES

REVIEW OF TRANSPORTATION ACTIVITIES

I. Introductory
  A. Reference should be made to the general discussion of Audit Guides, Chapter 11.

II. Preparatory Activities
  A. See standard Audit Guides, Chapter 11.

III. Organizational Factors
  A. See standard Audit Guides, Chapter 11.
  B. Establish that the transportation department is independent of the accounts payable department.
  C. Matters of special interest in the review of manuals will include:
    1. Standards of relationships with carriers.
    2. Extent of authority for local transportation arrangements.
    3. Coordination with user organizational groups.
    4. Authorized levels of approval.
    5. Restrictions on receiving of gifts.
    6. Follow-up responsibilities.

7. Handling of deviations from established procedures.

8. Jurisdiction over all arrangements with outside truckers.

IV. Authorization for Making Transportation Arrangements

    A. Review the procedures for making transportation arrangements. Points of special interest include:

        1. Who initiates?

        2. What approvals are necessary for particular types of arrangements and in what amounts?

        3. In what way is the making of the arrangement finalized?

    B. On the basis of actual tests, verify and appraise:

        1. The extent to which procedures are complied with. (Where they are not complied with to any significant degree, what are the causes?)

        2. Do the procedures appear to be adequate?

        3. When there are unusual types of arrangements, does it appear that these are questioned and discussed?

V. Internal Operations

    A. General

        1. Are the facilities adequate?

        2. Are the internal operations being carried on in a manner consistent with established organizational responsibilities, policies, and procedures? If not, what are the causes? What kind of corrective actions seems to be warranted? This part of the review would include such questions as:

            a. Should the organizational responsibilities be modified?

            b. Should operational policies be reappraised?

            c. Should operational procedures be revised?

            d. Do we need different people?

            e. Do we need better training and supervision of the existing people?

        3. To what extent do the operations reflect a high degree of efficiency and morale? Factors of special interest are similar to those of question 2.

        4. Are internal records and files of various types adequate in terms of special purpose and relation to other records and procedures? Are they being maintained efficiently?

        5. Is the operational cycle adequately controlled as to authorization, assignment to personnel, making of transportation arrangement, follow-up, and completion—so that the status of individual transportation assignments can be easily determined?

        6. Are official documents properly safeguarded and controlled?

    B. Relating to Carriers

1. Are adequate records maintained of business given to individual carriers?
2. What efforts are made to evaluate carrier performance?
3. How adequate are the efforts to work with individual carriers for cost-reduction possibilities?
4. How thorough is the effort to evaluate the value aspects of alternative routings and other transportation arrangements?
5. Is the selection of carriers reviewed and approved by a higher-ranking member of the traffic department with reasonable frequency?
6. Are records and controls adequate to minimize demurrage?

C. Relating to Approvals for Payment of Carrier Billings
1. Are procedures adequate to determine whether charges are for company account? Are portions chargeable to vendors or customers properly controlled?
2. Are billings in accordance with originally authorized transportation arrangements? If not, are proper deductions made?
3. Are weights properly confirmed?
4. If claims are to be made, are they adequately recorded for subsequent handling and control?
5. Is the follow-up of claims adequate?
6. Is adequate provision made for the more thorough post-audit of all freight bills?

VI. Special Audit Tests
A. In addition to such observations and queries as have been made relative to specific aspects, it is desirable to test a representative number of transportation decision actions, by following through all steps in the operational cycle. The sample should be picked at random from the original input of authorizations to make transportation arrangements. Points of special interest at all stages would include:
1. Compliance with all policies and procedures.
2. Reasonableness of timing at the various stages.
3. Evidence of care and maximum protection of company interest.
4. Evidence of good teamwork in the total traffic group.
5. All possible evidence of good value received in the decisions.
6. Effectiveness of internal records and related procedures.
7. Leads for matters to be investigated in the review of other operational activities.
8. Any evidence of favoritism to individual carriers.
9. Overall evaluation of the competence of the management of the department.

VII–IX. Not used.

X. Overall Approval of Transportation Effectiveness

A. See standard Audit Guides, Chapter 11.

B. Appraisal of relations with both carriers and company personnel should focus especially on reduction of transportation costs through development of new types of equipment, new conditions of shipment, use of company equipment to haul for others, and the like.

ILLUSTRATIVE AUDIT FINDINGS: PURCHASING AND TRANSPORTATION

Standardization of Parts Needed

The company could increase efforts to standardize electronic parts needed for production. This would reduce purchase costs, eliminate duplication in parts control efforts, and improve quality. The company had standardized parts in the heavy-equipment divisions, but had not attempted to standardize parts in the computers division.

Backlogs in Filling Orders

The purchasing department had significant backlogs in filling requisitions, resulting in delays in meeting production requirements and making deliveries to customers. A statistical sample of one month's requisitions indicated that the delays were caused by excessive time taken to process the requests and place orders with available suppliers.

Sole-Source Procurement

Purchases were being made from sole-source suppliers without adequate justification. In addition insufficient competitive bids were being obtained. As a result excessive prices were being paid for certain items.

Buying Items of Too High Quality

Controls over specifications needed strengthening to assure that the company was not acquiring a higher quality of items than needed. In a test of machine parts purchased it was found that parts with a useful life of 20 years were being acquired when the life of the equipment was only 5 years. By substituting machine parts with a lesser life, significant savings could be achieved.

Pinpointing Responsibility for Change Orders

Payments were being made for change orders that were caused by errors of suppliers rather than company design. Additional analysis and review of change orders as to cause were needed to prevent the unwarranted payment of additional costs that were the responsibility of the supplier.

Need to Monitor Subcontract Costs

Excessive prices were paid to subcontractors under cost-type contracts because there was insufficient monitoring of performance and costs claimed. Procurement personnel were not monitoring cost-type subcontracts any differently than they were monitoring fixed-price subcontracts.

Need for Private Fleet of Trucks

Savings in freight costs could be obtained by maintaining a private fleet of trucks to ship finished goods. This equipment could be used to haul goods for subsidiaries of the company and others under the new Interstate Commerce Commission (ICC) regulation granting contract carrier authority.

REVIEW QUESTIONS

1. What activities does the purchasing function typically cover in an organization? To the extent that some activities are excluded, what is the rationale?
2. To what extent should the purchasing function include the determination of needs? Why?
3. To what extent should the determination of needs include the authorization to purchase? Why?
4. Why is obtaining competitive bids, if practicable, important in terms of achieving effective internal control?
5. Under what conditions is it appropriate to procure something on a cost reimbursement basis? What are the disadvantages?
6. To what extent should the purchasing department be involved in the financial settlement for purchases? Why?
7. Under what conditions and to what extent should the purchasing activities be decentralized? Why?
8. How can we evaluate the effectiveness of the purchasing department?
9. To what extent is the procurement of transportation similar to the regular purchasing activity? To what extent is it dissimilar?
10. How is the transportation problem interrelated with other management problems?

CASE PROBLEMS

Problem 12-1

Fred Smith, purchasing agent of the Tower Company, was irate. He said, "Am I responsible for doing the buying in this company or not? The organization chart says I am, but in the last week there have been three bootleg purchases by people who know better. First, George Butts in advertising ordered some special promotional booklets for which he thought there was an emergency. The sales department went out and hired a new display group for their dealer show at an outlandish price, and now the head of accounting has just taken delivery on a specially made oversized desk. Alan (Alan Green, general auditor) will you review this situation for me and tell me how to get it under control."

Alan Green's first step was to get the views of the three other people involved. George Butts said, "It's very simple. The president wanted a promotional booklet to match the Wilson Company's surprise move and he wanted it fast. I just didn't have time to bother with Fred Smith's standard procedures." John Ross, sales promotion manager, told Alan Green that he had been searching for the right display group for years and he finally found one. He said there was no time to get purchasing in the act and that they couldn't have made a contribution in this matter anyway. Roger Rose, chief accountant, said, "I found just what I wanted and I bought it."

Required. Prepare a report for Alan Green to give to Fred Smith.

Problem 12-2

When John Colt, senior internal auditor, interviewed Lester Benson, transportation manager, Benson told him, "When President Welk set up our transportation department he thought I should report to Brian Jones, the vice-president–finance, to give me complete independence. But now I'm so independent that I don't get involved when I should. The purchasing department acts like I don't exist and gives our vendors a free hand. The result is that we are missing available savings on routings and commodity classifications. I'm doing my best to pick up the pieces, but there is a lot more I could do."

During a subsequent interview with Mason Kruger, manager of purchasing, Kruger said, "I really don't think, John, that the way Welk set up the transportation department is any of your concern; but in any event we are functioning and I suggest that you not rock the boat."

Required. Give your views as to how John Colt should draft his internal audit report.

CHAPTER THIRTEEN

Personnel Activities

Upon completing this chapter you should be able to:

☐ *Explain the relationship of the personnel function to line and staff managers*

☐ *Describe the scope of the personnel function*

☐ *Identify the activities of the personnel function in providing needed personnel resources*

☐ *Explain how the internal auditor can assist management in the personnel function*

NATURE OF THE PERSONNEL FUNCTION

This chapter is intended to deal primarily with the review of the activities of the personnel department. The name of this department may vary in individual situations, but it will be the department that is charged with the responsibility of assisting management in carrying out the personnel or people function. It is primarily a staff group since it is the basic responsibility of all managers to deal with people, although in certain situations the personnel department may administer service activities on a line basis. What is distinctive about this chapter, however, is that in discussing the areas where the personnel department is assisting management, we unavoidably are discussing matters of direct managerial responsibility. We will, therefore, be talking about a function that is carried out jointly and in a special collaborative manner.

Scope of the Personnel Department Role

Managers have basic responsibility for people

A proper understanding of the role of the personnel department must again start with the recognition that people problems are a major part of the basic responsibility of each manager. Managers accomplish things through people. Under normal circumstances, therefore, it is the responsibility of each manager to select, administer, develop, and reward people. But we know also as a practical matter that managers of the various line and staff activities in the company need assistance if they are to do their job effectively. In many areas there are opportunities for the utilization of professional counsel in the personnel area. It is also necessary that policies and procedures be developed on a company-wide basis so that there will be a proper standard of quality, an equitable application to all organizational components, and the protection of legal and broader social responsibilities. Certain personnel data also need to be developed on a company-wide basis. Finally also, there are frequently particular company service activities that can be best handled on a centralized basis. For all these reasons there is a proper and substantive need for staff assistance. It is the role of the personnel department to provide that staff assistance in the most effective manner possible.

What Is the Personnel Function?   The nature and scope of the staff assistance role can be viewed also in terms of the nature of the personnel function itself. One way of describing the personnel function is to say that it has to do with the relationships with all employees of the company from the time the employee relationship is first established until it is terminated in one way or another. This is, of course, a broad and far-reaching description, but it properly emphasizes the fact that the personnel function is all inclusive and that it is interwoven with the total management process. Still another way to describe the personnel function is that it has to do with the most effective matching of people with job needs. There is work to be done and people must be identified who can do that work. What "effective" means in this instance is a matching that strikes the balance that is most satisfactory from two points of view: (1) the needs of the company to achieve its established objectives, and (2) the personal needs of the people involved. Again it is clear that we have a broadly based function that goes directly to the heart of the total management function.

Personnel function interwoven with total management process

Special Problems of the Personnel Department.   What this all means is that the personnel department has a unique opportunity to assist management. Everything it does in one way or another affects managerial performance and success. But this close interrelationship brings with it a special problem. This special problem is that the department can very easily cross over the line of where its staff role should end and go on to assume a role that infringes on the basic responsibilities of individual managers at any level. A related special problem is that the personnel function can come to be an operation of policies and procedures that is unduly detached from the real operational conditions and needs. Too often the personnel department is accused of developing overly elaborate procedures that destroy an image of real workability in a partnership sense. At its worst the personnel department can develop gimmicks or shallow approaches that do more harm than good, and tend to operate in a kind of vacuum. The solutions here call for staffing the

Personnel department should assist managers, not take over

personnel department itself with people of adequate ability, judgment, and stature, and then to have these people work with other company personnel in a close and collaborative manner. There is, indeed, an important job to be done and the challenge is to find a way to do that job properly.

Major Areas of Application

In a general sense the area of application for the personnel function is people, whoever they are and whatever they do in the company. In its most important respect there is a common focus on people problems. At the same time the conditions of employment, the nature of the job performed, and the economic level of compensation result in significantly different problems. It is not possible to recognize all of these varying situations in any general discussion, but there are three major categories that need to be recognized. These are as follows:

Three major types of personnel

1. *Hourly Paid Labor.* This group of people is distinguished principally by the fact that the workers are paid on an hourly basis, and that in many cases they are unionized. The work done by this group is located mainly in the production area, but extends to other allied service and operational activities.
2. *Salaried Clerical.* This group is paid on a salary basis and is less likely to be unionized. The clerical work done can be scattered practically anywhere through the company.
3. *Management Personnel.* At some level in each company the salaried personnel are classed as management personnel. The distinguishing characteristics of this group are the scope of assigned responsibilities and the more complicated patterns of administration. The group covers gradations that run from lower levels up to the top management executives.

Because of the commonality of many of the principles of personnel administration among the three groups, the plan is to discuss the more basic considerations first as a whole, with only limited reference to the three separate groups. We then return to a further elaboration of some of the special problems, as they pertain to the individual groups.

OVERALL OPERATIONAL PATTERN OF PERSONNEL ACTIVITIES

Common Elements

Although the various needs of the company will cover a wide spectrum, there is a common operational framework for all types of personnel. This is:

1. The identification of personnel needs, both in terms of the current situation and the future at various points of time

2. The inventory, analysis, and appraisal of current personnel resources, for purposes of comparison with needs and determination of the existing gap

3. The various activities that pertain to the means by which the gap, as previously determined, is to be bridged

4. The many activities that have to do with the administration of the current work force

We propose to discuss the personnel activities in this sequence, and then to deal separately with certain special problems.

Identification of Personnel Needs

The company has presumably established an organizational structure that is applicable at the present point of time. This organizational structure reflects the managerial judgments as to how the work is to be broken up and assigned to particular individuals at all levels. From this basic organizational analysis the next step is the development of more detailed job descriptions. As we have seen previously, job descriptions become a key building block in the administration of any company activity. These job descriptions then become the basis for the development of specifications for the particular kinds of individuals that are needed. Each job has its specific requirements in terms of knowledge, skills, personality, and experience. When all of this is done on a company-wide basis we are able to determine what the total company requirements are for numbers of the various types of people.

Job descriptions the building block for personnel administration

The type of analysis described above, as applied to the current situation, is at the same time extended into the future. Sometimes this future projection is very limited in scope and relatively informal, but in a well-managed company it is done in a systematic manner and will extend at least through the planning period that is appropriate to the particular type of business. For this planning period the growth and changing nature of the business will be projected, the related organizational requirements will be determined as best possible, and personnel needs estimated. This is a process that will normally be carried on at all levels and by all managers on the basis of common company assumptions—growth, scope of business activities, and the like.

From a control standpoint the determination of personnel needs is basic. It is important that it be done on a careful and systematic basis, and that it be updated periodically to reflect changes in future plans. Unless this estimate is carefully made, all subsequent supporting implementation will lack direction. It is also important to note the close tie-in of the forward personnel determinations with the organizational planning and development discussed in Chapter 5.

Available Resources for Satisfying Personnel Needs

The next step is to take inventory of the available resources so that the company can determine the extent to which it is presently able to satisfy its personnel needs. This inventory again has both its current dimension and its projection through the same planning period as was used in identifying the future needs. Individuals are viewed first in terms of their capacity to fill designated jobs at this particular point in time, and then in terms of what the company thinks they would reasonably be capable of doing with further development in successive years through the planning periods. Thus needs and resources are compared through a time spectrum that encompasses the entire planning period and that discloses at each key point in that time spectrum the excess or shortage of resources. Normally a company will have a shortage gap that can exist at the present time and that will grow larger as needs grow at a faster pace than the resources. The identification of the gap during the successive years of the planning period provides the important information of what the company will face in the way of a people problem. It sets the stage for determining the nature and scope of the program which must be carried out to close that gap. As might be expected the importance of determining the gap and developing the needed action programs is greatest in the management personnel area, but it is important in the other two areas also. Illustrative would be shortages of particular types of technical personnel or special labor skills.

Evaluate existing personnel resources

From a control standpoint the assessment of available resources becomes the key backup to the earlier determined needs. Again, it is most important that the procedures for making this assessment and comparing it with previously determined needs be both well-designed and carefully executed. Again also, it is the responsibility of every manager to contribute his best possible input to this process.

Activities to Provide Needed Personnel Resources

The activities to bridge the current and projected gaps between personnel needs and personnel resources fall into two major categories. One means is through the recruitment of new personnel to the company. The other approach is to accelerate the development of the company's own personnel. The personnel department can provide assistance for both approaches.

Recruitment one way of expanding personnel resources

Recruitment and Selection of New Personnel.   The recruitment process begins with a judgment of where the prospective candidates are likely to be. Particular trade skills may tend to concentrate in particular geographical areas, managerial resources will generally be greatest in urban centers, and persons with modern business school training can best be found at the leading business schools. Closely related is the judgment as to how the potential employees can best be contacted. Typical methods are newspaper advertising, employee referrals, trade journals, employment agencies, and direct visitations to the colleges. Usually a reasonable amount of care and thought will determine the most appropriate approach for the particular kind of recruits being sought.

Once potential candidates have been identified, and recognizing that employment is always a two-way decision between the company and the candidate, one comes to the problem of how the actual selection shall be made. At this point there is no single approach and we have a combination of techniques and practices, subject always to the very important judgment factor. Typical approaches used include:

1. *Completion of Application Forms.* The usefulness of the application form is that needed information can be conveniently obtained along such lines as age, education, professional achievements, and work experience. There is something learned also by how an application form is completed. In the management category the applicant is more likely to submit his own résumé, and here especially is a basis of appraising the person by the way that résumé is prepared.

    Key approaches to screening potential hires

2. *References.* A second important method used in the selection process is the written or direct contact (usually by telephone) with references furnished by the applicant. The direct contacts provide an especially good basis for asking more probing questions about the candidate's qualifications. From a control standpoint, however, it must be remembered that the reference has usually been selected by the applicant, thus ensuring to a significant extent that the reference will be well-disposed toward the applicant. The company official, knowing this, must be all the more frank and persuasive to be sure that he is getting a truly objective report. Also where possible, the employer will seek to find independent references on whom he can more fully rely.

3. *Special Tests.* A variety of special tests have been developed to evaluate personality and particular types of aptitudes for different types of work. Clinical tests by psychologists are also sometimes used. These provide a useful supplementary bit of input but need to be used with caution, particularly in the psychological areas where the validity of the testing techniques is not as great as could be desired. However, progress is continually being made in the development of more effective testing.

4. *Personal Interviews.* Probably in most cases the major reliance is on the personal interview between the applicant and the company official or officials. Most managers have developed reasonable competence in sizing up an applicant on a face-to-face basis and determining whether he is likely to fit well into the particular job situation. It also works out best when the interviewer is able to induce the applicant to speak freely, thus involving the art on the part of the interviewer to be a good listener. Needless to say, however, it is easy to make mistakes and to be misled by favorable first impressions. Nevertheless the personal interview is a major means of supplementing the careful use of the other methods.

A major control oriented concern is that policies and procedures are in effect that will reasonably assure matching of the job opportunities with the best qualified candidates. This means that each major type of job need must be separately evaluated and handled. It means also that all available means of evaluation be utilized, but at the same time handled with great care. Interviews especially need to be made by a number of qualified persons to provide an adequate cross check.

Personnel resources can be expanded by training and development

Training and Development. In the normal company situation the employees recruited must be provided with additional training and development throughout the greater part of their career span. The general need for such training and development is recognized by all, the real problem being how much of it there should be and how it can be done most effectively. This training is initiated at the time of recruitment, and the extent to which it is needed is directly related to the qualifications of the new employee. As a minimum there will be the training that provides necessary instruction to carry out a particular job assignment. Thereafter the training may be of a remedial or supplemental nature to assist the employee in taking on a more advanced assignment. In other cases the training may be of a broader nature and pertain to the development of better human relations, providing administrative skills, or for other managerial purposes. The objective in all cases is to achieve a greater usefulness and capability on the part of the individuals to whom the training is made available. All of this training is over and above the development that comes about through normal job experience and as a result of the regular supervisory efforts of the various bosses.

Five key training principles

Fundamentals of Training. The achievement of effective training depends directly on the extent to which we can develop competence in the learning process. This is a professional area that cannot be reduced to precise formulas, but there are important principles that need to be understood and properly handled. These include:

1. *Receptivity on the Part of the Trainee.* A necessary first requirement is that the trainee recognize his need for training and want to receive the particular assistance that is being offered. The trainee must see the training as relevant and worthwhile in terms of his goals and objectives, thus giving him the motivation to take advantage of it.

2. *Quality of the Training Materials.* The training materials themselves must be sound in a professional sense. Ideally they have in fact been tested in that respect. At the same time they must be presented in a manner that is consistent with their quality. Especially must the materials have credibility to the trainee.

3. *Time Requirements.* The time requirements depend on the degree of

difficulty of the training to be imparted and the capacity of the trainees themselves. But within reasonable ranges the training must recognize these time requirements and respect them. Otherwise the training effort will be largely wasted.

4. *Participation and Involvement*. It is well known that effective training depends on a proper degree of participation on the part of the trainee. As learners we need to be involved and to have some kind of two-way interchange. In some situations it is possible to provide some type of feedback whereby the trainee can check on his progress. In the case method approach the trainee is able to participate directly in the discussion. These participative processes have been proven to be more effective than the conventional lecture approach.

5. *Reinforcement*. Closely related is the necessity for the trainee to perceive his definitive progress, and in some way to feel that he is being rewarded for that progress. This reinforcement can take place during the actual training session—as where a teaching machine program confirms the mastery of a particular increment of training—or it can be where the employer specifically recognizes the trainee's increased knowledge and competence which has come about through the training program.

Problems of Training.   For the most part the problems of training are where the previously outlined principles are not adequately handled. What is likely to happen is that training is carried out because of a higher-management-level edict, but without the development of well-planned and well-executed programs. Under these circumstances training programs become sterile, busywork-type programs that are not meaningful to trainees, but instead become a source of irritation and ridicule. The blame for such failures involves two major groups. The first group is the personnel department that is charged with the responsibility for planning and carrying out such programs. The second group is management itself in delegating too completely the training function. Here again it must be recognized that training is part of the direct responsibility of management at all levels, and that management must involve itself sufficiently in the training process to be certain that it is being carried out effectively.

Lack of meaning a common problem

Control Problems of Training.   The key control aspects of effective training can be summarized, as follows:

1. The need for continuous management involvement and support
2. The design of training programs that are both properly coordinated with operational needs and based on adequate professional standards
3. The careful and sensitive administration of the actual training programs to assure good motivation and interest

Key control aspects of training

Although effective training does depend on professional know-how to a considerable extent, the fact remains that much of it is good sense and conscientious administration. The review of training by the outside reviewer can, therefore, be most rewarding. The benefits achieved are especially important when one recognizes the amount of time and money that is expended in these programs and the impact on human productivity that is involved.

Utilization of Personnel

Managers attempt to achieve effective utilization of personnel in various parts of the company. This includes the proper assignment of personnel to jobs in accordance with abilities. Also sufficient subordinates and clerical staff should be assigned to assure that employees are working in accordance with job sheets and standards. Managers want the personnel function to be cost effective and are thus interested in personnel assignments.

Best utilization of people is basic goal

In recent years management has placed increasing emphasis on work measurement as a basis for improving the productivity of hourly employees. Work measurement programs are designed to disclose such factors as outmoded work routines, poorly organized systems, excess staffing, and duplication. Through time and motion study, work systems are reviewed to develop preferred methods, standardize systems, and determine the time required by the average worker to do the task. Various other systems are used, such as work sampling and methods time measurement. The latter analyzes operations into basic motions required to perform it, and assigns to each motion a predetermined standard. Work measurement is also being used in clerical office routine. The purpose is to reduce paperwork costs through improved work flow, methods, and layout. In addition, an effort is made to improve operating controls through establishing schedules, relating tasks, and measuring employee and supervisory effectiveness. Paper simplification and office mechanization are some of the methods recommended to increase productivity and reduce costs.

Management is also interested in controls to assure that there is not an excess of personnel in certain classifications and shortages in others. The timing and duration of excesses need to be reviewed, as well as whether hiring and transfers are based on actual need. Records of idle time need to be maintained and studied for trends and analysis of the causes. The use of overtime in the company should be well-controlled, with proper authorization in advance. Excessive overtime may be a symptom of improper scheduling of work, shortage of certain classifications of personnel, deficiencies in technical performance, and inordinate demands of customers, supervisors, and using departments.

PROBLEMS OF CURRENT PERSONNEL ADMINISTRATION

We come now to a wide range of current administrative activities that are carried out by a typical personnel department, supplementing the activities previously discussed. We will deal with these current administrative activities under the following headings:

1. Job analysis and evaluation
2. Compensation administration
3. Performance evaluation
4. Transfers, promotion, and termination
5. Employee records and reports
6. Personal guidance activities
7. Employee benefit programs
8. Employee services
9. Workmen's compensation and safety
10. Labor relations

Job Analysis and Evaluation

Reference has previously been made to the development of job descriptions and specifications as a basis for determining a company's personnel needs. From an administrative standpoint it also becomes necessary to rate the individual jobs in terms of relative difficulty and importance. This requires some kind of a yardstick that usually takes the form of a manual. In this manual various factors or dimensions are identified—as, for example, type of skill required, extent of responsibility, scope of effort, and nature of working conditions. These factors must then be measured in degrees of difference and some kind of weights assigned. These general measures are then available to be applied to specific jobs. At this point we require a detailed set of specifications to cover the individual job. At the same time appropriate job titles need to be developed.

Analysis of job first step

The most difficult part of the job analysis and evaluation procedure is now the application of the general criteria to the individual job on the basis of the particular specifications. This is generally accomplished by the assignment of points in recognition of the degree of application of the various criteria. The concern here is with relative rankings of individual jobs. It is a determination that is bound to involve a great deal of judgment and hence one that must be made with extreme care and objectivity. The individual jobs are normally grouped in a number of grades or other broad classifications. The number of such grades can be relatively large or small but it seems usually to work best when about 15 to 25 are used.

Compensation Administration

While the job analysis and evaluation process is technically something that stands apart from the matter of compensation, in practice the two processes are closely interwoven. The compensation phase actually begins with a determination of the general level of pay in the community and industry of which the company is a part. Here the company faces the first question of

Job analysis and compensation closely interwoven

its general approach to the meeting of that general pay level. On the one hand its own level of compensation must be sufficiently high to attract personnel of the quality desired and in the proper numbers. On the other hand an unduly high level of compensation will ultimately be reflected in excessive costs and noncompetitive product prices. Once the general level of compensation has been determined, the compensation levels must be fixed for the various job classifications and grades previously established during the job-analysis phase. In the case of each grade it is customary to fix a minimum and a maximum with the expectation that this will provide needed flexibility in the application to particular individuals. At the same time flexibility is provided for the giving of merit increases during the time span that an individual job falls in a particular grade.

The combined job classification and compensation grades together thus provide a necessary orderly framework by which a company can reasonably evaluate and control employee relationships. At the same time there are many troublesome problems that arise in actual practice. Specific individuals will, for example, feel strongly that the nature of their work calls for a higher job classification than has been assigned. In some cases changing conditions may provide legitimate support for that position. In other cases the problem may be that of a restless employee who is qualified to do more responsible work but where there is presently no opening for his higher-level skill. A more general problem arises when employees come to believe that merit increases periodically granted are due to them. Here management flexibility can be unduly restricted. In situations where unions are involved, the determination of the job classifications and the related compensation become a contested part of the contractual negotiations and the subsequent administration of the contract. Thus on many fronts the job classifications and compensation become the sensitive point in the resolution of conflicting individual and company needs.

Control Aspects of Job Analysis and Compensation. From a control standpoint it may be useful to summarize briefly the essential control requirements as they pertain to the combined processes of job evaluation and compensation administration. These include at least the following:

Controls for job analysis and compensation

1. A plan of job classifications that is based on a well-thought-out set of evaluation criteria
2. A level of general compensation, as applied to the various job classifications, that is reasonably competitive
3. Individual jobs carefully evaluated in terms of the existing criteria
4. Regular reviews periodically made as to the scope of compensation for individual employees
5. The overall plan of grades and related compensation as appraised at appropriate intervals for changes in existing conditions

Performance Evaluation

The administration of employees necessarily requires in one way or another some kind of evaluation of performance. This evaluation is in part a continuing process and in part a periodic undertaking. In its most basic sense it can be said to serve two key purposes. One of these purposes is to provide a partial basis for determining the best possible future utilization of the individual. This will include possible transfer, promotion, and increased compensation. The second objective also has to do with achieving the most effective future utilization of the employee, but concentrates more on what can be done to help the individual overcome any existing limitations and to increase his overall competence. It will again be seen that in both cases we are dealing with important direct management responsibilities. The personnel department role comes about in the way of helping to provide supporting procedures and policies.

Supporting Procedures.   The personnel department has typically provided assistance by establishing a policy whereby all managers and supervisors will be responsible for at least an annual performance review. Typically forms will also be provided for use at the several major supervisory levels that will detail the various factors to be considered and measures of performance to be evaluated. The factors will normally include job competence, personal qualifications, and the ability to work with people. Each of these factors will normally be evaluated on the basis of a scale or captions which run from unsatisfactory through acceptable, fair, good, very good, and outstanding. Provision will also be made for problems being encountered and consideration of what can be done to deal with such problems. The performance review is prepared by the immediate superior and is then reviewed and approved by the next-higher level of management. Under some procedures the completed review is shown to the person being reviewed, and his confirming signature may also be required. The completed forms are then placed in personnel files maintained by the personnel department, and are available to management personnel when wanted.

Procedures help managers discharge performance evaluation responsibilities

Problems of Performance Reviews.   The achievement of an effective performance review program begins with a comprehensive and well-designed review form. The problems, however, are much more deep-seated. Typically the individual supervisor or manager dislikes the role of playing judge over the evaluation of his subordinate. When it comes to reducing something like this to writing and sharing it with the subordinate it becomes all the more unlikely that there will be the needed degree of objectivity and candor. Most individuals also experience real difficulty in adequately perceiving their own shortcomings, and to cut through this natural resistance becomes both difficult and unappealing for a reviewer. As a result, reviews tend to fall far short of what they might to be in terms of overall usefulness. This is especially true as one moves up the managerial hierarchy, as it seems that the higher

Human limitations can block effective performance reviews

one goes, the less inclined managers are to complicate sensitive personal relationships by discussing performance evaluations. The answer is not to abandon the process. Rather, the best solution is to recognize the problem and to do the best possible to make an improvement. Generally this has come to mean that the coaching approach is most likely to be acceptable to all parties involved and at the same time has the greatest potential.

Transfers, Promotions, and Terminations

Key alternative of employee direction

In any ongoing company situation there is a changing pattern of personnel needs. Some of the problems relate primarily to individual situations, whereas others arise out of more broadly based changes in personnel requirements. In all of these situations the personnel department serves as a central source of information as to available personnel resources and as a planner and counselor in helping managers and supervisors solve their various problems. A particular individual is not working out well in his current assignment. What can be done to improve the situation or to find another situation where his contribution can be more effectively utilized? Or someone leaves the company, or a new job is created, thus opening up a new job assignment that needs to be filled. Who then are the individuals in the company who have the kind of experience and other qualifications that would make them eligible for consideration? The personnel department is uniquely equipped to provide a list of such candidates and to be able to help in making a final selection.

On a larger scale a new expansion of activity in a particular sector of the operations may bring with it the need for a substantially greater work force. Where are these people to come from and how can we best go about it to provide the people as they are needed? Or, conversely, there may be a major cutback of operations that will necessitate a substantial reduction of personnel in a particular department or division. Perhaps also a new computerized system may lead to a major cutback in certain clerical areas, but at the same time may mean expanded needs in certain other areas such as programming and system input. In all of these situations the personnel department can render major assistance in developing plans whereby the disruptive process can be minimized and whereby the company's ultimate needs can be best satisfied. Especially where terminations may be involved, there is the need to anticipate this aspect and to develop types of separation arrangements that will be both as equitable as possible and consistent with ongoing community responsibilities.

Employee Records and Reports

As we have seen, at various times the personnel department serves as a major central source of information regarding employees. When an individual joins the company, his original application and supplementary investigation becomes part of the basic company records. Subsequently, as individual job actions take place—transfers, new assignments, compensation changes, promotions, and so on—the papers pertaining to these job actions are processed by the personnel department and become part of the basic personnel records. As we have seen, performance reviews and evaluations become a part of these central employee records. Finally, when the employee leaves the company, or is retired or terminated, the circumstances of this final development are made a part of the records. The maintenance of these records thus becomes a primary responsibility of the personnel department. This enables the department to function as a major reference source to the entire company, and to be able to assist most effectively as a planning and counseling group.

The responsibility for all employee records and the processing of all changes in the employment status of the individual employees now sets the stage for a reporting responsibility along any lines desired by management. Information needed may relate to the composition of the work force and its changes over time—age, sex, religion, race, and the like—or it may relate to significant operational considerations. The particular interest may be for information as a basis for the control of overtime, absenteeism, or turnover. Or the information sought may pertain to levels of compensation and the trends in this area. How many merit increases are being granted and how often? What percentages of the individuals in the respective grades are at or near the upper and lower limits? How many people are being promoted from within as opposed to outside recruitment? What is the scope of the formal training activity in each sector of the operations? It is apparent that any of these needs can be served through the record resources of the personnel department.

Maintaining records is responsibility of personnel department

Personal Guidance Activities

The responsibilities of the individual manager in developing his subordinates have been stressed repeatedly. There are occasions, however, when the subordinate needs to have a place where he can go that is independent of his primary boss–employee relationship. The question may relate to the clarification of a particular personnel policy, and perhaps in its direct application to a specific aspect of the relationship with his boss. Or the need may be for counsel in working out some aspect of that boss relationship. In still other cases the employee may be interested in exploring alternative types of job opportunities in other operational areas of the company, or in appraising various types of career patterns. The personnel department can in these kinds of circumstances provide useful assistance to individual employees, both in the way of providing needed information and in acting as an independent friend and counselor. Needless to say, this requires a particular kind of professional competence and skill on the part of the individual representative of the personnel group. It requires also a high sense of confidentiality and integrity with respect to the kinds of matters disclosed by individual employees. Important also is the necessity to retain a friendly but neutral attitude and to avoid becoming a partisan advocate in opposition to the individual manager or higher-level management.

Employee Benefit Programs

In recent years there has been a widespread development of many types of programs which in one way or another supplement the basic wage and salary compensation paid to the employee. In some cases these programs have come out of union negotiations. In other cases they have been devised as means to provide better for the needs of the employees, thus enabling the individual employees to be relieved of problems that might otherwise threaten their efforts to serve the company effectively. In still other cases the objective seems to be to motivate the employee in some way to provide higher levels of service. In many cases the establishment of particular programs by other companies has brought with it the competitive necessity that one's own company do likewise. All of these supplementary programs are referred to loosely as fringe benefits. Needless to say, they all cost money and the cost of each must be appraised individually as to its worth in ultimately serving the company's interests.

Motivation key objective of benefit programs

The nature and scope of these supplementary fringe benefit programs cover a wide range. Some of them are very closely related to the basic compensation. Illustrative of this type would be bonuses paid out of profits, stock option programs, savings, and stock purchase plans where employee contributions are matched by the company in some manner, insurance coverage at no cost or at below-market rates, hospital and medical protection, vacations, paid holidays, and the like. Other programs, while still being of the same general character, are less significant and are not so closely identified with the basic compensation. Illustrative of these would be credit services, food services that are partially subsidized, recreational services, and special types of home management and counseling services. Some programs, while technically part of the employee benefits, are hardly thought of as compensation at all. Illustrative of these would be company newspapers, purchasing associations, and social centers. All of these programs, however, need to be developed in accordance with sound standards of design and then properly administered. It is the personnel department that typically assumes these responsibilities.

Control Criteria of Employee Benefit Programs. The various employee benefit programs not only cost a great deal of money but also are all the more important because they involve so directly the relationships with employees. The important control considerations that need to be carefully administered include:

1. The careful design of the program in terms of costs and expected benefits

2. The adequate communication of the way the program is to operate, including especially the basis on which available alternatives should be evaluated by each individual
3. The careful administration of all aspects of the program
4. Periodic reappraisal of whether the program is achieving its proper objectives, and what possible modifications should be made in it

Service Activities

In the typical company situation there are a number of activities of a service nature that can be carried out most efficiently and economically on a centralized basis. Illustrative of such activities are plant protection and security, maintenance of reception areas, local transportation, first aid services, safety, printing, photography, and communication services. The distinction between these activities and employee benefits is that they represent services that are necessary to the ongoing operations of the company, and when carried out on a centralized basis must be made the responsibility of some staff group. In some situations such responsibility is assigned to a separate administrative services group. In other cases the personnel department is selected to provide this role.

What happens in either case is that the particular activity needs to be handled as a kind of a special business. The objective on the one hand is to provide the particular types of service to all company users in the way that will best suit their various operational needs. At the same time the theory of the consolidated operation is that this will be done at the lowest possible cost to the company. The possibility that always exists, however, is that the service group becomes too secure in its kind of monopoly position and is not adequately motivated in the normal sense to do as energetic a job as it should in meeting the various user needs. In this connection the role of an independent outside reviewer like the internal auditor can be especially useful. Moreover, the existence of the regular outside review is in itself a useful kind of motivation to the service group to check more critically on its own operation on a day-to-day basis.

Individual services need evaluation

Workmen's Compensation Activities and Safety

The administration of the workmen's compensation program deserves special recognition as an important aspect of the total personnel department activity. The underlying safety problem as we have previously seen is a combination of effective engineering—that is, the design of good protective devices of a physical nature—and working with people for greater safety consciousness. It is the latter area where the skills of the personnel department can be especially effective. The people approach begins with the careful selection of people to avoid the type that tends to be unduly prone to accidents. It goes on to develop a staff type of service that educates and alerts all em-

Safety core dimension of workmen's compensation activities

ployees to the desirability of safety and the means of best achieving safety conditions. Finally, there is the need to reinforce the fact of each manager's responsibility for promoting safety in his own particular area of operations. Since the personnel department also administers the handling of all workmen's compensation claims arising out of actual accidents, the personnel department is in an excellent position to utilize these facts in the further efforts to develop an effective safety program. At the same time the facts in this area can be communicated to all interested parties in meaningful reports. The final test, of course, is the extent to which accidents are actually eliminated.

Labor Relations

Relations with unions critical part of personnel role

Any discussion of personnel department activities would be incomplete without some recognition of the role in the handling of labor relations and the day-to-day problems as they relate to the existing unions. It is of course natural that this close interrelationship with unions should exist since the personnel department is dealing with such a wide range of matters affecting every employee. At the outset these personnel relationships involve the conditions out of which union relationships emerge. Prior to the unionization of either hourly or salary workers it is the conditions of compensation and the conditions of other kinds of treatment which provide the foundation from which the proposals for unionization emerge. Here the personnel group serves both as the sensor to the developing problems and the counselor as to how the force of particular problems can be neutralized. Similarly, after a union is established, the process is repeated as the pressure for new types of contractual arrangements are generated. Here current actions continuously set the stage for the renegotiation and modification of union contracts. But irrespective of these future implications, the personnel department is also actively engaged in the current administration of the union relationships. Interpretation of and compliance with individual contractual provisions must be continuous. Rules must be enforced and actions pursuant to these rules properly documented. When grievances are asserted at any level in the work force, these must be dealt with in a manner that is fair and equitable. In all of these relationships with the union the personnel group has a major opportunity to blend the ever-basic managerial roles of other company personnel with the needed uniformity of company-wide policies and procedures.

SPECIAL PERSONNEL PROBLEMS FOR MANAGEMENT

The discussion of the functions of the personnel department provides an appropriate opportunity to touch on certain broader types of personnel problems with which management is currently being challenged. These further problems go beyond the previously discussed current operations of the personnel department, but do involve areas where there are major assistance potentials for the personnel group. At the same time the internal auditor can, through better understanding of these problems, be alert to the impact on operational problems that he is reviewing. We will deal very briefly with seven of these major types of management problems that involve the continuing effective utilization of people.

1. Increasing unionization
2. Minority-group development
3. Women in industry
4. Adapting to higher human expectations
5. Utilization of computers
6. Continuing management development
7. Achieving good morale

Increasing Unionization

The major development of unionization has, as we know, been in the so-called blue-collar or day-labor area. The basis for this development has been the belief on the part of labor that it was not receiving a fair share of the productive results made possible by its operational collaboration with management. Other contributing causes have probably also been the greater desire of laborers for self-expression and greater control over their own activity. At the same time enterprising labor leaders have recognized their opportunities to build up their own strength and power. The impact of all of this development on management has been primarily the constraints of union demands and the lesser degree of management flexibility. On the other hand there have been some benefits in the way of a more orderly process of dealing with labor needs. In most large companies the unionization of direct labor has become a fact and the management problem is how to deal with unions in an effective manner. Although there are still some situations where day labor is not unionized, there is continuing pressure on the part of unions for the further control.

Unionization a continuing part of management environment

The same forces that have generated the unionization of day labor now also appear to be operating to try to bring various types of salaried employees into the unions. Clerical-type salary workers have become increasingly a target for union organizers and some limited success has been achieved. More recently there has been some unionization of professional groups such as engineers. These developments again have effects similar to the earlier direct labor unionization in the way of widening the gap between the partners of the total company effort and in placing further constraints on management flexibility. Our own purpose is not to pass judgment on the very complex issues that are involved, but to recognize the problem as one where management needs all possible assistance. This assistance comes first in providing information and counsel about conditions where unionization may be developing as an issue, and then subsequently in dealing with existing unions.

Because of the internal auditors' continuous exposure to operations a special opportunity exists to render such assistance.

Minority-Group Development

Alertness needed to changing minority-group development

A major development of recent years has been the view that minority groups have not shared equitably in the economic and social progress of our society. To the greater extent this focus has been on the black portion of our population, but it has also extended to the status and progress of other racial and ethnic groups. The black dimension of this problem has, however, been the most volatile and has received greater attention because of the more violent type of protest which has often been associated with the problem. The basic complaint is that the blacks in our population have in total been substantially exploited, and that major corrective action is needed in providing better living conditions, better education, and better economic opportunities. This is a view shared not only by the blacks themselves but by a great number of others. The development has had a significant impact on the modern business company and its operations. It is a problem that every well-managed company is seeking to understand and to cope with more effectively. Suddenly the extent to which black persons are being utilized within the company is being carefully examined and new efforts are being made to accelerate the degree of utilization.

Again it is not our purpose to pass judgment on the causes and responsibilities of this very complicated problem. We are concerned primarily with the fact of the existing pressure for greater utilization of black personnel in higher-level jobs and the kinds of operational problems that are involved. These problems include the usually existing needs for more training, the often sensitive personal relations involved with the minority workers, the reactions of other company personnel, and the overall impact on the levels of product quality and customer service. Here the conflicts that normally exist between various internal management objectives pose major problems of evaluation and ultimate reconciliation.

Women in Industry

Equal jobs and pay for women

Another more recent problem has to do with the extent to which women are utilized as compared with male personnel. The concern here has two dimensions. The first of these is that women be given equal opportunity to have particular types of jobs, that is, that they are not discriminated against when they are equally qualified to do those jobs. The second dimension is that, when women are given particular jobs, they be fairly compensated. The standard here is especially the compensation given to a male when he does a similar type of work. The pressures to combat both types of discrimination have come primarily from associations of women. These associations have exerted their pressures directly on the management of various organizations, and have additionally made a strong appeal for general public support. The problem of management has been how to respond to these new pressures in an orderly and effective manner. One of the difficulties is the very frequently controversial judgmental question as to the extent to which the performance of the female employee really conforms to the ends of the job. There is also in many cases the counterpressures of male employees who feel that their earning needs have a higher priority. In all phases of the problem, management quite clearly needs the kind of assistance that can be rendered by the independent reviewer.

Adapting to Changing Human Expectations

The previously discussed problems of a more effective treatment of minorities and women extend also into the broader dimensions of changing human expectations and how management can best adapt to those changes. What has been the most basic development in this area has been the change in attitude of youth and the strong protest against certain conditions of our times. The general view of youth seems to be that in achieving economic and material goals, there has been an undue disregard for environmental factors and more basic human needs. The impact on business has been twofold. One result has been the new pressures to raise the standards of environmental protection to an extent that is both frequently very difficult in terms of feasibility and at very high cost. The other impact has been to divert many young people from an interest in business careers. Instead many of the brightest of the younger minds have been attracted to social causes and governmental activities. Business, while initially disregarding this change of attitude, or at least believing that it was a temporary phenomenon, has now begun more vigorously to find solutions to bridge the gap. For example, it is now much more common for business organizations to give the new younger employees the opportunity to participate more directly in the new causes. This trend has been helped also by the further recognition by companies of a higher degree of responsibility in these areas of greater social responsibility. At the same time the younger employees have been given more opportunities for personal self-expression and flexibility. In all of these ways modern business has sought to adapt itself more realistically to the greater expectations of modern youth. But the entire problem is very complicated, and management needs every possible assistance in working out the proper solutions.

All social expectations are expanding

Utilization of Computers

On various occasions reference has been made to the development of modern computers and the impact on particular types of operational activities. In Chapter 15 we deal more directly with the review of computers and the related processing and systems activities. Our interest at this point relates to one especially important type of application to the personnel activities and then more broadly to the total human problems of computers. As we

*Computers changing
personnel needs*

saw in our discussion of planning and placement activities relating to personnel, the identification of the existing human resources becomes of extremely great importance. Both in terms of effective personnel utilization and in providing maximum growth opportunities to the individual employees, it becomes most important to be able to determine accurately and promptly the kinds of talents and skills that are available in the company. This problem has always been dealt with in some fashion but often in a very inefficient manner. Now, however, the ability to develop computerized data banks, with immediate access and retrieval of pertinent personnel data, has made possible a new level of efficiency. What happens is that each individual's record is incorporated in the data bank with coverage of such factors as age, marital status, education, type of skills, kinds of experience, language capabilities, work preferences, and important personality traits. When a particular type of job needs to be filled, the data bank can then be tapped for an immediate listing of all individuals who meet designated requirements. A powerful type of tool is thus made available for better personnel utilization.

The broader impact of computers has been to automate many types of operational activity that were formerly carried out by specific individuals. In some cases the effect has been to restrict the number of personnel needed, and in other cases the nature of the job requirements has been significantly modified. Frequently, new types of skill are also required. At the same time the success of the particular computer application depends directly on the adaptation of the various individuals to the new requirements. What all of this means is that developing new computer systems, and putting them into operation, requires a collateral type of personnel planning and development that will anticipate the problems of adjustment, and deal with them effectively over an adequate time period. Individual companies have demonstrated that this can be done but there is still much room for improvement. The challenge to the personnel function is to assist operational management to exploit the benefits of the new computer technology, but to do it in a way that protects the necessary collaboration and cooperation of the various types of people involved.

Management Development and Motivation

While the activities relating to basic training and development have been dealt with earlier in the chapter, we continue this discussion of the personnel function with supplementary coverage of management development at the level of middle and higher management. Although people are important at all organizational levels, the maintenance of proper managerial standards becomes especially critical at the higher management levels. A number of important dimensions of this problem need to be recognized:

*Higher level management
also needs development
and motivation*

1. *There Is the Special Need to Provide Proper Motivation to Higher-Level Managers.* In part this can be done through imaginative programs of executive compensation which provide rewards that are re-

lated to their efforts to increase company profits. These programs can be made still more meaningful when they can be linked to organizational control of the operational factors determining profits, as in the case of profit decentralization. Still other kinds of motivation can be provided through effective leadership by superiors and the creation of the kind of climate that induces full utilization of talents.

2. *Changing Management Conditions Require New Types of Knowledge*. The greater use of computers and the new management sciences (which is made possible through computers) is illustrative of a kind of situation where new knowledge is needed. Similarly the new kinds of environmental and social issues that are emerging also bring with them the need for new knowledge and philosophies.

3. *A Greater Need Exists for Skills in Relating to Other Company Personnel*. Because of changing human expectations there is an increasing need for self-analysis and for the greater understanding of the complexity of human relationships. Higher-level managers especially need to be able to relate effectively to their colleagues at all levels.

These problems are illustrative of the changing needs and the increasing importance of providing continuing executive training and development. In some cases this is accomplished through in-house programs, whereas in other situations use is made of outside programs established to serve this kind of need. What is important is that the problem be recognized and dealt with in a comprehensive manner.

Achieving Good Morale

The effectiveness of any organization is directly related to the level of morale. Morale as here used refers to the extent to which employees are satisfied with the way they are treated and the enthusiasm they have for achieving established organizational goals. High morale thus not only makes for greater operational productivity, but also makes the efforts of individuals more rewarding to themselves. Hence it is something that is eagerly sought after by all managers at all organizational levels. The basis for good morale is a combination of many factors. Included here are soundness of organizational goals, good supporting policies, competent managers, evidence of fairness and integrity, functional facilities, well-designed operational procedures, a climate for self-expression, and a reasonable consideration for individuals and their problems. The managerial problem involved is to appraise continuously the success being achieved in doing things in a manner that promotes the highest level of morale practicable in the particular circumstances. There is also the related need to detect low morale and to determine its causes. The tie to people sets the stage for potential assistance on the part of the personnel department. The tie to operational conditions also makes it possible for the internal auditor to make useful observations and to develop

Productivity importantly linked to good morale

constructive conclusions and recommendations. Quite clearly, this type of contribution requires both special sensitivity and much good judgment on the part of the individual internal auditor.

Role of the Internal Auditor in the Personnel Function

We have gone to some length to describe the nature and scope of the personnel function and its unique blending of basic managerial responsibilities with needed staff assistance. We have done this because we believe that the review of the personnel department and its related activities provides a unique opportunity to serve management. In addition, every type of operational review carried out by the internal auditor relates in a number of ways to the activities of the personnel department. The combined insights gained by the internal auditor provide a useful basis for a number of specific types of contribution. These contribution potentials include at least the following:

Personnel function benefits by internal auditor input

1. The appraisal of the operational efficiency of the various types of programs, operational procedures, and records carried out by the personnel group
2. The extent to which the personnel group works in a collaborative fashion with the staff and line managers who have the primary people responsibilities
3. The appraisal of the soundness and operational effectiveness of the personnel policies adopted by the company
4. The extent to which otherwise sound personnel policies and procedures are being applied effectively in a managerial sense in individual operational areas of the company

Admittedly the total area is a sensitive one, and the internal auditor must proceed with extreme care. Clearly, however, the opportunities are there for important managerial service. Personnel activities, indeed, can be viewed as one of the new frontiers of internal auditors for management service.

AUDIT GUIDES

Personnel Activities

I. Introductory
   A. Reference should be made to the general discussion of audit guides, Chapter 11.

II. Preparatory Activities
   A. See standard Audit Guides, Chapter 11.

B. Because of the sensitivity of personnel activities, special care is needed on the part of the internal auditor.

III. Organizational Factors
  A. See standard Audit Guides, Chapter 11.

  B. Matters of special interest in the review of manuals will include:
    1. Personnel planning.
    2. Recruitment policies and procedures.
    3. Training policies.
    4. Job analysis and evaluation.
    5. Compensation policy.

IV. Personnel Planning and Development
  A. Personnel Planning
    1. Review and appraise the adequacy of the policies and procedures for the current determination and projection of personnel needs.
      a. Does each manager adequately participate?
      b. Is there proper coordination with all interested staff and line components?
    2. Review and appraise the adequacy of the assessment of currently existing employee resources and the developing expectations over the planning period.
      a. Does each manager evaluate the personnel for which he is directly responsible?
      b. Are results systematically matched with needs to show existing and projected gaps?

  B. Recruitment and Selection
    1. Is recruitment centralized and/or coordinated properly to avoid duplication of effort?
    2. Review and appraise the procedures followed for the various types of recruitment.
      a. Do organizational components being served participate adequately in the final selection?
      b. Are customer groups satisfied with the service being provided? If not, why not?
      c. Are records and files to recruitment being efficiently maintained?

  C. Training and Development
    1. What is the nature and scope of the training program?
      a. How adequate are the materials being used?
      b. Appraise the professional qualifications of the people administering the training program.

2. To what extent do other company line and staff managers participate:
   a. By demonstrating support for the program?
   b. By actually participating in the instruction and training?
3. Are company organizational components satisfied with the training being provided? If not, why not?
4. Are personnel being trained satisfied with the training experience? If not, why not?

V. Current Administration of Personnel Activities
   A. Job Analysis and Evaluation
      1. Review and appraise the design of the currently existing approach to job analysis and evaluation.
         a. How adequate are the criteria used?
         b. Are weighting factors reasonable?
         c. Is the number of classifications adequate?
      2. Are adequate specifications developed for individual jobs?
      3. Are the evaluations of individual jobs adequately made on the basis of the existing criteria and weights?
      4. Are job evaluations periodically reexamined for changing conditions?

   B. Compensation Administration
      1. Is the general level of compensation reasonably sound, and is it based on adequate surveys?
      2. Are individual job compensation levels adequately tested on a continuing basis?
      3. Are the individual cases of actual compensation reasonably distributed within the various job classifications?
      4. Are employees reasonably satisfied with the current job analysis and compensation administration? If not, in what respects is there dissatisfaction?

   C. Performance Evaluation
      1. Do adequate review forms exist for use at the several levels of organizational responsibility?
      2. Are policies and procedures reasonably adequate?
         a. Are reviews required periodically?
         b. Are reviews discussed with and approved by the next level of supervisory responsibility?
         c. Is there adequate evidence of the communication of review results to the affected subordinates?
         d. Are subordinates satisfied with the adequacy of the reviews being made by their superiors?
         e. Is there reasonable evidence that the reviews lead to specific developmental action on the part of the subordinate?

3. Are reviews available for later reference, and are they being used adequately for personnel planning?

D. Transfers, Promotions, and Terminations
   1. How effective is the coordination of individual organizational components with the personnel department when personnel changes come about?
      a. Are candidates identified for consideration before personnel actions are finalized?
      b. Is other assistance adequately rendered?
   2. Is the personnel group adequately advised when there are to be major expansions or contractions of volume in individual operational sectors?
   3. Does the personnel group take adequate measures to minimize the disruptive impact of personnel expansion and contraction?

E. Employee Records and Reports
   1. Are employee records adequate in terms of design, and are they efficiently maintained?
   2. Are individual personnel files kept up to date and available for current reference?
   3. Are job action changes—transfers, promotions, merit increases, new hires, terminations, and the like—promptly processed?
   4. Do reports rendered adequately cover needed information for the control of the various aspects of the personnel function?
      a. Are these reports satisfactory to company users?
      b. Are the reports reappraised periodically for scope of coverage, timing of release, and parties to whom distributed?

F. Personal Guidance Activities
   1. Are employees made aware of the availability of counseling services?
   2. Is there reasonable evidence that such personal counseling is being carried out in a professional manner?
   3. Are employees satisfied with the counseling services being made available?
   4. Is management being made adequately aware of the types of problems which are developing (over and above any violations of personal confidence)?

G. Employee Benefit Programs
   1. Appraise the adequacy of the total program of employee benefits, including consideration of programs carried on by competitor companies.
   2. Is the design and operation of each individual program sound and effective? If not, what are the areas of needed improvement?
   3. Are employees satisfied with the programs, both individually

and collectively? If not, in what respects is there criticism or complaint?

4. Are individual programs reappraised periodically?

H. Employee Services

1. Is the personnel department the most appropriate choice for the assignment of each particular type of employee service presently being handled?

   a. Are there other organizational components that might provide this service more effectively?

   b. Is the personnel department reasonably equipped to provide the particular type of service?

2. Is the individual type of service being provided in an efficient and effective manner:

   a. As to quality and availability of the service?

   b. As to economy of cost?

3. Are company users satisfied with the services being received in each case? If not, why not?

I. Workmen's Compensation and Safety

1. Is the scope of protective devices adequate? If not, in what respects is improvement needed?

2. Is a reasonable effort made to select personnel in such a manner as to avoid individuals who appear to be subject to greater than normal accident exposure?

3. Review and appraise the adequacy of the program to alert personnel to accident problems and to induce a positive approach to safety.

4. How adequately is the safety program related to individual managerial responsibilities?

5. Are workmen's compensation activities efficiently and promptly administered, including comprehensive reporting and utilization in the development of the broader safety program?

J. Labor Relations

1. Are personnel procedures closely attuned to labor relations requirements and implications:

   a. For conformance to existing contractual requirements?

   b. As a basis for possible changes in those contractual requirements?

2. Are grievance procedures adequate, and are they carried out effectively?

3. Do personnel department representatives participate adequately in the development of all aspects of the union relationships?

VI. Special Audit Tests

A. Detailed Reviews of Individual Employee Benefit Programs
   Over a period of time individual employee benefit programs should be subjected to detailed examination and review.

   B. Detailed Reviews of Individual Service Programs
      Similarly, the operations of individual service activities should be
      subjected to detailed examination and review.
   C. Testing of Particular kinds of Processing
      A particular type of job action—as, for example, getting a new hire
      into the records, or perhaps a change of job status—should be
      examined from the time of its inception to final completion. The
      focus here will be on types of problems encountered and time
      required for execution.
   D. Direct Employee Tests
      A useful type of special test is to review directly with representative
      groups of employees their satisfaction with selected types of per-
      sonnel activities.

VII. Special Personnel Problems for Management
   A. Special problem areas needing consideration:
      1. Increasing unionization.
      2. Minority-group development.
      3. Women in industry.
      4. Adapting to higher human expectations.
      5. Utilization of computers.
      6. Continuing management development.
      7. Achieving good morale.
         These problem areas were described briefly earlier in this chapter.
   B. Although no detailed audit guides are practicable to cover these
      broad areas, the internal auditor should be alert to the implications
      involved, and report significant observations and conclusions.

VIII–IX. Not used.

   X. Overall Appraisal of Personnel Activities
   A. See the standard Audit Guides, Chapter 11.
   B. The people aspect of personnel activities broadens the scope of this
      overall appraisal.

ILLUSTRATIVE AUDIT FINDINGS: PERSONNEL ACTIVITIES

Reductions in Administrative Personnel

Reductions in the number of administrative personnel were not made subsequent to a cutback in operations. As a result unnecessary expenditures
were made for administrative services no longer needed. The plant manager
was aware of the excess personnel but had not made reductions on the basis
that additional contracts might be obtained. At the time of our review the
plant manager stated that the plant had been unable to obtain the contracts,

and he agreed that cutbacks of personnel with annual salary costs of $125,000 could be made.

Better Assignment to Training Classes

The company did not have effective procedures for assigning staff to training classes, often selecting personnel based on availability rather than need. Some employees thus received extensive training, whereas others were not being given training courses needed for their work and for advancement.

Savings through In-House Courses

The company was incurring high tuition fees for enrollment of individual employees in courses sponsored by various organizations. Based on the number of enrollees, it was found that similar training could be provided on a group basis through company-sponsored courses, thus saving a significant amount in training costs. In addition, in some cases the individual taking a course outside the company could provide training to other members of the staff.

Using Idle Time

Based on time and observation studies of personnel in data processing, the auditor found that many employees had idle time throughout the month. The auditor recommended that these personnel rotate their functions to provide resources to run a new terminal being acquired. By better use of existing personnel there was no longer the need to hire an additional person to work on the new terminal.

Decreasing Overtime

Three departments of the company were incurring excessive amounts of overtime compared to other departments. Although some of the overtime was warranted because of backlogs, savings could be obtained if additional emphasis was placed on work-load planning, scheduling, and monitoring. Also in one department there was the need to hire two additional employees rather than granting overtime for extended periods.

REVIEW QUESTIONS

1. How does the responsibility of the personnel function relate to the responsibility of each line and staff manager at all levels?
2. Explain in your own words the total scope of the personnel function, including when and how it begins and ends.
3. How is the personnel function related to the planning function of the organization?

4. How is the proper balance arrived at between the nature and scope of the training program in relation to levels of people hired and other subsequent developments?

5. How can the personnel department effectively reconcile the needs of particular individuals with the total organizational needs?

6. To what extent does the existence of a union assist management rather than being an impediment?

7. To what extent should the personnel staff policies of the internal auditing department be determined and administered by the central personnel office and to what extent by the internal auditing department itself? Explain the rationale of your conclusion.

8. Explain how in various ways the personnel function challenges the internal auditor and provides opportunities for organizational service.

CASE PROBLEMS

Problem 13-1

Tracy Wyatt, general auditor for the Sturdy Corporation, wanted to build an internal auditing department that would make the maximum contribution to the welfare of the company. He knew that to do so he would have to find the right kind of people. He pondered some critical questions. What are the right kind of people for the job? Where should he get them? How should his departmental actions relate to the regular personnel policies of the company? His boss, Richard Trent, executive vice-president—staff services, had asked him the same questions. Trent suggested that Wyatt put his thoughts down in the form of a memorandum. Trent said, "Then we can sit down and come to a meeting of the minds."

Required. Help Tracy Wyatt prepare the memorandum.

Problem 13-2

"I give up," said Charley Somers, the Honey Bee Corporation's general auditor. "Every time I find a good person for my department, I have to fight with Personnel to get a sufficiently high job rating to interest my candidate. As long as Personnel's limited horizon is controlling, I see no hope of developing a really professional internal auditing department."

"I sympathize with you," said Somers' boss, Will Kern, vice-president–finance, "but right now all the president seems to want is to retrench and reduce costs. I'm having the same problems with the regular finance department hirings." Somers is discouraged but not really ready to give up his fight, but he doesn't know where to go from here.

Required. Analyze Somers' predicament and offer him your counsel.

CHAPTER FOURTEEN

Financial Management

Upon completing this chapter you should be able to:

☐ *Describe the functions of the financial management group in a typical company*

☐ *Explain the importance of sound cash management to a company*

☐ *Understand the role of budgeting in both the planning and controlling functions*

☐ *Discuss the process of making capital expenditure decisions*

☐ *Recognize the key elements in establishing price for a given product*

NATURE OF THE FINANCIAL MANAGEMENT FUNCTION

Financial group relates to all operations

In Chapter 11 we dealt with the basic accounting activities of a day-to-day operational character. In this chapter we are concerned with the higher-level activities that are carried out by a finance group in a modern company. Over the last several decades the finance function has emerged as one of the foremost types of support to top management. The function stemming historically from the accounting role has now gone on beyond the earlier base to encompass the responsibility for financial liquidity, the management of capital resources, and the coordination and integration of the total company effort for maximum profitability. This expanded role has been a natural result of the fact that all of the company operations have a major financial dimension. The development of new techniques combined with modern computer capabilities has also helped to make this new role possible. But perhaps the most dramatic development has come through the broader and more management oriented approach which has been adopted by finance managers themselves. Under these circumstances the internal auditor must similarly expand the scope of his own review so that he can effectively serve management. He must be able to review the finance group operations in the same way that he reviews any other company activity. At the same time also he must be able to identify and deal with the higher-level financial policy dimensions of the other company activities that he reviews. For all these reasons the modern internal auditor is vitally concerned with the area of financial management.

Organizational Setting for Financial Management

If the finance group is to effectively serve top management in the various financial areas, there must first be an adequate organizational setting. This organizational setting includes the level at which the finance group is placed in the organization and the related channels of relationship with the senior management group. It also includes the extent to which the finance group is integrated. In the normal situation the senior finance officer reports directly to the chief executive officer of the company. The senior finance officer will in these circumstances be a vice-president, a senior vice-president, or an executive vice-president, depending on the number of levels existing in the particular company. Under these conditions the senior finance executive will properly have direct access to the chief executive and be on an equal level with the other executives who report directly to that officer.

Senior finance officer should report to chief executive officer

In some companies the finance group is split between the treasurer role and the controller role, with the responsible heads of these two groups reporting directly to the chief executive officer. When this is done the chief executive officer himself has the additional responsibility of integrating the two important financial roles. However, this is likely to be a burden on the chief executive officer as he carries out his total management role. It is therefore believed to be more satisfactory to have one executive who coordinates and integrates the total finance role.

Internal Organization of the Finance Group. Assuming that there is a vice-president–finance who is responsible for the entire finance activity, the next question is how the finance group itself should be organized. Although practice will vary, it is normally desirable to separate the roles of the treasurer and controller. The treasurer's role will cover the responsibility for the cash received as soon as it can be brought under central control and the subsequent disbursement or other utilization of that cash for company purposes. It will also usually include responsibilities for bank relationships and investments. It may also include responsibilities for tax services, insurance, real estate, pension funds, stock purchase plans, and other financially based services. The controller's role, on the other hand, will normally be concerned with the accounting activities—including preparation of reports, analysis and interpretation of financial data, and development and administration of budgets and profit plans. Also, there may be other activities assigned—insurance, taxes, liaison with outside auditors, and so on. In some cases also, the data processing activities may be assigned here, although more will be said

Separate treasurer and controller duties

about this particular matter in Chapter 15. It may also be that some of the aforementioned responsibilities may be assigned to managers reporting directly to the vice-president–finance.

Plan of Treatment of Financial Management

The total financial management activities can be classified and discussed in various ways. Our own approach will be to deal first with the activities that pertain most directly to current operations. This will include major accounting policies, report interpretation, profit analysis, and cash management. The second major section will focus on the planning role. This will involve a consideration of the organizational relationships, budgets, and profit plans. In a third section we concentrate on problems of determining and administering the capital expenditures program. In the fourth section we turn to the problems of determining and satisfying the company's capital needs. Finally, we deal with some other matters not previously covered—taxes, insurance, and pricing.

ACTIVITIES PERTAINING TO CURRENT OPERATIONS

Accounting Policy

Accounting policies merge into financial and then management policies

When the basic accounting activities were discussed in Chapter 11, our interest centered primarily on the procedural and basic operational aspects. At this higher financial management level, however, we need to consider in more depth the accounting policies that underlie the basic accounting activities. Here accounting policy merges into financial policy and then into management policy itself. It is impossible to identify all such policy matters, but the important ones will at least include the following:

1. *Credit Policies*. There is first the determination as to whether credit will be made available to customers. For example, the motor companies have traditionally required cash on delivery of cars, but parts are payable on a monthly basis. Where credit is extended, the conditions must then be established for when and to whom such credit is to be offered and at what levels.

2. *Operational and Product Costing*. The policies as to cost allocation determine how costs flow to individual operations and then to products, affecting the values of inventories and what becomes cost of sales for the current accounting period. The problem of allocating the cost of the central company headquarters is illustrative. The use of direct costing is another example.

3. *Capital versus Revenue Expenditures*. Where and how the line is drawn between charges to expense and property accounts in the case of small items purchased or for various types of repair will substantially

affect the expense and profits for the accounting period. There is a trade-off here between theory and practical considerations.

4. *Depreciation Rates.* Once depreciable assets are acquired, these assets must be written off through allocations to current operations. But the manner in which this is done and the level of conservatism applied can vary greatly. The rates used may or may not be the same as those used for income tax purposes.

5. *Deferment and Accrual of Various Expenses.* The determination of what portions of cash expenditures are fairly applicable to future periods, and the accrual of expenses where cash has not been expended, involve many different types of questions and levels of conservatism.

6. *Treatment of Tax Credits.* The investment credit allowed by the federal government illustrates a kind of situation where policies will vary as to the accounting treatment to be followed. Under one policy approach the credits may be used in full as a reduction of the current year's taxes; whereas under a second policy approach they may be used to reduce the asset cost and thus be brought into the income account over the life of the asset via lower depreciation charges.

7. *Accrual and Deferment of Income.* In many cases income has not yet been received but is fairly accruable. On the other hand there may be book income which is properly applicable to future periods. In both cases the selection of methods and the level of conservatism creates important policy problems.

8. *Providing Reserves.* The possibilities of later liabilities or losses in existing assets may be so great that prudent accounting will require the creation of reserves. How these reserves should be set up and in what amounts can involve major policy determinations.

9. *Consolidation of Subsidiaries.* Although consolidation of subsidiaries is normally desirable when practicable, the determination of that practicability can reflect various degrees of judgment and conservatism.

In all these kinds of situations the internal auditor will be concerned with the reasonableness of the particular policy both in terms of generally accepted accounting principles and level of reasonable business conservatism. Although some of the issues involve decisions made at a very high level, the standing of the internal auditor in the accounting and financial field provides a special competence for making recommendations.

Report Analysis

Reports have been identified in Chapter 11 as a major dimension of the total accounting system. In our present discussion of financial management it can also be said that reports together with their supporting analyses can be a major means by which the management is given the information for effectively controlling and guiding the company. These reports take a great many

Reports should be adapted to management needs

forms to serve many different types of purpose. This comes about because of the varying needs of company managers and their particular levels of responsibility. Some reports will deal with specific operational aspects such as cost performance, product margins, changes in individual assets, and profit analysis. Other reports will be concerned with overall results of the individual profit center or of the company as a whole. The scope of the individual reports will range from a basic standard format to the inclusion of various kinds of standardized and special analysis. In some cases the data they contain will be predominantly financial, whereas in other cases the coverage will be a blend of operational and financial information. Although it is not practicable to cover all these variations in the present discussion, it will be useful to emphasize certain aspects of reports and their analyses which should be generally useful.

1. *Focus on User Needs*. The basic purpose of all financial reports is to serve the managerial needs of the particular users of those reports. Hence the starting point is an understanding of what those needs are. These needs arise out of the specific operational responsibilities of the users. The needs also are directly related to the level of responsibility and the amount of detail that is needed. Related also to this level of responsibility is the time element. The more detailed the scope of the information, the more quickly the report should be available. Admittedly some reports serve a number of different uses. However, there should be the constant effort to think of the scope of the report in terms of the person who is going to use that report.

2. *Ease of Interpretation and Use*. Although perhaps implied by the foregoing point, the objective of ease of interpretation and use needs special emphasis. There is a natural tendency for those who prepare reports unconsciously to develop them in terms of their own professional standards and capabilities. To some extent those reports may become satisfying to the makers, but not useful to the recipient. The key elements here that need attention are clearness and maximum simplicity of headings, arrangement, and supplementary analytical content.

Five criteria of good reporting need evaluation

3. *Respect for the Responsibility of the Individual Manager*. Each manager who has a given sphere of responsibility normally has a desire to have a reasonable opportunity to do his job before his superiors inject themselves into the problems involved. When reports covering these problems are exposed simultaneously to his superiors, he lacks the opportunity to assess the causes and to develop immediate or planned solutions. The proper approach is that there be some difference in timing of the release and scope of reports.

4. *Quality Analysis*. Reports quite commonly include analytical comments either as a part of the basic report as a separate attachment or as a later document. The objective here must be that such supple-

mentary analysis is really meaningful to the user. There is a tendency for such analysis to become stereotyped on a recurring basis. Again the needed approach is to seek to provide the user with additional information that will help him to understand his problems and to be able to take the best possible action.

5. *Emphasis on the Future*. One purpose of financial reports is to provide historical information for the record and for later reference. But the more important purpose is to be a constructive force for current action which will make possible a better future. The latter is in part accomplished by looking at the past and interpreting the implications of the past. This is also accomplished in part by developing forward estimates and projections. These forward estimates can also be combined with historical data. For example, the actual operational results for the months thus far elapsed can be used at each month end to provide a more enlightened basis for a new estimate of the year as a whole. The benefit here is that by recognizing the indicated future directions managers can know better what actions should be taken now to improve the future results.

Scope of Analysis.   The general objective of analysis to provide additional information which can be meaningful to managers has a number of important supporting dimensions.

1. *More Information as to What Actually Happened*. This is provided through additional details and through identification of relationships not otherwise apparent to the user of the reports.

2. *Identification of Causes*. The more specific objective here is to identify the different factors which were the causes of the larger results and to measure their relative significance.

3. *Comparison with a Standard*. Here the focus is on the evaluation of how good or bad the performance was in relation to some kind of an implicit or explicit standard.

4. *Guide to Action*. Finally, to the extent practicable, the purpose of good analysis is to provide guidance to the user as to what he might do to serve the larger organizational interest. The success at this stage depends directly on how well the preceding purposes have been achieved.

Four criteria for good analysis

Profit Analysis

The preceding general discussion of reports and report analysis leads directly into a brief examination of the basic concepts of profit analysis. Because profits and profitability become the central issue in so many operational and policy decisions, the financial manager is very concerned with all the means

Profit analysis limitations need understanding

by which he can better measure this aspect. At the outset, however, it needs to be recognized that profit analysis has certain limitations which need to be understood. One of these limitations is that profits frequently do not provide adequate recognition of other forces and developments that are of vital concern to the future welfare of the company. A given profit center may, for example, be showing adequate profits but may at the same time lose sales position, fail to provide adequate service support for products sold, be high-pressuring customers, and produce products of marginal quality. Although eventually these other factors will be reflected in declining profits, the current profit results may not be affected. Hence profit standards need to be supplemented by other types of operational standards. A second limitation of the profits concept is that it comes out of an accounting process which itself has certain basic deficiencies. Illustrative of these deficiencies is that costs of depreciable assets are on a historical basis rather than on a current value basis, that allocations of costs may be unavoidably arbitrary, and that average costs cloud the impact of fixed and variable costs and of incremental costs. What this all means is that normal accounting data are frequently not directly useful as a basis for decision making, and must be adjusted and restructured in various ways. All of this does not mean that accounting data are no longer important. It simply means that we must use them with special care and adapt them in a way that will eliminate the limitations as much as possible.

Volume–Cost–Profit Analysis. A very commonly used technique of profit analysis is the separation of fixed and variable costs and the projection of these costs at different levels of sales volume to show the resultant profits, including the point at which there is a break-even of profit and loss. In diagram form this appears as shown in Exhibit 14.1. Conceptually this chart illustrates that fixed costs and variable costs result in a varying total cost pattern under different sales volume conditions, and that profits are a func-

Break-even point guide to needed volume

EXHIBIT 14.1. Break-Even Profit Analysis.

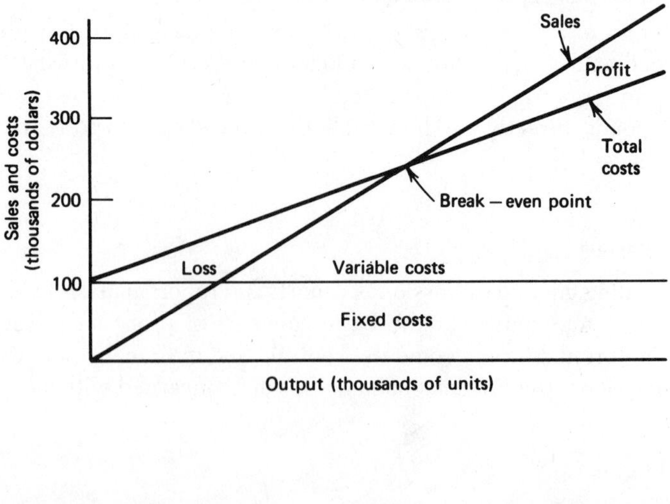

tion of the extent to which sales cover those total costs. In practice it is very difficult to measure fixed and variable costs accurately. This is because costs are variable to different degrees, and also because this degree of variability will vary over different periods of time. Also sale estimates represent a changing mix of products and prices over different levels of volume. However, the application can be useful to some extent.

Flexible Budgets. The entire subject of budgets is dealt with later in the chapter as a part of the planning activity. Flexible budgets, however, represent a special type of approach that pertains importantly to report analysis and control. Since costs have different degrees of variability under changing conditions, we need to study individual costs, and to determine what they should be at different volume levels. To the extent that this can be done, we have a better basis for profit analysis and control. Also, we have a means for measuring the extent to which actual cost variances are due to changing volume, thus making possible a more effective search for causes that are under the control of the particular activity. Again there are limitations as to how far one can go in this direction. There is an unavoidable judgment factor in estimating what costs should be at different volumes. There is also a practical limit to the number of volume levels that can be covered. However it is a useful approach when applied with reason.

Flexible budgets facilitate cost/volume evaluation

Incremental Profit Analysis. When analyses are made of the profitability of alternative decisions, the limitations of the usual types of cost data have been noted. What is pertinent to a particular decision is what *additional* revenues will be generated under the proposed course of action and what *additional* costs will be incurred. The extent to which these incremental revenues exceed the incremental costs is the measure of the worth of that particular course of action. Clearly the estimating of these incremental revenues and costs is very difficult, especially when the estimate must be projected over longer future periods. Nevertheless, it is an approach that is very useful in carrying out adequate analysis as a basis for decisions. Decision makers too often are unduly influenced by irrelevant past costs and thus fail to think in the necessary incremental terms. A good illustration of such a situation is when a determination is being made as to whether a particular machine or manufacturing process should be replaced.

Incremental profit analysis provides need decision basis

Cash Management

The management of cash is another one of the important activities of the financial manager of a current operations nature. It is the focal point of the broader problem of working capital management, which includes the management of receivables, inventory, and payables, thus involving the total problem of financial liquidity. It also relates to the problem of capital needs and how the desired funds will be obtained. In the simplest terms cash

Cash focal point for working capital management

management has to do with the most efficient utilization of cash, after consideration of all of the other related needs of the enterprise. It covers all the means by which one can increase cash availability, how the cash flows can be regularized to minimize the need for outside borrowings, and finally the investment of surplus cash to maximize supplementary earnings.

Increasing the Availability of Cash.   In the discussion of the cash and receivable financial processes, we discussed the types of actions that provided the most effective control. These same actions are closely related to the objectives of increasing the availability of cash. These and other types of action can be summarized as follows:

Ways to maximize cash availability

1. Billings to customers should be made as quickly as possible after a determination is made as to what is actually being shipped to the customer.
2. Every possible legitimate means should be used to accelerate payment by the customer.
3. Control over collections should be achieved at the earliest possible time, as, for example, routing collections to a regional center or using a lock box address to which the local bank has access for deposit purposes.
4. Transfers of cash balances need to be made promptly so that funds in excess of needed minimum balances are accumulated at key points for investment purposes.
5. Disbursements should be controlled so that the company meets but does not accelerate stipulated terms of payment.

To the extent that these types of action involve procedures under the company's control, the needed type of policies and procedures should be established and then effectively monitored. Where bank actions are involved, the counsel of the company's banks should be solicited. Assistance in achieving maximum availability of cash is a proper expectation as a part of good banking service.

Regularizing Cash Flows.   The operational requirements of each individual business will determine the relative cash inflows and outflows over the year. It is essential that the financial manager understand the nature of these various types of flow, and to be in a position both to appraise their relationships and the possibilities of modifying them. The starting point for this type of financial management is to develop a cash budget that identifies and summarizes the aggregate results. From such an overview it then becomes clear whether shortages exist at various points of time. With these special needs identified, consideration can then be given to what other courses of action might possibly be taken to eliminate the problems. It may be that there are securities which can be converted into cash. On the operational

Cash budget is starting point

side it may be possible to cut back temporarily on normal policies for the levels of inventories. Or a pending capital project might be temporarily deferred. Whether these are the courses of action that should be taken when consideration is given to the penalties involved, is something that will have to be determined on the merits. The important thing, however, is that the various possibilities are explored so that the company can decide on what is best. If then there are still shortages in the availability of cash, that need is known so that plans can be made most advantageously to obtain funds from banks or other lending agencies. Needless to say, such plans will be implemented only at the time the funds are actually needed. But the financial manager is aware of the potential needs and is prepared to deal with them.

Investment of Surplus Cash. Under the procedures previously outlined, all cash not needed to maintain minimum balances and established branch imprest funds will show up at the central cash depository or in a small group of banks that constitute the central cash depository. Determinations will now have to be made as to how large such balances should be to provide adequate support for the total company operations. Advantageous buying developments might lead to greater cash requirements or a pending strike might cause a major reduction in sales. Available cash beyond reasonable reserves, however, should now be used in a productive manner by investment in interest-bearing securities. The choice of the particular securities is determined to a major extent by the time it is expected that the money will be invested and the general state of the money market. Normally the objective will be to maximize the return within the constraints of an acceptable level of risk and an assured liquidity of the securities or money-market funds. In many cases this liquidity can be achieved with securities such as Treasury bills that have maturities corresponding to the expected time needs of the company. Here also the counsel of banks and other financial institutions is available to the company and should be utilized.

Profit from investing surplus cash

THE PLANNING ROLE IN OPERATIONS

Nature of the Planning Role

The activities pertaining to current operations merge into and overlap with the planning role now to be discussed. This planning phase is best exemplified in the development of the profit plan. Although the annual budget is a part of current operations, we wish to emphasize the planning aspect of that combined planning and control process. The capital budget covering forward capital expenditures is also clearly directly related to the financial manager's planning role. However, the planning of capital expenditures involves special problems and we will therefore defer this particular matter to the next section of the chapter. At this point, however, a preliminary word needs to be said about the financial manager's role in supporting management's policy of decentralization through the creation of profit centers.

Financial Control of Profit Centers

In Chapter 5 we discussed the possibilities of management decentralizing its responsibilities through the utilization of profit centers. When this is done the control exercised by the central management is effected to a major extent through budgets and profit plans. This in itself brings the finance group actively into the total managerial control carried out by that central management. In fact the very decision to create profit centers on a meaningful basis requires close collaboration with the finance group to determine the feasibility and practicability of profit measurement. The problem that frequently exists is that the profit centers share common facilities or services, and that, therefore, the accuracy with which profit center costs and profits can be determined becomes difficult or even impracticable. In other situations also, the profit centers sell products or furnish services to each other, and here there is the difficult problem of determining meaningful transfer prices. What this all means is that the finance group must play an active role, both in determining what profit centers should be set up and in developing the policies and procedures by which the profitability of their operations are measured and evaluated. The latter aspects become an integral part of the administration of both budgets and profit plans.

Finance group needs involvement when profit centers created

Annual Company Budget

If we go back in years, many companies made little use of the budgetary process, disregarding such usage altogether, or perhaps having the chief financial officer develop a projected profit and loss statement. Today it is unusual to find any large organization that does not make substantial use of annual operational budgets. A complete budget covers all the company activities, and comes together as an integrated final result in which all the individual pieces are linked. That is to say the expense budgets of individual cost centers and the revenue budgets of the revenue-producing components come together in profit center budgets—to the extent that such intermediate profit centers exist—and in turn come together in the total budget of the company. These detailed and aggregate budgets necessarily combine the operational and financial dimensions of the various activities, just as will the later reports covering actual performance. The responsibility for the total budgetary process in some cases is delegated to a special organizational component reporting directly to the chief executive officer, or to an intermediary such as a vice-president–planning or a vice-president–administration. More commonly, however, the responsibility for coordinating and administering the budget rests with the chief financial officer. This latter situation is a natural development when one considers the major role played by the finance group.

Role of the Budget Process. The budgetary process serves a number of important purposes, but one of the most important purposes is to assist the company to achieve better planning of its current operations. If the budget is properly developed, it provides an opportunity for individual managers to think thoughtfully and analytically about the effectiveness of the operations for which they are responsible and to then develop plans for improving the operational results. This is a type of action which, if properly achieved, can well justify the entire budget process. Once this planning has been accomplished, the budget becomes a major basis of control both for the manager who developed it and for the higher-level managers. Even then, however, as we shall see, the control must be carried out in a proper manner. Where the budget is viewed primarily as for control, or is improperly used as a control device, the planning role is likely to be significantly undermined.

Budgetary process helps operational planning

Relationship to the Accounting System. It is a basic requirement that the budget structure be the same as that of the accounting system. One aspect of this is that a well-designed accounting system and the supporting reports have recognized the scope of organizational responsibilities established and the related accountabilities. These same organizational responsibilities are then used in connection with the establishment of budgetary responsibilities and objectives. Although the line is always not as clear as we would like to have it between controllable and noncontrollable factors relating to those responsibilities, and although it is sometimes not practicable to eliminate all noncontrollable items, nevertheless we should seek in both the budgetary and accounting structure to focus on controllable responsibilities. The second aspect of the tie immediately follows, which is that actual performance as developed by the accounting system must be comparable with the budgetary data. If this were otherwise, there would be no practical possibility of using the budgetary process either as a useful planning or control purpose. When there is a high degree of decentralization of the company operations to individual profit centers, the accounting and budgetary structures combine especially to provide the basis for effective financial- and general-management control.

Budget structure must be like accounting

Developing the Budget

The question is frequently raised as to whether budgets should be developed from the top down or from the bottom up. The answer is that we need to do both. We know that eventually a budget should represent the mutual agreement of all levels of company management in a total integrated budget, insofar as the budget pertains to their respective mutual responsibilities. But in achieving this final result some things must come down from the top and some come up from the bottom. Where there are gaps, they must be negotiated on a mutually acceptable basis. The part that comes down from the top should in the first instance be the overall company objectives as to the level of *desired* improvement—sales objectives, cost productivity levels, and profit goals. Subsequently, certain assumptions must also be developed and approved on a company-wide basis. Illustrative would be such conditions as the level of expected general business activity, estimated industry sales, the expected level of inflation, assumptions as to labor cost levels, and the like. The individual company activities will then develop their own budgets within the framework of those assumptions. However, the latter development must proceed in a predetermined sequence. Thus sales budgets must be developed and agreed on before production and expense budgets can be developed.

All managers have own responsibility for budget development

Role of the Finance Group.   The development of budgets is clearly the primary responsibility of the line and staff organizational components which are responsible for the particular activities involved. This primary responsibility cannot be shifted to the finance group. On the other hand the finance group has a responsibility to provide assistance, to the extent possible. This assistance usually takes the form of providing needed historical data and in laying out forms and procedures for the development of the budgetary data. Personnel from the finance group should also be available to assist the operational managers in the analysis of pertinent data of all types as a basis for the development of meaningful operational objectives. It is absolutely necessary, however, that the finance personnel do not dominate the budget determinations and in effect themselves set the objectives. Otherwise the commitment on the part of the responsible managers is not a genuine one, and we end up with form rather than substance. There is always the very real danger that the special skills of the finance personnel and their eagerness to put together a budget that will be attractive to top management, will lead them to exert undue influence on the responsible managers.

Level of Budgetary Objectives.   In developing their respective portions of the budget, individual managers are always faced with the problem as to how much task and challenge they should take on. They can on the one hand opt for levels that will be relatively easy to achieve. On the other hand they can be too optimistic and set objectives that are unrealistically high. Or the objectives can be set somewhere in between. The question is what

Budgetary objectives should be at difficult but attainable levels

level best serves the total company interest. On balance, the right answer here is that objectives should be at levels that are difficult to achieve, but still attainable. A necessary condition here is that the objectives are backed up by sound plans to achieve those objectives. A second necessary condition is that the risks are adequately understood both by the individual managers and their superiors. The latter condition additionally involves the question of how the budget will be used later as a control device. If experience has demonstrated that the budget will be used in a rigid manner and that blame will be assessed in a punitive way when there are budgetary shortfalls, individual managers will tend to build protection into their budgets. If instead higher-level management uses the budget in a control sense with understanding of changing conditions, the individual manager will have the confidence to go on the line at budget development time with full disclosure and high-level objectives.

Reconciliation of Gaps. In developing the budget for a major operational activity, the detailed budgets prepared within the framework of certain company-wide assumptions will, as we have seen, move upward through the several organizational levels and eventually come together in the total company budget. But at any stage there may be gaps between the objectives proposed by the individual managers and those sought by the next higher-level managers. At this point the problem of the gap must be resolved in some manner. How this is accomplished is critical to the success of the budgetary process. Very often the wrong thing is done. This wrong thing is where higher-level managers either change the lower-manager budgets to match their own ideas, or where they put undue pressure on these lower-level managers to do it. Under proper procedure there is a meaningful joint probing of the issues, supplemented normally by a reexamination of the underlying buildup of the budget with the responsible manager's subordinates. What is essential is that if the budgetary levels are raised, there is a sound basis for the upward revision, as agreed to by the lower-level managers, who are going to be faced with the responsibility of performing in accordance with those higher objectives.

Administration of the Budget

If the budget has been properly developed along the lines just described, it now becomes a useful means of controlling operations at all levels. When managers are committed to the budgetary objectives they will themselves seek every proper means to achieve those objectives. It must be recognized, however, that conditions do change, and that the efforts toward compliance with the budget can become so intensive as to lead to actions that are not in the company interest. Thus if sales revenues decline because of changed economic conditions, such a shortfall should not necessarily be offset by cutting out an important training program. The budget must be viewed as having a reasonable amount of flexibility. It is guide, but not a straitjacket. In dealing with such situations there is special need for close relationships between the responsible manager and his superiors, coupled with a mutual concern for what can and what should not be done to reverse a current and projected budgetary deficiency.

Committed managers seek to achieve budgetary objectives

Formalization of Budgetary Adjustments. When conditions develop that are different from those existing at the time the budget was agreed on, there are various ways in which this kind of a situation can be handled in a procedural sense. One way is to adjust the budget to reflect the new conditions.

Budgetary adjustment procedures are critical

The revised budget objectives are then directly comparable with current and projected performance. The second approach is to leave the original budget objectives as they were, but to explain the effect of the changed conditions as a part of the supplementary variance analysis. In the case of deficiencies that are of a reasonably controllable nature—that is, essentially a measure of bad performance—the adjustment of the budget is normally considered to be undesirable. To do so would in effect relieve the responsible manager of his poor performance, and eliminate the pressure to recover this deficiency in the ongoing months. In the case of causes that are clearly noncontrollable, and where they are at the same time of a really significant nature, the case for budget adjustment has considerable merit. The use of the flexible budget to adjust for volume changes in a manufacturing operation is illustrative. At a higher level, the company might adjust the sales budget to reflect changes in industry volume, thus focusing on the level of penetration versus competition in an available market.

Internal Auditor's Relation to the Budgets

Budget department audit covers both procedures and operations

The interest of the internal auditor in the total budgetary process has a number of important dimensions. The first of these exists when he reviews the total budget procedure. This is done in depth when the internal auditor reviews the activities of the budget department. This will include the design of the basic policies and procedures, the scope of instructions issued, the timing of the development of the various parts of the budget, the manner in which the budget department coordinates the development of the budget, the way in which the budget is finalized, the types of reports used to evaluate budgetary performance, the more formal reviews that are made, the manner of adjusting budgets, and the general overall efficiency of the budget department itself. Since the budgetary process is such an important means of developing good management at all levels in the company, the internal auditor seeks in every way possible to identify specific ways in which that total process can be more effective.

The second kind of interest of the internal auditor in the budgetary process arises in connection with his review of any line or staff operational activity. At this point he is interested in the budget and the backup materials as a source of information about the plans and objectives of the particular operational activity. He is also interested in the later performance reports to find out about new problems and conditions that have been encountered. Finally he is interested in the manner in which the budget is being used as a basis for effective managerial control. What kinds of exposure is made down through the particular activity as to budgetary deviations? What kinds of review meetings are held, and what is accomplished at them? What evidence exists that a maximum effort is made to counter budgetary deficiencies at all levels?

Third, there is the direct interest that the internal auditor has in the budgetary process as he develops and administers his own budget covering the internal auditing department. This firsthand involvement has an additional benefit in that he has an opportunity to observe directly the way the total company procedure is designed and administered.

Profit Plan

In some companies the annual budget may be called *a* profit plan, and in those situations where there is no formal planning system beyond the one year it may be called *the* profit plan. Normally, however, the profit plan covers a longer period of time than the budget. The profit plan is like a budget in many respects, but is different in that it concentrates on long-term planning, and is not as detailed or precise as a budget. Moreover, it does not involve lower-level managers to the same extent as does the annual budget. As to its timing, there are various alternatives. It can be developed just prior to the development of the annual budget, in which case the annual budget then becomes the detailed implementation of the first year of the previously finalized profit plan. Or it can be developed simultaneously with the annual budget, in which case the profit plan can be viewed as a plan for the years after the budget year. Or the profit plan can be developed immediately after the finalization of the budget and cover the desired number of years beyond. The first approach appears to be preferable, as it can then be dealt with before people become so deeply involved in the more detailed budgetary process. A basis is also thus provided for a more meaningful budget.

Profit plan an extension of budget

Importance of the Profit Plan

The time horizon of modern business is being continually extended. One of the reasons for this is that we are able through the use of modern quantitative tools to probe the future more effectively. A second reason is that the development of our more advanced technology requires longer periods for design, construction, and to prove out from an operational standpoint. With this longer planning horizon, it becomes increasingly necessary that management think more carefully about its future directions. What new types of demand are developing? What new kinds of technology will be available? What new markets will exist? What new approaches in an operational sense will be possible? In short, where are the revenue opportunities, the possibilities for increased productivity, and the basis for continuing growth and increased profitability? Although these determinations are basically general management responsibilities, the considerations involve financial dimensions at every turn. What will the alternative types of action cost? What are the revenue potentials? What kind of funds will be required to support these endeavors? Thus the finance group must be actively involved in the total profit planning process.

Profit plan sparks needed broader planning

Development and Administration of the Profit Plan

The profit plan development begins at the highest management level. It normally consists of a statement by the chief executive officer of the scope of the total plan and how it is to be formulated. The supporting policies and procedures and the subsequent coordination of the total development process may in some cases be assigned to a vice-president–planning. In other cases this responsibility will be assigned to the chief financial officer. In any event the finance group must be closely involved both in working with other company activities and in developing the portion of the profit plan covering its own activities. Plans submitted by the individual line and staff operational activities will then be reviewed and discussed, and will finally come together as a total profit plan for the company.

Profit plan administration needs evaluation

The subsequent administration of the approved profit plan will vary. In some situations quarterly or semiannual reports of progress may be required. In other situations the interim reviews focus on the performance as covered by the annual budget. In either case the major formal review comes at the time the next profit plan is developed. At that time the new plan should be adequately reconciled with the plan presented the previous year and satisfactory explanations provided for changes and new directions. Again the well-developed planning materials become an important basis for high-level management control.

Internal Auditor's Interest in the Profit Plan

In most respects the internal auditor's interest in the profit plan process parallels the approach discussed in connection with the annual budget. He is interested in the basic central administration of the profit plan, he is interested in the profit plan as it pertains to the particular company activity which he is reviewing, and he himself should be participating directly in the process as he prepares a profit plan covering his own internal auditing department. It must be recognized, however, that the annual budget will have a greater impact on his current operational auditing. But at the same time we need also to recognize that the degree of involvement in, and concern with, the profit plan in its various phases is an important measure of how adequately the internal auditor will be able to understand management needs, and to service those needs effectively. For that reason he should make a special effort to be more concerned with profit planning.

PLANNING AND CONTROL OF CAPITAL EXPENDITURES

Capital spending has major long-term impact

In the development of the profit plans just discussed, the managers will necessarily be considering the kinds of facilities that they will be using in achieving the planned operational results. These facilities may be a major prerequisite for expanded operations, new product directions, or cost savings. Closely related also will be the cash budgets being developed and the resulting planning of needs for capital expenditures. This planning will reflect the greater cash needs at the time of constructing or purchasing facilities, followed by new cash availabilities when the investment in these facilities is being recovered in later years. It is, therefore, clearly very important that capital expenditures be planned carefully and with full consideration of all the various aspects of the total management effort. This planning process then merges into the controls that are necessary to assure that the definitive capital expenditure decisions are properly made and executed.

The finance group is very concerned with capital expenditures because of their major tie to the ongoing profitability of the company. A further type of concern arises through the impact of these capital expenditures on capital needs, both in terms of maintaining adequate short-term liquidity, and of the soundness of the longer-term capital structure. These concerns are all the greater because of the fact that decisions made covering capital expenditures have such a long-term impact.

Stages in the Development of Capital Expenditure Decisions

The decisions relating to capital expenditures normally come about through a series of stages, which are, as follows:

1. *As Reflected in the Determination of Company Strategy.* The choice of company strategy, as discussed in more detail in Chapter 3, if done on a sound basis, necessarily took into consideration the kinds of facilities, and their value, which would be required to support the particular strategy in a satisfactory manner. There was also presumably a consideration of whether providing the needed facilities was within the financial capabilities of the company. There exists at that point, therefore, a kind of general approval of a fairly definitive facilities program. This general approval then remains valid until there are developments that require a revision of the strategies to be pursued.

   Five key stages in decisions for capital expenditures

2. *Developing the Capital Expenditures Budgetary Plan.* During the period when the profit plans are being developed, the various types of forward action proposed will normally involve the replacement of or addition to facilities. It is then necessary for management to consider all of these needs for facilities as a total problem. This must be done to be sure that aggregate capital expenditures do not exceed the financial capabilities of the company. It must be done also so that the proper priorities can be evaluated as between the competing needs of individual operational components. Thus the development and finalization of the profit plans involve at the same time the development of the capital budget. This capital budget, as it is normally termed, consists of the total planned capital asset programs. These programs cover estimates of the total cost of the capital projects together with the funds required for the individual years during which the individual

programs are being completed. The applicable portions of this plan will then also be reflected in the annual budgets. However, none of these preceding actions constitutes authorization for actual capital expenditures.

3. *Delegation of Project Approval Authority*. Normally actual capital expenditures will be approved in the form of facilities or capital expenditure projects. In that connection determinations must first be made as to what approvals and concurrences will be required for projects at various dollar levels. The higher the level of responsibility of the individual manager the greater his authority. A particular divisional profit center might, for example, have an authority up to $50,000, and he might delegate an authority of $10,000 to a lower-level profit center department. It is then necessary in the subsequent control over these delegations to be sure that projects are not deliberately broken up to keep them within the authorized limits. There is also the possibility that expenditures of a capital nature will be charged to expense to avoid the restrictions of the delegated authorities. However, the counter-control to this practice is the resulting unfavorable impact on the profit performance of the particular organizational component.

4. *Development and Submission of Specific Projects*. Specific projects for capital expenditures are now developed and processed in accordance with established procedures. These projects are reviewed by the responsible line and staff personnel and unless rejected, and after possible modification, are approved by those individuals previously authorized. These projects will normally pertain to types of capital expenditures covered in the capital budget, and if not, should be supported by appropriate explanations of the special circumstances.

5. *Later Control and Evaluation*. The approved projects are now subjected to continuing control for progress and conformity with authorized cost levels. If and when it becomes evident that there will be overruns beyond a designated percentage, supplemental projects will be required. Postaudits should also be made after the completion of the projects.

Financial Evaluation of Capital Projects

Maximizing long-run profitability is key objective

Financial evaluation of individual capital projects centers around analysis of the level of expected profitability of the related capital assets. The first requirement will normally be that the expected profitability is consistent with established company objectives as to the level of return on investment (ROI). This established ROI objective constitutes a benchmark that is commonly used as a cutoff point for minimum acceptability of every proposed project. The second key aspect of the financial evaluation is the comparison of the expected profitability of competing projects so that they can be ranked as to their respective levels of attractiveness. The objective is to allocate the company's capital resources in a manner that will be most profitable. There will always be certain cases when a project will be approved for special reasons. Illustrative would be compliance with governmental regulations, safety requirements, or powerful competitive threats. All choices, however, are on the basis of maximizing long-run profitability.

Evaluation of Profitability. In the usual evaluation of profitability of individual projects there are two types of considerations involved. The first of these has to do with the accuracy of the estimates that go into the project. These estimates include the cost of the facilities and the time that will be required to make the facilities operational. The estimates include also the benefits that will be derived from the use of the facilities in terms of cost savings and/or revenues generated. The accuracy of these estimates is dependent both on the degree of difficulty inherent in the particular estimate and the competence of the people doing the estimating. Where new processes are involved, the estimates will necessarily be more difficult. Also when revenue projections extend a number of years in the future, the estimates unavoidably are subject to much risk and uncertainty. In addition, there is the very common problem of the objectivity of the estimates. When the management of a particular organizational component has concluded that a given facility is what is needed, it is very easy to yield to the desire to present that proposed capital expenditure in the most possible favorable terms. For all these reasons the supporting estimates and related analysis must be subject to especially careful review and appraisal.

Accuracy and objectivity of estimates key problems

Types of Evaluation. The second key aspect of the evaluation of profitability is the type of test applied. These tests vary as to their degree of complexity, and as to their relative merits. The most commonly used types are as follows:

1. *Payback.* This type of evaluation centers on the number of years required to recoup the investment covered by the project. It is not really a measure of profitability, but rather a measure of liquidity and risk exposure. Nevertheless, it is frequently used to measure the relative desirability of competing capital investment proposals. It is calculated by determining the number of years required for the cost savings or revenue benefits, on an "after-tax" basis, to equal the amount of the proposal capital investment. Assuming that the estimates are sound, it is a very simple and well-understood measure. Its limitations, however, are that it includes no consideration of how long or in what amount the ongoing benefits will be to the company after the payback point. This means also that there is no measure of overall profitability or return on investment. It is useful only as a crude measure.

   Payback is measure of liquidity and risk

2. *Accounting Method.* This type of evaluation attempts to project the profitability of the proposed investment through the existing accounting process. Here the estimate of the income to be generated is related

in percentage terms to the investment being made. In some cases the income estimate is before depreciation and taxes, in other cases after depreciation but before taxes, and in still other cases after both depreciation and taxes. On the investment side the amount used may in some cases be the original investment, and in other cases the average investment over the life of the asset. These alternative approaches lead to some confusion, and this is one of the disadvantages of using this measure. Moreover, the averaging of the investment may not fairly measure the use of the asset. The most important limitation, however, is that the method gives no consideration to the time element for the return of the funds.

Review methods consider value of money

3. *Time-Adjusted Methods.* The time-adjusted methods meet a major deficiency of the previously discussed accounting method by taking into consideration the value of money. These methods recognize the fact that dollars represent interest earning potential, and that the longer we hold on to dollars the longer they can have earning power. Similarly the sooner dollars are returned to us the sooner we will have an earning capability. This means that all dollars involved in the outflows and inflows processes pertaining to the project are adjusted in terms of current dollars. Once this is done, all projects can be put on a comparable basis.

The two commonly used time-adjusted methods are the discounted cash-flow method and the present-value method. The discounted cash-flow (DCF) method, also called internal rate of return, provides for the determination of the rate which when applied to the expected later inflows of cash (from the utilization of the asset) will make those inflows equal the original investment. This determined rate can then be compared with the rates calculated for other projects and with the required ROI rate. This rate should normally be higher than the company's cost of capital. The cost of capital is the combined cost of outside financing from debt and equity, where the cost of equity is induced through the relationship of the market price of the stock to current earnings per share.

In the present-value (PV) method the expected future cash flows are discounted at a predetermined rate, and the resulting present value is obtained and compared with the original investment. Since any difference will be in terms of dollars, those dollars must be related to the original investment to develop an index of profitability. The latter index can then be compared with the index for other projects. On balance the DCF approach is simpler and is more commonly used.

Role of the Internal Auditor Relative to Capital Expenditures

Internal auditor reviews adequacy of total process

The increasing concern of management that the decisions relating to capital expenditures be made on a sound basis has motivated the finance group to develop the policies and tools which will enable them to provide management with the guidance that is needed. Similarly, the internal auditor must now understand both the problems involved and the nature and scope of the newly developed techniques and procedures by which the financial implications of capital expenditure decisions are identified and evaluated. He is interested first that the new approaches are being used. It is no longer enough to rely on the older techniques and managerial intuition alone. The internal auditor is also interested that the new approaches are being used intelligently. We do not want to swing from one extreme to the other. What is needed is the competent use of the new approaches, but combined with the proper use of managerial experience and judgment. The internal auditor has a unique opportunity in his review of the financial management activity to make such a balanced judgment.

DETERMINING AND SATISFYING CAPITAL NEEDS

Responsibilities Relating to Capital Needs

A major responsibility of the financial manager is to evaluate the company's needs for capital. He does this at the beginning by participating in the determination of company goals and in the choice of the supporting strategies. At that time he helps provide information as to what the capital needs will be under various alternatives. That role is continued as capital budgets are formulated. It is continued also through his counsel and analysis as major policy and operational decisions are considered. Out of this background the financial manager is thus in a good position to estimate the company's total capital needs over the years of the planning period. These capital needs include the short-term needs—for current liquidity—and the longer-term capital needs, which, while involving different problems, are very closely related. Then with the knowledge of the existing and future capital needs it is the further responsibility of the financial manager to determine how those needs will be satisfied. The objective is to satisfy the existing needs at the lowest possible cost. However, all the different company interests must be considered, and the means finally utilized must be consistent with the total company welfare.

Evaluating capital needs

The foregoing role of determining and satisfying capital needs requires a great deal of special expertise on the part of the responsible officers of the finance group. It also requires the additional assistance of outside bankers and other financial institutions. Although it might seem that all of this would not greatly involve the internal auditor, we believe it is essential that a general understanding exist on his part of the major types of issues involved. Such a general understanding will especially enable him to review individual operational activities which in various ways relate to these higher-level responsibilities.

Short-Term Capital Problems

Short-term capital needs depend on operational factors

The short-term capital needs of the company stem to a considerable extent from the nature and scope of the particular business. A public utility has certain kinds of operations, while a retail merchandising chain has others. But even in the case of businesses in the same industry there can be substantial differences in the strategies followed. One company may have decided to provide its customers with special types of credit, whereas another may emphasize the savings that result from a no-credit policy. One company may emphasize supply availability and then establish more warehouse locations and more extensive inventories. Beyond these individual strategies there are then the many operational decisions that generate the need for various amounts of cash funds. Should a particular promotional program be undertaken? Should increased revenue be generated through a sale? Or should a particular staff activity be expanded?

Finally, there is the level of efficiency that is achieved in the management of each type of asset. This efficiency can be reflected, for example, in the cash management previously discussed, in a well-managed credit department, or in the more scientific determinations of inventory levels to be maintained. It can come also through the tight control of expenses. The objectives are to seek assurance that operational strategies are based on adequate study and that the levels of efficiency are the best possible under the circumstances. A sound basis is then provided through the cash budgeting process for the determination of the specific short-term capital needs.

Satisfying the Company's Needs for Short-Term Capital. At the same time that the company's needs for short-term capital are being determined, there must be consideration of the feasibility and cost of obtaining the funds needed to support the various policy and operational decisions. There is, therefore, a continuous interaction and trade-off. Needs in one area are also considered in relation to the possibility of generating funds somewhere else in the business to satisfy the first mentioned needs. At some point, however, a company determines that it does or does not need outside funds and the periods of time during which those outside funds will be required. At that point the company is ready to explore the manner of obtaining the needed funds. Typical sources will include:

Four ways to satisfy outside short-term capital needs

1. *Coverage via Long-Term Financing.* Quite often the company's needs for working capital will be included as a part of the long-term financing carried out for more basic capital needs. This approach has the advantage of avoiding a relatively short-term maturity.

2. *Use of Commercial Banks.* In the usual situation arrangements will be worked out with a commercial bank. The specific arrangements will include the scope of the total credit line, stipulations as to balances to

be maintained, the interest rate charged, the maturity of the loans, the larger credit line if involved, and the type of security provided. How liberal or stringent these specific arrangements will be depends on the availability of loanable funds and the credit standing of the particular company. Typical types of security will include marketable securities, accounts receivable, and inventory.

3. *Business Finance Companies.* In addition to the commercial banks there is another group of lending institutions which have tended to develop specialized financing techniques suited to the varying needs of the individual company. The approaches used include the purchasing of accounts receivable, advances on accounts receivable (with or without notification of the borrowing to the customer), and direct financing assistance to the company's customers.

4. *Other Financing Institutions.* This group includes a number of other types of financing institutions. These can be life insurance companies, leasing companies, or governmental or semigovernmental agencies of various types.

Long-Term Capital Needs

Initially at the time a company is created, and later as it grows and expands, the longer-run needs of the company must be determined and somehow provided. The basic needs again depend on the type of business that is involved, the basic strategies adopted, the operational decisions supporting those strategies, and the general efficiency of all of the total operational activities. The specific needs usually relate both to the capital expenditures planned and the increased permanent working capital needs resulting from new levels of operational growth. A major source of these capital needs will be the company's own internal operations. More specifically, there will be funds generated by profits, plus depreciation which is charged as an expense but not actually disbursed. Closely related also is the company's policy as to the level of dividends paid out. A profitable company that is growing has the basic justification of retaining earnings by being able to demonstrate that the reinvestment of those profits is in the interest of the corporation and its stockholders. Mention should also be made of the possibilities of a company divesting itself of capital assets, where particular operations are deemed not to be sufficiently profitable. There is the possibility also of selling certain assets under lease-back arrangements.

Satisfying Long-Term Capital Needs. When, however, all of the above-mentioned types of sources have been exhausted, and there is an indicated need on a sound basis for additional capital funds, the company must go outside to investors for such needed capital. The alternatives available relate to the type of security to be offered to investors and the manner in which the offering shall be made. The type of security depends in part on the state

Long-term capital needs choices depend on strategy focus

Outside capital approach needs evaluation

of the investment market, that is, the type of security wanted by investors. It depends in part also on the financial structure of the company and the feasibility of increasing debt as compared to equity. The manner of offering includes the question of whether the stock should be privately sold to a large investor or offered publicly to all investors. Included also is the possibility of offering rights to its own stockholders to acquire stock at a given price. The private placement has the advantage of avoiding registration with the Securities and Exchange Commission and in freeing the company from the risk that a public offering will not be completely sold. The financial manager will take into consideration all of the pertinent factors and choose the route that seems, on balance, to be in the best interests of the company.

Considerations of Financial Structure. In satisfying long-term capital needs the question of what is good for the company in terms of ongoing financial health and the question of what the market will accept, come together in the capital structure of the company as it exists before and after the proposed financing. This involves the amount of debt versus equity, with appropriate consideration to the types of debt and the types of equity. This requires some review of the nature of these different types of securities and their relative advantages and disadvantages.

Debt versus equity key policy decision

Traditionally debt has been preferred as a source of capital. The reasons for this preference include the deductibility for tax purposes of interest paid, greater market acceptability, preservation of ownership control, and the greater leverage.[1] The disadvantages and limitations are that a fixed obligation exists for both principal and interest. Where sales and earnings are subject to fluctuation the coverage of established interest requirements can involve considerable risk. The common stock type of equity in general carries advantages and disadvantages which are the counterpart of those for debt. Preferred stock is another kind of equity that ranks ahead of the common stock as a claim on assets and carries a designated rate of dividend, but not payable unless covered by earnings. There are additionally various types of bonds and stocks that embody different types of features. One of the most popular types of an intermediate security is the convertible bond. This is a bond in the sense of being a fixed obligation, but it is one that can be converted into common stock at a given price. Although the latter price is set above the prevailing market price of the common stock, it has the potential of extra profit if and when the stock price rises to and exceeds the conversion price. Because of this latter feature convertible bonds can be sold at a lower interest rate. Their disadvantage to the company is the potential dilution of the common stock equity.

---

[1]Leverage will exist where profit rates exceed the interest rates paid and the difference accrues to the benefit of the stockholders. The common stock in these circumstances is said to have leverage.

The decisions as to what the financial structure will be represent some of the most fascinating activities of the finance group. They do, however, represent an area where there are major opportunities for serving the company's total interests. The interests here involve particularly the cost of the capital obtained, the risks to which the company is subjected, and the impact on stockholder profits. A basic requisite to achieving these benefits is the special expertise of the financial manager, but augmented through the outside counsel that is normally available. The total benefit is achieved only, however, when this expertise is coordinated closely with the other operational activities of the company. Here too, it is the team effort that yields the greatest returns.

TAX ACTIVITIES

In different company situations there will be a wide variation in the range of activities carried out by the finance group. It will, therefore, clearly not be practicable to cover them all. We have, however, selected three areas that are of special significance from a financial management standpoint—taxes, insurance, and pricing. These are also areas where the internal auditor will be making both direct reviews and relating to them as a part of other audit reviews.

Scope of Tax Activities

The tax activities of a company cover a wide range of different types of taxes all of which are payable to many different governmental bodies. As to type, they include property taxes, use taxes, sales taxes, franchise taxes, and income taxes. The taxes may be payable to local municipalities, counties, states, or the federal government. Here again much specialized expertise is involved. But here again an important aspect is the way the effort is organized and administered. Important also is the dependence on good operational procedures, and especially a close linkage to the total accounting activity. All of this administrative and operational effort is of the type that calls for effective control. In addition, there is the major tie of tax activities to the development of operational policies and the making of various operational decisions. There are also great potentials of company benefit through a well-coordinated effort. We will look briefly at the more typical types of tax activities.

Effective controls needed for increasingly complex tax requirements

Property Taxes.   In most local jurisdictions the property tax is a major source of governmental revenue. Because it represents such a major operational cost it is essential that the company take every legitimate means to protect the fair assessment and administration of property taxes. The level of property taxes is normally one of the factors initially considered by the company when it buys or develops property in specific geographical locations. At that time the governmental unit with taxing power will often provide special tax-relief benefits as an inducement to the company. Subsequently, it is important to maintain good liaison with the taxing body so that changes in any initial arrangements are fairly considered. Similarly, the revision of assessed values needs to be monitored carefully to reflect changes due to capital additions and retirements, or for any other reasons. In most cases a kind of continuing negotiation takes place through which the company makes sure that its position is properly presented and fair treatment obtained.

Definitive tax bills subsequently give effect to the foregoing arrangements. These tax bills need to be examined for their correctness in all respects. Where accruals have already been made to reflect the correct operational costs for the accounting periods affected, these will be adjusted to the extent necessary and the obligation properly recognized in the accounts. Where there are questions of any kind, they will be referred to the proper parties for investigation. Major increases in the level of the tax billings would, for example, raise questions as to what were the causes and the degree of propriety. Effective controls are necessary to assure the identification of all developments where company action could be beneficial.

Sales Taxes. The pressure for additional revenues is leading more and more to the levying of sales taxes by cities and states. The first important issue here is the correct interpretation of the law to determine the types of items to which it is applicable. This applicability, in turn, determines the company's obligations as an agent of the government. The remainder of the problem has to do with the actual collection, the establishment of adequate records and accountabilities, the safeguarding of funds collected, the correctness of the later reporting, and the payment of the taxes owed. The reviewer of these operations must be sure that policies are clear, procedures adequate, and operational aspects well controlled.

Taxes have both legal and financial dimensions

Social Security and Unemployment Taxes. The social security taxes call for both deductions from the wage and salary payments made to employees and the payment of amounts which are the direct obligation of the employer. The unemployment taxes payable to the states in which the company has operations are also of the latter type. The deductions must be made in accordance with the provisions of the Social Security laws, and as a part of the payroll procedures discussed in Chapter 11. The tax liability that is directly the responsibility of the company must also be accurately calculated in accordance with the legal requirements. Reports must then be prepared and filed on the dates due, together with the actual payments. The review by the internal auditor should cover all aspects of the policies and procedures to assure both a correct compliance with the applicable legislation and that everything is done with maximum efficiency.

Franchise Taxes. There are a variety of taxes levied of a franchise nature. These taxes are levied principally for the right to do business in a particular area—city, county, or state. The basis of assessment will vary greatly and in some cases may become a special type of income tax. The first requirement is that the various reports to be prepared are properly identified and scheduled, thus minimizing the possibility that filing dates will be overlooked and lead to penalties. The second requirement is that the provisions of the report requirements are properly understood and carried out in preparing the reports. In preparing those reports a combination of legal and financial expertise is essential. In many cases there are options, or relationships with other company policies and decisions, that need to be identified and evaluated.

Income Taxes. In overall importance the federal tax, plus income taxes levied by other governmental jurisdictions, is clearly the dominant part of the total tax activities. This importance is the result of the heavy tax rate involved, and the related need to minimize this impact in every way possible through properly considered managerial decisions. The income tax activity is closely interrelated with the total accounting activity. This is true because all of the data used in the computation of income taxes payable flow directly or indirectly from the accounting system. Normally there is also an effort to design the accounting treatment of given types of transactions in a manner that coincides with the treatment for tax purposes. Where certain matters are treated differently than in the regular accounting system, the basic accounting data must be used as a starting point, and there must be a careful reconciliation with the figures used for tax purposes.

Accounting treatment directly affected by income tax needs

The tax department or other organizational group charged with the income tax responsibility is frequently headed by an individual who is both a qualified accountant and a lawyer. This is important because tax work is a blend of accounting and legal work. The tax group organizes the supporting data for the computation of income tax obligations, and then actually prepares the returns. Subsequently, as the governmental representatives make audits, the tax group deals with these representatives. If and when the need for adjustments is asserted the tax group handles these matters to a conclusion, including such tax litigation as may be necessary. Inasmuch as large amounts of money can be involved in the final resolution of the company's tax liability, there is a great need for the highest level of professional competence.

Impact of Income Taxes on Operations. In making any operational or policy decision of any significance, an important consideration in weighing the alternative approaches is what the income tax consequences may be, especially where the tax law may not be entirely clear. These questions have their first beginning when a company determines its corporate form of organization and continues on to include such matters as the manner in which inventory is valued, the types of sales arrangements, manner of purchase, depreciation of capital assets, retirement of plant, supplying capital needs,

Income taxes key consideration in operational decisions

corporate distributions, and executive compensation plans. In dealing with those various matters there are usually various opportunities for effecting tax savings, provided that the possibility is recognized on a timely basis and properly implemented. The tax group must, therefore, be aware of all of these operational developments and have the opportunity to provide information relating to the tax impact. This includes also the role of helping management to do what needs to be done in an operational way, but in a way that minimizes the income taxes payable.

Role of the Internal Auditor in Tax Activities

The internal auditor is first interested in the extent to which the tax group is administering its basic operational activities in an orderly and efficient manner. The second interest is in how effectively the tax group is working with other operational activities to assure proper consideration of tax issues in their respective policies and current decisions. Through the internal auditor's wide contacts in the company there is a continuing opportunity to contribute to the achievement of effective company coordination in all tax matters.

INSURANCE ACTIVITIES

Nature and Scope of Insurance Activities

Another important type of activity frequently carried on by the finance group has to do with insurance. The insurance function in its most basic sense is a major part of the total company effort to manage risk. The total business operations unavoidably involve risk. Profits are, indeed, the reward for the assumptions of risk in committing capital to the selected operational areas. But where risks can be eliminated or minimized through various types of action the prudent business manager weighs the cost, and determines what *Insurance is effort to* course of action appears to best serve the company interest. One of the ways *manage risk* to do this is by purchasing insurance for protection of various kinds. The most common form is the coverage of possible losses of assets like cash, inventory, and facilities. One can go further, however, to cover such items as the collectibility of accounts receivable, loss of profits from interrupted business operations, or life insurance on key officers. The responsibility of the insurance group is to develop policies for management approval covering the extent to which such insurance protection should be purchased. Subsequently then, the insurance group has the responsibility for administering the approved policies. Again a great deal of special expertise is required on the part of the people who administer this activity.

Developing Insurance Policy

Types of risk need The development of insurance policy starts with an inventory of the types
identification and evaluation of risks to which the company is subject. Although to some extent risks may

seem to be unavoidable, there is usually a way that they can be eliminated or substantially reduced if we are willing to pay the cost. In some cases we will pay that cost and in other cases the cost may be too high. For example, in the case of capital assets, the property may be so widely dispersed in a geographical sense that the company may conclude that it will assume directly the risk of fire and other similar hazards. In that case the company will either absorb losses directly into operations or it will accrue reserves at customary insurance rates and then charge actual losses to those reserves. Thus the insurance group appraises the types of existing risks and determines whether it shall seek outside insurance. This then leads into the more detailed determination of the particular features that are desired in the way of insurance coverage—what inclusions and exclusions, and what ranges of dollar limits. For example, do we want full coverage for auto damage or are we willing to accept a deductible provision? Do we want liability coverage at the $100,000 level, $300,000 level, or $500,000 level? In all these determinations a major level of professional competence is required and care in the identification and evaluation of the various issues and alternatives. To some extent also, additional counsel can be obtained from insurance agents and brokers.

Administering the Insurance Activity

The policies as now determined provide the basis for the actual procurement of the wanted insurance coverage. This first involves selecting the carriers to be used. In making that selection a number of factors are necessarily considered. This will include the range of the coverage that a particular carrier can offer, the financial resources of the carrier, the reputation as to the efficiency and fairness with which claims are settled, and the rates charged. Again insurance brokers, who usually represent a number of carriers, can be helpful in appraising the various alternatives. As a basis for the final negotiation for the purchase of insurance coverage, the insurance group will wish to have complete data as to the value and location of the assets, and other pertinent operational data. The objective will be to seek maximum coverage while achieving the most advantageous rates practicable. Out of these negotiations will then come definitive contracts for the agreed-upon coverage at mutually acceptable rates.

Special procedures needed for insurance administration

Ongoing Administrative Activities. During the life of the policy there will now be a varied range of ongoing administrative responsibilities. In some cases coverage should be adjusted periodically on the basis of regular reports as to the status of the insured assets. In other cases the changes in coverage are linked to other operational developments—as, for example, new facilities may be purchased and old ones retired. Usually coverage is automatically adjusted in such situations but there must be notification within a given period for the purpose of adjusting future billings. All these requirements must be complied with, and adequate procedures must be designed so that the various operational developments are identified and properly reported to the carriers. As billings are received for insurance coverage, they must be carefully reviewed both as to the accuracy of rates charged and the correctness of the coverage provided. All these review activities must also be closely tied into the regular processing of the invoices for actual payment, and the proper distribution of costs to the various operational activities affected.

Handling Claims. The insurance group will also normally play an active role in the reporting of all developments that provide a basis for a claim by the company under the existing coverage. This prompt reporting requires the proper cooperation of the operational activities directly affected. It is especially important because the carrier must usually be given the opportunity to take any steps that may assist it in reducing the final loss claim. The insurance group then works with the operational people in developing the actual claim, and after its submission to the carrier coordinates any later audit and negotiation that precede the ultimate settlement. At this stage the supporting data and related information must be provided as needed. However, it may also be necessary for the insurance group to provide additional pressure to assure a final settlement that is fair to the company. Again these settlement activities must also be closely coordinated with the accounting operations.

Educational Role of the Insurance Group

Insurance cost depends importantly on loss experience

The cost of insurance is very closely related to the loss experience of a particular company. If losses run at a very high level, higher rates must be charged by the carrier if it is to maintain its own profitable operations. In an extreme case of high losses the carrier may even elect to cancel the coverage completely. These possibilities make it very important that the company operations be carried out in a way that will minimize losses, thus reducing the amount of claims which will be filed. A well-managed insurance department recognizes this problem and endeavors to bring about the right kind of conditions. It does so by developing educational material that can describe the things that should be done. Departmental personnel can also make periodic field visits to ascertain firsthand what problems may exist. At the same time the insurance representatives can provide direct counsel to the operational managers. The liaison also makes possible a more up-to-date understanding of insurance needs and possible solutions.

Overall Appraisal of the Effectiveness of the Insurance Activity

Insurance considerations affect all types of operations

An impressive thing about the insurance activity is that it relates in some way to almost every phase of the company operations, and that it has to do with each level of those operations. This makes it a necessity that the insurance group maintain effective coordination with the highest level of management. It includes also the need to tie in closely with the basic accounting activities. The effectiveness of the insurance department is, therefore, dependent on combining professional expertise with good coordination with all company activities. The department must be prepared to respond to the needs of the various operational activities and at the same time to take the initiative in suggesting new possibilities and approaches. The appraisal of the insurance activity centers on the extent to which the insurance group is carrying on this total coordination. As it happens also the internal auditor comes across the insurance problem as he reviews the various operational activities, and this provides further input for the specific review of the activities of the insurance group. The internal auditor's interest is that the insurance department has developed sound policies and procedures and that they are being carried out in an effective manner.

PRICING ACTIVITY

Basis of Interest

The profits of a company, as we know, are determined by the excess of revenue over cost. In various chapters we have been concerned with the managerial efforts to control costs so that they will be at levels that make the greatest possible contribution to the success of the company. We have also considered at a number of points the need to maximize revenue. It is as a part of that latter concern that we look briefly at the problem of pricing. To a major extent this problem of pricing is part of the broader area of marketing management. However, pricing also has a major financial dimension and in most companies the recommendations to management for pricing action are finally determined by the finance group. We view pricing as a joint responsibility of the marketing and finance activities.

Pricing responsibilities shared with marketing

Factors Bearing on Price

Prices are the dollar figures set by the company for its products and services when offered to customers for purchase. How wisely these determinations are made quite obviously has a major impact on the company's profitability from both a short- and long-term standpoint. It is, therefore, most important that we understand the factors that need to be considered in establishing prices. It is also important that we understand how better information about those factors can be provided, as a basis for more advantageous pricing. In this connection there are three areas that need to be examined. One of these is the state of customer demand. A second is the competitive situation. The third is the particular company situation. Although all three areas are interacting, each has its specific type of influence, and we will look briefly at them.

Customers cast the final vote by purchase choices

Customer Demand.   We know that customers have various kinds of needs and desires. They also have different levels of economic capacity to make purchases that will directly or indirectly satisfy those needs. As products and services are then offered to them they will make some kind of evaluations and elect to make particular purchases. The extent to which they purchase the offerings of a particular company will depend on a variety of factors, of which one important factor is the price that company has established for the given item. From the company's standpoint an important consideration in price determination is the volume that will be purchased at different prices. If we can answer that question, we can project the revenue impact at particular levels of price, and give proper consideration to that dimension in our effort to achieve the highest possible level of profitability.

The answer to the question of what customers will purchase at various prices involves a number of matters—the design of the product, the quality achieved in production, the goodwill of the customer, the effectiveness of our salespeople, the advertising and promotional appeal, and the like. We also may have a great deal of experience as to how customers have reacted in the past to specific types of pricing action. Additionally, we need information of the kind normally now obtainable to a significant degree from modern marketing research. This research can take a number of forms. To some extent it will include the analysis of economic capability, including the levels of purchasing power and expected trends in the economy. To some extent also it will include surveys of customers' needs and preferences. In other cases it will include actual market tests in representative local markets. The objective in all cases is to contribute to the accuracy of the estimates that are made of the volume that will be purchased over time at various levels of price.

Competitive Situation.   The second area that needs to be examined is that of the competitive situation. The interest here is twofold. In the first place the extent to which customers are going to purchase the products and services of our own company at given prices will depend importantly on what competitors are doing in the way of offerings in terms of attractiveness of products, availability, and price. Our estimates of volumes at various prices must,

Customer options can be analyzed

therefore, take into consideration the number and types of options open to the customer. Involved also is our relative strength as respects basic product merit and effectiveness of various aspects of the marketing program.

The competitive situation also touches us in another very important respect. When a particular company sets prices it must take into consideration how competitors will respond to that price action in terms of their own prices. If our company is the leader in the industry, we may have less difficulty making this prediction. On the other hand, in a more equal competitive relationship we may, through our own pricing action, induce various types of retaliatory response. This retaliatory response will then change the scope of the options to customers previously discussed. Still another possibility is that a high-level profit margin may be so attractive that it will attract new competitors. In the short run this may not be a problem but in the long run it could be very serious.

Company Situation. The third area that needs to be examined is the particular company's own situation. At the highest level are the company's goals and objectives, and the supporting strategies—as, for example, an objective for more rapid growth through lower pricing. At the operational level are the conditions of existing stocks, production facilities, and the effectiveness of the production and marketing activities. The latter factors are reflected in current and projected costs. These projected costs will reflect the impact of new operational programs. Additionally, they will reflect the impact of different volumes that result from the various alternative price levels. This latter impact is due to the fact that all individual types of cost have different degrees of variability for different volumes. Thus to the extent that some costs are fixed (or not completely variable) unit-product costs will be lower for higher volumes. Therefore, the evaluation of various pricing alternatives must take into consideration the effect on profit of both the factors of cost and revenue levels.

Price decisions a two way evaluation of inside and outside factors

It is thus clear that cost plays an important role in the determination of prices. In specific situations it may even be the controlling guide. For example, some items are made to order on the basis of actual costs plus a given margin of profit. Cost is also a powerful psychological force in the short run when price reductions are being considered. Also we know that unless costs are covered on a long-run basis, we eventually want to abandon the type of business involved. But having said all of this as to the role of cost, it should be clear that sound pricing policy and action is based on an evaluation of all of the three areas discussed above—consumer demand, the competitive situation, and the company situation—and that these three areas have major interlocking relationships. It is because of these three factors that the determination of prices which best serve the total company interest is so difficult.

Typical Pricing Problems

The broad scope of the pricing policy decision can perhaps be best appreciated by an identification of a number of typical pricing problems.

1. *Product Differentiation.* If products can be differentiated from competitor products by some unique aspect that consumers value highly, prices can be higher than competitors as long as that differentiation can be maintained. Examples include unique styling, a special operational characteristic, or by being in the market first with a new product. Sound marketing policy, therefore, seeks to offer such product differentiation.

Eight major types of pricing problems

2. *Product-Line Relationships.* When there are a number of related prod-

ucts in a given product line, there is the question of whether profit margins should be uniform or to what extent they should be different. Illustrative would be a luxury model in an automobile line versus the standard model. Wider margins are usually sought for the more deluxe models, but there are practical limitations.

3. *Price Differentials.* A number of different types of price differentials normally exist. That is, different prices will be available to different kinds of buyers (like wholesalers versus retailers), for different quantities (quantity discounts), for promptness of payment (financial discounts), for purchases at different times (early orders before the season of normal demand), and the like. The question is the basis for such differentials and how they should be determined.

4. *Legal Constraints.* In all pricing action there is the ever-present potential threat that prices may in some way discriminate against particular buyers or groups of buyers. There is also the risk that the prices set may appear to reflect some agreement with competitors that can be interpreted as being of an antitrust nature. It is here that the assistance of competent legal authority must be utilized.

5. *Selling on the Basis of Price.* There can be many types of market strategy. One strategy, however, is to use pricing policy as a specific strategy. At one extreme prices may be set low to create special buyer appeal, subject always to the risk that competitors will meet those prices. At the other extreme high prices may be used to create the impression of special quality. There is the question, therefore, of the choice of strategy and then what specific prices support the selected strategy.

6. *Incremental Profit Pricing.* In many situations it may be possible to take on new business at lower-than-usual prices when the new business will still yield extra profit, without endangering the regular business. An example would be covering new markets overseas. Still another example would be a second brand to appeal to a lower-price market. A major question here is whether the additional sales, at the lower prices, will in some way undermine the market for the regular products.

7. *Sequential Pricing.* When a product with unique appeal is introduced, there is the possibility of initially exploiting this appeal through higher prices. This is especially applicable when production capabilities are still at relatively low levels. Subsequently, when production capabilities are expanded, the price will then be reduced to attract larger demand. Consideration must be given, however, to how the original buyers will react to the later reduced price. What seems to be in the short-run interest may not be the best policy in the long run.

8. *Standard Volume Pricing.* A company may decide to fix prices at a level which over a number of years at a reasonably expected volume will yield the desired level of profits. Although volumes over the

different years will yield different profit margins, the advantage is the stability of pricing policy that is thereby achieved. For the company that is the industry leader, this is an especially attractive policy. For other companies, however, this option is less available because of the fact that prices must be set at levels that are competitive with the industry leader.

Role of the Internal Auditor in Pricing Policy

The previous brief discussion of pricing clearly indicates that the problems in this area involve the highest levels of management and are linked to basic strategy policy decisions. It might, therefore, seem that the internal auditor has very little concern about what goes on in the pricing area. We believe, however, that the very fact that pricing is such an important management responsibility is why the internal auditor should seek to be of assistance. But if he is to be of assistance, the first step must be a general understanding of the issues that are involved.

Internal auditor has good overview of component pricing factors

When we turn more directly to the specific manner in which the internal auditor can be of assistance, we see two major ways in which this can be done. The first type of assistance can center about the kinds of factual input that are provided to management as a basis for policy development and actual pricing decisions. On the cost side the needed input is not only good historical cost data—a traditional concern of the internal auditor—but also estimates of future cost levels, developed for the different levels of volume that must be projected by management at various pricing levels. On the revenue side there is the needed input relating to the analysis and testing of market demand. There is also the necessary study of economic trends for the total economy and for the specific industry. In addition, there is the study and projection of possible action by important competitors. With respect to all these input factors, the internal auditor can be useful in appraising the scope and quality of the actual data developed. The objective here is to provide management with the best possible basis for pricing decisions.

The second major way in which the internal auditor can be of assistance is in the area of policy implementation. After the pricing policy has been determined, there should be adequate procedures for its extension throughout the company. Where the policies must be translated into specific prices, the procedures must cover that phase also. In some cases there may be in addition the need for particular types of deviations to meet specific types of situations. The internal auditor is concerned that the procedures and related controls are properly stated, and that they are adequate. Finally, there is the efficiency and care with which the pricing policies are implemented in terms of lower-level organizational performance. At the same time the problems of specific implementation may provide important information as to both the feasibility and desirability of specific pricing policies. The internal auditor can make significant contributions in all these areas.

Internal auditor helps assure compliance with pricing policies

AUDIT GUIDES

FINANCIAL MANAGEMENT ACTIVITIES

I. Introductory

    A. Reference should be made to the general discussion of audit guides, Chapter 11.

II. Preparatory Activities

    A. See standard Audit Guides, Chapter 11.

    B. To a considerable extent the individual financial management areas will be handled as separate reviews.

III. Organizational Factors

    A. See standard Audit Guides, Chapter 11.

    B. These organizational factors need to be adjusted to the particular subarea being reviewed.

    C. Matters of special interest in the review of finance manuals will include:

        1. Accounting policy.
        2. Financial reports.
        3. Profit analysis.
        4. Cash management.
        5. Budgets.
        6. Profit plans.
        7. Capital expenditures.
        8. Supplying capital needs.
        9. Taxes.
      10. Insurance.
      11. Pricing.
      12. Coordinative arrangements with other company activities.
      13. Handling of policy deviations.

IV. Activities Pertaining to Current Operations

    A. Accounting Policy

        1. Review and appraise the manner in which major accounting policies are developed, including depth of study and adequacy of coordination.

        2. Appraise the adequacy of the scope of existing policies, including those applicable to:

          a. Credit.
          b. Product costing.
          c. Capital and revenue expenditures.
          d. Depreciation.
          e. Deferments of expense.
          f. Treatment of tax credits.

      g. Accruals of expense.

      h. Creation of reserves.

      i. Treatment of subsidiaries.

B. Report Analysis

1. Review and appraise the total group of financial reports regularly issued, with particular reference to:
   a. Focus on user needs.
   b. Ease of interpretation and use.
   c. Respect for individual manager responsibilities.
   d. Quality of analysis.
   e. Adequacy of attention to the future.
2. Review the adequacy of analysis in the interpretation of financial reports.

C. Profit Analysis

1. Review and appraise the existing program of profit analysis.
2. Are adequate efforts made to recognize the limitations of profit analysis and to provide supplementary data?
3. Are flexible budgets used to the extent practicable?
4. Are incremental types of analysis utilized for guidance to management?
5. Is the total effort adequate, in the way of developing various types of profit analysis?

D. Cash Management

1. Is the importance of the cash management activity adequately recognized in terms of assigned responsibilities and quality of personnel?
2. What steps have been taken to increase the availability of cash? Are they adequate?
3. Have cash flows been studied for maximum possibilities of regularization?
4. Is a cash budget regularly prepared and released to all interested parties?
5. How effective is the program for the investment of surplus cash?

V. Planning Role in Operations

A. Annual Budget

1. Has top management established and provided adequate backing for a budgetary program? Appraise whatever is being done of an annual planning nature.
2. Is the responsibility for coordinating the development and later administering the budget placed at an adequate organizational level?

3. Is the organizational structure reasonably supportive of an effective budget program?
4. Is the planning aspect of the budget adequately emphasized?
5. Are there adequate procedures covering the manner in which budgets should be developed by the individual organizational components?
6. Does the finance group provide adequate assistance through providing historical performance data, explaining procedures, and providing any other needed experience?
7. Are the budget data developed along the lines of accounting reports, so that budgetary performance can be periodically measured and evaluated?
8. Are individual budgets as developed accepted by the respective managers as their own commitments and plans?
   a. Are existing gaps reconciled on a mutually satisfactory basis?
9. Review and appraise the extent to which interim performance reports are used for management analysis. What evidence is there of resulting corrective action?

B. Profit Plan
1. Apply the same guides as listed under the annual budget to the review of the profit plan activity.
2. Is the profit plan properly tied into the annual budget?
3. Review and appraise the adequacy with which new profit plans are reconciled with previous profit plans.

VI. Planning and Control of Capital Expenditures
A. Capital Expenditure Budget
1. Is a capital expenditures budget prepared? If not, appraise the extent of the existing need.
2. Review and appraise the adequacy of the manner in which the capital expenditures budget is prepared and administered.
B. Control of Individual Capital Projects
1. Is there an adequate and reasonable plan of delegations of authority?
2. Are projects processed, reviewed, and controlled?
C. Financial Evaluation of Capital Projects
1. To what extent are methods used which adjust for the different time value of money?
2. Are the results of these newer scientific methods adequately communicated to management?

VII. Determining and Satisfying Capital Needs
A. Short-Term Capital Needs
1. Does the determination of short-term capital needs reflect adequate coordination with all company activities and explo-

ration of merits of other actions that could minimize these needs?

2. Do qualified personnel effectively explore the various ways in which the determined short-term capital needs can be satisfied?

3. Are short-term needs properly coordinated with long-term capital needs?

B. Long-Term Capital Needs

1. Is the determination of long-term capital needs properly coordinated with the capital expenditures budget?

2. Do qualified personnel effectively explore the various ways in which the determined long-term capital needs can be satisfied?

VIII. Tax Activities

A. Policy

1. Are the tax implications of policy and major operational decisions given adequate visibility through effective coordination with all company activities?

2. What evidence exists as to the sufficiency of forward tax planning?

B. Operational Efficiency

1. Are the organizational responsibilities for the various types of taxes specifically assigned at a sufficiently high level? Is there adequate qualified staff?

2. Review and appraise the procedures for the development of required tax reports.

3. Are tax due dates adequately identified and scheduled?

4. Are relations with tax authorities effectively handled?

5. Are tax actions adequately coordinated with the accounting group?

IX. Insurance

A. Policy

1. Are the risk-reduction possibilities through insurance given adequate visibility to management by the insurance department?

2. What evidence exists as to the adequacy of the consideration of insurance factors?

B. Operational Efficiency

1. Review and appraise the effectiveness of the selection of carriers and the negotiation of specific insurance coverage.

2. Review and appraise the linkage and coordination of insurance matters with the affected operational activities, and with the accounting group.

3. Are claims efficiently handled?

4. Are adequate efforts made to carry out programs to reduce losses, to ultimately reduce insurance costs?

  X. Pricing
    A. Development of Pricing Policy
        1. What is the procedure for developing pricing policy? Does the finance department participate in a reasonable manner?
        2. Review and appraise the manner in which cost and revenue estimates supporting pricing action are determined.
        3. Is the coordination between the marketing and finance groups adequate?
    B. Operational Control
        1. Review and appraise the procedures by which price lists are developed and distributed.
        2. How adequate are the efforts to determine the propriety of prices actually used?
        3. Are procedures for the control of deviations adequate?

 XI. Specific Audit Tests
    Supplementary specific audit tests will be applicable in connection with the various operational phases of the areas discussed.

XII. Overall Appraisal of Financial Management Activities
    A. See standard Audit Guides, Chapter 11.
    B. The overall appraisal can be made separately for each financial management subarea, and also for the area as a whole.

ILLUSTRATIVE AUDIT FINDINGS: FINANCIAL MANAGEMENT

Needed Revision of Depreciation Methods

Modifications of depreciation methods were needed to obtain better valuations of capital equipment and to achieve savings on income tax. Depreciation policies established by the treasurer's office had not been modified under changed conditions. It was found that eight items of equipment were being depreciated over 10 years when the company's current plans for usage of the equipment were only 6 years. Improved coordination was needed between production, the accounting office, and the treasurer's office to assure that depreciation methods are periodically reviewed and changed as needed.

Delayed Deposit of Cash Receipts

A survey of two weeks average daily bankings of the five branches of the company indicated that delays were encountered in making deposits. Deposits by two branches were accumulated and made the next morning, even though total daily receipts from customers were as high as $200,000. Under the extended hours recently adopted by the bank, deposits made by 4 P.M.

would be credited that day. It was recommended deposits be made the same day as receipts, resulting in interest savings of $20,000 a year.

Inconsistent Methods for Developing Personnel Requirements

Procedures for developing budget requirements needed strengthening to provide management with more effective control of operations. There was no formal procedure which established the budget cycle from preparation through execution and evaluation of performance. Because of limited budget guidance, differences in forecasting methods existed. In forecasting personnel requirements the engineering research group relied on past historical performance only, whereas the economics research group developed more realistic requirements by using a combination of historical experience and an evaluation of each employee's anticipated performance.

Illustrative audit findings provide useful guides

Budgeting on an After-the-Fact Basis

In developing budgets there was no recognition of organizational changes during the year, resulting in budgeting partially on an after-the-fact basis. At the end of the first quarter a decision was made to consolidate two divisions. Experienced costs of the two divisions for the quarter were added together and used as a basis for the budget for the new organization, without change to reflect proposed economies.

Need to Identify Certain Overhead Costs

It was found that there was insufficient segregation of functional costs in overhead to serve as a basis for controlling costs. Costs of bidding, public relations, and downtime were not segregated in the accounting records; and operating groups did not separately budget for these functions. These costs should be identified in the records, and comparisons made with budgets that are sufficiently detailed to serve as cost control.

Coordinating Needs for Low-Dollar-Value Equipment

The company's policy required operating groups to submit budgets for the purchase of fixed assets with a unit cost of $500 or more. However, it did not provide for the separate budgeting of quantity acquisitions of capital-type items with unit values under $500, nor did it provide for coordinating the acquisition of annual capital item requirements of these items with the purchasing department. During the last year the company issued 341 purchase orders to acquire 754 items of desks, tables, chairs, and cabinets at a cost of $225,000. In addition to the inordinate number of purchase orders used, tests showed that over two-thirds of these purchase orders were issued to only three vendors. Better prices might have been obtained and substantially less costs incurred through separately budgeting for quantity acquisitions and coordinating the requirements with the purchasing department.

Invalid Data Used in Pricing

An analysis of losses and decreased profits for four product lines indicated that invalid data were used in pricing. For two of the products short-run factors were used for inflation, although prices were in effect for two years. For the other two products overhead rates had not been projected to reflect increases resulting from higher costs and decreased activity.

REVIEW QUESTIONS

1. What is "cash management"? Why is it important?
2. Should the budget be viewed as a planning or control activity?
3. To what extent is the budget related to the profit plan?
4. What is the relationship between the budgetary process and the accounting system?
5. Under what circumstances should the budget be modified during the budget year?
6. Discuss the importance of the sound administration of capital expenditure decisions.
7. How can "return on investment" serve as a useful guide for properly planning capital expenditures? What are the possible limitations?
8. What are the problems involved in deciding how needed capital should be obtained?
9. Who should be responsible for pricing? Why?
10. What factors need to be considered in making pricing decisions?

CASE PROBLEMS

Problem 14-1

Ron White, the chief executive officer of Black, Inc., had never been very excited about putting a lot of effort into the budget process, although the company did have one of a sort. But Clem Jones, the new vice-president–Finance, had been raising a lot of questions about how the company was missing out because of the lack of a really effective program. As general auditor, you believed the same as Jones and were now glad to welcome Jones as a new ally. The matter had come up again at White's weekly staff and this time White said, "I guess I have always felt that our problems are changing so fast that budgets really don't have enough continuing payoff. But maybe we have never really approached the problem properly. Anyway, Clem, I am willing to let you put it all down in a properly thought out manner. I would like to have both your ideas about the benefits we would gain and the scope of the administrative effort required to formulate and monitor an effective annual budget program. Because this closely relates to our overall control system, I suggest you also work together with our general auditor."

Required. Develop an outline of the written proposal to be developed by Jones and you for the chief executive officer, Ron White.

Problem 14-2

Capital expenditure decision making in the Binder Company was definitely a one-man show. Ross Meeker, the chief executive officer, considered all of that his personal prerogative. But now, after literally throwing half a million dollars down the drain for a new waste disposal system—covered in some depth in your last audit report—Meeker was having second thoughts. Meeker had just called Tom Winter, general auditor, to his office and said, "Well Tom, you asked for it. I know that this is actually John Miller's (vice-president–finance) responsibility. However, I have John tied up on a possible new acquisition, so I am turning to you. What I need is your ideas as to a practical program for making our capital expenditures. You can tie in with John later and then the three of us can talk about it in depth. Actually I have already discussed this with John and he is in full agreement."

Required. Help John Winter formulate a reply to Ross Meeker's request.

CHAPTER FIFTEEN

Computer Operations

Upon completing this chapter you should be able to:

☐ *Explain the importance of the internal auditor's involvement in computer operations*

☐ *Describe the phases of a Systems Design Life Cycle*

☐ *Understand basic computer operations*

☐ *Recognize the impact of distributed data processing on computer operations*

☐ *Describe the internal auditor's participation relative to developing a management information system*

☐ *Recognize approaches and techniques for auditing computer systems*

NATURE OF COMPUTER OPERATIONS

Planning, development, and processing are key functions

Computer operations are frequently referred to simply as EDP or electronic data processing. They are one of the most important operational activities in an organization in that they support the total management effort. Although a development of the last third of a century, computer operations have assumed a central role in the total spectrum of managerial and internal auditing practice. Computer operations involve three major functions. The first function is *planning* during which the kinds of uses to which computer capabilities will be put is determined. The second is *development* which consists of formatting and organizing the data to be processed. As a result of the activities in performing the first two functions, the computer applications will be identified and developed, and the proper computer equipment will be procured. The third function is the *processing* of data in accordance with the previously developed programs. The latter activity is directly operational in the conventional sense.

Because of the complex nature of data processing activities, it is often difficult for the internal auditor to cover all phases of the function. He is interested in such diverse areas as justification for type of equipment and application, lease versus buy considerations, design and planning, security, utilization and billing rates, controls over input, logistics and housekeeping, reports generated, and effectiveness of systems in meeting needs. Under these circumstances the internal auditor selects manageable segments of the function, performing reviews of various phases on a rotating basis depending on need and importance.

Wide range of concerns in planning

Importance of Computer Operations

Computer operations are of special importance to internal auditors for at least three reasons. First, the typical company has a total operational EDP group that is becoming increasingly large. Annual budgetary expenditures in many companies run into millions of dollars, and a large investment of capital is involved. With such a commitment of people and money it is to be expected that there is an increasing concern about the operational effectiveness of this effort. The second reason for the importance of computer operations is the direct relationship that exists between them and every other operating activity that is reviewed by the internal auditor. Third, our review of computer operations is important in that it further sets the stage for the internal auditor himself to use the computer as an audit tool in carrying out the various types of tests and inquiries—as discussed in Chapter 8.

Computers have multiple impact

Orientation of Chapter

The design of computer systems and the subsequent processing of data are highly specialized activities. It is not possible to provide such extensive and technical information in a single chapter of this book. Instead we will address the general nature of the major types of computer activities and their significance from an operational control standpoint. We will also consider the managerial implications, especially with regard to how computers can be useful to management. We believe that this approach will be most useful to the generalist, such as an internal auditor, who must look at computer operations as he would any other operational activity in a company. Although all internal auditors are necessarily learning more about the technical aspects of computer operations, it is assumed that there will be one or more internal auditors, usually referred to as EDP auditors, on the internal audit staff who will provide more specialized assistance. A 1982 study of 1300 companies indicated that management looked to internal auditors more than 70 percent of time for insuring adequate internal controls for computer applications. This management response suggests that all internal auditors must become involved in continuing education programs addressing audit issues related to their company's computer operations.

Computer operations need regular operational approach

Changing Character of Computer Utilization

Computer usage relatively new

Modern computers, as we have noted previously, represent a relatively recent development. Their real birth came about during World War II when the needs of our military establishment led to an acceleration of the underlying technical research and development. In the postwar period the new capabilities were then introduced into the commercial field. At this stage most commercial processing of data had been limited to the electromechanical types of equipment, and built around the use of punched cards. The immediate payoff was then to replace this older equipment with computers, retaining punched cards only as one of the means for preparing data for actual computer processing. In all of these installations the emphasis was on using the new capabilities of speed and accuracy to make clerical activities more efficient. At the same time computers made it possible to handle the increasing volume of such activities and thus avoid an almost impossible bottleneck that would have existed otherwise. Typical applications included the preparation of payrolls, billing of customers, handling of accounts receivable, and inventory records. These applications provided immediate and definitive benefits.

Computer usage accelerating

During the 1970s, there was an increasing movement toward the use of computers for a much broader range of business applications. A part of the new applications was recognizing that there can be a major range of benefits from using computers for managerial purposes. These broader applications were, to a considerable extent, linked to the use of the more complicated mathematical and scientific concepts (generally referred to as management science), which, with the new computer capabilities, made it feasible for the first time to make the necessary voluminous calculations and combinations on a timely and accurate basis.

New data base systems

Computer technology of the 1970s also led to introduction of data base systems. Prior to data base a separate program had to be designed for each individual business application and the data input for each program was considered as an integral part of that application. If there was a requirement to use this same data for another program, it was necessary to write a new program to reorganize or resequence the file in the computer. Data base technology has made it possible to manage data independent of the application programs which use the data. In this way, multiple users have access to specific items of data, assembled in the manner that each user wants to see the data. This is brought about through a Data Base Management System (DBMS) which is available as commercial computer software or may be developed by the company's own computer specialists. While not all organizations use data base systems yet, it is expected that by the late 1980s most will do so.

Minicomputers make possible distributed systems

Another innovation of the 1970s was the introduction of the minicomputer to meet commercial needs. This made possible the first use of distributed data processing which is discussed later in this chapter. The proliferation of the microcomputer in the early 1980s has also played an important role in the evolution of distributed systems. Other 1980 introductions include the expansion of computer communications capabilities in the area of electronic mail and linking of the office of the future with existing data processing systems. Thus computer operations as a field of operational activity now comes to have a much broader scope in terms of ongoing management interest and concern.

Management's Concern

Under these new circumstances the concern of management relative to computer operations can be more clearly defined. This concern has at least two major aspects. The first of these is whether the range of opportunities for using computers is being adequately exploited. Since business is competitive, no individual company can afford to lag behind in realizing the benefits that modern computer technology makes possible. At the same time there have been problems of overly ambitious uses of computers with the resulting excessive costs and operational disasters, all of which naturally make management cautious. The objective is therefore to find the level and range of computer use that is sound and profitable. There is also the related need to determine exactly what has to be done to achieve that objective. The second concern is more operationally oriented. Here the focus is on the day-to-day efficiency of computer processing. Are existing computerized systems functioning properly? Is the processing of data being done in a manner that provides the needed services on a timely and economical basis? Is the company relating to outside parties on an accurate and timely basis? All of these important management concerns help define the areas in which the internal auditor can make a contribution through his operational auditing effort. In essence we seek to determine whether management needs are being adequately served by existing computer operations and at fair and reasonable costs.

Proper level and range of computer use sought

PLANNING AND DEVELOPMENT ACTIVITIES

The Nature of Planning and Development

The process of developing computer systems is commonly called Systems Design Life Cycle (SDLC). SDLC is a systematic approach to systems design, which divides the task into phases and outlines the steps and procedures to be completed for each phase. For our purpose we will discuss the planning phase, the development phase, and the processing phase.

From a chronological standpoint the planning and development phases must precede the processing of data. That is, there must be operational instructions covering the processing to be done before the actual processing

Planning and development precedes processing

can take place. The range of these planning and development activities is of course very great. In the simplest form they can consist of the writing of a simple computer program for data processing; at the other extreme they can focus on long-range research projects. In total, however, they represent the foundation for computer operations. It has been said that the computer itself is a kind of robot, providing only the basic electronic impulse, and responding only to the instructions it receives. It is, therefore, through the planning and development phases that the process becomes meaningful. The planning and development effort are both the design of the physical means by which the data can be processed—that is, the operational features of the basic computer and the various types of peripheral equipment—and the software (programs that control operation of the computer) that direct the computer hardware to process data in a manner that will achieve the information objectives. In combination and properly integrated, these planning and development efforts provide the basis for the more specific operational activities.

Computer Applications

Operational systems first category of computer applications

In general there are two broad categories of computer applications. One of these categories has to do with operational systems of varying scope and the other focuses on providing specific information for individual decisions of various kinds. Although the two categories are interrelated and sometimes combined, the operational type is concerned with the handling of data as a definitive part of the operational activity of the company. It also commonly takes the form of a systems application. The term "systems" is used here to cover the situation where different operational activities or individual parts of a single operational activity are linked together in some manner. The complexity of a systems application depends on the complexity of the particular activity involved and the extent to which it relates to and includes other operational activities. The system can also be of a clerical processing nature or involve any type of production or other operational activity.

Computer Applications to Support Management Decisions

Supporting management decisions second category of computer applications

The second broad category of computer applications has to do with the support of management decisions. The support can take the form of making a specified calculation, answering a question, or providing some kind of analysis. In certain applications there may be data banks established where given types of information are stored and made available as requested. Of course, as discussed earlier, in a data base system data may be accessed through the DBMS as required. Illustrative would be a data base covering the specified qualifications of designated groups of company personnel.[1] When a person is needed for a given position, the necessary qualifications

[1]See Chapter 13.

are identified and the computer queried as to which company personnel possess the needed qualifications. Another important support for managerial decisions is where the results can be determined based on varying management assumptions. For example, the merits of a given capital project can be tested in relation to varying assumptions about the revenue that will be produced by the new investment. Similarly, the effect of alternative pricing decisions can be tested on the basis of varying sales estimates. It is recognized of course that the computer results are dependent on the merits of the assumption used. The value, however, lies in the way the computer capabilities can be used to provide a rapid cross check of the impact of the various assumptions, and thus help narrow the boundaries of the problems to which the manager must ultimately apply his judgment.

Organizational Setting of the Planning and Development Effort

The effectiveness of the planning and development effort for computer operations, as is true for every operating activity, depends to a major extent on where the responsibility is placed in the organizational structure. We know in principle that this planning and development effort has as its central mission the service of management needs. This means that it must have an organizational status that enables it to do that job at a level corresponding to its capabilities. This will include the ability to attract a person to head this activity who has the proper qualifications, plus a supporting staff of adequate numbers and qualifications. It means also that the personnel of that staff must have adequate access to the managers whose needs are being served. One question here is whether the planning and development of computer operations should be a part of one of the other staff groups or whether it should be entirely separate. In the past the practice has been to place this responsibility with the finance staff. However, there has been some question as to whether this resulted in a developmental effort that was too finance oriented and not as available to other company activities as it should be. For this reason some companies have created independent organizational units, frequently called management information systems (MIS) and have placed the developmental activity there.

High level organizational status necessary for computer planning/development

Centralization versus Decentralization.   A second organizational problem that is of great importance is whether the planning and development efforts should be centralized at the company headquarters or should be decentralized to the operating divisions. The argument for centralization stresses the company-wide character of the computer developments activities, and the possibility of exploiting the advantages of a more specialized and more professional computer development group. The argument for decentralization is that the divisional operations may be relatively unique and often large enough to justify their own efficient coverage of computer needs. The argument

Combination centralization and decentralization best

here also is that managers at this level will not be adequately served by a more distant and less directly involved central staff.

According to Perry in his book *Computer Control and Security*,[2]

> There is a strong technological movement toward the centralization of data. It has been estimated that during the 1980's most organizations will utilize the data base concept. With centralization of data goes centralization of administration of data.

Committee can provide effective coordination

Coordinating Committee. An approach sometimes used to coordinate the planning and development efforts in a company is through the use of a central committee. This particular approach has commonly been used in the transitional stages when the need for central coordination is first recognized but the company is not ready to establish a strong central computer group. Such committees are usually made up of representatives from the key central staffs and the major operations groups. They may deal with either or both the development of company-wide program applications and the acquisition of computer hardware by any individual organizational component. The committee may be advisory or have final approval authority in the designated areas. When used in a strictly advisory capacity they frequently lack sufficient authority to cope with the normal tendency of individual organizational components to go their own way. On the other hand, when they do have enough authority it is usually best to set up more formal organizational arrangements. Regardless, these committees have served a useful purpose by conditioning the internal groups to look at computer activities on a company-wide basis rather than in terms of the needs of individual units only. The mounting cost of computer operations has accelerated this trend.

Operational Phases of the Planning and Development Effort

A review and appraisal of the planning and development activities pertaining to computer utilization requires some understanding of the operational phases that are involved. We deal here with the situation as it is likely to exist in a relatively large company and with the problems arising in connection with the more complicated types of systems applications. It is indeed these more extended systems situations that present the major difficulties and risks. But it is this type of application that is becoming increasingly typical as the computer development effort seeks more rewarding opportunities.

Future use of computers needs study

General Research and Study. The planning phase begins when a company initiates studies on the future use of computers. This includes the forecasting of technological advancements and the types of computer equipment that may be available. Normally, broad company needs have been identified and a planning group is continually searching for the best approach to meet these

[2]William E. Perry, *Computer Control and Security* (New York: Wiley, 1981).

needs. There is increasing emphasis on the development of a coordinated management information system and the problem is how to proceed to develop such a system in a given situation.

Determining the Feasibility of Individual Systems Applications. Although there are some proponents for the view that a management information system should be approached as a total one-time problem, the more prevalent view is that priorities are established and that one then moves to the coverage of those priorities, with an evolving plan as to how various developments will eventually form a larger system. Assuming that such priorities have been established by management, the computer development group then moves to a conceptual plan for the specific systems application and to the more serious study of the feasibility of the proposed system. At this point there needs to be an in-depth examination of the affected operations as they now exist and the manner in which the proposed system will function. Normally there will be the requirement of covering the services presently provided, but also there will be the possibility of extending the role of the system to provide new types of services. The study at this point will take into consideration the transactions that take place, the information requirements, the operational needs of all interested parties, the impact on personnel needs, the types of equipment required, and the costs to be incurred.

View investment decisions for computer usage like other capital expenditures

The judgment of whether an investment should be made in a given systems application is in principle the same as any capital investment. The essence of that judgment is an evaluation of the operational benefits to be achieved versus the costs to be incurred, including an evaluation of the related risks. The time required for such an evaluation will depend on the complexity of the application, but it must be adequate to allow enough time for proper consideration of all the related factors. Of equal importance, it must involve the participation of all the key people who will be affected by the application. This participation is necessary both to get the proper input for a sound evaluation and to obtain their support for the new system. If the feasibility is properly established, the proposed application is ready for final management approval.

Feasibility evaluation must involve users

System Design and Specification. The materials developed in the feasibility study will now be used as a basis for a more in-depth determination all of the operational aspects of the systems application. Now the system must be developed in great detail, starting with the basic information inputs. What information will be collected, where, when, and in what form? How will this information input be received into the computerized portion of the system and with what equipment? What people will be affected and what will they do, and when? All of these details must be reflected in flowcharts supported by adequate notation as to the manner in which the operation will function. Similarly the stages of the later transfer and processing of the data must be covered, including finally the manner in which the results are to be made available as needed at all stages. Consideration must also be given to interim and final formal reporting, and to ongoing data retention needs. In this design and specification there is the need for close collaboration with all parties who will either be participating in the later operation of the system, or who will be using it for direct or indirect operational purposes. The great danger is that decisions will be made in isolation, without recognition of the practical operational problems. Also, there is no substitute for taking enough time to do the job right, despite the pressures that often exist for accelerating the completion of the application.

Programming.   Programming is converting designed program specifications into code that a computer can read and act upon. The first decision to be made is to determine the programming language that will be used. This determination should be made on a company-wide basis to assure maximum compatibility with existing and planned equipment and with current programs. Some of the more common computer languages are COBOL, BASIC, RPG, PL/1, AND FORTRAN. The next requirement is that there be a close collaborative effort between the programmers and the systems analysts to ensure a proper understanding of the system as designed and to provide a further check on the soundness of that design. The programmer will be concerned with how the capabilities of the computer equipment can best be used and how the programming instruction will assure an efficient processing of data. Although considerable progress has been made in simplifying the programming effort, this part of the development phase remains the most time-consuming activity.

Programmers and systems analyst must work together

In a well-managed programming activity there will be a major dependence on proper documentation in accordance with well-defined standards. These standards need to be set forth clearly in a manual. Such standards become the basis for training and for the development of adequate consistent documentation while programming activities are in progress. The documentation should normally move from the summary stage to the more detailed backup, with the total tie-in being clearly indicated. It typically includes program summaries, flowcharts, pertinent narrative explanations, diagrams of computer logic, identification of records developed at the various operational stages, codings, and supporting detailed instructions.

Documentation standards need coverage in manuals

Installation and Testing.   The system as designed and programmed is now ready for installation. This is a most critical phase because there is no absolute assurance that the total system will work satisfactorily, and, therefore, a transition from the old system must be effected in a manner that will not endanger the ongoing operational activities of the company. There is in addition the problem of getting operating people to adjust to the new system. In some cases the system can be phased in on a piecemeal basis, but in other situations this is not possible. In all other cases the problem is critical enough to work the two systems simultaneously for an appropriate overlap

Operating people need help to adjust to new system

period. Also every possible type of preparation should be made in the way of advance instruction and training. Despite the best of efforts, however, some difficulties and delays will normally be encountered. Accordingly, every possible provision should be made for backup support to protect the orderly continuation of the essential company operational activities.

Ongoing Operation of the System.   At the time the system is installed and before the key computer personnel move on to another assignment, it is important that all documentation be reviewed and put in order for possible use at a later time. Usually operational conditions will change and further modifications to the application will be required. In other cases experience with the application will demonstrate the need for some kind of improvement. It is important to have the basic documentation in the proper form for reference. It is also important that the modifications in the existing system be made with the same care as was exercised in the original design and then properly incorporated into the basic documentation.

Update documentation for future reference

Internal Organization of the Development Activity

The internal organization of the planning and development effort can vary greatly. It is not likely to be structured and rigid since personnel in the development group are high-level professionals who tend to operate in a more fluid and collaborative fashion. Nevertheless, as the group expands there is the need for a certain amount of organizational structure. In developing this structure there are two different dimensions of the activity. One of these relates to the varying time frame—for example, the distinction between long-range research, more immediate system development, and actual programming. The other dimension has to do with the type of systems applications and the extent to which the applications have to do with either particular functional areas or particular operating divisions. A typical organizational structure would be as shown in Exhibit 15.1.

Separation needed for research, development, and programming

Project Teams for Systems Development

Emphasis has previously been given to the need for close collaboration in systems development with the people who are going to be affected by the particular systems application. The people involved include the employees who will be relating directly to the system and the managers responsible for the various affected organizational groups. One of the ways this collaboration and coordination can be assured is through the use of project teams. Such teams can be used effectively both at the stage of determining feasibility (the planning phase) and at the subsequent design and installation stages. The project teams themselves include key representatives from the operational areas affected. In a given systems application, for example, the system might involve production, stores, marketing, engineering, and accounting.

Project team should include representatives from affected areas

EXHIBIT 15.1.   Organization of Planning and Development of Computer Operations.

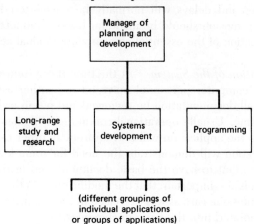

In such a situation each of these groups would designate a qualified person to work with the project leader—normally a member of the computer group. The team members can then provide needed operational expertise on the problems and requirements of their respective operational groups. The individuals can also provide needed liaison with the operational groups so that conclusions reached will be acceptable to those activities. The use of such project groups for the development of individual systems projects is most effective.

Relating Systems Development to Personnel Needs

In earlier chapters[3] we have stressed the need for understanding the human dimension of all operational relationships. This is especially true in developing computerized systems. The problem has two aspects that are closely interrelated. The first aspect has to do with assuring a needed level of cooperation to make an individual systems application effective in an operational sense. People tend to be apprehensive of the impact of a new system which can lead to a lack of cooperation or even to a degree of hostility. In many cases a major contributing factor to the failure of a particular systems application has been such resistance. The need, therefore, is to recognize the apprehension and deal with it properly. One of the ways that this is done is by adequate communication whereby people understand what is going to happen, when it is going to happen, and why. In that way distorted rumors can be dissipated and there will be time for mental adjustment. A second way to achieve the needed cooperation is by a clearly demonstrated

Users often resist new systems

[3]See especially Chapters 7 and 13.

intention to deal fairly with each affected employee. This leads into the second major aspect of the human problem—the effective use of people.

Effective use of people in new computer developments means proper planning of personnel requirements that come about as a result of the new system, and then taking actions to minimize the severity of the impact on existing personnel levels. Even though one of the purposes of a new systems application may be to reduce personnel requirements, two factors tend to counter such a reduction. One of these is that the new system normally contemplates an expanded range of services—which in itself can require more personnel—and the other is that volume of activity in the affected operations usually increases. It is true that different skills may be required for the new system, but again it may be possible to train many of the existing employees for the changed requirements. There is also the possibility that existing employees can be transferred to other company activities. If, however, in the most extreme case these efforts are not enough, the final resort must be to an equitable termination arrangement for the individuals affected.

Impact on personnel needs

Closing the Gap between Computer Personnel and Management

The importance of close collaboration between computer and operational personnel in the planning and development of computer applications has been emphasized. This collaboration becomes especially important in the case of the company managers. What frequently happens is that managers do not reach out sufficiently to work with computer personnel. This may be caused by the managers' perception that they are too busy or because they believe they have inadequate knowledge of computers and feel uncomfortable in the liaison relationships. At the same time computer personnel frequently live in their own private world, with their own special technical knowledge and jargon, and tend to be too concerned with the technical achievements of the system. They may even at times come to believe that they know best what the management problems are and how they should be handled. Unfortunately, their understanding of management needs is often not that good.

Operating managers and computer specialist must be a team

As a result of the existing gap, the computer effort is often misdirected. One of the greatest needs, therefore, is to bridge this gap and to establish a close working relationship between the responsible managers and the computer specialists. This problem has abated to some extent in recent years since the entire business community has become more computer literate and hardware manufacturers and software designers have made the computer easier to use.

Role of the Internal Auditor in Planning and Development

The foregoing review of the planning and development phases of the Systems Design Life Cycle sets the stage for an important role on the part of the internal auditor. We see at least two major contributions.

The Internal Auditors As a Participant.   Traditionally, the internal auditor has taken the position that he should not participate in the development of systems and procedures, lest he lose his objectivity in subsequently appraising the operation of the particular system. As we have previously seen, however, Guideline 120.03 of the "Standards for the Professional Practice of Internal Auditing" provides that "the internal auditor's objectivity is not adversely affected when the auditor recommends standards of control for systems or reviews procedures before they are implemented." Despite this conciliatory statement, the Standards go on to say that "designing, installing, and operating systems are not an audit function." In the case of major computer applications, it is highly desirable for the internal auditor to maintain participatory liaison with systems development personnel. The practical reasons are that systems are too costly and complicated to be modified on a post-operational basis. Therefore, if the internal auditor's contribution is not made during the developmental phase, it is likely to be too late to make the desired changes. It is a very real fact that through the internal auditor's knowledge of good internal controls and the total range of company operational activities, he is in an especially advantageous position to make important contributions.

Internal auditor needs participative liaison with systems development

If one accepts the soundness of utilizing the internal auditor's input during the development of EDP systems, the problem still exists of how that contribution can best be made. The practical problem is that the assignment of full-time liaison personnel by the internal auditing group may be too much of a drain on the internal audit resources. On the other hand the EDP group may otherwise be so occupied with their developmental work that they may fail to keep the internal audit group properly advised on a timely basis of the stage of the various types of important decisions. A practical compromise used successfully by many organizations is to establish in advance for each major development project appropriate milestone points, at which time the progress of the development of the system will be reviewed and evaluated in joint meetings. The internal audit group in this way is periodically alerted to the manner in which control aspects are being recognized and dealt with. Meanwhile the internal audit group can be concerned with its regular internal auditing program. The planning and follow-through of such milestone meetings is therefore strongly recommended.

Operational audit approach applicable to planning and development

General Appraisal of Planning and Development Activities.   The second major contribution of the internal auditor can come in the way of an overall appraisal of the computer development activities. Since the ultimate test of those activities is the accomplishments in the way of actual computer utilization the internal auditor should review the extent of the completed applications and compare the level of accomplishment, as far as is possible, with what has been done in similar business situations. At the same time consideration should be given to the nature and scope of applications currently in progress and under study. This phase of the appraisal leads naturally into a further appraisal of the professional competence and operational effectiveness. The basis of this further appraisal is the success of the development group in dealing with the various types of subactivities discussed earlier in this chapter, and in its handling of the related problems. Here a useful type of evaluation can come through the reported relationships with other company personnel. A really effective development group will have established a reasonable degree of both cooperation and professional standing with the key personnel of the various line and staff activities involved in previous studies and installations. In all these appraisal efforts the internal auditor seeks to be constructive since he knows that an effective planning and development effort in the area of computer operations is a basic essential for the ongoing welfare of the company.

COMPUTER PROCESSING OPERATIONS

The creation of specific programs as a part of the development phase has provided the basic instructions for the computer. These instructions will now be applied to transaction data for carrying out computer processing operations. This is the final step in the total computer operations to provide managers and other operational personnel with the information needed to do their jobs. Even though this final step does not involve the same degree of intellectual input as did the planning and development phases, it is still clearly an essential step, and therefore, one that needs to be carried out efficiently and effectively. The operations at this point are relatively more technical than most other operational activities, but they are subject to a large extent to standard administrative methods and criteria. There is also quite clearly a close relationship to the developmental activities since the efficient processing of data depends directly on properly developed programs.

Efficient processing needs good programs

Nature and Scope of Computer Processing Operations

There are three major steps in computer operations—input of the data to be processed, processing operations, and output of the processed data in some form. At the input stage the focus is on putting the particular transaction data in a form that will be acceptable to the computer. This input can be accomplished directly through consoles at the operations center or through terminals or other computers at remote locations. Data can also be recorded on punch cards or magnetic devices and input later. It should be noted, however, that for the most part, punch cards have given way to the magnetic devices such as computer tapes, cassettes, or discs. At the processing stage the data fed into the computer are analyzed, combined, and manipulated in the manner prescribed by the applicable program. During this process additional data may be drawn from various data storage areas and other data may be returned to those storage areas. Finally the processed data are

Input, processing, and output three major steps

released by the computer directly in the form of printed reports, visual displays, or as a magnetic device that will then be used to prepare reports. In some cases output will also be used as further input for subsequent processing.

Batch processing can be deferred

Batch and Real-Time Processing. The nature and scope of the processing operations will vary greatly depending on whether we are dealing with a batch or real-time processing. In the former case a package or batch of data is received for processing, and this batch can be processed later at a time when machine time is available. This availability takes into consideration the various priorities in the particular company. In the case of the real-time processing the user has direct access to the computer (or at least what seems to him to be direct access) and he will be able to receive an immediate response to his inquiry. Another type of real-time processing exists in the case of production processing where the production process is being immediately controlled on the basis of current data developments. The common characteristic here is that information is obtained from the computer on such an immediate basis that current operational activities can be continuously controlled and modified as needed. From a computer processing standpoint an important distinction is that computer capacity must be specifically provided so that it can be available to support the real-time demands that are made on the computer.

Organizational Setting of the Computer Processing Operations

We are again most interested in where the organizational responsibility for the computer processing operations is placed in the total company organization structure. Although it might be thought that the problem here is the same as exists in the case of the planning and development activity, this is not necessarily so. It is quite possible to regard the computer processing operations as an entirely separate service activity which can be available to users anywhere, like heat and electrical services, irrespective of where the planning and development effort is assigned. Nevertheless there has traditionally been some tendency for the computer processing operations to combine the developmental effort as an adjunct activity. This has been true especially when the developmental effort was relatively limited and confined to particular operational areas. Thus at a time when the emphasis of the computer operations was upon clerical-type activities—and when also those clerical-type activities were predominantly in the accounting area—the responsibility for computer processing operations plus the planning and development activities was most often placed with the accounting and financial group.

Separation from regular operational activities assures more objectivity

Because of the relationship of broader computer utilization to the location of the hardware, the assignment of the responsibility for the computer processing operations takes on special importance. In any event the responsibility issue is important because that responsibility carries with it to some extent the greater power to control priorities as to the way the processing time is allocated. Even when that power is administered on a statesmanlike basis there is always the possibility that some other operational activities will be skeptical. As a result it has become more common to remove the responsibility for computer processing operations from the finance group and to place it with an organizational component like a management information group where the neutrality of its use is more assured. In such a situation the central headquarters planning and development group and the computer processing operations group normally report to the same company officer.

Quite another issue is involved when one considers whether the computer processing operation should be centralized, or if decentralized, to what extent. The electronic data processing *function* is centralized in most companies today. This was brought about by the complexities of current technology creating the need to bring together a group of experts to deal with the attendant problems. This is not to say that all hardware and processing capabilities are centralized. Increasingly sophisticated communications links have made it possible to decentralize hardware and processing while keeping the function, as such, centralized.

Control Aspects of Computer Programs

Computer programming was discussed earlier as a part of the development phase. We return at this point to a further discussion of programs to focus on their control aspects. Programs can, when properly developed, provide effective controls over the quality and accuracy of the data processing. Fortunately the objectives of the systems development personnel and programmers are the same as for the internal auditor—efficient computer operations. The control considerations apply first in the basic design of the system with the determinations of where input data are to take place, under what conditions, and under whose responsibility. The problems are the same as in any operational situation, but focus more sharply on the requirements of developing accurate and complete input data for processing.

Programs provide controls for quality and accuracy

An important aspect of the effort to develop good input data concerns the editing controls that are built into the programs. The purpose of editing controls is to identify invalid data and to prevent the input of these data into the computer. There are two major types of editing controls. The first addresses the completeness and form of the data—whether proper codes were used, for example. The second type is concerned with qualitative and quantitative factors. Illustrative of the latter would be conformance to reasonable dollar limits of particular data, and conformance to specific company operational relationships. The scope of these editing checks will vary considerably, but they have the common purpose of avoiding the most common kinds of errors which can occur. Quite clearly these editing controls are valuable

Two types of editing controls

since they help prevent the processing of data which could otherwise contain errors.

Programs must be tested

Testing Computer Programs. All computer programs must be tested to insure that they work. The program testing, which is a part of the processing phase in the System Design Life Cycle, may take the form of processing data which are also being processed by another method and then comparing the results. Another method of testing is to process sample batches of live data or to inject erroneous data into the system to determine the accuracy with which the editing controls or other design features deal with the situation. In other instances a controlled answer, independently determined, can be used to check the performance of the program. Generally the objective is to determine whether the system works as intended and if not, to identify the problems and solve them before relying on the program to process production data.

Controlling Computer Processing

We will discuss computer processing of production data in terms of key considerations which are critical from a control standpoint.

Facility features provide needed protection

Facilities. Adequate facilities will protect computer hardware and software from fire, water damage, vandalism, and other potential sources of damage. Some of the important considerations are the extent of fire protection such as extinguishers, sprinkler systems, and alarms. Temperature and humidity controls are also important to protecting both the hardware and the software. A good security system which restricts entry to authorized personnel is also essential. The security system should also include passwords and other controls for remote data entry. The facilities should also have a source of backup power in the event primary power is interrupted.

Separation of duties required

Internal Organization. Computer processing, like any other operational activity, depends on good internal organization. The first requirement is that there be a clear separation of machine operations (either physically or through passwords for remote input devices) and other supporting activities. For example, programmers should not be allowed to operate the computer unless data files and production programs have been secured. This precaution will preclude the intentional or accidental manipulations of files or programs by a programmer. These supporting activities may report to the same manager, but they should be physically separated from computer processing. A typical operational activity is shown in Exhibit 15.2.

From an organizational standpoint it is important that the activities for which these subgroups are responsible be carefully defined, staffed with competent people, and supervised effectively.

EXHIBIT 15.2. Organization of Computer Processing.

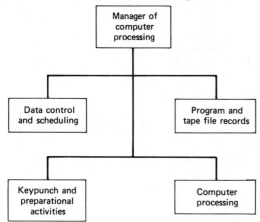

Input Controls. In each major computer application there are specific controls instituted to cover exactly what data are received for processing, that they are properly prepared, and that they are entered into the computer accurately. At the point the data are created there must be prescribed clerical procedures and well-designed forms. The person creating the data thus receives maximum direction, and possible errors are then more easily detected and minimized. In some cases it may be desirable also to provide for a specific review of these data before they are converted into machine-readable form. Clear instructions are also important when data are entered into the computer directly. When entering data on magnetic devices for later input, the problem centers on the accuracy of the keying operation. The accuracy here can be tested visually, statistically, or by a complete rerun verification. In other instances calculations have been devised to check the accuracy of specific critical portions of the data. In all these approaches the cost of verification must be balanced against the seriousness of the potential errors.

At the point where the data are entered into the computer the accuracy of that input in a real-time system will automatically be tested by the computer as it proceeds to develop the answer to the inquiry. In the case of batch operations, a test of the accuracy and completeness of the input can be tested through various kinds of control totals—as, for example, of total dollars, total numeric figures, number of individual documents, and the like. Programmed tests can also be used covering the valid use of coding, missing data, the proper combinations of specific data, and reasonableness of the aggregate totals. Various internal tests can also be devised to help ensure that the right tape files, and the portions thereof, have been used in connection with the data being received. Many of these same controls are also

Input controls assure quality and accuracy

applicable when data are later moved during the processing to provide input at a later stage.

Machine Controls. As the computer technology progresses more and more control capability is built into the computers themselves, thus reducing the necessary scope of programmed controls. A somewhat different kind of problem arises, however, in the possibility of the malfunctioning of equipment. The first attack on this latter problem is, of course, the proper level of quality in the design and manufacture of the equipment itself, including the subsequent installation. The second line of attack is through proper care and maintenance of the equipment. Beyond all this, however, is the fact that there are both electronic components and some parts which move mechanically, and which, therefore, are unavoidably subject to malfunction. Also there may be outside causes such as power failures, defective tapes, and improper equipment usage. The approach to equipment checks can be through the duplicate processing of particular lots of data and then comparing results. A common built-in control is through the use of "parity checking." Under this approach an extra parity bit is added to an identifiable group of data, and then at various stages of the processing a determination can be made as to whether a bit may have been erroneously lost or added. Other built-in controls, as developed by equipment manufacturers for their particular equipment, include such techniques as "read after writing," "echo readings," "duplicate circuitry," and the like. The internal auditor's interest here is primarily to know that such controls do in fact exist, and the type of cross check that is accomplished.

Receiving Data and Scheduling. In a batch-processing operation the first step is to receive the job from the user. At this point the essential control is to determine that the data received are in the proper form for processing. It is also necessary to determine whether the job is covered by an existing program. If a new program is to be used it should be checked to ensure that it is in proper form. The next step is to fit the job into an established operating schedule. The scheduler needs to use equipment as efficiently as possible while adhering to established priorities which apply to the various users. Computer operators should know the status of a particular job at any given point in time. This is made possible through the use of control logs and records of machine runs. For on-line operations provisions must be made for recognizing access priorities for using the system. Such priorities can be programmed to be administered by the computer automatically.

Running the Job. The processing of the individual jobs consists of mounting and dismounting data files, loading the programs, acting on requests from the computer (prompted by the program or the operating system) and assuring that supplies are available as needed. The processing by an individual

Controls built into computer reduce scope of programmed controls

Balance sought of equipment usage with user needs

piece of equipment is for the most part automatic. However, when there is a stoppage of any kind, there must be backup personnel to do whatever is necessary to determine the nature of the difficulty and correct it. Some limited control activities, such as maintaining accounting records, may be performed by the console operator.

Output Control.   Once the processing has been completed the results need to be released. In a real-time system this process is going on continuously but there may be periodic reports summarizing the activity or providing the current status of stored data. In a batch-type operation the results will be in the form of updated computer tapes and related reports. Normally, however, machine-generated materials will be arranged in a form that will better fit the user's needs. The control considerations are first, that the results developed are made available to the right people—the operational managers affected or their properly authorized representatives. The second and equally important thing is that the completed results are in satisfactory form. The final test of this is obviously the degree of satisfaction on the part of the user. It is, therefore, desirable that problems encountered be subject to a systematic review of the causes.

Library Services.   In normal operations there will be certain records of company users which will be kept on hand by the computer center for continuing use. Some of the applications programs may be kept on-line in mass storage devices. Other programs and records of company data will be stored off-line on magnetic tapes, disks, or disk packs. In a well-ordered operation off-line storage devices and related records will be under the exclusive control of a librarian and will be released for operational use as needed. From a control standpoint the important considerations are that they be properly labeled and stored in a manner where they are protected and can be easily found when needed. It is important also that these storage devices not be released except to properly authorized personnel. The computer center has a direct responsibility to the company for the careful custody of these valuable records.

Risks in Computer Operations Center

Our discussion of the key control areas for computer operations may also be conveniently reviewed in terms of risks.

Access Control.   To prevent unwarranted physical access, permission to enter the facility should be limited to those who are authorized and need access. Data processing facilities should be inspected and physical safeguards in place, such as guard service, locks, and a badge system. Programmers and systems analysts should not be allowed in the computer center. The location of the central computer facility should not be included in directory

Backup must exist to handle stoppage problems

Adequate protection of storage critical

Access to computer operations for authorized personnel only

listings or on maps. There should be a computer security administrator, and personnel should be trained on security matters. Sensitive activities should be independently authorized and duties should be assigned and records kept so that employees can be held accountable for their actions.

Fire and Water Damage.   There is the possibility of a major interruption in service due to destruction by fire or water. A disaster plan should be in effect and reviewed periodically to determine whether it is current and adequate. Fire protection should be in accordance with generally accepted standards. Appraisals of fire protection should be made by fire marshalls and insurance companies as appropriate. There should be adequate insurance covering the risks of natural disasters and sabotage. A secure off-site facility should be available for storing duplicate copies of software and other records, including those applicable to minicomputers. Building construction should be of noncombustible materials. The site should be located in a place to minimize the risk of flood damage or water leaks. Fire and smoke detectors and a sprinkler system should be installed.

Disaster plan essential

Interrupted Processing.   Temporary interruption of service through a power failure is a constant threat. If at all possible a backup power source should be available. Electrical power to the central processing unit should be separate and protected by special transformers to eliminate electrical surges. Insurance should be available for business interruption and extraordinary expenses due to interrupted processing.

Theft.   As with other assets there is the ever-present danger of theft. The theft can be of equipment, data, and programs. All of the security and control procedures mentioned previously will help to abate theft. Corporate policies should state specifically that employees may not sell, reproduce, or use company programs or equipment to their own benefit or for unlawful purposes.

Physical protection critical

Accidental Loss.   A common danger is that data will be lost or accidentally destroyed through confusion or errors. The protection against these risks lies chiefly in the proper assignment of responsibilities, adequate procedures, and effective supervision. Additional safeguards include proper labeling of all tapes, disks, disk packs, and records and to have adequate custodial control. Further protection against this kind of risk is to retain all basic files and records while updated files are being developed.

Distributed Data Processing

One trend in the development of computer technology has been in the direction of dispersing tasks among a group of geographically separated computers. This has been facilitated by moving minicomputers into commercial applications (as opposed to their initial uses in engineering and science) and the introduction of microcomputers into the office environment. Basically, distributed data processing (DDP) means locating computing units where the operational work originates, then establishing communications links (networking) among all units, and, in most cases, with the mainframe computer at the centralized data center. It is a form of decentralized computer operations, as discussed earlier in this chapter, with emphasis on increasing productivity through division of responsibility. According to Duff in reporting the results of a 1982 survey of 220 organizations, 86 percent had DDP systems implemented or had definite plans for implementing them before the end of 1982.[4]

Distributed data processing is locating computers where work originates

Advantages of DDP. There are functional, economic, and psychological advantages to using DDP. DDP systems can be more easily designed and developed with less complex software. In addition, growth can occur in smaller increments with less disruption to the system. Further, modules can be individually less complex under a decentralized system resulting in fewer failures. From an economic standpoint, personnel costs may be reduced because of improved system response and errors can be corrected more efficiently. Resources can be shared thereby reducing the amount of services. Less investment may be required to start a system and cost performance ratios can be improved by the economies of specialization in addressing the needs of specific user groups. The psychological advantages include the ability to tailor the system to meet the needs of specific users and the control which the user has over the computer. In addition, the system can be developed along organizational lines to facilitate meeting organizational goals.

Distributed data processing is highly advantageous

Disadvantages of DDP. The major disadvantage is that the standard methods of control for central-site computer systems, as discussed earlier in this chapter, are not adequate to control DDP. With DDP, computerized processes are operating in an office environment and at different geographic locations. Operating in other than a data center presents such problems as a lack of adequate separation of duties and the inability to control access to the equipment. With this lack of adequate control and since these processors have on-line, interactive processing capabilities, decisions have to be made whether to restrict certain high-risk systems (financial systems for instance) from processors at remote locations.

Distributed data processing control is challenging

Analysis of System. Although the analysis and evaluation of distributed data processing are complex, there are approaches that are useful to the internal auditor. He can review the design activities to determine whether they are comprehensive and relate to organizational objectives as well as to

[4]Larry J. Duff, *Audit and Control of Distributed Data Processing Systems* (Altamonte Springs, Fla.: The Institute of Internal Auditing, Inc., 1983).

available technology. An adequate system of documentation should be available as the result of the design process. There should also be program testing standards for reviewing test results based on specific criteria.

DDP audit problems
more complex

DDP presents some complex audit and control problems for which economical and practical solutions have not been found. For an excellent discussion on the nature and extent of these problems, the previously referenced study by Duff should be reviewed.[5]

Other Computer Operations

Up to this point we have dealt separately with three major phases of computer operations—planning, developing and processing activities. Although these three activities can be performed in different locations in the organization, it is quite common for them to be under the leadership of the same officer. Our interest in this final section of the chapter is to examine some of the problems that are encountered with this arrangement. It also provides an opportunity to cover certain operational matters that are common to the three activities.

Organizational Aspects of Integrated Computer Operations. One advantage to placing the planning and development, and processing activities in the same organizational unit is that it helps to assure better liaison between the two groups. The greater advantage, however, is that computer use will be considered on a totally integrated basis. Since development and processing perform related but different types of activity—requiring organizational separation—there is some risk that they may become too isolated from one another. Under such conditions there may also be some unnecessary expense due to the natural inclination for each group to develop special staff expertise in the area of responsibility of the other group.

Having one organizational
group has important benefits

In many companies the developmental and processing activities are themselves fragmented and dispersed in various organizational components. Such an arrangement is often found in a company where individual divisions have, in the past, been separate companies, and which still enjoy a high degree of autonomy. The creation of totally integrated computer operations can, in such instances, be the means of bringing all the computer-related activities together into one organizational group. This permits the development of a company-oriented approach and in most cases has proved to be beneficial. The integration also demonstrates the company's serious concern about computer utilization. Finally, total integration should justify high-level placement of computer operations in the company's organizational structure, demanding a top manager with exceptional managerial qualifications. It is common, at this point, to establish a vice-president in charge of a management information systems (MIS) group who reports directly to the chief executive officer and is independent of any other function.

[5]Ibid., pp. 193–125.

Planning and Budgeting for Integrated Computer Operations. The organizational integration and placement just described sets the stage for more definitive development of long-range objectives for computer utilization. Objectives can be developed and, after review by top management, can lead to establishing priorities and to more detailed operational plans. Long-range planning then leads to the development of profit plans which become an integral part of the total profit planning process for the company. These profit plans, in turn, are reflected in the annual budget. This is a highly desirable development because it better assures that the MIS group will do the planning that it should. It also helps to insure management participation in planning for computer operations.

Role of the Internal Auditor in Computer Integration. The internal auditor's role relates to both the development and processing phases. In a broad perspective, the special role would be to help the company achieve a properly integrated function. The act of integration is often a difficult one because the process itself is counter to the operating manager's desire to keep something he already has, as opposed to turning it over to a new separate organizational group. Top management, in such a situation, is often restricted in how far or how rapidly it can move toward integration. Top management is reluctant to take the risk of pushing the managers into a situation where their operations may suffer, or affording them excuses for not achieving established objectives. The independence of the internal auditor and his familiarity with operations puts him in a position to present evidence that will support the integration effort. Again it should be emphasized that proper computer use is a management need and it therefore must be a high priority consideration in the internal auditor's total effort to serve management effectively.

Internal auditor more objective about computer integration benefits

MANAGEMENT INFORMATION SYSTEMS

The direct relationship between computers and management information systems (MIS) makes it appropriate to consider in more detail some of the factors that contribute to effective systems. At the same time the role of the internal auditor in MIS will be developed. Improved data processing technology has made it possible to obtain large quantities of information at high speed and in the form desired. With the increase in computer storage and processing capacity, there is additional impetus toward developing a total information system for all activities of a company. Also with the increase in on-line systems, information is available as events occur. Financial statements, for example, are available soon after the end of the month and operating reports can be available on demand. The increase in the amount of information and the speed with which it is made available enables management to operate more effectively.

Internal auditor should review management information systems

The internal auditor reviews the MIS in light of its objectives, by evaluating its usefulness to management in conducting the affairs of the company. The audit review of the system is made whether the MIS is manual or a complex computer system.

Developing the Management Information System

Review all existing reports

Review of Past Information.   A management study to develop an information system should begin with a review of company information generated in the past. The study should identify information flows associated with decision-making activities throughout the business organization and evaluate the flows as a basis for designing changes. The internal auditor's initial activity in reviewing a MIS is to obtain a listing of major reports and any other information generated by the system and determine whether a study of the usefulness of the system has been made. He reviews the most recent study and follow-up action, if available, to determine whether there are indications that managers are working with relevant information.

Determining Requirements.   As a basis for evaluating a MIS, the objectives of the system should be identified. The need for data in one segment of the company's operations is identified and related to the decision-making process of management in the test segment. An attempt is then made to develop a model MIS to meet the specific needs of the organization. Such factors as the characteristics of the system, degree of sophistication, and cost should

How responsive is management information systems to management needs?

be considered. In some instances special research to identify the best system may be required. Discussions with managers are often needed to determine the nature of the decision-making process and the problems requiring solutions. The internal auditor, at this point, reviews management's analysis and conclusions to determine whether the system will be responsive to management needs and whether the objectives of the system will be met.

Responsibility for Developing the System.   In some companies information systems development is the primary responsibility of staff specialists. This is due to the complexity of today's large computer installations. The work of the specialist is coordinated closely with operating management in determining their needs. In other companies operating management controls MIS with the assistance of specialists. The leadership for systems design should probably be in the hands of operating managers who will be controlling the systems in their areas of responsibility. Regardless of who controls the development of MIS, it is vital that there be considerable involvement of operating management and close coordination of requirements where systems cut across departmental lines.

Collecting Data.   The final step in MIS development involves matching requirements with the sources of data. Data are classified and coded in a manner to allow storage for subsequent retrieval. The data are then transformed or transposed into specific information for planning or operating purposes. The internal auditor tests the procedures for originating, storing, retrieving, and transforming data which are part of the information system. He reviews the manner in which available sources of data are used to facilitate the preparation of needed information. He also tests the storage and retrieval system to assure that data are readily available.

Reports

The matter of reports as an element of internal control was discussed in an earlier chapter. "Reports . . . are a major means of control by management. Inadequate reporting can lead to unwise decisions or ill-considered action. As with records, reports must be prompt, accurate, concise and complete."[6] The timelessness of this quote is reinforced by the reporting criteria set forth in the *Standards for the Professional Practice of Internal Auditing*.

The internal auditor's review of controls extends to the total information system within the company. He is interested in the information available to executives in setting goals and evaluating performance. Without effective reports, management's ability to control operations is significantly impaired.

Total information system is internal auditor's concern

Proper Analysis. Data generated by the information system should be analyzed. In some instances sufficient data for analysis may be available as a part of the reports generated through the system. In other cases special studies may be required by management, to determine the causes of problems as a basis for recommending corrective action. The internal auditor examines reports and studies and evaluates whether data are sufficiently analyzed to meet management's needs.

Control of Reports. The internal auditor should evaluate the approval process for new reports. He should also determine whether periodic reviews of the types of reports and number of recipients are made. The review should involve questioning recipients as to their continuing need for various reports. One effective method is to ask the recipient to return a card if the report accompanying the card is still required. For some activities there may be a requirement for additional reports. As discussed elsewhere in this chapter, it is important that adequate information be provided management and the review of reports should take this into consideration.

All recipients may not need particular reports

Special Reports. The need for most reports can be planned in advance, but there are occasions when management needs a special report to solve a problem, to make a decision regarding a new product or expanding an

---

[6]Bradford Cadmus, *Operational Auditing Handbook* (New York: Institute of Internal Auditors, 1964, pp. 11–12).

activity, or to accomplish a short-term goal. Data may be available for the report, requiring only sorting and processing. In other instances detailed studies have to be made and sources of data determined. The internal auditor reviews the extent of special reports and the types of information requested. He should compare special reports with recurring reports to ascertain whether the data are already available in different form.

Timeliness. It is especially important that information be provided management on a timely basis. Historical reports that indicate past deficiencies are important, but of more use are reports which indicate current trends and problems. Such reports enable executives to make current studies and take timely corrective action. The internal auditor assures that reports are available in accordance with established schedules and that the timing is responsive to management needs.

Accuracy. The internal auditor reviews the accuracy of various reports as a part of the scope of the audit. The use of computers may simplify the auditor's traditional review of procedures for reviewing reports. For example, data already stored in the computer may be processed and arranged in a special format. Under these circumstances the internal auditor's general tests of the EDP system may suffice with a minimum of additional work.

Special audit work may be required on some interim financial reports to test their accuracy. Annual financial statements are audited by the external auditor, occasionally with the assistance of the internal auditors. However, management may require assurance that interim financial reports used for operating decisions are accurate, and may call on the internal auditor to help provide that assurance.

Usage of all reports needs testing

Use of Reports. If the objectives of the MIS are to be achieved, management must use the reports generated. The decision-maker requires information as a basis for selecting among alternatives; it serves no useful purpose to generate the information unless it is used. There are specific actions which can be taken by management to improve a situation once all the information needed is available. For example, management can provide guidance on training, supply better incentives, or make more personnel, facilities, and funds available. In some cases personnel are replaced, the goals are changed, and a new program is devised. Regardless of the subject matter or course of action, the internal auditor reviews, on a selective basis, the use management makes of the information provided. He notes instances where the information does not appear to be useful or is disregarded. He reviews the effectiveness of controls over the use and evaluates the extent to which proper analysis is made of the continuing need for the information. He also evaluates whether proper justification is included in the files when decisions are made that are not supported by information available through the MIS.

Cost of Information. The benefits of reports have to be weighed against *Cost and benefit a trade-off*
the costs involved and resources available. Some information can be obtained *evaluation*
by simply reclassifying data and reporting it in a different form. Other information may require extensive data gathering and computer programming,
making it more expensive. The internal auditor evaluates the extent to which
sufficient consideration is given to the cost of reports in view of their significance and operating objectives.

COMPUTER CRIME

We will discuss fraud and investigation in more detail in Chapter 16. However it will be useful to discuss computer crime in this chapter on computer
operations because of the impact of such crime on computer security.

Nature of the Problem

Management is becoming increasingly aware of the potentials for computer
crime with the growth of computer technology. Some of the more spectacular
crimes, shown in Exhibit 15.3, have dramatized the current dangers of
computer fraud. The risks for business are especially increasing with the *Computer crime now*
expanded number of employees who can get access to computers through *more tempting*
remote terminals. Also more people are learning how to use computers and

EXHIBIT 15.3   Examples of Computer Crimes

Case	Methods Used	Amount Taken
Wells Fargo	Funds were deposited in an account at one branch by using the bank's interbranch account settlement process to withdraw funds from a different branch; the account imbalance was hidden by making other fraudulent transfers later on, and the process continued	$21.3 million
Dalton School	Teenage students at Manhattan's Dalton School allegedly used their classroom computer terminals to dial into a Canadian data communications network and destroyed the files of two of the network's corporate customers	Zero
Union Dime	A teller at a New York savings bank used correction entries to embezzle money from accounts, transferring funds from other accounts to cover the shortages	$1.2 million
Equity Funding	Computers were used by management to report phony insurance policies that were sold to reinsurers	$27.3 million

are finding weaknesses in systems that enable them to break computer security. The greater availability of personal computers with communications capability has made it easier for individuals (commonly referred to as "hackers") to tap into data transmission lines. Hacking has caused serious breaches of security, resulting in such incidents as unauthorized transferring of money from one bank account to another and changing university students grades.

The incentive for computer crime is increasing because of the potential for a large take per crime—in some cases millions of dollars. In addition, computer crimes are often difficult to detect, and punishment may not be great even if management decides to prosecute. As a result, computer crime has become tempting as computer use expands.

Computer Security

The increased evidence of computer fraud has encouraged companies to develop improved security practices. Although these practices do not guarantee the prevention or detection of computer fraud, together they help to achieve increased computer security.

Key components of computer security

Design Emphasis. It is during the basic design of the computer system that data security should be emphasized. Often systems developed by computer manufacturers are extremely flexible and are thus difficult to control. To satisfy the concerns of management, security measures must be introduced during the program design phase, at the expense of flexibility and availability.

Separation of Duties. In accordance with good systems of internal control, sensitive computer duties should be separated wherever possible. Individuals should be accountable for their own actions and checks should be made on others. Access to other employees' areas of responsibility should be restricted. Some examples are, as follows:

Changes to a program library should be made by only one person

Programmers should not both specify and write a procedure, write and test a procedure, and write and execute a procedure

Employees should not have access to an asset and the records for control of the asset

Approval authority should be separate from initiating authority

Physical Security. Secret passwords are stored within the computer's memory system to prevent unauthorized use of the computer. In addition entrance to the computer building and to individual computer rooms is restricted to those needing physical access. Some companies use TV cameras to record personnel entering, with guards at a central location reviewing TV monitors. Also records may be kept within the computer's audit trail of all significant actions of users to get access to the computers. This serves as a means to detect unauthorized attempts to gain entry.

Scrambling Devices.   By encrypting or scrambling data during transmission from one computer to another, only a computer with a special device can unscramble the message. The need for encryption software and hardware has increased with the growth of personal computers, which make it easier to tap electronic funds transfer systems fraudulently.

Risk Analysis.   Studies can be made of a computer system to assess the risk of computer fraud. Estimates can then be made of the cost of measures to prevent fraud. These studies can be made either by personnel within the company or by outside consulting groups.

Audit Checks.   Special audit software packages, as described in Chapter 8, are now available to review computer data. These packages enable management as well as internal auditors to make computer inquiries that would be likely to uncover fraud. In addition special cross checks can be added to determine the reasonableness and consistency of transactions. For example, the computer can be programmed to disclose if individual salaries of workers are above a certain amount, or if the computer is being used in off hours.

Management Emphasis.   There has been increased involvement of top management in setting up sophisticated antifraud measures. The Foreign Corrupt Practices Act has added incentive to management efforts because of the penalties involved. In most companies management has relied on computer professionals to provide adequate control over EDP. They, in turn, were involved more in day-to-day operations than in developing preventive measures. Currently, however, management and professionals have worked together more closely to develop strong antifraud programs in the computer area, such as those described in the preceding paragraphs.

AUDIT GUIDES

REVIEW OF COMPUTER OPERATIONS

I. Introductory
   A. Reference should be made to the general discussion of audit guides, Chapter 11.
   B. The review endeavors to cover both the extent to which the company is fully utilizing computer application potentials and the operational effectiveness with which the various computer activities are being carried out.

II. Preparatory Activities
   A. See standard Audit Guides, Chapter 11.
   B. The familiarization with existing procedures and processes will be especially important.

III. Organizational Factors

    A. See standard Audit Guides, Chapter 11.

    B. Planning and development activities and processing activities need to be considered, both separately and as a total activity.

    C. Matters of special interest in the review of manuals include:

        1. For planning and development activities:

            a. Authorization of feasibility studies.

            b. Approval of actual program developments.

            c. Interim and final reporting.

            d. Standards of documentation.

            e. Planning of personnel impact.

            f. Planning of equipment requirements.

        2. For computer processing activities:

            a. Relations with other company activities.

            b. Priority policies.

            c. Operational standards.

            d. Security.

            e. Billing.

            f. Use of outside services.

            g. Records and reports.

IV. Planning and Development Activities

    A. Research and Long-Range Planning

        1. To what extent is a systematic effort being made to keep in touch with new developments in the field of:

            a. Basic computers?

            b. Mini and micro computers?

            c. Peripheral equipment?

            d. New types of applications?

        2. What internal effort is being made to appraise computer utilization potentials for the company?

        3. Has a long-range plan for company computer utilization been prepared? And is it adequate?

        4. Is this long-range plan being reviewed periodically with top management?

    B. Scope of Accomplishments

        1. Review and appraise the presently existing range of program applications.

        2. What are the specific accomplishments of completed programs in each of the past five years? What is the trend?

        3. What applications are currently under study?

    C. Operational Integration (Company-wide)

        1. Appraise the adequacy of the central coordination of planning and development efforts.

      a. Is there excessive overlap and duplication between various development staff units?

      b. Are company-wide systems developments being dealt with?

      c. Are computer personnel being properly utilized?

      d. Are staff efforts sufficiently consolidated to be able to attract needed personnel with special expertise?

   2. Appraise the adequacy of decentralization.

      a. To service management needs of individual staff and operational groups.

      b. To provide adequate input from local groups to the central group for broader company systems.

      c. To provide backup help from the central group to local groups.

D. Appraisal of Operational Efficiency

   1. How adequate is the staff in terms of numbers, types of expertise, and personal qualifications?

   2. Is adequate support being received from top management for investigative study activities involving various company operational activities?

   3. Are managerial coordination activities being effectively achieved?

   4. Is developmental work adequately documented?

   5. Are equipment needs adequately validated, and necessary procurement achieved most advantageously?

   6. Are installation plans properly developed?

   7. Are personnel implications fully discussed with management and the personnel group? Are adequate plans made?

   8. Are programming requirements being properly coordinated?

   9. How adequately are completed and installed applications monitored for later design improvement? Is documentation properly updated?

   10. How well is the internal administration of staff being done?

E. Miscellaneous

   1. What kind of training programs have been developed for management education?

   2. What kinds of internal training programs are being carried out?

   3. How adequate is the continuing liaison with the internal auditing group to permit its contribution on a timely basis? Are milestone review points established for individual programs to enable the internal auditors to use their time most effectively?

V. Computer Processing Activities at Individual Processing Centers

A. Operational Integration (Company-wide)

   1. Are computer processing activities consolidated adequately as a basis for reasonable achievement of potential operational economies, such as:

        a. Purchase of equipment of more efficient size and with most advanced operational features?

        b. Best possible machine utilization?

        c. Uniform programming and operational practices?

    2. Are users being properly serviced under the existing arrangements of operational consolidation?

B. Facilities

    1. Are quarters adequate in terms of physical operating requirements for current and anticipated volume?

    2. Are space costs reasonable (as compared with alternative possible locations)?

    3. Is proper provision made for controlling access to operational areas?

    4. Is there adequate protection from fire and other possible physical damage?

C. Procedures and Controls

    1. Are there adequate procedures covering the preparation of data for processing?

    2. Are procedures adequate for the review and approval of incoming jobs and related programs?

    3. Are priority policies clearly stated, and periodically reviewed?

    4. Do organizational arrangements adequately separate data input, processing, control, tape libraries, and data release?

    5. Are procedures and control adequate in such key operational areas as:

        a. Completeness and accuracy of data input?

        b. Scope of program controls?

        c. Utilization of machines?

        d. Status of individual jobs?

        e. Transfer of data as a part of the total processing?

        g. Protection of tapes during processing?

        h. Procedures for machine stoppages and interruptions?

        i. Custody of programs and tapes left on premises?

        j. Completeness and accuracy of output data?

        k. Authorized release of output data?

    6. Is there adequate security over:

        a. Access to computer room?

        b. Data transmission?

        c. Access to remote terminals?

D. Operational Efficiency

    1. How adequately are procedures and controls monitored and enforced?

    2. How adequate is the overall supervision?

    3. Are housekeeping standards well maintained?

      4. Are people being fully utilized?

      5. Are machines being adequately utilized?

      6. Is overtime excessive?

      7. Is the current work load being handled effectively? If not, what are the causes?

      8. Are costs reasonable in relation to available standards? What is the trend?

      9. Are operational manuals complete and up to date?

    10. Are operations consistent with the organization chart? If not, are organizational changes needed?

  E. Customer Relations

      1. Is work being processed in accordance with customer-agreed schedules?

      2. Are input and output customer relations satisfactory?

      3. Are customers satisfied in terms of:

        a. Processing time?

        b. Quality of processing?

        c. Cost?

  F. Leasing Arrangements

      1. Do current leasing arrangements appear to be reasonable?

      2. Is there adequate evidence that purchase/lease alternatives are being periodically reevaluated?

VI. Integrated Computer Operations

  A. Is the degree of integration adequate in terms of potential operating effectiveness? What are the specific problem areas?

  B. What specific road blocks exist for more effective integration?

VII. Specific Audit Tests

In addition to such audit tests as have been made in accordance with the preceding review of computer operations, it will be desirable in certain situations to carry out more elaborate tests. These tests can include:

  A. The detailed examination of one or more selected program applications from the first development to the operational stage.

  B. The development of special test decks to verify the accuracy of the processing of data with given programs.

  C. A more extensive survey of internal customer relationships in the areas of both development and computer processing. This will involve direct contact with these customer-users.

VIII. Continuing Involvement of Internal Auditor

  A. In Planning and Development Activities

      1. Is adequate liaison being maintained with planning and development group?

2. Are all possible contributions being made in building an effective control?

3. Is counsel being provided as to areas of development that have maximum company potential?

B. In Processing Operations

    1. Does the internal auditor receive copies of all current production and performance reports of the computer processing activities?

    2. Is adequate liaison being maintained?

C. For Total Computer Operations

    1. Is the internal auditor adequately supporting the organizational integration of all computer operations?

    2. Is the internal auditor aware of policy changes, and does he adequately participate in their determination?

IX. Not used.

X. Overall Appraisal of Computer Activities

A. See standard Audit Guides, Chapter 11.

B. The special importance of computer potentials calls for increasing attention to this overall appraisal.

ILLUSTRATIVE AUDIT EXAMPLES: COMPUTER OPERATIONS

Information Requirements Not Properly Defined

During the systems implementation phase of a new computer system, the internal auditor found that some departments were not making significant requests for new information. Review indicated that these departments had not analyzed their requirements in light of additional capabilities of the new computer. As a result, the planning did not assure that the potential of the computer for providing information could be realized for all activities of the company. In addition, the early determination and coordination of requirements would prevent untimely requests for changes in programs. It was recommended that controls be strengthened over the timely determination of information requirements in all departments.

Unused Reports

Reports were being generated that were no longer needed by company activities. In addition, excess quantities of reports were being distributed. A study of the condition indicated that activities were not notifying data processing of changes in requirements. Although the company had procedures for periodic circularization of report users, operating heads were not notifying data processing on an interim basis. In the case of one division, reports continued to be generated although a reorganization of activities eliminated the need for some of the reports. It was recommeneded that controls be strengthened to assure the timely elimination of reports no longer required.

Delays Caused by Inadequate Scheduling

Computer jobs were not being scheduled and prioritized effectively, resulting in delays in obtaining requested computer runs. It was found in some instances that an excessive number of jobs were being loaded with tape drives, exceeding the capacity of the computer. Additional emphasis was needed on scheduling job runs sufficiently in advance and assigning priorities based on importance.

Duplication of Information

Reviews of reports prepared in a department indicated that a manual report duplicated data available in a computer report. Analysis indicated that management required information in a different format, with more summary and trend data. These requirements had been superimposed after the request for the computer report. The internal auditor found similar manual reports and analyses prepared in other departments which could have been generated by the computer. It was recommended that consideration be given to additional or revised computer applications to meet the report requirements of management.

Computer Not Fully Utilized

Significant savings could be achieved by running the computer in two shifts instead of three. The internal auditor noted that the computer was not being fully utilized during the evening and night shifts. Discussion with computer personnel indicated that planned usage of the computer had not materialized because of the sale of a division of the company. As a result of a study recommended by the internal auditor, management decided to shut down the night shift, with an annual savings of $125,000.

REVIEW QUESTIONS

1. Why are computer operations so important to internal auditors?
2. Planning and development are two phases in a Systems Development Life Cycle. In summary, what are the primary activities which occur in these phases?
3. Where should computer processing operations be placed in an organization? Why?

4. Why should activities such as programming and systems analysis be physically separated from computer processing operations?

5. What are the five most common risks in computer processing operations?

6. What are the advantages of using distributed data processing?

7. In reviewing the number and types of reports generated, what are some areas for cost savings?

8. What security procedures should be in effect to provide computers protection against unauthorized use?

9. How do special audit software packages assist in achieving computer security?

10. What is the major advantage of using a data base system?

CASE PROBLEMS

Problem 15-1

The general auditor, Tom Jenkins, called in his two audit managers, Bill Spears and Jane Sarot, to discuss the approaches used in computer auditing. Jenkins told them, "I would like your opinion on computer auditing. Give me your views on what direction you think we should go."

Sarot responded with, "We have to get more involved in computer operations. We should review controls at the time of system development, study program logic and application surveys, and examine risks involved. We can no longer bury our heads in the sand; we have to train all of the staff in auditing computer systems."

Spears thought for a moment and said, "I think that we should take a more practical approach to computer auditing. Last year we sent Tim O'Brian to a two-week course in computer auditing, and he tried it on one of the audits. He prepared a 20 page audit program that was so detailed that it took 500 hours to complete and he came up with nothing. After that he didn't have an opportunity to further apply what he learned and now he has forgotten most of what the course covered. I personally think we should take another approach. In addition to using computer audit software packages, we can apply certain internal audit procedures which do not require a strong computer background. We can look at hardware use, security, computer generated reports, and user satisfaction. The staff won't need extensive computer training to cover these areas."

Jenkins then turned to Sarot and asked her to reply to Spears approach.

Required. Assuming the role of Jane Sarot, how would you respond to Jenkins?

Problem 15-2

In reviewing the number and types of reports generated in the purchasing department, the internal auditor contacted key users of reports. The internal auditor determined that twenty reports were generated and that in four instances the users either did not want the report or stated too many copies were being prepared. In two instances no one knew who had authorized the reports in the first place. Purchasing department employees generally had the attitude that it made no difference that a few extra reports were being prepared. Donald Good, head of the purchasing department said, "We really need other types of reports to get the information we require to do our job more effectively."

Required. How should the internal auditor respond to Good?

CHAPTER SIXTEEN

Fraud and Investigations

Upon completing this chapter you should be able to:

☐ *Explain the internal auditor's responsibility for the prevention and detection of fraud*

☐ *Develop methods and techniques for detecting fraud*

☐ *Recognize the impact of the Foreign Corrupt Practices Act on possible fraud and other corrupt practices*

☐ *Recall the organizational conditions and motivational factors which may indicate fraud*

☐ *Describe the major actions in a fraud investigation*

ROLES AND RESPONSIBILITIES

Fraud and the Internal Auditor

Fraud is an ever-present threat to the effective use of resources, and hence will always be an important concern of management and the board of directors. Existing fraud needs to be detected and potential fraud prevented (deterred) to the extent practicable. The primary responsibility in these areas is that of management—including its line and accounting personnel. However, management needs assistance and quite properly looks to auditors—especially to its internal auditors—for all possible assistance.

Preventing all fraud not possible
The question is then the extent to which the internal auditor is directly or indirectly responsible for fraud. It is impossible to prevent all fraud. Even if the internal auditor performed very detailed checking, there could be unrecorded transactions, forgeries, and collusion which might not be discovered. It is also too costly to go beyond reasonable levels of fraud prevention. As we have seen in earlier chapters, it is possible to overcontrol.

Judgment therefore becomes a basic ingredient in determining the nature and scope of fraud control efforts. It is a challenge to the internal auditor to give fraud the balanced attention it deserves, while achieving the total range of internal auditing services. This challenge also includes helping all parties of interest to understand the desirability of properly balanced fraud control efforts. We have consistently taken that position in all editions of *Modern Internal Auditing*.

Changing Concern for Fraud

In earlier days the internal auditing profession was more directly concerned with fraud. As discussed in our opening chapter this concern was part of the internal auditor's then existing major orientation to protective-type services—including compliance, accuracy, and preservation of physical assets. This orientation reflected the fact that management depended to a greater extent on internal auditors for fraud-type services, especially as to the detection of existing fraud. This situation began to change as the nature and scope of internal auditing services broadened. This change involved first a greater emphasis on fraud prevention versus fraud detection. It was wisely perceived that it was more beneficial to the organization to develop good systems and managerial capabilities that would reduce the possibilities of fraud.

The shift away from fraud detection through better systems then—among other factors—helped to make it possible for internal auditors to provide more constructive service to the organization via the new operational auditing. The fraud-oriented services then became proportionately a smaller part of the total work of the internal auditor. However, good internal auditors were always conscious of their very real responsibilities in the way of helping to prevent and detect fraud.

Good controls combine to reduce fraud possibilities

The pendulum has recently swung back to a greater interest in fraud prevention and detection by internal auditors. Management itself has been held increasingly accountable for various white-collar crimes such as embezzlement using the computer. The Foreign Corrupt Practices Act, with its related penalties, has added incentive to having better systems of internal control. In attempting to have a strong fraud prevention and detection program, management has called on finance personnel, internal auditors, investigators, and external auditors for assistance. The internal auditor thus often finds that an increased amount of his resources is presently being devoted to this area.

The current emphasis on fraud is reflected in the standards published by The Institute of Internal Auditors. In the 1978 "Standards for the Professional Practice of Internal Auditing," Section 280, it is stated:

> . . . In exercising due professional care, internal auditors should be alert to the possibility of intentional wrongdoing, errors and omissions, inefficiency,

waste, ineffectiveness, and conflicts of interest. They should also be alert to those conditions and activities where irregularities are most likely to occur.

. . . the internal auditor cannot give absolute assurance that noncompliance or irregularities do not exist. Nevertheless, the possibility of material irregularities or noncompliance should be considered whenever the internal auditor undertakes an internal auditing assignment.

The Institute of Internal Auditors issued the third Statement on Internal Auditing Standards (SIAS), Deterrence, Detection, Investigation and Reporting of Fraud, in June 1985. SIAS No. 3 is included as Appendix F. It should be studied as an integral part of this chapter. The major conclusions of the Statement relative to the deterrence or detection of fraud are as follows:

Deterrence of Fraud. The deterrence of fraud is the responsibility of management. Internal auditors are responsible for examining and evaluating the adequacy and the effectiveness of actions taken by management to fulfill this obligation.

SIAS No. 3 describes internal auditor's responsibilities

Detection of Fraud. Internal auditors should have sufficient knowledge of fraud to be able to identify indicators that fraud might have been committed.

If significant control weaknesses are detected, additional tests conducted by the internal auditors should include tests directed toward identification of other indicators of fraud.

Internal auditors are not expected to have knowledge equivalent to that of a person whose primary responsibility is to detect and investigate fraud. Also, audit procedures alone, even when carried out with due professional care, do not guarantee that fraud will be detected.

Approach of the External Auditor

The American Institute of Certified Public Accountants (AICPA) has similarly changed its approach to fraud, resulting in changes in public accounting standards. In the early 1900s there was strong emphasis by external auditors on the detection of fraud because audits were primarily involved with cash records. Auditing textbooks indicated that the detection and prevention of fraud errors were among the main objectives of an audit. This gradually changed over the next three decades, until the accounting literature emphasized that the external auditor did not assume any direct responsibility for fraud.

There were many reasons for the change in approach. The growth of business entities in size and complexity meant that the auditor had to use testing techniques rather than a detailed review of all transactions. This made it especially difficult to detect irregularities. In addition, the inability of the auditor to detect fraud involving unrecorded transactions, theft, and other matters made the profession more cautious. This became more important as lawsuits were filed against accounting firms holding them responsible for losses resulting from frauds. At the same time, there was a growing trend toward strengthening systems of internal accounting control, which could then prevent fraud and related deficiencies.

This led the AICPA to adopt a position on fraud, set forth in the codification of statements on auditing procedure published in 1951, which read:

> The ordinary examination incident to the issuance of an opinion respecting financial statements is not designed and cannot be relied upon to disclose defalcations and other similar irregularities, although their discovery frequently results. . . . If an auditor were to attempt to discover defalcations and similar irregularities he would have to extend his work to a point where its costs would be prohibitive. It is generally recognized that good internal control and surety bonds provide protection much more cheaply. . . .

This position was criticized by some for attempting to relieve the external auditor of the responsibility for the detection of fraud. In recognition of this, the AICPA issued Statement on Auditing Procedures No. 30 in 1960. This statement was incorporated in Statement on Auditing Standards (SAS) No. 1, along with all other statements on auditing procedure in November 1972. Section 110.05 of this Statement says:

AICPA describes external auditor's responsibilities

> The responsibility of the independent auditor for failure to detect fraud (which responsibility differs as to clients and others) arises only when such failure clearly results from non-compliance with generally accepted auditing standards.

In light of increased litigation against accountants and the concern of external auditors that there may be material misstatements as a result of fraud, the profession developed SAS 16. This superseded SAS 1 as it dealt with the auditors' responsibility for fraud. This states:

> . . . Consequently, under generally accepted auditing standards, the independent auditor has the responsibility, with the inherent limitations of the auditing process, to plan his examination to search for errors or irregularities that would have a material effect on the financial statements, and to exercise due skill and care in the conduct of that examination.

This Statement thus requires the auditor to look specifically for irregularities which may have a material effect on the financial statements.

The foregoing change of emphasis by the external auditors has in turn helped to relieve the internal auditor of direct responsibility for fraud in organizations.

Impact of Management Pressure

Regardless of differing opinions on whether or not internal auditors and external auditors have a responsibility to detect fraud, management tends to look to them in fraud matters. When a fraudulent act is committed the question is invariably asked: "Where were the auditors?" or "When was the last audit?" The burden is thus placed on the auditors as to why their last examination did not reveal the fraud or at least disclose the internal control

Management looks to all auditors on fraud matters

weakness that led to the fraud. The auditors' responsibility is thus seen as doing their work in such a professional manner that, if fraud exists the chances are that it will be exposed. In addition, management expects the auditors to perceive opportunities to provide more prevention, since prevention is preferable to detection where frauds are concerned.

There are of course limits to the ability of any organization to prevent fraud. No internal control plan can prevent an employee from stealing cash that he handles, and no controls can prevent a purchasing agent from colluding with a supplier. Also no control can be expected to disclose a fraud the instant it is committed. However, management looks to the auditors to be imaginative in the application of comprehensive and well-thought-out audit programs so that if fraud exists, there is a reasonable assurance that it will be discovered. Moreover, they look to the internal auditors especially because of the latter's deeper involvement in the total activities of the organization.

Responsibilities of the Internal Auditor for Fraud

The internal auditor's responsibilities in the area of fraud control in principle can thus be summarized as follows:

Internal auditor seeks balanced view of fraud

1. In the review of systems to help evaluate the extent to which fraud prevention and detection are given fair consideration along with other operational objectives.
2. To be alert to the possibilities of fraud in the review of operating activities carried out by organizational personnel—including the constructive evaluation of managerial capabilities.
3. To assist and cooperate with organizational and other personnel that have been assigned responsibilities in connection with the investigation of actual or suspected fraud.
4. To carry out such special assignments relating to fraud as may be requested by responsible members of the organization.
5. In all of the foregoing to seek directly and indirectly to achieve the balanced fraud oriented efforts that will assure maximum achievement of all other types of needed organizational services.

Priorities for Fraud Work

With the current increased emphasis on preventing, detecting, and investigating fraud, the internal auditor is often faced with the problem of resources to perform his other audit work load. Normal coverage of areas on a recurring basis may be disrupted by fraud efforts. In some instances internal auditors have had to curtail operational auditing and the resultant recommendations for cost savings. This may be especially frustrating when it has taken many years to develop an operational auditing capability with demonstrated results.

In order to accomplish overall audit objectives with available resources, it is necessary to set priorities carefully in coordination with management. Based on previous experience an estimated amount of time should be budgeted for fraud work. In some cases the functions performed by the internal auditor may be handled by others: for example, work by investigators, law officials, departmental personnel, and external auditors. In addition, to make time available for operational audits it may be necessary to lengthen the cycle for other coverage which may not be so productive. Overall, the internal auditor has to weigh the benefits of various audit efforts to arrive at the best utilization of audit time. The objective is that there will be time available both to perform operational audits and to carry out fraud responsibilities.

Agreement with management as to priorities needed

EFFECT OF FOREIGN CORRUPT PRACTICES ACT

In 1976 the Securities and Exchange Commission (SEC) submitted to Senator Proxmire's Committee on Banking, Housing and Urban Affairs a report on its investigations into questionable and illegal corporate payments and practices. The report recommended legislation to correct bribes and other illegal payments. In response to the recommendation, the Foreign Corrupt Practices Act (FCPA) was enacted on December 19, 1977. Excerpts from the act are included as Exhibit 16.1. The act contains provisions as to books and records, internal accounting control, and bribery prohibitions. We discussed in Chapter 4 the provisions of the act as they pertained to basic control concepts. Our focus here is the effect of the act on possible fraud and other types of corrupt practices.

Books and Records Required

This provision applies to issuers that have securities registered under Section 12 of the Securities Exchange Act of 1934 and does not apply to nonpublic companies. It was adopted as a result of SEC comments that illegal payments disclosed in SEC filings were often hidden by either falsification of records or maintenance of incomplete records. The provision requires that issuers keep, in reasonable detail, books, records, and accounts which are accurate and fairly reflect transactions. The phrase "in reasonable detail" was added by the conference committee to give effect to concerns by the accounting profession that no accounting system could achieve freedom from error. However, there is no definition as to the exact meaning of "in reasonable detail." Basically the intent of the rule is to cause the company to keep records to reflect transactions in conformity with accepted methods of recording economic events, preventing off-the-books slush funds and payments of bribes.

FCPA covers related requirements

EXHIBIT 16.1.   Public Law 95-213, 95th Congress

91 STAT. 1494   PUBLIC LAW 95-213—DEC. 19, 1977

An Act

Dec. 19, 1977

[S. 305]

To amend the Securities Exchange Act of 1934 to make it unlawful for an issuer of securities registered pursuant to section 12 of such Act or an issuer required to file reports pursuant to section 15 (d) of such Act to make certain payments to foreign officials and other foreign persons, to require such issuers to maintain accurate records, and for other purposes.

Be it enacted by the Senate and House of Representatives of the United States of America in Congress assembled,

Securities Exchange
Act of 1934,
amendment.
Foreign Corrupt
Practices Act of
1977.
15 USC 78a note.

TITLE I—FOREIGN CORRUPT PRACTICES

SHORT TITLE

SEC. 101. This title may be cited as the "Foreign Corrupt Practices Act of 1977".

ACCOUNTING STANDARDS

Assets, transactions
and dispositions.
15 USC 78m.

15 USC 78*l*.
Post, p. 1500.
Records,
maintenance.

Internal accounting
controls,
establishment.

SEC. 102. Section 13 (b) of the Securities Exchange Act of 1934 (15 U.S.C. 78q(b)) is amended by inserting "(1)" after "(b)" and by adding at the end thereof the following:

"(2) Every issuer which has a class of securities registered pursuant to section 12 of this title and every issuer which is required to file reports pursuant to section 15(d) of this title shall—

"(A) make and keep books, records, and accounts, which, in reasonable detail, accurately and fairly reflect the transactions and dispositions of the assets of the issuer; and

"(B) devise and maintain a system of internal accounting controls sufficient to provide reasonable assurances that—

"(i) transactions are executed in accordance with management's general or specific authorization;

"(ii) transactions are recorded as necessary (I) to permit preparation of financial statements in conformity with generally accepted accounting principles or any other criteria applicable too such statements, and (II) to maintain accountability for assets;

"(iii) access to assets is permitted only in accordance with management's general or specific authorization; and

"(iv) the recorded accountability for assets is compared with the existing assets at reasonable intervals and appropriate action is taken with respect to any differences.

Exemption
directive, issuance
and expiration.

"(3) (A) With respect to matters concerning the national security of the United States, no duty or liability under paragraph (2) of this subsection shall be imposed upon any person acting in cooperation with the head of any Federal department or agency responsible for such matters if such act in cooperation with such

EXHIBIT 16.1. *(Continued)*

head of a department or agency was done upon the specific, written directive of the head of such department or agency pursuant to Presidential authority to issue such directives. Each directive issued under this paragraph shall set forth the specific facts and circumstances with respect to which the provisions of this paragraph are to be invoked. Each such directive shall, unless renewed in writing, expire one year after the date of issuance.

"(B) Each head of a Federal department or agency of the United States who issues a directive pursuant to this paragraph shall maintain a complete file of all such directives and shall, on October 1 of each year, transmit a summary of matters covered by such directives in force at any time during the previous year to the Permanent Select Committee on Intelligence of the House of Representatives and the Select Committee on Intelligence of the Senate.".

File maintenance. Annual summary, transmittal to congressional committees.

FOREIGN CORRUPT PRACTICES BY ISSUERS

SEC. 103. (a) The Securities Exchange Act of 1934 is amended by inserting after section 30 the following new section:

"FOREIGN CORRUPT PRACTICES BY ISSUERS

"SEC. 30A. (a) It shall be unlawful for any issuer which has a class of securities registered pursuant to section 12 of this title or which is required to file reports under section 15(d) of this title, or for any officer, director, employee, or agent of such issuer or any stockholder thereof acting on behalf of such issuer, to make use of the mails or any means or instrumentality of interstate commerce corruptly in furtherance of an offer, payment, promise to pay, or authorization of the payment of any money, or offer, gift, promise to give, or authorization of the giving of anything of value to—

"(1) any foreign official for purposes of—

"(A) influencing any act or decision of such foreign official in his official capacity, including a decision to fail to perform his official functions; or

"(B) inducing such foreign official to use his influence with a foreign government or instrumentality thereof to affect or influence any act or decision of such government or instrumentality,

in order to assist such issuer in obtaining or retaining business for or with, or directing business to, any person;

"(2) any foreign political party or official thereof or any candidate for foreign political office for purposes of—

"(A) influencing any act or decision of such party, official, or candidate in its or his official capacity, including a decision to fail to perform its or his official functions; or

15 USC 78dd-1.
15 USC 78*l*.
Post, p. 1500.

EXHIBIT 16.1 *(Continued)*

"(B) inducing such party, official, or candidate to use its or his influence with a foreign government or instrumentality thereof to affect or influence any act or decision of such government or instrumentality,

in order to assist such issuer in obtaining or retaining business for or with, or directing business to, any person; or

"(3) any person, while knowing or having reason to know that all or a portion of such money or thing of value will be offered, given, or promised, directly or indirectly, to any foreign official, to any foreign political party or official thereof, or to any candidate for foreign political office, for purposes of—

"(A) influencing any act or decision of such foreign official, political party, party official, or candidate in his or its official capacity, including a decision to fail to perform his or its official functions; or

"(B) inducing such foreign official, political party, party official, or candidate to use his or its influence with a foreign government or instrumentality thereof to affect or influence any act or decision of such government or instrumentality,

in order to assist such issuer in obtaining or retaining business for or with, or directing business to, any person."

Internal Accounting Control Requirements

The act requires that companies with registered securities maintain a system of internal accounting controls. These controls should be sufficient to provide reasonable assurances that transactions are authorized and recorded to permit preparation of financial statements in conformity with generally accepted accounting principles. In addition, accountability is to be maintained for assets and access to the assets permitted only as authorized. Also recorded assets are to be physically inventoried periodically and differences analyzed.

Management can make cost/benefit control decisions

The cost of fully controlling each transaction in the face of existing risk would not be justified, and thus the term "reasonable assurances" is used. Management must therefore estimate and evaluate the cost/benefit relationships, exercising judgment as to the steps to be taken. Although a discussion of cost/benefit decisions is not mentioned in the act, it is included in the conference committee's minutes. Thus it is apparent that Congress intended that management have the right to make cost/benefit decisions as to controls.

Bribery Prohibitions

The bribery provisions, which are applicable to both issuers of securities and all other U.S. domestic concerns, prohibit bribes to a foreign official.

The maximum penalty for violation of the bribery prohibitions by a company is $1,000,000, and for individuals who participate in bribes the punishment is a fine of not more than $10,000, imprisonment not more than five years, or both.

The purpose of the payment must be to influence a foreign official to assist a company in obtaining business. The offer or gift must be intended to induce the recipient to misuse his official position, such as to direct business to the payer or his client. Excluded from the definition of foreign official are government employees whose functions are clerical or ministerial in nature. So-called "grease payments" to minor officials are permissible.

Role of the Internal Auditor

There are various groups involved in determining compliance with FCPA standards. The controller or vice-president–finance is responsible for the financial control system of the company. The external auditor is involved through reviewing management's representations of its control system. Legal counsel is interested because of the interpretations of compliance with the act. The internal auditor is involved because of his responsibilities for the evaluation of internal control. In some companies the board of directors and the audit committee have also taken an active part in directing reviews of internal controls to assure compliance with the act.

The internal auditor is in a unique position to work with these groups to accomplish the objectives of the act. The approaches described in this chapter for detecting fraudulent practices can be adapted to the company needs. In addition, the internal auditor's current reviews of internal control can play a strong role in preventing bribery and other acts.

Internal auditor evaluates FCPA compliance

Specifically with respect to bribes, the internal auditor would examine certain accounts for disguising the payment as a legitimate business expense. These may include entertainment, travel, advertising, consulting services, engineering services, selling costs, legal fees, and individual expense accounts. The examination of documents may give an indication of a bribe, such as the name of the bribe recipient appearing on copies of airline tickets or delivery tickets. This information may be compared with endorsements on checks. Loans made to individuals may in reality be bribes. Items such as automobiles and boats may be purchased by a company to be used as bribes. Significant events and transactions related to obtaining large sales contracts with foreign governments should be examined. Through these and other audit steps the internal auditor attempts to determine compliance with the act pertaining to bribe prohibitions.

WARNING SIGNALS FOR FRAUD

Although on occasion internal auditors carry out direct assignments in the investigation of suspected or actual fraud, the greater part of his fraud-oriented efforts are an integral part of a broader audit assignment. These fraud efforts may take the form of specific procedures included in a broader audit program. They also include all of the general alertness of the internal auditor as he carries out all parts of this audit assignment. This general alertness in turn includes various areas, conditions, and developments which provide warning signals.

Sensitive Areas

Internal auditor should be alert to sensitive areas

The internal auditor must be aware of the overall organizational climate and its potentialities for fraud. He should be especially alert for sensitive areas for review which may in some instances disclose wrongdoing. The following are examples:

Insufficient Working Capital. This may indicate such problems as overexpansion, decreases in revenues, transfer of funds to other companies, insufficient credit, and excessive expenditures. The internal auditor should be on the lookout for diversions of funds to personal use through such methods as unrecorded sales and falsified expenditures.

Rapid Turnover in Financial Positions. Loss of key accounting and other financial personnel may signify inadequate performance and result in weaknesses in internal control. Accountability for funds and other resources should be determined upon termination of employment.

Use of Sole-Source Procurement. Good procurement practices encourage competition to assure that the organization is obtaining the required materials or equipment at the best price. Sole-source procurement, if not adequately justified, indicates potential favoritism or kickbacks.

Excessive Travel Costs. In reviewing travel the auditor is on the lookout for unauthorized or personal trips, entertainment, costs in excess of those allowed by the organization, and unsupported travel and other expenses.

Transfers of Funds between Affiliated Companies or Divisions. A pattern of transfer of funds between companies or divisions may indicate unauthorized borrowings, coverup of shortages, or inadequate controls over funds.

Change in Outside Auditors. In some instances the change in outside auditors may indicate differences of opinion as to the appropriate method of handling certain transactions. There may be a reluctance on the part of management to disclose problems or events that are significant.

Excessive Consultant Costs or Legal Fees. These may be indicative of abuses in having services performed on the outside, favoritism, and undisclosed problems within the organization which require extensive legal work.

Downward Trends in Key Financial Figures and Ratios. The use of ratio, change, and trend analysis may indicate problems in certain areas which require follow-up. Downward trends may be symptomatic of significant losses, diversion of funds and resources, and inadequate controls over operations.

Reported Conflicts of Interest. The auditor should be aware of any rumors or allegations of conflicts of interest pertaining to outside employment, vendor arrangements, and relationships between employees. Company transactions with officers or employees should be carefully scrutinized.

Unexplained Shortages in Physical Assets. Inadequate physical storage may lead to pilfering or other diversion of assets. Shortages in assets should be analyzed carefully to determine their cause.

Decreases in Performance. One division of a company may be performing less adequately than other divisions. In addition, there may be a decrease in performance from prior experience. The reasons should be determined for indications of poor management or possible wrongdoing.

Management Control by Few Individuals. Domination of an organization by one or a few individuals may provide the opportunity for diversion of assets or other manipulations.

Collection Difficulties. Problems in collecting on receivables should be analyzed to determine whether there are fictitious sales or diversion of funds received from collections.

Many Bank Accounts. The use of a large number of bank accounts in excess of what is normally needed indicates possible diversions of funds or cover-up of illegal transactions. Transfers among these accounts and to personal bank accounts should be reviewed carefully.

Late Reports. Reports may be consistently delayed so that the preparer can manipulate data to cover up fraudulent actions.

Copies Used for Payments to Creditors. Rather than making payments based on original invoices, copies may be used to hide duplicate payments and kickbacks.

Shortages, Overages and Out-of-Balance Conditions. These may be symptoms of a larger problem and explanation should be obtained as to the variances.

Checks or Other Documents Written in Even Amounts. For example, a check might read $10,000 or $3500 when it might normally be expected to be in odd amounts, such as $10,261.34 or $3532.28.

Exhibit 16.2 is a list prepared by the American Institute of Certified Public Accountants of conditions or events that may signal the existence of fraud.

Personal Characteristics

There is no specific profile of the white-collar criminal that would identify him to the internal auditor. Although a prior criminal record would indicate the need for observation, many white-collar criminals have had no prior

EXHIBIT 16.2.   AICPA List of Fraud Signals

1. Highly domineering senior management and one or more of the following, or similar, conditions are present:
    - ☐ An ineffective board of directors and/or audit committee.
    - ☐ Indications of management override of significant internal accounting controls.
    - ☐ Compensation or significant stock options tied to reported performance or to a specific transaction over which senior management has actual or implied control.
    - ☐ Indications of personal financial difficulties of senior management.
    - ☐ Proxy contests involving control of the company or senior management's continuance, compensation or status.

2. Deterioration of quality of earnings evidenced by:
    - ☐ Decline in the volume or quality of sales (for example, increased credit risk or sales at or below cost).
    - ☐ Significant changes in business practices.
    - ☐ Excessive interest by senior management in the earnings per share effect of accounting alternatives.

3. Business conditions that may create unusual pressures:
    - ☐ Inadequate working capital.
    - ☐ Little flexibility in debt restrictions such as working capital ratios and limitations on additional borrowings.
    - ☐ Rapid expansion of a product or business line markedly in excess of industry averages.
    - ☐ A major investment of the company's resources in an industry noted for rapid change, such as a high technology industry.

4. A complex corporate structure where the complexity does not appear to be warranted by the company's operations or size.

5. Widely dispersed business locations accompanied by highly decentralized management with inadequate responsibility reporting system.

6. Understaffing which appears to require certain employees to work unusual hours, to forgo vacations and/or to put in substantial overtime.

7. High turnover rate in key financial positions such as treasurer or controller.

8. Frequent change of auditors or legal counsel.

9. Known material weaknesses in internal control which could practically be corrected but remain uncorrected, such as:
    - ☐ Access to computer equipment or electronic data entry devices is not adequately controlled.
    - ☐ Incompatible duties remain combined.

10. Material transactions with related parties exist or there are transactions that may involve conflicts of interest.

11. Premature announcements of operating results or future (positive) expectations.

12. Analytical review procedures disclosing significant fluctuations which cannot be reasonably explained, for example:
    - ☐ Material account balances.
    - ☐ Financial or operational interrelationships.
    - ☐ Physical inventory variances.
    - ☐ Inventory turnover rates.

13. Large or unusual transactions, particularly at year-end, with material effect on earnings.

EXHIBIT 16.2. *(Continued)*

14. Unusually large payments in relation to services provided in the ordinary course of business by lawyers, consultants, agents and others (including employees).
15. Difficulty in obtaining audit evidence with respect to:
    - ☐ Unusual or unexplained entries.
    - ☐ Incomplete or missing documentation and/or authorization.
    - ☐ Alterations in documentation or accounts.
16. In the performance of an examination of financial statements unforeseen problems are encountered, for instance:
    - ☐ Client pressures to complete audit in an unusually short time or under difficult conditions.
    - ☐ Sudden delay situations.
    - ☐ Evasive or unreasonable responses of management to audit inquiries.

Source: Reprinted from March 12, 1979 CPA Letter. Copyright © 1979, American Institute of Certified Public Accountants, Inc.

record of criminal activity. In many instances they are members of the middle-class, well-educated families with status in the community.

There are, however, certain early warning signals of personal behavior which require close watching.

Early warning signals need watching

Early warning signals of personal behavior:

High personal debts or financial losses

Expensive life-style

Extensive gambling

Heavy investments

Excessive use of alcohol or drugs

Significant personal or family problems

Close association with customers

Extensive overtime and skipping vacations

Questionable background and references

Excessive sick leave

Feeling pay is not commensurate with responsibilities

Strong desire to beat the system

Regular borrowing of small amounts from fellow employees

Refusing to leave the custody of records during the day

Common Fraudulent Practices

Fraud is so directly a product of the individual operational situation that it is impossible to cover all possibilities. Any list must also recognize that a particular type of fraud can perhaps be possible in one situation and not in another. However, it may be useful to enumerate some common types of fraud.

*Common types of fraud
should be understood*

1. *Nonrecording of Revenues.* When an employee has control over both the sale and collection of cash, it is relatively easy to pocket the cash without recording the sale. This can also occur when the employee handles receipts of cash and also does the record keeping.

2. *Withholding Receivable Collections.* There may be a temporary withholding of collections on account, or keeping the amount received and later writing off the account as a bad debt. In some cases shortages are made up by using new cash receipts and the latter shortage then covered by still later receipts. This type of action is known as "lapping."

3. *Theft of Materials.* Sensitive items of materials and equipment with high resale value may be especially susceptible to pilferage, especially if not adequately secured. Theft losses may be covered up by arbitrary write-offs, transfers between departments, and inadequate inventory-taking procedures. In some cases release passes are forged or there may be collusion of security guards with individuals.

4. *Diversion of Securities.* This could occur in a situation where there was unauthorized access or where the custodian was able to remove the securities without being detected.

5. *Padding Payrolls.* In some situations a payroll clerk or supervisor has been able to carry nonexistent or terminated people on the payroll and then later get the cash or check used for payment. In other instances the payroll clerk may overstate an employee's wages in return for a share of the excess.

6. *Misuse of Credit Cards.* Credit cards may be used to make personal purchases or may be lent to others in return for favors. Also expenses paid for by company credit cards may be simultaneously claimed and reimbursed by check.

7. *Falsification of Disbursement Documents.* Cash disbursements may be supported by documents that are false or improperly altered. Warehouse receipts may be forged or receiving reports may be falsified. Copies of invoices or receipts may be submitted for duplicate payments.

8. *Payment of Personal Expenses.* Miscellaneous expenses of a personal nature may be submitted which are not authorized by the company. These may include entertainment, expenses of spouse, equipment bought for personal use, and unauthorized travel expense.

9. *Purchase Kickbacks.* Arrangements may be made with vendors to purchase from them in return for special favors or money. In some cases vendors will specifically offer bribes to members of the purchasing department.

10. *Misuse of Petty Cash Funds.* Funds may be used for personal or other unauthorized purposes. In some cases supporting documents may be forged or falsified to cover the shortage.

11. *Transfers of Assets*. In some cases there may be transfers of funds between bank accounts in various divisions or affiliated companies. These transfers may be used to camouflage unauthorized expenditures or use of funds.

12. *Excessive Allowances to Customers*. In some instances sales allowances or discounts may be overstated. Also preferred customers may be charged less in return for favors.

13. *Conflict of Interest*. This may occur in various parts of a company, involving relatives, employees with an outside interest, or dealings with related companies.

14. *Bribes and Other Corruption*. Payments to obtain business may be made to a foreign officials, in prohibition of the antibribery provisions of the Foreign Corrupt Practices Act as discussed earlier in this chapter.

15. *Misappropriation of Receipts*. Through having incoming customer checks made payable to an employee rather than the company, the employee can cash the checks and have company funds available.

PROCEDURES FOR HANDLING FRAUD

Obtaining Leads

Fraudulent acts may be disclosed in various ways. The internal auditor may discover them during the course of his reviews. Documents may contain questionable items which when followed up disclose irregularities. Employees or outsiders may make allegations or bring up items of a suspicious nature during discussions. In some instances an employee who has committed or participated in a fraud may come forth and make a confession. In addition, management may specifically request internal auditors to review sensitive areas for possible wrongdoing, for example, conflict of interest. There may also be general warning signs which require close attention by the internal auditor as indicators of potential fraud. The internal auditor needs to be on the alert for any leads that indicate irregularities, assuring that staff members recognize and identify the leads when found. This often takes curiosity and imagination to separate the normal from the abnormal. Being independent from day-to-day operations and personnel, the internal auditor is in a good position to recognize irregularities.

Leads for fraud have varying sources

IIA Guidelines.   The major conclusions of SIAS No. 3[1] relative to the investigation of fraud are:

> *Investigation of fraud*. Fraud investigations may be conducted by or involve participation of internal auditors, lawyers, investigators, security personnel, and other specialists from inside or outside the organization.

[1]See Appendix F.

SIAS No. 3 describes
investigation responsibilities

Internal auditing should assess the facts known relative to all fraud investigations in order to:

Determine if controls need to be implemented or strengthened.

Design audit tests to help disclose the existence of similar frauds in the future.

Help meet the internal auditor's responsibility to maintain sufficient knowledge of fraud.

Informing Management

Notify appropriate members
of management when
fraud suspected

As soon as fraud is suspected, it should be reported to the proper company officials. Generally management is interested in obtaining information about fraud anywhere in the organization. This is important for alerting management at an early stage before there is unfavorable publicity. In addition this provides top officials an opportunity to provide input as to how the investigation will be conducted and to make key decisions as to the disposition of the case. Normally cases are not dropped without the concurrence of management. Also management becomes aware of control deficiencies that enabled the irregularities to occur. Employees should be informed that all frauds must be reported to management immediately. The official to whom reports are provided may be the president, vice-president, treasurer, controller, or other designated executive.

Usually a report is also made to the bonding company. This may be a requirement under the provisions of surety bonds. In addition, the bonding company may be of assistance in the investigation and determination of action to be taken based on evidence available. A report is also made to the legal counsel and to any special investigators in the company. The director of internal auditing should of course also be informed of all frauds.

In some instances the immediate supervisor of the employee for whom there is a complaint should be informed. The employee may be relieved of his duties to aid in the investigation or to prevent further manipulation. The employee may be assigned to other work or suspended. It may be necessary to take immediate control over the employee's records to prevent him from altering or destroying them.

Initiating Action

As soon as the preliminary facts are reviewed, a plan of action should be developed and an internal auditor or investigator designated to be in charge. It is especially important to start the investigation as soon as possible to prevent the destruction or alteration of records, obtain confessions, and gather evidence that can be used for interviewing witnesses.

Internal auditor participates
in initiating action

The internal auditor should determine the types of records and supporting documents that should be reviewed. To prevent the need for detailed checking, it may be preferable to interview key personnel and witnesses prior to performing the review. The type of evidence necessary to prove the case should be discussed to assure that the data obtained are pertinent.

Resources needed should be carefully reviewed. In some cases the work may require professional investigators because of the questioning involved or other factors. Discussions with law enforcement officials may be necessary. The role of the internal auditor should carefully be defined, both in performing the investigatory work and writing the report.

In planning the work, information should be gathered as to the number of persons involved and their positions. Personnel files should be reviewed to determine if background checks have been performed and whether there is any indication of personal problems.

Conducting the Investigation

Coordinating Efforts.   In conducting the investigation it is first necessary to coordinate the efforts of all parties involved. In an individual case this may involve the internal auditor who carries out various audit tests, including following the paper trails; the investigator, who conducts interviews, interrogates witnesses, and gathers other evidence; the legal counsel, who provides technical advice and support; and prosecuting attorneys, who perform early case review and provide guidance on evidence needed. Close communication should be encouraged among the internal auditor, investigator, legal counsel, and prosecutor during the investigation.

Guidelines for conducting investigation of fraud

Selecting Audit Procedures.   There are no audit procedures that are unique to fraud situations—each case is different and requires study and analysis to determine the best approach. In a case involving lapping in accounts receivable, in which the employee diverted collections to his own use during the early months of a year, confirmation of accounts was performed. In another case involving theft of sensitive equipment, a physical inventory was taken which the internal auditor observed. In both cases the internal auditor made inquiries of selected employees to obtain explanations of circumstances surrounding the irregularity. The internal auditor relies on his judgment in selecting the best procedures for gathering evidence. He must also be imaginative to detect such items as falsification of documents, forged signatures, and collusion. It should be emphasized that as soon as an internal auditor begins investigating fraud, his role changes. His normal cooperative role of reviewing controls as part of routine auditing is changed. He now assumes duties more like a detective, gathering evidence to determine whether there is a fraud, to ascertain who committed the fraud, to determine the extent of loss, and to find out how the fraud was perpetrated. He must investigate all discrepancies, believing no explanations until they can be proved. He must suspect transactions and consider possible collusion. Speed is essential in the investigation to prevent destruction of records and obtain evidence for interviewing witnesses and the suspected defrauder.

Determining Personal Gain. The internal auditor is on the lookout for diversion of funds to personal use. Although certain practices followed by an employee may be wasteful or not in the best interests of the company, the individual may not benefit personally and it may be difficult to prosecute him. Transfers of funds between accounts and divisions of the company are examined closely, as are personal withdrawals in various forms.

Isolating Specific Areas. The internal auditor attempts to concentrate his efforts on those areas that will provide specific evidence as to fraud. To conserve time and resources, his test checks should be limited as to detail and should emphasize areas of concern. Once fraud is uncovered, other activities of the employee may have to be examined to detect possible fraudulent actions. As the investigation proceeds, information obtained by interviews with employees is used to help determine audit emphasis. The internal auditor begins to develop answers to the following questions and plan his work accordingly.

Key survey questions

Have cash, securities, or other assets been stolen?

Can the defalcation be easily determined, or does it require extensive tracing of transactions through the records?

What documents and other evidence are needed to prove both shortages and intent?

How far back does the shortage go?

Do records indicate that there have been prior shortages which have not been thoroughly investigated or have been covered up?

Has management been aware of any wrongdoing and taken any action?

How many persons are involved?

What is known or can be learned about their habits and finances?

Do personal files indicate employment verification?

Interviewing Techniques. Interviewing and making inquiries of employees and outsiders become especially important procedures in conducting investigations. Information made available by a complainant, by employees and other witnesses, and by the suspected defrauder is often the key to the investigation. The internal auditor thus has to plan his interviews carefully to obtain the maximum evidence and benefit for the investigative effort.

Information from Complainant. The original complainant should be interviewed in depth as soon as possible. If the complainant desires secrecy, he should be informed that his identity and confidentiality of information will be protected. If the complainant has documentary support for this allegation, this should be requested at the time of the interview. If the allegation is general in nature, the complainant may be able to refer the investigator to other personnel or records for more information. In some cases the allegation should be put in writing. An evaluation should be made as soon as possible of the merits of the complaint. During the interview and preliminary survey of evidence, the internal auditor should attempt to determine action to be taken as follows:

Action dropped because allegation unsupported

Turned over to management for administrative action, because there was no intent to defraud

Full-scale investigation recommended and possible prosecutory action

Considered abuse or wasteful management action rather than fraud; recommendation made for improvement in procedures

Timing of Interview.   The auditor should make a determination as to whether interviews will be conducted early in the examination to enable him to pinpoint his approach and limit the extent of review of books and records. In some instances he may wish to perform preliminary auditing of the records in order to obtain information for conducting meaningful interviews. Generally it is preferable to conduct the interview with the suspect early in the audit, while he is still on the job and available to answer questions as the audit progresses. In some cases, however, it may be necessary to remove a suspected employee from his position because his duties involved handling assets or controlling records where there is a possibility of hiding the fraud or misappropriating assets.

Timing may vary

Rights of Employee.   Legal precedent supports the authority of the internal auditor to question individuals about company-related duties and actions while they are employed. This procedure is based on the employee's stewardship responsibility to the company. If an official investigation is begun to gather evidence for prosecution, however, the requirements for informing a suspect of his constitutional rights should be observed. When there are any questions on this or other civil rights, prosecuting officials or the legal staff should be consulted.

Employee rights important

Conduct of Interview.   The internal auditor should prepare an outline of the questions he wishes to ask. He should be prepared for both affirmative and negative responses to key questions. The auditor should avoid creating the impression that he is seeking a confession or conviction. It is preferable to appear in the role of one merely seeking the truth. The interviewer should be tactful when replies to questions do not agree with the facts obtained. He should point out the inconsistencies and ask for additional explanations. He should listen carefully to whatever the interviewee has to say, and relate questions to specific transactions and documents of interest. The skill of the interviewer is often a determining factor in obtaining information to use in the investigation. He must use one or more techniques, relying on his ability to size up the suspect and determine the approach that will work best.

There are various types of questions that can be asked, as listed below.

Open-Ended. This type of question is broad and unstructured, letting the interviewee give the answer as he sees it. Open-ended questions are intended to establish good communications and obtain the viewpoints of the interviewee. An example is: "Tell me about the internal control system."

Restatement. The purpose of restatement is to check the listener's understanding of what was said and to encourage the speaker to continue. An example is: "You say that the mail clerk sometimes hands envelopes to the accounting clerk without checking for receipts of cash?"

Right questions key to good interview

Probes. The purpose of probes is to obtain more specific information. The speaker is asked to explain in more detail when the responses are not sufficient. An example is: "Do you have any other information that would explain how this happened?"

Closed. This type of question is used when it is desired to lead the interviewee to express himself one way or another. An example is: "Do you record transactions daily or wait until near the end of the month?" The use of closed questions requires the interviewer to have background knowledge of the subject. This method is useful when it is desired to have the interviewee think through several alternatives and arrive at a conclusion.

Yes–no. This is a form of closed question which allows the interviewer to answer "yes," "no," and "I don't know." This type of question does not elicit much information, and should generally be replaced by questions that require more detailed answers.

Confession Statements. The employer has a right to ask a suspect to prepare a written statement explaining his actions, whether or not he confesses. A confession statement will be useful as evidence for prosecution and/or recovery. If there has been no confession, the suspect should be willing to explain his version of the facts. The confession, if made, must be voluntary and not under threat or promise of reward. The interrogation and subsequent confession may provide leads to additional fraudulent activities or to other individuals involved. If the confessed embezzler does not raise the question of restitution, the auditor should ask him when and how he proposes to make restitution.

Reappraisal of Internal Controls

Related internal controls need new look

At the conclusion of the investigation the internal auditor should make a careful analysis of the related internal controls. He should be concerned with the following:

Was the cause of the problem ineffective internal control, or controls not functioning?

Could the type of fraud committed occur elsewhere in the company?

Are additional preventive controls economically justifiable?

Would any proposed expansion fit into the normal pattern of the business and be accepted by employees, or would they be unworkable?

How could the audit program be revised to detect fraud of this nature?

Action against Employee

Based on the facts in the case, decisions have to be made on whether the employee will be dismissed, whether he will be prosecuted, and whether management will ask restitution. In addition, if the employee is prosecuted and found innocent, management must decide what his later position in the organization will be.

Action against employee up to management

The internal auditor must be aware that it is very difficult in some cases to get a district attorney to prosecute. Decisions as to whether or not to prosecute may depend on the amount of the fraud, type of crime, type of evidence gathered, and in some cases the work load of the district attorney and current political considerations. It is especially frustrating for the internal auditor to complete an investigation, provide the evidence to the district attorney, and then have him decline to prosecute.

The surety company should be consulted regarding restitution. This is generally desired to reduce the amount of the loss. Since any restitution may affect the criminal prosecution, the district attorney's office and the surety company should be kept well informed.

IIA Guidelines on the Written Report. SIAS No. 3 reaches the following conclusions regarding reporting fraud:

SIAS No. 3 describes reporting

> *Reporting of fraud.* A written report should be issued at the conclusion of the investigation phase. It should include all findings, conclusions, recommendations and corrective action taken.

Writing the Report. The final report of the investigation presents the evidence gathered and conclusions reached. It provides management with a summary of action taken as a result of leads and serves as a basis for decisions on how to deal with the employee. The report should contain a description of the process used in committing the fraud. The monetary value of the assets misappropriated and, when possible the dates of the misappropriation(s) should be included. All evidence gathered should be retained for possible future use. The circumstances which permitted the fraud to be perpetrated should also be in the report. In addition recommendations for improving any internal control weakness identified during the investigation should also be included. Exhibit 16.3 is an example of an investigation of purchasing fraud conducted by an internal auditor.

Issue a written report

EXHIBIT 16.3   Fraud in Purchasing

During a test of purchasing transactions the internal auditor noted that purchases of off-the-shelf items were being made without competitive bids. Further analysis of these transactions indicated that most were justified based on competitive bids obtained or technical and emergency needs. However, about $500,000 of purchases with one source, XYZ Company, which were handled by purchasing agent John Weston, did not have justification for sole-source procurement. The prices paid for these items were 10% above the going market prices based on quotes obtained by the internal auditor and prices paid by other divisions of the company. Examination of the files indicated that there was no review required of justification used for sole-source procurement.

Although it appeared that this was an example of waste and the internal auditor could make a recommendation in his report that would save in excess of $45,000 a year, he decided to go a step further and check for possible fraud. He therefore (1) reviewed the file for a history of purchases of the material, (2) checked for relationships of the purchasing agent with the company, and (3) questioned other employees about the life-style of the purchasing agent. He found that purchases of the material had been made from another company at a lesser cost until two years ago, shortly after the purchasing agent had been hired. During the past two years, the purchasing agent's expense vouchers showed periodic instances of mileage claimed in connection with luncheon meetings with the sales manager of the XYZ Company. When asked about the life-style of Mr. Weston, three employees commented that he had recently gone through a divorce, was making frequent trips to resort areas, and seemed to be spending a great deal.

The internal auditor then checked the employee's personal files for references. He found that references had been checked only for the last employer. When Mr. Weston's previous employers were contacted by telephone, it was found that he had been allowed to resign a previous job when questions were raised about his dealings with suppliers.

The internal auditor discussed the matter with the legal counsel, who recommended that Mr. Weston be questioned. After discussion of the facts obtained by the internal auditor, Mr. Weston confessed that he had received kickbacks from XYZ Company of $30,000 in the past two years. Since the purchases of material were made for use under a contract funded by the state, the matter was turned over to the State Attorney General's office for prosecution.

A review of internal controls over purchasing indicated that there was the need for more segregation of duties among the staff, including the review of all sole-source procurement by an independent official. In addition, there was a large backlog of unfilled purchase requisitions, requiring extensive emergency purchasing and bypassing existing procedures to expedite the work effort. Management had previously been made aware of the problems but had not taken corrective action. The internal auditor's report included recommendations to management for strengthening controls to correct the above.

Generally the written report should include the following:

1. How the fraud was discovered (regular audit, complaint, confession)
2. Nature of the fraud (theft of goods, misappropriation of funds, etc.)
3. Full identity of the perpetrator
4. Monetary value involved
5. How the act was concealed (lapping, forgeries, etc.)
6. Time period over which thefts occurred
7. Effect on financial statements
8. Recommendation to prevent recurrence of similar fraud
9. Prosecution (waived, pending, sentence, restitution)

FRAUD IN PERSPECTIVE

The need to assist management in the prevention and detection of fraud presents a real challenge to the internal auditor. To meet the need there must be sufficient time planned in the budget to provide this service. Because of its importance to management the prevention and detection of fraud often take precedence over other work. As such, careful planning and assessment of priorities are needed to assure that the broad responsibilities of internal auditing are met. For the short term it may be necessary to do fewer operational audits to handle investigations. It may also be necessary to devote significant resources to study the risk of fraud in a company and devise preventive measures. For the long term, however, the amount of time needed to be devoted to fraud measures should decrease. The internal auditor should also coordinate closely with management to assure that there are sufficient resources and time available to perform meaningful operational auditing. Demonstration to management of competence and beneficial findings in all areas of internal auditing will help in accomplishing this objective. It is thus important that the internal auditor and management work together to achieve the proper balance between fraud-oriented objectives and other broader needs and services. The internal auditor must then always be alert to the prevention and detection of fraud.

Budget should provide for fraud type services

ILLUSTRATIVE AUDIT FINDINGS: FRAUD AND INVESTIGATIONS

Double Reimbursement of Expenses

Expenses for meals and other services were being billed twice because an employee submitted original bills for items that had been charged to a company credit card. The company did not require support for the credit card purchases and did not review travel and expense vouchers of employees with credit cards for possible duplication. As a result, one employee received excess reimbursement of $3400 in a two-year period.

Accepting Entertainment from Vendor

A company computer specialist was terminated for accepting more than 200 dinners for himself and his wife from a computer firm that received a $12 million contract from the company. Since these dinners were not in connection with regular business meetings of the company, and the computer specialist was in a position to influence the award of the contract, the dinners were considered in the nature of kickbacks.

Stealing Company Pension Checks

A review of company pension checks issued to retired employees indicated inadequate control over returned checks. Through further analysis it was found that an employee who had access to the returned checks (returned primarily because of death) was forging the checks and cashing them.

Sale of Company-Developed Material

At one leading research organization a scientist was asked to resign after the internal auditor found that he had sold human cell cultures developed with company funds to other groups at a personal profit of $67,000. The scientist agreed to make restitution of the money.

FINAL PERSPECTIVE ON INTERNAL AUDITING

Internal auditing has expanding service potential

As we bring this book to a close, the reader should be aware that there is an increasing complexity of the organization and its activities and hence an increasing range of opportunities for the internal auditor. This means that there is a rich growth market for internal auditing services. The internal auditor is remarkably well positioned to exploit advantageously these opportunities. His position in the normal organization is unique, his credentials are excellent, and his prestige we believe is at the highest levels yet achieved. Admittedly things can change and there is always the danger that internal auditing will become unduly complacent and thus lose ground in relation to other company groups. But the total prospects on balance are most excellent for further progress.

Success based on demonstrated value

The progress of internal auditing has come about, for the most part, through the performance of individual internal auditing departments in business and governmental organizations. This performance has been the basis for success in the individual organizations involved. In addition, that success has spilled over to other organizations through writing and speaking, especially through the medium of The Institute of Internal Auditors. The future progress of internal auditing will also be achieved in large part through these broader professional efforts. In the main, however, the progress of internal auditing has its basic roots in the achievements in the particular organizational situations. Individual internal auditors will thus, we think, continue to be the key figures in developing new concepts, methods, and approaches to effective practice. It will also be the leaders in practice who provide the impetus for broader professional efforts such as The Institute of Internal Auditors. Fortunately, the profession has been unusually blessed by having a large number of leaders who have provided both substance and inspiration.

But in a broader sense the professional progress depends on the accomplishments of *every* internal auditor. The objective is, therefore, to increase the level of performance of each individual and department in every organizational situation. The total objectives of the profession must be to provide that individual help, and thus to add to the aggregate contributions to the needs of business, government, and society as a whole. At the same time each of us must do our part both in our own organizations and in the larger professional effort. By working together the further progress of internal auditing can thus be assured. The accomplishments to date and the vigor of the current outreach certainly indicate that internal auditors can face the future with high expectations.

Future progress a team effort

REVIEW QUESTIONS

1. Discuss the internal auditor's responsibility for the detection and prevention of fraud.
2. Why is there currently more emphasis on fraud prevention by both the internal and external auditor?
3. What are the internal accounting control requirements of the FCPA?
4. What are some organizational conditions which may indicate fraud?
5. What are some of the motivational factors that are warning signals of fraud?
6. Should an internal auditor rely on allegations or should he have an independent program for detecting fraud?
7. What are the major actions taken in initiating a fraud investigation?
8. Coordination is vital to the successful conclusion of an investigation. With whom should the internal auditor coordinate before and during an investigation?
9. What information should be obtained from a complainant?
10. After the investigation is completed the internal auditor's attention should turn to the related internal controls. What should his analysis consider?

CASE PROBLEMS

Problem 16-1

Peter Wright, president, was talking to the controller, Douglas Sentor, and the general auditor, Jamie Gomez, about a recent embezzlement. "I am really disturbed about all this newspaper publicity; we have a reputation to maintain, and it does not look good for our customers to read in the paper that an accountant ran off with $250,000. I look to you two for assurances that we have a good control system."

Sentor replied that the accountant had been stealing from customer accounts over a long period of time and was a trusted employee. Displeased with this response, Wright turned to Gomez and said, "Why didn't your people discover this in their audits? I know you have been spending more time on operational audits and I agreed to this because of the good work you have been doing. But I expected you to still do enough work on control to prevent something like this from happening?

Required. How would you advise Gomez to answer Wright?

Problem 16-2

Jack Smith, senior auditor, was complaining to his boss, Loretta Freed, that the district attorney had refused to prosecute a case on which he had been working. He said, "All that work for nothing; I spent 300 hours gathering evidence for this case. Our attorney told me I was on the right track, and I had five counts against the employee. If I had known that we could not get a conviction, I would have developed a procedural finding in about 100 hours and been through. It just isn't fair."

Required. How should Freed answer Smith?

APPENDICES

Statement of Responsibilities of Internal Auditing

STATEMENT OF RESPONSIBILITIES
OF INTERNAL AUDITING

The purpose of this statement is to provide in summary form a general understanding of the role and responsibilities of internal auditing. For more specific guidance, readers should refer to the *Standards for the Professional Practice of Internal Auditing*.

NATURE

Internal auditing is an independent appraisal activity established within an organization as a service to the organization. It is a control which functions by examining and evaluating the adequacy and effectiveness of other controls.

OBJECTIVE AND SCOPE

The objective of internal auditing is to assist members of the organization in the effective discharge of their responsibilities. To this end, internal auditing furnishes them with analyses, appraisals, recommendations, counsel, and information concerning the activities reviewed. The audit objective includes promoting effective control at reasonable cost.

The scope of internal auditing encompasses the examination and evaluation of the adequacy and effectiveness of the organization's system of internal control and the quality of performance in carrying out assigned responsibilities. The scope of internal auditing includes:

- Reviewing the reliability and integrity of financial and operating information and the means used to identify, measure, classify, and report such information.

- Reviewing the systems established to ensure compliance with those policies, plans, procedures, laws, and regulations which could have a significant impact on operations and reports, and determining whether the organization is in compliance.

- Reviewing the means of safeguarding assets and, as appropriate, verifying the existence of such assets.

- Appraising the economy and efficiency with which resources are employed.

- Reviewing operations or programs to ascertain whether results are consistent with established objectives and goals and whether the operations or programs are being carried out as planned.

RESPONSIBILITY AND AUTHORITY

Internal auditing functions under the policies established by management and the board. The purpose, authority and responsibility of the internal auditing department should be defined in a formal written document (charter), approved by management, and accepted by the board. The charter should make clear the purposes of the internal auditing department, specify the unrestricted scope of its work, and declare that auditors are to have no authority or responsibility for the activities they audit.

The responsibility of internal auditing is to serve the organization in a manner that is consistent with the *Standards for the Professional Practice of Internal Auditing* and with professional standards of conduct such as the *Code of Ethics* of The Institute of Internal Auditors, Inc. This responsibility includes coordinating internal audit activities with others so as to best achieve the audit objectives and the objectives of the organization.

INDEPENDENCE

Internal auditors should be independent of the activities they audit. Internal auditors are independent when they can carry out their work freely and objectively. Independence permits internal auditors to render the impartial and unbiased judgments essential to the proper conduct of audits. It is achieved through organizational status and objectivity.

Organizational status should be sufficient to assure a broad range of audit coverage, and adequate consideration of and effective action on audit findings and recommendations.

Objectivity requires that internal auditors have an independent mental attitude, and an honest belief in their work product. Drafting procedures, designing, installing, and operating systems, are not audit functions. Performing such activities is presumed to impair audit objectivity.

The *Statement of Responsibilities of Internal Auditors* was originally issued by The Institute of Internal Auditors in 1947. The current *Statement*, revised in 1981, embodies the concepts previously established and includes such changes as are deemed advisable in light of the present status of the profession.

Code of Ethics of The Institute of Internal Auditors

THE INSTITUTE OF INTERNAL AUDITORS, INC.
CODE OF ETHICS

INTRODUCTION: Recognizing that ethics are an important consideration in the practice of internal auditing and that the moral principles followed by members of *The Institute of Internal Auditors, Inc.*, should be formalized, the Board of Directors at its regular meeting in New Orleans on December 13, 1968, received and adopted the following resolution:

WHEREAS the members of *The Institute of Internal Auditors, Inc.*, represent the profession of internal auditing; and

WHEREAS managements rely on the profession of internal auditing to assist in the fulfillment of their management stewardship; and

WHEREAS said members must maintain high standards of conduct, honor and character in order to carry on proper and meaningful internal auditing practice;

THEREFORE BE IT RESOLVED that a Code of Ethics be now set forth, outlining the standards of professional behavior for the guidance of each member of *The Institute of Internal Auditors, Inc.*

In accordance with this resolution, the Board of Directors further approved of the principles set forth.

INTERPRETATION OF PRINCIPLES: The provisions of this Code of Ethics cover basic principles in the various disciplines of internal auditing practice. Members shall realize that individual judgment is required in the application of these principles. They have a responsibility to conduct themselves so that their good faith and integrity should not be open to question. While having due regard for the limit of their technical skills, they will promote the highest possible internal auditing standards to the end of advancing the interest of their company or organization.

ARTICLES:

  I. Members shall have an obligation to exercise honesty, objectivity, and diligence in the performance of their duties and responsibilities.

 II. Members, in holding the trust of their employers, shall exhibit loyalty in all matters pertaining to the affairs of the employer or to whomever they may be rendering a service. However, members shall not knowingly be a part to any illegal or improper activity.

III. Members shall refrain from entering into any activity which may be in conflict with the interest of their employers or which would prejudice their ability to carry out objectively their duties and responsibilities.

 IV. Members shall not accept a fee or a gift from an employee, a client, a customer, or a business associate of their employer without the knowledge and consent of their senior management.

  V. Members shall be prudent in the use of information acquired in the course of their duties. They shall not use confidential information for any personal gain nor in a manner which would be detrimental to the welfare of their employer.

 VI. Members, in expressing an opinion, shall use all reasonable care to obtain sufficient factual evidence to warrant such expression. In their reporting, members shall reveal such material facts known to them, which, if not revealed, could either distort the report of the results of operations under review or conceal unlawful practice.

VII. Members shall continually strive for improvement in the proficiency and effectiveness of their service.

VIII. Members shall abide by the bylaws and uphold the objectives of *The Institute of Internal Auditors, Inc.* In the practice of their profession, they shall be ever mindful of their obligation to maintain the high standard of competence, morality, and dignity which *The Institute of Internal Auditors, Inc.*, and its members have established.

Reproduced with the permission of The Institute of Internal Auditors.

Standards for the Professional Practice of Internal Auditing

Standards for the
Professional Practice
of Internal Auditing [1]

The Institute of Internal Auditors, Inc.
Altamonte Springs, Florida

ISBN 0-89413-073-9

IIA79040 Mar79

First printing, August 1978
Second printing, October 1978
Third printing, March 1979

Copies of the *Standards* may be purchased from The Institute of Internal Auditors, Inc., International Headquarters, 249 Maitland Avenue, Altamonte Springs, Florida 32701. The price is $2.50 for a single copy and $1.00 for each additional copy. Payment must accompany order. **Order No. 462**.

Foreword

In 1941, The Institute of Internal Auditors, Inc. (IIA) was created by and for internal auditors. Today, IIA is the only international organization dedicated solely to the advancement of the individual internal auditor and the internal auditing profession. Since 1941, IIA has been instrumental in helping its members meet the generally accepted criteria of a profession by:

- adopting a *Code of Ethics*
- approving a *Statement of Responsibilities of Internal Auditors*
- establishing a program of continuing education
- developing a *Common Body of Knowledge*
- instituting a certification program

Adopting professional standards is another vital step in the development of internal auditing. To accomplish this, IIA formed the Professional Standards and Responsibilities Committee in 1974.

The *Standards for the Professional Practice of Internal Auditing* are the result of nearly three years of effort by that committee. These *Standards* are meant to serve the entire profession in all types of business, in various levels of government, and in all other organizations where internal auditors are found.

The term "standards," as used in this document, means the criteria by which the operations of an internal auditing department are evaluated and measured. They are intended to represent the practice of internal auditing as it should be, as judged and adopted by the Board of Directors of The Institute.

As internal auditing adapts to the continuous changes taking place in business and in society, our *Standards* will be modified from time to time to meet the changing needs of auditors everywhere.

The Institute of Internal Auditors is grateful to those governmental agencies, professional associations, internal and external auditors, and members of management, audit committees, and academe who provided guidance and assistance in the development of these *Standards*. It is deeply indebted to the following individuals and members of the IIA Practice Standards Subcommittee and their employers for their dedicated services:

Roger N. Carolus, CIA, CPA, Chairman
Northwest Bancorporation

Michael J. Barrett, DBA, Vice Chairman
University of Minnesota

R. Glen Berryman, PhD, CPA
Consultant, University of Minnesota

i

LaVonne Carpenter
Northwest Bancorporation
M. A. Dittenhofer, PhD, CIA
Association of Government Accountants
Donald E. Friedlander, CIA
Honeywell, Inc.
Robert E. Gobeil, CIA, CA
Alcan Smelters & Chemicals Ltd.
Robert E. Rivers, CIA
IIA staff liaison
Lawrence B. Sawyer, JD, CIA
Consultant
John F. Stucke, CIA
The First National Bank of Boston
R. Scott Vaughan
Aluminum Company of America
H. C. Warner, CIA
IIA staff liaison

Organizations which already have established an internal audit function or are planning to establish one, are urged to adopt and support the *Standards for the Professional Practice of Internal Auditing* as a basis for guiding and measuring the function.

James R. Kelly, CIA, CPA
International President
1977-1978

W. J. Harmeyer, CIA, CPA
International President
1978-1979

ii

The Institute of Internal Auditors, Inc.
International Professional Standards
and Responsibilities Committee
1977-78

Roger N. Carolus, CIA, CPA, *Chairman* — Northwest Bancorporation, Minneapolis, Minnesota
Ernest W. Brindle, Standard Oil Co. (Indiana), Chicago, Illinois
Charles J. Doerner, CIA, The Penn Mutual Life Insurance Co., Philadelphia, Pennsylvania
William J. Duane, Jr., CPA, Manufacturers Hanover Trust Co., New York, New York
Charles L. Duly, MBE, CIA, FCCA, Standard Telephones & Cables, Cockfosters, Barnet, Hertfordshire, England
Donald E. Friedlander, CIA, Honeywell, Inc., Minneapolis, Minnesota
Clyde F. Haggard, Jr., CIA, CPA, El Paso Natural Gas Co., El Paso, Texas
Robert L. Jones, CIA, CA, Chartered Accountant, Calgary, Alberta, Canada
J. Cyrille Lavigne, CA, Department of National Revenue Taxation, Ottawa, Ontario, Canada
Robert P. Ness, CIA, Gamble & Associates, Pty. Ltd., Melbourne, Victoria, Australia
Stanley E. Petrie, CIA, CPA, Badger Meter, Inc., Milwaukee, Wisconsin
Charles E. Petry, CIA, Northwest Bancorporation, Minneapolis, Minnesota
Victor Phillips, CIA, FCA, Government of Canada, Ottawa, Ontario, Canada
Wilfred A. Ronck, CIA, Sun Oil Co., Dallas, Texas
John F. Stucke, CIA, The First National Bank of Boston, Boston, Massachusetts
Gordon A. Trew, CIA, John Swire & Sons (HK) Ltd., Hong Kong
R. Scott Vaughan, CIA, Aluminum Company of America, Pittsburgh, Pennsylvania

Board of Regents Representative
Robert E. Gobeil, CIA, CA, Alcan Smelters & Chemicals Ltd., Montreal, Quebec, Canada

IIA Staff
William E. Perry, CIA, CPA, Director of Professional Practice, The Institute of Internal Auditors, Inc.
Robert E. Rivers, CIA, Director of Certification, The Institute of Internal Auditors, Inc.
H. C. Warner, CIA, Manager of Professional Standards, The Institute of Internal Auditors, Inc.

Practice Standards Subcommittee — 1977-78
Roger N. Carolus, CIA, CPA, *Chairman,* Northwest Bancorporation, Minneapolis, Minnesota
Michael J. Barrett, DBA, *Vice Chairman,* University of Minnesota, Minneapolis, Minnesota
R. Glen Berryman, PhD, CPA, University of Minnesota, Minneapolis, Minnesota
Mortimer A. Dittenhofer, PhD, CIA, Association of Government Accountants, Gaithersburg, Maryland
Donald E. Friedlander, CIA, Honeywell, Inc., Minneapolis, Minnesota
Robert E. Gobeil, CIA, CA, Alcan Smelters & Chemicals Ltd., Montreal, Quebec, Canada
Lawrence B. Sawyer, JD, CIA, Consultant, Camarillo, California
John F. Stucke, CIA, The First National Bank of Boston, Boston, Massachusetts
R. Scott Vaughan, Aluminum Company of America, Pittsburgh, Pennsylvania

Administrative Assistant
LaVonne Carpenter, Northwest Bancorporation, Minneapolis, Minnesota

Staff Liaison
Robert E. Rivers, CIA, Director of Certification, The Institute of Internal Auditors, Inc.
H. C. Warner, CIA, Manager of Professional Standards, The Institute of Internal Auditors, Inc.

Contents

Introduction

Internal auditing is an independent appraisal function established within an organization to examine and evaluate its activities as a service to the organization. The objective of internal auditing is to assist members of the organization in the effective discharge of their responsibilities. To this end, internal auditing furnishes them with analyses, appraisals, recommendations, counsel, and information concerning the activities reviewed.

The members of the organization assisted by internal auditing include those in management and the board of directors. Internal auditors owe a responsibility to both, providing them with information about the adequacy and effectiveness of the organization's system of internal control and the quality of performance. The information furnished to each may differ in format and detail, depending upon the requirements and requests of management and the board.

The internal auditing department is an integral part of the organization and functions under the policies established by management and the board. The statement of purpose, authority, and responsibility (charter) for the internal auditing department, approved by management and accepted by the board, should be consistent with these *Standards for the Professional Practice of Internal Auditing.*

The charter should make clear the purposes of the internal auditing department, specify the unrestricted scope of its work, and declare that auditors are to have no authority or responsibility for the activities they audit.

Throughout the world internal auditing is performed in diverse environments and within organizations which vary in purpose, size, and structure. In addition, the laws and customs within various countries differ from one another. These differences may affect the practice of internal auditing in each environment. The implementation of these *Standards,* therefore, will be governed by the environment in which the internal auditing department carries out its assigned responsibilities. But compliance with the concepts enunciated by these *Standards* is essential before the responsibilities of internal auditors can be met.

"Independence," as used in these *Standards,* requires clarification. Internal auditors must be independent of the activities they audit. Such independence permits internal auditors to perform their work freely and objectively. Without independence, the desired results of internal auditing cannot be realized.

In setting these *Standards,* the following developments were considered:

1. Boards of directors are being held increasingly accountable for the adequacy and effectiveness of their organizations' systems of internal control and quality of performance.
2. Members of management are demonstrating increased acceptance of internal auditing as a means of supplying objective analyses, appraisals, recommendations, counsel, and information on the organization's controls and performance.
3. External auditors are using the results of internal audits to complement their own work where the internal auditors have provided suitable evidence of independence and adequate, professional audit work.

In the light of such developments, the purposes of these *Standards* are to:

1

1. Impart an understanding of the role and responsibilities of internal auditing to all levels of management, boards of directors, public bodies, external auditors, and related professional organizations
2. Establish the basis for the guidance and measurement of internal auditing performance
3. Improve the practice of internal auditing

The *Standards* differentiate among the varied responsibilities of the organization, the internal auditing department, the director of internal auditing, and internal auditors.

The five general *Standards* are expressed in italicized statements in upper case. Following each of these general *Standards* are specific standards expressed in italicized statements in lower case. Accompanying each specific standard are guidelines describing suitable means of meeting that standard. The *Standards* encompass:

1. The independence of the internal auditing department from the activities audited and the objectivity of internal auditors
2. The proficiency of internal auditors and the professional care they should exercise
3. The scope of internal auditing work
4. The performance of internal auditing assignments
5. The management of the internal auditing department

The *Standards* and the accompanying guidelines employ three terms which have been given specific meanings. These are as follows:

The term *board* includes boards of directors, audit committees of such boards, heads of agencies or legislative bodies to whom internal auditors report, boards of governors or trustees of nonprofit organizations, and any other designated governing bodies of organizations.

The terms *director of internal auditing* and *director* identify the top position in an internal auditing department.

The term *internal auditing department* includes any unit or activity within an organization which performs internal auditing functions.

SUMMARY OF GENERAL AND SPECIFIC STANDARDS
FOR THE PROFESSIONAL PRACTICE OF INTERNAL AUDITING

100   **INDEPENDENCE** — *INTERNAL AUDITORS SHOULD BE INDEPENDENT OF THE ACTIVITIES THEY AUDIT.*

    110   **Organizational Status** — *The organizational status of the internal auditing department should be sufficient to permit the accomplishment of its audit responsibilities.*

    120   **Objectivity** — *Internal auditors should be objective in performing audits.*

200   **PROFESSIONAL PROFICIENCY** — *INTERNAL AUDITS SHOULD BE PERFORMED WITH PROFICIENCY AND DUE PROFESSIONAL CARE.*

    The Internal Auditing Department

    210   **Staffing** — *The internal auditing department should provide assurance that the technical proficiency and educational background of internal auditors are appropriate for the audits to be performed.*

    220   **Knowledge, Skills, and Disciplines** — *The internal auditing department should possess or should obtain the knowledge, skills, and disciplines needed to carry out its audit responsibilities.*

    230   **Supervision** — *The internal auditing department should provide assurance that internal audits are properly supervised.*

    The Internal Auditor

    240   **Compliance with Standards of Conduct** — *Internal auditors should comply with professional standards of conduct.*

    250   **Knowledge, Skills, and Disciplines** — *Internal auditors should possess the knowledge, skills, and disciplines essential to the performance of internal audits.*

    260   **Human Relations and Communications** — *Internal auditors should be skilled in dealing with people and in communicating effectively.*

    270   **Continuing Education** — *Internal auditors should maintain their technical competence through continuing education.*

    280   **Due Professional Care** — *Internal auditors should exercise due professional care in performing internal audits.*

300   **SCOPE OF WORK** — *THE SCOPE OF THE INTERNAL AUDIT SHOULD ENCOMPASS THE EXAMINATION AND EVALUATION OF THE ADEQUACY AND EFFECTIVENESS OF THE ORGANIZATION'S SYSTEM OF INTERNAL CONTROL AND THE QUALITY OF PERFORMANCE IN CARRYING OUT ASSIGNED RESPONSIBILITIES.*

    310   **Reliability and Integrity of Information** — *Internal auditors should review the reliability and integrity of financial and operating information and the means used to identify, measure, classify, and report such information.*

3

320 **Compliance with Policies, Plans, Procedures, Laws, and Regulations** — *Internal auditors should review the systems established to ensure compliance with those policies, plans, procedures, laws, and regulations which could have a significant impact on operations and reports and should determine whether the organization is in compliance.*

330 **Safeguarding of Assets** — *Internal auditors should review the means of safeguarding assets and, as appropriate, verify the existence of such assets.*

340 **Economical and Efficient Use of Resources** — *Internal auditors should appraise the economy and efficiency with which resources are employed.*

350 **Accomplishment of Established Objectives and Goals for Operations or Programs** — *Internal auditors should review operations or programs to ascertain whether results are consistent with established objectives and goals and whether the operations or programs are being carried out as planned.*

400 **PERFORMANCE OF AUDIT WORK** — *AUDIT WORK SHOULD INCLUDE PLANNING THE AUDIT, EXAMINING AND EVALUATING INFORMATION, COMMUNICATING RESULTS, AND FOLLOWING UP.*

410 **Planning the Audit** — *Internal auditors should plan each audit.*

420 **Examining and Evaluating Information** — *Internal auditors should collect, analyze, interpret, and document information to support audit results.*

430 **Communicating Results** — *Internal auditors should report the results of their audit work.*

440 **Following Up** — *Internal auditors should follow up to ascertain that appropriate action is taken on reported audit findings.*

500 **MANAGEMENT OF THE INTERNAL AUDITING DEPARTMENT** — *THE DIRECTOR OF INTERNAL AUDITING SHOULD PROPERLY MANAGE THE INTERNAL AUDITING DEPARTMENT.*

510 **Purpose, Authority, and Responsibility** — *The director of internal auditing should have a statement of purpose, authority, and responsibility for the internal auditing department.*

520 **Planning** — *The director of internal auditing should establish plans to carry out the responsibilities of the internal auditing department.*

530 **Policies and Procedures** — *The director of internal auditing should provide written policies and procedures to guide the audit staff.*

540 **Personnel Management and Development** — *The director of internal auditing should establish a program for selecting and developing the human resources of the internal auditing department.*

550 **External Auditors** — *The director of internal auditing should coordinate internal and external audit efforts.*

560 **Quality Assurance** — *The director of internal auditing should establish and maintain a quality assurance program to evaluate the operations of the internal auditing department.*

4

100   **INDEPENDENCE**

**INTERNAL AUDITORS SHOULD BE INDEPENDENT
OF THE ACTIVITIES THEY AUDIT.**

.01 Internal auditors are independent when they can carry out their work freely and objectively. Independence permits internal auditors to render the impartial and unbiased judgments essential to the proper conduct of audits. It is achieved through organizational status and objectivity.

110 **Organizational Status**

The organizational status of the internal auditing department should be sufficient to permit the accomplishment of its audit responsibilities.

.01 Internal auditors should have the support of management and of the board of directors so that they can gain the cooperation of auditees and perform their work free from interference.

.1 The director of the internal auditing department should be responsible to an individual in the organization with sufficient authority to promote independence and to ensure broad audit coverage, adequate consideration of audit reports, and appropriate action on audit recommendations.

.2 The director should have direct communication with the board. Regular communication with the board helps assure independence and provides a means for the board and the director to keep each other informed on matters of mutual interest.

.3 Independence is enhanced when the board concurs in the appointment or removal of the director of the internal auditing department.

.4 The purpose, authority, and responsibility of the internal auditing department should be defined in a formal written document (charter). The director should seek approval of the charter by management as well as acceptance by the board. The charter should (a) establish the department's position within the organization; (b) authorize access to records, personnel, and physical properties relevant to the performance of audits; and (c) define the scope of internal auditing activities.

.5 The director of internal auditing should submit annually to management for approval and to the board for its information a summary of the department's audit work schedule, staffing plan, and financial budget. The director should also submit all significant interim changes for approval and information. Audit work schedules, staffing plans, and financial budgets should inform management and the board of the scope of internal auditing work and of any limitations placed on that scope.

.6 The director of internal auditing should submit activity reports to management and to the board annually or more frequently as necessary. Activity reports should highlight significant audit findings and recommendations and should inform management and the board of any significant deviations from approved audit work schedules, staffing plans, and financial budgets, and the reasons for them.

120 **Objectivity**

Internal auditors should be objective in performing audits.

.01 Objectivity is an independent mental attitude which internal auditors should maintain in performing audits. Internal auditors are not to subordinate their judgment on audit matters to that of others.

.02 Objectivity requires internal auditors to perform audits in such a manner that they have an honest belief in their work product and that no significant quality compromises are made. Internal auditors are not to be placed in situations in which they feel unable to make objective professional judgments.

.1 Staff assignments should be made so that potential and actual conflicts of interest and bias are avoided. The director should periodically obtain from the audit staff information concerning potential conflicts of interest and bias.

.2 Internal auditors should report to the director any situations in which a conflict of interest or bias is present or may reasonably be inferred. The director should then reassign such auditors.

.3 Staff assignments of internal auditors should be rotated periodically whenever it is practicable to do so.

.4 Internal auditors should not assume operating responsibilities. But if on occasion management directs internal auditors to perform nonaudit work, it should be understood that they are not functioning as internal auditors. Moreover, objectivity is presumed to be impaired when internal auditors audit any activity for which they had authority or responsibility. This impairment should be considered when reporting audit results.

.5 Persons transferred to or temporarily engaged by the internal auditing department should not be assigned to audit those activities they previously performed until a reasonable period of time has elapsed. Such assignments are presumed to impair objectivity and should be considered when supervising the audit work and reporting audit results.

.6 The results of internal auditing work should be reviewed before the related audit report is released to provide reasonable assurance that the work was performed objectively.

.03 The internal auditor's objectivity is not adversely affected when the auditor recommends standards of control for systems or reviews procedures before they are implemented. Designing, installing, and operating systems are not audit functions. Also, the drafting of procedures for systems is not an audit function. Performing such activities is presumed to impair audit objectivity.

200   **PROFESSIONAL PROFICIENCY**
                                  INTERNAL AUDITS SHOULD BE PERFORMED WITH
                                  PROFICIENCY AND DUE PROFESSIONAL CARE.

.01 Professional proficiency is the responsibility of the internal auditing department and each internal auditor. The department should assign to each audit those persons who collectively possess the necessary knowledge, skills, and disciplines to conduct the audit properly.

The Internal Auditing Department
210 **Staffing**

The internal auditing department should provide assurance that the technical proficiency and educational background of internal auditors are appropriate for the audits to be performed.

.01 The director of internal auditing should establish suitable criteria of education and experience for filling internal auditing positions, giving due consideration to scope of work and level of responsibility.

.02 Reasonable assurance should be obtained as to each prospective auditor's qualifications and proficiency.

220 **Knowledge, Skills, and Disciplines**

The internal auditing department should possess or should obtain the knowledge, skills, and disciplines needed to carry out its audit responsibilities.

.01 The internal auditing staff should collectively possess the knowledge and skills essential to the practice of the profession within the organization. These attributes include proficiency in applying internal auditing standards, procedures, and techniques.

.02 The internal auditing department should have employees or use consultants who are qualified in such disciplines as accounting, economics, finance, statistics, electronic data processing, engineering, taxation, and law as needed to meet audit responsibilities. Each member of the department, however, need not be qualified in all of these disciplines.

230 **Supervision**

The internal auditing department should provide assurance that internal audits are properly supervised.

.01 The director of internal auditing is responsible for providing appropriate audit supervision. Supervision is a continuing process, beginning with planning and ending with the conclusion of the audit assignment.

.02 Supervision includes:

.1 Providing suitable instructions to subordinates at the outset of the audit and approving the audit program

.2 Seeing that the approved audit program is carried out unless deviations are both justified and authorized

.3 Determining that audit working papers adequately support the audit findings, conclusions, and reports

.4 Making sure that audit reports are accurate, objective, clear, concise, constructive, and timely

.5 Determining that audit objectives are being met

.03 Appropriate evidence of supervision should be documented and retained.

.04 The extent of supervision required will depend on the proficiency of the internal auditors and the difficulty of the audit assignment.

.05 All internal auditing assignments, whether performed by or for the internal auditing department, remain the responsibility of its director.

The Internal Auditor
240 **Compliance with Standards of Conduct**

Internal auditors should comply with professional standards of conduct.

.01 The *Code of Ethics* of The Institute of Internal Auditors sets forth standards of conduct and provides a basis for enforcement among its members. The *Code* calls for high standards of honesty, objectivity, diligence, and loyalty to which internal auditors should conform.

250 **Knowledge, Skills, and Disciplines**

Internal auditors should possess the knowledge, skills, and disciplines essential to the performance of internal audits.

.01 Each internal auditor should possess certain knowledge and skills as follows:

.1 Proficiency in applying internal auditing standards, procedures, and techniques is required in performing internal audits. Proficiency means the ability to apply knowledge to situations likely to be encountered and to deal with them without extensive recourse to technical research and assistance.

.2 Proficiency in accounting principles and techniques is required of auditors who work extensively with financial records and reports.

.3 An understanding of management principles is required to recognize and evaluate the materiality and significance of deviations from good business practice. An understanding means the ability to apply broad knowledge to situations likely to be encountered, to recognize significant deviations, and to be able to carry out the research necessary to arrive at reasonable solutions.

.4 An appreciation is required of the fundamentals of such subjects as accounting, economics, commercial law, taxation, finance, quantitative methods, and computerized information systems. An appreciation means the ability to recognize the existence of problems or potential problems and to determine the further research to be undertaken or the assistance to be obtained.

260 **Human Relations and Communications**

Internal auditors should be skilled in dealing with people and in communicating effectively.

.01 Internal auditors should understand human relations and maintain satisfactory relationships with auditees.

.02 Internal auditors should be skilled in oral and written communications so that they can clearly and effectively convey such matters

as audit objectives, evaluations, conclusions, and recommendations.

270 Continuing Education

Internal auditors should maintain their technical competence through continuing education.

.01 Internal auditors are responsible for continuing their education in order to maintain their proficiency. They should keep informed about improvements and current developments in internal auditing standards, procedures, and techniques. Continuing education may be obtained through membership and participation in professional societies; attendance at conferences, seminars, college courses, and in-house training programs; and participation in research projects.

280 Due Professional Care

Internal Auditors should exercise due professional care in performing internal audits.

.01 Due professional care calls for the application of the care and skill expected of a reasonably prudent and competent internal auditor in the same or similar circumstances. Professional care should, therefore, be appropriate to the complexities of the audit being performed. In exercising due professional care, internal auditors should be alert to the possibility of intentional wrongdoing, errors and omissions, inefficiency, waste, ineffectiveness, and conflicts of interest. They should also be alert to those conditions and activities where irregularities are most likely to occur. In addition, they should identify inadequate controls and recommend improvements to promote compliance with acceptable procedures and practices.

.02 Due care implies reasonable care and competence, not infallibility or extraordinary performance. Due care requires the auditor to conduct examinations and verifications to a reasonable extent, but does not require detailed audits of all transactions. Accordingly, the internal auditor cannot give absolute assurance that noncompliance or irregularities do not exist. Nevertheless, the possibility of material irregularities or noncompliance should be considered whenever the internal auditor undertakes an internal auditing assignment.

.03 When an internal auditor suspects wrongdoing, the appropriate authorities within the organization should be informed. The internal auditor may recommend whatever investigation is considered necessary in the circumstances. Thereafter, the auditor should follow up to see that the internal auditing department's responsibilities have been met.

.04 Exercising due professional care means using reasonable audit skill and judgment in performing the audit. To this end, the internal auditor should consider:

.1 The extent of audit work needed to achieve audit objectives
.2 The relative materiality or significance of matters to which audit procedures are applied
.3 The adequacy and effectiveness of internal controls
.4 The cost of auditing in relation to potential benefits

200-3

.05 Due professional care includes evaluating established operating standards and determining whether those standards are acceptable and are being met. When such standards are vague, authoritative interpretations should be sought. If internal auditors are required to interpret or select operating standards, they should seek agreement with auditees as to the standards needed to measure operating performance.

300   SCOPE OF WORK

THE SCOPE OF THE INTERNAL AUDIT SHOULD ENCOMPASS
THE EXAMINATION AND EVALUATION OF THE ADEQUACY
AND EFFECTIVENESS OF THE ORGANIZATION'S SYSTEM OF
INTERNAL CONTROL AND THE QUALITY OF PERFORMANCE
IN CARRYING OUT ASSIGNED RESPONSIBILITIES.

.01   The scope of internal auditing work, as specified in this standard, encompasses what audit work should be performed. It is recognized, however, that management and the board of directors provide general direction as to the scope of work and the activities to be audited.

.02   The purpose of the review for adequacy of the system of internal control is to ascertain whether the system established provides reasonable assurance that the organization's objectives and goals will be met efficiently and economically.

.03   The purpose of the review for effectiveness of the system of internal control is to ascertain whether the system is functioning as intended.

.04   The purpose of the review for quality of performance is to ascertain whether the organization's objectives and goals have been achieved.

.05   The primary objectives of internal control are to ensure:

   .1   The reliability and integrity of information
   .2   Compliance with policies, plans, procedures, laws, and regulations
   .3   The safeguarding of assets
   .4   The economical and efficient use of resources
   .5   The accomplishment of established objectives and goals for operations or programs

310   Reliability and Integrity of Information

Internal auditors should review the reliability and integrity of financial and operating information and the means used to identify, measure, classify, and report such information.

.01   Information systems provide data for decision making, control, and compliance with external requirements. Therefore, internal auditors should examine information systems and, as appropriate, ascertain whether:

   .1   Financial and operating records and reports contain accurate, reliable, timely, complete, and useful information.
   .2   Controls over record keeping and reporting are adequate and effective.

320   Compliance with Policies, Plans, Procedures, Laws and Regulations

Internal auditors should review the systems established to ensure compliance with those policies, plans, procedures, laws, and regulations which could have a significant impact on operations and reports, and should determine whether the organization is in compliance.

.01   Management is responsible for establishing the systems designed to ensure compliance with such requirements as policies, plans, procedures, and applicable laws and regulations. Internal auditors are responsible for determining whether the systems are adequate and effective and whether the activities audited are complying with the appropriate requirements.

330 Safeguarding of Assets

Internal auditors should review the means of safeguarding assets and, as appropriate, verify the existence of such assets.

.01 Internal auditors should review the means used to safeguard assets from various types of losses such as those resulting from theft, fire, improper or illegal activities, and exposure to the elements.

.02 Internal auditors, when verifying the existence of assets, should use appropriate audit procedures.

340 Economical and Efficient Use of Resources

Internal auditors should appraise the economy and efficiency with which resources are employed.

.01 Management is responsible for setting operating standards to measure an activity's economical and efficient use of resources. Internal auditors are responsible for determining whether:

.1 Operating standards have been established for measuring economy and efficiency.

.2 Established operating standards are understood and are being met.

.3 Deviations from operating standards are identified, analyzed, and communicated to those responsible for corrective action.

.4 Corrective action has been taken.

.02 Audits related to the economical and efficient use of resources should identify such conditions as:

.1 Underutilized facilities

.2 Nonproductive work

.3 Procedures which are not cost justified

.4 Overstaffing or understaffing

350 Accomplishment of Established Objectives and Goals for Operations or Programs

Internal auditors should review operations or programs to ascertain whether results are consistent with established objectives and goals and whether the operations or programs are being carried out as planned.

.01 Management is responsible for establishing operating or program objectives and goals, developing and implementing control procedures, and accomplishing desired operating or program results. Internal auditors should ascertain whether such objectives and goals conform with those of the organization and whether they are being met.

.02 Internal auditors can provide assistance to managers who are developing objectives, goals, and systems by determining whether the underlying assumptions are appropriate; whether accurate, current, and relevant information is being used; and whether suitable controls have been incorporated into the operations or programs.

400   **PERFORMANCE OF AUDIT WORK**

*AUDIT WORK SHOULD INCLUDE PLANNING THE AUDIT,
EXAMINING AND EVALUATING INFORMATION,
COMMUNICATING RESULTS, AND FOLLOWING UP.*

   .01   The internal auditor is responsible for planning and conducting the audit assignment, subject to supervisory review and approval.

410 **Planning the Audit**
    Internal auditors should plan each audit.
    .01   Planning should be documented and should include:
       .1 Establishing audit objectives and scope of work
       .2 Obtaining background information about the activities to be audited
       .3 Determining the resources necessary to perform the audit
       .4 Communicating with all who need to know about the audit
       .5 Performing, as appropriate, an on-site survey to become familiar with the activities and controls to be audited, to identify areas for audit emphasis, and to invite auditee comments and suggestions
       .6 Writing the audit program
       .7 Determining how, when, and to whom audit results will be communicated
       .8 Obtaining approval of the audit work plan

420 **Examining and Evaluating Information**
    Internal auditors should collect, analyze, interpret, and document information to support audit results.
    .01   The process of examining and evaluating information is as follows:
       .1 Information should be collected on all matters related to the audit objectives and scope of work.
       .2 Information should be sufficient, competent, relevant, and useful to provide a sound basis for audit findings and recommendations.

          Sufficient information is factual, adequate, and convincing so that a prudent, informed person would reach the same conclusions as the auditor.
          Competent information is reliable and the best attainable through the use of appropriate audit techniques.
          Relevant information supports audit findings and recommendations and is consistent with the objectives for the audit.
          Useful information helps the organization meet its goals.
       .3 Audit procedures, including the testing and sampling techniques employed, should be selected in advance, where practicable, and expanded or altered if circumstances warrant.
       .4 The process of collecting, analyzing, interpreting, and documenting information should be supervised to provide

reasonable assurance that the auditor's objectivity is maintained and that audit goals are met.

.5 Working papers that document the audit should be prepared by the auditor and reviewed by management of the internal auditing department. These papers should record the information obtained and the analyses made and should support the bases for the findings and recommendations to be reported.

430 Communicating Results

Internal auditors should report the results of their audit work.

.1 A signed, written report should be issued after the audit examination is completed. Interim reports may be written or oral and may be transmitted formally or informally.

.2 The internal auditor should discuss conclusions and recommendations at appropriate levels of management before issuing final written reports.

.3 Reports should be objective, clear, concise, constructive, and timely.

.4 Reports should present the purpose, scope, and results of the audit; and, where appropriate, reports should contain an expression of the auditor's opinion.

.5 Reports may include recommendations for potential improvements and acknowledge satisfactory performance and corrective action.

.6 The auditee's views about audit conclusions or recommendations may be included in the audit report.

.7 The director of internal auditing or designee should review and approve the final audit report before issuance and should decide to whom the report will be distributed.

440 Following Up

Internal auditors should follow up to ascertain that appropriate action is taken on reported audit findings.

.01 Internal auditing should determine that corrective action was taken and is achieving the desired results, or that management or the board has assumed the risk of not taking corrective action on reported findings.

500   MANAGEMENT OF THE INTERNAL AUDITING DEPARTMENT

THE DIRECTOR OF INTERNAL AUDITING SHOULD
PROPERLY MANAGE THE INTERNAL AUDITING DEPARTMENT.

.01   The director of internal auditing is responsible for properly managing the department so that:

.1   Audit work fulfills the general purposes and responsibilities approved by management and accepted by the board.

.2   Resources of the internal auditing department are efficiently and effectively employed.

.3   Audit work conforms to the *Standards for the Professional Practice of Internal Auditing.*

510   Purpose, Authority, and Responsibility

The director of internal auditing should have a statement of purpose, authority, and responsibility for the internal auditing department.

.01   The director of internal auditing is responsible for seeking the approval of management and the acceptance by the board of a formal written document (charter) for the internal auditing department.

520   Planning

The director of internal auditing should establish plans to carry out the responsibilities of the internal auditing department.

.01   These plans should be consistent with the internal auditing department's charter and with the goals of the organization.

.02   The planning process involves establishing:

.1   Goals

.2   Audit work schedules

.3   Staffing plans and financial budgets

.4   Activity reports

.03   The *goals* of the internal auditing department should be capable of being accomplished within specified operating plans and budgets and, to the extent possible, should be measurable. They should be accompanied by measurement criteria and targeted dates of accomplishment.

.04   *Audit work schedules* should include (a) what activities are to be audited; (b) when they will be audited; and (c) the estimated time required, taking into account the scope of the audit work planned and the nature and extent of audit work performed by others. Matters to be considered in establishing audit work schedule priorities should include (a) the date and results of the last audit; (b) financial exposure; (c) potential loss and risk; (d) requests by management; (e) major changes in operations, programs, systems, and controls; (f) opportunities to achieve operating benefits; and (g) changes to and capabilities of the audit staff. The work schedules should be sufficiently flexible to cover unanticipated demands on the internal auditing department.

.05   *Staffing plans and financial budgets*, including the number of auditors and the knowledge, skills, and disciplines required to perform their work, should be determined from audit work schedules, administrative activities, education and training requirements, and audit research and development efforts.

.06   *Activity reports* should be submitted periodically to management and to the board. These reports should compare (a) performance with the department's goals and audit work schedules and (b) expenditures with financial budgets. They should explain the reasons for major variances and indicate any action taken or needed.

530   Policies and Procedures

The director of internal auditing should provide written policies and procedures to guide the audit staff.

.01   The form and content of written policies and procedures should be appropriate to the size and structure of the internal auditing department and the complexity of its work. Formal administrative and technical audit manuals may not be needed by all internal auditing departments. A small internal auditing department may be managed informally. Its audit staff may be directed and controlled through daily, close supervision and written memoranda. In a large internal auditing department, more formal and comprehensive policies and procedures are essential to guide the audit staff in the consistent compliance with the department's standards of performance.

540   Personnel Management and Development

The director of internal auditing should establish a program for selecting and developing the human resources of the internal auditing department.

.01   The program should provide for:

.1   Developing written job descriptions for each level of the audit staff

.2   Selecting qualified and competent individuals

.3   Training and providing continuing educational opportunities for each internal auditor

.4   Appraising each internal auditor's performance at least annually

.5   Providing counsel to internal auditors on their performance and professional development

550   External Auditors

The director of internal auditing should coordinate internal and external audit efforts.

.01   The internal and external audit work should be coordinated to ensure adequate audit coverage and to minimize duplicate efforts.

.02   Coordination of audit efforts involves:

.1   Periodic meetings to discuss matters of mutual interest

.2   Access to each other's audit programs and working papers

.3   Exchange of audit reports and management letters

.4   Common understanding of audit techniques, methods, and terminology

560   Quality Assurance

The director of internal auditing should establish and maintain a quality

assurance program to evaluate the operations of the internal auditing department.

.01   The purpose of this program is to provide reasonable assurance that audit work conforms with these *Standards*, the internal auditing department's charter, and other applicable standards. A quality assurance program should include the following elements:

.1   Supervision

.2   Internal reviews

.3   External reviews

.02   *Supervision* of the work of the internal auditors should be carried out continually to assure conformance with internal auditing standards, departmental policies, and audit programs.

.03   *Internal reviews* should be performed periodically by members of the internal auditing staff to appraise the quality of the audit work performed. These reviews should be performed in the same manner as any other internal audit.

.04   *External reviews* of the internal auditing department should be performed to appraise the quality of the department's operations. These reviews should be performed by qualified persons who are independent of the organization and who do not have either a real or an apparent conflict of interest. Such reviews should be conducted at least once every three years. On completion of the review, a formal, written report should be issued. The report should express an opinion as to the department's compliance with the *Standards for the Professional Practice of Internal Auditing* and, as appropriate, should include recommendations for improvement.

Statement on Internal Auditing Standards No. 1, Control: Concepts And Responsibilities

The Institute of Internal Auditors

**Statement on Internal Auditing Standards
No. 1 — July 1983**

CONTROL:
CONCEPTS AND
RESPONSIBILITIES

**Issued by
The Professional Standards and
Responsibilities Committee
THE INSTITUTE OF INTERNAL AUDITORS**
249 Maitland Avenue, P.O. Box 1119
Altamonte Springs, Florida 32701

Statements on Internal Auditing Standards are issued by the Professional Standards and Responsibilities Committee, the senior technical committee designated by The Institute of Internal Auditors, Inc., to issue pronouncements on auditing standards. These statements are authoritative interpretations of the *Standards for the Professional Practice of Internal Auditing.*

Organizations, internal auditing departments, directors of internal auditing, and internal auditors should strive to comply with the *Standards.* The implementation of the *Standards* and these related statements will be governed by the environment in which the internal auditing department carries out its assigned responsibilities. The adoption and implementation of the *Standards* and related statements will assist internal auditing professionals in accomplishing their responsibilities.

ISBN 0-89413-134-6
84282 MAY85
First Printing

Foreword

The Institute of Internal Auditors issued its *Standards for the Professional Practice of Internal Auditing* in 1978 "to serve the entire profession in all types of businesses, in various levels of government, and in all other organizations where internal auditors are found . . . to represent the practice of internal auditing as it should be . . . . " Experience and success have demonstrated the credibility of the basic principles promoted in the *Standards.*

The *Standards* states that internal auditing is to assist members of the organization in the effective discharge of their responsibilities by providing them with information regarding control. However, differences of opinion have existed regarding the nature of control and the roles of the participants in its establishment, maintenance, and evaluation.

This statement provides guidance on these issues by focusing on guidelines 300.02 and 300.03 and providing three additional guidelines.

Summary

This statement provides guidance to internal auditors on the nature of control and the roles of the participants in its establishment, maintenance, and evaluation. Major conclusions include:

- A control is any action taken by management to enhance the likelihood that established objectives and goals will be achieved.
- Control results from management's planning, organizing, and directing.
- The many variants of the term control (for example, administrative control, management control, internal control) can be incorporated within the generic term.
- The overall system of control is conceptual in nature. It is the integrated collection of systems used by an organization to achieve its objectives and goals.
- Management plans, organizes, and directs in such a fashion as to provide reasonable assurance that established objectives and goals will be achieved.
- Internal auditing examines and evaluates the planning, organizing, and directing processes to determine whether reasonable assurance exists that objectives and goals will be achieved. All systems, processes, operations, functions, and activities within the organization are subject to internal auditing's evaluations. Such evaluations, in the aggregrate, provide information to appraise the overall system of control.

Contents

Background

Controls were defined early in the evolutionary process of organizational management as mechanisms or practices used to prevent or detect unauthorized activity. The purpose of controls was later expanded to include the concept of getting things done. Current usage leans toward any effort made to enhance the probability of accomplishing objectives.

Examples of "controls" abound. A partial list relating to protection of cash highlights the diversity of opinions: a safe, a locked safe, a requirement to lock cash in a safe, a procedure directing the storage of cash in a locked safe, restricted access to a safe and its contents, assignment of responsibility for protecting cash, authorizing cash disbursements, a record of cash disbursements and receipts, and unannounced cash counts. This diversity should not be construed as indicating a problem; in fact, the opposite may very well be true. All of these may be regarded as controls, depending on circumstances and the specific activity being reviewed.

As illustrated above, control is used as a noun, a verb, and an adjective; the term is used to describe a physical device, a method of performing an activity, a step in a process, a means to an end, and an end in itself.

Differences of opinion exist regarding the term "system of internal control." This term was used in a 1949 American Institute of Certified Public Accountants study titled *Internal Control — Elements of a Coordinated System and Its Importance to Management and the Independent Public Accountants*. From the external auditor's viewpoint, the importance of the system of internal control was "to establish a basis for reliance thereon in determining the nature, extent, and timing of audit tests to be applied in the examination of the financial statement." Since then, the term has been used by auditors to describe the set of controls within a specific system, operation, or department; it has also been used in the context of the organization's system of internal control.

It is clear that management and internal auditors are interested in both specific controls in specific systems and in overall control. It is generally agreed that their scope of interest (and responsibilities) extends beyond that of external auditors. To clearly delineate the difference between the broader control concerns of management and internal auditors and the narrower control concerns of external auditors, the broader concept of control will hereafter be referred to as the "overall system of control."

Differences of opinion exist regarding the specific nature of management's role in the establishment, maintenance, and evaluation of control. For example, it is commonly stated that management plans, organizes, directs, and controls. Thus, at least conceptually, controlling has been viewed as a separate activity. However, specific actions taken by management to enhance the likelihood that objectives and goals will be achieved, such as the setting of standards, the monitoring for compliance to those standards, and the related feedback to those in a position to take corrective action, are ongoing and fully integrated with planning, organizing, and directing activities. Therefore, controlling can be viewed as a part of planning, organizing, and directing rather than as a separate activity.

There is also diversity of opinion as to how much of the management process is subject to internal auditing's review. Since such diversity of opinion regarding the nature of control and roles played by the participants may cause or contribute to less than optimum performance by internal auditors, the following concepts were formulated to serve the profession. These concepts guide the interpretations contained in the remainder of this statement:

● Management plans, organizes, and directs in such a manner as to provide reasonable assurance that established objectives and goals will be achieved.

- Internal auditors examine and evaluate the planning, organizing, and directing processes to determine whether reasonable assurance exists that objectives and goals will be achieved. Thus, all systems, processes, operations, functions, and activities within the organization are subject to internal auditing's evaluations.

- External auditors evaluate "internal accounting control" within the parameters stated in their **Generally Accepted Auditing Standards.**

- Audit committees have guidance and oversight responsibilities related to internal and external auditing's performance.

- Boards of directors have guidance and oversight responsibilities related to subordinate management's performance.

Note: As used in this statement, the term "management" includes anyone in an organization with responsibilities for setting and/or achieving objectives.

Interpretations of Existing Guidelines

Guideline 300.02

Guideline 300.02 states the purpose of the review for adequacy of the system of internal control is to ascertain whether the system established provides reasonable assurance that the organization's objectives and goals will be met efficiently and economically.

.1 Objectives are the broadest statements of what the organization chooses to accomplish. The establishment of objectives precedes the selection of goals and the design, implementation, and maintenance of systems whose purpose is to meet the organization's objectives and goals.

.2 Goals are specific objectives of specific systems and may be otherwise referred to as operating or program objectives or goals, operating standards, performance levels, targets, or expected results. Goals should be identified for each system. They should be clearly defined, measurable, attainable, and consistent with established broader objectives; and they should explicitly recognize the risks associated with not achieving those objectives.

.3 A system (process, operation, function, or activity) is an arrangement, a set, or a collection of concepts, parts, activities, and/or people that are connected or interrelated to achieve objectives and goals. (This definition applies to both manual and automated systems.) A system may also be a collection of subsystems operating together for a common objective or goal.

.4 Adequate control is present if management has planned

and organized (designed) in a manner which provides reasonable assurance that the organization's objectives and goals will be achieved efficiently and economically. The system-design process begins with the establishment of objectives and goals. This is followed by connecting or interrelating concepts, parts, activities, and/or people in such a manner as to operate together to achieve the established objectives and goals. If system design is properly performed, planned activities should be executed as designed and expected results should be attained.

.5 Reasonable assurance is provided when cost-effective actions are taken to restrict deviations to a tolerable level. This implies, for example, that material errors and improper or illegal acts will be prevented or detected and corrected within a timely period by employees in the normal course of performing their assigned duties. The cost-benefit relationship is considered by management during the design of systems. The potential loss associated with any exposure or risk is weighed against the cost to control it.

.6 Efficient performance accomplishes objectives and goals in an accurate and timely fashion with minimal use of resources.

.7 Economical performance accomplishes objectives and goals at a cost commensurate with the risk. The term efficient incorporates the concept of economical performance.

Guideline 300.03

Guideline 300.03 states the purpose of the review for effectiveness of the system of internal control is to ascertain whether the system is functioning as intended.

.1 Effective control is present when management directs systems in such a manner as to provide reasonable assurance that the organization's objectives and goals will be achieved.

.2 Directing involves — in addition to accomplishing objectives and planned activities — authorizing and monitoring performance, periodically comparing actual with planned performance, and documenting these activities to provide additional assurance that systems operate as planned.

.2.1 Authorizing includes initiating or granting permission to perform activities or transactions. Authorization implies that the authorizing authority has verified and validated that the activity or transaction conforms with established policies and procedures.

.2.2 Monitoring encompasses supervising, observing, and testing activities and appropriately reporting to responsible individuals. Monitoring provides an ongoing verification of progress toward achievement of objectives and goals.

.2.3 Periodic comparison of actual to planned performance enhances the likelihood that activities occur as planned.

.2.4 Documenting provides evidence of the exercise of authority and responsibility; compliance with policies, procedures, and standards of performance; supervising, observing, and testing activities; and verification of planned performance.

New Guidelines

Guideline 300.06 — Concepts of Control

Guideline 300.06: A control is any action taken by management to enhance the likelihood that established objectives and goals will be achieved. Management plans, organizes, and directs the performance of sufficient actions to provide reasonable assurance that objectives and goals will be achieved. Thus, control is the result of proper planning, organizing, and directing by management.

.1 Controls may be preventive (to deter undesirable events from occurring), detective (to detect and correct undesirable events which have occurred), or directive (to cause or encourage a desirable event to occur).

.2 All variants of the term control (administrative control, internal accounting control, internal control, management control, operational control, output control, preventive control, etc.) can be incorporated within the generic term. These variants differ primarily in terms of the objectives to be achieved. Since these variants are useful in describing specific control applications, participants in the control process should be familiar with the terms as well as their applications. However, the methodology followed by internal auditing in evaluating such controls is consistent for all of the variants.

.3 The variant "internal control" came into general use to distinguish controls within an organization from those existing externally to the organization (such as laws). Since internal auditors operate within an organization and, among other responsibilities, evaluate management's response to external stimuli (such as laws), no such distinction between internal and external controls is necessary. Also, from the organization's viewpoint, internal controls are all activities which attempt to ensure the accomplishment of the organization's objectives and goals. For the purpose of this statement, internal control is considered synonymous with control within the organization.

.4 The overall system of control is conceptual in nature. It is the integrated collection of controlled systems used by an organization to achieve its objectives and goals.

Guideline 300.07 — Management Responsibilities

Guideline 300.07: Management plans, organizes, and directs in such a fashion as to provide reasonable assurance that established objectives and goals will be achieved.

.1 Planning and organizing involve the establishment of objectives and goals and the use of such tools as organization charts, flowcharts, procedures, records, and reports to establish the flow of data and the responsibilities of individuals for performing activities, establishing information trails, and setting standards of performance.

.2 Directing involves certain activities to provide additional assurance that systems operate as planned. These activities include authorizing and monitoring performance, periodically comparing actual with planned performance, and appropriately documenting these activities.

.3 Management ensures that its objectives and goals remain appropriate and that its systems remain current. Therefore, management periodically reviews its objectives and goals and modifies its systems to accommodate changes in internal and external conditions.

.4 Management establishes and maintains an environment that fosters control.

Guideline 300.08 — Internal Auditing Responsibilities

Guideline 300.08: Internal auditing examines and evaluates the planning, organizing, and directing processes to determine whether reasonable assurance exists that objectives and goals will be achieved. Such evaluations, in the aggregate, provide information to appraise the overall system of control.

.1 All systems, processes, operations, functions, and activities within the organization are subject to internal auditing's evaluations.

.2 Internal auditing's evaluations should encompass whether reasonable assurance exists that:

    a. objectives and goals have been established;

    b. authorizing, monitoring, and periodic comparison activities have been planned, performed, and documented as necessary to attain objectives and goals; and

    c. planned results have been achieved (objectives and goals have been accomplished).

.3 Internal auditing performs evaluations at specific points in time but should be alert to actual or potential changes in conditions which affect the ability to provide assurance from a forward-looking perspective. In those cases, internal auditing should address the risk that performance may deteriorate.

Acknowledgments

We wish to acknowledge the contributions to the literature on control made by various professional organizations, internal and external auditors, members of academe, firms, and individuals. We especially want to thank those experts in the field who voluntarily contributed their time and effort in reviewing the preliminary work and related drafts of this document.

Task Force on Control

William P. Viggiano, CISA, Chairperson
Michael J. Barrett, DBA, CIA
George Cirasuolo, CIA
William E. Dolan, CPA
Richard Allan White, CIA, CPA, CMA, CAM

Professional Standards and Responsibilities Committee: 1982-83

William J. Duane, Jr., CPA, Chairperson
Herbert D. Barbour, CIA, CPA
Donald R. Baumunk
William E. Dolan, CPA
Ellis J. Glenn, CIA
William F. Henderson, Jr.
Odd Hunsbedt, CIA, CPA
Herbert D. Miller, CPA
Richard M. Morris, III, CIA, CBA
Donald J. Nelson, CIA
Stanley E. Petrie, CIA, CPA
S.A. Murali Prasad
John G. Sayers, CIA, FCA
Thomas D. Trobaugh, CIA
William P. Viggiano, CISA
Graeme Ward, FIIA, FCCA, IPFA
H.C. Warner, CIA, CPA, CISA
John K. Watsen, CIA, CPA
John J. Willingham, PhD, CPA

Statement on Internal Auditing Standards No. 2, Communicating Results

The Institute of Internal Auditors

Statement on Internal Auditing Standards
No. 2 — July 1983

COMMUNICATING
RESULTS

Issued by
The Professional Standards and
Responsibilities Committee
THE INSTITUTE OF INTERNAL AUDITORS

The Institute of Internal Auditors is an international association dedicated to the continuing professional development of the individual internal auditor and the internal auditing profession. Founded in 1941, it now serves more than 28,000 members through 175 chapters and 102 countries.

The Institute of Internal Auditors

Statement on Internal Auditing Standards
No. 2 — July 1983

COMMUNICATING
RESULTS

Issued by
The Professional Standards and
Responsibilities Committee
THE INSTITUTE OF INTERNAL AUDITORS
249 Maitland Avenue, P.O. Box 1119
Altamonte Springs, Florida 32701

Statements on Internal Auditing Standards are issued by the Professional Standards and Responsibilities Committee, the senior technical committee designated by The Institute of Internal Auditors, Inc., to issue pronouncements on auditing standards. These statements are authoritative interpretations of the *Standards for the Professional Practice of Internal Auditing.*

Organizations, internal auditing departments, directors of internal auditing, and internal auditors should strive to comply with the *Standards.* The implementation of the *Standards* and these related statements will be governed by the environment in which the internal auditing department carries out its assigned responsibilities. The adoption and implementation of the *Standards* and related statements will assist internal auditing professionals in accomplishing their responsibilities.

ISBN 0-89413-135-4
85325 MAY85
First Printing

Foreword

The Institute of Internal Auditors issued its *Standards for the Professional Practice of Internal Audting* in 1978 "to serve the entire profession in all types of businesses, in various levels of government, and in all other organizations where internal auditors are found . . . to represent the practice of internal auditing as it should be . . . ." Experience and success have demonstrated the credibility of the basic principles promoted in the *Standards.*

The *Standards* establishes a basis for the guidance and measurement of internal auditing performance. For Communicating Results, this basis is delineated in the *Standards* by seven guidelines related to the types, contents, and attributes of audit reports. This statement interprets guidelines 430.01 through 430.07.

Summary

This statement provides guidance to internal auditors in communicating audit results in the form of oral and written reports.

It includes interpretations of Standard 430 (Communicating Results) related to types, contents, and attributes of audit reports; discussion of findings, conclusions, and recommendations with management; and audit-report approval and distribution.

CONTENTS

Interpretations

Guideline 430.01

Guideline 430.01 states: A signed, written report should be issued after the audit examination is completed. Interim reports may be written or oral and may be transmitted formally or informally.

.1 Interim reports may be used to communicate information which requires immediate attention, to communicate a change in audit scope for the activity under review, or to keep management informed of audit progress when audits extend over a long period. The use of interim reports does not diminish or eliminate the need for a final report.

.2 Summary reports highlighting audit results may be appropriate for levels of management above the head of the audited unit. They may be issued separately from or in conjunction with the final report.

Guideline 430.02

Guideline 430.02 states: The internal auditor should discuss conclusions and recommendations at appropriate levels of management before issuing final written reports.

.1 Discussion of conclusions and recommendations is usually accomplished during the course of the audit and/or at postaudit meetings (exit interviews). Another technique is the review of draft audit reports by the head of each audited unit. These discussions and reviews help ensure that there have been no misunderstandings or misinterpretations of fact by providing the opportunity for the auditee to clarify specific items and to express views of the findings, conclusions, and recommendations.

.2 Although the level of participants in the discussions and reviews may vary by organizations and by the nature of the report, they will generally include those individuals who are knowledgeable of detailed operations and those who can authorize the implementation of corrective action.

Guideline 430.03

Guideline 430.03 states: Reports should be objective, clear, concise, constructive, and timely.

.1 Objective reports are factual, unbiased, and free from distortion. Findings, conclusions, and recommendations should be included without prejudice.

.2 Clear reports are easily understood and logical. Clarity can be improved by avoiding unnecessary technical language and providing sufficient supportive information.

.3 Concise reports are to the point and avoid unnecessary detail. They express thoughts completely in the fewest possible words.

.4 Constructive reports are those which, as a result of their content and tone, help the auditee and the organization and lead to improvements where needed.

.5 Timely reports are those which are issued without undue delay and enable prompt effective action.

Guideline 430.04

Guideline 430.04 states: Reports should present the purpose, scope, and results of the audit; and, where appropriate, reports should contain an expression of the auditor's opinion.

.1 Although audit-report format and content may vary by organization or type of audit, they should contain, at a minimum, the purpose, scope, and results of the audit.

.2   Audit reports may include background information and summaries. Background information may identify the organizational units and functions reviewed and provide relevant explanatory information. They may also include the status of findings, conclusions, and recommendations from prior reports. There may also be an indication of whether the report covers a scheduled audit or the response to a request. Summaries, if included, should be balanced representations of the audit-report content.

.3   Purpose statements should describe the audit objectives and may, where necessary, inform the reader why the audit was conducted and what it was expected to achieve.

.4   Scope statements should identify the audited activities and include, where appropriate, supportive information such as time period audited. Related activities not audited should be identified if necessary to delineate the boundaries of the audit. The nature and extent of auditing performed also should be described.

.5   Results may include findings, conclusions (opinions), and recommendations.

.6   Findings are pertinent statements of fact. Those findings which are necessary to support or prevent misunderstanding of the internal auditor's conclusions and recommendations should be included in the final audit report. Less significant information or findings may be communicated orally or through informal correspondence.

Audit findings emerge by a process of comparing "what should be" with "what is." Whether or not there is a difference, the internal auditor has a foundation on which to build the report. When conditions meet the criteria, acknowledgment in the audit report of satisfactory performance may be appropriate. Findings should be based on the following attributes:

Criteria: The standards, measures, or expectations

used in making an evaluation and/or verification (what *should* exist).

Condition: The factual evidence which the internal auditor found in the course of the examination (what *does* exist.

If there is a difference between the expected and actual conditions, then:

Cause: The reason for the difference between the expected and actual conditions (*why* the difference exists).

Effect: The risk or exposure the auditee organization and/or others encounter because the condition is not the same as the criteria (the *impact* of the difference).

The reported finding may also include recommendations, auditee accomplishments, and supportive information if not included elsewhere.

.7 Conclusions (opinions) are the internal auditor's evaluations of the effects of the findings on the activities reviewed. They usually put the findings in perspective based upon their overall implications. Audit conclusions, if included in the audit report, should be clearly identified as such. Conclusions may encompass the entire scope of an audit or specific aspects. They may cover but are not limited to whether operating or program objectives and goals conform with those of the organization, whether the organization's objectives and goals are being met, and whether the activity under review is functioning as intended.

Guideline 430.05

Guideline 430.05 states: Reports may include recommendations for potential improvements and acknowledge satisfactory performance and corrective action.

.1 Recommendations are based on the internal auditor's findings and conclusions. They call for action to correct existing conditions or improve operations. Recommendations may suggest approaches to correcting or enhancing performance as a guide for management in achieving desired results. Recommendations may be general or specific. For example, under some circumstances, it may be desirable to recommend a general course of action and specific suggestions for implementation. In other circumstances, it may be appropriate only to suggest further investigation or study.

.2 Auditee accomplishments, in terms of improvements since the last audit or the establishment of a well-controlled operation, may be included in the audit report. This information may be necessary to fairly represent the existing conditions and to provide a proper perspective and appropriate balance to the audit report.

Guideline 430.06

Guideline 430.06 states: The auditee's views about audit conclusions or recommendations may be included in the audit report.

.1 As part of the internal auditor's discussions with the auditee, the internal auditor should try to obtain agreement on the results of the audit and on a plan of action to improve operations, as needed. If the internal auditor and auditee disagree about the audit results, the audit report may state both positions and the reasons for the disagreement. The auditee's written comments may be included as an appendix to the audit report. Alternatively, the auditee's views may be presented in the body of the report or in a cover letter.

Guideline 430.07

Guideline 430.07 states: The director of internal auditing or designee should review and approve the final audit report before issuance and should decide to whom the report will be distributed.

.1 The director of internal auditing or a designee should

approve and may sign all final reports. If specific circumstances warrant, consideration should be given to having the auditor-in-charge, supervisor, or lead auditor sign the report as a representative of the director of internal auditing.

.2 Audit reports should be distributed to those members of the organization who are able to ensure that audit results are given due consideration. This means that the report should go to those who are in a position to take corrective action or ensure that corrective action is taken. The final audit report should be distributed to the head of each audited unit. Higher-level members in the organization may receive only a summary report. Reports may also be distributed to other interested or affected parties such as external auditors and audit committees.

.3 Certain information may not be appropriate for disclosure to all report recipients because it is privileged, proprietary, or related to improper or illegal acts. Such information, however, may be disclosed in a separate report. If the conditions being reported involve senior management, report distribution should be to the audit committee of the board of directors or a similar high-level entity within the organization.

Acknowledgments

We wish to acknowledge the contributions to the literature on communicating results made by various professional organizations, internal and external auditors, members of academe, firms, and individuals. We especially want to thank those experts in the field who voluntarily contributed their time and effort in reviewing the preliminary work and related drafts of this document.

Task Force on Communicating Results
William P. Viggiano, CISA, Chairperson
George Cirasuolo, CIA
William F. Henderson, Jr.
Otto K. Kalok, CPA
Beverly E. Levy, CISA
Jack C. Liddie, CIA, FLMI
Hanan Rubin, PhD, CIA
Thomas J. Ryan
Peter Villani
Richard Allan White, CIA, CPA, CMA, CAM

Professional Standards and Responsibilities Committee: 1982-1983

William J. Duane, Jr., CPA, Chairperson
Herbert D. Barbour, CIA, CPA
Donald R. Baumunk
William E. Dolan, CPA
Ellis J. Glenn, CIA
William F. Henderson, Jr.
Odd Hunsbedt, CIA, CPA
Herbert D. Miller, CPA
Richard M. Morris, III, CIA, CBA
Donald J. Nelson, CIA
Stanley E. Petrie, CIA, CPA
S.A. Murali Prasad
John G. Sayers, CIA, FCA
Thomas D. Trobaugh, CIA
William P. Viggiano, CISA
Graeme Ward, FIIA, FCCA, IPFA
H.C. Warner, CIA, CPA, CISA
John K. Watsen, CIA, CPA
John J. Willingham, PhD, CPA

Statement on Internal Auditing Standards No. 3, Deterrence, Detection, Investigation, and Reporting of Fraud

The Institute of Internal Auditors

Statement on Internal Auditing Standards
No. 3 — May 1985

Deterrence,
Detection,
Investigation, and
Reporting of Fraud

Issued by
The Professional Standards and
Responsibilities Committee
THE INSTITUTE OF INTERNAL AUDITORS
249 Maitland Avenue, P.O. Box 1119
Altamonte Springs, Florida 32701

Statements on Internal Auditing Standards are issued by the Professional Standards and Responsibilities Committee, the senior technical committee designated by The Institute of Internal Auditors, to issue pronouncements on auditing standards. These statements are authoritative interpretations of the *Standards for the Professional Practice of Internal Auditing.*

Organizations, internal audit departments, directors of internal audit, and internal auditors should strive to comply with the *Standards.* The implementation of the *Standards* and these related statements will be governed by the environment in which the internal audit department carries out its assigned responsibilities. The adoption and implemention of the *Standards* and related statements will assist internal auditing professionals in accomplishing their responsibilities.

ISBN 0-89413-135-4
85326 MAY85
First Printing

Foreword

The Institute of Internal Auditors issued the *Standards for the Professional Practice of Internal Auditing* in 1978 "to serve the entire profession in all types of business, in various levels of government, and in all other organizations where internal auditors are found . . . to represent the practice of internal auditing as it should be . . . ."

The *Standards* has been widely accepted and remains current despite continuous changes in business, society, and the profession of internal auditing. Promoted widely in management texts and used extensively in professional and technical symposia, such increasing acceptance and use demonstrate the credibility of the principles established by the *Standards.*

Fraud is a significant and sensitive management concern. This concern has grown in recent years owing to a substantial increase in the number and the size of the frauds disclosed. The tremendous expansion in the use of computers and the size of and publicity accorded computer-related frauds intensify this concern.

The internal auditor's responsibilities for deterring, detecting, investigating, and reporting of fraud have been a matter of much debate and controversy. Some of the controversy can be attributed to the differences in internal auditing's charter from country to country and from organization to organization. Another cause of the controversy may be unrealistic expectations of the internal auditor's ability to deter and detect fraud.

While several standards and guidelines directly or indirectly address the issue of internal auditors' responsibilities in cases of fraud, the following directly address these responsibilities:

Standard 280 — Due Professional Care

Internal auditors should exercise due professional care in performing internal audits.

280.01 In exercising due professional care, internal auditors should be alert to the possibility of wrongdoing, errors and omissions, inefficiency, waste, ineffectiveness, and conflicts of interest. They should also be alert to those conditions and activities where irregularities are most likely to occur.

280.02 The possibility of material irregularities or noncompliance should be considered whenever the internal auditor undertakes an internal auditing assignment.

280.03 When an internal auditor suspects wrongdoing, the appropriate authorities within the organization should be informed. The internal auditor may recommend whatever investigation is considered necessary in the circumstances. Thereafter, the auditor should follow up to see that the internal auditing department's responsibilities have been met.

Standard 300 — Scope of Work

The scope of the internal audit should encompass the examination and the evaluation of the adequacy and the effectiveness of the organization's system of internal control and the quality of performance in carrying out assigned responsibilities.

330.01 Internal auditors should review the means used to safeguard assets from various types of losses such as those resulting from theft, fire, improper or illegal activities, and exposure to the elements.

Summary

This statement interprets the *Standards* and establishes guidelines for internal auditors regarding their responsibility for deterring, detecting, investigating, and reporting of fraud. It does not provide guidance on specific audit procedures used in performing audits; rather, it establishes guidelines by which internal auditors conform their activities with the stated concepts of due professional care.

Major conclusions of this statement are:

DETERRENCE OF FRAUD

Deterrence of fraud is the responsibility of management. Internal auditors are responsible for examining and evaluating the adequacy and the effectiveness of actions taken by management to fulfill this obligation.

DETECTION OF FRAUD

Internal auditors should have sufficient knowledge of fraud to be able to identify indicators that fraud might have been committed.

If significant control weaknesses are detected, additional tests conducted by internal auditors should include tests directed toward identification of other indicators of fraud.

Internal auditors are not expected to have knowledge equivalent to that of a person whose primary responsibility is to detect and investigate fraud. Also, audit procedures alone, even when carried out with due professional care, do not guarantee that fraud will be detected.

INVESTIGATION OF FRAUD

Fraud investigations may be conducted by or involve participation of internal auditors, lawyers, investigators, security personnel, and other specialists from inside or outside the organization.

Internal auditing should assess the facts known relative to all fraud investigations in order to:

- Determine if controls need to be implemented or strengthened.
- Design audit tests to help disclose the existence of similar frauds in the future.
- Help meet the internal auditor's responsibility to maintain sufficient knowledge of fraud.

REPORTING OF FRAUD

A written report should be issued at the conclusion of the investigation phase. It should include all findings, conclusions, recommendations and corrective action taken.

Contents

Characteristics of Fraud

.1 Fraud encompasses an array of irregularities and illegal acts characterized by intentional deception. It can be perpetrated for the benefit of or to the detriment of the organization and by persons outside as well as inside the organization.

.2 Fraud designed to benefit the organization generally produces such benefit by exploiting an unfair or dishonest advantage that also may deceive an outside party. Perpetrators of such frauds usually benefit indirectly, since personal benefit usually accrues when the organization is aided by the act. Some examples are:

a. Sale or assignment of fictitious or misrepresented assets.

b. Improper payments such as illegal political contributions, bribes, kickbacks, and payoffs to government officials, intermediaries of government officials, customers, or suppliers.

c. Intentional, improper representation or valuation of transactions, assets, liabilities or income.

d. Intentional, improper transfer pricing (e.g., valuation of goods exchanged between related entities). By purposely structuring pricing techniques improperly, management can improve the operating results of an organization involved in the transaction to the detriment of the other organization.

e. Intentional, improper related party transactions in which one party receives some benefit not obtainable in an arm's-length transaction.

f. Intentional failure to record or disclose significant information to improve the financial picture of the organization to outside parties.

    g. Prohibited business activities such as those which violate government statutes, rules, regulations or contracts.

    h. Tax fraud.

.3 Fraud perpetrated to the detriment of the organization generally is for the direct or indirect benefit of an employee, outside individual, or another firm. Some examples are:

    a. Acceptance of bribes or kickbacks.

    b. Diversion to an employee or outsider of a potentially profitable transaction that would normally generate profits for the organization.

    c. Embezzlement, as typified by the misappropriation of money or property, and falsification of financial records to cover up the act, thus making detection difficult.

    d. Intentional concealment or misrepresentation of events or data.

    e. Claims submitted for services or goods not actually provided to the organization.

Note: As used in this statement, the term "management" includes anyone in an organization with responsibilities for setting and/or achieving objectives.

Deterrence of Fraud

.4 Deterrence consists of those actions taken to discourage the perpetration of fraud and limit the exposure if fraud does occur. The principal mechanism for deterring fraud is control. Primary responsibility for establishing and maintaining control rests with management (See SIAS No. 1, *Control: Concepts and Responsibilities*).

Internal Auditing's Responsibilities

.5 Internal auditing is responsible for assisting in the deterrence of fraud by examining and evaluating the adequacy and the effectiveness of control, commensurate with the extent of the potential exposure/risk in the various segments of the entity's operations. In carrying out this responsibility, internal auditing should, for example, determine whether:

a. The organizational environment fosters control consciousness.

b. Realistic organizational goals and objectives are set.

c. Written corporate policies (e.g., code of conduct) exist that describe prohibited activities and the action required whenever violations are discovered.

d. Appropriate authorization policies for transactions are established and maintained.

e. Policies, practices, procedures, reports, and other mechanisms are developed to monitor activities and safeguard assets, particularly in high-risk areas.

   f. Communication channels provide management with adequate and reliable information.

   g. Recommendations need to be made for the establishment or enhancement of cost-effective controls to help deter fraud.

Detection of Fraud

.6 Detection consists of identifying indicators of fraud sufficient to warrant recommending an investigation. These indicators may arise as a result of controls established by management, tests conducted by auditors, and other sources both within and outside the organization.

Internal Auditing's Responsibilities

.7 In conducting audit assignments, the internal auditor's responsibilities for detecting fraud are to:

a. Have sufficient knowledge of fraud to be able to identify indicators that fraud might have been committed. This knowledge includes the need to know the characteristics of fraud, the techniques used to commit fraud, and the types of frauds associated with the activities audited.

b. Be alert to opportunities, such as control weaknesses, that could allow fraud. If significant control weaknesses are detected, additional tests conducted by internal auditors should include tests directed toward identification of other indicators of fraud. Some examples of indicators are unauthorized transactions, override of controls, unexplained pricing exceptions, and unusually large product losses. Internal auditors should recognize that the presence of more than one indicator at any one time increases the probability that fraud might have occurred.

c. Evaluate the indicators that fraud might have been committed and decide whether any further action is necessary or whether an investigation should be recommended.

d. Notify the appropriate authorities within the organization if a determination is made that there are sufficient indicators of the commission of a fraud to recommend an investigation.

.8 Internal auditors are not expected to have knowledge equivalent to that of a person whose primary responsibility is detecting and investigating fraud. Also, audit procedures alone, even when carried out with due professional care, do not guarantee that fraud will be detected.

Investigation of Fraud

.9 Investigation consists of performing extended procedures necessary to determine whether fraud, as
suggested by the indicators, has occurred. It includes
gathering sufficient evidential matter about the specific
details of a discovered fraud. Internal auditors,
lawyers, investigators, security personnel, and other
specialists from inside or outside the organization are
the parties that usually conduct or participate in fraud
investigations.

Internal Auditing's Responsibilities

.10 When conducting fraud investigations, internal auditing should:

a. Assess the probable level and the extent of
complicity in the fraud within the organization.
This can be critical to ensuring that the internal
auditor avoids providing information to or obtaining misleading information from persons who may
be involved.

b. Determine the knowledge, skills, and disciplines
needed to effectively carry out the investigation.
Assess the qualifications and the skills of the
internal auditors and of the specialists available to
participate in the investigation to ensure that it is
conducted by individuals having the appropriate
type and level of technical expertise. This should
include assurances on such matters as professional
certifications, licenses, reputation, and that there
is no relationship to those being investigated or to
any of the employees or management of the
organization.

   c. Design procedures to follow in attempting to identify the perpetrators, extent of the fraud, techniques used, and cause of the fraud.

   d. Coordinate activities with management personnel, legal counsel, and other specialists as appropriate throughout the course of the investigation.

   e. Be cognizant of the rights of alleged perpetrators and personnel within the scope of the investigation and the reputation of the organization itself.

.11 Once a fraud investigation is concluded, internal audit should assess the facts known in order to:

   a. Determine if controls need to be implemented or strengthened to reduce future vulnerability.

   b. Design audit tests to help disclose the existence of similar frauds in the future.

   c. Help meet the internal auditor's responsibility to maintain sufficient knowledge of fraud and thereby be able to identify future indicators of fraud.

Reporting of Fraud

.12 Reporting consists of the various oral or written, interim or final communications to management regarding the status and results of fraud investigations.

Internal Auditing's Responsibilities

.13 A preliminary or final report may be desirable at the conclusion of the detection phase. The report should include the internal auditor's conclusion as to whether sufficient information exists to conduct an investigation. It should also summarize findings that serve as the basis for such decision.

.14 SIAS No. 2, *Communicating Results,* which expands on Specific Standard 430 and provides interpretations, is applicable to internal audit reports issued as a result of fraud investigations. Additional interpretive guidelines on reporting of fraud are as follows:

a. When the incidence of significant fraud has been established to a reasonable certainty, management or the board should be notified immediately.

b. The results of a fraud investigation may indicate that fraud has had a previously undiscovered materially adverse effect on the financial position and results of operations of an organization for one or more years on which financial statements have already been issued. Internal audit should inform appropriate management and the audit committee of the board of directors of such a discovery.

c. A written report should be issued at the conclusion of the investigation phase. It should include all findings, conclusions, recommendations, and corrective action taken.

d. A draft of the proposed report on fraud should be submitted to legal counsel for review. In those cases in which the auditor wants to invoke client privilege, consideration should be given to addressing the report to legal counsel.

Acknowledgments

We acknowledge the contributions to the literature on the subject of this statement made by various professional organizations, internal and independent auditors, members of academe, firms, and individuals. We especially thank those experts in the field who contributed valuable time and effort to review the preliminary work and subsequent drafts.

Task Force on Deterrence, Detection, Investigation, and Reporting of Fraud

William F. Henderson, Jr., Chairman
Donald J. Nelson, CIA
H.O.C. Southwood-Smith, CPA
Thomas D. Trobaugh, CIA
John J. Willingham, PhD, CPA
Richard Allan White, CIA, CPA, CMA, CAM

Professional Standards and Responsibilities Committee: 1984-1985

John K. Watsen, CIA, CPA, Chairman

Robert M. Atkisson, CIA

Donald R. Baumunk

William E. Dolan, CPA

Joanne E. Duncan, CIA

Ellis J. Glenn, CIA

Paul E. Goodburn, CIA

William F. Henderson, Jr.

Michael J. Holmes, CIA, CISA

Odd Hunsbedt, CIA, CPA

Harold J.M. Izzard, FIIA

Donald K. Kitchen, CIA, CGA

Joseph P. Liotta, CPA

Marjo N. McEwen, CIA, CPA

Herbert D. Miller, CPA

Richard M. Morris, III, CIA, CBA

Donald J. Nelson, CIA

Stanley E. Petrie, CIA, CPA

Gerald A. Saunders, CIA, CBA,
   CPA, CISA

H.O.C. Southwood-Smith, CPA

Thomas D. Trobaugh, CIA

William P. Viggiano, CISA

Graeme Ward, FIIA, FCCA, IPFA

H.C. Warner, CIA, CPA, CISA

John J. Willingham, PhD, CPA

APPENDIX G

Manual Supplement

Department of the Treasury
Internal Revenue Service

September 27, 1978

STATISTICAL SAMPLING PROCEDURES IN THE EXAMINATION OF ACCOUNTING RECORDS

Section 1. Purpose

This Supplement provides general guidelines and procedures to be followed whenever statistical sampling techniques are employed in an examination.

Section 2. Background

.01 For some time, the Service has been exploring the use of statistical (probability) sampling techniques in tax examinations, where effective use of resources make it uneconomical to audit voluminous accounting data. Statistical sampling techniques are permitted under the generally accepted auditing standards of the accounting profession. Also, several Revenue Procedures have been published which specifically allow its use by taxpayers in certain situations (e.g., trading stamps and revolving credit plans); however, the Service has not, up to now, made general use of scientific statistical sampling techniques in its examinations.

.02 The Office of the Chief Counsel and the Department of Justice have jointly analyzed the legal ramifications of utilizing probability sampling techniques in the examination of large accounts, and have concluded that substantial authority exists for the determination of tax deficiencies based on statistical samples.

.03 The application of statistical sampling audit techniques should be confined to those revenue agents who have received training in the principles and use of statistical sampling. The application of these principles to tax examinations holds the potential of substantially increasing both the efficiency and quality of IRS examinations.

Section 3. Scope

.01   The instructions contained herein are designed to:

1.   Ensure that estimates of adjustments to tax liabilities resulting from statistical samples are statistically sound and legally defensible; and

2.   Ensure the fair and equitable treatment of taxpayers examined by using statistical sampling techniques.

.02   A comprehensive discussion of statistical methods and procedures is beyond the intent and scope of this document. Such information is presented in Training Course 3172, Statistical Sampling for Audit Personnel, and Course 3174, Advanced Statistical Sampling for Audit Personnel. As problems arise in the area of statistics which are beyond the knowledge and expertise of field personnel, they should be referred to the Director, Examination Division, National Office, Attention CP:E:E:C

Section 4. General Instructions

.01   Projections obtained from examination of statistical (probability) samples of accounting records may be used as the basis for proposing adjustments to items reported on a tax return.

.02   Statistical sampling should be considered whenever a group of accounting entries or transactions has sufficient adjustment potential to warrant examination, but the examination of the totality of all such transactions is prohibitive in terms of time and resources. In any audit situation where it is reasonable to examine 100% of the items under consideration, statistical sampling techniques should not be used.

.03   In most sampling situations, it is possible to estimate, with some degree of reliability, the incremental beneficial effect of increasing the sample size. This may be obtained by determining the variability of the items in question. The decision on sample precision and thus on sample size is to be made after performing such an analysis.

Section 5. Determination of Proposed Population Adjustment

.01   As a general rule, the proposed population adjustment will be determined, such that, 95% of the time, it will not be greater than the actual adjustment obtainable by a 100% examination of the population. This applies regardless of whether the adjustment favors the government or the taxpayer.

.02   The above result will be attained by using the lower limit of the estimated population adjustment at the 95% confidence level. (The estimated population adjustment is also referred to as the point estimate.) This lower limit will generally be computed by subtracting the sampling error (the standard error of the estimated population adjustment multiplied by 1.65) from the population adjustment. (The population adjustment is derived by multiplying the average adjustment for the sample by the number of items in the population.) In making the computation, the following specific rules should be applied; in applying these rules, an adjustment which reduces an expense or increases income is considered positive in sign.

1.   If the point estimate is positive and greater than the sampling error, the proposed population adjustment is obtained by subtracting the sampling error from the point estimate.

2.   If the point estimate is positive and is less than the sampling error, either select additional sampling units to attempt to reduce the sampling error or abandon the sampling plan and propose only those adjustments specifically identified.

3.   If the point estimate is negative, and the sampling error is less than the absolute value of this adjustment, the proposed population adjustment is obtained by adding the sampling error to the point estimate.

4.   If the point estimate is negative, and the sampling error is greater than the absolute value of this adjustment, either select additional sampling units to attempt to reduce the sampling error or abandon the sampling plan and propose only those adjustments specifically identified.

.04   An exception to the general rule, stated in .01 above, occurs whenever both of the following occur:

1.   The Code or Regulations provide for determination of portions of a tax liability on what may of necessity be an estimated value (e.g., certain determinations of fair market value or inventory values), and

2.   The sampling error at the 95% confidence level is less than 10% of the point estimate.

.05   Under such circumstances as stated in 1 and 2 above, it is appropriate to use the point estimate as the basis for the proposed population adjustment.

.06   Whenever two or more accounting populations for a particular tax return are examined, a stratified sampling situation exists, and statistically the sample result and sampling errors can be combined according to the rules for a stratified sample. However, combining strata which cross natural account categories will cause difficulties for Revenue Agent Report (RAR) and Notice of Deficiency purposes. Therefore, examiners are restricted to the combination of strata within a line item category on the tax return. For example, if a travel and entertainment account, and a repair and maintenance account are sampled, separate projections of the population adjustment for each type of account must be made. (These projections cannot be combined.) But if the travel and entertainment accounts in a number of separate divisions are independently sampled, the results from each division should be combined to arrive at an overall adjustment to the total travel and entertainment expense claimed on the tax return. (The word "projection" as used in this Supplement is synonymous with the proposed population adjustment applied only to the sampled population.)

Section 6. Sampling Procedures

.01   Sampling units should be selected for the sample based on random number selection techniques. Systematic (nth item) selection methods should not be used.

.02   Any unusually large transactions should be grouped into a separate stratum and examined in their entirety. Transactions should only be considered unusually large in terms of magnitude.

.03   In stratified sampling situations, a stratum could be deleted or added to the population without affecting the validity of the sample; however, there should be sound reasons for doing so.

.04   The examiner must come to a conclusion as to the correctness of each item in the sample. It is never valid to replace a sample item that is included in the sampling design with another sample item which is not included in the sampling design, merely because documentation is unavailable or difficult to obtain.

.05   The decision reached as to the validity of any sample item must be the same as the conclusion which would be reached if that item were encountered in a 100% examination.

Section 7. Related Entries Originating from a Sampled Transaction

.01   All business transactions generate a minimum of two accounting entries. Frequently, multiple entries are generated. The correctness of a particular entry, whether sampling is used or not, can only be determined by reviewing the transaction in its entirety.

.02   In analyzing individual entries generated by a transaction, the examiner must deal with two types of problems: determining the validity of an entry, and determining the associated adjustments to other accounts when errors are encountered. These problems must be properly dealt with in any audit; however, if sampling techniques are being used, special care must be taken. The following principles should be observed when using sampling methods.

1.   Adjustments with Sampled Accounts:

a.   The examiner should review the basic documents supporting a sample entry in order to determine how the taxpayer handled the entire transaction. If the examiner feels the transaction was handled improperly, it must be decided how it should have been handled.

b.   The way the examiner allocates adjustments among the various entries must not be influenced by which entries are drawn in the sample and which are not.

c.   If, within a population which is to be sampled, errors in specific entries are known to exist beforehand, these entries, if substantial, should be separated into a separate stratum and examined in their entirety. However, if after the sample is drawn, specific adjustments to items not part of the sample are discovered, projections must be based only on items selected in the sample. This does not preclude making adjustments to related entries in other accounts that are not subjected to sampling; nor does it preclude the option of abandoning the sample and proposing only those adjustments specifically identified.

d. No adjustment to a sample entry should be made unless that particular entry can be shown to be in error. The amount of the adjustment to a sample entry should not include any adjustment that properly belongs to some other entry.

e. In those instances where an adjustment applies not to a specific entry, but to a group of related entries, it is appropriate to allocate the total error in the group over all involved entries in proportion to the reported value of each entry.

f. A sample entry that has been totally offset by a reversing entry anywhere in the same account is considered to be correct and is not to be adjusted.

2. Associated Adjustments to Other Accounts:

a. When adjustments are made to sample entries in an expense account, the normal procedure for making associated adjustments to asset accounts, depreciation, investment credit, etc., cannot be followed. As the adjustment to the sample items will be projected to a larger total, so must the associated adjustments be projected to a corresponding level.

b. When an examination of sample items results in the capitalization of amounts for which the taxpayer is entitled to an allowance for depreciation, two separate projections must be made—one for adjustments resulting from the capitalization of items for which depreciation is allowable and one for all other adjustments. The sampling errors must be computed independently and separate adjustments determined as described in Section 5 above.

c. Since the projected adjustment from capitalized items will generally be based on the lower confidence limit of the estimated population adjustment, the ratio of the lower confidence limit to the amount of adjustment in the sample (before projection) is to be used to derive the projected value of the associated adjustment characteristic. It must be remembered, however, that these projected adjustments represent aggregate values rather than specific identifiable assets.

d. Projected depreciation write-offs in subsequent years can be determined by first computing the depreciation which would be allowable on the items in the sample (without projection) and then applying a multiplier to project the write-off to the total amount actually capitalized. The multiplier is derived by computing the ratio described in Section 7.022c above for the amount capitalized; i.e., the total projected adjustment for items capitalized (lower confidence limit) divided by the actual amount of capital items in the sample (before projection).

Section 8. Coordination with Appeals Division

Upon receipt of cases containing issues which involve statistical sampling techniques, the regional Appeals offices should notify the Director, Appeals Division, Attention: CP:AP:SS, so that appropriate coordination can be maintained.

Section 9. Effect on Other Documents

.01   This supplements IRM 42(13)0.

.02   This also supplements IRM 8240, and this "effect" should be annotated by pen and ink, beside the text cited, with a reference to this Supplement.

/s/ John L. Wedick, Jr.
Director, Examination Division

Index